FEB   2008

MISTRESS of WINTER

ALSO BY
Giles Carwyn and Todd Fahnestock

Heir of Autumn

MISTRESS
of WINTER

GILES CARWYN

and

TODD FAHNESTOCK

An Imprint of HarperCollinsPublishers

MISTRESS OF WINTER. Copyright © 2007 by Giles Carwyn and Todd Fahnestock. All rights reserved. Printed in the United States of America. No part of this book may be used or reproduced in any manner whatsoever without written permission except in the case of brief quotations embodied in critical articles and reviews. For information address HarperCollins Publishers, 10 East 53rd Street, New York, NY 10022.

HarperCollins books may be purchased for educational, business, or sales promotional use. For information please write: Special Markets Department, HarperCollins Publishers, 10 East 53rd Street, New York, NY 10022.

FIRST EDITION

Eos is a federally registered trademark of HarperCollins Publishers.

Designed by Joy O'Meara
Maps and drawings by Langdon Foss

Library of Congress Cataloging-in-Publication Data has been applied for.

ISBN: 978-0-06-082977-3
ISBN-10: 0-06-082977-X

07 08 09 10 11 DT/RRD 10 9 8 7 6 5 4 3 2 1

GILES'S DEDICATION:

For my Samwise, who kept her promise to Gandalf.

TODD'S DEDICATION:

For Lara, my Brighteyes. Your gaze upon me lights my way.

Pronunciation Guide

Arefaine—ÄR-e-fān
Astor—AS-tôr
Baedellin—bā-DEL-in
Baelandra—bā-LÄN-drä
Brezelle—bruh-ZELL
Brophy—BRŌ-fē
Caleb—KĀ-leb
Celtigar—SEL-ti-gär
Efften—EF-ten
Emmeria—e-ME-rē-uh
Faedellin—fā-DEL-in
Faradan—FE-ruh-dan
Fessa—FE-suh
Floani—flō-A-nē
Galliana—ga-lē-Ä-nuh
Heidvell—HĒD-vel
Issefyn—IS-e-fin
Jesheks—JE-sheks
Kherif—KER-if
Koscheld—KÄSK-held
Koscholtz—KÄSK-holts

Lawdon—LÄ-dun
Lowani—lō-ä-nē
Mikal—mi-KÄL
Morgeon—MÔR-jē-un
Natshea—NAT-shā
Necani—ne-KÄ-nē
Ohndarien—on-DÄ-rē-en
Ohohhim—ō-HÄ-him
Ohohhom—ō-HÄ-hum
Ossamyr—OS-uh-mur
Phandir—FAN-dēr
Phanqui—FAN-kwē
Physendria—fi-SEN-drē-uh
Reignholtz—RĪN-holts
Shara—SHÄ-ruh
Suvian—SOO-vē-un
Vallia—VÄ-lē-uh
Victeris—vik-TER-is
Vinghelt—VING-helt
Vizar—vi-ZÄR
Zelani—ze-LÄ-nē

The Opal Palace•

OHOHHOM

VIZAR

The GREAT

Kec Salum•

KHERIF

Upper Kec Lyn•

Kec Lyn•

EFFTEN

•The Fallen City

UPPER
KHERIF

Kec Naster•

•Slavers

THE
SILVER ISLANDS

Kec Rostric•

THE SOUTHWYLDS

Lone Hill

THE VASTNESS

The Cinder

...AN

FARADAN

Port
Royal

Ohndarian

THE
PETAL
ISLANDS

Physen

Sitha

Hyphlus

THE
SUMMER

Vinghelo

PHYSENDRIA

SEAS

Koschelo

Syllse

Heidhelo

Ardhelo

Gildhelo

Reignhelo

Munkhelo

Book One

A FORTRESS OF LOVE AND SHADOWS

Ohndarien

Fortress of Light

Prologue

The rain finally stopped, and the goddess went outside to play.

Grandfather Lewlem followed the sleeve of three-hundred-year-old Arefaine Morgeon through the Opal Gardens. The child's bare feet stepped delicately along the rain-slicked mosaic path. An opalescent silk gown, bordered in black, covered her from chin to ankles, and her dark brown hair fell down her back like the single stroke from a giant brush. She walked as if her toes could read the songs of Oh that had been painstakingly wrought beneath her.

Little Arefaine turned her powdered face upward, transfixed by the May Dragon trees towering above her. Their thick trunks twisted into the sky as if each day they decided to grow in a different direction. A hundred feet overhead, the branches stretched to the horizon, their thick, spiny leaves still dripping from the morning rain.

"Why are the trees so tall?" she asked.

"It is in the nature of trees," said Lewlem.

"No," she replied. "These trees are taller than outside."

It had only been two years since Arefaine had awoken, and Lewlem knew better than anyone what horrors the child had endured during the three hundred years that she slept. Was it any wonder that her eyes were fascinated by the towering trees, that her feet were enthralled by the mosaic path?

"Ah," he said. "The imperial gardeners cultivated these trees for many years to grow so tall."

"Culti . . ." she tried the word.

"Cultivated," he said again.

"Cultivated," she mimicked.

"Very good."

She grinned up at him and was, abruptly, a three-year-old child again. "Come play with me?" she said, tugging on his hand.

The pain in Lewlem's hip protested, as it often did these days, but he took a deep breath and forced himself to kneel beside her. "These bones are too old for playing."

Arefaine frowned. "Bones not old. Come play."

Lewlem shook his head, but she yanked her sleeve away and stuck out her tongue at him.

"Arefaine ... Decorum follows grace, grace follows dignity, and dignity follows inner peace—"

"And inner peace leads to the voice of Oh," the girl finished in perfect mockery of the familiar phrase. At a frown from Lewlem, she burst into giggles and scampered away, disappearing around a bend in the path.

With a slight exhalation, Lewlem struggled to stand and started after her. Every day presented a new ache, but he had one task to accomplish before he took his final walk.

In these last years, the shadow of Oh's cave beckoned to Lewlem more and more. He looked back on his life and knew he was not a wise man. When he was young and unmarried, he dreamed of a life by the sword, longing to serve the Emperor as a Carrier of the Opal Fire. Then he married and came to aspire to a life of great wealth, many children, and at least five wives. But the plague took his wives and children, leaving him with an empty house until he lost his heart to a young widow with a face that shone like moonlight. He took the girl, already heavy with child, for his third wife and hoped they would share a few happy days before the fevers claimed them all.

The plague ended when the old Emperor took his last walk into the welcoming darkness of Oh's cave. A few days later a line of three hundred priests appeared at Lewlem's doorstep. They identified his newborn son as Oh's chosen, the new Emperor, and Lewlem knew that dreams were foolish. He did not dream anymore, but instead listened closely to the quiet voice of Oh. His destiny was to raise an emperor and after, this little girl who held the fate of the world in her tiny hands.

Lewlem tracked the child's giggles through the rain-soaked gardens and took a shortcut through the ferns to a row of sunberry bushes. The girl huddled between two thorny shrubs, grinning back along the path where she expected him to emerge. Lewlem slipped around the bushes and came up behind her. He stood there for a long moment, then whispered, "Caught you."

She shrieked and leapt away, scurrying down the path. For the life of him, Lewlem saw nothing more than a vital and precocious child. She wasn't the dreaming child, the infant goddess who held back the night. She was just a little girl. His little girl.

"Old bones," she called from behind a tree. "Your bones not old."

"Not true. My bones are old, but a quick mind can make up for old bones."

She laughed, then looked at the nearby row of sunberry bushes. Quite deliberately, she plucked a berry from the bush.

"Arefaine," he said in a stern voice, walking toward her. She popped the berry into her mouth and grimaced at the bitter taste. Though it pained him, he descended slowly to his knees. "Arefaine, I already told you, the berries will hurt you if you eat them. You must wait one more week until they are ripe."

"No," she protested. "I will ... cultivate them to be ready now!" Again, she said the word with Lewlem's exact tone and inflection, a perfect mockingbird who never forgot anything. She reached for another berry.

Lewlem gently took her wrist and pulled her hand away from the bush. "Come away. They will make you sick."

"No!" she shouted, yanking back with all her might. "They're mine! Mine!" Her feet slipped on the wet path, and she fell, smacking her head on the ground.

Lewlem scooped her up and held her close, fearing a howl of anguish that never came. Pulling back, he looked to see how badly she was hurt.

Black tendrils seeped from the edges of her eyelids, creeping across her pale blue eyes. "Put. Me. Down," she hissed through clenched teeth.

Lewlem took a swift breath. "Arefaine, no ... You must—"

Arefaine's nostrils flared, and she reached out one little finger, stabbing him on the shoulder. Pain flared through Lewlem's arm into his chest. He gasped and stumbled backward. His bad hip buckled, and he fell to the ground.

Arefaine fell on his chest, rolled to the ground, and stood up next to him.

Lewlem struggled to breathe, he tried to reach for her, but his arm wouldn't move.

With her hands calmly at her sides, Arefaine touched her toe to his cheek. Fire spread through his face, down his neck, lodging again in his heart. His frail body convulsed, and he felt something rip inside his chest.

"Please, child!" he tried to say, but no words came out. "Don't do this to yourself. Please ..."

❄

The roaring inside Arefaine's head slowly calmed. The little girl blinked, and the howling voices faded into the distance.

Frowning, she crouched next to the old man, and poked him with a finger. He didn't move; his unblinking eyes stared at the trees above. Frowning again, she toddled back to the bushes. Plucking several berries, she popped them into her mouth as quickly as she could.

"Now," she insisted. "I want them now." She smiled as the bitter juice ran down her chin.

CHAPTER 1

Ossamyr's father called her a queen the day she left home.

She could still see the frightened little man kneeling before her in the vast foyer of his new home. His wispy hair hung limp over sunken cheeks still pallid from his long imprisonment. The emaciated man wore the blue, feathered cloak she'd just bought for him. It made him look like a very expensive scarecrow.

"Thank you, my daughter," he'd whispered to her feet. "You bring honor to us all."

His words were sincere, but the depth of his bow could not hide the look of relief—and pity—in his eyes.

That was Ossamyr's wedding day, the day she had sold herself into royalty. She'd done it to save her family, to save that shadow of a man from the Wet Cells. She'd lied, seduced, betrayed, and murdered her way into the bed of a man she despised. And when she reached that bed, she had put on a performance the likes of which the king had never seen.

Ossamyr closed her eyes against her memories, plagued by a past she couldn't seem to escape. She stood at the heart of the most beloved city in the world, within the most respected school in the world. She was surrounded by lovers, friends, and devoted pupils, but she had never felt so alone, so naked and exposed.

Ossamyr's hand lay frozen on the curled piece of yellow paper. A bottle of Siren's Blood pinned the edge of the note to the table, the swirling colors casting little rainbows on the paper, on her skin. The bottle had drawn her curiosity, but the page had captured her. Her fingers covered the words that revealed what she truly was, exposed her to the only person she could claim to have loved since Brophy sacrificed himself.

Ossamyr had stepped into Shara's room for just a moment, to borrow a book. It was something she had done a dozen times before. She noticed the bottle on a dusty shelf with other unwanted gifts from Shara's flatterers and admirers. It was unopened, but there was a slight tear in the parchment, and she noticed a strange glow coming from inside. Curious, Ossamyr unwrapped the bottle and was amazed to find an exquisite bottle of the Silver Islander's spirit wine. The extravagant gift of Siren's Blood had surprised her, but the message that accompanied it left her unable to speak, unable to move.

She tore her gaze from the message and looked out the window, trying to guess who could have sent such a venomous warning.

The mighty Ohndarien battlements glowed like the edge of a sword. The sun was setting beyond the Windmill Wall, throwing orange and red across the waters of the bay, painting the blue-white walls of the buildings with a golden glow. Nearby rooftop gardens fluttered in the early-spring breeze. Children shrieked in the streets below, pretending to be Zelani and Lightning Swords. Merchants in the Long Market rushed to pack up their wares before the lanterns in the Night Market were lit, twinkling with the sultry promise of pleasures to come.

In the center of it all, the Hall of Windows shone like a dome of jewels. A single torch burned atop that magnificent building. Its feeble light was lost amid the grandeur of the setting sun, but the mere thought of that flame burned right through her. That light stood as testament to the freedom one boy had bought for everyone and as a reminder of the prison that Ohndarien had become.

Ohndarien was no longer the Free City, no longer the jewel of the known world. Her citizens now called her the Fortress of Light, all because of that one torch and the boy who lay beneath it.

Ohndarien's days of thriving as the crossroads of the world had ended shortly after the Nightmare Battle. Merchants still paid dearly for the right to ferry their ships through her locks, but few stayed to trade in the city's famous Long Market. Only the stoutest of heart lingered within Ohndarien's blue-white marble walls any longer than they had to.

They had won the Nightmare Battle, but the war against the Legacy of Efften continued. The black emmeria called to its own, and the boy who had been the beacon of Ohndarien's salvation was now a beacon for the corrupted. All that was vile in the world had come south. As the profane creatures once sought the baby and the music box, now they sought the boy. Those transformed by the foul magic of Efften scratched and clawed at Ohndarien's walls, desperate to get in, yearning to set loose the shadows that everlasting torch held at bay.

Those few Ohndariens who stayed within the cursed city fought for their lives beside their fellow merchants, sailors, cobblers, and butchers. The battlements were filled with Lightning Swords, Zelanis, and former Physendrian queens.

Ossamyr closed her eyes. The mysterious message felt hot under her fingertips and that word came again, unbidden, to her mind. Queen...

"You are a queen among queens, my love," Phandir had said, kneeling at her feet. Her former husband was flush with victory, drunk on the adulation of the crowd and reveling in his power over her. His hand slid beneath her dress and up her thigh as he looked up at her with mock reverence as brutal as his smile. He knew she had tasted real love, and that she had murdered it for him.

"You're just like me," he continued, squeezing her to him, his eyes glistening with triumph. "My perfect queen." He beamed at her, clenching her soul between those perfect white teeth.

And he did have her. She might as well have been in the Wet Cells for all the control she had over her life. She marched with him, all the way to the walled city. She curled her lips in a smile for him, spread her legs for him, whispered how powerful he was. She played the perfect queen, marching into the conquered city by his side until the black emmeria swept across them like a blizzard of despair.

And then she tore his throat out with her own claws.

She would never forget that feeling, the exultation, the freedom, as that black ooze surged through her limbs, filling her with more power than she had ever dreamed of.

She tore her husband limb from limb until no two bones still clung together. She could still feel the flesh parting between her claws; could still feel her grinning teeth awash with hot blood.

The black emmeria knew who she was, it called her home, and she had spun into that dark abyss, lost and elated. She had killed Phandir, and she would have continued killing, rending, tearing.

Then *he* came along and saved her. He came along and saved them all.

Him.

The boy.

Brophy.

He sacrificed himself, drew all of that evil into his heart and locked it within his dreams. He was only sixteen, just a child, but he knew more about love than Ossamyr ever would. He gave her that first taste back in Physendria, and she had ripped out his heart for it, betrayed him when he needed her the most. It seemed to be her fate with those she claimed to love. As soon as they were sure she was theirs, she tore them to pieces.

Her fingernails dug through the paper into the desk below, making five tiny holes. Her arm vibrated. The colors in the bottle of Siren's Blood seemed to swirl faster, as if sensing her anger. The words on the page were burned on her mind.

You must not wake the Sleeping Warden. You must not let the child take him from the city.

Drink this. Drink it all, and the truth will be revealed to you.

And beware the former Queen of Physendria. She longs for your death and will soon betray you.

Ossamyr swallowed hard. She longs for your death, it said. Whoever wrote those words had stuck a dagger in Ossamyr's soul. She had worked tirelessly to save the boy, but there was no escaping the truth. In some small way, she did long for Shara's death, or rather for her place at his side.

Shara was probably atop the Hall right now. Sitting by his side, sharing his dreams. Ossamyr could see it all too clearly. His arms around Shara's back. Her hands running through his blond curls, the love shining in his deep green eyes.

Ossamyr tried to draw a calming breath, tried to use her training, tried to be a better person than she was.

Could a person truly change? Could a scorpion withhold its stinger before it poisoned all those who came close, lover or husband, friend or rival? Could a serpent ever become a falcon? A lion? A phoenix?

Ossamyr should have been executed for her role in the Nightmare Battle. She had walked into Ohndarien at the head of an invading army, but Shara and Baelandra had accepted her as one of their own. They'd shown her nothing but respect and compassion.

But someone knew that Ossamyr was still the "perfect queen" in her acid heart, where betrayal came as easily as breathing. All this time she had told herself that she had changed, that the boy had changed her, that Zelani had changed her, that Shara had changed her. But she was just pretending, masquerading as something she barely understood: a decent person.

"When the moment came to choose between love and hate, you chose love," Baelandra had once told her, explaining how she freed herself from the black emmeria. "Always remember that you chose love at the moment when it mattered most."

The former Physendrian queen smiled tightly, drawing her fingernails out of the paper and meticulously rolling it back up. Had Baelandra herself written it? Or the Physendrian rebels who constantly asked her to return to Physen and lead them against their enemies? It could have been anyone.

Ossamyr stared at the single torch glittering atop the Hall of Windows. The sun had just dipped behind the walls, and the boy's torch seemed to grow brighter and brighter as the world grew dark.

That torch was why she was here. Freeing the boy was all that mattered, no matter the cost. Her new boat was ready, sitting at anchor just beyond the Windmill Wall. She would find her storm and sail into the teeth of oblivion if she had to. And damn the rest of them. Damn herself and who she had been.

A sudden tap on the door jerked her out of her thoughts. Fear spiked her heart, and she stuffed the note into her pocket. Snatching the Siren's Blood off the windowsill, she looked around desperately for a place to hide it.

The door opened just as she thrust the bottle behind Shara's wardrobe. She swiveled as she rose, holding her hands in front of the pocket containing the damning message.

Caleb stood in the doorway, calm and alert. The slender man with the boyish face and close-cropped sandy hair simply looked at her, saying nothing.

Twin rushes of relief and fear flooded through her. He wasn't here because of the note. He was here because of—

"The corrupted," she breathed.

"Yes."

"When?"

"Now."

Ossamyr stepped forward. She took a deep breath, and Caleb matched her. He reached out his hand, and she took it. A jolt of energy shot between them as they touched.

Tingles ran up her arm, through her body, as energy cycled between them. Their fingers entwined, hot with energy. Ossamyr channeled her churning emotions into the spell, transforming them into a flood of raw sexual power.

Within moments they were full to bursting. "Ready?" Caleb asked her.

Ossamyr nodded, using her scant Floani training to shift the energy into her legs, eyes, and ears. Caleb squeezed her hand, and they began to run. The hallway flashed by. They took the stairs together five at a time, stepping in perfect timing.

"Reports have them close to the quarry ridge," he rasped, the energy threatening to boil over.

He shuddered, stumbled. She calmed his desire, held him upright even though her body ached, desperate for him to throw her against the wall, surge between her legs and inside of her. But they ran. They kept running, hand in hand. There was no time. There was never enough time.

They raced across the courtyard. The gardens were a blur. Many of the other Zelani were already ahead of them, rushing through the school's open gates.

"Has Shara been told?" Ossamyr shouted, barely able to contain the energy coursing through her as they surged through the gate and into the Ohndarien streets.

A warning bell had already begun to toll atop the Quarry Wall. A frightened woman held her door open as her children rushed inside. She watched Ossamyr run past with a pained expression trapped somewhere between gratitude and pity.

"She's with Brophy," Caleb yelled back.

Good, Ossamyr thought, tossing the parchment behind her into an open storm drain. She kept her legs pumping, practically dragging Caleb along with her. *She belongs by his side.*

And I belong at the wall.

CHAPTER 2

Brophy's feather fluttered in the breeze, bound to his neck by a leather thong. Shara stood behind him, just out of sight, watching the silky black feather twist and twirl amid his golden curls. He needed a haircut. He always needed a haircut.

He stood atop the Hall of Windows, leaning against the torch still burning for the lost Brother of Autumn and soaking in the view of Ohndarien in all her splendor. He was only ten feet away. And impossibly far out of reach.

The faint sound of singing hovered around them like mist, coming and going with the wind. Shara wore one of Brophy's long, loose shirts from the Kherish ship. It fluttered in the breeze, rippling against her thighs. She smoothed it, like she always did. Fingertips brushed bare skin, like they always did.

Her eyes traveled the length of his naked body. Broad shoulders, muscled back and legs. The sun made his bare skin glow. Her jaw trembled, seeing him this way again. Again, again, and again. How could a heart overflow with joy and twist in pain at the same time? How could she still feel this much, after all this time?

The words caught in her throat. She knew exactly what words she would say, knew exactly what would happen next. And what wouldn't happen. But she said the words again. There were no other words to say.

"She is worth fighting for," Shara whispered, walking up beside him on silent feet. "Worth dying for."

Brophy turned and saw her next to him. And he smiled. Oh, how she knew that smile, how she lived for it. He looked down at his arms, his hands. "What is this?"

"A dream, my love. Your dream."

The same dream.

She turned and stepped backward onto the air, reaching out for him, touching his hands.

Brophy laughed, and she tried not to wince. There was so much love in his eyes. So much wonder, so much joy.

She tugged his hands, pulling him beyond the sloping edge of the Hall. "Shara!"

"Come. Let's fly," she whispered, every part of her aching for him.

Tentatively, he took a step into thin air. Such faith. It lifted her up and cut her to the quick.

Shara held tight to Brophy's hands and floated backward, leading him farther out. The Wheel passed below them. "How are you doing this?" he asked, his face alive with green-eyed wonder.

"Magic." She winked, willing herself to forget. Willing herself to fall into the moment.

"Wait." He grinned. "Why are you wearing clothes and I'm not?"

She forced a smile. "It's your dream."

He touched her shirt, and it dissolved in a shimmer of sparkles. Shara took a deep breath and let it go, let it all go, sinking into the joy of the moment, this shining moment.

She spun away from him and dived toward the bay, feeling the salty air whip through her hair. He chased her, reaching to grab a toe but never quite getting there. She pulled up at the last moment and streaked along the tips of the waves. He caught her and drew her toward him. Their bodies entwined, his hands on her back, his hips sliding between her thighs. They flew upward again, spinning, kissing, her body enveloped in his. The Spire whipped past them.

"I never want to wake up," he murmured, tasting her neck, her ear. Shara's chest seized, and tears welled in the corners of her eyes. She buried her hands in his floating hair.

"Then sleep, Brophy." Somehow she kept the quaver from her voice. "Sleep and love me. We will take what eternity we can find in your dreams."

The familiar words wrenched her heart as she spoke them, just as they had every day and every night for the last eighteen years.

He kissed her. Hungry lips turning desperate. Strong arms crushing. Trembling legs spread wider as he slid inside her, and they flew together on and on and on.

CHAPTER 3

Ossamyr and Caleb kept the energy racing between them, holding hands as they flew northward through the city's twisting and winding streets. The streets were packed, as Ohndariens fled home to their families to find what little protection they could behind locked doors.

The frantic crowd parted for the two Zelani. A few Lightning Swords were seen amid the throng, easily spotted in their blue tunics with the golden slash across the front. One of them rushed through his front door, barely pausing to kiss his wife and daughter good-bye before raising shield and spear and joining their mad dash for the wall.

Ossamyr heard Faedellin's deep voice before they rounded the final corner to the wide street leading to the Quarry Gate.

"Form ranks! Form ranks!" the captain of the Lightning Swords thundered. "The Quarry Rim has been breached! Two large corrupted are headed this way."

Baelandra's husband was a slender man with a long nose and thin face. He was neither tall nor powerfully built, but his voice carried like rolling thunder. The former steward was the heart and soul of the Lightning Swords, Ohndarien's citizen soldiers who took their name from the legendary mercenary army of J'Qulin the Sly.

Ohndarien was once defended by a professional army of foreign swordsmen. The few of those soldiers who had survived the Nightmare Battle had watched, mesmerized, when the first few corrupted came south and flung themselves against the wall, frantic for a way in. Those soldiers kept to their ramparts, secure in the knowledge that the city's celebrated wall would stop the vile beasts.

It didn't.

The boy was almost lost that first attack, the black emmeria almost freed. A lone corrupted nightcat swam under the Sunset Gate, climbed the sheer walls of the Wheel, and attacked the Hall of Windows. It sliced its way through a pair of guards and the two novice Zelani as they sang to the boy before Shara managed to slay it with the Sword of Winter. Her forearm still bore the scars from the creature's teeth.

The next day, Faedellin called the blood of J'Qulin together and re-formed the Lightning Swords. The hired soldiers left for easier money and the 'Swords had manned the walls ever since, joining their dedication with the power of Shara's Zelani.

Faedellin's men arrived from every direction, quickly forming orderly rows. The golden lightning bolts on their shields glimmered in the torchlight. A ragged pack of Zelani stood behind the orderly Lightning Swords, their tight, wispy clothing a stark contrast to the bronze and leather armor of the soldiers. The Zelani kept to themselves, each staring into the eyes of a partner, building up the energy they would need for the battle. There were barely sixty of them altogether, and Ossamyr couldn't help wondering how many would die tonight.

"Control is the key," Faedellin reminded them. "We establish control before anyone moves in." The words were ingrained in the minds of every Lightning Sword, every Zelani, but Faedellin repeated them before each skirmish. The Lightning Swords kept their swords sheathed and carried long, pronged spears designed to pin their enemies from a safe distance. Once the monsters were restrained, someone with a gemsword did the actual killing.

Gavin and Gareth stood to Faedellin's left. The young twins of the House of Winter held two of Ohndarien's five gemswords. Ossamyr had helped Shara create the magical weapons, imbuing each with a shard of the Heartstone. They could not match the original Swords of the Seasons in power or beauty, but they were effective at killing the corrupted.

To Faedellin's right stood his son, Astor, who also bore one of the magical swords. Except for his wavy brown hair, the new Heir of Autumn was the spitting image of his cousin. Ossamyr found it difficult to look at him without thinking of Brophy.

Astor was humble and brave, quick to smile and talented with a blade, but he had only recently come of age and had just been accepted into the Lightning Swords. Ossamyr could see the doubt and fear written on the boy's face and sent a gentle caress of energy to ease his racing heart.

"Look at the man beside you," Faedellin shouted. "Look at the lass to your right." His troops did as they were told, their grim faces full of love. Ossamyr looked to Caleb and squeezed his hand. Their Zelani magic hummed through them like a swarm of bees.

"We do not go out there alone," Faedellin continued. "We stand together for our families, for each other, for Ohndarien, for the light!" Ossamyr kept the energy playing back and forth between herself and Caleb, and sent a steady stream of it toward Faedellin, adding power to his voice.

"Will we fail those standing beside us?" he shouted.

"No!" The Lightning Swords shouted as one, and she could feel their voices thrumming through her chest.

"Will we run from the face of darkness?"

"No!"

He pointed behind himself to the Hall of Windows. "Will we let that light go out?"

"No! No! No!" they shouted, and Ossamyr added her voice to their song.

Faedellin gave the signal, and the Quarry Gate began to open. Huge metal gears ground together as the counterweights moved. The metal doors swung outward. With a united cry, the Lightning Swords and Zelani moved as one. They rushed into the darkness of the tunnel that cut through Ohndarien's massive wall.

They emerged in the quarry on the far side of the wall. Ten of the Lightning Swords held torches, creating a ring of light twenty feet out. Cunning metal dishes directed torchlight down from the wall above them, casting murky shadows along the stretch of flat marble. The quarry floor continued to the perfect stair-steps of blue-white stone that extended up the side of the mountain and out of sight.

The Lightning Swords rushed forward over the well-known ground and spread out in a precise arc, with the Zelani behind them. Pronged spears bristled.

Silence greeted them, but everyone remained tense and ready. Corrupted could come from the sky, the water, or overland, and they took every shape imaginable. Faedellin counseled constant assessment to his Lightning Swords. Assess, attack, reassess, attack again. Defend yourself first, he'd told them over and over again. Patience was their greatest weapon against the mindless beasts. Patience and discipline. There was no such thing as a predictable enemy.

Magic hummed in Ossamyr's ears as the Zelani all around her let their power flow into the soldiers, adding to their strength, their speed, their conviction. Astor was the closest man to her with a gemsword. She concentrated her power on him, and he turned back to give her a manic grin, his whole body shaking with energy.

Ossamyr closed her eyes, sending out a tendril of her awareness. Her magic rushed up the carved cliffs, up into the darkness beyond the rise.

"There," she pointed. "Two large ones. Coming fast!"

"Separate them!" Faedellin shouted, his deep voice ringing across the distance. "Those on the flanks hold back, watch for others!"

A gurgling roar thundered down the quarry, echoing off the wall behind them. Two hulking shapes rolled over the lip of the quarry and dropped to the stair-step of rock just below. She could barely see them in the darkness until they gathered their bulk and launched themselves forward, flapping their tails as if swimming in water.

The massive black shapes flew down half the quarry steps before hitting the stone and rolling the rest of the way. They crashed to the quarry floor and slid into the midst of the Lightning Swords, scattering them like pebbles.

Ossamyr ran to one side, losing hold of Caleb's hand. She dodged around the retreating soldiers, desperate to stay on her feet. The defenders gathered their courage and plunged their fifteen-foot spears into the thrashing black shapes.

"By the Seasons, they're sharks," Astor said, right next to her. His eyes were wide, but he still held his gemsword at the ready, waiting for his chance.

Ossamyr could barely recognize the creature, so complete was its transformation. Hundreds of thin tentacles had sprung from every possible place on the fish's body. They slapped at the slick marble, desperate to propel the beast forward, but the barbed spears held it solidly in place. Crimson eyes flared behind clusters of teeth as long as Ossamyr's fingers. Its jaws were the only part of it that still looked like a shark.

"Contain!" Faedellin shouted. "Contain and wait for the opening!"

Ossamyr fed Faedellin's emotions into his warriors, and the soldiers split into two groups, driving the sharks back with their spears, forcing them apart.

The beast closest to her thrashed its tail frantically, knocking one soldier aside. Ossamyr sent her magic to his aid, but it was too late. A tentacle lashed out and wrapped around the man's leg, throwing him into the monster's mouth.

Teeth chomped, and the soldier screamed. Red blood splashed across the quarry floor.

"Contain!" Faedellin roared, but Astor charged forward. Ossamyr sent a rush of pure energy into his body as he leapt over one of the spears and sank his sword into the side of the beast's head.

The shark's teeth blurred in the half-light. Its jaws snapped shut on nothing, scraping Astor's leather greaves as he leapt out of the way.

Black blood poured from the wound in the shark's head, and the air filled with a thousand distant voices screaming in rage.

The beast whipped about, frantic in its death throes. A hundred tentacles flailed against the ground, reaching out like fingers. The howling voices grew louder, then faded as the beast slumped to the ground, its tentacles twitching.

Ossamyr took a deep breath and turned her attention to the other shark, which had already thrown three of the Lightning Swords to the ground. Gavin and Gareth lurked at a distance, waiting for their moment. The spearmen who had pinned the first shark turned to the second one. Dozens more spears pierced its flesh. The beast would be overwhelmed in moments.

Ossamyr was about to help them when she saw Astor down on hands and knees panting uncontrollably.

She rushed to his side. "Are you all right?" she asked, checking for corruption with her magic.

"That was so dumb, so dumb," he panted, shaking his head. "I should have waited."

Ossamyr helped him to his feet, sending a stream of reassurance toward him.

The other beast roared, and she glanced over to see Gavin and Gareth stabbing repeatedly as fifty Lightning Swords held it down.

"You did fine," she said. "The beast is dead, that's all that matters."

He nodded, dazed. "I should get my sword."

Ossamyr walked with him as he put a foot against the dead beast's head and yanked his sword out with both hands. Ribbons of pure black emmeria tainted the glowing gem in the pommel, enough to infect a hundred people.

Ossamyr reached out to take the sword. Astor's job was done. Only a Zelani could add the few drops of emmeria to the malevolent ocean trapped in the boy's dreams—

A thunderous crash shook the quarry. The ground rocked, and she nearly fell.

An earsplitting bellow shook the night, driving Ossamyr to her knees.

By the Nine! What was—

"Above! Look to the quarry!" Faedellin shouted.

An immense shape rolled over the quarry's rim, stark black against the stars overhead. It was as big as the Hall of Windows and shook the earth when it shoved its girth over another stair-step, slamming down to the next level below.

Ossamyr's breath left her as she stared. She had seen all manner of corrupted: men, women, children, twisted rock lions, horses, bears, dogs, oxen, but this ...

"I think ..." Astor whispered, his voice catching in his throat, his sword held in a slack grip. "I think it was a whale."

Ossamyr fought to regain her composure, fought to gather the fleeing threads of her magic. She needed Caleb. Where was he?

"It doesn't matter what it is," she said, swallowing down a dry throat. "We have to stop it."

"How?"

She looked to Faedellin and saw him frozen in disbelief as the mountainous black shape undulated down the steps toward them. She sent him a jolt of energy, and he snapped back into action.

"Form ranks," he bellowed. "Form ranks!"

The Lightning Swords slowly started forward, forming a line of bristling spears. Astor hesitated a moment, glancing back at Ossamyr.

The whale thundered toward them, levering its body forward. Its flesh was worn away by its long trek across dry land. Dirt-caked yellow bones stuck out of its sides, and a trail of black ichor followed in its wake.

The Lightning Swords slowly retreated from the whale's path. None had the courage to rush forward to engage it.

Ossamyr gathered her energy, wishing Caleb were closer.

"Ossamyr, look out!" Astor shouted, a second too late.

Searing pain shot up Ossamyr's leg. She staggered backward as a tiny black fish wrapped barbed fins tightly around her calf. Its teeth burrowed into her leg again and tore away a chunk of flesh.

"No!" she roared, and fell to the ground.

"Ossamyr!" Astor rushed forward and skewered the fish with a deft flick of his blade. His gemsword blazed in the darkness. Anguished voices howled, and the beast died.

Ossamyr bit back a second scream and glanced down at the gaping wounds on her calf. Her blood was already turning black as inky tendrils crept up her leg.

"Are you all right?" he asked, falling to his knees at her side.

Ossamyr looked into Brophy's face, his green eyes filled with dread.

No! Not Brophy! Astor! Astor! She fought her way back to her senses. The tendrils sped beneath her dress; her entire leg was black and starting to ripple.

Ossamyr shook her head, trying to clear it. Her leg was on fire, and she was starting to like it, like it a lot. She remembered her claws ripping through Phandir's flesh; she could taste his blood pouring down her throat.

Someone else crashed down next to her, and she felt a surge of energy rush into her body, pushing the flames back down her leg. She snarled at him to stop and found Caleb kneeling next to her, adding his strength to her own.

Slowly, her head cleared. The corruption slowed, and she fought it with everything she had. Together they began to force it out of her body.

Astor looked at Ossamyr, his brown eyes full of compassion. But there was resolution, too. The pommel of his gemsword glowed. If she turned, he knew what had to be done.

"You go," Caleb assured Astor, reaching for the pommel of the sword. "They need you over there. Leave the sword with me. I'll see to her."

Reluctantly, Astor nodded and ran toward the battle, snatching a discarded spear off the ground. Beyond him, the whale loomed across the entire horizon, blotting out the stars. The soldiers' spears weren't going to stop it; they wouldn't be nearly long enough. Each of beast's flippers was thirty feet long. It swung them from side to side and soldiers screamed as they were thrown about like leaves.

"Go," Ossamyr said to Caleb through her teeth.

"Your leg—"

"Forget my leg! We'll all be dead if you don't help them!"

"You can't—"

"Yes I can! Leave me the sword. I'll do what needs to be done if I can't hold it back."

Caleb's lips set in a straight line before he nodded tersely.

"Connect to the Heartstone," he said. "Use her strength to bolster yours."

"Of course."

He stood up, paused only half a second, then ran toward the battle.

Ossamyr turned to her wound, throwing her full concentration into purging the emmeria from her body.

It fought back tenaciously, refusing to give up its hold on her life.

A dull spike of fear shot through her as she realized how much Caleb had been helping her. The black tendrils moved back up her leg toward the hem of her gown. Closing her eyes against the shouting soldiers, against the thundering whale and its foul stink, she pulled strength from the glowing gem in the sword. She could feel its connection to the mighty Heartstone high atop the Hall of Windows.

The earth jumped, and a boom split the air. Ossamyr jerked her head to the side. With a dozen spears buried deep in its hide, the whale had thrown itself against Ohndarien's wall.

Soldiers shouted from the battlements. Rocks hailed down on the thing, tearing chunks from its ravaged flesh, but it didn't seem to notice. It drew its massive tail back and slammed it against the wall once more. The world shook, and a crack appeared between the massive stones.

I know you. A throaty voice spoke in her head. *We've danced before.*

The seductive voice curled around her like a lover. The sound of it caressed her skin, making her feel warm and powerful. Ossamyr laughed, feeling stronger and stronger by the moment. She looked back to her wound and realized she'd dropped the sword. She reached for it, but it burned her, and she yanked her hand back.

Remember what we did together? You've never felt so good. You've never felt so free.

An image of Brophy's sleeping body flashed in her mind, and she clung to it.

"No!" she whispered, pushing the voice away, but it was like fighting the ocean, trying to push back the water with your hands. She fumbled for the sword, nearly screaming as it seared her hand. Gritting her teeth, she placed the gem back on her wounds.

You don't need that. Together we have all the power you'll ever need. Together we can wake Brophy. He could be in your arms tonight. Yours, all yours.

No. She whimpered.

Yes . . .

A harsh white light flared in the distance, and she shielded her eyes. A lithe form clothed in gossamer silks flew past her, bearing a burning sword.

She has come. She will take Brophy from you. You will never get him back.

Ossamyr pulled the sword from her leg and rose to her feet.

Like a pinpoint of light in a sea of darkness, Shara stopped in front of the huge, black whale, the Sword of Winter held high above her head. The immense creature turned from the wall and bellowed at her, knocking people down with the force of its voice.

A wave of energy shot out from Shara's chest into the warriors who fought for Ohndarien.

"The head!" Shara shouted. "Attack the head."

The Sword of Winter flared, and the light enveloped the scattered Lightning Swords. Astor charged at the monstrosity, planting his spear in the creature's eye. The whale flicked its snout, and he went flying. A dozen others rushed in after him.

Ossamyr's lips pulled back away from her fangs as she shuffled forward. She raised the sword in both hands and crept behind Shara.

Yes, yes. She will take away the one you love.

Gavin and Gareth charged the whale as more defenders rushed in, pinning the beast's head against the wall. The twins grabbed ragged flesh, protruding spears, whatever they could reach and clambered up its side. No normal human could move that fast.

The beast thrashed, trying to dislodge them, but they clung stubbornly. It yanked itself free of the spearmen, but the gemsword warriors worked their way closer and closer to its huge head.

The mistress of the Zelani held the Sword of Winter high in front of her, pommel up like a ward. Gareth's and Gavin's gemswords glowed in response as they stood on the creature's neck and plunged their swords into its blubber, hacking toward the spine. The whale thrashed again, slamming its head into the wall.

Kill her, and he will be yours. He will wake, and you will have him for eternity.

A feral purr rolled out of Ossamyr's throat. She stepped silently toward her quarry, claws sliding out of the tips of her fingers—

Shara turned, shouting a command that cut straight through her. Ossamyr froze. Sweat beaded on Shara's brow, and her eyes were bare slits of concentration, but she turned a tight smile on the former Queen of Physendria.

"A moment, my friend," she whispered through clenched teeth. "I will be with you shortly."

Shara sent a surge of energy into Ossamyr, a scant diversion of the power she was funneling into the twins.

A wave of pain rushed through her, and Ossamyr dropped to the ground. Her entire body felt like it was on fire, but she could hear the Heartstone's voice again. She fumbled toward it, searching for that voice in the darkness.

The whale's howl twisted into a high-pitched keening. Wind whipped through the quarry, shrieking like a multitude of death screams. With one last mighty thrust against the wall, the whale crashed to the ground and lay still.

Shara slumped to her knees. The Sword of Winter clattered to the stone and dimmed like a guttering candle. The Heartstone's song faded.

Now is your moment. Rise. Take what is yours before she takes it from you.

Ossamyr rolled drunkenly to her feet. One quick swipe. Just one, and Shara would never rise again. She lurched forward, eyes on the back of Shara's neck.

A pronged spear hit her arm like a manacle. She snarled, turning toward her attacker, but another spear struck her from the right. They shoved her backward, off-balance, slamming her into the ground. Two more Lightning Swords pinned her legs with the prongs of the spears. She struggled, howling, but they held her with grim determination.

Faedellin approached, his gemsword gripped in one hand, glowing hatefully as it dripped with black blood.

"She's gone," someone said. "It's taken her."

Faedellin nodded resolutely, taking a deep breath. "Forgive me, Ossamyr-lani." He raised his sword.

She hissed at him.

"Stop!"

Faedellin stopped his blade in midswing. Shara staggered up to him and grabbed his forearm to keep from falling. Her long raven hair hung down on either side of her face, and she gasped for breath as if she had just run the wall.

"Shara-lani," Faedellin insisted, his sword lowered to point at Ossamyr's chest. "She is infected. It is a mercy."

"She is my friend."

"There is nothing you can do. You can barely stand."

Shara held up an abrupt hand.

He fell silent.

She turned to Ossamyr and gave a thin smile. "You're looking a little dark, sister."

Ossamyr hissed. "I'll rip your heart out, bitch. The boy is mine. He loved me first."

Shara took a deep breath. "We'll worry about that later. But not tonight, not tonight."

Shara closed her eyes and put a hand on Ossamyr's chest. Her powerful magic rushed in like a wave. Ossamyr fought back, clinging to her power, clinging to her rage.

You've done this before, Shara's voice said in her head. *You can do it again. I am here with you. I will not let the darkness have you.*

Ossamyr saw her father crying at her wedding. She felt Phandir's ribs snap beneath her fingers. She saw the look on Brophy's face as she betrayed him.

You chose love, a tiny voice whispered in the back of her mind. *Always remember that you chose love at the moment when it mattered most.*

With a cry of anguish, she let go of her power, her freedom, and Shara's magic flooded through her.

Ossamyr began to weep.

CHAPTER 4

A gentle touch pushed at Shara's shoulder. She opened her eyes and drew a long breath. Her back ached from falling asleep in the chair. A thin ray of sunlight slanted across the infirmary through the half-drawn curtains, illuminating the former Sister of Autumn. Baelandra's legendary red hair was frosted with snow. Crow's-feet bordered her lively green eyes, but those eyes still bore the same fire they had a quarter century ago.

Baelandra pressed a steaming cup of Saelen tea into Shara's hands and sat down on the edge of the bed. Shara thanked her with her eyes as she inhaled the tea's sleepy aroma. Ossamyr was sleeping peacefully on the bed next to them. The nightmares that had plagued the former queen all night seemed to have faded, at least for the moment.

Faedellin walked up behind Shara's chair, placed his hands on her shoulders, and kissed the top of her head. Bae and her husband had come a long way from the Nightmare Battle. Faedellin had once been the gracious and gregarious host at the Midnight Jewel, but that restaurant was long gone and so was that man. Baelandra had abdicated her place on the council a few months after the Nightmare Battle and married Faedellin the next day. Less than a year later, Astor was born. At first Shara thought their marriage was a foolish match, hastily made under the shadow of grief. But nearly two decades down the road, the two were still living life side by side.

Shara loved how the two of them were always together, rarely talking because they always knew what the other was thinking. She had always wanted that with someone. Someday she would have the same thing. Someday soon.

"You fell asleep," Baelandra said.

"Just a quick meditation," Shara insisted, looking over at Ossamyr. Her chest rose and fell with a slow, steady rhythm. Her skin was once again bronze and healthy, not black. Not bubbling.

"You've been up all night with her?" Baelandra asked.

Shara gave a tired smile. "Actually, I was only up half the night helping Ossamyr. The other half I was wrestling a whale."

Faedellin chuckled, but Baelandra wasn't amused.

It had been a grim night. Besides Ossamyr, the infirmary in the Palace of Summer held half a dozen people with broken ribs or dislocated shoulders from trying to pin the whale. Shara had done what she could for the wounded, infusing their bodies with the energy they would need to heal themselves.

"How's Astor doing?" she asked. Baelandra's son was in a bed on the far side of the room with a major concussion and deep gash over one eye.

"He'll be fine," she said, but Shara could see the lines of worry etched in her face.

"That blackie threw him a long way," Faedellin added, "but luckily, he landed on his head."

Baelandra frowned again and pushed the cup of tea toward Shara's mouth, forcing her to take another sip. The Saelen tea warmed her throat and belly.

"Why don't you go home?" Baelandra asked. "I'll take over here. You need sleep just like anyone."

"We both know that's not true," Shara said. "I want to wait until Ossamyr wakes up." She turned toward the blade lying on the small table next to her. The pommel stone of the Sword of Winter swirled with inky tendrils. "And then there are a few things I need to take care of first."

"You push yourself too hard," Baelandra insisted.

Shara looked at her again, and Baelandra finally let the matter drop.

"How is Ossamyr?" Baelandra asked.

Shara stood, taking pains to make the movement seem graceful and effortless, as though she'd slept the entire night. She touched two fingers to Ossamyr's temple. "She's resting quietly now, but she'll wake soon."

"Good," Baelandra murmured. "Gavin said Ossamyr was nearly lost. She tried to kill you."

"The black emmeria tried to kill me," Shara corrected her. Again, she felt a chill at the speed with which the tainted ani was evolving. It was constantly working to unravel the spell she'd cast around Brophy. It wanted to escape, wanted it more than any mortal could want something. Shara wasn't sure how much longer she could hold it.

Last night had shaken her to the core. She had never seen a corrupted creature of that size. The swath of corruption in the Vastness that started when Copi's music box broke must have already grown beyond the shore. Shara had always been convinced that they could cleanse it someday. Now she had her doubts. The corrupted were becoming more ferocious, more co-ordinated, with every attack. They needed a permanent solution. Needed it fast.

Baelandra was silent a long moment. She reached out a hand, and Shara gave her the cup of tea. "Get some rest, please. Do it just to shut me up, if need be."

Shara smiled. "I'd be happy to, if it would work, but it never does."

Baelandra gave her a sad smile that turned into a little frown as Faedellin led her to Astor's bed on the far side of the room.

Shara heard a slight mummer and turned back to Ossamyr. Her eyes fluttered open, and she reached out, groping for something. Shara forced a cup of water into her hand and helped her drink.

Ossamyr barely took a sip before pushing it away. "Wine," she croaked. "I took your wine ..."

"No, water," Shara insisted, giving her another drink.

"No ... You need the message ... I'm so sorry ..."

Shara gave her a little nudge with her magic, and Ossamyr's eyes fluttered closed. A few moments later her breathing was rhythmic and steady once again.

With a sigh, Shara picked up the Sword of Winter and headed for the Hall of Windows.

❄

Shara took deep breaths as she made the long climb up the staircase that led to the top of the Hall of Windows. Two perpendicular arches of blue-white marble were the only supports for the vast amphitheater. The rest of the dome was a vast latticework of copper and stained glass that shimmered in the morning sun. She walked toward the rising sun that burnished the clouds yellow and orange. The growing light sparkled across the shifting waters of the bay. Clouds darkened the sky to the east, and the air smelled like rain. A storm was coming and, by the looks of it, it was going to be fierce. Shara cast a quick prayer of thanks to the Seasons that Ossamyr was slumbering in her bed. She wouldn't be riding this storm into the teeth of the Silver Islanders. Her crusade would have to wait.

The stairs grew less and less steep as she neared the apex, and soon she could see the smoke from the torch burning atop Brophy's gazebo. The top of the Hall of Windows had been re-created following Brophy's sacrifice. Loving artisans had expanded the small platform, which once held four torches burning in constant vigil for the four Lost Brothers. Those torches were long gone, faded into history like the four men who had never come home to see them. The pinnacle of the stained-glass dome now held an elegant gazebo for a different kind of Lost Brother.

As Shara drew closer, she could hear two young Zelani singing. Their voices rose together in the wordless melody that held Brophy in his endless slumber. Those same haunting notes had once come from the silver music box that kept the Child of Efften locked in her eternal slumber. Singing for Brophy was part of a Zelani student's training, and the best and brightest competed for the honor. Every few hours, when their voices grew tired, two more would climb the staircase to take their places. The tune continued unbroken, day bleeding into night, night into day.

Shara felt her fatigue, but also the undercurrent of exhilaration at another battle won. Their vigil over Brophy hadn't faltered, not yet.

After that horrible night when Shara barely saved Brophy from a corrupted nightcat, a silver gazebo had been built around Brophy's bier. At first glance the gazebo appeared to be decorative, but it was the also an enchanted cage that kept Brophy safe from the corrupted. Shara and the silversmiths had incorporated the Heartstone into the structure, using her power to keep Brophy safe and repel anyone or anything with the faintest hint of black emmeria.

The gazebo's poles curved upward at each of its six corners, and the walls between were a filigree of molded brass that twisted like vines, forming pictures. Scythe stood in one, sword raised to ward off the corrupted. Baelandra knelt in another, hands clutching the Heartstone just before she placed it upon Brophy's chest. The third and the sixth were arched, locked doors. The fourth wall showed Mother Medew, the silent Ohohhim sword matron, cradling the Child of Efften against her chest. The last depicted Shara, long hair twining behind her, Brophy's head cradled in her lap. She seemed to look out at the viewer and inward at Brophy at the same time.

Closing her eyes, she took a deep breath of the fresh sea air that blew in from the west. Despite her assurances to Baelandra, Shara was painfully tired. She didn't want to linger this time; she would transfer the corruption into Brophy's dream and head straight back to the school.

As she drew closer, a solid young woman with blond hair and a round face peered down the steps toward her. Shara didn't know the girl personally, but the blue and gold tunic made it obvious who she was. Just like the two Zelani who sang the song, four Lightning Swords always guarded the platform as a last line of defense against any threat that slipped past the walls. One of the defenders always held the Sword of Autumn. It never left Brophy's side, just in case.

Shara nodded to Brophy's guardians as she reached the top of the hall. They nodded respectfully and stepped aside to let her pass. Shara's heart caught in her throat when she saw Brophy lying on his bier. It always did.

She walked up to the gazebo and placed her hands against the delicate silver bars. Brophy was dressed in a sleeveless coat of red and gold over a milk-white silk shirt. His curly blond hair shimmered in the sun, shifting as the light breeze played with it. His closed eyelids haunted her. She still remembered those green eyes, intense, quick to shine, quick to mirror the laughter in his face. But that light was lost, hidden beneath darting eyelids.

The four Lightning Swords patrolling outside the cage and the two Zelani singing inside it tried not to stare as she hovered just outside the gazebo door. Shara had grown used to never being alone with Brophy outside the dream. Just as she had grown accustomed to the compassionate pity in everyone's eyes.

How many hours had she lingered by his side, watching him sleep, holding his hand, telling him things he couldn't hear? Like a moth to a flame, she seemed drawn to the pain of his presence.

Despite the tumble of years since Brophy's sacrifice, Shara couldn't help feeling that time had stopped in Ohndarien. The whole world seemed frozen, unable to move forward until Brophy returned to them. It was like a brief and glorious autumn had passed her by, and she was trapped in an endless winter.

Shara chuckled and shook her head, banishing the too-familiar melancholy thoughts. Fortunately, the irony had never been lost on her, and she could still laugh at herself. The teenaged girl who burned to be free of any father, husband, or cruel-eyed Zelani master had ended up searching half her life for the one man who could make her whole. Despite all this time she still loved him, still longed for his touch more than anything she had ever known.

*

"Shara-lani?"

Shara blinked twice and turned as Galliana ran up the last few steps of the staircase. Shara must have fallen asleep on her feet. She had no idea how long she had been standing there, but she woke when she felt the girl's presence on the steps behind her.

The young woman's black-and-silver gown rippled in the breeze, revealing the length of her young legs. Her platinum blond hair blew back away from her face in the light breeze that presaged the coming storm. The girl's eyes were dark and intense, easy to mistake for black at a distance. In truth, they were a deep, rich blue.

"Yes, Galliana?"

Shara tried not to have favorites among her students, but her niece always filled her with a special pride. The poor girl fled her home in Faradan after her father beat Shara's sister to death. She made the perilous journey to Ohndarien all on her own. It was a desperate undertaking for a ten-year-old, but Galliana was an extraordinary young woman, easily the best student of her class.

"I am sorry to bother you, but Issefyn sent me with news," Galliana said.

"What news?" She looked to the Quarry Wall. Another attack? The bells had not rung.

"Captain Ghafta's ship has returned from the Southwyldes."

For a moment, Shara didn't understand what Galliana was saying, then it rushed in like a hurricane wind.

"The crystal?"

"Yes."

Shara's chest swelled, and her hands clenched into fists.

"Mistress Issefyn is speaking with the trader captain now," Galliana said. "She promised to meet us at the base of the Wheel."

Excitement thrilled through Shara. She looked down at the swirling black emmeria in the sword's pommel stone. Suddenly, she had another, more important use for it.

She stole a quick glance at Brophy and couldn't help grinning. *Soon, my love,* she thought, *soon,* and began running down the stairs.

Galliana hurried to catch up with her, and the women's slippered feet padded down the steep marble stairs side by side. A stumble at this height would surely mean death, but joy lent wings to Shara's feet. She ached to run, but held herself back for Galliana's sake.

The girl matched her pace down the stairs, and the two of them headed across the Wheel. They rushed through the verdant gardens splashed with the morning light.

They wound their way around the plateau's torturously long spiral staircase down toward the quiescent Night Market. Along the way, they passed a group of sailors from Kherif wearing shabby sheepskin vests. The reeling sailors must have been kicked out of the taverns at dawn and decided to explore the city.

The two women rushed past them, and Shara couldn't help noticing how the men's gazes fixed on Galliana. Shara couldn't blame them, the girl was radiant, but it still stung a little.

Shara was still an alluring woman. She still turned her fair share of heads, but they didn't stare like they used to. Every now and then she missed flaunting that thing that Galliana didn't even know she had.

Shara could have kept herself young, could have stayed that nineteen-year-old woman who first held Brophy in her arms. It was an advanced spell, but well within Shara's power. But no matter the years that passed, she would never forget the Wet Cells when Brophy had pulled her back from the edge of self-destruction.

That was the first time she'd truly felt the strength of the black emmeria. That voice was always with her now, always beckoning. One easy step, and she could slip down that slope so quickly she would never know it was happening.

It no longer mattered, though. All of her waiting could end tonight. Her mind raced ahead to the enchantment she would craft. Was everything in place? What could possibly cause a delay?

As they reached the bottom of the steps, Shara spotted Issefyn waiting for them. The older woman's dark hair curled in ringlets to her shoulders. She turned her gentle brown gaze upon Shara. The two of them grasped hands, and Shara went up on tiptoes to kiss her friend on both cheeks. Issefyn was one of the tallest women Shara had ever met, and her stately bearing made her seem more like a queen than a humble teacher.

"Dignity, child," Issefyn chided her. "A Zelani does not rush in the bedroom . . . or out of it."

Shara laughed at the words she had spoken countless times to red-faced children caught running in the halls of the Zelani school.

"Bugger my dignity," Shara replied, and Galliana raised her eyebrows. "Have you seen it? Will it work?"

Issefyn nodded. "It is the finest stone we have ever seen. It is everything the merchant promised it would be."

"Where is it?"

"I have asked the Steward of the Long Market to escort the crate to the school. It will arrive there before we do."

Shara clenched her teeth before nodding. That made sense. Of course it made sense. Issefyn was always so practical about these matters. Shara would never have been able to run the school without her.

Issefyn's arrival in Ohndarien six years ago had been an unforeseen blessing. She had grown up on a merchant galley, a direct descendant of mages who escaped the destruction of Efften. Issefyn herself was not a great sorceress. Ninety percent of Shara's students had more raw talent. The woman simply could not hold a powerful concentration of ani within her body, but that did not stop her from being an excellent teacher. Her knowledge and perceptiveness were unparalleled. She arrived in Ohndarien knowing the broad strokes of all ten of the lost arts of Efften. Over the years, she had taught Shara everything she knew about creating and manipulating ani, and now they worked side by side to expand that knowledge. It had been Issefyn who had taught her the term "ani," the word the mages of Efften used for the essence of emotion and spirit they molded with their ten schools of magic.

Issefyn had also been the genesis of Shara and Ossamyr's quest to find or create a second Heartstone. The mages of ancient Efften had used ani-imbued containment stones to store black emmeria, the vile refuse born of their selfish and hateful magic. Issefyn believed there were still stones hidden in the ruins of the shattered empire.

Before Shara began experimenting with her own containment stones, she and Ossamyr had nearly lost their lives trying to sneak past the fanatical Silver Islanders who guarded Efften.

Their attempts had failed miserably. The tattooed pirates were always waiting, guarding the destroyed empire as though it were the gate to hell. On their last attempt, Shara and Ossamyr had brought a full crew of senior Zelani, determined to use their collective magic to slip past the fanatics. But before they even caught sight of the mythical island, the steel prow of an Islander warship had appeared out of the darkness and rammed their vessel to splinters. Half of Shara's crew died in the attack, and most of the others succumbed to thirst and exposure after drifting on the wreckage for days before finally washing ashore on a tiny island off the coast of Vizar. Laren had died in Shara's arms within sight of shore.

Shara had vowed never to take that path again and turned her attention to making her own containment stones, but Ossamyr refused to give up on reaching the shores of Efften.

"Galliana, dear," Issefyn said, turning from Shara to the girl standing by her side. "Would you hurry ahead and inform Caleb-lani that the stone has arrived and to begin making preparations for its arrival?"

Shara bit her lip. With Ossamyr injured, she would have to rely on Caleb to be her second in the upcoming spell. Shara had complete trust in Caleb; he certainly had the magical ability. But she wasn't sure if he had the backbone to do what needed to be done if Shara should fail. It was always something that had to be considered.

"Of course," Galliana replied with a slight curtsy, and hurried ahead.

Shara and Issefyn continued east through the Night Market.

"What's wrong?" Shara finally asked. "Why did you send her away?"

"I didn't want to discuss finances in front of a student."

Shara nodded, bracing for the bad news. "How much did he want?"

"Seven thousand."

Shara clenched her teeth. "Seven thousand? Is he mad?"

Issefyn shook her head. "The man said he had a buyer in the Opal Empire who would pay him seven thousand five hundred for a flawless crystal of that size. But due to his great respect for the legendary Zelani of the Free City, he would go as low as—"

"Right, right, right. What did you tell him?"

"I told him yes."

"What? How?"

"I looked into the man's eyes. He spoke the truth. He had another buyer. We had no choice but to pay his price."

Shara grimaced. Issefyn would never pass the Fifth Gate and become a full Zelani, but she could certainly spot a liar.

"Where did you get the rest of the money?"

Issefyn turned to her, then shrugged. "Baelandra."

Shara closed her eyes. She should have known.

"I invited her to come with me," Issefyn explained. "I suspected we would not have enough."

"But she's given us so much already, gold for half my failed experiments, Ossamyr's new ship, the buyers she's sent all over the world looking for relics of Efften, anything that might help."

Issefyn nodded again. That was all the emotion Shara could expect to see from her.

"Where does she get the money?" Shara asked.

"She's borrowing heavily. She has been for years."

"But we can pay her back, if this one works, if this is the last time?"

Issefyn shook her head. "Even if we cancel the planned expansion of the school, it would be fifteen to twenty years before we could pay her back."

Shara sighed.

"We still receive offers for assignments with recently graduated students."

"No," Shara insisted. "I won't run my school like its former master. My students will always choose their own assignments. The ten percent they send back to us is payment enough."

"But so many choose assignments that don't pay."

"That is their choice and always will be."

"Of course."

With nothing left to say, the two of them wended their way through the Night Market. There were still plenty of taverns and restaurants, but the place had simply never been the same since the Nightmare Battle. They left the empty market and crossed Donovan's Bridge before trekking up the hill to the Zelani school.

Ossamyr met them at the rose-colored marble gates of the school. Shara sighed at the sight of her, twin floods of relief and guilt mixing in her belly. Ossamyr had bathed, changed, and wrapped her calf in fresh bandages. She looked refreshed and ready, but no one recovered from the black emmeria that quickly.

The former queen was twenty years Shara's senior, but looked like her younger sister thanks to her Zelani magic. She looked younger now than she did when Shara first met her eighteen years ago. Ossamyr's sun-browned arms made a striking contrast to her white Zelani gown, belted with gold at the waist and slit high up the sides of her thighs. She had never adopted the calm radiance of a Zelani and always looked like a woman about to rush into battle, every inch the Physendrian queen she had once been.

"What are you doing out of bed?" Shara asked.

"I made a promise. I intend to keep it."

Ossamyr had agreed to stay and make one last attempt at creating a containment stone if Shara's crystal arrived before the first storm of the season. From the look of the black clouds rolling in from the east, the gem had barely arrived in time.

"You aren't strong enough for this," Shara insisted. "You should be resting."

"So should you." Ossamyr's green eyes flashed.

Shara said nothing, and Ossamyr did not move from the doorway. Issefyn waited patiently, seemingly oblivious to the tension in the air.

"Caleb has prepared your chambers," Ossamyr finally broke the silence.

"And he should be the one—"

"No." Ossamyr held up her hand for silence. "We both know what Caleb can and can't do. And this is something he can't do."

Shara could still see Ossamyr pinned to the quarry floor, howling in rage, her blackened flesh bubbling like boiling pitch. The woman was hanging by a thread, but for this job, Shara still trusted Ossamyr at her worst more than Caleb at his best.

"Fine, enough," Shara said, moving past her. "Prepare yourself. We will start tonight."

They passed into the center of the school. More than a dozen Zelani students waited under the eaves that bordered three sides of the open courtyard. News traveled fast. Everyone knew what was about to happen. Shara felt a slight pang of regret seeing all of the eager faces.

Careful to maintain her dignity around students, Shara gave them a smile and a nod before moving through the foyer and up the steps to her chambers.

Shara's and Ossamyr's feet touched the same steps at the same time as they rose together. They had climbed these steps so many times that they moved with the same rhythm. "How is the boy?" Ossamyr asked on the way up.

Ossamyr called Brophy "the boy." She loved him as much as Shara. She had carried and lost his child, and she still called him "the boy."

"The same as always," Shara said. "But if all goes well, you can ask him yourself in a few days."

Ossamyr snorted with her usual die-hard pessimism. She couldn't have survived the last eighteen years without some hope locked somewhere deep inside, but you would never know it to talk to her.

The former queen refused to climb the Hall of Windows to visit Brophy. She hadn't been up there since the very first time. It was too painful for her. She'd dedicated her entire life to waking him, but she couldn't look him in the face.

They reached Shara's room together and found a crate the length of her arm lying open in the center of the room. It was packed with dried moss, and a depression in the center showed where the huge crystal had rested just a moment ago. Caleb must have already taken the stone to her workroom at the top of the tower.

Shara took a quick look around her bedroom to make sure he hadn't forgotten anything. To her left, her shelves were piled with stacks of books, some thin, some thick, all old. A stained quill lay on her latest page of notes next to an open bottle of ink. A Floani scarf and staff leaned against the tallest stack of books. Pots and jars containing the psychotropics used in the Balani form were clustered on the floor. A silver dish packed with sand and the stubs of Pinani incense lay next to them. These were the trappings of Shara's life.

Some people gathered pleasant memories. Some collected seashells. Some built a family. She collected bits of lost power, hints of secrets burned in Efften centuries ago.

Forcing herself to go slow, Shara climbed the ladder to the open trapdoor in the ceiling, to her tiny workspace above.

Caleb met her at the top, offering his hand to help her up the rest of the way. He was already naked in preparation for the spell. His body was lean and hard, his smile gentle.

Everything had been laid out. The floor had been cleared, all the furniture and rugs moved away. The rat sniffed the air from its cage, and a silver dagger lay sheathed beside it. The tall, thin stand stood at the center of the room with a glimmering crystal resting between its three prongs.

Shara hurried over and touched it with trembling fingers. Caleb held his lamp closer so she could get a better look. The shifting light projected shimmering rainbows onto Shara's hand. There were dozens more drifting across her body, across Caleb's tan skin, on the floor, the ceiling, and walls.

The merchant had not lied. The gem was huge, easily the size of both of Shara's fists. It was the largest she had ever seen, save the Heartstone herself. On the day of the Nightmare Battle, Ohndarien's Heartstone had been nearly large enough to contain all of the black emmeria released from the baby. Nearly, but not quite. So Brophy had sacrificed himself to make up the difference, taking everything the Heartstone could contain and more into himself, draining the legendary diamond until it was clear again, swirling with vibrant rainbow colors. It had been Shara's dream from the beginning to make up that difference somehow, so the Heartstone could finish the job it was created for, containing the black emmeria forever.

At first Shara had tried to destroy the excess, but that was like trying to destroy the ocean by drinking it. Later, when Issefyn arrived, her hopes had shifted to building a second Heartstone, a smaller, lesser stone, to finish the job the Heartstone could not complete alone. Six times she tried. Six times she had failed. But she knew so much more now than she did then. And she had never had a flawless gem like this to work with. As perfect as love, as they said in the Summer Cities. As perfect as she must be this night if she wanted to see Brophy open his eyes again.

Shara looked up as Caleb placed his hand on her shoulder. She returned his smile and turned to Ossamyr.

"Go, you two," Shara told them. "Get some rest. I'll send Issefyn to wake you a few hours before I need you. Then go do what you do best. Love well. Love true. Fill your hearts. Fill your bodies, and bring me every mote of ani a human body can contain. We'll need it. We'll need it all."

She picked up the silver dagger, drew it slowly. "We'll start as soon as you are ready."

CHAPTER 5

Shara held her hand over the Sword of Winter's pommel. She could feel the ravenous power locked within. Intangible fingers of emmeria strained against the edges of their prison, reaching for her, desperate to ride her flesh to freedom.

Shara knelt before the newly constructed containment stone. She could hear Ossamyr's steady breathing behind her, giving her strength. An alabaster bowl rested between Shara's knees, and the unsheathed Sword of Winter lay across her naked thighs, its blade shimmering in the candlelight.

Her long black hair was bound back tightly, and she wore only the belt of her office. The big blue stone glowed softly against her hip, grounding her. The facets of the giant crystal twinkled in the faint light.

A fierce wind whistled through the city just outside the slender tower, strangely akin to the tortured voices that howled inside the pommel stone. Distant thunder rumbled through the walls of the windowless room. The storm Ossamyr had been waiting for had finally arrived. But she wouldn't need it. Not this time.

Shara had worked all through the day to imbue the crystal. The dream space within was vast, almost incomprehensible. It could hold all the power of every spell Shara had ever cast, could hold them all a hundred times over, a thousand times over. It was her masterpiece.

It would hold. It must hold.

Shara's gaze strayed to the small cage at the very edge of the candlelight. A rat scurried about in its tiny prison, desperately looking for a way out. It could sense the black emmeria emerging.

Shara closed her eyes and focused again on the sword. *Do not think about the rat. We will not need it.*

Shara took a deep breath, accepting the waves of fear that washed over her, making them part of herself. Visions of the night in the Wet Cells flashed through her mind. She heard her laughter as Victeris crawled naked through his own filth before her. She had felt so powerful in those moments, so oblivious to what she was doing. She didn't want to walk that path ever again. Without Brophy at her side, she would never be sure she could say no a second time.

The black emmeria swirled through the pommel stone. It felt as if it were already crawling through her belly. Shara didn't want to do this. Absorbing the black emmeria was like pushing a dagger into her own eye. Every part of her screamed to run, hide, find an easier way.

"It's time," Ossamyr said, placing a light hand on Shara's shoulder. She nodded, took a deep breath, and let go.

She went slowly at first, letting the corruption leak from the gem into the palm of her hand. Her skin started to tingle, and fiery pains shot up her arm. A whirlwind of hateful voices blew through her body, threatening to overwhelm her thoughts.

A single purring voice rose over the cacophony of the others. *Hello, my love, I've missed you.* Shara knew that voice, knew it well. She had never responded to it and never would.

Concentrating on the black emmeria crawling into her skin, she kept her hand on the sword, absorbing the putrid ani until the pommel was clear and bright again.

Where is the radiant woman I once embraced? You have withered in my absence, a shadow of your true self, and all for the sake of another?

Shara's forearm roiled and bubbled as inky stains rose to the surface of her skin and submerged again. The black emmeria worked its way through her body, desperate to puncture the thin veil of her willpower and consume her.

Ossamyr reached over her shoulder and grasped the Sword of Winter. Taking it in both hands, she raised it, ready to end everything if the need should arise. Shara was suddenly very glad that it was Ossamyr standing behind her and Caleb waiting one story below.

This is not who you are. You were meant for so much more.

With Ossamyr's help, Shara kept the surging blackness confined within her arm. The polluted ani writhed and twisted, threatening to rip her flesh from her bones. She focused on Ossamyr's steady breathing, leaning on her friend for strength.

You never used to be afraid of yourself, afraid of who you could become.

Shara fought for control, her stomach lurched, and she nearly vomited on the floor. The retch doubled her over, and she swallowed back searing bile, breathing hard.

"I'm all right," Shara assured her friend, and she could sense Ossamyr's grip on the sword relax.

Ossamyr and Caleb had spent hours making love while Shara prepared the crystal, and the heat still radiated from Ossamyr's body. She held the sexual energy like a contained inferno, an inferno that Shara could tap at a moment's notice.

You are a shadow of what you once were, a withered husk fleeing from your beauty.

Shara carefully reached to her side and picked up the small silver dagger. She drew the blade and placed it against her boiling skin. Her arms burned as if a swarm of bees fought beneath the surface, trying to sting their way out. Her hands started to shake.

How long has it been since you've been touched? How long has it been since you let go?

With a quick stroke, Shara sliced deep. The black emmeria erupted from the wound, and she cried out at the pain, cycling it back into her spell. The raging voices of the black emmeria roared into the room. Her vision swam, but she managed to direct the flow of blood into the bowl between her knees. Globs of black liquid splattered into the basin. The fluid undulated up the smooth sides of the container, trying to escape.

Shara had learned long ago that blood could be used to stabilize the black emmeria. The corruption latched on to the living tissue, but could not grow to horrific proportions without a living mind and soul to bend to its will.

This is not what you want. Let go of this prison. Let go.

Shara gritted her teeth and forced the Emmeria out of her body. The corruption resisted, but with Ossamyr's help they forced it into the bowl until her skin stopped bubbling, and the wound ran clean and red. With one last plaintive whisper, the voice faded away.

Shara reached for the bandage on the floor next to her and quickly bound her wound. Blood soaked the white linen, but she would deal with that later. When the bandage was secure, Shara took a shuddering breath and prepared herself for the most difficult part.

"Are you ready?" she asked Ossamyr.

Ossamyr squeezed her shoulder in reply, sending a steady stream of energy into her body. Shara closed her eyes and kept breathing, accepting everything her friend had to give.

With her head swimming, she reached out and grabbed the containment stone from its pedestal. Solid. Smooth. Flawless. Holding it over the porcelain bowl, she pulled the black emmeria up into the stone. Black filaments rose from the pool of roiling blood to the bottom of the crystal. As soon as they touched, the filaments passed into the crystal, spreading out like ink.

Shara kept pulling and pulling, forcing the malignancy into its cage. Her breathing grew heavy and ragged, breath hissing through her teeth. Behind her, Ossamyr grunted with the strain, giving all she had and more.

Shara finally gasped as the last of it was sucked from the bowl into the stone. Letting out a single sob, she set it back on the tripod and slumped forward.

The black cloud swirled inside the crystal, looking for a way out. Shara wanted to hold her breath, but forced it to stay steady and even as she watched.

"Yes," she murmured, sitting back up again. Her heart beat faster, daring to believe. Ossamyr slumped next to her and grabbed her hand.

It held. They had done it. They had finally found the right—

The crystal exploded.

Shards of sharp rock peppered Shara's skin like a thousand needles. It threw her backward, and she slammed into Ossamyr. They slid across the floor and crashed into the wall.

The voice returned.

You cannot contain me. I will not be held back from my prize.

Shara pushed the voice out of her mind. Her body was a terrible weight, a huge boulder she couldn't move.

Get up, get up . . . she thought.

With a weak cry, she struggled to roll over onto her stomach, pushed herself to her hands and knees. Her braid drooped limp across her face. She tried to draw a breath, but it ended in a sob.

The walls and ceiling on the opposite side of the room were splattered with tiny droplets of the blackened blood. Somehow Ossamyr had deflected the emmeria away from them and kept them alive.

You will be mine, my child, my sister, my bride.

The droplets of black emmeria slowly started moving toward one another, coalescing into larger and larger drops. It dripped like oil onto the blasted floor, moving together, gathering into a pool.

Panting, Shara spared a quick glance for Ossamyr. Her friend lay sprawled against the wall, her limbs splayed across on the stone like a cloth doll.

The ever-growing pool of emmeria oozed toward them, trickling around the shards of crystal as though the room were on a slant.

Shara forced her lungs to draw breath, struggled to control her thoughts.

She emptied her mind, cloaking it from the voice that ran through her thoughts like greasy fingers.

Her emotions were more difficult to shut away. Despair fought with frustration. Only her years of Nilani meditation came to her aid. With steady concentration, she purged herself, and the fire of her passion ceased to be.

Shara ... It searched for her. *I'll set you free.*

The black ooze stopped flowing toward her. It hesitated for a moment, unable to find her. Then it changed course, as though the angle of the room had shifted.

Shara looked at the rat. It scuttled back and forth in its cage, gnawing desperately at the bars. Sensing the creature's fire, the black ooze flowed toward it across the flagstones. It entered the cage, and a questing rivulet touched the rat's claw. The creature leapt away, cowering into a corner. The black liquid rushed forward, washing over the rodent and soaking into its body. The rat shrieked, gyrating frantically around the cage. Bones popped, and its skin bubbled. It shrieked again. The furry flesh surged and expanded, filling the tiny space.

"Shara! Are you all right?" Caleb shouted from below, pounding on the locked trapdoor.

"Stay away!" Shara screamed, staggering across the room, snatching up the Sword of Winter and standing between the rat and the unconscious Ossamyr.

With another shriek that deepened into a roar, the rat burst from its cage. It bubbled out to the size of a dog, then to the size of a bloody, twisted boar. Gnarled limbs curled underneath it, and its great head swung about.

Claws scraped the floor. Fangs the size of daggers poked from beneath leprous, whiskered lips. It howled again, shaking the room.

"Shara!" Caleb shouted again.

"Stay back!" Shara screamed

The corrupted rat was as big as Shara now, but she stood fearless in front of it. It crouched, preparing to pounce, and she began to sing. The magic of the Lowani flowed from her voice and took control of the creature's tiny, tortured mind. Its monstrous body shivered and bubbled as the black emmeria fought her influence. But while the emmeria was strong, its host was weak.

The corrupted rat shivered, paralyzed. Shara held the long, smooth note. The rat hissed and shook its head, fighting for its freedom. Its blackened claws dug into the stone floor, but it made no move to harm her.

Continuing to sing, Shara walked forward and slit the rat's throat with the Sword of Winter. The diamond flashed in the darkness as it tasted the corrupted blood.

The monstrous rat shivered as the blood drained from its neck, but it stayed where it was. Howls of rage rushed from the wound, whipping Shara's hair out of her eyes. She held the rat steady as the ravenous voices whipped around the room and slowly faded to anguished whispers. Finally, the rat's muscles could no longer hold it upright. The corrupted vermin slumped to the floor and died.

Shara stared at the monster until the creature's tail stopped twitching and fell limp to the floor.

With a wretched sob, she dropped the sword. It clattered across the wood, and she rushed to Ossamyr's side. Shara's fingers fumbled for a pulse on her friend's neck and found it. She gasped, slumped back against the wall, closed her eyes.

Ossamyr was alive, breathing shallowly. Shara breathed in time with her, sharing what small strength she had, but she couldn't hold the breath, she couldn't keep it up.

"Shara!" Caleb called again, searching for her with his mind. "Are you all right?"

A shuddering sob wracked her body. She wrapped her arms around her naked chest and stared numbly over her destroyed workshop, the shards of her containment stone, the ruins of her life.

CHAPTER 6

I won't let you do this," Baelandra said to Ossamyr. Thunder boomed, and the rain poured down. Clouds darkened the sky. "I won't let you throw your life away."

Ossamyr jumped to the dock and winced at the impact. "How do you plan to stop me?" she asked, grabbing a sack of apples from the wheelbarrow on the dock and tossing it aboard her waterbug.

Her wound still burned, and Shara's spell had sapped what little energy she had left. She needed a few days to rest and heal, but she needed this gale even more. She might not see another one this size until next year.

Her ears had not stopped ringing since the ritual, and her vision had been fuzzy for a full hour afterward, as Galliana served tea, and Caleb cleaned up the mess. Ossamyr tried not to think about Shara's emotionless expression as the Zelani mistress stared at the wall, her steaming cup tilted carelessly, tea scalding her bare thigh.

Baelandra stood defiantly in Ossamyr's path. "There's no shame in abandoning a hopeless task."

The Zelani laughed harshly and moved around her. "Tell that to Brophy."

"Brophy knew exactly what he was doing when he took the black emmeria into himself. Can you say the same about this voyage?"

Ossamyr threw a second bag into the little boat and jumped after it. "That boy never knew anything. That's what made him so beautiful. He had a vision in his head, and he followed it until he made it real."

"Brophy did what he had to."

"As do I."

Baelandra gave her an imperious look, the one she saved for when everything else failed.

Try your wiles elsewhere, Ossamyr thought. *You were not the only one who was raised at court.*

"You can barely stand," Baelandra said. "This is a fool's errand."

"And I am a fool. We were made for one another."

The rain pelted their faces as they stared at each other. Baelandra and Fae-dellin must have followed her all the way from the Zelani school. The leader of the Lightning Swords was a lion on the battlefield, but the second his wife showed up, he shut down and followed her around like a hound on a leash. She could sense him now, standing in the rain at a respectful distance, waiting for the women to handle the important matters.

Ossamyr turned away and did a quick recount of her provisions. They should be stowed better, but she only needed the waterbug to get her beyond the city wall. The ship she'd had specially built for this voyage was tethered just beyond the Sunset Gate. She needed to shuttle her supplies out there and pull anchor before the crest of the storm passed her by. This squall had to carry her all the way to Efften, or she'd risk being becalmed until the next gale struck.

"You've sailed this course three times before," Baelandra persisted, step-ping back into Ossamyr's line of sight. "You know where it leads. Your death might end your pain, but that's all you will accomplish."

Ossamyr let out a breath, slumped over her baggage. The rain was get-ting stronger every minute. She was losing her storm. Still, she turned to look Baelandra in the eye. "We can't defend Brophy forever," she said. "Ohndarien's walls were breached before, they will be breached again. The containment stones on Efften are our best hope to end this for all time. If we can save Bro-phy, then we can cleanse the Vastness as well."

"That is a pleasant theory," Baelandra said tartly. "But there is no reason to believe you would succeed now when you have failed so many times before."

"The Islanders would be crazy to brave a storm like this."

"On that we agree," Baelandra said pointedly.

Ossamyr ignored her and started to double-check the rigging, yanking each rain-soaked line to make sure it was secure. The desert queen had be-come a consummate sailor in the last ten years. The ironies of her life never ceased to amaze her.

"Please stay, Ossamyr," Bae said, dropping the imperious veneer that clearly wasn't working. "Brophy's sacrifice saved your life. He saved all our lives. Don't throw that gift away. Find some joy in the time he has given you."

"You mean abandon him?"

"No! Stay. Stay and help us defend him even if we can't wake him. Shara needs you. She loves you. And she can't do this alone."

Ossamyr knelt and untied the stern line, leaving a single half hitch looped over the cleat on the dock. "Shara will be fine. Shara is always fine," she said, wanting to believe it.

"No. Shara's not fine. She's hanging by a thread, and you know it. She needs you. As a friend and an anchor to her spells. She couldn't do them without you."

Again, Ossamyr laughed. "Don't you understand how far beyond me Shara is? I cannot even fathom some of the things she does." She shook her head. The heavy rain matted her dark hair against her scalp. She had always doubted that this latest spell would work, but somehow their defeat had stung far more than she'd expected. "Shara does not need me to help her fail."

"Without you, she would be dead tonight. Caleb said so."

"Caleb knows even less than I do."

"You are one of the finest Zelani in Ohndarien."

"Yes!" Ossamyr said emphatically, her eyes flashing. "Yes ... Now hear what I'm saying. Shara is beyond me like the archmages of Efften are beyond her. Me helping Shara build a containment stone is like a newborn helping a five-year-old build the Hall of Windows."

Baelandra walked up to the little boat. "You don't want to do this."

"Of course I don't want to do this. Do you think I want to go out there? Those madmen destroyed my ship! They killed my crew!"

"Are you sure you aren't going out there to let them finish the job?"

"Gods, Bae!" Ossamyr shook her head. "How can you even say that?"

"I say what I see."

"Well let me tell you what I see. I see that boy. Every moment of my life. Even when I sleep, I see him." She stabbed a finger in the direction of the Hall of Windows. "I put him up there in that gilded cage as surely as I put him in the Wet Cells. And the key to that prison is sitting on Efften. Just sitting there! The only thing standing between me and victory are those damned Silver Islanders."

Baelandra knelt and released the stern line, but kept a tight grip on the ragged hemp rope. "Brophy put himself in that cage, not you. It's not your job to save him."

Ossamyr untied the sail, letting it luff in the heavy wind. The only thing stopping her was Baelandra's hand on the mooring line. Ossamyr raised an eyebrow and looked from Bae's hand back to her face.

"What would you have me do? How would you prefer that I spend my time? Should I fuck the first waiter that comes along? Squeeze out his babies and wait for the end of the world?"

Baelandra looked quickly over her shoulder, but Faedellin was well out of earshot. Her green eyes flashed as she looked back. "Unfair, Ossamyr."

Ossamyr turned away, regretting her words. She took a deep breath, reining in her own turbulent emotions.

"I'm tying to save your life," Baelandra said.

"I know," she said in a softer tone. "You shouldn't. But I appreciate it. It's . . ." Her voice caught in her throat. She forcefully cleared it. "Thank you." She paused a long moment, then said, "Now let go of my ship."

Baelandra was silent, but did not release her hold on the mooring line. The rain poured down her face, and she licked it off her lips. Finally, she set her jaw and spoke, her words muted by the storm. "Even if you succeed, do you think it will get you what you want?"

Ossamyr did not reply.

"Imagine these winds carry you all the way to Efften, and you slip past the Silver Islanders in the storm. And let us believe that Issefyn was right, and the containment stones are actually there. And let us further imagine that you somehow return with them, what then? What will you have when he wakes? A friend?"

Ossamyr swallowed hard. The boom bounced against her leg in the heavy wind.

"Will he be grateful to you?" Baelandra continued. "The last time he saw you, you betrayed him. You lied to his face and led him to the slaughter. You sacrificed him to save yourself. That may have been eighteen years ago to you, but it was yesterday to him."

Ossamyr pressed her lips together, fighting the surge of despair in her chest.

"It was Shara who found him in the Wet Cells, Shara who saved him. And it was to Shara that he gave his heart."

"Yes," Ossamyr said slowly. "I won't deny him anything. Brophy is free to follow his heart." She leaned forward, bringing her face within inches of Baelandra's. "And I am free to follow mine. Now let go of my ship before I rip your eyes out."

The two women stared at each other as lightning slashed across the sky. Ossamyr's hand clenched into a fist, and she swallowed back the nausea rolling in her belly. But she stopped, looking past Baelandra.

A cloaked apparition appeared through the driving rain, and Ossamyr's hand dropped to her side. Baelandra turned to see what Ossamyr was looking at and stepped back.

Ossamyr let out a breath through clenched teeth as Shara walked up and gently took the mooring line from Baelandra's hands. Ossamyr wondered if

Baelandra had maneuvered her after all. Was the point only to stall until Shara arrived?

The former Sister of Autumn backed away, fading behind the curtain of rain.

"Leaving without me?" Shara asked softly. The wrinkles around her eyes were tight as she fought to keep herself on her feet. Anyone else would have seen a beautiful woman, soaked by the rain. But Ossamyr saw the strain that it took for Shara to stay upright.

"You wouldn't come if I asked," Ossamyr said.

Shara shook her head. "No, and you know why."

Ossamyr looked away. The rain dripped from her cheeks and nose. *Beware the former queen of Physendria.* The words echoed through her mind. *The boy is mine. He loved me first.*

Ossamyr would have killed Shara that night in the quarry. If they hadn't stopped her, she would have stabbed her best friend in the back. She wanted to tell Shara about the wine, about the note. She wanted to scream that it was all a lie.

She looked back at Shara, opened her mouth to speak, but the words wouldn't come. And Ossamyr knew she couldn't stay any more, she had to go. It was best for everyone.

"Why did you come here," she whispered.

"For this."

Shara leapt from the dock to the waterbug and threw her arms around Ossamyr. A whimper escaped from her throat, and she returned the embrace fiercely, letting it linger as they both shivered in the rain.

"Go," Shara finally whispered. "Ride this storm of storms and bring back his salvation."

Ossamyr looked north, toward the Hall of Windows. She couldn't see Brophy's flame through the squall. But she knew it was there, sheltered under a storm shield, burning on, ever on.

Shara held tight for another long moment. When she let go and stepped back, she was smiling. Hopping off the boat, Shara untied the bowline and tossed it to her.

Even without a sail up, the wind caught the little craft and pulled it away from the dock. Ossamyr raised a few yards of the main sheet, and the water-bug lurched forward over the waves. She looked behind her and watched until Shara slowly disappeared into the rain.

It was best for everyone.

CHAPTER 7

You've sent her to her death," Baelandra said, walking up beside Shara as the waterbug's white sail faded into the darkness.

"Perhaps," Shara murmured, barely hearing her own voice over the patter of the rain. "But I didn't set her on that path, I simply knew that I couldn't keep her from it."

Baelandra turned to look at her. The dim light and rain-soaked hair made her look older than Shara had ever seen her before. "How can you condone such a pointless waste of life?"

"I don't condone it, but I understand it."

"Then explain it to me. How can her death solve anything? You don't actually think she can return with another Heartstone?"

"She's not looking for a Heartstone. She's looking for forgiveness."

Baelandra opened her mouth to disagree, but the words never came.

Shara reached over and took her friend's hand. "Sometimes we have to seek out horrendous pain to save our souls."

"Is that what you are doing then?" she asked. "Killing yourself to make these stones?"

Shara turned away and stared into the falling rain, but she didn't answer.

"I'm sorry," Baelandra finally said. "You didn't deserve that."

Shara squeezed her hand.

"I went to the Zelani school when you were casting," Baelandra continued. "I saw Caleb cleaning up. Do you know what went wrong?"

Shara shook her head. Her throat was tight when she tried to speak. She swallowed hard, then said quietly, "No. It should have worked."

She closed her eyes and opened them again, fighting to breathe. Did Brophy lose hope when he looked into his future at that last moment atop the Hall of Windows?

He had such love in his eyes that moment before he shut them forever. How could he love so much in the face of such despair?

How could she do any less?

"You take too many risks," Baelandra said, standing on her tiptoes and kissing Shara on the cheek. "The emmeria is dangerous. How many times can you dive into those waters and not drown?"

Shara pulled back and offered her a weak smile. "You never drown until you stop swimming."

Baelandra's green eyes flashed, and her voice was thick with emotion.

"Listen to me, Shara. I've never said this before, but it's something you need to hear. You are like one of my own. My sister. My daughter. I long to see you and Brophy reunited, but you need to accept that it may never happen. You and Ossamyr have given up your entire lives waiting for him to return."

"Baelandra, please, not now."

"Shall I wait until you are ripped apart by a corrupted of your own making, wait until you are overwhelmed yourself?" Baelandra shook her head. "No, you will listen to me now. Now may be the only time I have. I wasted too much of my life waiting for Krellis to *wake up*, waiting for him to become the man I thought he should be. Life is too precious. Seize joy whenever you can. Life is for living."

Shara closed her eyes, waited for the weight of the wasted years to rise and fall within her chest. "I know, Bae, but I'm not you. And Brophy is not Krellis. I do not seek to change his nature. I seek to unlock his prison. I have the power to do it."

"Shara, child, no matter how powerful we are, some things are just beyond us." She touched Shara's cheek. "We all live in the shadow of Brophy's sacrifice. Every one of us owes him our lives, but that was a gift he chose to give. Not a debt he expected to be repaid."

Shara shook her head, and Baelandra drew her into an embrace. "You are not alone. This entire city has pledged to share your burden."

Shara pushed her away. "I know. But it's not just a matter of holding the wall against the corrupted. The bonds of my spell are weakening, and that foul voice within the emmeria is getting stronger, smarter, more determined."

"What do you mean? You said you weren't worried about that voice, that Brophy was safe."

"I wasn't worried then. I am worried now."

Baelandra's eyes tightened. "How worried?"

"Very worried."

"Why didn't you tell me this before?"

Shara gave her a sad smile. "You seemed so happy."

Baelandra bit her bottom lip as it began to quiver. She pulled Shara into a fierce hug. "You do too much, child. You do too much. You are not alone."

A single sob escaped from Shara's throat as she returned the tiny woman's embrace. "I miss him, Bae. I miss him so much."

"I know you do. We all do."

They stood like that for a long time until Faedellin walked up and kissed them both on them top of the head. "Let's get out of this rain," he said in his deep voice.

Shara broke the embrace and backed up. Faedellin shrugged off his fur-lined, leather cloak and set it over her shoulders. Shara pulled it tight around herself, grateful for the warmth.

"I'm all right," Shara assured them. "You can go. I'll be fine."

"Don't go back to the school," Baelandra begged her. "Come and spend a few days with us."

"I'll make mussels in cream sauce," Faedellin assured her. "And I just bottled a new batch of plum wine. It's not too bad if you mix it with enough fruit juice."

"That sounds wonderful. I'd love to see you and the kids again, but I need a few days alone first."

Baelandra started to say something, but Faedellin put his hand on her back and began to lead her away. He looked back at Shara and offered a sad smile. Shara smiled in return.

She watched the two of them hurry away, then turned back to stare at the rain. The golden feather Brophy had given her a lifetime ago sat tight in the sheath of a silver comb in her sodden hair. She touched it, closing her eyes for a moment, thinking of that day on the Kherish sailing ship so long ago.

"At least you are safe in our beautiful dream, my love," she said. "If nothing else, I know that you are happy."

CHAPTER 8

W ake up, my love. It's time to go home."

Brophy slowly opened his eyes and smiled to see Shara leaning over him. The setting sun painted her face with a golden glow. A small comb held her hair back behind her ear, and the golden feather attached to it fluttered in the slight breeze.

"I must have fallen asleep," he said, reaching up to touch her cheek.

"You've been asleep for a very long time."

"Then it's time to wake up." He pulled her toward him, her breasts pressed against his chest as their lips met. His desire swelled as she overwhelmed him with the smell of her skin, the heat of her touch.

"Shall we fly again?" he asked.

"Yes," she breathed, her voice thick with emotion. "Let's fly again, one last time."

Shara rose and helped him to his feet. They stood atop the Hall of Windows, on a warm autumn night. The four torches flickered all around them. "You won't need that anymore," Shara said, touching his wrist. "You can leave it here."

Brophy looked down and saw the Sword of Autumn in his hand. He gripped it tighter as tendrils of doubt crept into his belly.

"I can't leave my sword," he said, looking around for his belt, scabbard, and the rest of his clothes, but there were none to be found.

She smiled, shaking her head. "Come on," she said, taking his hand, and together they ran off the edge of the platform. Brophy spread his arms wide, sword in one hand, Shara's wrist in the other. They dived past the dazzling glass of the Hall of Windows. They swept low over the gardens, laughing as they barely dodged the trees and bushes. In moments they flew beyond the edge of the Wheel and over the bay. Shara led him east over the Night Market, rising higher and higher.

"Where are you taking me?" he asked.

"I have a little surprise for you, just on the other side of those clouds."

He looked up at the fluffy white clouds just above them. A chill crept up his back, prickling the hairs on his neck.

"I can't leave the city."

"You can now. This dream is over, Brophy. You've done what you needed to do. Let's go home."

A rush of cold fear coursed through him, and he slowed down. She'd said that before . . .

"No." He shook his head. "No, I can't."

Shara pulled on his hand. "Just a little farther. We're so close."

Brophy glanced at the buildings far below. His lip trembled, and he felt sick to his stomach. "Shara, please," he whispered. "I can't go."

The air grew colder as they entered the wispy edges of the clouds. She smiled down at him, her eyes filled with love. "Come on, Brophy!"

"No!" He yanked his hand out of her grip and tumbled away from her.

"Brophy!"

He clutched his sword, plummeting toward the ground. Shara swooped down and caught him under the arms. Their bodies pressed together as she held him tight.

"What are you doing? I have to get you out of here." She slowed their descent and began to rise back toward the clouds. He struggled against her, but he could not break her hold.

"Let me go," he demanded, filled with a sudden revulsion.

"Don't fight me, Brophy." Wisps of mist swirled all around them. "It's me. It's Shara."

Lightning arced across the sky.

"You're not Shara."

He plunged the Sword of Autumn into her body, ramming it through her chest and out the other side. A gout of black blood gushed from the wound, burning his arm.

She screamed and lashed out at him, slashing his face with her nails. Her eyes turned solid black, midnight orbs filled with rage.

Brophy reeled backward. The sword slipped from her wound, and he began to fall. He spun head over heels, clinging to his sword. Black clouds rushed in, blotting out the sun. Angry voices whipped around him, buffeting him about, trying to yank the sword from his grip.

He clutched the blade to his chest, hanging on with both hands. The ground rushed toward him faster and faster.

He screamed just before he hit the ground.

❄

Brophy woke up screaming. He leapt to his feet, the Sword of Autumn in hand. A flood of rage swept through his body, and he was ready in an instant, ready to run, ready to kill.

He crouched naked in the Night Market. Black clouds crowded the sky, locking the city in perpetual gloom. The wind carried angry voices, like distant screams not quite heard. Successive flashes of lightning revealed ghostly shadows hunched between the buildings. This was how it began. This was how it always began.

Brophy gripped the Sword of Autumn more tightly, aching for something to use it on. His lip curled into a snarl as he remembered the dream. It was all lies. Dreams within dreams. A labyrinth of deception.

The Fiend was out there somewhere, waiting for him, baiting another trap, crafting another torture he could not escape.

Gritting his teeth, Brophy jogged forward. The streets were clogged with bodies, Physendrians in full armor, slaughtered Ohndarien civilians, Ohohhim soldiers with open eyes and painted faces. The dead meant nothing. They weren't real.

The Sword of Autumn glowed red in his fist, its scant light illuminating the streets with a bloody glow. The sword was connected to the Heartstone, the only thing that held back the night. If the sword still glowed, then the Heartstone lived on. Ohndarien lived on. That was all that mattered.

A flash of lightning split the darkness, and Brophy saw a man walking toward him, picking his way through the contorted heaps of corpses strewn across the ground. The man was slight, narrow-shouldered, with a curved sword and a sour frown.

Scythe paused and gave him a Kherish salute with his blade. Brophy swallowed his turbulent emotions. He gripped the pommel of his sword in both hands, dreading what was to come, knowing there was no way to avoid it.

"Are you ready to be the Heart of Ohndarien?" the Kherish assassin hissed. "Are you ready to protect your own?"

Brophy refused to respond as Scythe spun his blade in a lazy circle. With a sneer, he charged. Brophy met the curved blade with two quick parries. He danced back, barely avoiding the flashing sword.

The thing looked like Scythe, sounded like Scythe, even fought like Scythe, but it was all part of the lie.

Brophy backed up, tripped over a corpse, and went down. The curved blade lashed out and cut him across the chest.

Brophy gasped and spun back to his feet.

"Open your eyes, Brophy," Scythe said, twirling his sword. "The world is an ugly, brutal place, and you are alone in it."

"Shut up, Fiend," Brophy snarled. Tendrils of corruption seeped from his wound, flowing around his heartstone like a stone in a river. Brophy felt like he was swelling, growing larger and more powerful.

The thing with Scythe's face attacked again, and Brophy met it with a roar. New power rushed through his arms, and the Sword of Autumn slammed the creature's blade aside, slicing deep into its shoulder. Brophy yanked his weapon out and swung it again and again.

It was over in seconds. Scythe's double lay dismembered in the street, soaking the cobblestones with inky blood.

Brophy looked around, wanting more. There was always more. He sprinted past Scythe, leaping over corpses as he crossed the square.

The dream hadn't always been like this. The Fiend hadn't always been there. It started with little nightmares, brief interruptions to the blissful time he spent with Shara. He'd wake up screaming, not remembering where he was. The nightmares grew longer and longer, one dream fading into the next, until Shara faded away entirely, never to return. He never knew if the Fiend locked her out or if she'd abandoned him. Either way, Brophy was alone.

He'd tried running at first, tried to flee across the Long Market, into the bay, or up the Wheel. But there was nowhere to run. And he could not leave the city; he would never leave the city. So they always found him, surrounded him, overwhelmed him. They flayed the flesh from his arms, trying to rip the sword from his grip, but he'd never let go. Not yet.

Brophy ran to face his tormentor, seeking out the cause of his pain. He could sense the Fiend nearby, watching, waiting. It was a deadly game they played, locked together in endless nightmare, neither able to escape until the other gave in. His nemesis was getting stronger, but so was Brophy. Each time he woke more angry, less frightened than the time before.

He rounded one corner, then two, wending his way through the corpse-strewn streets. His adversary was that way. In the main square.

He ran between two buildings and skidded to a stop as he reached the plaza. The Fiend stood on the lip of a fountain, amid a crowd of blackened and twisted creatures. His enemy's white face was a ghostly light in the darkness. Robes like black oil flowed from delicate shoulders to the ground.

A mob of corrupted lay between them, their contorted bodies bristling with spikes and claws. The Fiend waited for Brophy, taunting him from behind a wall of tainted flesh.

Ready to try again? You can't resist me forever.

The voice slipped into his mind like a blade into a sheath. Brophy gagged on bile water and forced it back down his burning throat.

The corruption had spread across his chest. His flesh twisted and bubbled. He could already feel it seeping into his bones. He didn't have long.

He had cut through almost all the lies, but he'd never reached the Fiend itself. All others died on his sword. Corrupted friends, family, but never the Fiend. He had never come within a blade length of his opponent, and with each failure, Brophy's rage grew.

"I'll gut you this time," he whispered.

You want me, little brother. Here I am. Come claim your freedom.

Brophy heard a sound behind him and looked back. Multiple shapes ran toward him through the shadows.

He rushed into the square, and the dead bodies around him began to move. Corpses writhed in pain, their limbs twisting and elongating, sprouting spines, scales, and spurs. Dead flesh split, folded in on itself as the corpses struggled to rise.

With a growl, he rushed into their midst, hewing left and right. He burst through them and spun like a madman, following the serpentine path cut by his sword. Phanqui, Tidric, Lewlem, Medew, Garm, and Femera all fell before his sword.

Is that the best you can do? You are a lone, pathetic candle in a growing storm.

Claws caught his ankle, and Brophy fell. He rolled back to his feet, rammed his shoulder into a hulking beast with Athyl's face, and kept on running.

He charged left into a tavern, kicking the door open. Running across two tables, he leapt for the stairs, landing in stride. A dark shape vaulted over the balcony, and he caught Celinor's neck in midair with his hand. Twisting his body, Brophy threw the creature over the rail. Its claws raked through his forearm as it fell.

Brophy gasped, his legs pumping up the stairs. That was another wound. There would be more. He had to reach the Fiend before they overwhelmed him.

He charged up two more flights, bounded off a wall, and headed down a side hallway. Ossamyr sat on the railing, with her legs wrapped around Phandir's waist. Her back arched as the king kissed her neck. "I'm sorry, Brophy," she said, laughing. "Forgive me. I had no choice."

Brophy shouted and cut them both down without breaking stride. Heavy feet pounded up the stairs behind him.

He burst through another door. His aunt Baelandra fought four Ohndarien soldiers who pinned her to the bed. Her dress was in tatters, her face contorted in anguish. A fifth man strained on top of her, his pants around his thighs. He turned to Brophy with a smile. "Hey, Broph," Trent said. "You want a turn?"

He cut Trent down with a single blow, and the others grabbed him. Brophy twisted out of their grasp, lashing out with his knees and fists until he had room to use his sword. He'd barely cut them all down before Baelandra leapt naked upon his back and sank her teeth into his shoulder.

He flung her away and dived out a window. Landing on his feet, he slid down a red tile roof, struggling for balance. At the last moment he jumped toward the roof garden on the next rooftop.

He cleared the gap and landed in a thorny hedge. He ignored the scrapes and ran toward the Fiend. All he needed was one chance, one brutal stroke of his sword.

Brophy's wounded arm was already black and shriveled. Jagged bone sprouted from the tips of his fingers, leaving his skin in tatters. The dark power coursed through him, driving him toward his goal. He would catch him this time, claw his way to his enemy's throat, and crush it with one hand.

Lightning flashed, throwing harsh shadows between the buildings. Krellis leapt out of the bushes behind him, tackling him and driving him to his knees.

"You'll never make it, boy," the corrupted said, its weight crushing Brophy to the roof. It ground forearms against the back of Brophy's neck, forcing his head downward. "No point in trying."

Brophy rammed his elbow into Krellis's face, knocking the creature back. He flipped around and smashed his fists into it over and over. The beast's claws raked Brophy's flesh until it finally lay still.

Come to me, little brother. Come and face me. Show me what you can do.

Searing pain spread through Brophy's guts, but his body sang with the agony, and it made him stronger. He would kill and kill and kill until the Fiend's heart lay beating in his hand.

Brophy scrambled to the edge of the roof. Lightning flashed again, illuminating the street below. It was so packed with corrupted he couldn't see the ground. They swarmed like worms in a bucket. The plants behind him rustled as the pursuing creatures closed in. He turned and leapt across another alley, landing hard on a peaked roof one story down. The red tiles cracked under him. He clung there for a moment, breathing furiously. His panting was loud in his ears, and howling voices rushed upon the wind.

He could see the Fiend just below—one more jump, and Brophy would be there. His enemy's white face was a ghostly light in the darkness, framed by curly black hair that blended with the night. Robes like black oil flowed from his shoulders to the ground. It waited for him with a mocking smile.

What are you waiting for? Let's finish this. Finish it now.

Something behind Brophy howled, and he spun around to meet it. He slashed with all his might as Baelandra barreled into him from the adjacent building. Brophy's blow struck true, but the creature's momentum knocked him flat.

Roof tiles broke, and they slid. Brophy grabbed a handhold, but his aunt clung to his leg. He kicked her in the face, and a thrill ran through him. He kicked her again, and she let go.

Laughing, he ran across the roof and leapt off the edge. He landed in the midst of the writhing corrupted just a few feet from his foe. He knocked a swath of them to the ground as their bodies broke his fall.

Brophy scrambled over the fallen creatures, drawing back his sword to land the killing blow.

Claws pierced his flesh. Barbed tentacles wrapped around his arms. Fangs sank to the bone. He screamed as a wave of enemies swept him away from the pasty face of his foe. They twisted his arms behind his back, pinned his legs together. He screamed and tried to head-butt those around him. Their slimy fingers grabbed his hair and pulled his head back. Powerful hands gripped the blade of the sword, trying to rip it out of his grasp. Needlelike claws ripped at his fingers.

"No!" Brophy howled, jerking his arm free. He swung the blade, slaying anything within reach. His sword arm was free, but the rest of him was held fast, his feet off the ground, his head in a vise grip.

The Fiend strolled slowly toward him. He pulled a bone-white hand from the depths of his robe and motioned the corrupted aside. The horde parted for him, making a precise aisle. His oily black robes left a trail of slime, and he stopped just beyond the reach of Brophy's sword.

Have you come so close, only to fail again?

Brophy swung his blade wildly, missing his enemy's powdered face by inches. He felt the power surge within him. He could throw the blade. He couldn't miss at this range. One thrust, and it would all be over.

Is that the best you can do? Victory is in your reach.

Brophy drew his arm back to throw.

The Fiend watched him with its glittering black eyes.

No. He couldn't. Not the sword.

Brophy's arm went limp. He let out a wail that echoed across the square. He started sobbing, and collapsed in the arms of his foes.

The Fiend sneered, then his face relaxed into a patient smile. His hand descended slowly to his side, and the oily robe enveloped the white skin once again.

Very well then, little brother. We shall try this once again. One way or the other, you will be mine.

He nodded to the beasts holding Brophy.

"Take his sword," the Fiend commanded.

The corrupted wrenched at the Sword of Autumn. They plunged their hands into his belly, ripped out his entrails, and clawed his eyes from their sockets.

Brophy held on to the sword with all his might. He wouldn't let go. He would never let go.

❄

"Wake up, my love. It's time to go home."

Brophy slowly opened his eyes and smiled to see Shara leaning over him. The setting sun painted her face with a golden glow. A small comb held her hair back behind her ear, and the golden feather attached to it fluttered in the slight breeze.

"I must have fallen asleep," he said, reaching up to touch her cheek.

"You've been asleep for a very long time."

CHAPTER 9

Ossamyr spat salt water from her mouth and tightened her grip on the tiller. The wind shifted, and the boom whipped about as if to strike her down. She ducked it and blinked away the spray, peering into the sheets of rain as her little craft rode up the next mountainous wave. This storm was what Ohndarien sailors called a splinter storm, one that shivered your ship to splinters. Every wave was her death, and every time she bested it she cheated that death. But her arms ached with the strain. Her back burned with her exertions, and she didn't know how much longer she could fight the tiller to guide her lumbering ship. Each new wave was a desperate battle.

Just a few more, she thought. *I'm so close.*

Efften was within her reach, and with it the containment stones and the boy's salvation.

The little ship started up the next wave. Her arms wavered, and she missed her mark.

Stupid! she thought, even as she braced herself. *Stupid stupid stupid!*

The water hammered into the side of her boat. The ship rocked dangerously to port, and Ossamyr slipped, going down to one knee. A deluge of salt water rushed over her, but the rope around her waist held her tight in place. She cried out, hanging on and finding her feet again. The heavy ship leaned dangerously but did not capsize. Ossamyr gasped, wrenched at the tiller, and pointed herself into the worst of it. The little craft fought its way up and over, breaking the crest of the wave. She started down the far side. An endless series of watery black hills stretched out in front of her, throwing white froth into the air.

One more, she thought. *Just one more.*

As she started up the far side, she thanked the Seasons, all nine Physendrian gods, and the surly shipwright who had built this heavy, sturdy ship. She remembered the conversation with longing as she threw her back into angling the ship toward the next crest. She wished she were back in Ohndarien, haggling with the city's finest shipwright.

He had scoffed at her, looking at her designs.

"This keel is half-again as long as the ship," the shipwright said.

"I know. And I want it bound in sheets of lead."

"Lead? You're crazy, that's what you are. Who builds a ship with lead? She'd be a wallowing pig."

"Just as long as she doesn't tip over."

He frowned at her, smacked the back of his fingers against her drawing. "It's a waste of wood, m'lady. This mast and those sails are too small. It would take a typhoon to get her out of the harbor."

"Exactly."

The shipwright spat on the ground and walked away from her, but he came back the next day, took her silver, and started building her ship, scowling every step of the way.

This was her fourth attempt to reach Efften. The first two times she and Shara had tried to sneak to Efften in the dark of night. Each time they were forced to flee when warships appeared out of the darkness, headed straight for them. The third time they brought a crew of Zelani, and together they cast a glamour over the entire vessel. It didn't matter. The Islanders still found them, crushing their little craft without warning or mercy.

No one knew why the Silver Islanders guarded Efften with such fanatical devotion. They rammed and burned every ship that came close to the island ruins. To sail the waters of Efften was to die at their hands.

But Ossamyr had solved that problem. Even those bloody-minded pirates wouldn't sail in this storm. This horrible, blessed storm that was Ossamyr's only hope. It would take her to Efften, or it would take her life. Either way, her debt was paid. The ship was built to weather a storm like this, but it would never sail under calm skies. If this storm failed before she reached Efften, she would be left stranded, bobbing helpless in the sea waiting to see if her supplies ran out before the Islanders ran her down.

Again she rode up to the top of the wave. Again, her aim was imperfect and the ship rocked dangerously.

I am slipping, she thought. *I am flagging.*

Her memory flew back to the conversation she had with Baelandra and Shara on the docks. That was only days ago. It seemed like years.

And now it looked like Baelandra was right. She would die here. She couldn't feel her hands anymore. Her arms had gone numb. She rode the next wave, fighting for every inch. Somehow she made it and started down the far side. She slipped and fell to her knees.

She struggled to her feet, looked up. Through the rain she glimpsed something gray and solid in the distance. Land!

Ossamyr yelled as her boat skimmed down the backside of the wave, and the horizon disappeared. With renewed strength, she brought the ship about, pointing it toward her salvation. She crested the next wave, and they were directly in front of her. Broken, shadowy minarets. Water crashing on rocks. Lightning lanced to the waterline just off Efften's coast, revealing the ruined city in sharp, white relief—

—and glinting off the silver prow of an Islander warship to port.

"Pig-fucking bastards!" Ossamyr shouted into the wind.

The sleek warship disappeared behind a swell for a moment, and Ossamyr turned her craft as fast as she could. But the warship reappeared moments later, closer, slicing through the water like a dagger.

The storm had been her only protection, and the crazy pirates had braved it.

The warship's steel prow appeared over the next wave, huge and ominous as a falling axe. It skimmed down the wave far too fast to escape. Bulky, tattooed warriors armed with bows lined the rail, grim and ready. Ossamyr barely had time to turn away before the ships collided, slamming her against the deck.

The steel ram crashed through the side of her boat. Wood shattered. Decking planks splayed as her ship was torn in half. Desperately, Ossamyr cut free from her line. Two arrows thunked into the deck next to her chest. She rolled over, launched awkwardly over the edge of her dying boat, and splashed into the black waters.

Arrows fell with the rain, seeking her flesh. One grazed the back of her thigh, and she cried out, precious bubbles of air escaping. Twisting, she swam with the last of her strength, deeper, down where their arrows could not reach her.

Keeping tight control on her breath, Ossamyr calmed herself, stroked steadily toward Efften, stroked and stroked until her lungs felt like they would burst. Only then did she rise to the stormy surface and gasp for air. The choppy waves tried to drown her, but she fought them and looked for the warship. It cruised on the swells, the wind carrying it swiftly away. The wreckage of her tiny boat was visible for one scant moment, then it dropped beneath the waves.

Ossamyr swam drunkenly for the dark shore. She threw herself against the incessant waves for an eternity. The towers of Efften appeared and disappeared as the waves crested over her. She gasped for air. She was so close, but her arms could barely move. Her legs were as leaden as the keel of her ship, dragging her down.

Brophy, she thought as she foundered. *I tried. I tried so hard.*

CHAPTER 10

The sky was blue, and the clouds had cleared away to the east. The four-day storm had finally passed. Tree limbs littered the side streets and alleys of Ohndarien, and pockets of water lingered in every dip and basin, but the walkways were already clear and dry.

Astor hiked the bundle of wood up and swung it over his shoulder. He hoped that Brophy's torch had managed to stay lit. He'd hate for it to have gone out.

Quinn, the Sister of Summer, had quietly hinted to Astor that hauling wood to the top of the Hall of Windows was no longer proper etiquette for his station, especially since he'd officially been initiated into the Lightning Swords. But these days, a young man grew up quickly in Ohndarien, especially a Child of the Seasons. Astor had long since developed his own ideas on proper etiquette.

He turned and looked back. His younger sister Baedellin straggled behind him, running her hand along the edge of the Wheel as they approached the top of the steps.

"You're slower than a turtle," he told her. She was nine years old, but this morning she had chosen to walk like a two-year-old.

She leaned her head one way, then the other, looking up at the early-morning sky as though she hadn't heard him.

Astor shook his head with a smile. She was such a brat.

"You need to get to your history lesson," he said. "You know how Vallia gets when she's cross."

"I don't want to listen to Vallia talk for five hundred thousand hours."

Astor ignored that and kept on toward the steps. "Come on," he said.

"I *know* where the Palace of Winter is," she said. "I don't need *you* to show me."

"And yet you always seem to get 'lost' every time you go to your lessons alone."

"Says who?"

Astor reached out and ruffled her bright red hair. She hated that. "Says Mother."

She swiped at his arm. "She did not!" she said, trying to smooth out the mess he'd made.

He jumped up the steps, and she pursued. "Yes, she told me this morning, 'Astor, take care of your little sister. She is short and funny-looking, and no one will ever love her.'"

"She did not!" Baedellin caught him and punched him in the arm.

Astor threw himself against the wall as if he'd been socked by a giant. The wood he was carrying clacked on the steps as he collapsed.

"Did too," he said, rubbing his arm as if it hurt. "And Father warned me to keep you away from the other children because red hair attracts fleas."

"Does not!" She punched him again.

"And you can't go swimming because your feet stink, and all the fish will die."

Baedellin leapt at him. Astor laughed and protected himself from the rain of tiny blows.

"Careful, careful, I'm wounded." He kept her wild blows away from his black eye and the bandage over his temple where his head had cracked the quarry floor.

"Not wounded enough," she said, hitting him even harder.

"All right, all right, I take it back! I take it back!" he laughed. "You're tall and gorgeous, with feet that smell like roses!"

"And red hair is the best. Just like Mother's," she said, sitting back on her heels.

"And red hair is best. Just ask the fleas."

Baedellin squealed and struck at him again, but he slipped to the side, grabbed the bundle of wood, and sprinted up the stairs. She chased him until he almost reached the top. He ran slower and slower, then slumped to the stairs, feigning exhaustion.

She jumped on him, straddling his stomach and pinning his arms under her bony knees. She thumped him on the chest with her finger.

"Ha!" she said. "I win."

"You win."

"I always win."

"You always win."

She eyed him suspiciously while he maintained his look of innocence. Finally, she stood and held out her hand. He took it, and she helped him up.

"Do I really have to go to the lesson?" she asked.

"What do you think?"

Ignoring his little sister's pout, he turned and continued up the stairs. A pair of swallows zipped past their heads, chasing each other around the Wheel.

As they reached the top, the sculpture of the Kher came into view. It was carved from the red granite of the man's homeland, a larger-than-life depiction of Ohndarien's ultimate defender. No one knew where the man came from, or what his real name was, but he was there when the Fortress of Light needed him the most. The foreign warrior crouched to the left, a curved sword in his right hand that dipped so low it almost touched the ground. Flowers decorated the base. Wreaths hung from his arms, some from around his neck. Little candles, tiny wicker boxes, and bowls filled with seashells dotted the ground around the statue.

The Kher looked as though he was about to pounce on whoever ascended the stair. Thick eyebrows over deep-set eyes gave him a look of implacable intensity. He stared down the stairs as though death was coming for him, and he was ready, even eager to meet it. Astor was always struck by it. He wondered if he could face a man like that, so intent, so dizzyingly fast. No wonder the Physendrians had balked, if this was the sight they faced. Astor couldn't imagine being able to stop his foes with a glance.

Quinn told her students that the Heartstone had called the Kher all the way from his homeland, the only warrior who could hold off an entire army, giving Brother Brophy the moments he needed to contain the black emmeria.

But Astor knew differently. Mother knew the man, knew his real name, though she never talked about it. The taciturn Sister Vallia had mentioned him once, then went silent at a glance from Mother, but Ossamyr-lani didn't care what anyone else thought and could occasionally be badgered into telling her stories. She had known him when she was queen of Physendria, and he went by the name of Scythe.

She said that the man had single-handedly kept the Physendrian army at bay during the Nightmare Battle, slowly retreating up the steps to the Wheel, killing scores of Physendrians before they overcame him at the top. But he hadn't been alone. Mother had been with him every step of the way, holding a shield to protect them from Physendrian archers.

When Astor asked Mother about that, she had just smiled and told him that Ossamyr always had a flair for the dramatic. Which was no answer at all.

"Do you ever wonder what it would have been like to be in the battle?" Baedellin asked, peering over the edge of the Wheel. "With Physendrians all below?"

"Only every time I come up here."

"We beat them so badly, they don't even have a country anymore. The Summer Cities took it."

Astor nodded. "They should never have come north."

"Do you ever imagine you're Father, leading the Lightning Swords from here, throwing rocks and spears on the army down below?" Baedellin said.

"Sometimes."

She was quiet for a moment, and Astor was content to look out over Ohndarien, blue marble shining in the sunlight, diamonds sparkling in the bay, the Night Market asleep for the day. Some called Ohndarien "The Cursed City" now, but Astor felt that the Fortress of Light shone all the brighter for the darkness that wanted to overwhelm it. The last few days had been quiet, though. No new corrupted had appeared. It was a blessing.

"I think Mother loved him," Baedellin said softly.

"What?"

"The Kher. I think Mother loved him. She never talks about him. She won't."

Astor fell silent, amazed that his flighty sister had put those pieces together.

"What would have happened if Mother had married the Kher instead of Father?"

That was about enough of that, Astor decided. He stood up and held out his hand.

"You'd have a funny hook nose to go with your funny red hair," he said.

Baedellin leapt to her feet and punched him. He caught her fist in his hand. She tried to punch him with her other fist, but he forcibly turned her body, and she missed him.

"Baedellin, it's time for you to go to your history lesson," he said sternly, and she knew the game was over. She yanked her hands away from him, pouting, but she started walking toward the Winter Palace. He followed until her flame-colored head disappeared around a curve in the marble path.

Readjusting the bundle of wood, he continued toward the Hall of Windows. The gardens were quiet today, the council was not in session, and he didn't meet anyone until he'd climbed the blue-white marble steps up the outside of the hall. It was a tricky climb, but he'd done it so many times it was second nature.

Astor was pleased to see the trail of smoke rising from Brophy's fire. It looked like the flames had burned down to coals, but they had survived.

"Greetings, cousin," said the Lightning Sword on duty at the top of the steps. He left the other three guards and reached for Astor's bundle of wood. "Let me help you with that."

"That's all right. I like to do it myself."

The man nodded and turned back to his conversation with the others.

As always, two Zelani sat on either side of Brophy's cage, singing to him. This time it was Galliana and Fyrallin.

Galliana smiled at him, but didn't stop singing. Fyrallin didn't even notice him. She always sang with her eyes closed, lost in her song. She had one of the most beautiful voices Astor had ever heard. It was high, clear, and as smooth as honey. He thought she would have made a fortune at one of the theaters in the Night Market, but she had passed the tests and entered the Zelani school instead.

Shara-lani sat next to Brophy inside the cage. She looked weary and sadder than usual. Mother hadn't given Astor any details, but he knew something had gone wrong at the Zelani school. Yet nothing seemed to keep Shara from her lover's side. She was almost always holding Brophy's hand whenever Astor arrived to feed the brazier. Some people said she never slept, that the Brother of Autumn slept for both of them.

"Good morning, Astor," she said, wiping a finger underneath her eye and smiling. Her smiles always made him want to cry, so he nodded quickly and looked up at his destination, then back at her.

"Good morning, Shara-lani," he said. "I won't be long." He set most of the wood into the elaborately carved box at the base of the dais and carefully closed the lid, then he climbed the narrow steps to the top of the gazebo. He removed the storm shield and added a few pieces of wood to the coals.

Before he went south to Physendria, Brother Brophy had maintained the torches for his father and uncles, the Lost Brothers. Shara-lani was still looking for a way to wake Brophy, but until he returned, Astor would make sure his flame burned brightly.

And if they hadn't found a way to wake him by the time Astor took the Test, then Astor had plans of his own. He would make sure that Brophy's sacrifice was not an eternal one.

He watched the fire for a moment, then looked out over the Great Ocean and saw an unexpected sight. A small fleet of ships approached the Sunset Gate. His heart beat faster.

He squinted, making sure his eyes weren't playing tricks on him. But no, they were Ohohhim ships.

The Emperor wasn't due to arrive until later in the week, and Mother said the storm might slow them down even more. But there they were, black ships with triangular sails, tacking toward Sunset Gate. They must have sailed through the teeth of the storm.

The Emperor came back to Ohndarien every year, but this time Astor heard the legendary Arefaine Morgeon, the Sleeping Child herself, the baby that Brophy had brought back with him from the Cinder, was coming with him. The child who started the Nightmare Battle was returning to Ohndarien for the first time since she had awoken. He had heard that she was quite a beauty.

He jumped over the side of the gazebo, slid his hand down one of the brass rails, and landed on the platform with a thump. Galliana and Fyrallin looked up, though they both continued singing.

"The Ohohhim have arrived," he said, far more excited than he expected. There was much to be done.

CHAPTER 11

Somewhere in the kitchen, a dish shattered. Issefyn suppressed a flash of annoyance, keeping all emotion from her face. The lessons of poise and calm were best taught through example.

The Ohohhim had arrived earlier than anticipated, and the entire school was a beehive of activity this morning, making certain that everything was in its finest form for the Emperor's visit.

Issefyn finished the floral arrangement she was working on and headed for the kitchen to make sure there wasn't an important part of the Emperor's dinner on the plate that just broke. His Eternal Wisdom spent an evening dining with Shara every time he visited Ohndarien. The man was constantly trying to entice Shara to become his mistress. He seemed to enjoy taking no for an answer.

As Issefyn strode into the kitchen, she was surprised to find it empty. Gathering herself, she sent out her awareness to see where the plate breaker might have run off.

At first she didn't sense anyone, but she concentrated harder and realized she wasn't alone.

She turned to face Suvian, who leaned against a pantry doorway.

"That is an impressive glamour. Almost as impressive as your plate-shattering skills."

"I learned from the best," he replied. His glittering gaze devoured her, lingering on her cleavage.

Suvian was a beautiful young man who had recently emerged as a full Zelani. He had deep brown eyes, dark hair, and a handsome face that could have belonged to the House of Spring. In reality, though, he was a Farad peasant.

"I was being sarcastic," she said. "Any talented novice could see right through that."

"But I wanted to be seen," he said as he sauntered toward her. "Hence the plate."

"That is recklessly bold for someone forbidden to enter this building ever again."

"Why are the best things in life always forbidden?" he asked.

Suvian had been expelled from the Zelani school for his overexuberance with one of the younger students. Shara had named it attempted rape.

Issefyn waited, back straight, arms folded across her chest. He touched her arms, unfolded them, and began to pull her toward the pantry. She raised an eyebrow at him but didn't resist.

The storeroom was deep enough to be shadowed, but it was still open to the kitchen. It held three shelves of food, a stout table, and two unlit lanterns on the walls.

"Exactly why are you here, Suvian?" she asked. "The Emperor will be dining here tonight, and there are things that require attention—"

"I require attention," he said, trailing his hand along her arm as he walked around her. His chest pressed against her back, and his fingers wrapped around the curve of her hip. He was taller than her. That was one of the things Issefyn always liked about him.

Suvian slipped his fingers inside the lip of her neckline and moved slowly down, touching the edge of her breast. "Aren't you the one who said we must always make time for joy, Issefyn?"

She smiled, and her hand closed over his gently. She took it away from her breast. "You shouldn't be here," she said, turning around and stepping back from him.

He grabbed her hands. She shook her head, but didn't resist as he leaned close, his smooth cheek touching hers as he whispered in her ear, "Tell me you don't want this, that you don't want me. Tell me, and I shall leave."

His hands slid up the sides of her arms and held her firmly just above her elbows.

"You are forbidden to be here, Suvian. We had a bargain. I overlooked your past indiscretions when I chose to complete your training. And in return, you agreed to keep your distance from this place. If Shara found you here, it would go badly for both of us."

For a moment, the cocksure glimmer in his eyes faltered. His hands loosened their grip, but only for a moment.

"You're right," he said, smiling wider. "We made a bargain." He pushed her suddenly, forcefully, backward. With a little gasp, she stumbled, sat down hard on the table. He moved forward, pushing his way between her legs. "And yet, here I am. Here you are."

"Suvian . . ." she admonished, breathing harder, matching her breath to his. She tried to close her legs, but he forced his hips between them and slammed her down on the table. Her head hit the wood, and she gasped.

His hands pushed at her knees and, after resisting for a moment, she let her legs drift apart. He hiked her gown up.

"Is this really what you want, Suvian?" she asked.

"Yes," he said in a husky voice. His trembling hands ran the length of her legs, drinking in the sight of her. She wore no undergarments. She never did.

He unlaced his breeches and let them fall. Pulling her to the edge of the table, he spread her legs farther, baring her to him. Hot flesh touched hers.

"Do you want me?" she whispered.

"I already have you," Suvian said, putting his hands on her hips and leaning on them.

"Do you?" she asked, slowly sitting up on her elbows.

"Yes I do." He started to push inside her.

She sat up a little more, pivoting her hips away from him. She glanced down and saw, with satisfaction, the newly healed scabs on his knees. "Do you?" she murmured again, feeling a rush at the memory of those scabs, feeling her power over him. "I want you to show me exactly what you have."

Suvian stopped, his brow furrowed.

"You heard me, Suvian."

His hands eased their pressure a little. He blinked, turned his head as if someone was calling his name from far away.

Removing his hands, Issefyn shifted backward, brought one leg slowly past him, then slid off the table. Her gown floated back down into place, and she walked around behind him. He turned with her, dazed.

"Now, my *big, strong* man," she purred. "I want you to crawl."

His knees buckled, and he fell to the floor on hands and knees. His forehead wrinkled as his brows came together. His shoulders shook as he tried to resist. "You . . ." he panted. "Bitch . . ." But he didn't move.

Issefyn smiled. The lovely boy was made of sterner stuff than she anticipated. She had known kings who succumbed more easily.

She knelt next to him, placed a finger on his trembling lips. "When I call," she intoned, "you will come to me. When I speak, you will obey."

With a growl, Suvian swung out blindly. His wrist cracked against the leg of the table, and he fell forward on his belly. He lay there, breathing hard for an excruciating moment before all of the struggle drained from his face. His muscles relaxed, and he lay peacefully on the stone floor, his mouth open.

"Take off your clothes, my darling," she whispered. "And crawl for me. I want to see you crawl." He woodenly pulled his shirt over his head and pushed his pants the rest of the way off his legs.

Issefyn pressed a hand against her breast, felt the rising tide of her desire. Suvian rolled to his hands and knees and began crawling across the floor.

Issefyn leaned back against the table as he moved around the tiny space, carefully dodging the shelves and table legs. She smiled wide as the rush of her own power flowed through her. She might take him later, she might not, but that didn't matter. This was the moment in life that she truly loved.

She felt the emmeria seeping from her bones, swirling through her body. It was so wearisome to hide her power day after day, year after year. The fools here had no idea who their sweet little teacher truly was.

Issefyn looked longingly at Suvian's body, his penis still hard despite her hold on him. Taking him here wasn't safe. Someone could come into the kitchens at any moment, but the thought of discovery was intoxicating. She was sick of being patient. She needed this. After years of fawning over insipid Zelani students like a mother hen, she needed to remind herself who she was. The emmeria rolled in her stomach, and she wanted to laugh. The charade was almost done. Morgeon's daughter had arrived. The little bitch's plan would soon unfold, and Issefyn would finally get what she came for. Her prize had been locked within that gaudy cage atop the Hall of Windows for decades, but Arefaine would fling those doors wide forever. And after that, the fun would begin.

In honor of Victeris, Issefyn would shatter Shara's will. The sanctimonious whore would crawl her knees raw then and fling herself from her own putrid pink tower.

Then Issefyn would reward Phandir's betrayer by letting the corrupted rip Ossamyr limb from limb.

And last, Issefyn would shove a sword into Baelandra's stomach. Perhaps she would even hang the former Sister of Autumn from that vulgar statue of Krellis's murderer.

The women who murdered Issefyn's three sons would suffer before they died, and they would know why. It would be the sweet cream on top of her victory here. Ohndarien's walls would come tumbling down, and Issefyn would build her monuments upon this city's ashes.

But first, she needed a taste of the power flowing through the Awakened Child's precious veins.

CHAPTER 12

All of Ohndarien gathered by the bay to welcome the Ohohhim ships.

The Emperor's arrival and the celebration to follow was the greatest event of the year in Ohndarien. Everyone stayed on alert during the week beforehand, dropping business on a moment's notice to rush to the docks.

Shara took a deep breath and watched the sleek, black ships come through the Sunset Gate. She stood with Baelandra and other prominent Children of the Seasons at the edge of the dock waiting to receive their guests.

The crowd swelled as the ironwood ships sailed between Stoneside and the Long Market. The joyous crowd gathered along the shore, cheering and throwing flowers. They cheered even louder than usual this year. It was common knowledge that Arefaine Morgeon, the mythical child from the Nightmare Battle, was coming with the Emperor.

Arefaine was revered as a goddess among the Ohohhim, second only to the Emperor. Temples and shrines were built in her honor. Women went on pilgrimages in her name, stayed up for weeks at a time, huddling together and turning the handles of music boxes to better appreciate the price of keeping evil at bay.

The Emperor's ship docked. Her black masts towered high overhead. Great white sails luffed in the soft breeze. Ohndarien's port masters threw thick ropes aboard, and the efficient Ohohhim sailors made the ship fast. The Carriers of the Opal Fire, personal guardians of the Emperor, were dressed in black with white-powdered faces. They extended a polished black gangplank, and marched down single file, fanning out unobtrusively across the dock. Once set, they stood as still as posts. The Carriers were the greatest warriors in the Opal Empire, and they went everywhere with the Emperor.

The double doors to the aft stateroom opened, and the Emperor, His

Eternal Wisdom, the Embodiment of Oh on earth, emerged from the darkness within. The cheering of the crowd surged as the man nodded politely to the hundreds who had gathered to greet him. His Eternal Wisdom was a handsome man with a long straight nose and commanding cheekbones. His calm dark eyes saw everything. He had the black curly hair of all Ohohhim, and the white-powdered face of nobility. Black robes covered him from shoulder to toes, with pearlescent embroidery along the stiff neck and wide cuffs. The huge opal amulet of Oh's Chosen rested against his chest.

The Emperor paused in the doorway, focusing on each of the Sisters in turn, then on Shara. She met his gaze and smiled.

After a few moments, the Emperor stepped forward, and Arefaine appeared just behind him, holding his sleeve. The crowd noise swelled as people fought to get a look at her.

The nineteen-year-old girl looked just like the few paintings that Shara had seen. Her dark brown hair had been oiled until it shone. Her features were difficult to see at a distance under her white powder, but her blue eyes burned like ice caught in the sunlight. Her intense gaze moved quickly over the crowd until it came to rest on Shara. A surge of power crackled between them, and Shara took a deep, strong breath, cycled it through. *By the Seasons* . . .

She wanted to flick a glance at Caleb on her left. He had to have felt that. The girl's power preceded her like a trumpet blast. Shara felt a surge of hope and gave Arefaine a brief nod. If she was truly as talented as she appeared, she might be able to help Shara find the missing pieces to her disastrous spell. The young woman's gaze lingered on Shara. Was that a hint of a smile?

The Emperor continued forward across the deck toward the gangplank. Arefaine followed, pinching his sleeve, and was in turn followed by the Opal Advisor, and so on until fourteen of the Emperor's entourage stood on the dock, just behind the semicircle created by the Carriers of the Opal Fire.

As patient as the Great Ocean, the Emperor waited as his entourage formed up behind him, then he transformed from a rigid Ohohhim god to perfect diplomat, greeting each of the Sisters of the Council, beginning with Vallia, the Council Elder and Sister of Winter, and ending with Baleise, the youngest member and Sister of Spring.

Not one of the Emperor's advisors so much as twitched, but Shara could feel their discomfort. The Emperor did not speak to mortals. His divine voice was reserved for the twelve chosen who surrounded him. It was the Opal Advisor's place to pass the word of Oh's Chosen down the divine queue.

Once the greetings had finished, the Sisters stepped back, and the Emperor moved to stand before Shara.

He took her hands in his. "Though Ohndarien grows more radiant every time I visit, I confess that she still pales in comparison to you, Shara-lani."

"You are kind to say so, Your Holiness," she replied.

"I would be delighted if you would take dinner with me sometime during my visit."

"I would be honored, Your Holiness."

The Emperor turned to Baelandra and her family. Faedellin wore his finest uniform, and Astor bore his recent wound like a badge of honor. Except for his darker hair and eyes, the boy could have been Brophy. They even moved the same. Shara looked away.

"Sweet Baelandra," the Emperor said. "Motherhood becomes you, and your children grow with the strength of their father and the allure of their mother."

Little Baedellin was hiding behind her mother's skirts, but beamed at the Emperor's words.

"Ohndarien welcomes her liberator, Your Eternal Wisdom," Baelandra said. "You do great honor to us. Our city rejoices with your presence."

He nodded, and no one spoke for a long moment.

"Come," Vallia broke the silence, standing aside and bowing at the waist, "I know there is one place that you would visit before the festival begins, Your Holiness."

He nodded. "Yes. I could not enjoy the comforts of your great city without giving my respects to the Sleeping Warden."

Vallia led her Ohndariens in a line parallel to the Ohohhim through the Long Market. The stalls were packed with spectators, who cheered at the procession and threw flowers. As always, the drinking for that night's festival would begin before noon.

The dual procession continued along the base of the Wheel to the great stairs and started up side by side. They wound around the ceremonial steps, leading a sea of people behind them. Shara found herself staring at the back of Arefaine's head a little way ahead of her. She was intensely curious about the young woman born on Efften and raised in the Opal Palace. Shara had been the child's guardian for a short time, turning the music box that kept her asleep. Did she remember anything from all those years locked in nightmare? Could anyone truly leave such a tortured past behind her?

The Opal Advisor let go of Arefaine's sleeve when the procession reached the base of the Hall of Windows, disconnecting the entourage from the Emperor. His Eternal Wisdom usually went up alone to pay his respects to the man who once freed him from the grip of the black emmeria, but this year he paused at the bottom of the steps and turned to Shara and the others.

"I would be honored if the Sisters, Baelandra, and Shara would join me as I pay my respects. My ward, Arefaine, has a gift she wishes to bestow upon the Sleeping Warden and the people of Ohndarien."

A Carrier of the Opal Fire stepped forward, holding a lacquered wooden box in his arms.

The Emperor started up the steps, followed by Arefaine, the Sisters of the Seasons, Shara, and Baelandra. The Carrier of the Opal Fire brought up the rear, with the mystery box in his hands.

As they neared the top, the sweet, lilting duet of the Zelani's song surrounded them. The singing seemed to descend from the sky until they reached the top and could see Fyrallin and Kirette singing. Shara had handpicked them for the Emperor's visit—they had the most beautiful voices of all her Zelani.

As they reached the gazebo, the Emperor dropped to one knee. Arefaine seemed mesmerized by the sight. Her perfectly expressionless Ohohhim mask dropped for the first time as her powdered features winced. Breaking protocol, she let go of the Emperor's sleeve and walked forward, reverently sinking to her knees next to Brophy's cage. He was dressed in a rich velvet doublet of crimson and orange, with his hands on the pommel of the great Sword of Autumn, its huge red gem and stylized branches glimmering in the sun. His eyes darted frantically under his closed lids.

Arefaine touched the intricate brass bars and blinked. Shara stepped forward, stood behind her, and put a gentle hand her shoulder. Arefaine looked up. Two thin tear streaks marred the powder on her cheeks.

Shara couldn't imagine what it must be like to meet the man who had given his life for yours.

Keeping her breath slow and steady, Shara found it difficult to speak, but she forged on. "I put him in his favorite dream so that he might have some comfort until we find a way to release him." She paused as Arefaine looked up at her, only the tear streaks betraying her impassive Ohohhim expression. Shara swallowed. "It is a small thing, I know, but at least his dreams are pleasant," she said.

Arefaine looked back at Brophy's pulsing eyelids, his eyes darting frantically underneath. Her tears had stopped, and she spoke just loud enough for Shara to hear. "He has kept us safe with his strength all of these years," she said. "And you have helped him, for which you are to be revered." She paused. "But do not deceive yourself, Shara-lani. He lives in a nightmare."

Shara's eyes widened, and her breath left her. Arefaine rose, so close that Shara could have kissed her.

"I am sorry," Arefaine said. "I have dreamed those dreams, and they are unbearable." She rose to her feet and nodded to the Emperor. Shara's hand fell nerveless to her side.

"The Lady Arefaine has brought a gift for the Sleeping Warden," the Emperor said. "If you will allow us to present it."

The Carrier of the Opal Fire brought forward the ornate chest encrusted with three huge opals. They set the heavy box down and stepped away. Arefaine crossed to it, knelt, and opened the lid.

Shara gasped.

Within lay three crystals, each the size of a fist. Muted colors swirled within. They were perfect, miniature replicas of the Heartstone.

CHAPTER 13

All of Ohndarien celebrated, but none so much as Astor, Heir of Autumn. The Grand Feast of the Opal Festival was about to begin. The Emperor was in the city and Arefaine the amazing, the wonderful, was with him. Astor's thoughts had been thrown into a delicious confusion from the first moment he saw her stepping off the ship. He had never seen anyone so radiant, so mysterious in her distant beauty. She almost seemed sad or lonely at the front of the long line of powdered faces. He'd spent the whole walk up the Wheel trying to think of some way to talk to her, to make her laugh so he could see the smile in those pale blue eyes.

Astor hurried down the hallway to his mother's room. Like always, his mother and Baedellin were slow getting ready, but even that could not dampen his mood. He would get them there on time. He paused at the doorway, collecting his thoughts and slowing his breathing before poking his head inside.

Mother sat in her dressing robe on the short bench in front of her vanity. Baedellin sat next to her as both gazed into the huge oval mirror. Mother dabbed a tiny bit of red paste on Baedellin's lips, and the girl tried to spread it evenly with her finger.

"Slowly, dear," Mother said. "The art of a lady's preparation is in the subtlety. We want to elevate our appearance, but we don't want anyone to think we spend time doing so."

Baedellin giggled.

"Father says we'll be late," Astor said from the doorway. Baedellin craned around, then swiveled back as if she hadn't heard him. Mother never moved, but she said, "I'm no longer the Sister of Autumn. I'm allowed to be late."

"That's right." Baedellin giggled. "You men will just have to wait for us. It takes time to be beautiful."

"No, being beautiful is easy. It takes time to stop being ugly."

Baedellin spun around, gave Astor a withering stare, but she noticed that Mother had said nothing, calmly continuing to apply her makeup. Baedellin paused, then turned back into the mirror and spoke in her best adult voice. "Astor is just grumpy because he wants to see his girlfriend."

Looking at Astor in the mirror, Mother raised an eyebrow. He felt his face grow hot but didn't say anything.

"Oh, it's true," Baedellin continued. "He wants to kissy kissy kissy and do the naked dance and have her babies."

"That's enough," Mother said, trying to suppress a smile. "Go get dressed, or your father will eat all the tarts before we get there."

With a last look at her makeup, Baedellin pressed her lips together critically, nodded, and stood up. As she walked toward Astor, she stuck her tongue at him.

"Kissy. Kissy. Kissy," she said.

Astor pretended to lunge at her. With a squeal, she dodged and smacked into the doorjamb. It spun her halfway around, but she giggled. "Kissy, kissy," she said, and darted out the door.

Despite his embarrassment, Astor smiled at her retreating back, then turned to look at his mother.

"She reminds me more of you every day," Mother said.

"I was never that bad," Astor said.

"No. You were twice as bad and half as sweet."

Astor sketched a quick bow. "That must be why you always loved me best."

Mother gave him a disapproving frown before rising and crossing the room to the wardrobe near the bed. She untied her robe and tossed it onto the bed.

"Are you as anxious to get to the feast as Baedellin says?" Mother asked as she pulled two dresses out of the wardrobe. She appraised them for a moment, then laid them both on the bed.

Astor poked at the jewelry box on her dresser, picked up a hairclip shaped like a golden butterfly. Many things came and went from Mother's dresser, but the golden hairclip had been there as long as he could remember.

He nodded. "I am."

"Do I know the girl?"

"Mother, Baedellin is a girl. Girls my age are called women."

Mother laughed softly. She picked the dark crimson dress. "And at my age, all women seem like girls. I apologize. Do I know this woman?"

"No more than I do."

"Are you being mysterious?"

"Mother, I'm embarrassed. Let's not talk about it. She doesn't know who I am." Then he added, "Not yet."

"That is hard to believe," she said, stepping into the dress. She slipped it up over her waist. "You are a Child of the Seasons. Chances are she knows you better than you know her."

"Let's stop."

"As you say."

Astor looked at the space between his mother's breasts for a brief moment before she pulled the dress the rest of the way up. There was a tiny white scar where her shard of the Heartstone was once embedded, testament to her time as Sister of Autumn. He didn't know where she kept the red diamond that used to go there. Once again, Astor felt the call of the Heartstone, always soft in the back of his mind. He would have a gem in his chest someday. And with the arrival of Arefaine and the containment stones, someday soon.

Anxious to change the subject, Astor said, "When do you think Arefaine and Shara will use the containment stones to awaken Brophy?"

Mother tied the long strings of her dress around her neck. "Soon."

Astor thought of Brophy sleeping on the top of the Hall of Windows. When Astor was fourteen, he would sometimes sit and watch Brophy's face for hours. It was like staring into a mirror. That was three years ago. Now Brophy seemed like a mirror to Astor's childhood.

"What was Brophy like as a child?"

"A lot like you."

Astor smiled.

"Except he was polite, well-mannered, thoughtful, conscientious, humble ..."

Astor shook his head.

She crossed to the dresser, twisted her hair up onto her head. She didn't say anything for a moment. Her hands cast about among her jewelry. Astor handed her the golden butterfly hairclip.

"No, not that," she murmured. "Give me that one."

He handed her a golden comb encrusted with rubies, and she tucked it in her hair with a sigh. "Brophy was very similar to you," she murmured. "But he had a seriousness, a focus that frightened me sometimes. I couldn't stand the thought of him in harm's way and protected him as long as I could, but events took him away from me. I wasn't there when he really grew up. I was there for his childhood, but the Physendrian Nine Squares made him a man."

Astor thought about Brophy playing that brutal game. Neither the game nor the country existed anymore, but the legends of both remained. Brophy had been three years younger than Astor when he climbed that burning tower, wounded, exhausted, making himself a god to a nation of his enemies.

"I barely spent ten minutes with him after he returned, before he did what he did, and ..." She drew a long breath. "He was so young." She shook her head a little.

She looked at herself in the mirror over the dresser for a moment, adjusted the front of her dress.

"I wanted to take his place, you know ..." Astor said. "When I was younger."

Mother turned to look at him.

"I even asked Shara to switch us." He looked down, then returned her intense gaze. "I must have been nine or ten."

"I didn't know that," she said softly.

Astor remembered Shara's sad, sad smile as she gently refused him. Looking down at his mother, he coughed. "Well," he said, shrugging and holding his hands out. "There were always these beautiful women singing to him, and nobody ever told him what to do." He smiled. "It seemed like a good trade."

Mother simply watched him for a long time. He thought she was going to say something, but instead she took his head in her hands and bowed it, kissed him on the brow.

"Find my orange scarf with the red embroidered leaves, will you?" she murmured. "It should be in the tall wardrobe."

"When will Shara try to wake him?" he asked as he fetched the scarf from the wardrobe, brought it back to her.

She took it and laid it lightly on her shoulders. "I don't know. The council must discuss it first."

Astor's brow furrowed. "Why?"

She paused as she always did when they talked about council business. "It's your question. Why don't you see if you can answer it?"

Astor rolled his eyes. These questions always became lessons, her way of preparing him for the Test.

"Because they think it is dangerous."

"Don't you?"

"Maybe."

She arched an eyebrow, slipped a bracelet on her wrist.

"All right," he said. "If the corruption gets loose inside the city, we may not be able to defeat it again."

"Exactly. If Arefaine's stones fail to contain the black emmeria, all of Ohndarien could be lost. Or worse."

"Isn't Brophy worth that risk?" Astor said.

"That is what the council will debate. Is one person's life worth taking that chance?"

He wanted to give the quick answer, the answer his heart yelled, but he hesitated. Mother had taught him that his heart was only one of several inner voices. Sometimes the mind spoke the truth, sometimes the body. The key to wisdom was deciding which voice to listen to.

"I would take him to the Heart to minimize the danger. Or move him somewhere where there is nobody around. The Vastness, or the Cinder."

She nodded. "And yet, it is still a huge risk, if what we believe about the black emmeria is true."

"But we have to try," he insisted. "You think we should try, don't you?"

"I am not on the council. It is not a decision I have to make anymore, but I understand their hesitation. I love you and your sister just as much as I love Brophy. And there are thousands of mothers in Ohndarien who love their children as much as I love you. I made these kinds of decisions for long enough. I'm very happy for someone else to make them now." She paused, looked up at him. "But it doesn't matter what I would do. The important question is what would you do if you were on the council?"

Could he risk Baedellin's life, or Mother's, to awaken Brophy? Brophy had gambled with the entire world to save Ohndarien, but could Astor do it? And if he didn't, who would? Who saved the heroes when they needed saving?

Baedellin burst into the room, twirling in her red dress.

Thankfully distracted, Astor smiled. "You look beautiful, like a little spinning bit of fire."

Baedellin screwed up her lips, trying to find the insult. When she couldn't she beamed at him and nodded emphatically. "Thank you, good sir," she said in her adult voice, and curtsied.

"You look lovely, my dear, absolutely lovely," Mother said. Baedellin twirled again.

"Come, it's time to go," Mother said. "We'll have plenty of time to discuss this later."

"Discuss what?" Baedellin asked as they left the room.

❄

The feast was amazing. It always was. The Opal Festival was Ohndarien's greatest holiday, and the feast was its zenith. Tonight, Ohndarien's wealth ran through the city like water through the locks. The party covered the whole top of the Wheel. Entire pigs and oxen were roasted on huge spits, and garlands of flowers hung from every tree in the gardens. Torches taller than a man bordered the festival area, and it seemed as though everyone in Ohndarien had come to celebrate their victory at the Nightmare Battle, and to honor the Ohohhim who made it possible. People talked and ate. Ate and talked. Children scampered through the gardens, as their parents gathered together to discuss art, politics, or the past. Astor saw his father among an aging group of the Lightning Swords, reminiscing about the old days. This was the only night of the year that no one brought up the subject of the next attack.

This was the first year Astor had been allowed to wear his Lightning Sword uniform at the feast. He was proud to wear the deep blue tunic that always drew the eyes of pretty girls, but tonight he found himself lingering at the edge of the crowd. He wasn't normally timid, but that night his feet were heavy, and he kept finding reasons to delay.

The dancing was about to begin, and everyone knew it. Slowly but surely the crowds migrated to the huge bonfires outside the Hall of Windows. The band always started the evening playing slow and stately Ohohhim music to honor the Emperor. The melodies were lovely, sad and lingering, but the Ohohhim never danced to it, and no one in Ohndarien knew how. When the musicians switched to faster more playful Ohndarien tunes, the party would really begin.

The Emperor's entourage sat at the edge of the dancing space on an iron-wood dais that had been specially built for them years ago. Arefaine sat to the right of His Eternal Wisdom. She was a pale vision of beauty, with striking blue eyes. Besides nodding formally to the Sisters of the Council, she hadn't so much as twitched an eyelash since the festival began.

Ten Carriers of the Opal Fire stood around the dais, managing to seem unobtrusive and threatening at the same time. Their tall, black helmets looked like sharks' fins, obscuring everything but dark eyes and grim mouths. Each wore loose, black silk clothing, tied with sashes at the waist, ankles, and wrists. Black-handled long swords lay across their backs, short swords hung at their waists. The center of each of their tunics was embroidered with a white flame. From what Astor could tell, the Carriers were all the same height, the same weight, the same size. They could have been the same person, duplicated over and over.

If Astor didn't do something soon, he would end up standing there all night gazing at Arefaine from a distance. But with the Emperor and everyone else around, there was no way he could just walk up and talk to her. Even if he had the courage to start a conversation, what would he say to her? What would impress her?

Astor let out a breath and ran a hand through his long hair. He wished this was something easy, like sword practice, or reciting the Ohndarien treaties, but Ohndarien's walls weren't built with wishes. If he wanted to talk to her, he'd have to go make it happen. Taking a deep breath, he ran a hand through his hair again and adjusted his doublet. He'd wait till the music changed, then he'd talk to her.

Half an hour later the last lingering note of an Ohohhim ballad faded away and the band launched into a popular new tune called "Two Cats in a Bag." The crowd roared in approval, and people rushed forward to join the dancing.

Suddenly, a little hand grabbed his. Startled out of his reverie, Astor looked down at his sister.

"Come on," she said, hopping up and down. "Come dance."

Astor frowned at her. "No. Not right now."

Her beaming expression faded to a pout. She tugged at his arm. "Come on. We always dance this dance."

"I don't want to dance right now. Maybe later." Ohndariens and a myriad of visiting foreigners began spinning and stepping around the bonfires. Astor looked over the heads of the growing crowd at the Emperor's dais. He regretted it immediately. Baedellin jumped straight up, trying to see where he was looking. She caught a glimpse of the Imperial party, and a mischievous smile crossed her face.

"Oh, you want to dance with your girlfriend. I'll go ask her for you."

Astor grabbed for her arm and missed. Slippery as a snake, she disappeared between the dancing people. He charged after her and ran into a dancer, almost knocking her down. Setting her gently on her feet, he mumbled apologies and lunged through the crowd again.

He almost caught Baedellin at the far edge of the dance circle, but she shrieked and twisted out of his grip, leaving him holding only her scarf. With a growl, he jumped after her—

And pulled up short.

Baedellin stood on the first wooden step of the Ohohhim dais, ten feet away from the Emperor. She stood frozen to the spot. The Carriers of the Opal Fire hadn't moved a muscle, but two of them focused completely on her while the others watched the crowd.

Baedellin swallowed, taking a few steps backward.

Astor nodded to the Emperor and reached out for Baedellin's arm, intending to apologize for her behavior, but she dodged his arm and fled into the crowd, leaving him standing alone in front of the Emperor and Arefaine. Suddenly bereft of any reason for being there, Astor's hastily prepared speech dried up. He swallowed.

At that very moment, the first song came to an end, and the band paused. Silence fell.

"Uh," said Astor. Both the Emperor and Arefaine watched him.

He should just leave, mumble an apology, disappear into the crowd, and go back home to curl into a ball and die. But his feet wouldn't obey him. He couldn't just leave. He had to do something.

Arefaine gave him the barest hint of a smile, and Astor's eyes went wide. A rush of heat filled his chest. He took one step up, then another, then he knelt before her chair. The Emperor watched his approach with the same detached expression as always, but the rest of his entourage shifted, sitting up straighter or leaning forward. One even cleared her throat. Two of the Carriers had moved closer, though their hands did not reach for their weapons. Yet.

Raising his head, Astor looked into Arefaine's dazzling blue eyes. Her brief smile shone in his memory. He offered his hand to her.

"May I have this dance?"

The music started up again at that moment, and Astor smiled.

The Emperor raised his hand and gave a barely perceptible shake of his head. Astor's heart dropped.

But Arefaine stood. Her shimmering white dress flowed down her body like water, straightening without a wrinkle. She extended her hand.

"That would be delightful," she said, her voice lightly accented. Astor glanced at the Emperor, at his attendants. The rest of the Ohohhim had wide eyes, but none spoke. The Emperor's impassive mask reasserted itself, and he looked out over the crowd.

Astor led her down the stairs toward the dancers. Two Carriers followed at a polite distance.

Astor leaned toward her, and asked in a low voice, "I didn't just start a war, did I?"

"Any other day, perhaps," she said. "But not tonight."

"Good," he said, and held out his hand for her to take. She didn't move.

"Um, do you know the steps?" he asked.

She looked over his shoulder at the others dancers. "I think I can follow it."

He held out his hands again, and she took them. A charming smile curved the corner of her mouth, and she looked down briefly as he began the steps.

Astor could scarcely believe it was happening. His heart soared as he turned and stepped with her. She was light on her feet, just as graceful as he imagined.

Suddenly, Baedellin spun in close, turning up her face and making loud kissing noises at them. Then spun away, giggling, and disappeared into the crowd.

"Your sister?" Arefaine asked, arching one of her dark eyebrows.

Blushing from his neck to his hairline, Astor said, "I've never seen that child before in my life."

Arefaine laughed, and a soothing calm washed over him. "I must confess to you. I have never danced before." Again, she spared a brief glance down at their feet. Beneath the white powder on her face, she was blushing, too.

"You are doing wonderfully," he said.

"It is exhilarating."

The two Carriers continually followed them, walking brazenly across the dance floor. They would not let more than ten feet of distance between themselves and Arefaine in the crowded space. Soon, other dancers simply gave Astor and Arefaine a wide berth. The two of them danced alone within their own little space.

They finished the rest of the steps in silence, simply enjoying the movement and the music. Arefaine laughed twice more, each time after she stepped on his foot as the beat changed, and Astor laughed with her. They were both breathless when the song ended.

"This is the moment where everyone stops and looks silly while they wait for the next song," he said.

She smiled, looked over her shoulder.

"Everyone is so open," she said, "They laugh aloud as if no one can hear them. They bare their arms, their legs as if there is no one to see." She nodded toward a pair of Zelani. Bashtin was stripped to the waist, his muscular torso glistening in the firelight. Lovely Galliana was his dance partner for this song, her light blond hair a shimmering curtain across her back. She wore the filmy attire of a Zelani student, the skimpy bodice revealing the curving tops of her breasts, the split-sided wisp of a dress exposing lithe thighs. The girl met his gaze. He nodded and smiled.

"We don't consider legs to be something to hide," Astor said to Arefaine. "They look very nice, I think."

"Yes," she said. "They do." She looked down at herself. "Shall I take shears to my dress?"

A thrill went through him. "I think that *would* start a war."

She smiled at him. The music started again, another jaunty tune that Astor recognized well.

"You'll love this," he said. "Come on!"

All of the couples formed a circle, with the women on the inside and the men on the outside. During the first cycle of the tune, Astor showed Arefaine the steps, then the circle shifted, the men going to the right and the women to the left. Partners changed, and the tune cycled through again. The Carriers kept pace with Arefaine around the outside of the circle.

She danced with everyone, but she kept looking back at Astor. He longed for the dance to come full circle.

When it finally did, he took her warm hand in his, and they spun through the last cycle of the song together. When it was finished, he led her to the edge of the dancing area. They both laughed breathlessly. The musicians started up again with another song.

"Thank you. I've never ... Never done anything like that before," Arefaine gasped, looking at the Emperor's dais briefly, then back at him.

"Surely they have dances back in the Opal Palace," Astor said.

"Not for me," she said softly. He almost didn't hear her over the music.

Astor swallowed, and an awkward silence fell between them. A sudden flush swept his cheeks as he realized he'd never introduced himself.

"I should have already ... I mean to say that I'm Astor. I'm the—"

"The Heir of Autumn. I know. I saw you on the docks."

He smiled. "You did?" He thought he'd caught her gaze for a moment, but he hadn't been sure.

Her face was as composed as the Emperor's, but her eyes sparkled. "Of course." She kept his gaze for a long moment, and he could think of nothing to say. Finally, she spoke again.

"What happened to you?" She reached for the bandage around his head, but didn't quite touch it.

Astor shrugged, not wanting to talk about it. "I slipped in the bath."

"I know who you are. I know what you fight. The entire world owes you a debt of gratitude."

Astor felt a surge of heat rising though his chest. He felt proud and sick all at the same time. "Thank you," he mumbled, "But I think they owe you a whole lot more."

He saw something pass across her face, but he couldn't tell what it was, and he suddenly felt like he'd said the wrong thing.

"Could you show me the Heart?" she finally asked, breaking the awkward silence. "I've heard about it, but never seen it."

Astor nodded. "I will. I mean, I can't take you inside, but I can show you the entrance."

"I'd like that very much."

Moving through the crowd, Astor led her around the Hall of Windows to the Spring Gate. The two Carriers followed them at a polite distance, mute but powerful presences. Astor glanced back at them, then said in a low voice to Arefaine, "Do they follow you everywhere?"

"Only when I'm surrounded by dangerous foreigners." She gave him a sidelong glance.

He smiled.

"Don't worry about them," she said. "They won't bother us."

"Don't they get tired of just following and standing stiff like that?"

She shrugged. "That is what they do."

They entered the Hall. There were no braziers or torches inside on this night, but the moonlight outside filtered through the stained glass, throwing cool blue colors of night on the archways and pillars.

They headed down the steps and passed a couple kissing fervently in the shadows, hands groping. Astor coughed, looking forward as they continued. Arefaine watched the amorous couple until they were obscured by a pillar, then glanced at Astor before she turned forward again. Astor felt his face go hot.

They walked to the center of the amphitheater in silence and stopped in front of the hole in the center of the floor.

"That is where the Heartstone resided until the Nightmare Battle?" Arefaine asked quietly. Gathering her heavy, floor-length dress in one hand, she swept it artfully to the side and descended to her knees, sat back on her heels. The fabric flowed out around her, shimmering like liquid pearls.

"Yes," he said. "Deep in the catacombs. Even I don't know exactly what is down there."

"I can hear her song from the top of the Hall, but it also lingers in this place. Echoes."

He looked at her sharply, and she returned his gaze. As always, he heard the music of the Heartstone thrum through him, an ethereal woman's voice singing from a distance. The Heartstone sang in a language spoken nowhere else in the world, a language of which Astor knew not a single word, and yet he somehow understood. It was his birthright as a Child of the Seasons. As far back as he could remember, even as a small child, he had always heard that singing in the back of his mind. He could almost see his future when he heard it, could feel those notes pulling him forward.

"I've never heard anyone say that." He broke the gaze and stared at the hole, then looked back at her. "Anyone who wasn't a Child of the Seasons. Even some of the Blood can't hear it very clearly, those who aren't likely to take the Test."

"The blood that flows in your veins responds to her magic. Some people's blood is stronger than others."

"I was never told why."

Arefaine nodded. "That is why. But you see, I am more closely related to her than you are."

"Related to a stone?"

"She is my sister," Arefaine said.

Astor's brow furrowed. Arefaine gave him one of her sad smiles. "My sister gave her life to create the Heartstone. You know about the containment stones I brought, yes?"

Astor nodded.

"That's what the Heartstone is. What she was meant to be. After she fled Efften, my sister crafted the stone as a way to free me from the burden our father was forced to lay upon me. She tried to make a vessel strong enough to hold all of the black emmeria, strong enough to release me. She sacrificed herself in the enchantment, creating a containment stone of more beauty and power than the world had ever seen."

Arefaine held out her hands, palms up. "My beloved sister gave her life to save me, but it was not enough. And my fate was set for another three hundred years."

"Is that true?" he murmured softly. Mother had never said anything about it. "I've never heard that tale."

She nodded. "It is true. Few know, but I do."

"How could you know?"

"My sister kept a journal. The Emperor collected it with many other artifacts of Efften. When he was very little, His Eternal Wisdom had a vision about the holy island, about Efften. He has followed that vision ever since. He sent agents to scour the world for any stories, artifacts, or information about the City of Dreams. My sister's journal was one of many items he found." She nodded, a small smile on her lips, and she looked at him. "Your Donovan Morgeon kept journals, too. Sometime you must read his earliest entries, when he first dreamed of Ohndarien. He speaks of my sister there, of her sacrifice. His Eternal Wisdom has the original copies."

"I knew the Heartstone was from Efften, brought here when Ohndarien was founded, but I thought the stone was created by the great archmages a thousand years ago."

"No. It was created in a mud hut in the Vastness, and brought south by

Donovan. He built Ohndarien to house the stone, and hoped that eventually I would be brought here and released from my vigil. But he ran into his own problems trying to build and hold the city. He would be happy to know that his plan finally worked, if much later than he had hoped."

"I've never heard any of this," Astor said.

"Perhaps it is something you learn when you take the Test." She smoothed the front of her dress across her legs, though there wasn't a wrinkle to be found. "I only learned it because I spent my childhood in the library of the Opal Palace. I read and reread every book that mentioned Efften by the time I was ten."

Astor whistled softly. "I think I could count the number of books I'd read at that age on one hand." He smiled sheepishly.

"They called Efften the City of Dreams. It was the height of civilization," she murmured as if she hadn't heard him. "A place where anything was possible. Did you know that they built silver towers that rose a thousand feet into the sky?"

"That's amazing," he said, watching her face. Her gaze was distant.

"Magic made everything wondrous. The Illuminated Scions elevated their people beyond mere mortality. Even the servants had magic to assist them in their menial tasks, and they could study in the great public libraries like everyone else." She looked at him, and her eyes glinted. "It is a crime that envy and petty jealousies can destroy the beauty for all of us. The Silver Islanders were once allies of Efften, left to live in peace so close to the heart of the world. They were given secrets that made them the greatest mariners on the Great Ocean. They showed their gratitude by betraying that trust and attacking Efften at her weakest moment. They slaughtered the old and the young, citizens and servants alike, even mothers with unborn babes in their bellies. Did you know they strung the heads of children across the docks to scare away any who might try to return?"

Astor swallowed hard at the venom in her voice. "I did not know that," he said quietly.

She stared down at the hole that led to the Heart and took a deep breath, then she closed her eyes. "I am going back there someday," she said. "I will return Efften to her former glory."

Several alarming questions leapt to his mind, but her fiery gaze made him pause. He left them unsaid.

"I have heard such different stories about Efften," he said politely.

Her face became impassively Ohohhim again. She nodded. "You heard that it was a horrible place of injustice, overcome by its own greed and lust for dark magic."

He couldn't gauge her emotions, so he nodded hesitantly. "Something like that."

"And yet you did not know that the Heartstone contains the soul of my sister."

"I . . . no."

"The stories you know are lies. Those Silver Islanders wanted to steal the glory of Efften, but you cannot steal power, you cannot steal wisdom. It must be freely given. So they destroyed what they could not dominate. I admit that Efften was in a difficult time just before she fell. But all great cities have such difficult times. Ohndarien has. The Opal Empire has had many. But clearer heads like my father's would have prevailed if we had been given time, if we had not been betrayed."

She stopped, drew a long breath, then watched him closely. Astor kept his face as neutral as he could manage. With a small smile, she waved a hand. "Look at this beauty, all of the loveliness of Ohndarien. Efften had ten times this beauty. It had ten times the majesty of the Opal Palace. What the Ohohhim know of grandeur they learned from Efften. The splendor of Ohndarien is but a reflection of its parent city. Efften's Illuminated Scions were the pinnacle of what humans could accomplish, and they would have gone farther. Their magic was a gift to the world, a tool for creating beauty. Now it is scattered. Destroyed. Poured into the ocean like so much dirt."

Her eyes glowed in the purple light. Astor's pulse raced as she stared at him.

"I am sure you would feel the same way about Physendria if they had succeeded in destroying Ohndarien," she said, raising her voice.

"I'm sure I would," he said, trying to put a convincing tone in his voice, but she wasn't fooled. She looked like she was about to give him a scathing reply, but a little firefly appeared from behind her ear and began to float around her head. It seemed to distract her for a moment, and her gaze softened.

Astor looked closer at the tiny ball of incandescent light. "By the Seasons!" he whispered. "What is it?"

"Not 'it,'" she said, holding her hand up so the light circled her wrist. "He."

Reaching out, she touched Astor's hand. The little light landed on his fingertip.

"He buzzes," Astor said, unable to contain a grin.

"His name is Lewlem, and he is one of my oldest friends. He has always been there when I needed him."

The little glowing ball flew off his finger and disappeared up the sleeve of Arefaine's gown.

Astor felt the loss immediately, like a fire going out. "How did you do that?" he asked.

She smiled at him differently than before, a sly, mischievous smile. "Magic." She winked at him.

Astor couldn't do anything more than stare as she rocked back on her heels and rose. Her gown flowed back down her legs. She glanced over her shoulder at the two Carriers of the Opal Fire, standing like statues just out of earshot. "Thank you for the dance; you are very kind, but I should return now."

"It was no kindness." Astor winced. "I mean, I am the grateful one, that you should dance with me." He shut up. He didn't want the evening to end.

"I am sorry to burden you with the anger of a girl who lost her family before she ever knew them. You have more than your own share of troubles."

He shook his head. "When will I . . . I mean will I see you again?"

"So sweet," she murmured, and took him by the hands. She stood on her tiptoes and kissed him on the lips.

His eyes went wide. Before he could even think about what to do, the kiss was over. She let go of his hands and stepped back.

"Something else I have never done," she murmured with a little smile. "I will cherish this moment. Thank you."

She turned and rejoined the Carriers, who escorted her from the Hall of Windows. Astor watched her leave, his pulse pounding in his ears.

CHAPTER 14

Ossamyr coughed. A thin thread of seawater drooled from the corner of her mouth. Sharp palm fronds scratched her cheek, and she tried to raise her head. The back of her throat was brittle parchment, and her head felt as though it were trapped between two rocks. She did not try to sit up, but instead opened her gummy eyes and looked across the sand and rocks of the beach. Bits of broken wood lingered in the white foam at the edge of the ocean. The last remains of her boat.

How am I alive? she thought, unsure how her desperate swim through the black waters could possibly have succeeded. She didn't recall making it to the beach. All she remembered was swimming, swallowing more water, losing track of her breathing as she tried to push her body further and further. But somehow the storm was over, and she was here.

She shivered as the sun baked her and the breeze chilled her by turns. A thick cloud of bloodsucking flies buzzed about her, clustering on her cuts. With a feeble gesture, she brushed at them. They buzzed away before settling once again on her wounds.

Through a haze of half-formed thoughts, she got ahold of herself. She wasn't out of danger yet. Trying to control the pain in her head, she ignored the flies and concentrated on her breathing, trying to gather her strength. The steady cadence of her breath lulled her.

Yes. That was better. She could just stay here for a while. The pain wasn't so great if she just lay still. Go back to sleep. Yes. She could sleep a while longer.

"Your Majesty, you have awakened at last," a gentle voice said to her.

Her eyelids flickered open again. Agony rose to the surface. Enemies! The Silver Islanders! Had the bastards come ashore? She could not fight them. She could not even sit up.

She rolled over, and the world wobbled as she panted with the exertion. Every breath was fire against her ragged throat. Her canvas sailor's breeches were stiff, crusted with salt, and her shirt was in tatters. Climbing to hands and knees, she craned her head upward.

Less than twenty feet away, a middle-aged man sat on the moss-covered ruins of an ancient building. The wall lined the edge of a great city, rising against the encroaching jungle like a shield thrust into a patch of weeds. The man was bare-chested, wearing a shimmering green sarong, and he stood and bowed with an elegance that belonged at court.

"I am so pleased. You lay there so long, I feared for your life."

Her tongue was so swollen that she could only croak. She tried to swallow, but could not, and bowed her head.

"Please, don't speak," the man said, coming closer. He stopped a few feet away from her. "You must be parched. There is a fountain nearby, filled with fresh water."

Ossamyr clenched her teeth and, leaning on a curved palm tree, levered herself to her feet. She finally managed to swallow.

"Then this is Efften?" she rasped, regretting it immediately. Her throat burned.

The man had a well-trimmed mustache and a long, pointed beard, both streaked with gray. His pale blue eyes sparkled in the sunlight. "Oh yes. What is left of her."

She took a hesitant step forward. Pain lanced into the back of her thigh, and her leg gave. She pitched forward onto the beach.

Feebly spitting sand from her mouth, she rose to her knees again, looked up at the man. He stood a polite distance away without offering to help. Finally, she managed to stand on her own and shuffled forward. Her arrow wound throbbed.

"This way," the man said, motioning for her to follow.

She did, one labored step at a time. "Who are you?" she rasped.

"Ah," he murmured, pursing his lips. "A shadow of what once was. A thought that refuses to die. An apology for a beautiful dream gone astray."

Ossamyr wondered if she was hallucinating. How could the man be here? Was it a trick? He acted so calm, as if he lived here, but no one had lived on Efften for centuries.

I am dying, she thought. *This is the last fancy of a dying woman.* She stopped, put her hand against a moss-covered wall. Closing her eyes, she willed reality to assert itself. She evened her breathing. A tiny wisp of her power lifted her spirits. It was pitifully weak; the thrum of her Zelani was very far away, but not entirely gone.

She opened her eyes.

The man in the sarong stood at a distance, waiting politely. Ossamyr's knees wobbled, and she locked them straight.

"It is this way, Your Majesty," he said.

With a tiny grunt, Ossamyr pushed herself away from the wall and staggered onward.

He led her across the sand to a path between two ruined buildings. The jungle had reclaimed the city, moving in and covering everything that had once been tall and grand.

Ossamyr stayed silent as they wended through the broken walls of the buildings. He led her to a shattered, defaced fountain that must once have been breathtaking. Broken pieces littered the lichen-spotted courtyard, bearing exquisite carvings. A trickle of water poured from the center, finding its way through the cracks until it soaked into the green ground between the flagstones.

Ossamyr slumped onto the fountain, wincing at the pain in her leg. She put her cracked lips to the tiny stream. It went through her like a cold jolt of lightning. She sucked the cool, clear water into herself, forcing it past her ravaged throat.

"Slowly, please," the man said. "Not too fast."

Despite her dire need, Ossamyr knew he was right. She would vomit if she wasn't careful. Forcing herself away from the delicious, life-giving water, she blinked up at him.

She spoke again, wincing against the pain. "You are ... one of the Illuminated Scions?" she rasped. "An archmage of Efften?"

"I am Darius Morgeon, once an archmage of Efften and now just a very old, very lonely man."

Ossamyr paused. Everyone in the world knew that name.

"Darius Morgeon?"

"The same."

"How?"

The man chuckled politely. "You don't believe me."

She wished she was fresh, ready for this conversation, wished she could be sure that it wasn't a fever dream. "You'd have to be almost four hundred years old," she said.

"Something like that, yes."

Her head swam. Could it be true? All of the archmages had been slain. Despite herself, a tiny flicker of hope rose within her. She leaned over the fountain and took another mouthful of water, then sat upright and wiped her lips. "I am Ossamyr-lani."

"I know who you are, Queen of the Golden City. My daughter has seen you in Brophy's dreams."

"Your daughter?" she asked quietly, pursing her lips doubtfully, but her hands gripped the edge of the fountain tighter.

"Yes, my eldest daughter, Jazryth. She gave her life to create Ohndarien's Heartstone."

"But she's dead."

The man shrugged. "Only the body dies. Ani is eternal, surely you know that."

A hundred questions came to her mind.

"How is he? How is Brophy?"

But Darius Morgeon only smiled. He inclined his head. "Come, let me show you what remains of the City of Dreams. And I will take you to the artifacts you seek."

Her heart leapt. "You have the containment stones? They are actually here?"

"Oh yes. Dozens of them."

The warmth of triumph spread through her. She stood up, feeling somewhat stronger because of the water. She extended her hand to him.

"Please, show me the way."

He held up a hand in a formal gesture, declining the offered touch, and she lowered her arm.

"Obtaining the stones will not be a problem," he said. "Taking them from the island will be."

"One step at a time," Ossamyr said, echoing the words of her dear friend. It was fitting Shara's words came to her now, when she was so close to her prize. But Ossamyr was well prepared for the next step. Months ago, Ossamyr had stashed a small boat on one of the many tiny islands just to the south. The Silver Islanders patrolled the waters around Efften fanatically, but they were looking for ships. Even they should not be able to find an individual swimmer in the vast ocean. It would be a hellish journey, but after some rest and food, her magic should be enough to carry her through.

"Yes," Darius echoed. "One step at a time."

He led her through the ruins into the heart of the city. Despite the crumbling walls, the vines that snaked across and the trees that grew straight up through the flagstones, majesty breathed from the buildings all around her. High, thin arches crossed the wide streets. Some of the arches served as walkways between the third and fourth stories of taller buildings. Some were free-standing decorative structures, triumphant testaments to a culture that had loved power and beauty for its own sake.

The buildings gave way to a huge square, and they started across. A knee-high wall sketched a meandering shape in the center of the square. It must have once been a pool with a series of fountains. The individual fountains had been reduced to rubble, and even the short wall was broken in places. There was no water in the place anymore. Ossamyr tried to imagine what the square had been like at Efften's height of power, filled with colorful banners and art, the latest fashions worn by the citizens as they bustled about, buying and selling.

She kept thinking of the Water Wall in Ohndarien, of the great locks. Each building in Efften contained the same mastery, but there was a flowing elegance to these buildings that Ohndarien lacked, as if they had grown up in relation to one another, built by a dream rather than human hands.

"Is this the main square?" Ossamyr asked, looking around at the wide expanse.

Darius laughed. "No. This is Gibling's Square, the fourth largest in the city. If you like, I can take you to see the Silver Wharf, easily three times this large. That is where most of the trading happened." He waved a hand around. "This was a servant's market."

Ossamyr kept the awe off her face, walking slowly, trying to take it all in. As she moved around the dry, meandering fountain, she looked up between two tall buildings and caught a glimpse of a towering spire in the distance. She stopped, her neck craning as her gaze followed it up into the sky. In a daze, she moved toward it.

The pearl-and-silver tower spiraled straight up, the tallest building Ossamyr had ever seen. It made the Citadel look like a stack of children's blocks. Vines gripped and twisted up its base, but even they could not grow as tall as the grandiose structure and left off a third of the way up. Impossibly high in the air, at the very top, the tower fanned out into a wide atrium.

She stopped, breathless.

"Beautiful, isn't it?" Darius nodded. "There are five of them, actually."

"The silver towers of Efften."

He smiled. "Yes."

"It looks as if it is made of metal. I can't believe I didn't see it before now, it is so tall."

"From a distance, you can see them all, but they are obscured inside the city unless you're standing right next to one, or unless you catch a vantage point like this."

"This is what I saw as I was sailing in," she breathed. "In the storm."

"No doubt. That one is my tower." He nodded at it.

"Of course," she murmured.

"Well, I had family and servants who lived with me." He smiled. "So I wasn't all alone."

"The Silver Islanders pulled down so many other buildings. Why did they leave these standing?" she asked.

Darius chuckled. "Well, they tried to raze them. But there is a bit more to those towers than granite and silver." He paused, then beckoned to her. "Come, that is where we are bound. I will show you."

But Ossamyr remained in the middle of the square, her eye fixed on the lofty tower. Finally, she looked at Darius. "Why are you helping me?"

He raised an eyebrow. "Because you defied those hateful savages. Because you bested them. Anyone who has the courage to do that, I will help until my last breath."

She nodded, gazing up at the tower, then asked, "Why did you stay? There is nothing here for you. You have no family, nobody else to talk to, to live with."

Darius lowered his eyes, his long beard drooping just a little. "I am waiting for my daughters to return."

"You mean—"

An arrow hit the man, and he exploded in a flash of light. The blast threw her to the ground, sending her sliding across the stones. Multicolored fire showered her. Another arrow flew, passing through the space Darius had occupied a second ago. But he was gone. Completely destroyed. The arrow clattered on the stones, sparking from the tip.

"By the Nine!" Ossamyr swore, lurching to her feet. Two stocky men and a burly woman burst from behind the cover of a low, crumbling wall. Their long, bound hair was streaked with silver paint. Black and silver tattoos covered their bare skins and faces. They shot their bows again as they ran, and Ossamyr tried to duck, but all three arrows hit her. Two in the chest and one in the side.

She stumbled to her knees, gasping at the pain. She bled from where she'd been struck, but the arrows had not penetrated. One of the shafts fell into her lap. It wasn't sharp. It was tipped with a small, blunt crystal shining with swirling multicolored lights.

The hunters raced across the square, dropping their bows and pulling short spears from sheaths across their backs. Ossamyr summoned power as best she could, but barely heard the whisper of the magic that usually sang through her body.

"Stop," she commanded, rising, letting the magic flow into the three murderers. She made the motion with as much grace as she could muster, but still she shook, as weak as a newborn. She had to be quick.

The largest man paused, his eyes going glassy. But the other two stabbed her with their spears.

The blows slammed her backward onto the ground in a shower of multicolored sparks. Just like the arrows, the spears were blunt and tipped with those strange crystals. Her magic vanished, and she moaned at the loss. The pain felt as if someone had pulled her stomach out through her belly button.

"Try that again, witch, and I'll stab out your eyes," the woman said.

Through a haze of pain, barely able to breathe, Ossamyr's mind raced. She had to think of something. She was so close to her prize. The three brutes stood around her, gripping their spears. Rainbow colors swirled in the tips.

"She is not of the darkness," said the largest of the three, a broadshouldered man with a silver and black crescent painted on his chest. "The stones had no effect."

The woman's arms were painted with spirals of dark silver all the way to her shoulders. "She still must die. Reef says she is one of the Warden's witches, dedicated to waking him."

The third Silver Islander seemed content to defer to the other two. He remained silent.

Spiral Arms raised her spear, and the third Silver Islander copied the action, but Crescent Chest held up a hand.

"Wait," he said.

"But Reef says—" the woman began, but Crescent Chest made a chopping motion with his hand.

"Reef is not here."

The woman frowned, but she and the other Islander lowered their spears.

Crescent Chest turned to Ossamyr and crouched, putting them nose to nose. "Why are you here? This place is forbidden."

Breathing hard, she stared into his dark eyes.

"I am here for love."

He grunted, rocked back on his heels. "Love?" He rolled the word around in his mouth. "You are one of the Sleeper's witches."

"I don't know what you mean."

"You are from the Blue City, the second Efften?"

"I am from Ohndarien."

He nodded impatiently as though she'd just repeated what he had said.

"And you love the Corrupted One, the Sleeping Warden?"

"His name is Brophy," she said. "He protects us all, and I'm here to help him."

"There is no help for him." Crescent Chest grunted, his thick, muscled legs rippling as he stood up again. He turned to the others. "Bring her. We must not linger."

Ossamyr looked up in time to see Spiral Arms' crystal-tipped spearhead coming at her. It struck her between the eyes.

The world went black.

CHAPTER 15

The black-lacquered walls of Arefaine's stateroom glistened as if wet, as though she were trapped inside a shard of obsidian.

She stood silently in the center of her room as six attendants prepared her for bed. She stared into the mirror fixed on the wall over her chest of drawers, watching as the young women transformed her from Ohohhim goddess to nineteen-year-old girl. Their deft fingers sponged off the white powder that had been mixed with crushed opals. Slowly the servants revealed Arefaine's true face, large azure eyes, straight nose, and high cheekbones, the features she shared with the legendary Illuminated Scions of Efften. She was her father's daughter, a true child of the great race.

Arefaine had been confined to her quarters all day. She had displeased the Emperor at the celebration the previous night, and he quietly suggested that she spend the day meditating in her quarters, listening for the voice of Oh. Despite her anger at being treated like a child, she had made good use of her time in confinement, going over each moment of the previous day, savoring it like a rare delicacy.

When the bath was ready, the silent women removed her samite gown. One attendant held her left arm, and one held her right as she stepped into the steaming hot water. A slight pain ran through her as she knelt and lay back against the copper rim.

Arefaine closed her eyes as they delicately filed and removed the paint from her nails, brushed and meticulously removed the oil from her hair. They scrubbed her pale skin until it was pink. She did not move as they worked on her, did not say anything. There was no point. Her attendants never spoke to her. That would be rude, above their station. The only details Arefaine knew about them were their names, so she might call upon them if she had a need.

Only the Emperor and the priests of Oh were allowed to speak directly to her, and it was a privilege they seldom used.

Arefaine was told that the people of Ohohhom loved her. They called her beautiful. They called her a goddess. They called her mystical, mysterious, magical, anything but friend.

When she was younger, Arefaine had dreamed of fleeing from her stewards to live a brutal life on the dusty steppes of Kherif, or to make a mud mask, run away, and hide among the Vizai, or perhaps even to sail away to the fiercely beautiful Fortress of Light, the last reflection of Efften in the world.

She had shared her feelings with the Emperor once, demanding to be set free. He simply nodded and reminded her of those few unfortunate incidents from her childhood. It was best for all concerned if she remained where she was. "Wait for the voice of Oh," he told her. "He will show you when it is time to move on."

The only glimpse of the world Arefaine had been allowed was through books. The only strangers she had contact with were a few foreigners whose ambiguous place in the divine queue allowed them greater freedom than the Ohohhim.

When Arefaine was seven, an artist from the Summer Cities visited Ohohhom. He quietly sketched her with bits of charcoal on a canvas as tall as a man. When he had finished, he knelt before her, bowing his head. "I have never seen anything so pure, so flawless," he said. She reached out and touched his head, as the priests of Oh did with pilgrims. Two Carriers of the Opal Fire immediately rushed forward and escorted him out of the room. She never again saw the man or his half-finished portrait.

She did not touch anyone after that.

For years, Arefaine had played the goddess in Ohohhom, visiting temples erected in her honor, but never once setting foot in another person's home. But now she was in Ohndarien. The Fortress of Light. The place that was once called the Free City, the one place in the world with no laws, no locks on the doors, no endless line leading to Oh. She had been here once before when she was just a baby, and a young man took pity on her, taking her crushing burden upon himself, granting her freedom at the cost of his own. It was time she returned the favor and emancipated herself in the process. The containment stones she brought would be the key to Brophy's prison, and hers.

With the help of her attendants, Arefaine rose from the bath and stepped onto a plush rug. They wrapped her in soft towels, drying the water from her body. Two of them held out the sleeves of her dressing robe, but Arefaine shook her head and ushered them from the room. They seemed confused at first, but she insisted, and they slowly formed a short line and shuffled from the room.

Brazen in her nakedness, Arefaine spun about the room as if she were dancing with Astor again. She could still feel the touch of the young Heir of Autumn's lips, the warmth of his hand on her back as they danced. It was still strange that they had stolen away and talked just like two young people. She'd wanted to kiss him again, to watch that eager young man widen his eyes. She'd wanted his hands on her, wanted to feel what was forbidden.

But she knew that was impossible. The Carriers would have leapt forward in an instant if she had dared such a thing. The Emperor had lengthened the chains that held her, but he was not ready to release her. And she was not yet ready to force his hand.

No. She would allow the chains for the time being. She would even use them to her advantage. After so much waiting, planning, the time had come, and it all began with her gift to the Sleeping Warden.

She needed the ani that young man held locked within his dreams. If Arefaine was going to go home, if she was going to rebuild the City of Dreams, she needed the power that Brophy held.

Her father still waited for her on the isle of Efften. He'd entrusted her with the task of returning the Heartstone to the City of Sorcerers filled with the emmeria, the Legacy of their ancestors. Together they would purify that dark magic. Together they would cleanse the sins of the past and rebuild a world of light, beauty, and endless possibility. Together they would release the entire world from her chains.

CHAPTER 16

Shara stalked from the Hall of Windows, seething with frustration. The council chambers had been packed for the past two days. Most people seemed to support Brophy's immediate release, but everyone had the right to speak before the Ohndarien Council, and the obnoxious minority always seemed to eat up the majority of the time. Shara had sat through an endless stream of self-centered caution and petty cowardice as the citizens debated when—or if!—the Brother of Autumn should be released. She finally had to leave, unable to maintain her composure any longer.

She took a deep breath of the cool night air, thick with the scent of flowers, and headed down one of the secluded garden paths. Shara could sense Baelandra behind her, hurrying to catch up with her. Shara kept walking. She needed to be alone.

Eighteen years. She had never felt the time more heavily than now. The containment stones were here, waiting useless in her tower. Brophy should be free by now.

Her walk became a quick stride, and she broke into a run, blazing past fountains and glades of fruit trees in full blossom. Eighteen years of pent-up emotion surged through her body, and Shara channeled all that power into her legs.

She reached the edge of the Wheel and leapt over the rim. Magic burst from her heart as she fell. It surged into her limbs, tingling across her skin. Flinging her arms out, she whirled into the Spinning Fall pose, the edges of her dress whipping about her. The energy of the Floani form coursed through her as she fell fifty feet to the base of the Wheel. Her charged body took the impact, and she rolled twice across the ground. She danced to her feet, spinning seamlessly into a run, then slowing to a walk. The energy crackled about her, ready for more, ready to leap again, but she cycled it through her breath.

A single waterbug bobbed in the water not far from where she had landed. The man in the boat stood up, straining to get a better look at her through the darkness.

Shara ignored him and broke into a jog. She knew just where she needed to go.

❄

Fifteen minutes later she stood atop the city's ramparts, gasping for breath. A steady breeze pushed the hair back from her face, and she let the wind pass through her, cooling her anger, calming her racing mind. She leaned against the battlements until her breathing was back under control. Beyond her the Summer Seas were a black abyss flickering with sketches of scant moonlight.

The touch of the cool stone beneath her forearms was reassuringly familiar as she looked east from highest point of Ohndarien's walls. Shara had come to this spot many times over the years. It made her sad, but the sorrow was tinged with hope.

There was a smattering of exposed reefs to the east of Ohndarien called the Petal Islands. Most were just jagged rocks, but a few were covered with verdant meadows and cypress groves. The islands drew their name from a poem written long ago that described them as "a wind dance of flower petals cast upon the moon-kissed waves." The famous verses told the story of a man who fought with his wife and drove her into the arms of another man. When he heard the new couple had sailed from the city, the man forgot his anger, raced to the top of the wall, and threw himself into the ocean, vowing to swim out and catch his wife before he lost her forever. The poem never said whether he succeeded.

Shara could barely see the westernmost of those islands through the darkness, but she imagined one in particular. Her special one. Their island.

Long ago on a Kherish sailing ship headed for the Cinder, she and Brophy had dreamed of building a cottage in the Petal Islands. In the early years of Brophy's sleep, she had built that little cottage to surprise him when he finally awoke. With every stone she added to the little cottage's walls, Shara imagined the glorious days she and Brophy would spend making love and the endless nights they would lie in each other's arms, catching up on everything they had missed through the long, lonely years. It was meant to be their little haven away from the pressures and duties of Ohndarien. No one would clamor for their attention. There would be no decisions more pressing than which berries to pick for dessert. They could finally have their happy ending.

Shara sighed. That island seemed closer than ever but still just out of sight.

She pressed her palms against the blue-white marble of the battlements, trying to cycle her frustration out through her breath, trying to find patience with the council's hesitation.

What if the council refused to release Brophy? Would she use the containment stones regardless? Would she go behind the backs of the people who had become her family?

After three days of clear skies, another storm was passing them to the south. The dark clouds made her think of Ossamyr, wherever she was. She could really use a dose of the queen's bitter sarcasm right now.

"So you are the spider at the center of the web."

Shara turned so suddenly she nearly lost her balance. Gripping the parapet with one hand, she stared at the man who'd just spoken. She hadn't sensed his presence. And what was worse, she still didn't.

To her magical senses, he didn't exist.

She took a step back. "Who are you?"

The man was not tall, he stood at eye level with her, but he was massive. His shoulders stretched the fabric of his rough-spun, sleeveless shirt, and his arms were as big around as her thighs, covered with an intricate network of tattoos. He wore the loose blue leggings of a sailor, stained by salt water and worn by use, and his legs were tree trunks underneath. Shara had never seen a man so thick, so solid. He looked like he could row a boat from Ohndarien to Kherif and barely break a sweat. His eyes were an eerie golden color.

"I am Reef," he said, walking up and putting his thick, hairy forearms on the battlement next to her. He had short-cropped black hair going gray at the temples. A deep scar puckered his face, starting at the bridge of his nose and curving to his ear. He looked in the direction she had been staring and spat over the edge.

Shara appraised him through slitted eyes. Most men knew enough to leave a Zelani alone. "If you're looking for a good time, Islander, you won't find it here. You'd best move along, I'd like to be alone."

He gave her a sidelong glance. "Islander? That's being polite. Most call me pirate or sea scum."

"Believe me; I have good reason to distrust Silver Islanders."

He shrugged. "Can't say I blame you, I don't trust most of them either. But I would wager you've never met a real Silver Islander before."

He was goading her, but she refused to take the bait. "That's absurd."

He smiled mirthlessly, just a slight widening of his mouth. "The world is full of absurdities." He spat over the edge again and turned around. "You're prettier than I thought you would be."

"I'm flattered."

"We heard you were fair from some of the Gold Islanders, but I didn't believe them. I thought they had fallen under your spell."

Shara tried to probe him with her power, tried to feel his heat, his emotions, anything. He simply wasn't there. It made her fingers itch to reach out and touch him, to make sure he was real. At least she could smell him, a faint masculine smell mixed with the sea. It was chilling to realize how much she had come to rely on her magical senses.

His smile curled the corners of his mouth. "You won't get your hooks into me, witch."

"Don't be so sure."

"I'm sure."

"What do you want?"

"I came to give you a chance. To see reason."

"This coming from a Silver Islander?"

He shook his head. "We are the sane ones. It's the rest of the world that's crazy."

"Siren's Blood drives people mad. I've seen it."

"Not the strong ones."

"And you, of course, are one of the strong ones."

He bored into her with his odd golden eyes. "Don't wake the boy."

She gave a short, sharp laugh. "I hope you didn't come all the way from Slaver's Bay just to tell me that."

He paused, running his fingers behind the rough-spun sash wrapped around his waist. It was burdened with several pouches, a small sack, and a seaman's knife. His fingers rested lightly on the pommel. "I could kill you," he said.

"You'd have to."

He sneered. "Without your magic. It's your arms against mine. Your speed against mine."

Shara gathered her energy, ready to respond. "Somehow I doubt it will come to that."

"You shouldn't."

"And yet there you stand."

The muscles in his square jaw worked for a moment. His forearm twitched, and she watched him struggle with the idea of stabbing her.

Finally, he smiled ruefully and shook his head. "That is the problem with you people. You children of Efften have always lacked the capacity for self-doubt. You refuse to see the whole picture." He looked her slowly up and down. "But you will. If you refuse to listen, the truth will be forced on you just like it was forced on them."

Shara remembered the tapestries depicting the burning of Efften that once hung in the Zelani school. She imagined Ossamyr out there alone somewhere, trying to slip past men just like this. "The last man who tried to force something on me came to regret it."

Reef snorted. "I'm sure he did." He spat over the wall. "You are not what I expected. I'll give you that. I'd say you've cast an enchantment on me if I thought it was possible."

He pulled a sculpted green bottle from the sack tied to his waist. It glowed, filled with tiny lights of every color of the rainbow. He held it out to her.

She glanced at it, but did not take it.

"It would be a lot easier just to kill you," he said in a low voice. "But I'm a softhearted fool. Drink this, and you'll see the whole picture."

She raised an eyebrow. "What is it?"

"You should know. I already sent you a bottle."

"I have no idea what you are talking about."

Reef scowled and held the bottle out to her. "It's Siren's Blood. The real thing. Not the watered-down swill the Gold Islanders sell to foreigners."

"I don't know what a Gold Islander is."

"Yes you do. You think they're Silver Islanders. So do they, but all they care about is flesh, wine, and gold. Much like the fools in the Summer Seas."

She reached for the bottle and brushed his fingers as he gave it to her. His skin was warm, rough. He wasn't a phantom.

"And what will drinking this show me?" she asked.

"The truth."

Shara looked at the man doubtfully, but there was no trace of mockery in the Silver Islander's face. He was deadly serious. With a firm nod, he stood up and backed away.

"I may have been wrong about you," he said. "I hope so. But I'm not wrong about the boy. He must not wake until the time is right."

"And when is that?"

"Certainly not in my lifetime. Perhaps in yours."

He continued backing up until the shadows obscured him, and all Shara could see was his hulking silhouette.

"Keep that bottle away from the Awakened Child of Efften and the black-hearted crone from Physendria. They are conspiring to bring the Summer Fleet through your locks. That must not happen." He continued walking backward, though his deep voice still carried to her.

"Drink the wine and all will be made clear," he said. "Drink it all."

Shara looked down at the ancient bottle with the swirling points of light trapped inside. It felt strange in her hand, too heavy for its size. There was a subtle but unmistakable power trapped behind that glass. She could feel it without even trying. When she looked up again, Reef was gone. She searched for him with her magic one more time, but there was nothing, only darkness and the storm in the distance.

CHAPTER 17

Issefyn stood on the Long Bridge watching the Emperor's flagship in the distance. The market was deserted this time of night, and a simple glamour easily kept her hidden from the two fin-helmeted goons standing guard on the docks.

Arefaine had been in the city nearly three days, but the two of them had not had a chance to speak yet. Issefyn had been waiting for an opportunity to catch the girl alone, but that was proving much more difficult than she imagined. Their eyes had met briefly when the girl first disembarked, but that was all. They had a lot to discuss after all this time.

Seeing Arefaine again had reminded Issefyn of herself at that age. The court of Physendria had been a gilded brothel. Young women from every house schemed their way into the beds of highborn noblemen, each certain that the treasure she held between her legs was more precious than the next. But Issefyn had always been a survivor. She knew how to mark her quarry, run it down, slit its throat.

Arefaine resembled a young woman Issefyn had known long ago. Sessepha had been Issefyn's primary rival for the king's interest, a sleek little bitch with impeccable manners and mastery of every courtly nuance. She swung her beauty around like a whip, wounding or entangling as she chose. The king practically salivated whenever she was around. Sessepha would surely have wed the fool if she hadn't perished when her father's ship sunk off the coast of Physen. There had been only one survivor of that crash, Sessepha's best friend and confidante, Issefyn, who emerged half-drowned on the beach.

Issefyn learned the most important lesson of her life from her friendship with Sessepha. Your enemy's trust is the best dagger with which to slay her.

I will sink you, too, Child of Efften, she thought. *I will swim in the waters that birthed you and claim your secrets for my own. Then we will see which of us deserves to sit on Efften's throne.*

Morgeon's daughter finally emerged on deck for an evening stroll. She walked to the prow of the ship and watched the moon setting over the Citadel. The child sorceress was backlit by the silvery orb, and her silhouette reminded Issefyn of the first time she had ever seen the Awakened Child of Efften.

The tiny girl had stood before one of the impossibly tall windows in the pretentious throne room of the Opal Palace, only a slim shadow against bright moonlight as she looked out to sea. The child had worn the black gown of Ohohhim nobility, her face powdered, her long dark hair combed and oiled to perfection.

Had it only been six years since that moment? It seemed like a hundred. At the time, Issefyn had recently joined the Zelani of Ohndarien. She had barely begun to spin the web that would entrap her son's murderers. She didn't want to kill the women quickly, artlessly. She intended to take her time, savor the moment. At Shara's request, Issefyn and Ossamyr traveled to the Opal Palace to seek an audience with the Awakened Child of Efften, to search for any clues that would awaken her precious Brophy from his eternal sleep. They stayed in the palace for months, honored guests of the Emperor. Several times, the Emperor received them. Several times, Ossamyr requested an audience with the Awakened Child. Every time they were politely received and politely ignored. Ossamyr's feeble patience was quickly spent, but Issefyn had her own plans. She wasn't about to let propriety—or the pathetic Carriers of the Opal Fire—keep her from her quarry.

Using her magic, Issefyn easily slipped past the guards, following the scent of power through the labyrinth of the Opal Palace. In the cold, empty throne room, she found Arefaine standing by that tall window, gazing out at the surf. Issefyn could still hear the arrogant child's first words.

"A warm welcome to you, my sister," Arefaine said, never taking her eyes from the moon.

"You don't belong here, child."

"I know. And you believe you have come to liberate me?"

Issefyn had been irked at the tone in her voice, but continued without a ruffle. "These sleeve-chasers are afraid of you. They hold you back, keep you locked in the shadows when you were meant to outshine the sun."

"Yes." The child paused for a moment, then said, "You are a descendant of Efften."

"My grandmother's grandmother was born there," Issefyn admitted, wondering how the girl could possibly know.

"Tell me about it."

"It would take me years to teach you the secrets of Efften. I could take you as my apprentice if you wish to learn. We could leave tonight. No one would know until you were already gone. I can show you more than your chalk-faced monks could possibly imagine."

Arefaine turned, her pale blue eyes looking calmly into Issefyn's soul.

"But I'm already stronger than you."

Issefyn laughed, a genuine laugh at the arrogance of youth. But Arefaine's calm, steady gaze rattled her confidence, and she stopped laughing. The young sorceress's first lesson would have to be humility. When Arefaine found herself dancing like a puppet on Issefyn's strings, she would keep a civil tongue around her new master.

Issefyn reached out with her mind to infiltrate the girl's thoughts. Suddenly, Issefyn was under siege. She gasped and stumbled under the onslaught. The press came from all around her like undeniable claws, grabbing, crushing, rending. Issefyn found herself in the battle of her life. She pushed back viciously, but she might as well have been trying to throw the Great Ocean off her back. She was enveloped, smothered, and could not find her compass. Darkness covered her eyes, and Arefaine disappeared from sight.

"I could kill you now." The little bitch's voice floated at her from every direction at once. Issefyn lashed out, flinging her will into the darkness. "The Carriers would find you here, cold and dead. They would merely think an old woman died of a sudden strain."

Issefyn groped about the room again, blind, desperately seeking the girl's mind. But it wasn't there. Nothing was there. Just empty darkness.

"Now, you were talking of masters and apprentices," Arefaine said. "I have a proposition for you ..."

The memory faded, leaving an acid taste in Issefyn's mouth.

The sting of defeat had been Issefyn's constant companion for the last six years. Taken off guard, she had not been prepared for a thirteen-year-old to have that much power. The next time would be very different. The child had spent hundreds of years entombed in the black emmeria; it had changed her in ways Issefyn had never anticipated. Arefaine was neither slave nor master of the dark power. The two had become one, fused in a fundamental way that Issefyn did not yet understand. But she would, and very soon.

Once she learned how to tame the power of the emmeria, she would twist it—and the girl—to her own uses. All it took was patience, time, and observation. Eventually, Issefyn would find the means to transform the bitter taste of defeat into something far sweeter.

Until then, she played the part of the faithful servant, a fawning sycophant dazzled by the girl's plans of resurrecting the Doomed City. At Arefaine's request, she'd returned to Ohndarien to guide Shara's training and lock the Zelani mistress's sights on the creation of the containment stones.

Issefyn had planned on the trip being a short one. She originally intended to steal the emmeria from the sleeping fool's dreams and teach herself how to use it. But she could never get past that wretched Heartstone and the gilded box they'd locked him in.

So she had waited, hiding in the guise of a bootlicking matron, biding her time until the child returned to Ohndarien to claim her birthright. This time Issefyn would not be caught unaware. This time Morgeon's daughter would be the one stumbling helpless in the dark.

Issefyn returned from her musings and realized that the girl had left the prow of the ship. She briefly considered intensifying her glamour and sneaking aboard, but there was no need to push that hard yet. Their time would come. She was about to leave when she stopped suddenly and turned around.

The child stood at the edge of the bridge, her long black robes fading into the darkness. If not for her white-powdered face, she would have been impossible to see. Issefyn felt an immediate rush of fear and revulsion and struggled to keep them hidden from her rival.

The Awakened Child glanced at her and raised an eyebrow. Issefyn smiled as if she belonged there, biding her time, skulking like a rat in the shadows.

"Let us talk," Arefaine said, her quiet voice somehow carrying across the distance.

Issefyn nodded and walked over to meet her.

"I was waiting for you to come see me on the ship," Arefaine said.

Issefyn paused. Her magical touch had been so soft. How had the little bitch detected it? "My apologies. Watching from the shadows has become a habit of mine."

She waited for the girl's reply, a dismissive bit of forgiveness for the humiliating role the girl had condemned her to. It did not come. Issefyn hated herself that she even paused to look for forgiveness from this girl. Ohndarien had changed her. The city had a hard shell, but the people within were soft-hearted and weak. She had spent altogether too much time here.

"Time is short. I shall be missed," the white-faced child insisted. "What news of the Summer Cities?"

Issefyn fought to control her emotions. After six years of being Arefaine's eyes and ears in this cursed city, the corrupted whelp was treating her like a servant, a basket of information to be emptied and discarded. Careful to shield her thoughts, Issefyn saved her anger and related what she knew.

"Lord Vinghelt will be leaving Physendria shortly. He plans to rally the fleet as soon as he returns to the Floating Palace. They should be here by midsummer."

"What of his opposition?"

"A man named Reignholtz is the leader of those who oppose him."

"Is he strong enough to hurt our cause?"

"Not without winning a duel, but I just received word that he sent one of his captains to Ohndarien."

"Who?"

"His adopted daughter, a horse-faced peasant girl by the name of Lawdon. She's had ties to Shara and Baelandra since before the Nightmare Battle." Issefyn's man in the Summer Cities had better be right about that. If that fat sadist was letting pieces slip, she would be forced to pay him a visit.

"Make sure she doesn't speak with anyone, especially the council."

"Of course."

"And what progress have you made with the council? They are critical."

"My apprentice has been in several of their beds. They will not be a problem."

Arefaine said nothing, did not commend her for keeping the most powerful people in Ohndarien so artfully under her thumb. Issefyn smoldered in silence, keeping her breathing even.

"All of the fish are in my net except Shara," Issefyn continued. "I have withheld dominating her at your request."

"You've withheld because Shara is stronger than you," Arefaine said.

Issefyn's jaw tightened, but she kept her thoughts placid.

"Do not worry about Shara-lani. I will bring her to our side," Arefaine said. "If I give Brophy back to her, she will see reason, and Ohndarien will follow her lead. We will take the other road only if necessary."

Ohndarien will never join you without deception or force, Issefyn thought. But she did not say it. "I have carefully dissected Shara's mind in my years here," Issefyn said. "She may fawn pathetically over that dead Flower she barely bedded, but she is not a fool."

"Watch your tongue. That dead Flower is my kinsman."

Issefyn bowed her head. "My apologies. I have been trapped in one place too long. It tests my temper. I'm sure you know what that is like."

Arefaine did not respond to the bait. Issefyn continued. "The fact remains. The Farad peasant will never join our cause willingly. She is no child of Efften. We must eliminate her before our plans can proceed."

"I will draw my own conclusions about the Zelani mistress. She was instrumental in my release from the nightmare. I will give her every opportunity to find the truth for herself."

Issefyn scoffed inwardly. The self-deluded child's grasp of "the truth" was laughable. She still planned to use the black emmeria to build a paradise on earth.

"I will find a way to make Shara our sister," Arefaine said softly.

She may bow to you, Issefyn thought. *But she will fly for me.*

"Brophy is the key," Arefaine continued. "Shara's love for him, this city's love for him, these are the levers I will use to pry Ohndarien's gates open. After that, our path leads straight to Efften."

Issefyn nodded. *My path may lead to Efften,* she thought. *But yours leads to the bottom of the ocean.*

CHAPTER 18

Y ou're not going to drink it, are you?" Baelandra asked, holding the bottle of Siren's Blood. The multicolored lights swam around Shara's chambers as she peered through the glass.

"Of course not," Shara said, taking the bottle back from her. It made her nervous to have it in someone else's hands.

She'd asked Baelandra over to the school as soon as she'd come back from the wall. She'd wanted a second opinion on her mysterious visitor.

Baelandra shook her head. "I can see why he'd try and turn you away from Arefaine—the Islanders have always hated magic—but why would he poison you against Ossamyr?"

"I have no idea. Maybe he drank a little too much of his own truth."

Baelandra smiled. "He actually called Ossamyr a crone? If he thinks she's a crone, I hate to hear what he says about me."

"Exactly. And what's the nonsense about the Summer Fleet in Ohndarien?"

"That might actually have a kernel of truth to it," Baelandra said. "The occupation of Physendria is going badly for the Summermen. I've heard one of their princes is pushing to launch a massive counterattack against the rebels. With the mountain passes held by the resistance, they couldn't do that without sending troops through Ohndarien."

"Vallia would never allow that."

"I know."

Shara looked at the bottle again, suspicious of the way she was drawn to it.

"You've never tried this stuff, have you?"

Baelandra tried to keep a straight face, but Shara couldn't help noticing the tinge of embarrassment creeping into her cheeks. "Bae?"

The older woman shrugged. "It was a long time ago, I was very young."

"What was it like?"

A distant smile crept across Baelandra's lips, and she let out a long breath. "Let's just say that I was very lucky I didn't come home pregnant that night—"

"No—"

"Because I wouldn't have known who the father was."

Shara laughed, trying to imagine Baelandra in a drunken tryst. "You're a walking scandal."

"There wouldn't have been a scandal if I'd kept walking."

Shara's laughter was cut off by a faint knock at her door.

Shara felt a twinge of disappointment. She didn't get to just relax and joke with a friend nearly enough. "Come in," she said to Galliana.

Her niece opened the door and entered the room, giving a small bow.

"Shara-lani, Arefaine of the Ohohhim is here at the school to see you."

Shara raised her eyebrows and glanced at Baelandra. An unannounced visit from an Ohohhim? That was certainly odd, though not unwanted. Shara had extended Arefaine an open invitation to visit the school after she had revealed the containment stones. There was a great deal she wanted to talk to the young woman about.

"Thank you, Galliana. Please escort her up to my room."

Galliana left, and Shara's gaze fell on the Siren's Blood.

Keep that bottle away from the Awakened Child of Efften . . .

"I'd better leave you two," Baelandra said, giving her a kiss on the cheek as she headed for the door. "Be careful of that wine. It's good. Too good. I never touched it after that one time."

Shara nodded and Bae gave her a parting smile before closing the door behind her.

Taking a deep breath, Shara took the bottle to her wardrobe, set it on the top shelf, and closed the door. There was only one reason the young sorceress could have come for a visit this evening. The council had still not decided about Brophy, but Arefaine had. She didn't come all this way to see her gift scorned.

Another knock at the door. This time, Shara crossed the room and opened it.

The Ohohhim goddess stood on the far side, her hands tucked into the long sleeves of her robes. Her black clothing covered her from neck to floor. Its high, stiff collar framed her powdered face, serene as a statue's. Issefyn stood at her side, without any other attendants. Somehow Arefaine had convinced the Carriers of the Opal Fire to remain downstairs.

"Lady Morgeon," Shara said, bowing at the waist. "You honor me by your presence."

The girl nodded in response. "It is I who am honored. I apologize for the lateness of the visit, but there was much that we need to discuss.

Shara smiled. "I understand. Please, come in." She nodded at Issefyn, and the teacher bowed and left.

Shara led Arefaine inside. "Would you like to sit down?" Shara asked.

"No, thank you," Arefaine said. She had a pleasant voice, calm and soft-spoken without being timid.

"I'm afraid my rooms are not in a state to receive visitors."

A desk on the far left-hand side of the circular room stood buried under stacks of books and magical implements. Combs, hairbrushes, two hair clips, and a brooch lay carelessly on her vanity.

Arefaine gave a ghost of a smile. "If I had such a space for my own studies, I wouldn't embellish it to please others, either."

Shara paused a moment, trying to judge the young woman's inscrutable face. "I imagine finding any privacy at all has been difficult for you."

"Yes," Arefaine nodded. "The Ohohhim can't even seem to visit the bathroom in groups of less than ten."

Shara smiled, surprised that the girl made a joke. Her old, dear friend Father Lewlem was the only Ohohhim she'd ever met who seemed to have a sense of humor. She still missed him. The news of his death had touched her deeply.

"I wish to discuss the containment stones and Brophy's slumber," Arefaine said.

Again, Shara was surprised at her directness. It just seemed wrong coming from the powdered face of an Ohohhim. Even Father Lewlem had been far more circuitous in his conversations.

Arefaine crossed the floor and stopped in front of a basket containing the shards of crystal that remained from Shara's failed spell. "You have been trying to imbue a containment stone." Arefaine looked over her shoulder.

Shara nodded, her lips pressed together for a moment. "I have not been successful," she said, pulling each word up from the bottom of her lungs.

Arefaine nodded.

"How did you acquire the ones you brought?" Shara asked.

"I didn't acquire them. I made them."

Shara stared at her, then dropped her gaze to the floor. Strands of her long black hair slipped forward across her flushed cheeks. Her voice was barely a whisper when she spoke. "How?"

"Diligence, frustration, sleepless nights, pain ..."

Shara swallowed. "Then you are the better magician. I gave all this and more ... but I failed."

Shara looked up at the young woman, standing so thin and so still. Not even an eyelid twitched, but her gaze was soft.

"There is no need to be unkind with yourself," Arefaine said. "Sometimes an entire tower can collapse because of one misplaced stone."

"Sometimes."

Arefaine touched the tattered, leather cover of a thin book on the edge of Shara's worktable. Flaked blue writing told the title: *The Illuminated Personification of Objects*, by Hestorn the Blind. She lifted the book and opened it to a dog-eared page. She laid a slender finger upon the words Shara knew so well she could recite it from memory.

"*... progeneration requires utter commitment to the transfer of quintessence into a vessel ...*" she read from the book.

"Yes," Shara said. "I did. I gave the stone as many of my heartbeats as I could, right up to the last one before I lost consciousness."

"*The unbroken string of heartbeats must be given with grace and conviction,*" Arefaine read. "*The last heartbeats ...*"

"Yes."

"Not your heartbeats."

Shara's breath stopped, and her mind raced through the passage she'd read a hundred times. She closed her eyes and clenched her teeth. "A sacrifice," she murmured. "Another's sacrifice. I thought it meant my own."

"The passage can be read that way. Hestorn was vague at best. In my first attempt, I did the same." She extended an arm to reveal the smattering of tiny white scars. Shara glanced at the similar marks on her own arms. "But self-sacrifice was not what Hestorn meant. As you know, magic comes back to one basic principle, again and again. Only the living can wield it or be affected by it." She closed the book and pushed it back on the table. "That is the heart of the Alcani form," Arefaine continued. "A living spirit must be transferred for an inanimate object to come to life. Not part of a living spirit, its entirety."

Shara put her fingers to the bridge of her nose, drew a deep breath. "All of those years," she said. "All of those stones. All for one conclusion I could not draw." She took another long breath, then let it out. Her eyes burned when she looked back at Arefaine. "And you did it."

Arefaine nodded.

"What did you use?"

"The condemned, of course."

Shara drew a quick breath. "People?"

Arefaine arched an eyebrow. "What would you suggest? A squirrel?"

"Yes! Or some other animal."

"That would never work, and you know it. A stone made from such a primitive soul would never have the strength to contain that much emmeria."

"Then we make more."

"Adding a thousand brittle bars to a cage does not make it any stronger."

Shara strode toward her, grabbed Hestorn's book from the table. She flipped open the well-used pages. "But you can't. The sacrifice must be a willing participant."

"Of course."

"But no one would willingly ..." Her statement petered out.

Arefaine watched her carefully, then said, "Condemned men will often jump at a chance to redeem themselves, to take a few steps closer to Oh before the end," she said. "I found many willing to give their lives to avoid being put to the sword, alone and ashamed, before their Emperor's eyes."

"You tricked them."

"Of course I didn't. They cannot be tricked or coerced. They must commit to the transfer with no doubt or hesitation. The released soul must fight to complete the transformation."

"But you actually took their lives?"

"No. Their lives were already forfeit. I simply changed the manner of their deaths."

"That cannot be the solution," Shara insisted. "A mage should never resort to violence—"

"And the emmeria should never have been corrupted in the first place," Arefaine said, but not without sympathy. "Magic requires power, and true power is not cheaply bought."

"Not at that price. Arefaine, believe me, we are defined by the paths we refuse as much as the ones we choose. Brophy taught me that in the Wet Cells. I will never again use my magic that recklessly. There are some things I will never do."

"Not even to save Brophy?"

Shara winced. "Not even for that."

Arefaine smiled. "Truly?"

Shara nodded, searching the woman for any hint of lingering black emmeria. But there was nothing. She was clean.

"The strongest stone I made," Arefaine said, "was created from the life of a young woman who killed her husband's mistress in a jealous rage. The mistress was farther up the Divine Queue, a higher caste, if you will. If the husband had married her, it would have elevated the entire family, but it would also have made the murderess the second wife. It was a crime of *asris*, a term only used in the Opal Empire. It means greed for status and is the greatest affront to Oh's loving example. In Ohohhom, those guilty of *asris* are put to the sword. But death was not what the woman feared the most. She begged for a way to remove the shame from her husband's name."

"But that is no excuse to cut her throat and pour her lifeblood into a stone, to imprison her for eternity."

"The mind is not transferred, just the essence. There is no sense of self. She remains unaware of what happened. The stone has been personified, but it is not a living creature. Only one archmage was able to transfer even some of her consciousness into an object: my sister, Jazryth, when she created the Heartstone."

Shara raised an eyebrow in admiration. The girl had studied. That bit of information was not widely known.

"That is why that stone is ten times more powerful than any ordinary containment stone," Arefaine continued. "That is why she can choose the Children of the Seasons and offer a piece of herself to lend them her strength."

"And the Emperor knew you were doing this? Making these stones?"

"Of course he knew. He owes as much debt to Brophy as any of us."

Shara paused for a long time.

"Your stones . . . Can they safely contain all of the black emmeria?"

"With the help of the Heartstone, yes."

Arefaine paused. For the first time, true emotion showed through the young woman's carefully powdered face. "The long wait is over," she said hoarsely. "For both of us."

Shara looked away, suddenly caught up in the other woman's emotions.

"My only wish," Arefaine said, struggling with the words, "is that the two of us could have met earlier. How much easier would this task have been if we had been allowed to work together? The Sleeping Warden might have awoken years ago."

Shara nodded, thinking again of all the time wasted by one simple misunderstanding.

"We mages need a place to gather," Arefaine continued. "If there was a place for us to learn, think of the good we could accomplish. Think of how we could help the world."

"That's what the founders of Efften said."

Arefaine smiled. "Yes. And think of the secrets simply left on that island.

What could we learn from what the archmages left behind? Look at how far you have come with just a few crumbs that escaped the island before its fall. Together, we could bring back the best of what the world could be."

Shara's brow furrowed. "Efften was the best and the worst. They almost destroyed the world."

"Some of Efften's mages were reckless. Some of her leaders weak. But we would not make that mistake. People call the tainted emmeria the Legacy of Efften. But our people's legacy is far more than our mistakes. The emmeria in Brophy's keeping is simply raw power tainted by misuse. That power could be cleansed, redeemed, and put to work in the world."

"Arefaine, the world does not need that kind of power. The emmeria is evil, pure evil, born of hatred, abuse, and pain."

"But evil can be redeemed, hatred set aside, pain healed. We must be careful, very careful. But there is no reason we must repeat the sins of the past. Look what you have already done with Zelani in Ohndarien. Your school is a beacon in the night to those like us. Would you rather your students went back to being simple craftsmen and breeding stock, born and raised to produce dowries?"

Shara shook her head.

"People say that power corrupts, that a desire to reach beyond what you have been given is inherently evil. Then why don't we put out our eyes to avoid being corrupted by the power of sight? Why don't we cripple ourselves before we are undone by our greed for movement?"

"That's not a valid comparison. The emmeria is not a simple tool. It lives, it thinks, it yearns to unleash its plague upon the world. You cannot tap its strength and simply walk away. If you make that kind of thieves' bargain, you will be looking behind your shoulder for the rest of your life."

"You did it. You walked away."

"No I didn't. I have never been free of its call. I am forever diminished by the path I walked long ago."

Arefaine winced and turned away. Her slender hands were balled into fists.

"I too have done some ..." She struggled with the words. "Some horrible things in my life. But I have to believe that we can move past those things. There's nothing wrong with us, Shara," she said, almost pleading. "We're just different than everybody else."

"You're right. There is nothing wrong with us, but we are not different than anybody else. Just because you can do magic doesn't place you above the laws of common decency."

"Think of Brophy," Arefaine persisted. "He is not the only one who suffers. Many are locked in nightmare, frightened of their own powers, confused at the voices that call to them, never knowing why. What if we could build a home for those lost souls?" Arefaine paused, but Shara said nothing. Finally, Arefaine continued, her voice softer. "We have been given amazing gifts. All I want to do is use them."

"You can use them, we will wake Brophy, just not before everyone has had their voice heard in council," Shara said, struggling to defend the arduous process.

"Such a debate could last for months. Even years. Would you let Brophy continue to suffer any longer than he had to?"

"Brophy doesn't suffer," Shara insisted, an ache in her chest. Arefaine's words on top of the Hall of Windows had shaken her, but she couldn't believe them. Arefaine hadn't been in Brophy's dream. She didn't know. "He is happy where I left him. I have seen it in his eyes."

Arefaine shook her head slowly. "I am sure that is easier to believe, but it is simply not true. I spent ten lifetimes in that place. The emmeria lies. The only thing it wants is to escape, and the only thing stopping it is Brophy. You can't imagine what pressure it is putting on him, twisting him until he breaks. It is a miracle that he has not already been shattered."

"I have been there," Shara said stubbornly.

Arefaine let out a small breath. "We will wake him regardless. No one need know until Brophy walks into the council meeting tomorrow morning. Why wait, why prolong his suffering?"

"Because it doesn't have to be tonight," she said. It took all of her breath to say it. Every part of her body ached to agree with Arefaine.

"If you knew what I knew," Arefaine said, "you would not say that."

Silence fell in the chamber, and Arefaine waited.

Eighteen years . . .

"No," she said quietly. "The council rules in Ohndarien, not I," she said in a dead tone. "I will not betray my friends to wake my love."

Arefaine watched her with cold blue eyes for a long moment. She did not frown at being denied. She did not let out a frustrated breath. Her face betrayed no emotion at all. Finally, she nodded.

"I understand. You honor yourself and your city. It is I who am guilty of *asris*. Fortunately, they do not execute anyone for that in Ohndarien."

Shara gave her a weak smile. And Arefaine returned it.

"Let's put this argument behind us. I would still love to talk with you about so many things. Would you consider joining His Eternal Wisdom and me for a late dinner?"

The tension seemed to drain from the room.

"I would be delighted," Shara said, feeling like she'd just taken a beating. "Just let me grab a few things," she said, opening her wardrobe doors to grab a shawl.

Arefaine smiled. "Of course. I will—"

She shoved Shara out of the way and snatched the bottle of Siren's Blood out of the wardrobe.

"Keep that bottle away from the Awakened Child of Efften."

Shara lunged for the bottle, but Arefaine spun away and hurled it against the wall. The crystal shattered, splattering deep red liquid across the rose-colored wall. A hoard of colored lights scattered into the air, zipping about the room. Arefaine charged into their midst, waving her arms about her, snuffing each little light she touched.

Shara leapt to stop her, grabbing Arefaine's wrist. The last three lights shot through the open window and escaped into the darkness.

"Are you mad! What are you doing?"

The room reeked of wine, and the smell made Shara dizzy.

"Where did you get that bottle?" Arefaine demanded.

Shara narrowed her eyes, refusing to let go of the girl's wrist. "Someone gave it to me," she said, ice in her voice.

"Do you have any idea what that was? It's poison, the vile brew of a vile people. Drinking that would have been a fate worse than death." Arefaine's eyes continued to search Shara's. Looking for ... what?

"I know what Siren's Blood does."

"Not this kind. If you had drunk that, the villain who gave it to you would have owned you body and soul. That was the brew that destroyed our people. They were all swimming in it when the pirates attacked Efften. It's why our magic didn't work on them."

Shara backed up, letting her go.

"You didn't seek this out yourself?" Arefaine asked.

"No. It was an unexpected and unwanted gift."

The girl paused. "A gift? When did you receive it?"

"About an hour ago."

Arefaine's jaw dropped, then her lip curled into a snarl. "They're here now, in the city?"

"Yes."

"Then they mean to take the Sleeping Warden!"

"What?"

"The Sleeping Warden. If they couldn't get to you, they'll take him from us!"

CHAPTER 19

Shara couldn't get up the stairs fast enough. The energy of the Floani form surged unbidden through her body. Her muscles ached, yearning to run ahead, but she had to hold herself at the pace of the others.

Arefaine looked as anxious as Shara, craning her neck to see around the curve of the stairs. Scant moonlight filtered through the spotty clouds, and the sculpture of Scythe loomed in the distance

Arefaine's bodyguards showed no signs of strain from their mad dash across the city, but Baelandra and Issefyn were panting heavily as they approached the top of the Wheel. The older women were obviously struggling, but neither showed any signs of slowing down.

Baelandra had been chatting with Galliana when Shara and Arefaine came down the tower stairs. The former sister instantly knew something was wrong, and once Baelandra heard that Brophy might be in danger, she insisted that she come along. Issefyn had also offered to help. Shara was happy to have them along, but she would have gotten here much faster if she had just used her magic to race across the city alone.

Shara had also sent Galliana to the Citadel to warn Faedellin and ask him to send a squad of Lightning Swords. Even if Arefaine's fears turned out to be unfounded, Shara wanted extra guards around Brophy as long as that Islander was in the city.

They reached the top of the stairs, and Shara finally got a clear view of the Hall. Brophy's torch still burned atop the amphitheater, but she couldn't see anything else at this distance. Shara waited for the others to catch up, starting to wonder if she was going to feel very foolish when this night was done.

"I told you it was probably nothing," Shara said, resting the box of con-

"Why?"

"Because they're mad!" Arefaine cried, rushing to the door. "There isn't a moment to lose."

"*If you refuse to listen, the truth will be forced on you just like it was forced on them.*"

A chill ran up Shara's spine. That Islander was invisible to magic. He could get past the Heartstone's cage.

"I think you might be right."

Arefaine opened the door, then stopped. "Wait. The containment stones. Where are they?"

"The stones? Why?"

"Who knows what could happen?"

Shara nodded and hurried across the room to the ironwood chest that held the containment stones.

tainment stones on one hip as Baelandra reached her side. The former Sister struggled to catch her breath.

"Nothing wrong . . . with a little moonlit stroll . . ." she managed to get out. "I rather enjoyed—"

The shatter of distant glass cut her off in midsentence. Moments later a young woman screamed.

"They're here!" Arefaine shouted.

Shara handed the box to Baelandra and invoked the Floani form. Her legs surged with power, and she rushed toward the sound. Arefaine smoothly kept pace with her, using the same magic, and they left the others behind. Together they flew down the dark pathway.

Arefaine reached into the sleeve of her robe and tossed a little glowing ball in the direction of the hall. It shot into the distance, leaving the path and heading into the gardens. "Follow the light!"

Shara swerved to her left, following the little spirit. She'd read about the mages using Elani magic to create the luminous orbs from the souls of the departed, but she had never tried to do it. Once again she was vexed and awed by Arefaine's skill.

The two women flew through the night, following the tiny light as it whipped across the Wheel. They weaved around trees and fountains, leaping hedges and ducking low-hanging branches. Shara spun around a stone bench as Arefaine lifted her skirts and hopped over it. The two sorceresses rounded the marble steps of the Palace of Winter to the sound of clanging steel. Blood wet the grass. A pair of tattooed Silver Islanders lay sprawled on the lawn next to three Lightning Swords, all dead.

Reef and the last of Brophy's four defenders circled each other, swords striking and parrying. The veteran Lightning Sword frantically defended himself with the Sword of Autumn. The red glow from the sword's pommel stone lit their grim faces. Beyond them, a tattooed woman held Brophy under the armpits, dragging him toward the edge of the Wheel. She clutched the Heartstone in both hands, pressing it against Brophy's chest. Shara felt the power of the Silver Islander's voice, maintaining the spell that kept Brophy asleep.

Reef spotted their arrival and cursed, pressing his attack with a deadly barrage. The Lightning Sword fell back, nearly overwhelmed.

Arefaine skidded to a stop and clenched her teeth in fierce concentration. She pointed an imperious finger at Reef.

"Die," she whispered, and a flood of magic more intense than Shara had ever seen engulfed the burly islander. Nothing happened.

"No!" Arefaine shouted. Her teeth showed, and she tried again.

The magical assault flowed around Reef as if he were a rock in a river. The man continued his ferocious assault, driving his opponent back.

"You are invincible," Shara whispered to the Lightning Sword, sending a stream of ani toward him. "Your blade strikes the heart. Your strength cannot be matched."

The Ohndarien defender swelled, his tunic tightening against his arms. He bared his teeth and bulled forward. With a growl, Reef stumbled away. The soldier followed, his sword flexing with the speed of his blows. Reef fell to one knee, and the guard brought his sword down in a fierce downward cut, smashing through Reef's parry. His sword tip nicked the Islander's chest and buried itself into the ground. Seizing the moment, Reef lunged, driving his blade through the soldier's stomach. With a feral roar, the soldier slumped to his knees.

Reef discarded his bent sword and drew a knife. He started toward them. "I warned you," he growled, looking at Shara.

Reef's eyes flicked behind them, and Shara heard the pounding of booted feet on the steps of the Winter Palace just behind them. The two Carriers of the Opal Fire rushed past Shara and Arefaine, heading straight for Reef.

The Islander's huge biceps twitched, the tattoos seemingly alive as he backed toward his companion and placed his dagger against Brophy's neck. "I'll kill him!" he shouted. "Stay back."

The Carriers swerved right and left, coming at Reef from opposite directions.

"No! Wait!" Shara shouted. "Do what he says!"

The Ohohhim guardsmen paused a few feet away from Reef and the woman holding Brophy. The Islanders continued backing toward the edge.

"It's a bluff," Arefaine whispered. "He'd never harm the Warden."

The Islanders reached the edge of the Wheel where it extended out into the bay. There was water directly below them, but they'd be fools to jump with Brophy from that height.

"Don't do it!" Shara called to them. "You'll destroy us all."

"Start singing," Arefaine whispered. "I'll handle the rest."

"No. Just wait," Shara begged her.

Reef pointed at Arefaine. "Don't let that witch drag you into the abyss."

"I'll drag your entire race into the abyss," Arefaine shouted back at him.

A flicker of a smile crossed Reef's features. "We'll see about that, daughter of Morgeon."

"Reef," Shara shouted. "You don't want to do this."

"You leave me no other choice," Reef insisted. "You had your chance to see the truth, now these deaths are on your head."

"Start singing," Arefaine insisted.

"No."

Reef took the Heartstone from his companion. A tender look passed between them, and she bent her knees to jump.

"Now!" Arefaine shouted, and the Carriers attacked.

"Wait!" Shara screamed.

One of the Carriers attacked Reef. The other threw his sword, piercing the tattooed woman through the throat.

"No!" Shara screamed.

Reef swatted aside his opponent's blade with his bare hand and spun around to aid his companion. She slumped forward, landing on Brophy. Without a second's hesitation, Reef turned and leapt from the edge of the Wheel. At the top of his arc, he spun and threw his dagger straight at Arefaine. With a shout, Shara lunged for it. She meant to catch the knife by the handle, but missed, hitting the blade instead.

The knife spun past Arefaine's shoulder. She never flinched.

Shara clutched her bleeding hand and started singing. Desperately, she reached out with her magic, grabbing the unraveling threads of her spell and wove them back together. She could feel the black emmeria surge within Brophy, but she held it back, keeping Brophy safely within his dreams.

Arefaine strode to the edge of the Wheel and glared down where Reef had disappeared. Shara would have screamed at the woman if she could. The bloodthirsty fool had nearly gotten Brophy killed.

"Mistress!" one of the Carriers called, leaning over Brophy's body. "Come quick!"

Shara knelt next to Brophy, ignoring the terror in the Ohohhim guard's voice. A foul wind hit her in the face.

"Look," the Carrier said, his voice tight.

The Islander woman lay slumped over Brophy, impaled through the neck. The Ohohhim blade had pierced Brophy's shoulder as she fell forward. Black blood was frothing up from the wound. Shara nearly screamed. She nearly dropped the singing and lost her spell.

A chorus of tortured voices swept around them, gaining in intensity as the flood of tortured souls fled their prison through Brophy's wound.

It's the Nightmare Battle all over again, Shara thought. *All over again.*

CHAPTER 20

Keep singing," Arefaine shouted, grabbing the Heartstone off the grass. She threw the woman's tattooed corpse to the side and pressed the stone against the gout of hungry, black blood surging from Brophy's shoulder.

Shara wanted to cry, to rage, to smack the girl for her reckless arrogance, but she couldn't. She kept singing.

The torrent of screams swirled around the glade. The sounds grew louder and louder until they became a deafening cacophony all around them. Shara's hair blew back, and she closed her eyes against the tormented wind. Her ears rushed with the noise, and she sang louder to compensate.

A single voice rose above the others, drowning out the cacophony with its laughter. *You have failed, Morgeon, I am free at last!* Shara hid her face and covered her ears, singing at the top of her lungs.

Shara felt Arefaine taking a deep breath, gathering her power. She held the magic trapped within herself for a moment, then seemed to explode, flooding the area with a rush of ani so intense it nearly blinded Shara. Arefaine's magic spun around them, catching the foul voices in her net. Within moments she had contained all of the black emmeria that had escaped from Brophy.

I made you. I made you! You cannot deny me.

Shara stared at the girl. She could never have created and mastered so much raw energy. It didn't seem possible.

Arefaine pitted her will against the black emmeria stemming the flood rushing out of Brophy's body at the same time that she fought to repress the energy that had already escaped. Her brown hair blew loose and whipped across her white cheeks. Lines of strain appeared at the edges of her eyes where the white powder had smeared away, and her lips pulled back from gritted teeth.

The surge of magic was like a trickle of deep water forcing its way through a crack in the rock. Shara could feel the pressure. A malignant blackness surged from Brophy's shoulder into the crystal.

This power is yours, Daughter of Morgeon. It is your birthright. Set us free!

Shara split her attention, concentrating on her singing and sending Arefaine a flood of power at the same time. Together, they forced the emmeria into the Heartstone, staining the crystal black at an alarming rate.

Arefaine turned away from Brophy and looked behind them. "Issefyn! Baelandra!" she called, using the Lowani form to amplify her voice. "I need those stones!"

Shara looked from the blackened Heartstone to Brophy's face. The air of serenity that had surrounded him all those years had been shattered. His brows were knitted in pain, and his eyes pulsed frantically back and forth between his crinkled lids. She groped in the grass for the discarded Sword of Autumn and placed the pommel stone against his wound. She began channeling energy through the crystal, willing his flesh to knit back together, but it was too slow, too difficult with the polluted ani rushing though the gash.

Arefaine continued to imprison the black emmeria in the Heartstone. The gem was already pitch-black, and Shara could sense that it was dangerously close to its capacity.

Shara heard footfalls behind them and turned to see Baelandra running toward them, still holding the box of stones. Her frantic eyes took in the scene at a glance.

"I need the stones, now!" Arefaine hissed, shaking with the strain.

Baelandra looked to Shara for guidance. Shara nodded, and Bae rushed to them, sliding on the grass right up to Brophy's side. She opened the box and handed Arefaine one of the stones.

Do not listen to their lies, their petty fears. We will resurrect Efften together, you and I.

Arefaine leaned the Heartstone away from Brophy's wound and immediately replaced it with the much smaller containment stone. The multicolored stone instantly filled with an inky darkness. Shara willed the stone to work, dreading that it would explode just like all the ones she had made, but it held.

"How . . . can I help?" Baelandra panted.

"You can't," Arefaine replied, her face rigid with concentration.

"I've done this before." Baelandra insisted.

"I know, but you no longer carry a shard of the Heartstone. She cannot protect you."

Slowly, Baelandra nodded. "Be careful," she whispered. "Be sure." Shara didn't know if she was talking to Arefaine, to all of them, or to no one in particular.

Issefyn finally caught up with them, staring at the saturated Heartstone with wide eyes.

Arefaine set the Heartstone on the grass and continued to channel the black emmeria from Brophy's wound into the smaller crystal. Issefyn reached for the Heartstone, but Arefaine shook her head.

"Stay back. Only Shara and I can handle the stones, you must not touch them for any reason." Issefyn pulled her hand back, and Baelandra nodded.

When the first stone was nearly filled, Arefaine reached for the second. Most of the black emmeria had been purged from Brophy's body, but there was still enough left to corrupt thousands.

Do not let caution hold you back. Claim your birthright, and I will share this treasure with you.

Arefaine swapped the stones and continued the process. She handed the pitch-black stone to Shara. The emmeria ate at her fingers, desperate to escape its crystal prison and invade her flesh. Shara sheathed herself in her own ani, forcing the blackness back where it belonged. She carefully placed the stone in the box.

Brophy's head jerked from side to side, and his legs twitched as if he was trying to run. Shara had longed for years to see him move again, but she never wanted it to be like this. Was this how Brophy would wake? Covered in blood, surrounded by brutal murder and near cataclysm?

Shara unbuttoned Brophy's shirt and vest, revealing his heartstone, gray and cloudy. It still struck Shara as wrong every time she saw it. That gem should be red, blazing red like the sunset. She used the hem of her dress to wipe the blood from his chest.

"We're nearly done," Arefaine told them. "Whatever you do, Shara, do not stop singing. Keep him asleep until we have it all."

Beads of sweat appeared on Arefaine's forehead, creating tracks through the powder. She panted, her hands like bird's claws as she swapped the third stone for the second. The last gem filled much more slowly than the others. It darkened, then blackened.

Poorly done, little one. You have held me for now, but it is you who has been denied. I will wait for now. I will wait for you.

The black blood frothing around Brophy's wound slowly calmed, then disappeared altogether. The howling faded to nothing until Shara's steady voice was the only sound in the moonlit night.

With a gasp, Arefaine held the last containment stone out to Shara. Shara transferred the stone to the case, and Baelandra put her arms around Arefaine, who suddenly seemed skinny and frail. Sweat streaked her cheeks, but she smiled.

"It's done," she said. "It's out. All of it." Brophy's heartstone gleamed a brilliant red.

Shara pulled Brophy to her chest.

"Oh Brophy," she wept, cupping his head in her hands. "It's over. We did it. You're free . . ."

But he did not wake. He did not stir.

Shara pulled back. Brophy twitched in her arms. He jerked his head to the side as if writhing in pain while his eyes darted frantically back and forth beneath their lids.

Enjoy your lover while you can, Shara-lani. I am sure you will appreciate what I have made of him.

CHAPTER 21

Issefyn stared at the Heartstone lying on the grass a few feet in front of her. She could feel the power within it, warm on her face, drawing her forward. After all this time the emmeria was finally within her grasp, and it was physically painful to keep her distance. She needed time alone with the stone. She needed a safe place to explore the mysteries locked within, but she couldn't risk anything with all the others around.

None of the other women held the slightest concern for the treasure that lay before them. They all clung to Brophy, whimpering like starving puppies huddled around their dead mother.

Issefyn braced herself for the disgusting reunion scene, but the seconds passed, and the fool never opened his eyes.

"What's wrong?" Shara bleated, shaking him. "Why won't he wake?"

Issefyn wanted to laugh. Only the archmages of Efften had shown true mastery over emmeria. These three played with it like apes poking a fire.

The Ohohhim girl sent her magic into Brophy, searching for the reason. "There's something still there," she said.

Issefyn saw right through the girl's feigned surprise. *She probably knew this would happen. It must all be part of her little plan.* Issefyn itched to probe the girl, but didn't dare. Not yet.

"More black emmeria?" Baelandra asked, a toothless dog still trying to seem in charge.

"It's not the emmeria. We are safe from that," Arefaine assured her. "There is something else that holds him."

"What?" Shara asked.

"I am not sure, but I think it is his own will, his own refusal to wake up."

Issefyn narrowed her eyes, wondering what the girl's game was. Where would her lies lead?

"He might not realize it is safe," Arefaine said, wearing her pathetic mask of urgent sincerity. "I will go into his dreams and bring him out."

"No." Shara insisted. "I put him in the dream. I should be the one to bring him out."

How sweet, Issefyn thought. *She's going to rescue her damsel in distress.*

"Are you sure?" Arefaine asked slowly.

Does that not fall in with your plans, dear girl? Do you want the pretty boy all for yourself?

"I'll do it," Shara whispered, comical in her pretty anguish. She slowed her breathing and began her spell.

Issefyn moved a step closer to the Heartstone. *Soon,* she reminded herself, *soon.*

❄

Shara closed her eyes and focused on her breath. She drove the fear from her body, the shock and disappointment. She banished her anger at Arefaine's bloody-minded impatience, concentrating on her breath, in and out, nothing but the breath.

Her jitters faded, the fears and doubts passed away as she fell into the bittersweet routine she had gone through so many times before. She reached out for the sleeping Brophy, mingling her ani with his life force. She matched her breath to his, and slowly the two became one.

Shara felt herself falling, tumbling through mist as she entered Brophy's dream. She felt her body changing, becoming lighter, leaner, as she transformed into the nineteen-year-old girl he expected to see.

Opening her eyes, she drifted through the clouds, falling gently without fear. The cool wisps of vapor faded away, and she could see the city below. The setting sun glinted off the Hall of Windows and danced across the waves of the bay. The Water Wall stood massive in the distance, a trellised curtain of stone that had kept Ohndarien safe all these years.

Shara sank lower, seeking her lover. A surge of emotion filled her as she saw him sleeping atop the Hall of Windows. Her fears melted away in the warmth of relief. Arefaine was wrong. Brophy still lived in the dream they had built together. He was safe and happy here.

She drifted lower and lower until she alighted without sound on the blue-white marble beside him. Brophy's feather twirled in the breeze, bound to his neck by the leather thong. His golden curls shifted, tickling his cheeks. He still needed a haircut.

The sun made his bare skin glow. Seeing him sleeping there, Shara felt a sudden rush of nostalgia. This would be the last time they shared this dream. As painful as visiting him had always been, now that it was over, she felt a loss. Part of her didn't want to let it go.

She knelt next to him and drank in the sight of his naked body, then placed a hand on Brophy's chest. He stirred in his sleep, taking her hand in his.

"Wake up, my love," she whispered. "It's time to go home."

Arefaine had been wrong, so very wrong.

❄

Shara lay across Brophy's chest, her face nuzzled into his neck. Her body shuddered, and Arefaine turned away, looked at Baelandra. The old Sister of Autumn was watching the dreaming couple with a worried intensity.

Arefaine glanced at the scene around her. The two Carriers hovered at a distance, their swords drawn. Issefyn knelt nearby, keeping her thoughts carefully hidden. The dead zealot lay crumpled in the moonlit grass, her chest soaked with blood.

Arefaine looked at the woman's glassy eyes and didn't know what to feel. She hadn't caused anyone's death in a very long time, not since she was a little child. The Islander deserved to die, but Arefaine's orders had nearly cost them everything. Was she right to take such decisive action? Could she have risked allowing the savages to jump into the bay with the Sleeping Warden, then tried to capture them later?

Arefaine banished her thoughts, her brow wrinkling. She wasn't staying focused. It would be the death of her.

"You," she said to one of the Carriers. She had never been told their names.

He bowed slightly in acknowledgment.

"Run and find an Ohndarien soldier. Raise the alarm. The Islander must not be allowed to leave the city."

The man hesitated. "Your Grace, we have orders not to leave your sight."

"You have new orders now."

The man hesitated only a moment, then nodded and took off running.

Arefaine refocused on Shara's heavy breathing, her twitching body, her grasping hands. She feared what her new friend might have found in the Warden's dreams. Distant memories of her time in the emmeria drifted back to her. She shut her eyes against the past, suddenly feeling small and helpless, like an abandoned child calling out into the darkness. She'd never escaped those lingering feelings of isolation and despair, and her chest clenched at the thought of going back there. But if Shara needed her, she would have to be ready.

❄

Shara's entire body trembled as Brophy slowly opened his eyes and smiled. Golden light played across his face, making his green eyes sparkle.

"I must have fallen asleep," he said, reaching up to touch her cheek.

His touch was soft and warm, she melted into it. "You've been asleep for a very long time."

"Then it's time to wake up," he said, pulling her down on top of him. He crushed her against his chest, and she nearly gasped at the contact. Hungry lips met, and she lost herself for a moment, diving into him like a pool.

"Shall we go flying again?" he asked.

"Yes," she whispered, wanting him desperately. "Let's fly again, one last time."

Shara took his hand and pulled him to his feet. She paused, looking up at his boyish features. She loved the size of him, the width of his shoulders, the strength in his arms. Those arms would soon be wrapped around her. So very soon.

She led Brophy to the edge of the platform. His feather twirled in the breeze, and she felt her own fluttering against her hair.

"You won't need that anymore," Shara said, touching his wrist. "You can leave it here."

Brophy looked down and saw the weapon in his hand.

"I can't leave my sword," he said, looking around.

Shara smiled. On second thought, the sword seemed perfect, it just looked right in his hand. "Come on."

She took his hand and ran with him off the top of the Hall. They spread their arms wide, Brophy's hand locked on her wrist. They flew past the shimmering glass and swooped over the trees. Brophy laughed as they brushed against the leaves. She led him beyond the Wheel and over the glittering water. Shara pulled him to her as they flew across the city, rising higher and higher.

"Where are you taking me?" he said, looking around.

"I have a little surprise for you, just on the other side of those clouds."

Brophy looked up, his eyes crinkling. "I can't leave the city."

She squeezed his hand, understanding his confusion. "You can now," she explained. "This dream is over, Brophy. You've done what you needed to do. Let's go home."

Brophy shook his head, resisting her grasp. "No. No I can't."

Shara held on tighter. "Just a little farther. We're so close."

He fought her grip. "Shara, please, I can't go."

"Come on, Brophy," she shouted over the wind. It was just a few feet more.

"No!" He yanked his hand away and plummeted toward earth.

"Brophy!"

She dove after him, caught him under the arms. He fought her grasp as she struggled to slow their plunge.

"What are you doing? I have to get you out of here."

"Let me go," he cried, writhing in her arms, but she held tight to him. She dashed for the clouds as quickly as she could. She hadn't expected this, hadn't expected anything like this.

"Don't fight me, Brophy. It's me. It's Shara!"

"You're not Shara," he hissed. Sunlight flashed on metal, and a searing pain tore through her. She screamed, choking on a sudden rush of blood in her throat. Gaping down, she stared at the Sword of Autumn, plunged to the hilt in her stomach.

Her arms went limp, and Brophy's fell away from her. The wet blade emerged from her flesh, spraying blood into the misty air.

Shara screamed again as she lunged for him, but he slipped through her hands. She plunged after him, barely able to control her own flight. *Why? What was he thinking? What had she done wrong?*

Her chest seized with the pain. She couldn't draw breath, and the world grew black. Hateful voices knocked her off course, pushing her away from Brophy. She fought the wind, willing herself closer to him.

He clung to his bloody blade with both hands, not even trying to save himself. The ground rushed toward them faster and faster.

Brophy screamed just before he hit.

Shara landed right on top of him.

❄

Arefaine knew immediately that something wasn't right, knew it before Shara's body jerked like she'd been stabbed.

"What's wrong?" Baelandra asked.

"I don't know." Arefaine was already trying to sense where the imbalance lay, but she couldn't find it. As far as she could tell, Shara was still in the same dream she'd entered.

Shara's entire body convulsed and a black stain appeared in the center of her dress.

"What's happening?" Baelandra cried, looking into the rift. "By the Seasons, what's happening to her?"

Arefaine ripped the dress open and revealed an ugly black slash on Shara's stomach, just above her belly button. The parted flesh was torn and ragged, but there was no blood. Dark tendrils of emmeria sprouted from the wound, slithering across her skin.

"She's being corrupted!" Baelandra cried, reaching for Shara.

"Don't be a fool," Arefaine's command cracked like a whip.

Baelandra jerked her hand away, immediately touching the place between her own breasts that had once held a heartstone.

Arefaine dived into the wound with her magic, following it back to its source. "The emmeria is coming from Brophy," she said, not knowing how or why. "He's still corrupted."

"What do we do?" Baelandra asked.

"We have—"

"It's spreading!" Baelandra shouted. "Look!"

Ribbons of black emmeria snaked up Shara's body, darkening the flesh. It oozed past the neckline of her dress, moving closer and closer to her head.

"Issefyn!" Arefaine shouted. "Use a containment stone. Pull the infection out of her."

The former queen stepped forward, chin high.

"Issefyn?" Baelandra asked, looking around. "But Issefyn isn't—"

"The stones are so full already ..." Issefyn began.

Arefaine fixed the old sorceress with an unmistakable gaze. "Just do it."

Issefyn gave her a wooden smile.

"But she ... She can't," Baelandra insisted. "She doesn't have the power ..."

"She can do it," Arefaine said, ripping Shara's dress in two, exposing the black lines creeping over her pale flesh. Arefaine grabbed the last containment stone and placed it on Shara's wound.

Issefyn hesitated. Arefaine hated to trust the bitter and secretive old woman, but there wasn't any other choice.

"Help me, or we all die," she insisted.

With a cautious nod, Issefyn knelt next to Shara and grabbed the stone.

"I must follow her," Arefaine said. "Get her away from Brophy, fight the corruption at the source."

"We may have to use the blade on her," Issefyn said, nodding toward the Sword of Autumn.

Arefaine's eyes narrowed. "Only as a last resort."

Baelandra looked shocked, but she nodded slowly, pulling the blade closer. A Sister of Autumn would not be a stranger to the need for drastic measures. "But what would happen to you, if you are still in the dream?"

"Just keep her from turning," Arefaine said

Issefyn concentrated on the containment stone, relaxing the veils that hid her true nature and shifting her ani toward the task at hand. Arefaine watched for a scant moment, just long enough to see the black tendrils on Shara's chest slow and stop.

With a terse nod, she knelt next to Brophy and put her head next to his. She felt the turmoil inside him, felt the echoes of her three-hundred-year captivity. She did not want to go back to that place. Clenching her teeth, Arefaine banished her fears. The dream did not own her; this time she would be the master.

With one last deep breath, Arefaine plunged in.

❄

Issefyn kept her hands on the crystal, feeling its sluggish acceptance of Shara's corruption. She felt like she held the Great Ocean in her hands, an entire sea of power for her to command. She'd been cautious at first; careful to shield herself from the emmeria's influence, but keeping her boundaries intact was even easier than she'd thought it would be. Under her expert guidance, the flood of black emmeria rushing into Shara dwindled to a steady trickle, nothing more.

Issefyn's mind spun with the possibilities. Her patience had finally been rewarded. All the black emmeria in the world lay at her fingertips. All she had to do was pick it up and claim it.

Arefaine's body lay limp alongside Shara, as if the two of them and Brophy had just collapsed after a tawdry little threesome. They were pathetic...

Pathetic. And helpless.

She glanced at Baelandra, her fat face a mask of bovine concern. Issefyn's gaze bored into the redheaded trollop.

The Nine were just. It was suddenly so clear. Two of those responsible for her sons' deaths were here, their necks exposed. And the misguided freak who had dared to place herself above Issefyn had trussed herself for the slaughter.

Issefyn had savored a thousand scenarios where she turned the tables on the Awakened Child in a moment of weakness. She had never imagined it would be so simple. Why risk a dangerous confrontation when Issefyn could just slit the girl's throat now and be done with it?

She flicked a quick glance at the mindless Carrier of the Opal Fire who remained, standing vigilant guard. He would be tricky, but surely no more difficult than playing the motherly teacher for half a decade. This was the moment for which she had been born. Her season of triumph was about to begin. The ultimate feast of power and knowledge lay before her, and it would begin with a small appetizer of revenge.

She looked back at Baelandra.

It will begin with you.

❄

Brophy woke up screaming. He leapt to his feet, the Sword of Autumn in hand. A flood of rage swept through his body, and he was ready in an instant, ready to run, ready to kill.

He crouched naked in the Night Market. Black clouds crowded the sky, locking the city in perpetual gloom. The wind carried angry voices, like distant screams not quite heard. Successive flashes of lightning revealed ghostly shadows hunched between the buildings. This was how it began. This was how it always began.

"Brophy," a soft voice said from above him.

He whipped around and saw a stunning woman with pale blue eyes floating down from the sky.

He hurried back a few steps, keeping the Sword of Autumn between them. For some reason the red diamond in the sword's pommel no longer glowed. Brophy shook his head at the strange sight. It had to be another trick. Another lie. It was always a lie.

The woman hovered above the corpse-strewn street, just out of reach of his sword. Like an Ohohhim holy man, she wore black robes that hugged her waist, tight around her figure. Her long brown hair fluttered in the wind, half-covering her powdered face.

"Hello, Brophy," she said. Her voice was a soft contralto, soothing, but his lip curled. She looked like a female version of the Fiend.

He gripped his sword tighter, preparing to charge.

"A new dream, Fiend. A new face," he said. "But you don't fool me."

"No," she said softly. "The dream is over. It's time to come home."

He scoffed, keeping the sword between them. "It's never over. It never will be." He flicked a gaze around the street, looking for the others closing in.

"No, Brophy, nightmares do end. You ended mine, now I'm ending yours."

She looked down at him with a deep, deep sadness in her eyes. His breath caught in his throat. They were blue eyes, not black, and he had seen them someplace before.

"Who are you?"

"I am your kin, Brophy. Arefaine Morgeon, the sleeping child you gave up your life for so many years ago."

Brophy stopped moving. "No," he said, shaking his head. "You lie. That girl is an infant."

"Eighteen years ago I was an infant."

His sword dipped as he tried to remember. Could it have been so long?

She nodded. "The emmeria is safe, held by the Heartstone as she intended. Now I can guide you out of here. It is time for you to wake."

His head snapped up, and he looked at her through narrowed eyes. The Sword of Autumn rose again. "That will not happen."

"I admire your will, but it is no longer necessary. We have contained the black emmeria. Ohndarien is safe."

"No." He looked around, waiting for the claws, waiting for the twisted faces of his past. They should be here by now. "You're wasting your time, Fiend. I will never give you what you want. I will never set you free."

"I'm sorry, Brophy," she said. "But we don't have time for this. Shara could be dying right now."

She drifted closer, landing softly on the street. He snarled, rushing forward to cut her down—

Light flashed around her, and she blocked his sword with her hand. The edge cut deep into her palm, and she twisted the blade out of his hand. It clattered to the street.

"No!" Brophy screamed, diving for it.

She grabbed him by the hair and yanked him upward. "Your will is strong, Brophy. But so is mine."

Brophy swung at her blindly, kicking, screaming. His fist bounced off her pale flesh as if it were stone.

They hurtled into the sky, higher and higher. Light flashed all around them.

He spun upside down in her grip and slammed both heels into her chin. Again, light flashed, and his blow bounced aside.

"Hush, Brophy," she said. "Calm yourself. It is almost over."

They hurtled into the black clouds.

"No! I can't! I can't wake!" he screamed, punching her with all his might.

"You can, Brophy. You will."

The darkness engulfed him.

❄

Brophy's body twitched violently in the grips of the nightmare, and Baelandra bent over him in a flutter of concern. She held Shara's palm in one hand and Brophy's in the other as if the power of her worry could hold back black emmeria.

Issefyn glanced at the Carrier twenty feet distant and chose her moment. With sweat beading on her forehead, Issefyn slid the containment stone across Shara's stomach until it was nearly touching the back of Baelandra's hand. The corruption began to spread across Shara's body once again. Issefyn closed her eyes and brought the full power of her mind to bear. Instead of pulling the corruption out of Shara and guiding it into the Heartstone, she latched on to Baelandra's wrist and shoved the stone against her hand, funneling the hungry malice straight into her.

Baelandra's eyes shot open, and she tried to yank her hand away, but Issefyn clung to her like a bird of prey.

"What are you doing?" Baelandra gasped, jumping back like a jackal. Issefyn fell on top of her, pinning her to the ground.

She fought. Oh, it was delicious. The plump, redheaded matron fought for all she was worth, but she was not the Sister of Autumn anymore. The Heartstone no longer lent her strength, if it even had any strength left to give.

The black tendrils shot up Baelandra's arm, groping like black worms. She screamed in despair, and it was the sweetest music. Issefyn leaned close, put her mouth near Baelandra's quivering ear.

"This is how Physendria rewards betrayal."

Baelandra grabbed the Sword of Autumn and lashed out, striking Issefyn across the temple with the pommel. She fell back, and Baelandra scrambled to her feet.

Krellis's whore clutched the sword to her arm as if that would stem the flood. Her wide-eyed horror made Issefyn laugh.

Corkscrew spikes sprouted from the bubbling black skin of Baelandra's arms. The emmeria sensed the trembling heart of its victim, the birdlike shaking of her limbs, so desperate. So fragile.

Arefaine's bodyguard rushed up behind the beast and cut her down. But the flawless strike bounced off the scales that had grown across Baelandra's back and only knocked her to the ground.

Baelandra dropped the sword and leapt upon him. Long claws burst through her shoes, and she raked the Carrier's belly with them while holding tight to his shoulders. He roared and staggered to his knees. His sword fell from nerveless fingers. She spilled his entrails across the grass and turned away, blood splattered across her torn gown.

The Carrier gaped like a fish, and died.

Baelandra spun around, her smoldering red gaze locked on the Heartstone.

Issefyn scrambled to her feet, the containment stone still in hand. "Not so fast, my pretty," she whispered. "The stones are mine."

The corruption had not taken Baelandra's face yet, but her features were twisted in rage. She hissed, staggered closer, crouching low.

Issefyn reached out with her magic, grabbing hold of Baelandra's fragile mind.

The bitch froze, struggling. Her arms bubbled as she resisted.

Issefyn hurried forward and pulled the box of containment stones out of harm's way. She pulled them to the Heartstone and crouched over her prize.

Baelandra hissed, struggling against the mental bonds. The helpless bodies of Shara, Brophy, and Arefaine lay between them. "You smell their flesh, don't you?" Issefyn hissed. Baelandra snorted, her hair hanging over her red eyes. "You're hungry, aren't you? Feast, my beauty. Feast on them."

Baelandra looked from the sleeping idiots to Issefyn. With a long hiss, she reached for the Sword of Autumn and wrapped her claws around the hilt.

Issefyn sucked in a breath, as she felt her control lurch. "Too late for that," she said. "You're mine now."

Baelandra kept the sword tight in one claw. A thrill of terror rushed through Issefyn. Half of Baelandra's body was twisted into a blistered and blackened beast, but her face was still human, except for the red eyes that swirled with pure malice. She leaned over and sniffed Brophy's hair. With a mewling roar, she broke free.

She lunged forward, slamming into Issefyn, snarling and clawing.

They rolled to the ground, and Issefyn gave a powerful Lowani shriek, stunning the feral Sister for an instant. Issefyn scuttled backward and stood up, clutching the single containment stone to her chest. Baelandra crouched between her and the swirling black Heartstone. Issefyn had lost her prize. She had to get it back.

She grabbed hold of her rage and flung it at her enemy, hammering the bitch's mind with her will. Issefyn had to finish the job. Arefaine and Shara were helpless. She would never have a better chance to kill them both.

With a snarling grunt, Baelandra broke the spell again. A fierce grin spread across her lips, and she leapt after Issefyn. Again, Issefyn used the Lowani shriek to halt her; but Baelandra fought her like a demon, creeping closer and closer.

Issefyn's gaze flicked to the blackened crystal clenched in her fist. *One is enough for now,* she thought. *When I master this, I will come for the rest.*

Channeling her power into her legs, Issefyn ran.

Baelandra charged after her.

❄

Arefaine found Shara broken and bleeding on a dock at the edge of the Market. Her body was crushed, her skull cracked open. Corruption covered her naked body from neck to midthigh, and unseeing eyes stared at the black clouds far above.

Barely able to draw breath, Arefaine knelt next to Shara's twisted body. She touched the Zelani mistress's hair, soaked with blood.

"Well done, my child, well done."

Arefaine turned toward the familiar voice behind her.

He looked exactly as she remembered, bare-chested in a shimmering green sarong. His graying hair was cropped close, and she could see him smiling between his thin mustache and long, pointed beard.

"I have waited for your return," he said, his light blue eyes sparkling. "How beautiful you have become."

"Father ..." she murmured, and rushed into his arms.

"Now, now, child, our time here is short. You've done well. Brophy awakens as we speak."

"But ... What will happen to her," Arefaine asked, pulling back from his shoulder. "What about Shara? Is she dead?"

"How can she be dead? This is only a dream."

Arefaine nodded.

"You can take her with you when you go."

She nodded again, "But what—"

Her father held up a hand for silence. "I know you have questions. All will be answered in time, but for now, I need you to listen very carefully."

Arefaine looked over at Shara. "Please, Father. Just a moment." She knelt beside Shara, placing a hand on her friend's lifeless flesh. Reaching out with her magic, she found the flicker of ani locked within Shara's shattered body. Shara's tortured spirit clung to the illusion of death, unable to find its way back to the light. Arefaine lent her strength to Shara's feeble life force, drawing her out of the darkness and setting her free. Shara's corpse slowly disappeared as she was released from the dream.

The simplicity of the spell wrenched Arefaine's heart. How many other souls were still trapped in nightmare, lost in despair, when the tiniest speck of magic could lead them back home? There were so many wrongs she could make right.

Her father knelt by her side, placed a warm hand on her shoulder. "You must bring the Sleeping Warden to Efften. We will need more young people like him if we are to rebuild our city."

"I will, but we must get you out of here. Why have you lingered so long?"

"That is a question for later; right now I need you to do exactly what I say."

She paused, then bowed her head, and said, "Yes, Father."

❄

Brophy woke up screaming. He leapt to his feet, scrambling away from the bodies that lay on top of him. He was ready in an instant, ready to run, ready to kill.

There were corpses scattered all around, but this was different. All different. And that meant . . .

He backed away, looking to the sky overhead. A night sky, but no storm. And his sword was gone. Where was his sword?

Brophy spotted the glowing red pommel on the grass a few feet away. He leapt upon it, clutching the weapon to his chest. Was it too late? Had he failed?

He winced at the pain in his shoulder and looked down at his wound. There was no sign of corruption anywhere on his body. Where were the corrupted? Where was the foul wind destroying everything in its path?

He looked around and saw the woman from his dream lying on the grass, her pale face turned to the sky. A second woman's features were hidden by a curtain of black hair. With a hammering heart, Brophy reached out, pushed the hair away, then snatched his hand back.

It was Shara. Or what Shara's mother might have looked like. The hair slowly fell back across her face. Was the black emmeria loose, or was this another twisted dream concocted by the Fiend?

The familiar howl of a corrupted shattered Brophy's hopes.

Snarling, he rushed after the noise. They weren't far. Behind a stand of trees, two corrupted creatures battled in the darkness.

Brophy leapt upon them. He lopped the head off the first one, and cocked back for a follow-up thrust for its friend.

"No!" the woman cried, holding an arm up for defense. A normal woman. Gray hair at her temples, wrinkles, not a monster.

Brophy's brow furrowed. His heart thundered in his chest. His head hurt. He waited for her to change, waited for her to leap upon him, but she just fell backward and scrambled away.

Something rustled behind him. He spun around, bringing the Sword of Autumn up. The gemstone pommel flared as the thing lurched out of the trees.

Brophy attacked.

CHAPTER 22

Astor and his father had just left the Citadel when Galliana found them. At first he feared an attack on another part of the city, and ran to greet her. She breathlessly told him about Shara's fears, and Astor left her at a full sprint. Father would send a full squad, but Astor wasn't willing to wait. If someone meant to harm the Lost Brother, Astor had to get there first.

He was nearly across the Night Market when a sudden terror gripped his chest. The ever-present voice in the back of his mind had gone silent. The Heartstone had stopped singing.

He doubled his speed, taking the steps up the Wheel four at a time. His joints ached; his muscles felt like jelly by the time he rounded Scythe's statue and headed for the Hall of Windows. The torch still burned on top of it, but that was all he could see.

Sweat dripped from his cheeks, and his chest pumped like a bellows. Something moved to his left, and he instinctively grabbed his sword hilt, stumbling away. Trees rustled, and Astor's sword rang against the sheath.

No Silver Islanders lunged from the shadows. It was a squirrel, or a rabbit, or maybe just the wind. Gritting his teeth, he slammed his blade back into the sheath and ran on, willing his feet to keep pounding the gravel path.

The thought of running to kill another person made it even harder. As an Heir of Autumn, Astor had practiced swordsmanship for years. He'd fought battles beyond the wall. But Astor had never even struck another person in anger. Could he actually look another man in the eye and swing his sword if he needed to?

He flinched at a guttural roar off to his side. He swerved from the path and headed for the sound. Another howl shattered the night, more gut-wrenching than the first. He swerved around a fountain and burst through a copse of trees. A woman cried "No!" just ahead of him.

Astor slashed his way through a flimsy hedge and burst into the open. A huge figure blocked his path. He was the biggest man Astor had ever seen, wreathed in a burning red glow. Astor tried to stop, slipped on the grass, and almost went down.

The glowing sword flashed toward him, deadly and unerring. Astor snapped up a quick parry, but the crushing blow knocked his blade back into his own chest and drove him to the ground.

Astor gasped at the pain, rolled away. The figure loomed over him, raising the burning sword again.

"No!" Astor yelled.

"Stop!" Another voice charged the air with undeniable force. Astor froze. So did the fearsome warrior standing over him.

Shara limped into the glade, holding together the tattered edges of her torn dress. Her face was a mask of pain. "Brophy!" she cried. "It's over, my love. It's over."

Astor looked up at the bestial man towering over him and saw his own face, tortured and twisted.

"It's all right," Shara murmured, staggering up to him. She put a hand on his shoulder—

Brophy's heartstone flared crimson. In the sudden light, Astor saw that Brophy's eyes were as black as night.

He lashed out, his fist smashing into Shara's head. She flew into a tree and dropped like a sack of wet meal.

Astor gasped, suddenly free from Shara's spell. Brophy turned back around, raising the sword above his head. Astor scrambled backward.

"Cousin!" he blurted, preparing to die.

But the strike didn't fall. Brophy hesitated, staring at something on his hand. He lowered the sword, looking at the back of his knuckles.

He glanced at the prone Shara. Astor couldn't tell whether she was alive or dead. Was she breathing?

"It's red," he breathed, looking back at Astor. "The blood is red."

Astor's heart thundered in his chest. Should he try to run? Could he hide?

Those black eyes peered at Astor, and slowly they cleared, revealing the whites and Brophy's green irises.

"Your blood is red."

Astor nodded dumbly.

"By the Seasons . . ." He choked out the words.

All the fury left Brophy's face. He looked at Astor, and for the first time Astor saw deep, horrible fear in his cousin's gaze.

"What have I done?" Brophy murmured. "What on earth have I done?"

He dropped the Sword of Autumn and sprinted into the night.

Astor watched him go, the sound of his own breath roaring in his ears. He nearly threw up, but forced himself to crawl over to Shara.

"Thank the Seasons," he breathed as he found her pulse. She was unconscious, but at least she was alive.

Astor staggered to his feet, not sure what to do, how to find help. He squinted into the darkness. Another prone figure lay a short distance away.

He stood there for a long moment. That dress. He knew that dress, even torn and smeared with dirt and blood.

He lunged forward, tripping over something in the dark and fell to his knees next to the headless body. *No. Oh no.* He rolled it over. Delicate, wrinkled hands. His mother's hands.

The front of her dress had been ripped open, exposing the white scar where her heartstone had once been. Bile surged up his throat. He leaned over his mother's body and retched into the grass. He couldn't feel his face. Couldn't feel his hands.

Turning slowly, he looked at what he had tripped over. It was his mother's head, one eye closed. The other eye was open, staring blankly. The ends of her fiery red hair were stained dark, and her face bore a frozen grimace of pain and rage.

His plaintive yell swelled into a heartrending scream.

CHAPTER 23

The smell of the rain had already faded, and the swirling dust returned, stinging Phanqui's eyes. The storm had come and gone as quickly as a glimmer of hope. The parched earth of Physen devoured the moisture, tantalizing her populace with a moment of stolen joy, the promise of better days that never arrived.

Phanqui remembered a time when the rains had left happiness in their wake, but memory was Phanqui's curse from the Nine. He recalled everything, every moment of his life in exquisite detail, over and over again.

He limped along the King's Highway, flanked by his Summermen body-guards. He had given up trying to speak to them a decade ago. The guards' names changed, but their faces stayed the same. They were the dustborn, the peasants of the Summer Seas, and the only people lower than them were Physendrians. All of his guards were sullen young men, sailors by craft and blood, exiled to a foreign desert. Phanqui's protectors hated him. They hated Physen, hated the entire country of Physendria.

At first the occupiers had just been soldiers, hired swords trying to force order down the throats of a shattered people. But subduing a foreign land had changed the Summermen and the would-be liberators became reluctant tyrants. The last few years had been the worst, ever since Lord Vinghelt was named governor. Only the lowest sort of men were recruited to serve under him, and the reluctant tyrants were gradually replaced by vicious thugs.

Phanqui hobbled forward, dodging a pile of offal and trying not to think about it. Golden chariots once bore Physendrian royalty swiftly down the wide trench that shaded them from the brutal sun, but now the King's High-way was a midden heap. Back then, no one would have dared throw garbage into the path of the king. Those were the days when there still was a king.

Phandir had been a terrible monarch, a brutal man who led them to ruin. But he had been their king. One of their own.

Phanqui stumbled, the old wound in his leg cramping suddenly. He paused, wincing, and massaged it so that it would work again.

"Get your ass moving," one of the dustborn growled, warily scanning the edges of the trench. He was right to worry. The King's Highway was not safe for Summermen or their Physendrian lapdogs at this time of night.

"A moment," Phanqui said, working the muscle roughly. The wound had never completely healed after Phee had stabbed him through the thigh in that last Nine Squares competition. It might have, but all of Physen's physicians had gone north with their king and died with him there. Phanqui had been left to heal on his own, battling an infection that had nearly taken his leg.

Their defeat in the Nightmare Battle left Physendria as dry as the southern badlands. The Summermen rushed into that vast emptiness, filling it like the Summer Seas and washing away the nation that had once been Physendria. They were now the Summer Deserts, and to speak the word "Physendria" to the wrong person meant your life.

Still, if the Nine Squares competition were to begin tomorrow, Phanqui retained the right to begin at the Scorpion stone. It made him smile, the idea of his cowardly heart and broken body running the desert again, like he had run with Brophy so long ago. Phanqui could still smell the swirling dust during that glorious moment when he and his kinsmen ran side by side with the Ohndarien prince. That day had been the finest of his life, and it truly seemed that everything would finally change for the better. How wrong he had been.

The Nine Squares games ended the night Brophy flew, burning like Phoenix. Now the great volcano was home to countless refugees, packed into the galleries like roaches. Some children had spent their entire lives in that horrid place, some had—

"Look out!" one of his guards shouted. Phanqui turned just as the rock struck him. With a gasp, he fell to the garbage-strewn road, clutching the gash in his head. Another rock arced down, but he managed to get his arm up in time to deflect it.

The heads of three youths poked briefly over the lip of the trench. "Traitor!" one of them called. "Ass-spreader!"

They threw more rocks, then disappeared.

Phanqui's guards left him on the ground, running for the nearest ramp leading up to the surface. Both pulled little silver whistles from their tunics and blew in unison, filling the air with a piercing shriek. Half a hundred Summermen would swarm over this area in moments. There was a handsome reward on the head of any rebel, no matter how young.

Phanqui sent a brief prayer to Falcon for the fleeing boys. "Lend wings to their feet," he whispered. "Fly away little ones. Keep running, keep throwing your rocks until we're free of them forever."

He remained on his knees, holding one hand to his bloody head as the shrill whistles of other Summermen crisscrossed the surface above them. Part of him wished the rock had been a spear that would have ended his part in this endless nightmare.

He shook his head. Is that what Brophy would have done? When an entire country stood against him, did he lie down and wait for the spear? No. He broke the game, threw off the shackles, escaped the inescapable prison. He soared like Phoenix.

Phanqui rose to his feet and continued toward the Catacombs. He still lived in the subterranean palace, surrounded by the officers and soldiers of the new regime. In exchange for a full belly and feather sheets, Phanqui had become the hatchet man of the invaders. Or their shovel man, rather. The Summermen buried their enemies alive.

As a subcaptain of Physen's Black Watch, Phanqui ate as the officers did, attended some of their planning sessions, and was afforded some small luxuries, the best food, a physician's care when his wife fell ill, things that his starving countrymen no longer knew. In exchange for these things, Phanqui had the simple job of arranging the arrest and execution of anyone who raised a finger against the foreign invaders.

Here in Physen, the rebellion was little more than children throwing rocks. The Summermen held all the major towns, but it was a different story in the deep desert. His countrymen had seized the mountain passes and many of the smaller towns in the south. The Summermen could only move men and supplies by ship, sailing through the Ohndarien locks. The Waveborn were losing their grip. They would have to leave soon, or ... If Lord Vinghelt had his way, come back with the combined might of the Summer Cities and wash them from the face of the earth.

Phanqui entered the Catacombs, nodding at the two Summermen who stood sentry at the archway. He wound his way through the dimly lit passages until he reached his door.

Drawing a deep breath, he tried to banish his brooding thoughts, tried to banish the faces of the Physendrians he had condemned today, two men and a woman. He tried not to think about how they might even now be struggling to breathe under six feet of desert, their hearts beating out of their chests as they scratched at their sandstone coffins, screaming words that none would ever hear.

Phanqui's fingers became a claw on the door, and he cursed his perfect memory. He had known the woman, had seen her once while riding on Governor Vinghelt's chariot through the city above. Her arm had been wrapped protectively around a skinny young boy. The woman he'd condemned to death tonight had had a son.

For hours afterward, he had dwelled on the hateful gaze she had given him. She never once looked at their Waveborn oppressors as they passed. Her hatred was for Phanqui alone. Everyone despised a traitor, an ass-spreader bending over for their foreign lords.

Phanqui pushed the door open and crept into his chambers.

His wife, Shafyssa, lay sleeping on the circular bed that hung from chains in the middle of the room. Their one-year-old daughter lay cuddled tight in the curve of her body, as if the mother could protect the child from the world outside their door.

Swallowing, he crossed the room and knelt silently at the bedside. He touched the child's tiny palm, and she reflexively grabbed his finger, squeezing twice.

Shafyssa's eyelids flickered.

"Hello, beautiful," he said softly.

"Hello, gimpy," she mumbled, still half-asleep.

Their marriage had been arranged by their parents, and neither of them had wanted it. But sometimes the Nine were generous, and the two of them had fallen in love. It was about the time that she had started using that nickname that he had lost his heart to her.

Slowly waking up, she opened her eyes and saw his forehead.

"What happened?" she cried, jolting upright and waking the baby. She gathered Brepha into her arms, holding her against a breast. The little girl began sucking immediately.

"Rebels," he said. "Children. Got me good with a rock." He smiled wryly.

Shafyssa lowered her voice to a whisper. "Are they all right? Did they get away?"

"I don't know," he whispered back. Phanqui doubted he was important enough to spy on, but secrets slipped through the Catacombs like water slipped through sand. "I hope so. I sent a prayer after them. With any luck, they were fast enough to stay ahead of it."

Brepha had fallen back asleep as quickly as she woke, and Shafyssa laid her gently on the bed. She rose and went to fetch a basin of water. Kneeling next to Phanqui, she began washing his cut.

"I buried three more today," he said. He rarely talked about his work, but he couldn't help himself. The woman had had a son.

She winced and nodded. "You did what they made you do."

"But I said the words. I was the one they looked at with such hatred—"

She grabbed his chin, forced his gaze to meet hers. "Don't say that." Her gaze flicked to their baby, asleep on the bed. "You know who you are; you know why we're doing this."

"Yes, but sometimes I just wish . . ." he said, then stopped. He wished they had never had Brepha. She made them so vulnerable, so afraid every moment of their lives. How could he ever explain this to his daughter? How could he look at her and tell her what he'd done, tell her why he had done it?

Phanqui banished the thoughts from his mind and silently begged forgiveness from the Nine. It was profane to wish away a child.

"Stay strong, my husband," Shafyssa whispered. "You are the only one who could do this. The information you feed the rebels is invaluable. Your timely whispers have saved hundreds of lives."

"But my accusations have also buried hundreds."

"That blood is on their hands, not yours. If you fled your post, ten lesser men would line up to fill it. You do the Nine's work."

"Explain that to the son of the woman I just condemned to death."

Shafyssa fell quiet for a moment, then said, "That boy is the reason you are doing this." Her voice was hard, angry. "Hold his face in that flawless memory of yours. Hold that boy close to your heart with all of the others. Because one day we will make Vinghelt and all of his minions pay for every death, for every orphan who cries because her mother dared to believe in Physendria."

Phanqui turned away. He wanted her words to rekindle the fire in his soul, as they had done so many times in the past; but after tonight, he would need more than her words.

Leaning close to her, he whispered in her ear, so quiet that she could barely hear him. "That day may be very close at hand. One of my contacts has asked me to join a plan to assassinate Lord Vinghelt."

She drew back, her eyes wide. She swallowed, and he could see the fear and excitement mixing in her heart. "Is this the new one? The—"

"Yes. The spy sent by the Kherish crown."

"The fat one with the red eyes?"

He nodded. "He is posing as a weapons merchant and needs me to arrange a meeting with Lord Vinghelt on his ship. With my help, it would only take a few men to bring him down."

"Do you trust the fat man?"

Phanqui paused, then said, "The Kherish have no love for the Waveborn, that is certain."

"But you want to trust him. You want to swing a sword for the Nine once again."

Phanqui glanced at little Brepha. His hand moved, then stopped. He longed to touch her, to run a finger down her smooth cheek, but he held back.

"You must remember our pact, Phanqui," she whispered, catching his glance. "Remember that night in the desert."

"I cannot forget it."

"We made that choice together. We bought the worm's milk that would have thrust her from my womb, but we both held that cup and poured that tea into the sand. We promised we would not let a child hold us back. We promised we would still take this step when the time came."

Phanqui nodded, reliving the moment. He could still feel the stinging sand blowing against his legs. He could still smell the acrid stench of the tea. He had never been so scared. Or so in love.

He looked at his wife. He looked at his daughter.

"We're running out of time," she told him, and she was right. Vinghelt would return to the Summer Cities soon to gather his army.

Phanqui watched Brepha's tiny chest move up and down as she slept. Shafyssa gently forced him to look back at her. "You fear they will bury us. But we are already buried, my love. They squeeze the life out of us."

Shafyssa turned toward little Brepha. Silence fell for a time, then she whispered, "Every time I nurse her, I'm afraid the hatred and bitterness will seep into her, crushing her heart before she even has a chance to really live. We cannot allow her to grow up as a slave, as a worthless child of a defeated people."

Phanqui shook his head, walking away from her. She followed, grabbing his hands, squeezing them tight.

"I still remember the moment I fell in love with you," she said.

His heart wrenched as the memory came back to him as clear as if it had happened an hour ago. In the weeks before the Summermen descended upon them, the fifteen families were desperate to unite their feuding factions against the foreign invaders. They made several royal matches in one week. Phanqui's had been one of those.

"We'd just made love for the first time," she said, smiling ruefully. "And it was bad. So bad." She chuckled softly, squeezing his hand. "I had never felt so awkward, so lonely. I hated you at that moment, and I despaired for my life."

He kept his gaze on the floor.

"But then you started to talk. You told me about that horrible wound in your leg. You told me about the last Nine Squares contest. You told me about your friend, Brophy, about the day you stabbed him in the back. You did it for your family, you said. For your mother, your father, your sisters and cousins. You saved your family."

"I lost my soul."

She shook her head. "I did not believe that then, and I do not believe that now. At that moment, I saw the man you really are, even if you couldn't. I saw the gods in you that night. I saw the Nine shining through your eyes."

She placed her head against his chest, holding him tight.

"This is another moment, just like that first," she murmured against him. "The Nine are in the room with us. You've been touched by the gods, and the lives of the men they choose are rarely happy, rarely long. But this is your burden, and only you have the strength to bear it."

She paused.

"If Brophy was here right now," she whispered, "he'd be on that Kher's ship. He'd take his stab at Vinghelt's heart, with nothing but a sharp stick if need be. And you would be with him."

Phanqui didn't say anything.

"Wouldn't you?" she pressed.

Slowly, he nodded. "If Brophy was here, I would be with him."

"Then go," Shafyssa whispered. "Fight for us. Fight for her." She looked at their sleeping daughter. "If the Nine claim the highest price, I will pay it before I see you—before I see any of us—truly lose our souls."

He nodded, then whispered. "And before our country disappears forever."

CHAPTER 24

"Must we drag ourselves through the filthy streets of these dusteaters," Mikal said to Lawdon, flashing his winning smile. "When it looks to be such a beautiful day?"

"If the simple act of walking pains you so much," Lawdon replied, "why didn't you stay on the ship?"

"I would sooner die a coward's death than be cleft from your side," Mikal said as he trudged along Canal Street next to her. "You wound me with the mere suggestion."

"When I wound you, you'll feel it," Lawdon said, walking down the deserted street with long strides. She had spent most of her childhood on Ohndarien's streets and waterways scheming up her dinner for the night, but the city had changed more than she'd expected.

"I would bare my breast to receive your knife, my steel dove," Mikal said. "Simply give the word."

Lawdon considered handing him her dagger, just to see what he would do, but suppressed the urge.

Lawdon had docked her ship, *Summer's Heart*, in Cliff Town late last night. She'd considered heading to Baelandra's house immediately, but decided that would be rude and forced herself to wait until dawn before heading to the far side of the city. It had been years since she had climbed the four hundred steps alongside Ohndarien's underground waterway. Those locks usually ran day and night, but they seemed to be shut down for some reason, and Lawdon hadn't seen another soul since they entered the tunnels.

Climbing the famous Foreplay Steps used to be a chore most sailors looked forward to, as every step brought them closer to the Ohndarien brothels on Canal Street, but those brothels had closed down years ago leaving this part of the city practically empty on this lovely morning.

A bell began to toll in the distance. The deep ring came from the west and carried across the city. Lawdon felt a swift chill up her spine. Her first thought was a fire, but that was never a problem in a city made of stone. The sound continued clear and steady, and she paused, looking toward the Hall of Windows.

"Are we being invaded?" Mikal asked.

"Let's hope not." The attacks of the corrupted on Ohndarien were well-known in the Summer Seas. Lawdon had seen Shara once when she had embraced a tiny whiff of black emmeria. She had no desire to see a full-fledged corrupted.

Mikal tried to usher her back toward the ship. "Please, my love, my life, my light. Let us away from these desiccated—and ridiculously steep—shores with all haste. An ocean of delight awaits us back in the Summer Seas."

Lawdon ignored his efforts and continued down the street, increasing her pace, just to spite him. "Don't you realize that Ohndarien was once called the Jewel of the Known World? She is renowned for her beauty."

"Farad oxen are renowned for the size of their dumpings," Mikal replied. "It does not change the nature of the oxen. Or their dumpings." Mikal dramatically dodged a pile of dung that steamed in the street.

She glanced back and couldn't help but smile, wondering if he arranged these moments. He was a poet duelist, after all; even if his reputation implied that he enjoyed the sound of his own voice much more than the heft of his blade.

Mikal grinned back at her, showing flawless white teeth. "You see?" he said. "No matter how glorious a dusteater city may be, it still squats upon the land. Such vile necessities have nowhere to go. And so they sit in plain view. It is not the fault of these fine Ohndariens. I'm certain they are a very ... clean people." He wrinkled his nose. "But surely you must feel the indignity of being land-bound. You are Lord Reignholtz's captain, master of the prince's flagship! Not a sheep. A hoofed ox. A ... a dusteater."

"No one made you come with me," Lawdon replied. "In fact, I don't think you were even invited."

"My dear, my heart, my savior, your recent kindness has put me forever in your debt. You know I must attend upon you every moment until the last breath drifts from my mouth." Mikal scissor-stepped quickly to catch up with her, facing her as he walked backward.

"You have taken the most tender parts of me and kept them cruelly in hand, and I cannot leave your side until I melt your fist into a tender embrace, until we spin with abandon, shedding our outer defenses and leaving naught but your skin ..." He looked at her, eyes brimming with hope. "My skin ... Our skin ..."

Lawdon snorted. "I have a task, Heidvell. All that skin might be pleasantly distracting, but I must meet with Baelandra, as charged by my lord. It is a matter of duty. Surely you must remember what duty is?"

"I believe it was a word my mother used every time I embarrassed her, but the memory comes and goes."

Lawdon turned onto a bridge across the canal and headed for the bay. "If your memory comes and goes, perhaps you should drink less and eat more vegetables."

"Sound advice, but somehow there always seems to be a drink about when I'm wanting a vegetable."

Lawdon chuckled. She found it impossible to be as angry with Mikal as he deserved. He had a way about him. His mother was Lady Heidvell, the widow of a lesser prince of the Summer Cities. Unfortunately for the Heidvell shiphome, Mikal's reputation as a feckless philanderer did nothing to improve their modest standing. Yet somehow, his sincere blue eyes made you want to overlook that. His handsome face and curly black hair made you wonder if his reputation had been concocted by a few petty, jealous women who only wanted to defame his character.

If she had met Mikal in a port of the Summer Seas, she would certainly have let him tumble her, but he was on her boat, and a captain didn't lay down for anyone, passenger or crew.

"Come, my heart's fire, my sparkling hammer of love," Mikal said, taking her arm. She paused in the middle of the street, letting him hold her hand for a moment. "I cannot stand for your beautiful feet to endure this indignity any longer. Come with me back to the deep blue sea. We'll even sail west if we must. We can seek our fortune on the Lesser Ocean amid tattooed pirates and fat Kherish merchants with their dog-headed scows."

"Shouldn't you be kneeling for this sort of thing?"

He glanced down, and his brow furrowed. "On *land?*"

Lawdon took her hand back. "Ah, if you cannot handle me on land, my fickle prince, you'll never handle me at sea." They left the bridge and headed down a residential street. "I should have left you on that island. A bit more starvation would have been good for you. I'm still not sure how I spotted your pathetic signal fire."

"Divine intervention, my cherished one," he insisted, running to catch up. He put a hand to his chest and waved to the sky. "I prayed to Fessa of the Deep, and our benevolent goddess sent a sprite of the sea to my rescue. It is her divine will that brought us together."

"Was it divine will that got you marooned in the first place?"

"Certainly, that and an error of my misguided heart. The Lady Amalitz has a cold, unforgiving disposition. Unfortunately, I did not see it until—"

"The Lady Amalitz found you humping her maid."

"She was not—"

"In her own bed."

Mikal spread his hands. "I was seduced."

"At knifepoint, no doubt."

They continued down the hill. Hastily dressed people were filling the streets, talking quietly among themselves. From their pained expressions, Lawdon guessed that somebody must have died.

"You know," Mikal said, oblivious to everything around him, "I cannot quite put the tip of my tongue upon the reason why you captivate me so. There's something haunting about the icy mystery at the depth of your un-welcoming hearth. Something haunting about the chilly caress of your conti-nence." He shivered. "Something haunting about—"

Lawdon rolled her eyes. "There is certainly something haunting about a poet who relies on his looks more than his words. The chilly caress of my continence? By Fessa, what's your next poetic pinnacle? 'The warm caress of my incontinence'?"

"My lady, you wound me!" Mikal stopped walking, then hurried to catch up with her. "My words are all I have. I birth them with as much love as a mother births a child."

"You certainly bring them screaming into the world."

They turned another corner and Lawdon saw the familiar row of blue-white mansions along the bay. They walked closer, and Lawdon smiled. That was Baelandra's house. She was sure of it. She looked for that tree she had climbed so long ago to reach Baelandra's window. She shook her head. That wouldn't do. If that tree was still there after two decades, it certainly wouldn't look the way she remembered it.

Mikal was correct in one respect. The land was not her home anymore, and she longed for the open sea, for the natural rolling of her ship on the waves. Lawdon had grown up in Ohndarien, but she had a difficult time think-ing of it as her childhood home and not just another port. She remembered Ohndarien's bay as a vast ocean of adventure for a waterbug. Now it seemed like a dirty puddle that real ships reluctantly passed through to unload their cargo.

They walked up to Baelandra's gate, and Lawdon wondered if her friend would be awake this early. Her mission grew more urgent with every day that passed. High summer had nearly begun, and Lawdon desperately needed to warn Baelandra about the danger behind Lord Vinghelt's plans. The upstart prince was only one duel away from starting a bloody war that would eventually consume every nation bordering the Summer Seas. Ohndarien must be convinced to bar her gates to the Summer Fleet.

As they reached the front gate, Lawdon's smile faded. The garden was mobbed with people, mostly soldiers and a few civilians still dressed in their nightclothes. Many of them were crying. The bells across the city continued to toll, and Lawdon got a sinking feeling.

One of the soldiers spotted Lawdon and hurried over to greet her. "Sad days, my friends," the heavyset man said. He wore a blue tunic with a gold slash across the front.

"What happened?" she asked, trying to spot Baelandra amid the crowd.

"Murder. We are still looking for a man who did it. He is about this tall." The soldier held out his hand. "The fellow is burly as an ox. Silver Islander, with tattoos all over. Have you seen him?"

She looked at Mikal. He shrugged. Lawdon shook her head. "Who was killed?"

"He and his band tried to steal the Sleeping Warden. They killed three guardsmen, an Ohohhim bodyguard, and the old Sister of Autumn."

Lawdon's thoughts froze. The current Sister of Autumn was barely Lawdon's age. Not old at all.

"What?"

"Killed her. Cut her head right off, but the city will stay locked down until we catch the fiend. I promise you that."

"Killed who?" Lawdon murmured, but her breath had been taken from her body. She knew who he meant. Before he even responded, she knew.

"The old Sister. Baelandra. The bells ring for her. They're gathering in the Hall of Windows already."

"No . . ." she murmured.

"Lawdon?" Mikal put a hand on her shoulder.

"Oh Fessa, no." Lawdon began running toward the Wheel, leaving a bewildered Mikal behind her.

CHAPTER 25

It had been suggested that Arefaine stay in her room until His Eternal Wisdom called for her.

It was not a command, of course. A command was an artless, barbaric method of control, something only a mortal would do. The Emperor was the voice of Oh on earth. He made polite suggestions. And who would not heed the words of a god?

Of course, those who did not follow this softly spoken advice soon came to regret it.

Outside the ship, a single mourning bell tolled atop the Wheel. Arefaine did her best to ignore the sound and everything it implied.

Her attendants had left her just before dawn. She was prepared, her face powdered, her dark hair oiled and curled, and she had been made to wait. Her hands were folded neatly in her lap, her back straight as if she were going to rise and open the door at any moment. She had been sitting like that for two hours. It was the first time she had ever been made to wait for an audience with the Emperor.

Finally, the tap came at the door.

Arefaine stood, crossed to her black dressing table, and lifted the heavy, silk-wrapped bundle. She went to the door, and it opened at the sound of her footsteps.

The procession had just reached her. The timing was perfect as always. Arefaine started to take her place in front of the Opal Advisor, ready to offer her sleeve to him and lead the procession to the Emperor.

But the Opal Advisor did not look at her, did not reach to take her sleeve. Behind him, the Chief Carrier of the Opal Fire let go of the Advisor's sleeve, implying that Arefaine should take the second place in line.

Arefaine hesitated only an instant, then smoothly stepped into the gap and pinched the sleeve in front of her.

So, I have been removed one step further from Oh, dropped below an ordinary mortal. It did not matter. She knew this had been a possibility. She had begun this dance, and she would see it through.

The procession snaked through the passageway of the great ship to the Emperor's stateroom, a tiny replica of the towering chamber in the Opal Palace. A cunning bit of engineering, the lacquered black walls sloped inward toward the ceiling, giving the illusion of greater height. The Emperor sat on a tall-backed, obsidian throne on a black dais, an exact replica of his throne in the Opal Palace.

The procession moved forward, and the Opal Advisor stopped, clapped his hands quietly, just once, in front of his stomach. Everyone released their sleeves and fanned out to the left, creating a perfect diagonal line to the edge of the room. They descended to their knees, starting at the back and moving forward like a softly falling wave. The Opal Advisor was the last to kneel, putting his head to the floor.

Arefaine set her heavy bundle by her knee and genuflected, keeping her forehead pressed against the cool wood. After a moment, she could hear the Opal Advisor's robes rustle as he straightened. No doubt that had been prearranged. Arefaine did not take that as her cue to rise. Only the Emperor could give that permission.

Silence fell over the audience chamber. There was only the slight creaking from the shifting ship and the faint sound of the distant bell.

The wait was intended to be a punishment, a torture. For most Ohohhim, the shame of making the Incarnation of Oh on earth wait this long simply to show his displeasure would have been unbearable.

Arefaine kept her breathing slow and steady, sending her turbulent emotions into the swirling well of magic at the center of her being.

If the Emperor had listened during their increasingly infrequent talks back in Ohohhom, he would not be so surprised. He would not wonder at how important this was to Arefaine. Still, it hurt to wait, to suddenly be the subject of the Emperor's calculated wrath. If he could not understand why she must stay this course, no one would. But she would make him see. He must see.

For a fleeting moment, as the silence dragged on, Arefaine began to fear that the waiting itself would be the entire lesson. There would be no opportunity to explain. The Emperor had brought her here simply to be ignored, then have her led away again, locked in her stateroom. She didn't fear the token captivity. There wasn't a room in all of Ohndarien that could hold her, but the real punishment was the humiliation before one of the few people she had once called friend.

But the Emperor cleared his throat, and Arefaine felt a prickle of release across her scalp and clenched her teeth immediately. She shouldn't care so much what the Emperor thought. If he couldn't see reason, she had to proceed without him.

She waited for his soft, even voice, but it was the Opal Advisor who spoke in his stead, another humiliation, a sign of the Emperor's inexpressible rage.

"Would the Awakened Child be so kind as to help a humble man grow in the wisdom of Oh?" the Opal Advisor said.

The tone of voice was deferential, a supplication, but Arefaine was not fooled. He would order her death just as politely. For the first time, she found herself hating the Opal Advisor. His black, curly hair had never grayed, though his face was creased with the wrinkles of an old man. She could picture those wrinkles twitching as though wanting to smile at her shame.

When Arefaine spoke, she remained calm and respectful, like all good Ohohhim.

"I would be delighted to share what little wisdom I possess," she said, still keeping her forehead pressed against the floor. She could not look upon the Emperor's face until he gave her leave to do so.

"You are too gracious," the Opal Advisor said, sounding like he meant it. "I wish to understand something my simple mind cannot seem to comprehend. Why did you choose to leave your chambers last night and infringe upon the hospitality of our respected hosts?"

And more importantly, ignore the express orders of His Eternal Wisdom, Arefaine thought. That was what they were really talking about, but it was something that could never be mentioned. After all, when the Emperor spoke, reality must follow.

Arefaine had been prepared for this moment ever since she nudged the minds of the two Carriers of Opal Fire and convinced them to accompany her to the Zelani school. She had played this inevitable conversation over in her mind a hundred times, refining what she would say. But that did not keep her from pausing to consider her words carefully one last time. She chose them precisely.

She could not explain her reasons. The Emperor held the power of Oh on earth and had never been wrong in five thousand years. One did not attempt to convince him of the error of his ways.

She had to take a different route.

"I was following the sleeve of Oh as best as I was able."

She waited for the words to sink in. The Opal Advisor took some time in formulating his reply.

"Your wisdom still eludes me. I humbly beg that you explain further."

Arefaine allowed herself a small, inward smile, though it didn't show on her hidden face or her body language. This was not the response the Advisor had been expecting.

"Oh granted me the knowledge and power to repay a great act of kindness that was once granted to the Opal Empire. I was given the ability to awaken the Sleeping Warden, and I felt honor-bound to use the power I had been given."

"I understand the wisdom of your actions once the Sleeping Warden was abducted. It is the timing of your actions that led to that moment that are unclear to me."

"I understand your confusion," Arefaine said, seeing the direction of the conversation now. Still, she must be careful. The best-laid traps were unseen. "You could not know that I was also given the gift of impatience. I felt a sense of urgency about this issue so profound, it must have been sent directly from Oh. I knew that I needed to speak with Shara-lani last night. I could not see my destination, but that did not stop me from following the sleeve in front of me."

The man was caught. The voice of Oh spoke through the Emperor, not through his subjects. But the Ohohhim had touted Arefaine as someone nearly divine. To deny that she might hear the voice of Oh would make them liars. Arefaine could sense that the Opal Advisor desperately wanted to take counsel from the Emperor, but he could not. His drooping mustache quivered as he opened his mouth, licked his lips.

She waited until she thought he finally found something to say, then took the upper hand.

"The wisdom of Oh in this matter became apparent to me when we came upon the Silver Islanders. If He had not instilled that sense of urgency, I would not have been there to prevent the inevitable disaster. I was led to that place at that time, and I knew in my heart what must be done. My only regret is the tragic loss of Lady Baelandra and the others."

Arefaine paused. Her heart was heavy about that. The image of the handsome young Astor sobbing next to his mother's headless body still lingered in her mind. She needed to discover how such a thing had happened. She understood why Brophy attacked his aunt. What Arefaine didn't understand was why Baelandra had been corrupted. Was it a mistake? Was Issefyn a bigger fool than she imagined? Releasing the emmeria so close to the Heartstone was perhaps the most profoundly stupid thing a person could possibly do. A fully corrupted creature could have released the emmeria in moments.

Her father had insisted that Issefyn be allowed to keep the single containment stone that she took with her. It had been her father's suggestion that she recruit Issefyn and the albino in the first place. His plans for them showed both cunning and wisdom. Spirits had access to knowledge that the living did not, and she would simply have to trust him until his grand vision was completely revealed.

After a respectful silence following the mention of the recently deceased, Arefaine continued. "I apologize for my sorrow at the Sister's passing. Such unenlightened emotion only proves that I cannot yet see the whole of the divine queue and the place that each of us must stand within it."

Silence descended again, and Arefaine wondered if the Opal Advisor would soon be facing his own painful silence at the Emperor's feet for failing to meet her explanations with insightful refutations to put her in her place.

"I wish to speak alone with the Daughter of my Heart," the Emperor finally said in his soft voice.

The Opal Advisor's robes rustled as he knelt and rose quickly. His slippered feet padded away quietly, followed by the Chief Carrier of the Opal Fire, and on and on until the entire throne room had been quietly and efficiently emptied.

"Rise, child, and look upon the face of Wisdom," the Emperor said a long moment after the door had been closed.

Arefaine rose, keeping her face impassive as she looked at him. This was her true judge, not the Opal Advisor. This was the man she must convince, whose mind she must change.

"You speak with a tongue of honey," the Emperor said, unmoving except for his black eyes, which looked deep into her own. "But sweet words do not always lead to wisdom. Remember the lesson of the sunberries. Sometimes the easiest path is the most dangerous."

The memory came swift upon his words. As a child, Arefaine had eaten so many unripe sunberries that she nearly died. She had been so ill that she missed the funeral of her first guardian, Father Lewlem. Visiting his grave for the first time was one of the earliest memories of her awakened life outside the nightmare. It lingered in her mind like an unhealed wound. Though Father Lewlem was still with her in spirit, she missed what she remembered of him as a man.

Arefaine did not contradict the Emperor. She did not want to push him to any rash decisions. He was using the same extremely formal tone of voice that he had adopted shortly after she realized he had grown afraid of her. Since then, he had stopped talking to her and started talking at her. She had always lived in a prison of solitude, but that was the day the last door was shut and barred. She always held hope that this man would open that door again and welcome her back into his heart.

Finally, the Emperor spoke again. "One of the first steps to wisdom is to pay very close attention to the sleeve you are following . . ." He paused. "And to make certain that it is not your own."

Arefaine felt a tightness in her belly. Her face burned, and she was thankful for the makeup that hid the moment of uncertainty. She breathed through it, enduring the unpleasant emotion until she was clean once again.

"I thank you for your lesson. I will take it to heart."

"I hope that you do," the Emperor said. "We will return to Ohohhom soon, and you will have plenty of time on the voyage to meditate on these recent events." The reprimand had been delivered. The audience was over.

Arefaine nodded. But she was not finished. There were other things that had to happen first.

"I look forward to doing so, but before we go, I feel compelled to seek out the Sleeping Warden. His body has been freed, but his mind is lost in darkness. I know exactly what he has endured these last eighteen years. I am sure that I can turn his face toward the light of Oh."

"I am sure that you could, but it might be best to return to your room for now and quiet your mind so that you might better hear the voice of Oh."

The Emperor never commanded, only made suggestions.

Arefaine tensed and forced herself to draw an even breath. She calmly spoke the words she had never had the courage or the need to speak before now.

"That is an excellent suggestion," she said. "I will be certain to do that, once I have eased the mind of the Sleeping Warden. We owe him a great debt of gratitude, which has not yet been fully repaid."

The Emperor's gaze left hers, and he calmly stared over her head. His face was the perfect, impassive Ohohhim mask, but one did not defy the Emperor. He could order her death with a nod of his head, but would he? Was he considering his words as carefully as Arefaine had considered hers today? Was he prideful enough to make an enemy of the Heir of Efften?

If anyone else had been present, Arefaine had no doubt the Emperor would have "suggested" that she might better serve Oh standing next to him in the afterlife.

But a private audience gave him a different option, and he said nothing.

Arefaine suppressed her smile.

"There is one other matter I feel compelled to bring under the light of the wisdom of Oh," she said. "I beseech your guiding hand in bearing this burden."

She knelt next to the silk-wrapped bundle at her feet, picked it up, and approached him. She set the bundle at the edge of the dais and unwrapped it, revealing the blackened Heartstone within.

The Emperor's impassive stare turned to the prize. She expected some hint of surprise beneath the man's perfectly powdered face, but he glanced at the stone as if he had expected it to be there all along.

A simple glamour was all she'd needed to remove the stones from the Wheel and return with them to the ship. In all the confusion, they might not even be missed.

The stone must go to Ohohhom. Arefaine gambled that the man who spent his boyhood obsessed with the lost treasures of Efften could not resist the ultimate artifact from the Fallen Island. The Heartstone was also a person, filled with the spirit of a woman who had lived during Efften's peak. He could not pass up such a prize. His Eternal Wisdom could not believe that such a powerful and deadly object should be in the hands of anyone other than the Incarnation of Oh on earth.

If the Emperor refused her gift and returned the stone to the Ohndariens, the next few days would become very complicated.

"This stone and the box of three others in my chambers are too great a burden for mortals to steward," she said, avoiding mention of the missing stone. Who would be foolish enough to open that box and look for it? "I am certain that His Eternal Wisdom will know what must be done with them."

Without being dismissed, Arefaine rose and walked quietly from the room.

CHAPTER 26

Lawdon ran across the Night Market. Her lungs burned, and her legs ached, but she dodged through the somber crowd as fast as she could go. The bells continued to toll, and a steady stream of people were making their way toward the Wheel. The entire city was gathering to grieve this death.

The stairs winding around the Wheel were packed with the grim procession. Dangerously close to falling, Lawdon ran along the outside edge. The Ohndariens looked up at her in surprise as she bumped past them, but no one stopped her.

The line of mourners circled around the Wheel, spiraling counterclockwise toward the Autumn Gate, but Lawdon headed straight for the Hall, cutting across the gardens. The Spring Gate was the closest. Her feet fell into the rhythm of the tolling bells, and she felt like she was in a dream. She reached the flower-draped entrance and paused.

Inside the Hall, stained glass glittered in the morning sun, the dazzling beauty she remembered so fondly from her childhood seemed foreign and cold. Underneath that impassive light was a sea of crying people. A flower-covered bier lay at the center of the Hall, surrounded by a crowd of mourners. Lawdon hovered just inside the Spring Gate, her chest hollow and light.

A boot scuffed on the marble behind her, and she turned.

"Heaven knows I am a scion of propriety," Mikal huffed, breathing hard. "But isn't it criminally early for a funeral?" He leaned over, putting his hands on his knees and trying to catch his breath. "This is yet another reason to stay away from the land. Do they really run everywhere like this?"

Lawdon turned back, trying to ignore him. He was the last person she wanted to see at this moment.

"Who was the withered old dusteater anyway?" Mikal gasped, straightening up and laying a light hand on her shoulder.

She spun, striking his arm away with all of her strength. It was all she could do not to punch him in the face. He stepped back, wincing and holding his wrist.

"A woman who saved my life," she said. "A woman who showed me the first true respect I ever had. Something you know nothing about."

Mikal's eyes were wide, and for the first time he seemed unable to come up with something to say. "I ... I'm sorry," he stammered, massaging his wrist, "I didn't—"

"Apology accepted. Now get out of my sight." She turned away from him and marched into the Hall of Windows.

Her anger seemed to spill out of her, and Lawdon couldn't hold back the tears any longer. She weaved her way through the somber crowd toward the bier at the center of the room. The other mourners all threw flowers into the stone pedestal as they passed. But Lawdon hadn't brought one. She stopped, put a hand on the stone. Only Baelandra's face was visible. The rest of her was covered with an ocean of blossoms. A red silk scarf had been wrapped around her slender neck.

Beheaded, the soldier had said.

Baelandra was revered as much for her beauty as for her wisdom, as much for her courage as her cunning. The long years had barely touched the Sister's beauty, but death had snuffed it out in an instant.

Lawdon's fingernails scraped against the stone. Her lip trembled, but she held herself still. The Sister's face had been subtly painted to give the illusion of life in death. Her red hair shone as lustrous as ever in the multicolored light. Lawdon looked for Baelandra's hands, but they were covered in flowers.

She thought about the first time they'd met on Baelandra's balcony. Lawdon had been selling information. Baelandra had bought it and more.

Born in the slums of Gildheld, Lawdon had grown up as a street rat, human refuse. She'd fought and scratched her way from the ports of the Summer Cities to become a waterbug on Ohndarien's harbor. If she kept scratching, kept fighting, one day she could have risen to the lofty height of a fishing boat captain, but she had been guided to a different fate. All because of the Sister of Autumn.

Baelandra had sent Lawdon away from the danger of the Physendrian invasion to become a ward, then the adopted daughter, of a Summer Prince. With that one kindness, countless doors of opportunity opened for Lawdon. Lord Reignholtz had given her a family, a home, a life, and finally a ship to sail.

If Lord Reignholtz was Lawdon's adopted father, then surely Baelandra was her mother. Another woman had given her birth, but the Sister of Autumn had given her a life.

The long line of people waiting to pay their respects looked at Lawdon with a mixture of concern and impatience. Blushing, she gave a last long look at her friend and walked away.

She hovered among the crowd. In the front row of mourners sat three unmistakable people: a grim-faced man holding a sobbing redheaded girl in his arms. A teenage boy with a white bandage around his head sat next to them. He was as distant from his father and sister as the Summer Seas from the Great Ocean. He stared blankly at the dais, his eyes glassy.

The Sisters of the Seasons stood nearby, talking with the other mourners. Lawdon spotted Vallia, the only one of the four whom she recognized. The rest were mere girls, but Vallia was eternal, looking just as gaunt and stern as she had a decade ago.

Lawdon needed to know what had happened. What kind of monster could do this? She moved toward Vallia.

A very handsome, dark-eyed and dark-haired Zelani standing near the Sisters locked eyes with Lawdon, and she paused. A sudden warmth rushed through her body, and a little huff escaped from her lips. The man slipped through the crowd with elegant grace and approached her.

"Excuse me," he said in a rich voice, still half-smiling. "Are you Captain Lawdon, master of *Summer's Heart?*"

"Who wants to know?" she asked, taking a step back, but she paused as he smiled wider, a gentle smile, with just a hint of danger. It drew her into his gaze. She swallowed down a dry throat and found her eyes straying to his muscled chest, pressing against the blue fabric of his robe.

"My apologies. I am Suvian. I thought I recognized you," he continued, his voice thrumming through her chest. She put out a hand to steady herself, and he took it in his. His grip was firm, but also soft and warm. "Would you care to take a walk in the gardens with me? I have a proposition for you."

He placed a hand on the small of her back. Her skin thrilled at his touch, and she breathed a little faster. She nodded, unable to say anything. He guided her through the crowded hall and out the Spring Gate, ushering her along a sculpted path through the gardens.

"I understand you just arrived from the Summer Cities," he said.

"Yes." She wanted him to move his hand up, along her spine, touch her neck. "I grew up in Ohndarien, but I haven't been back since."

"Really? Why come back now?"

"I came to see Baelandra," she said, unsure if she should be telling strangers about her mission. But she could trust this man. She felt it in her bones. And his hand was moving, just as she longed for, up her back. She closed her eyes and took a deep breath.

"Is that so?" he said, his low voice surrounding her. "Baelandra's death is a horrible tragedy. Why did you need to see her?" He steered her into a thick grove of trees, away from the crowds, away from prying eyes. His hands barely touched her shoulders, bringing her to a stop. Lawdon brushed his fingertips with her own as he smoothed the tension out of her shoulders.

He leaned close, and she could feel his warm breath on the back of her neck. "Yes . . ." she murmured, and let out a gasp as he kissed her.

"Why did you need to see Baelandra?"

Her mind was fogged. Why didn't he stop talking? "The Summer Fleet . . . My . . . My patron, Lord Reignholtz, sent me north to convince the council to stop the fleet. Physendria . . . It's an invasion . . . a plot . . ."

"That's terrible," he said. "Who could be behind such a thing?" His hands slid down her body, caressing her breasts through her sailor's tunic.

"By the Seasons," she whispered

"Who is crafting this plot?" he asked again.

"Prince Vinghelt . . ." She swallowed, trying to rally her thoughts. Her head was light, dizzy, and she slumped against him. "He's gathering the other princes. Possibly with magic, we think . . ."

"Really?" He held her up with one hand. The other slid down, across her ribs, over her belly. She closed her eyes as his fingers slipped under the band of her pants.

"Please . . ." she gasped softly, reaching behind her and grabbing the back of his neck.

"Tell me more," he said. His finger slid inside her.

She shuddered. "I need . . . I have to find Shara . . . She needs . . . I need . . ."

There was a sudden crack, and Suvian stumbled against her. They fell to the ground, and he landed on top of her.

The fog over Lawdon's mind cleared instantly, and a cold fear lanced through her. What the hell had she been doing? She yanked his hand out of her pants and kicked him away, rolling to her feet.

With a low growl, Suvian staggered to his knees, hand cupped over a bleeding head wound. A fist-sized rock with a spot of blood on it lay in the thick leaves next to his knee.

Lawdon looked around, but saw nothing but trees. She stepped forward, ready to kick him, but Suvian glanced up, and his rage-filled eyes locked on hers.

"Hold still," he commanded.

Lawdon froze. A horrible, swirling pain filled her gut. She wanted to run away, wanted to vomit, but she couldn't move. She couldn't even breathe.

She fell to the grass like a statue, and he leapt on top of her, pinning her. He grabbed her by the throat and drew his dagger. Lawdon wanted to scream, but she could only stare at him with wide eyes.

Then Mikal was there. He grabbed Suvian by the hair, yanking him back.

Suvian staggered, ripping his hair out of Mikal's grip and swinging around with the dagger. Mikal danced back, looking horrified as the blade missed him by an inch.

Lawdon gasped, and her muscles relaxed. She rolled away from the combatants.

Panting, Suvian snarled at Mikal. "Hold still!" Mikal froze just like Lawdon had, his eyes wide with shock.

Lawdon leapt forward, drew her dagger, and buried it in Suvian's spine. He crumpled to the ground with a shout. His own knife fell from his hands as they scrabbled at his sides like frantic spiders. His eyes rolled up into his head, and he lay still, Lawdon's dagger sticking out of his back.

Lawdon collapsed to her knees, hunched over like an ape. She tried to get her breathing under control, tried to keep from retching. The vileness swirled in her belly, but it was slowly receding.

"Are you all right?" Mikal said, his voice trembling. The duelist's eyes were locked on the dead Zelani. He looked on the verge of running away.

"Yes," Lawdon said, swallowing down her bile. "I . . . I haven't killed a man in a long time." She let out a huff and steadied herself, forced her hands to stop shaking. "And I hate it. Every time."

"I wouldn't know," Mikal said. All the color had gone from his face, and his skin was soaked with sweat.

They both stared at the body.

"Who was he?" Mikal asked.

"A Zelani. I have no doubt. I think he was trying to get information out of me. Fessa of the Deep, could Vinghelt have influence among the Zelani?" The thought scared her more than she could say, but it could explain a lot. Lawdon pressed her hands to her face, trying to put it together. If Vinghelt sent Suvian after her, then the man already had his hooks into Ohndarien.

"We need to get out of this city right away," she said.

"But this was self-defense. He was—"

"I stabbed the man in the back, who's going to believe that was self-defense?"

"But—"

"Mikal, this is Ohndarien. You can't spew a few lines of poetry and get away with murder here. They stone people to death in this city."

Mikal nodded.

"Can you hide the body under those leaves? Then tell the crew to prepare for departure," she said.

"Of course, but . . . Where are you going?"

"I have to find Shara. She has to know about this. If Vinghelt . . ." Lawdon caught herself, shook her head. "Just do it."

"Will you be all right alone?"

Lawdon paused a long moment. "I thought I was," she murmured. "Until today."

Mikal stood there looking like a lost child. "Just go tell the crew," she assured him. "I'll hide the body. You warn the crew."

He nodded, but his brows were furrowed in concern. "If you're sure—"

"Mikal," she warned.

Reluctantly, he turned to go.

"And Mikal," she said. He looked over his shoulder. "Thank you for being there."

With some of his old smile, he nodded to her. "My lady told me to stay out of her sight, and that's where I stayed, just out of sight."

She nodded and looked at her dagger, sticking straight up.

"Staying out of sight sounds like a really good idea right about now."

CHAPTER 27

Shara winced as she awoke. She couldn't see anything, her vision swam white and unfocused as splitting pain hammered through her head. "By the Seasons . . ." She tried to sit up, and someone pushed her back down.

"Lie still, Shara-lani," someone murmured. "You are hurt."

Shara reached up and found a cold cloth wrapped around her forehead. She winced as she felt her own eye swollen beneath the wet cloth. What had happened—

"Brophy!" she shouted, jerking upright. The cloth fell to her lap. Shara gasped, shielding her eyes from the painful light streaming through her chamber window.

"Where is he? Where's Brophy?" she said, fumbling for the covers, trying to get out of bed.

"Don't worry about him," Galliana said, pushing her back down gently but firmly.

"No, no," she protested, trying to sit back up, but her body barely responded. "Where is he?"

"He ran away," Caleb said. Shara turned her head. The world spun, and she clenched her teeth.

When it settled, she could see him sitting in a chair on the other side of her bed, breathing a steady cycle, sending magic into her body. She felt his ani flow through her in a gentle stream, helping her body knit together the broken places. Already, her headache was diminishing.

Galliana, seated on the mattress next to her, picked up the cloth and set it back against Shara's forehead.

"He's hurt," Shara murmured. "He needs—"

"You're hurt," Galliana said, her dark blue eyes solemn. Her smooth cheeks were slightly flushed, and her placid expression seemed brittle.

Shara closed her eyes and breathed strength into herself. Galliana was right. She was hurt, badly hurt. The memories came slowly. She couldn't remember anything after that terrifying fall in the dream. She thought she had died, but somehow she woke up on the blood-soaked grass, lost and confused. She'd never felt so adrift, so disconnected to her mind and body. Mutilated corpses lay around her; Arefaine was still unconscious, but Brophy, Baelandra, and Issefyn were gone. She heard Brophy shout, and she ran after him, tried to stop him . . . And he had hit her, struck her so hard she must have blacked out.

"I need to find him," she said, struggling against the hands that held her down.

"Not yet, Shara," Caleb said, holding her hands still. "We will find him. I have sent Zelani to sweep the city, and, of course, the soldiers are searching, too."

Shara shook her head. "No, he's not himself. He's dangerous."

"Then lock him in a cell," Galliana said, her eyes flashing.

Shara glanced at her, pausing at the force in Galliana's voice. "He needs help. He needs time to—"

Galliana's nostrils flared, but she said nothing. Carefully folding the cloth and putting it on Shara's nightstand, she stood up, smoothing her dress.

"Gallian—"

"He nearly killed you," she said. "You should see your face."

Shara reached up and touched her eye again. Her cheek was swollen from her ear to her nose.

"You don't understand. He's confused. He didn't—"

"—didn't mean to hit you," she interrupted, staring at the wall. "It was an accident? My mother used to say the exact same thing."

Shara wanted to laugh, or to cry. "This isn't the same; you can't imagine the place he has been for the last eighteen years."

"And that means he can beat you?"

"No, no. It was my fault. I should have seen it. I should have been more careful."

"She used to say that, too." Galliana turned and walked stiffly to the door. "Just before she died."

"Galliana."

Shara's niece paused with the doorknob in her fist. In a calm, even voice, she said over her shoulder, "Did he ever hit you before?"

"No, of course not!" Shara said, as the image of Brophy's sword plunging into her belly flashed through her mind. She closed her eyes, fought her throbbing head, and pushed the image from her mind.

"If he did it once, he'll do it again. If you don't believe that, you're a bigger fool than my mother."

Shara winced, remembering the image of her sister's battered face, plucked from Galliana's mind when the girl first arrived in Ohndarien.

"Brophy would never do that on purpose," she assured her niece.

"Then the black emmeria has him, and you should lock him up. Or kill him." She slammed the door behind her.

Dread crept into Shara's heart, as she remembered those last seconds before Brophy hit her. He hadn't looked like himself at all. His face was contorted with a mindless rage. He was about to kill Astor.

Looking at Caleb, she said, "Is Astor—?"

"Alive," Caleb said. "Grieving for his mother."

"What?"

"Brophy killed her."

"What?" The room spun. Shara couldn't draw a breath.

"She was nearly corrupted, and he cut her down from behind."

Shara brought her hands up to her face. "Baelandra . . ."

"Those bells are ringing for her funeral," Caleb said, pulling her into an embrace.

She heard the mourning bells now, faint outside the window, echoing throughout the city. Sweet Baelandra, gone forever . . .

She pushed Caleb away. "Does Brophy know? I have to find him!"

"You should rest, Shara," Caleb said softly, still feeding her energy.

"No." Closing her eyes, she wrenched power from her tumultuous emotions, bending her pain to her will. She sent her awareness out of her room, through the walls of the Zelani school, and out into the city. Her stomach lurched against the strain, and her head began to throb immediately. Bearing down with her will, she forged on. With an effort that brought stabbing pain to her head, she forced her thoughts into focus and reached across the city, searching.

Ohndarien was in an uproar. Shock, grief, and anger assaulted her from a thousand directions at once. That was how they would remember the day the Sleeping Warden finally woke. It was not the beginning of another Nightmare War, as the council had feared, but it was far from the dream that Shara had envisioned. The mourning bells tolled steadily, telling Ohndarien's citizens the price that had been paid for Brophy's return. A life for a life. The most beloved Sister in a century was dead.

Shara shielded herself from everyone's feelings and surged ahead, looking for that one lost voice amid the chorus of anguish. She knew where to find

him, knew where he must have gone. Focusing her magic, she sent her awareness east, up the ridge. If Brophy was hurting, he would find someplace lonely,
someplace high.

Her ani reached the upper end of the last street where the ground became
too steep and too rocky to build houses. The last few homes butted up against
a hopeless jumble of boulders that jutted upward at a sharp angle all the way
to the top of the wall. Shara had explored those boulders with Brophy and
Trent when she'd run away from the Zelani school so long ago. It seemed a
hundred years. *Those days are lost now,* she thought. *A vague memory of someone else's
life, and barely that.*

She flowed through the narrow gaps between the vast boulders until she
found him huddling in a narrow crevice like a frightened animal. He was so
young, so lost that it made her heart ache. Had Arefaine been right? Had
Shara abandoned him to years of torture and misery?

The Brophy she had known would never have cut someone down from
behind. The Brophy she knew was a gentle soul. She barely recognized the
bundle of rage and despair that huddled in torment, hiding from a world he
saw as his enemy.

"Brophy," she said softly.

He leapt to his feet so fast she started. His emotions surged, flying around
him in an inferno. Waves of pain crashed into Shara. Her concentration
lurched, and she lost him.

"Shara," Caleb said, shaking her gently. "Stop. You'll hurt yourself. You
don't have the strength."

She opened her eyes, still in her bed. Her heartbeats pounded against
her skull, and she felt her consciousness ebbing. "Brophy ..." she murmured
weakly. "He's there ... The boulders ..."

"He'll be all right. But you need rest." Caleb's gentle magic flowed into her,
easing her pain, ushering her toward sleep. She fought him for a moment, but
his ani swept her away like a leaf in the wind.

Caleb's lips brushed her cheek, kissed her softly. "Rest, my love. Rest and
regain your strength. Brophy can wait."

CHAPTER 28

B rophy," Shara's voice said softly.

He leapt to his feet, smacking his head against the cold stone. His fists clenched at his sides, the knuckles white and hard as marble.

Brophy had crammed himself deep into a tiny crevice between two cliffs. Sweat streamed down his face, and his arms twitched. He whirled around, looking for the source of the voice, but there was nothing around him except cold stone and deep shadows. The voice was in his head, like all the others.

He could still feel the side of his fist smashing into Shara's skull. He'd lost her in the nightmare, never believing that she would return? He'd needed her so badly through those dark times, yet the moment she returned, he struck her down.

Brophy pressed his hands against the reassuringly solid stone and pounded his skull against it twice. He had to get control of himself. He had to shut out the distant screams, the sudden floods of fury.

He was hungry, thirsty, tired, but he couldn't go into the city. The damage he'd already done . . . He couldn't bear to think of it.

This wasn't just another dream. He knew that now with agonizing clarity. The bells tolled for the Sister of Autumn. Aunt Baelandra. He knew. He'd seen the red hair on that head lying on the grass.

He slumped back against the rock, sliding into a crouch. He jammed the heels of his hands against his brow. He'd killed her without the slightest hesitation. Cut her down from behind!

The dream was over, but the nightmare continued. He was trapped, imprisoned in someone else's hate, someone else's rage. His body was free, but the Fiend somehow still had a hold over him. Somewhere deep in Brophy's soul, he felt the rot of corruption slithering, spreading. He couldn't root it out, couldn't purge it, couldn't escape it.

Even worse, a part of him didn't want to escape. He ached to embrace his feelings, run with them. He longed to feel the power coursing through his arms, his legs. He could ride that wave of power to a place past all fear, all doubt, all caring. He'd just killed his own aunt, and all he wanted was to let go and kill more and more and more. That was freedom, that was joy!

Brophy slammed his forehead into the stone again, leaving a little smear of blood. *I'm not free of it. I'll never be free of it.*

He looked through the narrow fissure at the boulder-strewn slope rising above him. He could climb the hill all the way to the wall overlooking the Summer Seas. He could go there. He could jump. Wouldn't that be better? For him? For Ohndarien?

Brophy closed his eyes and leaned his head against the cold stone. He concentrated on his breathing. *Just keep breathing*, he told himself. *Just keep breathing.*

❄

Brophy woke again, leaping to his feet. He'd heard something. Someone was coming.

He looked to his right and left along the narrow crevice, ready to run, but not sure which way to go. He saw a faint light in the distance and ran in the opposite direction. He wanted his sword back, wanted to use it, wanted to make the monster pay.

The light came closer and closer, and Brophy doubled his speed, scraping his shoulders against the narrow sides of the fissure. He reached the end of the constriction between the two cliffs and leapt onto an unstable scree slope between boulders the size of houses. He spun to face his pursuer.

The tiny floating light drifted toward him. He picked up a rock, hurled it. The stone passed right through the glowing ball and clattered off the rock walls behind it. Brophy slowly backed away, his breath coming faster.

It approached slowly, and Brophy hesitated. The glowing ball was no bigger than a pebble, but he could feel its gentle warmth on his face. He backed into a little alcove between two boulders. The light stopped a few feet away from him, and its faint glow seemed to seep into his chest, soothing his pounding heart. Brophy held out his hand, and the light gently landed on his palm, filling his arm with a welcome glow. He drew a shuddering breath as the warmth spread throughout his body. He sank to his knees and drew the little light to his chest, pressing it against his heartstone with both hands.

"I see you two have met," a woman's soft voice said from around the corner, just beyond the edge of the alcove.

Brophy jumped up, his hand reached reflexively for the Sword of Autumn, but it was gone.

The woman's thin silhouette appeared at the narrow entrance to the alcove. The tiny light flew back to her, and his heart ached as it left him. It spiraled around her head, illuminating her long dark hair. Her ice-blue eyes shone in the shadows.

"You're the one from the dream," he said, retreating until his back was pressed against the chilly stone.

"Yes."

"You did this. You woke me up."

"Just as you did for me so many years ago."

The young woman with the powdered face stepped closer, trapping him in the narrow dead end with no escape.

"Stay back," he warned. He wanted the light back. He needed the light back. Glancing down, he picked the stone he would throw if he needed to.

"I'm here to help you, Brophy." She took a step forward, her long robes flowing over the jagged stones.

"Stop," he warned again. He looked at the stones. His fingers ached to snatch one up, to crush her skull with it, paint the rocks with her blood.

He shook the image from his mind. He had get away, run into the wilds of Physendria or the Vastness, away from everyone; until he could control it, learn to fight it. "Get out of here while you still can," he growled, barely able to get the words out. His arms twitched. He could gut the bitch, steal the light from her.

"No. I'm not leaving you, Brophy. I know where you've been, and I know the path back home. We're going to walk out of here together." She approached slowly and crouched a few feet away.

"Please, just go." He clenched and unclenched his fists. The howling voices grew louder, making it harder to think. "It still has me. I won't be able to stop myself."

"You can't hurt me," she said.

His arms trembled, and he took a step toward her. He stared at her delicate neck, imagined it snapping in his hands. "Oh, yes I can," he said, his voice deep and husky.

The voices raced through his head, and his entire body began to vibrate.

He would rip her chest open; taste her beating heart. With a snarl, he leapt upon her. The voices screamed in triumph.

She slipped to the side, lithe as a shadow. Brophy caught his balance on the loose rocks and spun, lashing out with his fist. She caught his wrist in her hand. Her gritted teeth glimmered white. Her thin arm trembled, but she held his arm with inhuman strength.

He wrenched his arm free and lunged for her neck. She let out a powerful, melodic note. He froze for an instant, arms outstretched.

She slipped past him and vaulted to the top of a boulder in three goatlike jumps. "You can't hurt me, Brophy. I'm as strong as you are."

With a grunt, he broke free of her spell and turned to face her. He snatched up a rock and pulled his arm back to throw.

Her blue eyes met his, calm and unafraid.

He squeezed the stone, imagined it smashing into her powdered face, splattering her brains across the rocks behind her. His arm vibrated, aching to throw.

"No," he screamed, and hurled the rock away from her. It shattered against the cliff, pelting him with shards of stone.

Brophy sank to hands and knees, panting uncontrollably. For a few moments his mind was blissfully empty, but only for a few moments. The voices slowly crept back into the far corners of his mind. He fought to control them, fought to keep them back in the shadows.

"You see?" she said. "You can master it. You are so much stronger than you think. It took me years to do what you just did. The emmeria is only a tool. Like any other tool, it can be mastered by a strong hand."

"I can't ..." he said, gripping the stones under his hands. "I killed Bae! I almost killed Shara. I almost killed you." He slammed his fists into the rocky ground.

"It's all right," she said. She nimbly leapt down the rock and came to his side. He looked up into her bright eyes. "I've been there," she said softly. "I've come back from there. I know the way out."

"How?"

She knelt before him and brushed the sweaty hair out of his eyes. "I had help. A lot of help."

The little light drifted out of the sleeve of her robe and descended onto his palm. He raised it to his face and breathed in the warmth. His mind slowed, the constriction in his chest relaxed a bit, making it easier to breathe.

"What is this?"

"An old friend of yours. His name is Lewlem."

Brophy looked up at her. "This isn't actually—"

She smiled. "Yes. It is the same Father Lewlem that helped bring the two of us to Ohndarien."

"How?"

"Magic," she said with a wink, and helped him to his feet. "That little light has watched over me through some very dark times. I lived in nightmare far longer than you, and was just as lost when I emerged. You saw the Nightmare Battle in your dreams; I saw the Fall of Efften. Everything I knew and loved was ravaged before my eyes. Even now, when I'm awake, I still see Silver Islanders with glowing red eyes, raping, killing, destroying everything that is beautiful in the world.

"My body did not age in that place, but my mind did. I grew up in that nightmare world. If not for Grandfather Lewlem's love, I would never have escaped it."

"You're really that baby I carried all the way from the Cinder?"

"Yes. I told you before, you and I are kin, linked by blood and by fate. I came here to save you the way you saved me."

Brophy turned away, not wanting to see the depth of emotion on her face. The anguished voices were returning. He could not keep them at bay. "I don't think I can be saved. I don't think it's possible."

She laughed. "You, who have held all the evil magic in the world at bay, are very quick to point out what is not possible."

"Just go, please," he said, clutching the light to his chest.

She looked at him for a long time with a sad smile, then said, "Very well, if you insist, but I have something for you first." Her fingers slipped into the neck of her robe.

She withdrew two silver chains. Each had a crystal shard dangling from it, one white, one red. Brophy touched the hard, red diamond in his own chest. Lewlem slipped through his hand and flew back to Arefaine.

She held up one of the two heartstones. Lewlem's light danced along the crimson facets as it twisted on its chain. "This one was your father's."

"Where did you get that?" Brophy asked, his gaze never leaving the stone.

"You gave it to me."

"Me?"

"When I was still a baby. You bound these stones to my wound to slow the spread of the emmeria. They've been with me ever since, but I'm sure your father would want you to have his stone."

She held it out to him. Hesitantly, he took it, holding it tight in his fist. "I never met my father," he said.

"Would you like to?"

He glared at her. "What do you mean?"

"Magic, Brophy." She nodded at his fist. "His spirit lives on in that stone. It is alive with his essence."

He opened his hand, looked down at the glowing diamond. "How can he still be alive?"

"He isn't, but ani is never destroyed, even in death. It simply changes form. Sometimes when extraordinary people die with a task unfinished, they cling to this world. Your father was a very extraordinary man, and he left a great deal undone."

Brophy stared at the shard.

"I can draw him out if you wish. I can free him, and he'll be with you always."

He swallowed down a dry throat, looked up at her. "I can see him? Talk to him?"

She shook her head. "It's not the same as being alive. He can't say anything to you, but you'll know how he feels about you, about what you do. Just like Lewlem did for me."

Brophy squeezed the diamond shard. He could feel the warmth inside.

"May I?" Arefaine asked, placing one slender hand on his chest. He flinched, tensing. She wrapped her other hand around the fist that held the crystal shard. Closing her eyes, she settled her breathing into slow, rhythmic cycles, and Brophy found himself breathing in time to it. The hair on his arms and the back of his neck stood on end, and he could feel her magic hovering around them like mist.

He had a brief flash of the first time he made love with Shara in the tunnels below the Wet Cells. The sensations were similar, but Arefaine's touch was much more subtle, much less affectionate.

The stone in Brophy's chest tingled, and the shard in his palm throbbed. Slowly, a tiny red glow slipped from between their fingers. Brophy gasped, and Arefaine opened her eyes with a smile. The light flew about the maze of boulders like a crimson firefly. It finally settled, hovering a foot in front of Brophy's face. Moving much more slowly, it approached and came to rest on Brophy's hand.

He sank to his knees. A warm rush of emotion coursed through him. Love, strength, longing fulfilled. Clutching the light to his chest, Brophy began to sob as he heard the gentle whispers of his father.

CHAPTER 29

The Farad seamstress brought another dress from the back of her shop and held it up for Lawdon's inspection.

"No, no, no," she said, waving the dress away.

Lawdon hadn't worn a dress in years and had never spent good money on one. The few she had were gifts, worn once to please the giver.

"This is the last one that will fit you, dear," the exasperated seamstress said. "You are so slender through the bust. If you were willing to pad a little, I could show you—"

"No, no padding," Lawdon insisted for the third time. "Just give me that green dress you showed me, and the white shirt."

"The blouse with those lovely ruffles on the sleeves?" the grandmotherly woman asked.

"Yes," she growled.

"I'll have to take the skirt in a bit, dear."

"Fine, just do it quickly."

Time was running out for Lawdon in every way. She felt like she was on a tiny island with the water slowly rising. In a very short while, she would have nowhere to turn.

She hated being trapped in the city and couldn't help feeling that a hundred eyes were watching her from all around. People in this place could slip their fingers into her mind, or any other part of her, and there was nothing she could do to stop them.

If she was lucky, no one had found Suvian's body yet, but the way things had gone since Lawdon arrived in Ohndarien, she was not keen on trusting her luck.

She had spent half the day in a dark corner of a tavern along the locks, gathering eyes and ears. Before long, she had a trio of waterbugs under her employ. She'd sent one to Cliff Town to check on *Summer's Heart*. The Ohndariens still hadn't found the missing Islander, and the city had been locked down. It wouldn't have helped if the gates were open; the mother of all storms was rolling in from the Summer Seas. Right now it was bunched on the far side of the ridge, threatening to engulf the Arridian Mountains as it moved northwest. Even if she talked to Shara tonight, they still couldn't leave until sometime tomorrow. *Summer's Heart* couldn't sail into the teeth of a storm like that even if she wanted to.

Lawdon was determined to speak with Shara before she left. Things in Ohndarien were going badly. If Vinghelt had at least one Zelani under his thumb, Shara needed to know. Could his influence really reach so far?

Ohndarien had once been Lawdon's haven in a dangerously shifting world, but now she had committed murder. If Vinghelt had infiltrated the Zelani school, he could easily have done the same with the council or the Lightning Swords. Who knew how the crime would be viewed? Murderers were still stripped and stoned just outside the city walls. If they'd done it to Brophy, they'd do it to her. Only one murderer in a hundred escaped the stones. And Lawdon was no Brophy.

Which led her to this place. If she was going to stay in the city, she needed a disguise. And what better disguise than to make herself look like a girl? Luckily, this seamstress was a recent immigrant from Faradan. Only a Farad would be callous enough to keep her shop open on a day of mourning.

Lawdon picked up a small mirror, and she ran her fingers through her tangled mess of black hair, combing it, trying to make it look fuller. She'd sent one of the waterbugs looking for midnight plum juice and washed her hair in it. It made her smell like a dessert.

The seamstress returned from the back of the shop with the dress and blouse.

Stripping off her sailor's tunic, Lawdon grabbed the flimsy shirt and pulled it over her head. After contorting her arms in an attempt to fasten the tiny buttons along her back, she gave up and let the other woman do it for her. What kind of insanity caused a person to make clothing that could not be put on without help?

With a sigh, Lawdon unbuckled her belt and pulled off her breeches, then stepped into the skirt. She felt naked, her bare thighs open to the air, but after a glance in the mirror, she nodded in satisfaction. It produced the desired effect. She looked like a prude old spinster, not the captain of *Summer's Heart*.

"You look lovely dear, just lovely," the woman said. "It must be terribly exciting sailing the Summer Seas, dancing at grand parties on the Floating Palace. When I was a girl, I always imagined being swept off my feet by a dashing duelist."

"I'd recommend staying on your feet when duelists are around."

"Oh, posh, dear," the woman said. "Where is your sense of romance?"

Lawdon was saved from further conversation by a tap at the shop door. She hurried to flip the latch and let one of her waterbugs inside.

The young informant had a broken tooth and a cagey look about her.

"Well?" Lawdon prodded her.

"I hid on a rooftop across from the school. Lots of people coming and going, but no one seen me though."

"Is the Zelani mistress awake yet?"

"Saw her through the tower window, heading down the stairs. She's well enough to walk."

"Where is she now?"

"Don't know. I left. You told me to come get you as soon as I saw her."

"Any other news?" Lawdon asked.

"You mean 'sides the Lost Brother waking up, that Flower getting her head chopped off, and every soldier in town looking for the tattooed madman?"

"No other deaths?" Lawdon pressed, remembering her woeful attempt to hide Suvian's body in the leaves.

The girl shook her head.

"Stay close then. I may have more work for you later." She slipped the girl a few coins and sent her back out into the street.

The seamstress shook her head as Lawdon closed the door. "I don't trust those wharf rats. There's a reason they don't work a proper trade. They'll cheat you every chance they get."

Lawdon ignored the woman and picked up her knife belt. She fastened it on, but shook her head. That would never do. What kind of maiden walked around with a captain's dagger strapped to her waist?

She tried to tuck the knife under the blouse, but it showed right through. After a moment's contemplation, she raised her dress and wrapped the belt around her thigh twice and cinched it tight. The squeeze was uncomfortable, but not as uncomfortable as the thought of going into the city without a weapon. It made a slight bulge just below her hip, but under the flowing skirts it might not be noticed.

"That's a dangerous-looking knife to be carrying," the seamstress said.

Lawdon slapped some coins on the counter. "The extra is for forgetting you ever saw me." She turned to go. "But don't forget, my friends will be watching you for the next couple of days."

"No need to be nasty, dear. I just don't see any reason for a woman to carry a knife like that."

"Well," Lawdon said, her hand on the door's latch, "I've already been half-raped once today. I have no intention of letting it happen a second time."

She left the seamstress gaping in shock and stepped into the street.

Outside, a bell was ringing. Lawdon wrinkled her brow. This was not the slow, sad tones of the mourning bell, this sound was loud and urgent like a warning bell. The few people in the street hurried along their way as if they suddenly had someplace to be.

Lawdon paused, looking at the orange sun, low in the sky. She went back into the seamstress shop. "What's that? The bell?"

The seamstress clutched a dress to her chest.

"An attack," she said in a low voice. The wrinkles around the woman's face were tight with fear. "The corrupted are attacking again."

CHAPTER 30

Shara slipped out of the thin silken robe and let it fall to the warm bathhouse floor. She unfastened her Zelani belt and gently set aside the hair comb with Brophy's feather in it.

She didn't have time. After eighteen years of frustration, eighteen years of waiting, of yearning, she had no time at all.

But she pushed back the urgency that screamed in the back of her mind and dipped her toe in the steaming bath. Caleb stood naked in the waist-deep water next to her. He reached out a hand and helped her into the steaming bath. With a deep breath and slow exhalation, she tried to calm her spinning thoughts. Caleb led her to the deeper water. He placed one hand against her back and another behind her thigh. She leaned back, allowing him to lift her up until she was floating. Shara smiled as the water enveloped her. The sensation brought her back to her childhood when she and Caleb had often bathed together, leading each other further and further into the mysteries of Zelani. The two of them had loved riding the razor's edge, always pushing their arousal to the very brink of release, but never taking that final step. Shara hadn't bathed with Caleb, or anyone else, since leaving to rescue Brophy from the Wet Cells.

She let herself drift on the steamy torchlit pool, relaxing into Caleb's expert touch. He matched his breath with hers and sent his magic to bolster her own. After the tumultuous storm of the last few days, Shara was so drained she could barely find her own compass.

Brophy was awake, but he was, if anything, in more trouble than when he slept through the years. He needed stability, balance, a steady hand to help him. If she was going to help Brophy, she needed to find her own center; she needed to be strong enough for both of them. He needed someone to come to him with hope, with solutions, with a heart full of love. When he remembered himself, when he came to his senses, then she could cry on his shoulder and tell him how hard it had been without him for the last two decades.

Shara let the heat from the water seep into her aching muscles. Caleb's sure hands moved across her skin, coaxing the power back into her body.

Clear the thoughts. Empty them like a cup of water poured into the ocean. There was always a way.

She let out another long breath. Caleb's fingers brushed her breasts, and magic hovered around her so quickly that she smiled. It shimmered like the air right before a lightning storm. Yes. This was what she needed.

I will take care of you, she thought. *We have come this far. We can finish the journey, and I will protect you until you can protect yourself.*

She let her mind drift out over the city of Ohndarien. A storm gathered in the southeast, headed toward them. Shara spread her awareness over the city like a blanket, soaking up the ani, the life force of the world around her.

Slowly, a sense of calm descended, and her mind quieted enough to hear the voices of others. Shara went searching for Brophy, just checking to make sure he was all right, to make sure he was still where she had left him.

Shara's awareness drifted farther and farther away, seeking high ground, surrendering to the vast power of the magic. She brushed the boulder field with her thoughts, searching for Brophy's familiar presence. She missed him at first and increased her concentration. Her relaxed overview became a quick, focused search. But he wasn't there, he was nowhere amid the stones.

Her first thought was the wall. Surely he had gone to the top of the wall. She scanned farther and farther out, but he was gone. The magic dissipated around her as her mind raced. Where was he?

Caleb's breathing faltered, and her concentration shimmered like a mirage. He lifted her out of the water and quickly brought her back to the present.

"What's wrong," she asked, standing up, shaking the water out of her ears.

"Warning bells. Another attack."

Shara's heart sank. The corrupted had come again.

Caleb pulled himself out of the bath and snatched his tight breeches, pulled them on quickly. "Shara, the bells," he said.

Shara felt like she'd been punched in the stomach. Again. "But—"

"Shara, we have to go. With Faedellin and Astor in no shape to fight, they'll need us at the wall more than ever."

She clenched her fist, then nodded. "All right. Let's go."

Standing up, she sloshed to the edge of the pool and pulled herself out. Dripping wet, she hastily grabbed her feathered comb and robe, shoving her arms through the sleeves. She quickly fastened her Zelani chain around her waist and followed Caleb as he rushed up the stairs from the baths and into the foyer. Several Zelani had already arrived; they looked to Shara for orders.

"Gather every Zelani you can find," Caleb told them. "Even the students, anyone who has passed the Third Gate or higher. Get them to the wall, now!"

Without a word, they rushed to follow his instructions. Caleb took Shara's hand and ran with her toward the front gate. "You and the young ones stay back," he insisted. "I only want you there as a reserve, Shara. You're not ready for anything more."

Shara followed him through the gate and into the street. She could already feel her energy ebbing, but she spared a quick moment to search for Brophy again. Her attention flashed frantically through the streets, back toward the Zelani school.

She found him.

The bonfire of Brophy's emotions was close, just a few blocks away, but he wasn't alone. Arefaine was with him, her cold presence obvious because of the complete lack of emotions. The young sorceress's formidable magical protections made her stand out like a flickering fire with a hollow space cut from the center. Shara felt her temper flare. She didn't want Brophy anywhere near that child sorceress.

Shara dug deeper into his turbulent thoughts. Her breathing faltered, and she stopped running.

"He's leaving . . ." she murmured.

"What?" Caleb stopped as she let go of his hand.

"He's going to the docks. With her."

"Who?"

"Brophy."

"Shara, we're under attack. Brophy can wait. I need you to look after the young ones."

"I'm sorry," she murmured, backing down the hill, away from the wall. "He's leaving, Caleb. I have to . . ."

Shara left him standing there as a group of Zelani ran up to join him. She barely turned the corner when she passed a black-haired woman in a green dress. The woman yelled at her to stop, called her name. Shara ignored her and used the Floani form to lend strength to her legs.

She rushed through the gloomy streets. The sun was low in the sky, and the storm was almost upon them. The thin robe clung to her wet body. Her bare feet slapped the flagstones, and a stiff wind blew her hair into her face. She passed a pair of Lightning Swords rushing toward the wall. They turned and stared at her as she sped down the street.

Shara rounded a corner and found her quarry walking slowly down a side street a few blocks from Donovan's Bridge. Brophy, Arefaine, and four Carriers of the Opal Fire. Shara slowed as she approached. Two of the Carriers turned toward her, and the procession slowed. Arefaine spotted her and looked at her curiously. Brophy looked at her for a brief moment with such longing that her heart soared. But he turned away, his fists clenched.

Shara tried to control her breathing, her heart aching. She looked down at herself, felt heat in her face. Her nipples pressed against the sheer, wet fabric of her robe. She swallowed hastily and tugged the front of the clinging robe.

"Brophy ..." she said, moving toward him. The two Carriers facing her stepped forward, blocking her way. Shara's brows furrowed, and it was only with an effort of will that she didn't fling them out of her way.

No, she thought. *Calm. He needs to see me calm. Needs me to be steady for him.*

"Shara-lani," Arefaine said. "I am so happy to see you."

"What's going on here?" Shara demanded, then realized how petulant she must sound. Breathing evenly, she said more quietly, "Where are you taking him?"

Arefaine took a slow steady breath.

"Brophy has decided to sail for Ohohhom with the Emperor."

CHAPTER 31

Lawdon hurried up the crowded street toward the Zelani school. Frantic people were running all around her, civilians toward their homes, soldiers toward the wall. She felt disaster in the air, and the hairs on the back of her neck prickled. Brophy waking, Baelandra's death, Suvian's rape, an assassin loose in the city, Ohndarien's lockdown, the corrupted attacking the city at this moment; everything was aligning against her.

A raindrop splattered on her nose. A few more spattered against her blouse.

And the storm had come.

Clenching her teeth, Lawdon looked up and saw two people arguing farther up the street. Both of them wore white robes and silver belts with the blue stones of the Zelani. Lawdon's hand dropped to her side, grabbed a fistful of her skirt over the dagger hidden there.

The woman broke away from the man and ran toward her. She had a gruesome black eye; the whole side of her face was swollen. It looked like she'd taken a terrible beating.

"Shara!" Lawdon shouted as she suddenly recognized her friend. What had happened to her? Lawdon stepped forward, into her path, but Shara ran right past. She was practically naked in a wet, silk robe.

Lawdon spun around and sprinted after her. "Shara! Stop!"

The Zelani mistress flew down the hill and cut into an alleyway. Lawdon had never seen anyone run so fast. She tried to follow and slipped on the dusty paving stones, ripping her dress. Cursing, she jumped back to her feet and chased Shara down the alley.

When she emerged on the far side, there was no sign of Shara anywhere. Trying to slow her heart, Lawdon jogged to the center of the street, trying to see where Shara had gone. A young man in a blue tunic with a long spear ran up the street toward her.

"Did you see anyone run this way?"

The young man shrugged and kept on going. Thunder cracked overhead.

Lawdon shook her head and doubled back. Any man who'd seen Shara run by in that robe would have noticed. She tried a different street, jogging slowly. How could anyone be so fast?

She slowed at the next intersection as she heard a muted conversation.

"You can't be serious," a woman said.

Shara's voice! Lawdon rounded the corner onto a street that looked out over the Ohndarien bay and stopped in her tracks.

Lightning boomed in the distance.

Shara was arguing with an exquisite young woman wearing long black robes. Brophy stood just beyond them staring at the ground. He hadn't aged a day since Lawdon had last seen him twenty years ago.

The three of them were surrounded by a handful of the Ohohhim swordsmen with the shark-fin helmets. Lawdon suddenly realized to whom Shara was talking. That had to be the Ohohhim goddess, Arefaine Morgeon, the child who had started the Nightmare Battle.

Lawdon took a step toward them, and two of Arefaine's guards marked her, hands on the hilts of their swords. She didn't go any closer. She froze at the corner of the building and listened.

"Shara-lani," Arefaine said in a kind voice. "Brophy needs help. My help."

Shara ignored her, looking at the back of Brophy's head. "I can help you here," she said. "This is your home, this is where you belong." Light drops of rain dotted the dry stone.

"Brophy does not agree," Arefaine said.

Shara's nostrils flared. Her hand twisted her wet robe at her side. "Brophy, talk to me. This isn't necessary."

"Sister, it is best if he comes with us for now," Arefaine said. "Give him some time to regain his bearings. You can follow after you have set your affairs in order. His Eternal Wisdom and I have longed for you to visit the Opal Palace for many years now. We would greet you with open arms. A sorceress of your power has much to teach."

Shara clenched her jaw, stepping around Arefaine, trying to get closer to Brophy, who still refused to look at her. The shark fins moved closer together. Shara's eyes flashed, but Arefaine motioned with her hand, and the guards stood aside.

"Brophy," Shara said. "Please look at me."

He stared stubbornly down at the bay. The rain fell harder. His yellow curls bounced as the rain hit them.

Lawdon felt her face turning red. She felt like she was prying, intruding on this too-intimate moment, but she couldn't leave.

"I can help you," Shara said, holding out her hand, inches from his, but he did not move. "Like you helped me in the Wet Cells?"

"Please, just leave me alone. I need to be alone." He fell silent.

Shara swallowed slowly. "Together, we can find a way, just like we did—"

"I can't stay here," he said tersely. His hands were clenched into fists at his side, and he took a step away from her. "I can't hurt anyone else."

Shara blinked, her jaw muscles working. "Please, Brophy. Just look at me . . ." Her voice quavered. She tried to take his hand. He stepped away.

She followed, moving into his line of vision. This time, he did look at her. He winced and looked away again. "Look what I did to you! What I did to Bae! You have to get away from me, Shara," he said, his face contorting. "There are voices . . . And I see the blood . . . I can't stop myself. I can't."

"Yes, you can. Together, we could—"

He turned to her, lips pulled back in a snarl. Lawdon took an involuntary step back, fingers touching the hilt of her dagger.

"Enough!" he shouted, the veins bulging in his neck. "Don't you under-stand? You can't help me! It's got me, and you can't stop it!"

Shara backed up, put a hand to her heart.

"Eighteen years I waited for you to come save me, and you never did! She did!" He pointed viciously at Arefaine. "You left me in there! And she's the one who saved me! She's the only one who can help me now!"

He turned and walked away. She caught his arm.

"Brophy—"

He shoved her violently backward. She slipped and fell, smacking her head against the street.

Brophy looked down at her, eyes wild. With a low, animal noise, he turned and ran down the slope.

Shara's fingers trembled where her nails scraped into the rock. Her mouth opened, trying to form words, but nothing came out. Her flimsy robe did nothing to hide her nakedness.

Lawdon rushed forward, but two of the Ohohhim guards blocked her path.

"Just give him time," Arefaine said, kneeling at Shara's side and speaking so softly that Lawdon could barely hear.

"All these years . . ." Shara whispered.

"Shara," the Ohohhim girl said. "Follow us later. A month. Is it so very long to wait?"

"No," Shara said, her eyes unfocused.

"I understand where he's been. I can help him and then—"

"No," Shara breathed through trembling lips. "I can't do it anymore."

Arefaine touched Shara's cheek. Shara jerked back and leapt to her feet. With a sudden burst of energy, she knocked Arefaine out of the way. Shara's robe fell open as she raced past the Ohohhim guards and ran up the street.

Lawdon leapt after her, tried to block her path, but Shara shoved her aside and kept on going.

"Dammit!" Lawdon stumbled, regained her balance, and gave chase. Thunder boomed, and the rain paused for a short moment, as though the sky was taking a deep breath. Then the clouds opened up. Sheets of stinging rain poured down on Ohndarien as Lawdon chased Shara up the hill. The Zelani mistress flew over the wet paving stones, heading toward the ridge that towered over them.

Lawdon followed as fast as she could, house after house, block after block. Her burning lungs begged for respite, but Lawdon wasn't going to let Shara escape this time. She shouted after the Zelani mistress, but the raging wind whipped the words back into her face.

Shara slipped once, fell, and got back up again. Lawdon reached the spot where she fell and found Shara's Zelani belt, the delicate twist of silver chain with a smooth blue stone that marked her office, lying on the wet stones. She snatched it up and kept running.

They sped past the uppermost houses, across a bridge and onto a narrow path that cut switchbacks up the mountainside. The path ended at the base of Ohndarien's wall. Shara darted into a dark archway cut into the immense fortifications. Lawdon followed, sprinting up the spiral staircase and chasing her all the way to the top of the wall. They emerged on the highest part of the battlements that looked over the Summer Seas. Thunder rumbled, and lightning forked to the waterline.

Through the driving rain, Lawdon saw Shara standing on the edge of the parapets, leaning dangerously into the wind over the sheer drop. The rain beat on her naked skin as her robe flapped behind her like a ripped sail.

Lawdon wanted to call out, but she couldn't catch her breath. Her legs trembled, and she felt dizzy. She leaned over, sucking in precious air as she staggered forward.

The Zelani mistress faced the fury of the storm, oblivious to the wind that tried to tear her from her perch. Shara put her hands in front of her. Slowly, she began to glow, and Lawdon paused, mouth open, words unspoken.

The rain veered around Shara's body, creating a wedge of calm in the raging storm. The light increased until Shara blazed like a bonfire, throwing wild shadows across the battlements.

Lawdon screamed through the wind. "Shara! What are you doing?"

Shara looked over her shoulder, her dark eyes glistening with an inner light. Her gaze only lingered on Lawdon for an instant before she turned back and spoke to the storm. Her voice was low, the voice of a much older woman, and somehow Lawdon heard it over the storm. It seemed to be coming from every direction at once.

"The Archmage Rellana wrote that love and hate are illusions," Shara said. "Pain and pleasure are one. Only the limitations of our minds make them different."

"Shara! It's me! It's Lawdon!"

"'Seek out the storm,' Rellana said. 'Build the highest tower and stand atop it. Invite the lightning to strike you. Only the power itself is real. Any meanings we attach to it are as fleeting as a gust of wind.'"

"She sounds like a fool without the sense to come in out of the rain!" Lawdon shouted. "Now get down from there before you kill yourself."

Shara knelt, and Lawdon felt a wash of relief. She moved forward, holding out her hand, but the Zelani mistress did not come down. She pulled something from her wet mass of black hair and stabbed it viciously between the stones of the wall. It was a comb attached to a small, golden feather. The feather fluttered frantically in the wind and rain.

Shara caught Lawdon's gaze then, black eyes flashing, as dark as the midnight ocean. She moved closer to the edge.

"Don't," Lawdon cried, reaching out, but she couldn't reach Shara's foot.

Turning her face from the wind, Lawdon climbed up on the slick parapet after her friend.

"It's only another form of intensity," Shara said, and released her spell. The wind hammered into both of them. It threw Lawdon backward onto the battlements.

Dazed, Lawdon stared up as Shara leaned far over the killing edge, held up by nothing but the force of the ferocious wind.

Shara spoke. Once again, her voice came from all around, from inside Lawdon's head.

"'There is only one way to be free,' Rellana said. 'To be truly free. Surrender to the pain, to the pleasure, to the storm.'"

"The woman was a lunatic!" Lawdon screamed. "Get off the fucking wall!"

Shara spread her arms. The flapping robe slipped off her shoulders and vanished into the darkness.

"Shara!"

A sudden flash blinded Lawdon, and a crack of thunder struck her with a hammerblow. She ducked into a ball, hiding her eyes and covering her ears. When her vision returned, Shara was gone.

"Shara!" Lawdon shouted. She threw herself onto the parapet and scrambled to the edge. Clinging to the windswept stone, she stared into the swirling abyss far below.

Book Two

A SEASON OF
WINE AND STEEL

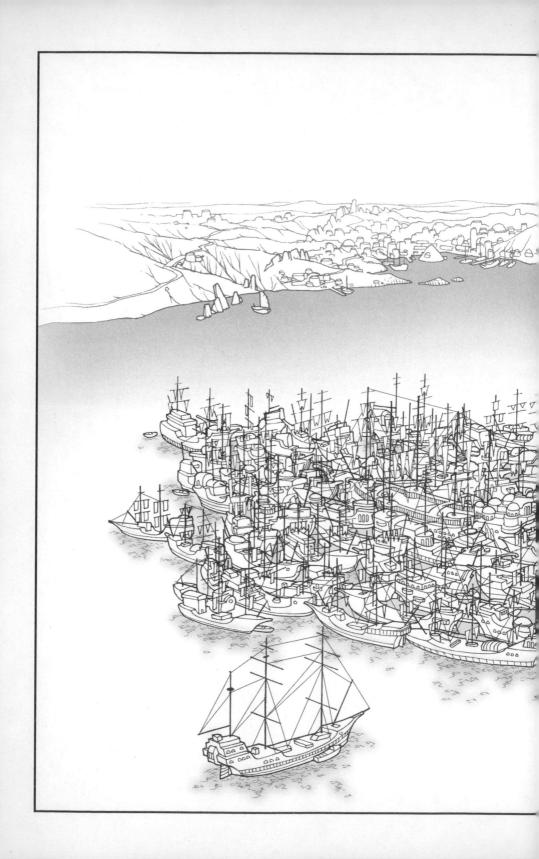

The Glory of Summer

The Floating Palace

Prologue

Prince Vinghelt flailed against the hands that forced his head underwater. His feet churned the wet sand, but the two men twisted his arms behind his back and held him under the surf. He thrashed wildly and felt his bladder give way, warming his legs in the cold water.

He didn't deserve this! It wasn't his fault! None of this was his fault! He could explain everything!

His chest spasmed as cruel hands ground his face into the sand. Sparkles floated in front of his eyes, and his lungs threatened to burst. He made the mistake of opening his mouth. Cold, salty sea flowed in, down his throat. He coughed, then sucked in a bigger gulp.

Seawater spewed from his mouth as they pulled him out of the waves. He fell limp in their arms sobbing.

"Please ..." he sputtered. "By Fessa's blackness, I'm a Summer Prince," he coughed up more seawater. Salty sand poured from his nose and burned the back of his throat. "I pay my debts. I pay my debts."

A third man splashed into view. Vinghelt blinked, trying to bring the thick, blue leggings into focus. Rough hands grabbed him by the hair and yanked his head up until he was nose to nose with the pockmarked face and gold teeth of Lord Faugher. The petty dustborn moneylender insisted that his debtors call him Lord. Vinghelt owed him a small fortune, and he hadn't paid on time. No one ever gave him enough time.

"My lord," Vinghelt croaked. "Surely we are civilized men. This is no way to do business."

Faugher cleared his nose and spat in the water. "No, my lord. This is exactly the way I do business."

"The other princes will not stand for this."

"Actually, they will stand and cheer for this, Lord Vinghelt. They hate you as much as I do."

"A prince always pays his debts. I just need more time."

"You had more time, and you don't pay your debts."

"Just kill him," Grouner, Faugher's ape of a son, said.

"No! No! I have a plan. I can pay you back!"

"Shut up, you drunk fishlicker." Grouner squeezed Vinghelt's wrist until the bones ground together. "Enough of this, Father, let me end it. We drown one Summer Prince, and the rest of those wretches will come running to settle their marks."

"With interest! I'll pay you back with interest!" Vinghelt whined.

"You can't pay anyone back," Faugher said, flashing his gold teeth. "You drank and gambled away every star you've ever had. There are a hundred other traders swimming in gold from the Summer Deserts. It's been thirteen years since we invaded, and you still don't have a flake to show for it. Thirteen years you've been buying good wine with bad lies. I'm not selling any more."

Faugher twisted a tuft of Vinghelt's hair and pushed his head under. Vinghelt struggled, but Faugher didn't keep him under for long.

Coughing and sputtering, Vinghelt squeaked, "I'll double your money, double it!"

"How?" Faugher asked, putting his wide, squashed nose right up to Vinghelt's. "Three months ago I gave you two hundred barrels of the finest red on the Summer Seas. That's worth twenty thousand silver stars! And you just drank up the last flake you have to your name." Faugher nodded at his ugly son and the henchman they'd brought along. They yanked Vinghelt upright, and Faugher slugged him in the stomach.

Vinghelt fell face-first into the water, gagging until they hauled him out again. He needed time. Time to think. The money was somewhere. He could get it. He just needed time.

"I can pay you! I swear!" he sobbed.

"Don't insult me, Lord Vinghelt. I'm not the senile fishlicker you tricked into marrying you."

"That's right. That's right. My wife has lands. Money. I can pay you as soon as the next harvest is in."

"That would be an interesting offer . . ." Faugher caressed the top of Vinghelt's head, then jabbed a thumb into the tender spot behind his ear. Vinghelt screamed.

"If you hadn't already sold that harvest and the next five as well."

Vinghelt sagged in their arms, salty snot gushed from his nose. Faugher looked at his son and shook his head. "This fish thinks I'm a fool, Grouner."

"Kill him, Father."

"I think you're right," Faugher said.

"No, my lord, you're not a fool!" Vinghelt cried. "Only a fool if you kill me! I can get your money. If I die, there's nothing."

"Then where's my two hundred barrels!"

"I sold it!" Vinghelt said. "Sold it to the governor of Physen just like we agreed. I got a good price. A great price! Thirty-five thousand silver stars!"

Faugher pressed their foreheads together. His garlic breath washed over Vinghelt, and he could see the man's rotting teeth beneath the gold caps. "Then where's my money?"

"Zandish!" he sputtered. "Zandish took it. His boys met me at the dock. They took it all! Your money and mine. I only owed him twenty-five, but he took it all!"

Grouner grunted. "Enough with this worthless drunk. Let's just kill him. I told Bian I'd meet her at high moon."

"Don't push me, boy, or you'll get the same." Grouner fell into a sulky silence, and Faugher looked back at Vinghelt. "Zandish took it, eh? Took it all, you say?"

"Yes." Vinghelt breathed hard, wobbling as a little wave hit him in the chest. "It's Zandish you want. Zandish took your money."

Faugher nodded to Tanik and Grouner. "Stand him up."

"No ..." Vinghelt whimpered. They pulled him upright, twisting his arms so hard Vinghelt was sure they would break.

Faugher hammered a fist into Vinghelt's gut. The breath whooshed from his lungs. "Zandish ..." Faugher said as he slugged Vinghelt in the face. "Is not my ..." And in the stomach. "Fucking ..." And in the face. "Problem!"

Vinghelt whimpered, feebly twisting his head away from the next blow, which never fell. "Please ..." he coughed.

"Just drown the filth and be done with it," Grouner growled.

Faugher grabbed Vinghelt's bloody face and turned it toward him. "My son wants to see you die. Give me one good reason why I shouldn't let him."

Vinghelt managed a drunken nod, finally found his tongue. "I just need one more run. Just one more. The run to Physen is dead. Too much competition. We need to think bigger," he slurred. "The real profit's across the Great Ocean." Faugher was listening. Oh, by Fessa, he was listening. "Yes. They're dying for good wine in Kherif. I can sell a barrel of your red for three hundred in Kec Lyn. And ... And buy swords and spear tips for a song. They're always short of good steel in the Summer Deserts. I could quadruple your money in three months."

"Quadruple my money."

"Yes, yes. I swear." Vinghelt nodded, exhausted.

"And all you'd have to do is slip past the Silver Islanders."

"Yes ... No! I mean no, no! I'd go far to the south, go around them."

"In three months."

"I would ... Well, with good winds. Yes. Yes, three months."

"That's it," Faugher said. "I've heard enough. Drown this piece of shit."

"No!"

With a happy whoop, Grouner plunged Vinghelt's head under the surf. Again, Vinghelt struggled, but he had no strength. The sea stung his split lips, and his seared lungs screamed in agony.

Gods, no! Oh Fessa! I beg you! I'll stop drinking. I'll give up my lands. I'll pay my debts.

The blackness of the water surged around him, waiting until he opened his mouth.

Dear Fessa! Please, I'll change. Just let me live!

He continued to struggle, until one of the thugs reached between Vinghelt's legs and squeezed. Vinghelt screamed and water flooded into his mouth and lungs. Fessa! He coughed, but only bubbles came out.

A strange lethargy took his limbs. He stared unblinking into the deep blackness of the sea—

And saw a light.

It floated forward, growing and growing.

A wave of calm swept through him, and the pain faded away. His lungs were still heavy with water, he still felt the crushing grip on his testicles, but there was no pain. No pain at all.

The arms let him go. The incoming surf pushed him toward the shore, then pulled him out again. Vinghelt found the strength to stumble to his knees. He vomited seawater upon the sand. Convulsions wracked his body, but there was on pain, no fear.

He turned to look at his attackers. They retreated up the beach, looks of terror and revulsion on their faces as they stared at the sea.

Vinghelt turned and gaped.

The goddess herself rose from the waves. Her pale skin glowed in the darkness, outshining the moon. Shimmering waves of green hair poured from her head like a fountain, cascading down her breasts, thighs, and flawless curves, flowing into the sea.

"By the deep!" Faugher said with disgust.

"He's hideous," Grouner said. His lip curled as he drew his knife.

Fessa smiled at Vinghelt as she strode from the water, and he felt her power rush through him. He knelt before her, but he couldn't bow his head, couldn't take his eyes off her magnificence.

"I don't know who you are, Whitey, or what you want," Faugher said, also drawing his knife. "But if you don't swim back out to sea, I'll gut you like a pig."

"There is no need for that," Fessa said, her voice haunting, like music played underwater. *Vinghelt sobbed at the beauty.*

"Stay back, you bloated—"

The goddess narrowed her eyes and frowned. Faugner stumbled back, his face contorted in pain.

"You seem to have an infected hangnail," Fessa said, her voice swirling around them. "That can be very painful."

Faugher fell to his knees in the shallow surf, clutching at his left boot.

Grouner looked down at his father with wide eyes, then turned a murderous gaze on Fessa. "I'll kill you, you fat fuck!" *he snarled as he charged.*

Calmly, the goddess turned to Tanik, and whispered, "Kill him."

The thick-necked thug lunged forward, tackling Faugher's son just before he reached the goddess. The two brutes tumbled into the surf, sending up a spray of water.

Fessa walked slowly to Vinghelt, and the men's struggles and cries faded into the background. Extending her slender, beautiful hand, she helped him to his feet. Her touch vibrated through his entire body.

"Are you ready to start your new life?" she asked in her unearthly voice.

"What?" He could gaze at her forever.

"The man you were is dead," she said. "A new man has been reborn in his place."

"Why? Why did you save me?"

"You called to me."

"But ..." he stammered. "I'm nothing. Nobody."

"Not for long, my prince. Not for long."

Grouner and Tanik thrashed by them, grappling at each other's throats, smashing their heads into each others' faces. They fell into the surf and fought to hold each other underwater. With a powerful surge, Tanik rolled Grouner underneath him and jammed his thumbs into his partner's eyes. Grouner fought back, plunging his knife into Tanik's side over and over again.

Faugher writhed on the beach. He had removed his boot and clutched frantically at his foot.

"Make it stop!" he shouted. "For pity's sake, make it stop!"

"It might feel better if you cut it off," Fessa whispered to him.

"Yes," Faugher slobbered as he crawled to his discarded knife. "Yes." He snatched up the blade and drove it into his ankle.

Fessa turned back to Vinghelt and gave him a loving smile. "Are you afraid?" she asked him.

"No. No, I'm not."

"Good. Put your faith in me, and you'll never be frightened again."

"What do you want me to do?"

"I want you to learn, to grow. I want you to become the man you were meant to be. My children need a king, a man with the vision and strength to lead them."

"A king on the Sea of Princes? How?"

Fessa turned away from him and walked back into the sea. Her green hair spread across the water behind her, flowing over Grouner and Tanik where they floated facedown in the surf.

"There is a Kherish merchant with pale skin and unusual eyes. The man is a mage, a student of the lost arts. He will teach you everything you need to know."

Fessa looked over her shoulder, smiled. A wave broke against her chest, and Vinghelt felt a loss as she left him standing on the beach.

Vinghelt stepped forward, reaching to her. "But ... How will I find him?"

Fessa was nearly underwater, but her voice carried to him as though it were inside his head. "He will find you. Everything you need will find you."

Her glowing body disappeared beneath the waves. Vinghelt's fear at her departure only lasted a moment, then he was filled with a glorious purpose. His heart swelled with more strength than he'd ever known.

Vinghelt strode out of the water and stopped next to Faugher, who lay whimpering in the sand. He clutched a bloody knife and a severed foot to his shuddering chest. Blood poured from his stump, making a black swath on the moonlit sand.

"It still hurts," Faugher whined. "It still hurts."

"I can pay you now," Vinghelt said in a quiet voice. It was hard to believe that moments ago, he had been terrified of this pathetic dustborn gold peddler. But that was a different life. He had been a different man.

"It still hurts," Faugher whined. "Please make it stop ..."

"If you like."

Vinghelt brought his foot up and smashed it onto Faugher's face. It felt so good that he did it again, and again, and again.

He felt bones crack under his bare feet, but there was no pain. No pain at all.

Faugher finally stopped writhing, and Vinghelt continued up the beach. For the first time in years, he didn't feel the need for a drink.

CHAPTER 1

Lawdon cursed her slowness. She cursed the damned optimism that had her chasing a crazy Zelani through a thunderstorm while her crew had been captured.

She and Mikal hunched on the garden-topped roof of a warehouse in Cliff Town peering through the waning storm. *Summer's Heart* was empty. No sign of anyone. Even in a storm, someone should have been standing watch, but there was no movement, no life aboard.

"You see?" Mikal asked.

"Yes."

If Mikal hadn't been waiting for her at the bottom of the Foreplay Steps, she would have walked right into the Ohndariens' trap .

How had everything gone so wrong? Baelandra was dead. Shara was dead. Lawdon was running from a murder. All her hopes in Ohndarien had dried up. There would be no help for the Summer Cities. She felt storm-tossed and betrayed, as if someone had cracked off her rudder.

Now she must return to her lord and report complete failure. They would have to find another way around Lord Vinghelt's strange powers before the assembly of the Floating Palace.

"I found her that way," Mikal continued. "I returned to the ship straight-away, but somehow the soldiers arrived before me."

Lawdon hissed. She hated magic, hated it. What hope did they have against Zelani?

"Hours later, twenty armed Ohndarien soldiers crept onto the ship, followed by twenty who crept off," he said, wiping his brow, blinking away rain.

"Changing of the guard," she said in a monotone.

He nodded, water dripping from his chin. Lawdon squinted up at the sky. It was impossible to tell how long the storm would last, but she was now willing to risk just about anything to get the hell out of this city.

"We have to—" Lawdon started, but Mikal jerked. She spun around and saw a figure in a blue robe standing behind them.

Hissing through her teeth, Lawdon drew her dagger, ripping her skirt in her desperation to free the blade. She ran forward and whipped her dagger up, just underneath his chin, "Don't try it. I'll gut you, I swear I will," Lawdon hissed, sounding braver than she felt.

The man studied Lawdon briefly, without fear. "Did you really think you could hide from the Zelani?" he asked.

She just about cut his throat at that, but she couldn't bring herself to do it. He hadn't so much as raised a hand against her.

"My apologies if I startled you. I am Caleb-lani, a good friend of Shara-lani's, and I have no intention of harming you."

Mikal hadn't moved from the edge of the roof, ten feet away. "Just cut his throat," he said without any real conviction.

"I would prefer that you didn't," Caleb said, pushing Lawdon's blade away from his neck.

Mikal took a hesitant step forward. "Don't listen to him. We'll take him in a rush, just like the other one."

Lawdon hissed, wanting to stab Mikal for being such an idiot.

"So it was you who killed Suvian," Caleb said.

"Yes," Lawdon admitted.

"Why?"

Her eyes narrowed, and she felt a flicker of hope. Why would he question her if he could just enchant them?

"He wanted to play a game I wasn't interested in. He got pushy. I pushed back."

Caleb paused for a moment, but his expression did not change. "If that is what happened, I need to be sure you are telling the truth. Will you allow me to look into your memories?"

"Don't let him get his hooks into you, " Mikal said, moving a step closer, but still keeping his distance.

"Shut up, Mikal!" Lawdon shouted back at him.

Caleb smiled, still completely calm. "I would like to believe you. But I need to be sure."

"And if I refuse?"

"I'll walk away."

"And within five minutes those twenty men on my ship will 'magically' appear to arrest me."

"Almost certainly," Caleb said.

"And if those soldiers catch us, then you will look into my memories whether I wish it or not."

Caleb paused again. He swallowed. "I hope that would not be the case—"

She scoffed. "You hope—"

"I would not walk that path unless it was absolutely necessary," he finished.

Lawdon breathed for a moment. The rain slackened even more, and she felt exposed on the flat rooftop. She wanted to stab the Zelani and be done with it, but why would he bother talking to them if he meant to arrest them?

She hesitated, hating the idea of this man messing with her head, but she didn't really have a choice. She couldn't hide from the Zelani, and it was too late to run. She would have to prove her innocence somehow.

"You may look," she said, then held up a hand as he started forward. "But I want two things in return."

"Yes?"

"First I want to know what happened to my crew."

"They were taken to the Citadel and questioned by a Zelani. None of them knew where you were."

"What will happen to them?" Lawdon asked.

"They have committed no crime. They will be set free as soon as the council learns the truth about Suvian's death."

"There's something you're not telling me."

Caleb paused. "Perhaps. What is your second wish?"

"Mikal puts a dagger at your back before you muck with my head. You do something we don't like, you die. I'm not taking another chance with you people." She cleared her throat. "That's the condition."

"As you wish."

Reluctantly, Mikal moved behind the Zelani and put a dagger against the back of his neck.

"Are you satisfied?" Caleb asked.

Lawdon's heart thundered in her chest. She nodded tersely.

Caleb moved closer. "May I touch your face?" he asked softly. "It will make it easier for both of us."

Again she nodded. She forced herself to stand firm. "What do I do?"

"Relax." He laid a hand on her cheek. His touch was light, warm. "I will not hurt you. I will take nothing that you do not allow."

"Just hurry," she said.

"Recall what happened. Everything, from the beginning."

That was not hard. She hadn't been able to get it out of her mind. She thought back to the first moment Suvian walked up to her in the Hall of Windows.

Caleb's touch was nothing like the other Zelani's. Suvian had forced his way into her mind, dominated her. All she felt of Caleb was light, feathery whispers moving through her thoughts. The images rushed through her: walking with Suvian into the trees, his hands on her body, his death. Once again, the memories filled her with revulsion, helplessness and, afterward, rage.

She gasped as Caleb withdrew his hand. The images vanished.

Caleb's brow was deeply furrowed. "It is as I feared," he murmured. "Suvian was not of our order. He was cast from the school in disgrace. This never should have happened." He stopped, looked up at her. "I am so sorry for what you were forced to endure. Shara-lani is adamant about this perversion. It is not allowed."

"Well someone isn't following your rules, then," Lawdon said, rubbing her arms. The echoes of Suvian's touch lingered on her skin, on her mind.

"May I ask you one more question?"

She nodded.

"Did you see Shara-lani? Before she left?"

Lawdon turned away. She drew a long breath, remembering that last moment, screaming at Shara to come down off the wall. The lightning strike. Staring at the empty, swirling rain.

"I'm sorry, Caleb," she said hoarsely. "She didn't leave. She's dead. She threw herself from the top of the wall."

Caleb searched her eyes for a moment, then started chuckling.

Lawdon glared at him. Her hand twitched on her dagger.

He held up his hands, stepping to the side, away from Mikal's blade. "I apologize."

"You find her death funny?"

"Only her nature. Even in defeat, she does what others only dream of."

"I don't understand."

"I'm sorry if she frightened you, Lawdon. Shara is lost right now. I knew she had left the city, but I didn't realize she had left in such a fashion."

"What are you saying?" Lawdon said. "No one could survive that fall. I don't care how—"

"Shara-lani could survive that fall. She has survived worse."

"No." Lawdon shook her head, but her heart surged with hope.

"Shara is the master of several paths of ani," Caleb explained. "Such a leap is not beyond her."

"How can you be sure?" she asked, but she felt rejuvenated, and there was suddenly hope for both of her failed missions. Perhaps she could still make a difference in their struggle for the Summer Seas.

"I have watched her from a distance for a long time now." He paused. "It is a duty I have taken upon myself. Believe me. If she had perished, I would know." He closed his eyes and raised his chin, as if smelling the wind. When he turned back, he looked straight into Lawdon's eyes.

"Time is short. Great events are moving," Caleb said quietly. "I have seen your memories, and I believe I can trust you. If you will make a bargain with me, perhaps we can both get what we want."

"What do you mean?" Lawdon sheathed her dagger and waved Mikal away. Slowly, he stepped back from Caleb and put up his weapon.

"I would go after Shara," Caleb said. "But there are too many things happening right now. We barely escaped the latest attack from the corrupted; luckily, it was relatively minor. But with Shara gone, we are too vulnerable for me to leave. And now—" He drew a breath, and for the first time Lawdon could see the lines of concern at the corners of his eyes. "The Emperor has stolen the Heartstone."

Lawdon drew a swift breath.

"Yes." Caleb nodded. "The Ohohhim ships fled the city during the attack. Arefaine Morgeon took over the minds of our men guarding the Sunset Gate. The Heartstone was taken beyond the walls just as we were defeating the corrupted. In one night, we have lost our two strongest protectors."

"Why would the Emperor do that?" Lawdon asked.

Caleb shook his head. "I do not know. He has always been Ohndarien's staunchest ally."

"It will mean war," Mikal said.

"Perhaps," Caleb said. "But there is nothing I can do about the Heartstone right now. My duties have shifted. My heart longs to follow Shara, but I am now the senior Zelani in Ohndarien, and that duty comes first. Suvian's re-emergence troubles me, and must be investigated. The theft of the Heartstone cannot be kept a secret for long, and the city will be in an uproar when they discover the truth."

"What is your bargain?" Lawdon asked.

"I get you out of the city, and you find Shara. Help her."

"Why not send another of your Zelani to bring her back?" Lawdon asked.

"Shara does not wish to come back. She made that very clear last night. I just want to make sure she is not alone, wherever she is going next. You are one of her oldest friends. She desperately needs someone like that right now."

"Where is she?"

"The Petal Islands. There is one particular island close to the city with a large grove of cypress on the southern shore. It is very important to her."

Lawdon shot Mikal a quick look, then peered back at Caleb. "So you're just going to let us go? Just like that?"

"You've done nothing wrong," Caleb said in his soft voice.

"You'll give us back our ship?" Mikal asked. Lawdon flicked him an annoyed glance. *Our* ship?

"That is beyond my power, I'm afraid. The council would insist you face a full trial. That could take months, with everything else that is happening. But I can get you out of the city."

Lawdon was silent for a long moment. She had to report to Reignholtz. She wanted to help Shara, and she needed the Zelani's advice about Vinghelt. If the man was truly a mage, they had to find a way to match him.

"What about my crew?"

"They will be treated as honored guests until they are released. They can come south to find you afterward."

"I came north to warn the council. I must—"

"Yes. I saw your memories. I will bring your message about Lord Vinghelt and his plans to the council's attention. They have many weighty matters to consider right now, but I will do everything I can for you in that regard."

There were only hard decisions, no matter which way she turned. Slowly, she nodded.

"I will go after Shara. How do we help her?" she asked.

"Just be there for her. Don't let her grieve alone. Send her back to us when she is ready. Ohndarien needs her now more than ever." Caleb smiled. "Simply use the tenacity you have shown so far."

Lawdon couldn't help but return a small smile of her own.

"How do we get out of the city?" Mikal asked.

"I have a friend manning the Sunrise Gate. Don't draw attention to yourself, don't hail the guards, just sail straight for the center of the gate, and the doors will open for you."

"What exactly are we supposed to sail?" Mikal demanded.

Caleb shrugged lightly. "I am sure you'll find something." He touched Lawdon's cheek again. This time she did not flinch. The fear in her heart had eased. Was this what a real Zelani was meant to do?

"I could ease your pain," he said softly. "I could erase the fingerprints Suvian left behind. You should never have had to bear that burden."

She swallowed. "Thank you, but I think I'll keep my past right where it is."

His eyes held hers for another moment, as though silently offering her a chance to change her mind. "A wise choice," he finally said, removing his fingers.

She felt the loss immediately, like a smooth, warm rock taken from cold hands. She noticed for the first time how incredibly attractive Caleb was. He had a boyish face, which wasn't usually what she liked, but the warmth of his eyes made him feel genuine and reassuring. He was a good man, with all the power Suvian possessed but none of the desire to abuse it. What would it be like to have such a man touch her, to welcome him into her arms?

Caleb smiled at her, gave Mikal a brief nod, then jumped off the roof.

Mikal rushed to the edge and looked down. After a moment, he let out a small huff.

"Nice trick, for a dusteater," he mumbled, turning to look at Lawdon.

Still feeling the kind touch of Caleb's hand on her cheek, Lawdon snorted at Mikal. "I wish we could stay here another month and let that man teach you something about women."

Mikal bowed with a flourish. "And destroy the single perfect mystery in this world? Never."

"Enough," she said, moving to the edge of the roof. A thick growth of vines clung to the wall. She swung her legs over and started down.

Mikal followed her. When they stood on the street in the deep shadows between the two buildings, Mikal brushed his hands on his breeches, looked ruefully at her ship, half-visible down the alley.

"How, exactly, shall we be going?" he asked.

"Well." Lawdon chewed her lip. "We can walk or sail."

Mikal give her a scornful look.

She chuckled. "I thought as much. Then we sail."

"Splendid. You plan to take your ship back in a rush? We could overwhelm them with our army of two."

"No."

"Then what shall we be taking?"

"Ever sailed an Ohndarien waterbug?"

CHAPTER 2

Phanqui struggled to keep the hatred off his face as Lord Vinghelt's men rowed them across the harbor. Little waterfalls still poured from the cliffs on either side of them. Last night had brought the largest storm he had seen in years. The life-giving deluge seemed like an omen, a promise from the Nine that they would wash the foreigners from the face of the earth.

Vinghelt laughed with his men as he spun a silver chain around his finger. He was never without the chain holding the jade pendant of his beloved fish goddess. He wore it everywhere, along with the jeweled broach and one of a hundred silk cloaks embroidered with the image of the bare-breasted mermaid. Her likeness was carved into the prow of this runabout, from her flowing tresses to her long, scaly tail.

Your goddess won't save you here, Phanqui thought. *This land still belongs to the Nine.*

Death waited for the Summer Prince inside old wine barrels on the Kherish albino's ship just a few hundred yards away. Nearly twenty years of struggle came down to this single moment. His daughter's future came down to this single moment. Phanqui could not let victory slip though his fingers.

He turned his face into the sea breeze as the dustborn swordsmen rowed the sleek runabout toward the Kherish merchant's ship.

Vinghelt continued lazily spinning his chain like a man who thought himself invincible. The dark-haired man oiled his graying beard to a point below his chin. He would have been handsome if his smile didn't make your skin crawl. He claimed to have magical powers, but Phanqui doubted his mystical arts were anything more than a steady supply of gold to traitors and informants.

"Three more days, lads," he said to his men. "Three more days of kicking the desert rats back into their holes, and we'll be on our way back to the Eternal Summer."

His men pounded their feet on the hull in approval.

"You've done right by your families, by your lords, and by the goddess herself. Each one of you will be drinking from the sweet breast of Fessa before the moon turns. I'll see to that myself."

His men burst into grins and rowed even harder.

Phanqui's stomach turned. Vinghelt's men were like dogs pissing themselves over a scrap of their master's food. He'd once heard two of them bragging about a Physendrian girl they'd kept tied to a bed for a whole week. And now they expected a goddess to thank them for their work?

It was ironic, the hold Lord Vinghelt had over his men. Stories about the summer prince said that five years ago the man had practically drowned himself in the bottom of a wine barrel. They said he still bore the scars from an angry creditor's knife. But Fessa of the Deep saved him from himself, and he had been reborn. He stopped spilling wine and started spilling blood, bragging the entire time about being drunk on Fessa's love, the sweetest vintage in the world.

Surely the Nine could not allow such a man to live. The Physendrian gods did not miraculously forgive the weak and the wicked. They punished you until you changed your ways.

In a very short while, that punishment would finally reach the Summer Prince. When Phanqui spoke the words, "Kherish blades are the strongest in the world," seven loyal Physendrians would leap from their wine barrels with blades in hand and send the tyrant back to his beloved waves. He could pray to Fessa all he wanted as he sank to the bottom of the sea, bleeding from a dozen holes.

They approached the Kherish trading ship painted in gaudy reds and blues and bearing a dog-headed maiden on her prow. Phanqui searched the deck for a sign of the pink-eyed merchant. It was the fat man's lure of high-quality, inexpensive weapons that had drawn Vinghelt here. Greed had brought him high, and greed would bring him low.

"Look sharp, lads," Vinghelt said, as they pulled up alongside the ladder dangling from the Kherish ship. "These Khers would sell you a night with their mother for a whiff of gold."

Phanqui looked up to see if the albino or his men were within earshot, but no one came to the rail to greet them.

Two of Vinghelt's guards climbed up first and made the runabout fast. Two more followed, with Phanqui trailing. Vinghelt was the last one out of the boat.

"Where is this Kherish weapons merchant?" Vinghelt asked mildly as he climbed up next to Phanqui.

"I'm not sure," Phanqui said, looking around. The man swore he would be here. "I'm sure he will be along shortly."

"Will he?"

The tone of Vinghelt's voice prickled the hairs on the back of Phanqui's neck, and he felt a sinking feeling that the albino was not coming.

"He has a hold full of weapons to sell," Phanqui said casually. "He didn't come all this way just to sail back with them. Perhaps he did not hear us arrive."

"Or perhaps Kherish blades are not the strongest in the world," Vinghelt said, looking over at Phanqui. A thin smile spread across his lips.

Phanqui's blood froze. The code phrase.

"Kherish blades are the strongest in the world!" he shouted, and launched himself at Vinghelt. He had no weapon, but he was still strong enough to snap the man's neck if he could just—

Two guards tackled him before he took the first step. The three of them tumbled across the deck. Phanqui elbowed one in the face and put the other in a chokehold. He struggled to grab the man's chin and snap his neck.

Solid steel cracked into the back of his head. He grunted and tried to roll away with his hostage, but another dagger pommel slammed into his head, and another.

Phanqui screamed as they pried his arm away from the man's throat. Someone hit him in the face. His nose crunched, and he sprawled onto the deck.

They hauled him upright in front of Vinghelt. His heart raced, and he couldn't catch his breath. Who had betrayed them?

"You treacherous little rat," the governor said. "You have eaten from my table since the day I arrived, and this is the thanks I get in return?"

"You are the ones eating from our table," Phanqui spat, spewing flecks of blood on the governor's tunic.

One of the dustborn slammed a fist into Phanqui's stomach, and he doubled over. A grunt of pure rage escaped from his paralyzed lungs.

Vinghelt shook his head in disappointment. "It has been a full generation since we liberated your country," he explained as if to a child. "And still you resist. One begins to think there is something fundamentally wrong with you people."

"The gods will punish you for this," Phanqui wheezed.

"No, they will stand up and cheer me for this. They hate you as much we do."

Phanqui choked on his own blood. He was on the verge of vomiting. How had they known? Had they killed the albino? Had the Kher betrayed them? And what about his wife? His daughter? They had left the city last night, but if Vinghelt had known ahead of time... What if the man was truly a mage?

Breathing hard, he looked up at Vinghelt. At that moment he would have ripped out one of his own ribs if he could have stabbed the man with it.

Vinghelt smiled at him. "Come, see what's become of your petty little assassins."

Three dustborn dragged Phanqui across the deck to one of the barrels. The lid had been nailed shut, and the wooden stopper removed. The barrel was filled with water, and he heard a man moving inside, struggling to breathe.

"Looks like the little jumping rats are trapped in their holes," the Waveborn governor said with an indulgent smile. "Isn't that the lowliest of your false gods? The jumping rat? You see? I've done them a favor." He chuckled. "I've turned them into crocodiles. Maybe one day, I'll light them on fire and turn them into phoenixes."

Phanqui struggled in vain against the men who held him. "Careful whom you burn, fishlicker. The Phoenix rises again to take her revenge."

Vinghelt shook his head with a grimace, then turned to his men. "Do it," he ordered.

Phanqui screamed like the desert wind as they hefted him off the ground. He yanked his arm free and struck one of them in the jaw, elbowed another, but they overwhelmed him, wrenching his arms behind his back. They stuffed him into another barrel and quickly hammered shut the top.

The cork plug squeaked as it was removed. Through the tiny hole of light, Phanqui saw Vinghelt's perfectly oiled goatee.

"Fessa has claimed these lands," he said. "You are but a rat dumped into the Summer Seas. You can try and try, but you can never best the waves. The goddess is too strong."

"There are thousand of us rats," Phanqui shouted. "Millions! One of us will find his way to your throat in the middle of the night."

Vinghelt's chuckle echoed in the barrel.

"You should be careful what you say to a student of the lost arts. The goddess has taught me the magic of Efften. I knew about this little conspiracy before you ever joined it. I've known about them all. Remember, little rat, the goddess whispers in my ear. You don't want to end up like your pasty fat friend."

"My children will dance on your grave!"

Through the tiny hole of light, Phanqui saw Vinghelt's nose, mouth. "Children?" he whispered. "But you only have one child. A dear, sweet little girl. At least for a few more hours, anyway."

Phanqui slammed his shoulder against the lid of his tiny prison. He kicked fiercely, rocking the barrel, but the guards held it still.

Vinghelt walked away, and his men began pouring seawater into the hole. One bucket at a time.

"This should make you feel right at home, maggot," one guard whispered, as the others laughed. "Just imagine this is your own private Wet Cell." Phanqui threw curses at his captors, struggling in vain as the water rose higher and higher.

CHAPTER 3

Shara stood naked on a hilly slope, her back to the cypress trees that blocked Ohndarien from view. Last night's fierce storm had blown itself out, leaving fluffy patches of white stretched across the sky. Her mind was clear and focused, her heart felt swept clean, unburdened and empty.

A herd of goats milled about. It had been a while since Shara had visited the island, but the animals still flocked around her. One of them nuzzled her hand, and she petted it absently.

It had been more than a decade since she'd first started building the cottage. The goats had been her only neighbors, and she brought them chunks of apple whenever she could. They soon became fast friends.

Then one day she'd arrived to find all the goats sheared and half of them slaughtered by shepherds from Faradan.

She squinted at the sun, framed by last night's scattered storm clouds. That was life for you. A few sunny days rolling in the grass, a few bites of apple, and then a knife across your throat. She stared at the light until her eyes watered with the pain.

"I will not wait for the knife," she said aloud, looking away. A couple of the nearest goats glanced up, chewing grass. She reveled in speaking aloud, not concealing her thoughts for propriety or diplomacy. For so long she had watched over Brophy, protected Ohndarien with her magic, watched over the Zelani, advised the Ohndarien Council and assuaged their fears. For too long. Any debt she owed to him or that city had been paid a hundred times over.

"I am finished there," she announced to the goats. "Brophy has chosen his life. It is high time I did the same."

She looked down at her body. Frowning, she slid her hands across her naked belly. Thin hands. Her breasts were slightly smaller, a bit lower. Her hips were wider, her belly no longer perfectly flat.

With her constant Floani training, she looked much younger than her years, but she was hardly the nineteen-year-old girl she had been, bursting with vitality, at the peak of her flowering.

How did I let it get this far?

"You do not care how I look, do you?" she said, glancing down at the goat as it nuzzled her leg. She scratched its head.

Again, she looked to the sunrise. Gold and orange light reached across the Summer Seas, warming the islands and blending with the ripples of the water.

"But I do," she murmured.

She thought about who she had wanted to be before she passed the Fifth Gate of the Zelani, before Victeris got his hooks into her. Oh, the dreams she'd had about her life, what she would do as a Zelani.

But it had turned out so differently. First, the twisted battle to free herself from her master. Then the insanity of breaking into the Wet Cells. The impossibility of breaking out. The Cinder. The Child. Brophy's sacrifice. And all the life-risking spells in between. What of that had been part of her original dream?

She was supposed to have walked with kings, whispered in their ears, and changed the course of nations. She had planned to travel to every known land, dine on exotic foods, wear the finest clothes, converse with the keenest minds, take the most powerful men to her bed and make them her own.

And what had she done? Played nursemaid to fledgling magicians, a bickering council, and a boy who couldn't stand the sight of her?

"Enough," she said softly. The goats did not even look up this time.

What had happened to that girl? How many years had she lost waiting for the return of a man who had been her lover for barely a month?

"Enough!" she shouted to the sunrise. Some of the goats started, trotting a few steps away before turning back to the grass.

Shara brought her hands up across her belly, across her breasts. A lover had not touched her for almost two decades. She pushed her hands down into her pubic hair, stiff with salt water. A gray strand glistened there, catching the morning light. With a frown, she pinched it between her fingers and yanked it out.

"That is the first thing I'll have to change," she said, turning and leaving the goats to watch the sunrise without her.

She started boldly up the hill to the place she had avoided since she swam ashore. The cottage was nestled in a grove of cypress atop a small rise. The steps that Shara had carved into the hill were still there, topped with flag-stones and elegantly curving up to the porch.

She used to sail here in the leaky old waterbug that Lawdon had left behind. As she stepped up the hill, she thought of those first trips, walking the shore alone, looking for stones to add to the foundation. She'd mixed the sand, clay, and dried grass she used to build the walls with her bare feet. This was where she first practiced the Floani form, running up and down the hills, carrying the heavy stones on her shoulder, never growing tired, never doubting for a moment that she and Brophy would make a life here, start their family here.

Twenty-seven steps took her to the porch, and she paused there, look-ing into the little cottage that had no door. She could see the meticulously crafted fireplace against the far wall. The sunrise cast a slanted rectangle of light across the mortared stone, and the rest lay in shadow. But she could see it all in her imagination. She had built it. The wide hearth of blue marble from the Ohndarien quarries. The granite chimney, six feet across and tapering to a sturdy flue. She had placed every stone while envisioning Brophy and her making love by that fireplace.

Realizing she was hesitating at the doorway, she strode into the cabin, plunging into cool darkness. Her eyes adjusted slowly, and she looked around. A bed frame without a mattress filled the southwestern corner, and a small breakfast table with two chairs sat on the opposite side. A wooden box full of stone-working tools sat by the door, next to a pickaxe, a hoe, a sledgehammer, and a dirt rake.

She snorted. She could have finished the cabin five years ago, but the neatly stacked tools remained at-the-ready, gathering cobwebs. There was no door because she kept coming up with an excuse not to make one. If the tools remained, if there wasn't a door, then the job wasn't done. The house couldn't feel empty if the work wasn't finished.

It was a pretty little cottage, built like the walls of Ohndarien. A hurricane couldn't knock it down.

Shara had never taken another lover, not even to fuel her magic, but she'd made love to Brophy countless times in his dream. She'd taken the energy they created there and brought it back to her studies, back to this island. Hours of keeping vigil over him created this place. Hours of sharing his dream, loving him again and again.

But that dream had been a lie, her magic birthed from a lie.

What did that make this house?

"Was I wrong?" she murmured.

She reached back across time, summoning a sweet moment outside the Hall of Windows during their innocence. She remembered telling him that she would take her final step and pass the Fifth Gate with Victeris. Brophy had blushed.

Shara let out a laugh, ended in a sob. He had blushed. She remembered thinking how immature that was, but he'd loved her even then. And then he brought her out of darkness in the Wet Cells, when he was beaten, broken, exhausted. He had summoned the last of his strength to save her soul, taken her hand and pulled her back into the light.

And that last moment atop the Hall of Windows, when the howls of demons swirled around them and storm clouds bunched overhead like black, muscled beasts, his last glance had been for her. "Stay close. I need you close," he had said. Three times he'd said it as they rushed headlong toward their destiny. And then he looked into her eyes before he passed into the dream.

No one could deny that he had loved her in that moment, loved her more than any woman could hope for.

Yet now he sailed west with Arefaine Morgeon, the little girl he had snatched from an eternal doom, the child who had accomplished in a few days what Shara couldn't manage in eighteen years.

Shara could see them on the prow of the Emperor's ship, looking toward the dark horizon as the sun rose behind them over the city he had forsaken. Arefaine stood at his side, perhaps even putting her pale hand over his.

They'll be lovers before they make landfall, Shara thought. *Arefaine will catch him during a vulnerable moment, perhaps in his quarters, sitting on his bunk. She will sit next to him, and he will finally cry, finally release all of the pain inside him, and she will kiss away his tears. He will resist at first, but she will kiss him again, and he will slowly kiss her back. His hands will slide inside the folds of her robe, pushing it open. Her hands will slip into the front of his breeches, and his back will arch. Soon her naked thighs will be sliding across his body, lowering herself down onto him...*

Shara screamed. She turned and snatched up the pickaxe. The rake clattered to the ground as she spun and smashed the axe on the mantel of the fireplace. The metal bounced off with a sharp pang, and a lone chip of stone ricocheted off the ceiling.

Letting out a long breath that became a wail, Shara channeled her rage, calling upon strength that no ordinary person could possess. She swung the pickaxe down on the mantel with a thundering blow.

Metal clanged against stone, and the handle splintered. The axe rebounded, spun past her ear, and clattered across the floor. She hissed, falling to her knees. Blood seeped down her fingers from a deep gash on her palm.

One drop. Two. Three, four. Blood dotted the stone, and she thought of the slaughtered goats, bleeding their lives onto the grass that had nurtured them.

Tears welled in her eyes. *Is that my fate? No matter what I do, am I marching toward my own sacrifice?*

What could she do? Rush after him? Stop Arefaine, kill her if need be, make Brophy...

Make him what? Make him look at her that way again? *You can't help me!* he'd said. *Eighteen years I waited for you to come save me, and you never did. You left me in there! And she's the one who saved me! She's the only one who can help me now!*

A footstep scuffed the landing outside. Shara leapt to her feet, throwing a glamour over herself, covering her nakedness, covering the blood.

"Hello?" a man said, squinting against the darkness as he filled the doorway. Blinking, he spotted her, caught his breath.

"Are you all right?" he asked. His voice was young and rich, full of false confidence. "I heard a scream."

Shara watched him for a long moment, his cocksure grin, his broad shoulders, tanned skin, sun-kissed black hair, sea-blue eyes. He moved like a fighter, stood like royalty.

He was Waveborn, perhaps a prince's son. He wore a thin sword at his hip. A duelist.

She touched the man with her magic. He had come here looking for her. And, already, he lusted for her.

The silence stretched, and Shara felt as if she stood upon a pinnacle. Fall one way, and she stayed on this island forever, waiting for the knife. Fall the other, and ... What?

The man smiled, and Shara drank it like a cup of cold water.

"Are you Shara-lani?"

Slowly, she smiled, suddenly knowing which way she would fall.

"I was," she murmured in a throaty voice. She didn't consciously command it, but she felt the magic at work around her, enhancing her glamour. He looked her up and down, his eyes lingering on her body. He cleared his throat.

Shara blinked lazily, and time slowed for her. This time she did not teeter with indecision. She owned this moment. She knew exactly what was going to happen now. And tomorrow. And the day after that, and the month and the year. Kings and exotic dishes. Dazzling gowns and conversations with the most brilliant minds of the age.

She let her magic surround them both. With every breath, she breathed him closer. With every heartbeat, she bound him to her.

"What are you doing here?" he asked.

"Looking for an answer. And I just found it." She smiled wide, touched him on the shoulder. He twitched.

"Do you want me?" she whispered.

He opened his mouth, half-drunk on her magic, and managed to nod. "Come closer."

He stepped into the room, cleared his throat again. She caressed his muscled arm, bringing him close.

"I don't understand," he whispered, barely able to make a sound.

"Kiss me," she said, touching her lips to the tip of his chin. "Kiss me, and you will."

He crushed her to him, finding her mouth with his, her tongue with his. Shara ripped open the back of his shirt, smearing his skin with her blood.

With a grunt, the stranger lifted her in his arms. He strode into the cabin and laid her on the wooden table. She gasped, turned her face to the dark ceiling as his hands grabbed at clothes that weren't there. She dissolved the glamour, let him see all of her.

With a guttural grunt, he ripped at the front of his pants, tearing the laces away. A roaring filled her ears, a wave of power curled over her, vast as the Great Ocean. She closed her eyes and leapt into it, just like Rellana said.

She guided him to her, guided him inside her, and they both gasped at the union. His body crashed down on top of her, crushing her against the table, and she wrapped her legs around him, held him to her.

He shuddered inside her, lost in climax almost immediately. She let out a deep-throated laugh and held on to him, didn't let him spill over the edge. She grabbed his orgasm, wrested it from his control, and stretched the moment into a never-ending scream.

She refused to let him go, and the stranger rode her, a beast in thrall to her will. Shara came with him suddenly, powerfully. Her laugh turned to a moan and joined his animal keening. She cycled her breath through all of the gates. One. Two. Three. Four. Five. The energy burst through her, filling every extremity. She turned it to work, bid it fulfill her vision.

Shara glanced over the stranger's shoulder at her bloody hands, shivering as the magic flooded her. Her thin fingers grew thicker, smoother. Wrinkles disappeared before her eyes. The skin grew tight and plump and glowed with energy.

Her laughter echoed in the small cabin.

"Shall I make you a god?" she asked him.

"Yes, yes, yes," he cried, throwing himself into her over and over again, faster and faster, as if it would never end.

CHAPTER 4

Brophy faced east watching, waited for night to fall. The blue-white walls atop Ohndarien's ridge were almost lost in the distance. He gripped the stern rail with iron fingers, feeling as if his heart was slowly being pulled from his body. His arms vibrated with strength. He wanted to rip the ship apart, wanted to tear his own hair out in bloody clumps.

The little red light circled his head and landed on his shoulder. Brophy felt the subtle presence of his father's soul, like a cool cloth on a fevered brow. He sighed and relaxed his grip on the rail.

Brophy hadn't meant to say those things to Shara. He wanted to tell her how much he loved her, that the mere thought of her saved him over and over again during his nightmare, that he was doing this for them, but someone else's words had spilled from his mouth. Someone else's hand had knocked her to the ground.

Leaving is the only gift I can give her, he thought. *My only gift.*

The four Ohohhim ships rode a strong tailwind away from Ohndarien, the Emperor's flagship in the lead. The ocean stretched out on all sides, a blank parchment ready to hold new writing, but all he could think about was Shara and the thin hope that he would someday return to her.

He did not want to make this trip to Ohohhom with Arefaine, but he had to learn how she survived the corrupted sleep. He had to escape the voices in his head, the malice in his heart. Only then would he allow himself to return to where he belonged.

He hated being trapped on the tiny ship with so many people. He wanted to flee into the wilderness, run from any human contact. His body longed for action, release. He'd been running through his nightmares for years. Standing still was unbearable.

Craning his neck, he glanced up at the crow's nest. But no, he couldn't go up there. The memory of Shara and him standing together in the crow's nest of the Kherish trader stood out sharply in his mind. That was *their* place. He would not go there. Not alone.

The sails billowed full, and the ships charged over the waves. He turned his gaze back to the churning wake behind them.

Wind whipped through Brophy's blond curls. Swallowing, he reached inside his tunic, touched the leather thong that held the straight black feather Shara had given him on that Kherish ship so long ago. He'd worn it since their trip back from the Cinder. His hand tightened on it. What would have happened if his life had taken a different turn from that point? Who could he have become if they'd never gone to the Cinder and found the sleeping baby? Brophy shut his eyes to the past. There was no point. That boy, that life, was long gone. He could never feel that way again.

Brophy's thoughts were interrupted as someone crept up behind him. Quiet as the night, Arefaine joined him at the rail.

"You're missing a beautiful sunset," she said, facing into the wind with him. Her long brown hair streamed behind her like a feathered cape. The orange glow of the sunset behind her brushed the swirling tresses with gold highlights.

He wanted to grab the dark strands, yank her over the rail, and throw her in the sea. He gripped the rail tighter. He didn't trust his hands.

"I'm watching Ohndarien fade," he finally said.

"Does it make you sad?"

"I don't want to talk about it," he growled. One twist of the body, and he could crush her windpipe with his elbow. She'd never have time to stop it.

"You need to rest, Brophy."

"I've been sleeping for eighteen years."

"That was not sleep."

"I lost an entire lifetime there," he said through gritted teeth. "I don't want to lose any more."

She smiled. "Imagine how I felt when I woke up."

He said nothing.

"I could teach you the secrets of Nilani meditation."

He continued staring at the churning surf of their wake.

"My teacher, Father Dewland, is the true master of the form, but he taught me how to lead someone into the trance. Once you've made the connection, you can always find your way back. It's like losing your virginity." She cleared her throat. "Or so I've been told."

Her pale hand closed over his, warm in the cold wind. "Shall we try it together?"

He pulled his hand out from underneath hers and gripped the rail an inch away. He wanted to smash her face into the railing until the wood shattered, and she fell overboard. "Please go away. I'd really just like to be alone right now."

Arefaine's chin rose slightly, and she swallowed. She withdrew her hand, and it hovered uncertainly before falling to her side.

"Of course," she murmured, nodding as she took one step backward. "I know you are in pain," she said softly. "I only want to help you."

He nodded once.

"There is food in the galley, if you are hungry," she said, then left.

Brophy stared at the swirling water until she had gone back belowdecks. He knew he should be kinder to her, but how could he? Everything was wrong. He had to put it right. He had to find the key.

A window opened in the back of the ship underneath him. Narrowing his eyes, Brophy peered over the railing and saw a pair of pale, robed arms resting on the windowsill of the stateroom below. Brophy leaned farther over the rail and watched as the powdered face of the Emperor emerged, craning his neck around to look up at Brophy.

Brophy's brow wrinkled. The rest of the Ohohhim prostrated themselves before this man if he so much as looked their way. But the man was no god. Why should Brophy kneel to some pasty-faced weakling? He could rip the man in half with a single wrench of his hands.

Brophy's father circled around his head, and the howling voices faded into the background. With an effort of will, Brophy nodded graciously to the Ohohhim ruler.

The Emperor smiled up at him with reserved warmth. Brophy could not read the man's expression, but there was no pity in those black eyes. And no fear, either.

"I've heard that a man who stands at the back of a ship doesn't want to reach his destination," the Emperor said.

"Then why are you looking out the stern?" Brophy replied.

The Ohohhim's smile became more genuine. For a moment, he looked like a normal man with a powdered face. "Because my shipwright, in his infinite wisdom, built my stateroom at the widest part of the ship."

Brophy nodded. He felt that he should smile. Before all of this, he probably would have.

"I will leave you to your thoughts," the Emperor said. "I remember what it is like to wander in the darkness, casting about for the sleeve of Oh to lead me into the light."

Memories from Brophy's previous life flickered in his mind. The Emperor had once been corrupted, a feral beast hanging from chains in the bowels of this very ship. Was this the same man? He must have been saved somehow by what Brophy had done in the Nightmare Battle. He thought of that night in the catacombs beneath the Hall of Windows when he nearly succumbed to the corruption. The voice of the Heartstone had called out to him then, had brought him safely into her presence. But there was no voice now. He had not heard her in all those years of nightmare and she was silent now, lost in her own sea of corruption.

"I've never followed a sleeve before," Brophy said. "But I've followed a voice. A beautiful voice."

The Emperor nodded. "And now you've found another lovely voice to lead you out of the darkness."

Brophy narrowed his eyes, catching the odd tone.

"There are many different kinds of voices," the Emperor continued. "Some lead us to the light. Some are lost souls who need our help as much as we need theirs. Are you sure you know where this beautiful voice will lead you?"

Brophy's brow furrowed. He couldn't read anything in the man's powdered expression. With a slight nod, the Emperor withdrew into his stateroom and closed the window, leaving Brophy alone, staring at the walls of Ohndarien slipping below the horizon.

CHAPTER 5

hat's my luck these days," Lawdon grumbled, fighting her way through the twilight underbrush. *A grove of cypress,* Caleb had said.

Well, it had looked like a grove from a distance, but the damned thing was a forest once you got inside it.

She and Mikal had beached the little waterbug on the west side of the island over an hour ago, and Lawdon had told Mikal to secure the boat while she searched the interior.

Lawdon didn't think it would take long to find Shara. But that was a laugh. Now it was getting dark, and she wished she'd tied Mikal to the boat. He was obedient enough when they were under sail. She'd have him flogged if he wasn't. But once they set foot on land, she wasn't his captain, and he was quick to remind her of it. She had little confidence that he'd stayed with the boat. And if he found Shara before she did . . .

During the boat ride here, Mikal had been practically salivating at the prospect of meeting the distraught and vulnerable mistress of the Zelani.

The more lost and entangled Lawdon got into this godforsaken jungle, tramping through endless brambles full of clinging thistles, the more likely it was that Mikal had abandoned their boat and begun his own search.

With a growl of frustration, Lawdon yanked her dagger out of its sheath. Her pants were covered with clinging burrs that scratched her every time she took a step. She leaned against a tree and tried scraping off a few of the tenacious things.

This was ridiculous. She was playing the pincushion, and Mikal was likely off—

The knife slipped, slicing her through her pants. "Ow! Dammit!" she yelled, then turned and stabbed the tree in frustration, yanked out the dagger and stabbed again. And again. "Damned, stupid hunks of—"

"Are you lost?"

Lawdon nearly swallowed her tongue as she spun around. A rock turned her ankle, and she went down, her arm jerking as she refused to let go of her dagger. It stuck for a second, holding her up, then tore free. She stumbled back and sat down heavily.

A figure emerged from the shadows between the cypress trees. Tall, svelte, black-haired, and stark naked.

"Shara!" Lawdon gasped, jumping to her feet. "Are you okay? I've been looking for you."

"And I have been looking for you," Shara said, her voice smooth and rich. She gave a sweet smile. "I already met your friend."

Lawdon opened her mouth and shut it. Fessa damn that man!

"We followed you after . . . After you jumped."

"Really?" She arched an eyebrow, a little sardonic curl to the corner of her mouth. A chill scampered up Lawdon's spine.

"Well, uh, a fellow from your school—"

"Caleb told you where I'd be." She nodded. "Good. I'm glad he did."

Lawdon paused. This wasn't what she had expected, and she felt like she was having to row backward all of a sudden. This was not the ragged, crazed woman who had leapt from the top of Ohndarien's walls. She was poised, calm, and exuding an unmistakable strength. And she was . . .

By the Seasons! It was as if Lawdon had stepped back in time. This was not the mature Zelani mistress Lawdon had chased through the rain. This was the Shara that Lawdon first ferried across Ohndarien's bay more than eighteen years go.

Lawdon struggled to find something to say, but Shara suddenly stepped closer and wrapped Lawdon up in a soft hug. Her arms stuck out straight as Shara's naked body pressed against her. Shara's black hair enveloped Lawdon's face. "My dear friend," Shara murmured into her ear. "I'm so glad to see you. Thank you for coming here to find me." The woman smelled of the sea. And sex.

Fessa damn that man!

Lawdon pushed her back. "Shara, look—"

"Please forgive me," the Zelani mistress said softly, her fingers keeping a warm grasp on Lawdon's arms. "I'm so sorry for the way I treated you the other night."

Shara looked deep into Lawdon's eyes, and together they let out a deep breath. All the tension drained from Lawdon's back and shoulders. The knot in the pit of her stomach loosened. "I was so worried for you," she murmured.

"I was in quite a state," Shara admitted. "I had some very difficult decisions to make." She leaned forward and kissed Lawdon, leaving a tingling bit of euphoria on her cheek. "But as it turns out, they were not so difficult to make after all."

Lawdon nodded.

"I've decided to come with you to the Summer Cities. I have always wanted to see the Floating Palace."

A wave of relief flooded through Lawdon's body. That was what she needed to hear. It was going to be all right. Everything in the Summer Cities was going to be set right. Shara was with them now. "By Fessa, it's good to see you again, Shara. I didn't realize how much I missed you."

"It is good to be seen," Shara said, then spoke in a softer voice. "I look forward to being seen much more." She stepped away, her graceful feet barely making a sound on the forest floor.

"Mikal is right behind me." Shara pointed back to the trees. "I long for a swim. I will meet you at your boat." She turned and began jogging down the slope. "See you soon." The jog turned into a run, and she disappeared into the trees.

In a daze, Lawdon watched her leave. The joy of seeing Shara again slowly faded, and Lawdon remembered the order she had given Mikal. As though blinking away sleep, she found her anger again. She weaved her way through the trees in the direction Shara had pointed.

She found Mikal almost immediately. He was wandering through the cypress, looking at the leaves as though it was the first time he'd ever seen them. Hearing Lawdon, he smiled briefly, then touched one of the branches.

"You pathetic, skirt-chasing fop!" she shouted at him. "I told you to stay with the boat!"

She walked right up to him, and he finally focused on her, the skin around his eyes tightening, but he did not let go of the leaf.

"Hmmmm ..." he said. He chuckled then, shaking his head. "You did warn me."

"Is it really so hard for you to keep your pants on?"

"Hmmmm ..." He looked back at the leaf.

"Hey! I'm talking to you."

"I can hear you."

The smug bastard. Lawdon slugged him in the jaw—

Lightning quick, he caught her wrist and spun her to the side. Her mouth opened at his strength; he hadn't even seen the blow coming. His gaze found hers again, piercing but odd. It took Lawdon a moment to understand what his little frown meant. He wasn't angry with her. He was concerned. For the first time since she'd known him, he looked serious.

"I had no choice," he said simply.

"Oh, yes you did," she said, twisting her wrist. He held it for a moment, then let her go. "You could have done what you were told, or at the least said, 'Shara, come with me. Lawdon wants to see you.' How hard is that?"

"Hah ..." he said softly.

"Mikal—" she hissed, but she was beginning to feel that nothing she said could possibly threaten this man. It was like suddenly seeing Shara as a nineteen-year-old. He was Mikal, but he wasn't.

"I'm a liar," he interrupted her. "And a cheat and a thief."

Lawdon's mouth was open to speak. She closed it. Her brow wrinkled, then she said, "You sound surprised."

"I am. I don't think I truly saw who I was until this moment."

"And suddenly you care? How about we go back an hour and try this whole thing again with you caring?"

"I had the best intentions," he murmured, finally letting go of the leaf he was caressing. He faced Lawdon.

"We came to help Shara," Lawdon said. "And now you've jumped in prick first, and we have a whole new set of problems. Did you see—?"

Quick as a snake, Mikal snatched her wrist again. She jumped, tried to yank her arm back, but he held it like a vise. He had never been faster than her before.

"I. Had. No. Choice," he said, each word like a tiny hammer hitting her chest.

He stared at her as an eerie silence fell in the glade. The leaves rustled with the sea breeze, fragrant from the storm.

"What happened up there?" Lawdon finally asked.

"What do you think happened up there?"

Lawdon swallowed. "She made you? Like Suvian?"

He gave her his charming half smile, but it was stiff, forced.

"Oh, she was a lot nicer about it. But other than that, I suppose it wasn't much different." He released her, and she stepped back. He ran both hands through his black hair, let out a breath. "I meant to bring her back to the boat. I really did. But she seemed in so much pain and I was ..." He glanced at her. "I was going to toy with her. Kiss her and bring her back with my arm around her. Make you jealous ..."

She frowned, and her lips tightened into a line. "I told you—"

"You told me. You didn't tell me enough."

"Mikal—"

He waved a hand. "It wouldn't have mattered, anyway. Not if I was a sexless eunuch. I've never experienced anything like that before."

"Are you all right?" Lawdon asked, her voice softening.

"All right? I'm a changed man. An hour ago I was a frivolous wastrel with a heart full of fear. But right now, I believe I could outduel the great Natshea herself." He lunged and poked two fingers between the branches of the trees. "With my left hand."

"Do you trust her?" she whispered. "Should we let her come with us?" The rush of euphoria Lawdon felt had seeped away in Shara's absence. It made Lawdon cold to the bone to think that Shara had used magic on her, just like Suvian.

Mikal chuckled. "Now there is a funny question. She's your friend. I don't even know her."

"And yet you slept with her."

"Indeed I did," he laughed softly, looking at his fingers as if they were some foreign object. After a moment, he said, "I will tell you one thing." He focused on her again. "There is nothing I wouldn't do if she asked me."

Lawdon swallowed slowly. She felt like she'd just stepped into a deep, slow pit of mud. Her pulse raced. "That's the Zelani magic speaking," she said, trying to sound derisive, but it came out as fear.

Mikal didn't notice. "It could be the winds, the water, or an ape in court dress speaking. It doesn't change a thing."

Lawdon's heart thumped painfully in her chest. "Come on," she said, leading the way. "Let's get back to the boat."

"Lawdon," Mikal said.

"Yes?" She turned around.

"The beach is that way." He pointed.

She clenched her teeth. "Fine. Whatever. You lead." She fell in stride behind him. "That woman has some explaining to do before I let her set foot on any boat of mine."

"Ah . . ." his voice floated back to her, though he did not turn around. "I'm sure she'll be very convincing."

CHAPTER 6

Astor frowned as the corrupted snake threw itself against the bars of its cage. The mutilated creature's severed entrails dangled behind it, staining the cage with a filthy black sludge. The reptile had been chopped in half during the last corrupted battle three days ago, but black emmeria kept it alive. It repeatedly slammed its head against the delicate silver bars of the birdcage they had trapped it in, mindlessly struggling to rejoin its foul creator. Its frantic quest led perpetually toward the northwest, where the Ohohhim had taken the Heartstone. Where they had taken Brophy.

Astor watched the snake dispassionately. Once upon a time, he might have felt sorry for the twisted creature. But he was done feeling sorry. Once upon a time, he had felt sorry for Brophy, too.

He could still see the inky-black shadow that slithered over Brophy's eyes after he'd slain Mother. He'd told the Sisters exactly what happened, but they still let a corrupted murderer sail right out of Ohndarien, just as they'd let the Emperor steal the Heartstone. It had been three days since the Opal Empire betrayed them, and the council continued to debate. With every hour that passed, the Heartstone moved farther away from Ohndarien, and still the Sisters argued.

The women feared war. They were paralyzed at the thought that the accidental death of the Emperor would bring the entire weight of the Opal Empire down upon them. Astor didn't care. Without the Heartstone, the Fortress of Light was nothing more than a half-empty city led by a pack of cowardly old women.

It was high time for the men of the Blood to take matters into their own hands. The Heartstone belonged in Ohndarien. On that issue there could be no compromise.

And so the fastest ship in Ohndarien sat ready to sail with thirty of the finest Lightning Swords aboard. Astor had sold his mother's jewels and pooled the money with the other warriors to purchase the craft. She had a long keel and a shallow draft, built to outrun Silver Islander pirates on the dangerous trading routes between Kherif and Faradan.

Catching the Emperor's flagship wouldn't be easy, but they could still do it if they left soon and pushed day and night all the way to the Opal Empire.

The corrupted snake would lead them straight to Brophy better than any compass. They were ready, they only waited on the twins.

Astor kept an eye on the harbor, resenting every moment of delay, until he finally saw a waterbug leave the Night Market and head toward them.

He paced the deck as Gavin and Gareth crossed the harbor. He could tell from their expressions that the news wasn't good. They finally tied off at the wharf, and Astor met them at the gangplank. "What news from the council?" he asked.

The two brothers from the House of Winter stopped at the foot of the plank. "No news," Gavin said. "Vallia is committed to our cause. The others continue to debate. They have adjourned for the night and agreed to continue the discussion tomorrow."

Astor let out a disdainful breath. He secretly believed those women were glad to see the stone go. They were probably happy to cede their sacred charge to the chalk-faced Ohohhim, and would drag their feet until it was too late to stop the theft.

"That's it, then," Astor said. "We sail." He nodded to the Lightning Swords on the dock, and they began untying the lines.

"Astor," Gareth said, "this is not what the Lightning Swords were created for."

"We were created to shield the black emmeria from all enemies. *All* enemies, not just the corrupted."

Gareth looked at his brother. It was plain that they were torn. Astor knew they felt the same rage he did about the Heartstone's theft.

"What would Captain Faedellin say?" Gavin asked.

The pain rose within Astor. The monster with Brophy's face had taken more than one life with his mother's murder. Astor shoved the feelings down with a wave of anger. "My father hasn't left the house in four days. He's welcome to cry over my mother's death, but I intend to do something about it!"

"I thought this was about the Heartstone," Gavin said quietly.

Astor clenched his teeth. "It is about the Heartstone."

"Astor—"

"No!" he shouted. "No more debate! No more second thoughts. Are you with us or not?"

Gavin let out a long breath and looked at his brother. Gareth turned to Astor with sad eyes. "Not," he said.

"Fine! Then get off my ship."

The two men who had cast off the lines moved past the twins and clambered up the gangplank. The two brothers continued to watch Astor as the plank was hauled up.

"Don't try to stop us," Astor warned them. "Or there will be needless bloodshed."

"Our hearts go with you, Astor," Gavin said. "But we belong in Ohndarien. The people of this city are what matter. Not the stones."

Astor gritted his teeth, but refused to be taken in by cowardly sentiments.

"Please be careful," Gareth added. "You must not kill the Emperor, no matter what. The Ohohhim will tear our walls down with their bare hands if that man dies."

Astor put his hand on the pommel of the Sword of Autumn and stared at his lifelong friends. The Emperor was not the one he planned to kill.

The boat began to move away from the dock. Astor stood watching as the twins grew smaller and smaller. Finally, he raised his hand, waving good-bye. They returned the gesture.

A young girl's scream broke the silent moment.

Bendrick, the first of the Lightning Swords to join Astor's crusade, strode from the stern carrying a screaming, flailing child in his arms. He held Baedellin at arm's length as she tried to kick him. Her fingernails dug into his coarse hands, but he did not drop her. "I caught her trying to climb aboard, sir. She was clinging to the rudder."

"Put her down," Astor said, a lump in his throat. "I'll deal with this."

Bendrick set Baedellin on the deck. She ran to Astor, but drew up short at the look in his eyes. His sister swallowed, bedraggled hair hanging in her face, wet clothes dripping onto the deck.

"You shouldn't have come," Astor said.

"You can't go," she said, a sob catching in her throat. "Not now."

"I have to," he said, remembering his mother's body, remembering the blood on Brophy's sword. He cleared his throat.

Her narrow shoulders trembled, and she held up a hand, but he didn't reach out to her. She let it fall to her side. "You have to stay ..." she whispered, her lip trembling. "I have this feeling ... that if you go ..."

"Baedellin—"

"If you go, you'll never come back." She bit her lip to keep from crying.

"That doesn't matter anymore," he said in a flat tone.

"Please," she whispered. "Don't leave us, not now. Dad won't talk. Shara's gone. We need you."

She held out her arms. The gesture was pitiful, her scrawny arms stretching up to him. Astor sighed and knelt in front of her. He reached out to her, and she wrapped herself around him.

"I'm sorry," he said. He held her for just a few seconds before stepping to the rail and tossing her overboard.

"Asssssstorrrrrr!" Her scream was cut short as she splashed into the bay. None of the soldiers on deck said a word. Astor watched his little sister as she spluttered to the surface. "Astor!"

"Go home!" he shouted.

"Astor, no! Wait!" She tried to grab the side of the boat, but it slid past her.

"Go home!"

He walked to the stern as she desperately tried to catch up with the ship and grab hold of the rudder. Baedellin was a fantastic swimmer, but she wasn't that fast.

Astor watched from the rail, the wind ruffling his hair, until his sister was just a dark blot of red hair swimming furiously through the choppy bay. He could still hear her screaming at him.

Swim to shore, you idiot, he thought. *Swim to shore.*

But she just kept paddling after him as the ship pulled farther and farther away.

CHAPTER 7

Shouts overhead woke her, and Ossamyr opened gummy eyes. Another sailor called out, the words muted by layers of wood. Something was happening.

Putting her hands to her face, she tried to clear her jumbled thoughts. She was curled up in the pitch-black and numbing cold. She still wore her clothes, but they were stiff and scratchy, coated with filth. The reek of her own vomit and feces stung her nose. She could taste it when she breathed. *Why am I still here? How long has it been?*

Her head pounded as though someone was lightly kicking her skull over and over. She shifted and cried out in pain. Her joints were stiff, locked in place. She was hemmed in on all sides, trapped in a tiny space. There was no way to sit up, no way to stretch.

I've thought this before, she realized suddenly. *All of this, all over again.* Her thoughts were clearer than they had been in a long time, but she still felt as if she was waking up after a week of drinking.

They drugged me, she thought sluggishly. It chilled her to think of it.

She had vague memories of a terrible thirst and a foul-smelling soup. She could have been down here for weeks.

The ship lurched sideways, and her stomach flip-flopped. She leaned over and vomited into the darkness. The foul liquid ran down the slope of the hull and pooled warm against her leg. She shifted to avoid it and bit back another cry, as pain lanced through her crippled joints.

Her misery was cut short by a grating scrape that rumbled along the length of the hull. Hope surged in her chest. *We've docked,* she thought. A dock meant land, and land could mean escape, if only she could get off the ship. She had to be ready, had to prepare before they came for her. *Begin with the breath,* she thought. *Just breathe.*

She controlled her inhalation, evened out her exhalation, but all it did was reawaken her nose, and the stench made her gag.

Take yourself away, she thought, *away from this place.*

Ossamyr closed her eyes and breathed, falling into the spell in moments. Slowly, a wisp of power scampered through her body, then another. The power began to swell. She imagined she was back in Physendria with Brophy.

She woke up in his arms and immediately felt a stab of panic. Ossamyr had never fallen asleep with a man before. She'd crept away from all the other boys long before dawn. The queen always slept alone, with guards at every door. But somehow she had let herself slip with this one.

"I think I'm falling in love with you," he said, when she stirred. He pulled her back tighter against his chest.

They were words she'd heard many times before. Words she'd never once believed.

"It was different tonight," he whispered. "You didn't seem so far away."

She pretended to be asleep.

"I liked that. I liked seeing you when I looked in your eyes." He paused, searching for words. "But it made me sad too. I hated seeing how lonely you are ... Behind your eyes ..." he murmured, drifting back into sleep. "So sad, locked in there all by yourself."

The queen had nearly leapt from the bed, nearly called for the guards and ordered them to chain him to a chariot and drag him down the King's Highway until the flesh peeled from his bones.

But instead she just closed her eyes, bit her lip, and prayed that the dawn would never come.

A fist pounding on wood crashed through her dream.

Ossamyr jolted awake. The darkness of a cell. The reeking filth.

She kept her breathing steady, and the magic hovered around her in a thick fog. She held the power close, readying herself. She might only get one chance.

"Wake up, witch," a husky voice called from outside her prison.

Heavy tumblers clicked, and a rusty squeak grated in the door's lock. She could throw a glamour over herself, make herself irresistible—

No, let them see a half-starved, shivering woman. Let them underestimate her.

The thick slab of wood swung outward. Harsh light stabbed her eyes.

"What a stench!" the deep, rough voice exclaimed.

Ossamyr pushed her magic into the man, sinking her tendrils into—

Nothing. He wasn't there.

"Get the hell out of there so I can shut this door," he growled.

She hesitated. That wasn't possible. Again, she tried to touch the man with her magic.

"I said get out of there."

A meaty hand grabbed her arm and dragged her through the doorway, toss-ing her across the ship. Ossamyr's head smacked against hard wood, and she crumpled to the floor. Her breathing faltered as she cried out. She couldn't make her legs work. Her arms were limp sticks, unable to push herself upright.

Calm, she thought. *Cycle the breath. In and out. In and out . . .*

She was still blinded by the sudden light, but she reached for the man again with her magic. He simply wasn't there. She reached beyond him, searching the crew above. Yes, they were there, men and women on the dock outside, on the deck overhead. But not this man.

"Don't test my patience, witch!" He was enormous, with a voice that rum-bled like the beating of distant drums. "You'll probably die for what you've done," he said. "No need to reach that shore any quicker."

Ignoring the giant, Ossamyr turned her energy inward, letting her ani flow into her arms and legs. She clenched her teeth and managed to force her-self to a sitting position, trying to maintain a scrap of dignity. Her eyes slowly adjusted to the lanternlight.

Her captor had a square jaw, shadowed by at least a week's worth of beard. His nose was bent, and a deep scar twisted from the bridge of it to his ear. Like all Silver Islanders, his arms were scrawled with tattoos. The size of the man was unreal. He had legs like tree trunks and arms as thick as a ship's mast. If Ossamyr could have reached into his chest and crushed his heart with her magic, she wouldn't have hesitated.

A rough, mirthless chuckle erupted from the man as he studied her ex-pression. "Save the poison stare. If your smell didn't kill me, those devil eyes won't either." He paused, about to rub his chin, but stopped, looked at his hand with a sour expression, and dropped it to his side. "My name is Reef, and I'll decide in the next few hours whether you live or die."

Ossamyr bit back a venomous reply. She had to get off this ship and back to Efften. All that mattered was the containment stones. Getting to them. Getting them back to Brophy. She had sailed through that killing storm. She could sail through this.

She tamed her gaze. Clearing her throat, she rasped, "I would prefer to live."

"No doubt. What mage ever cared about something more than her own skin?"

He was baiting her, testing her temper, but she didn't care. She kept her tone civil. "Why am I here? Why did you capture me? Drug me?"

He shrugged. "Crew had to keep you that way. No doubt you'd have killed them if they let you form a steady thought."

With each passing moment, her head cleared a little more. Keeping part of her attention focused on Reef, she sent her magic into her arms and legs, easing the tortured, tightened muscles. Her body responded, but she did not untangle herself. She felt she could rise if she had to, but this barbarian didn't need to know that.

The hulk crouched, resting his massive forearms on his knees. "I'm going to ask you a few questions. If I don't like your answers, you'll be swinging from my foremast before dawn."

Reaching behind his back, he fumbled with something, jerked his arm, and brought out a small lump of leaves wrapped in a leather thong. He tossed it on the deck at her feet.

"Eat it. Eat all of it."

Ossamyr looked him in the eye.

"You don't need that," she said. "I have nothing to hide from you. I'll tell you the truth."

He snorted, and his mouth curved up on one side in a half smile. "Whatever you say, witch. I'll listen to your truth. Then you'll eat it anyway, and I'll find my truth."

She clenched her teeth. Her arms vibrated, and it was all she could do to keep her anger in check. Picking a fight with this arrogant savage would avail her nothing. Not now. Once she figured out how to use magic on him, then the story would be different.

"What do you want to know?" she said evenly.

"You're one of the Sleeper's witches, aren't you?"

"His name is Brophy—"

"I don't care about his name. You're from the Blue City, yes?"

"If you mean Ohndarien, then yes I am."

He shook his head, frowning. "What were you doing on Efften?"

"I went there looking for containment stones. There are rumors that Efften has stones that—"

"I know what the stones do. I've seen them."

Ossamyr paused, holding her breath. It was infuriating. This man had had the stones in his grasp the entire time and refused to use them.

"What did you want them for?" he asked.

"To wake Brophy."

He shook his head, growled. "You arrogant fools have no idea what you are doing, what kind of power you are tampering with. Wasn't the Nightmare Battle enough of a warning?"

Ossamyr's lips set in a straight line. She didn't answer.

"It's arrogance like yours that destroyed Efften in the first place."

"That's funny," Ossamyr hissed. "I thought it was your people that destroyed Efften." She inwardly cursed herself the moment she spoke. She could not afford to lose her temper with this man.

But he didn't seem angry. Instead, his half smile returned. "They signed their own death orders. We just swung the axe." He paused, and his smile disappeared. "They got what they deserved."

He made a brief gesture as though tossing something over his shoulder. "Doesn't matter. Your trip there was for nothing."

"What do you mean?" she asked.

"They woke him seven days ago. Your witch mistress and the Awakened Child."

Time slowed for Ossamyr.

"They released Brophy?" Could it be true? Was this barbarian lying to her?

He nodded. "The Child of Efften brought your precious containment stones from Ohohhom. Between her and your mistress, they've damned us all."

Ossamyr closed her eyes. *Shara found a way. Thank the Nine. Thank the Seasons.*

"I warned her," Reef said. "Wrote it down plain as the day, but she ignored me."

Her heart soared, and despite herself, a little sob escaped her. She couldn't help it.

"Don't start crying just yet. The boy is mad, as we knew he would be. He is as much a tool of the black emmeria as any corrupted, and twice as dangerous. Just like that baby who should never have been awakened."

"Mad?"

"No one can survive being immersed in black emmeria for five minutes without being corrupted. You think that boy could be immersed in it for two decades and come out unchanged? The first thing he did when he woke up was kill his mother."

"His mother died a long time ago."

Reef shook his head. "The other one. The old Sister of Autumn."

"Baelandra . . ." Ossamyr said slowly. No. He was lying. He had to be lying.

"That one."

Ossamyr shook her head. Her thoughts were reeling, refusing to take form. Brophy free? Baelandra dead? An image came to her mind of Baelandra standing in the rain as they fought on the docks.

"What happened?" she murmured through numb lips. "Where is he now?"

Reef spat on the door of the tiny room they had trapped her in. "What do you think? You mages can't even conceive of the notion that you are the villains of the world. They didn't kill him, like they should have. They had a party for him, sent him off to Ohohhom with the ice-eyed witch, just like she wanted. They even sent the Heartstone with him. That's like handing a child a red-hot coal on an oil-soaked boat."

"What? Why would she want Brophy?"

"It's not Arefaine. It's the black emmeria that wants him. The Awakened Child is just a fool dancing to the emmeria's song, led by the nose just like the wizards of Old Efften."

Reef snorted. "The black emmeria drove your precious Brophy to madness, and it twisted that poor sleeping girl into what she is today."

He leaned closer. She could see his teeth; smell his breath as he spoke in a deadly voice. "The black emmeria thinks, witch. It is alive. And it will consume everything. You, me, everything. And arrogant idiots like your boyfriend and his new lover are taking it right where it wants to go."

CHAPTER 8

Issefyn's hand twitched on the door handle. It felt as if there were a dozen roaches scuttling across her arms, her back. They would start, then stop, then start again. She had to get home, but she kept a smile plastered on her face. Her eyes sparkled with interest.

"... just dreadful, really," Quinn was saying as they hovered outside her front door, locked in a conversation that refused to die. Ever since Lord Vinghelt passed through the locks yesterday, Quinn had brought the subject up a dozen times.

Quinn was a tall woman with pronounced curves. The voluptuous Sister of Summer towered over the rest of the birdlike council.

"This rebellion in Physendria must be stopped," she prattled on. "Those radicals are tearing the country apart. I can't stand the thought of all those suffering children. If the Summer Cities can keep the peace by sending their fleet into the Great Ocean, we really ought to help."

Talking to Quinn was like having honey poured down your nose. The woman was so sweet, so caring it made Issefyn want to gag.

"I agree, we cannot abandon the children to war and deprivation," Issefyn said, her headache growing steadily worse. "But I am certain that the Sister of Winter has her reasons for denying the Waveborn passage."

"Vallia is a brilliant woman with a heart of gold," Quinn said of the crusty old bitch. "But Physendria is in need. Shouldn't we help everyone we can? Perhaps we could send some of our own men as well."

"I had not thought of that," Issefyn lied. They were her own words, whispered in Quinn's ear by Ceysin as he pushed up her skirts.

Ceysin was Issefyn's latest plaything. He'd taken over the duties abandoned by that idiot Suvian after he blundered his way onto that redheaded peasant's knife. Ceysin had been hastily schooled to accomplish the tasks meant for Suvian. Since Shara had run away to blubber over her broken heart, it would be much easier to recruit the helpers she needed.

Issefyn could picture Ceysin's head lying on Quinn's plump thigh, feeding those thoughts into her mind after stuffing the woman like a honey-roasted piglet. The boy had done remarkably well for only having a week to work. It had taken him the first four days to get into her bed. Since then he had laid the Sister twice, and was taking her well in hand if she was parroting his words back so accurately. Issefyn wondered what Quinn's husband, the Master of the Citadel, would think of her afternoon indiscretions.

"I only want to do what is right," Quinn continued. "We must make Vallia see that people are more important than traditions. Doing what is right is more important than doing what is safe."

Ever since Arefaine had flooded the Heartstone with black emmeria, it no longer protected the Sisters of the Council, something that delighted Issefyn to no end. The sheep could no longer hear their shepherd's call, which made Ceysin and Issefyn's tasks sinfully easy.

"Vallia will see in her own time," Issefyn assured her.

Unfortunately, Vallia remained as intransigent as ever. Issefyn could only guess at what was balking her magic. Was the old woman really so strong?

"It might be too late by then," Quinn urged. "Really, Issefyn, you must take a stronger hand in these meetings. Shara-lani was never shy to offer strong counsel."

Issefyn shook her head and paid the price immediately. The headache seemed ready to split her skull in half. She forced her lips into a smile. "It is not my place, dear. I am merely an advisor. I do not want to push the council in one direction or another."

Quinn's forehead creased in frustration, and she banged her fat fist on the doorjamb. "It's just so frustrating when the obvious solution is right in front of everybody's face, and they refuse to see it."

"Consensus is often difficult to achieve, but it is the heart and soul of Ohndarien."

"Tell that to those foolish boys who went running after the Emperor." She bit her lip. "I know I keep repeating myself, but poor Astor's grief has put us in a very difficult position. A war with Ohohhom would be—"

"Captain Shindin and his crew will return with the boy and his rogue Lightning Swords."

"Yes, but before they do irreparable harm?"

"The Emperor is well protected, Quinn," Issefyn said, wishing she could twist the insipid Sister's head off and end the painful conversation. "Captain Shindin was less than a day behind. He will overtake those boys before they reach Ohohhom and bring back the errant Heir of Autumn."

Quinn sighed. "You are right, of course." She glanced up, her vapid blue eyes looking deep into Issefyn's. "Thank you so much, my friend. You are very kind to take this time to help me get my thoughts in order." Quinn squeezed her hand. "I will see you tomorrow."

And more importantly, you will see Ceysin this afternoon. "Good day, dear. Don't hesitate to send for me should you need anything." The pounding in her head drowned out Quinn's parting words as Issefyn strode down the garden path, heading for the front gate.

The moment Quinn shut the door, Issefyn's stately walk became a quick stride. Everything was moving too slow and too fast at the same time. If her man in the Summer Seas did his job, the Summer Fleet would arrive at the Sunrise Gate within a month. Once that would have been music to Issefyn's ears, but a stubborn stone had dammed up the river, and her name was Vallia.

Illisa, the Sister of Autumn, was a reasonable young woman, and she listened well to Issefyn's council. She wasn't the problem. And after a week of Ceysin's gentle ministrations and constant suggestions, Quinn and Baleise were wet to the knees and aching to spread Ohndarien's legs to the Summer Fleet. Without the protection of the Heartstone, the Sisters of Autumn, Summer, and Spring were ready to do whatever Issefyn wanted.

But Issefyn would dearly love to rip out Vallia's throat.

Arefaine needed the Summermen to join Ohohhom's fleet in the Great Ocean just after the end of the stormy season. Unfortunately, Issefyn had missed her opportunity to end Arefaine's life during the spell that woke Brophy. And so she must continue to play the loyal lackey. But the Summer Fleet would take her to Arefaine's side once more, and more importantly to the emmeria-filled Heartstone. One way or another, Issefyn would gain the power—and the revenge—she deserved.

But the withered old Sister of Winter adamantly refused to break with tradition. Ceysin had already tried his hand at seducing her, but the hag's dusty cunt seemed impregnable. And Issefyn had to be careful. The Sister's eyes were hard, suspicious, and they didn't miss much. If either Quinn or Baleise let word of their secret affairs slip to Vallia, Issefyn could easily find herself facing a squad of soldiers ready to toss her out the Physendrian Gate.

She could not afford to give Vallia more than one week to see reason. After that, well, there was more than one way to remove an obstacle.

The worst part was that all of this nonsense was keeping her from the only thing that really mattered.

The sun beat down on her, too bright. She squinted and wended her way up to the school. A badly turned stone tripped her, and she almost fell. Recovering with a whispered curse, she set out again just as fast. She had to get back to her room at the school. Her conversation with Quinn had taken far too long. The squealing pig had wasted half the day.

Issefyn finally reached the pink eyesore that she had come to loathe so much. Hurrying through the front gate into the courtyard, she noticed Baedellin sulking in one of the alcoves. It gave Issefyn a little thrill every time she saw Baelandra's homely orphan blubbering in some corner. She had generously offered to foster the girl at the Zelani school while her father wallowed in his boundless grief. She had delightful plans for the little troll as soon as she found the time.

Hurrying across the courtyard she entered the school.

And drew up short.

Caleb stood there. His brown eyes caught her, held her for a moment. Usually, the man hovered at a distance like a castrated rabbit. But he lacked his usual emasculated air.

"Issefyn," he said, standing in her way. "We must talk."

She broke the intense stare and stepped past him. "Not now." He touched her shoulder, and it jolted her.

"Yes. Now."

She brushed past him, reaching the base of the stairs. "I cannot," she said over her shoulder. "Perhaps later?"

He said nothing, but she felt his eyes on her back until she reached the next floor and passed from his sight.

She broke into a run, racing up the spiral staircase that led to Shara's room. She yanked open her door and slammed it behind her, throwing the bolt.

Her heart hammered in her chest, and her gaze immediately fell on the wardrobe across the room. With her last scrap of willpower, she summoned the Floani form, filling her arms and legs with power. She grabbed the four-poster bed and dragged it toward the door. She could not afford to be interrupted. The situation might turn ugly if she was disturbed, and it was not yet the time for that. Not yet.

Once the bed was in place, she flew across the room and flung open the wardrobe doors. Sinking to her knees, she opened a drawer and removed the silk-wrapped bundle hidden beneath her clothes.

The blackened containment stone shimmered in her hand, humming with all the power of the world.

She laid a shaking hand upon its surface and gasped. Her mind cleared. The pounding headache drained from her skull. The itching on her skin soothed as if a cool cream covered her body. Her heart slowed, beating steadily.

The stone was fathomless, holding entire oceans. Once Issefyn learned to master it, she would no longer need Arefaine.

She took the stone to bed, crawled under the covers, and held it close to her chest. The howl of distant voices swirled all around her, blocking out the rest of the world, drawing her into their embrace. The stone had already spoken to Issefyn's heart, teaching her to harness its power, make it her own.

She concentrated on the darkness within, calling it forth. A distant roaring filled her mind, like a great storm of ani coming closer and closer. She let the power flow through her, riding the beast, forcing it to serve her.

"Hello, Mother."

She smiled, turning.

Victeris leaned against the windowsill. His obsidian eyes glittered, and his lips curved up in that sardonic smile that turned down slightly at the corners.

Ah, my beautiful boy, she thought. *The strongest of my sons. Only you had the will to follow in my footsteps.*

"You are looking well, younger than ever," he said.

"I do what I must. There are many arts I never had a chance to share with you."

He chuckled, a dark and dusky thing. "You will find that I am much more knowledgeable in death than I was in life." He glanced at the window, traced the sill with his finger. "This is where I died, did you know?" he said, looking down. "Well, at the bottom, actually."

"I know. The students still talk about it."

"Brag about it, you mean?"

"Small minds tell small lies. They idolize Shara for betraying you. But we will pay her back, my son. You and I."

He waved his long-fingered, delicate hand. "Small minds have small goals. Is this the mother I remember?"

Issefyn's brow furrowed.

"The woman I knew would have wanted to see this entire city on its knees, the entire world," Victeris said.

He crossed the room and crouched next to the bed.

"Why take them a piece at a time, when we could have them all at once?" Victeris whispered, running a slender finger along her cheek.

His touch sent a cool thrill through her, but she pulled her head away. "You forget yourself," she said, fixing him with an imperious gaze.

He laughed, throwing back his head. "You summoned me, Mother. You called me back from the howling dark. We were born from the same soul, you and I. Play coquette with your reflection in the mirror, if you like, but I know the truth."

"Perhaps." She climbed out of bed, walked past him to stand at the window. She held the stone close, kissed it. "But I choose when and where to take my revenge. Not you. Not anyone else—"

"Certainly not a whelp like Arefaine," Victeris mused.

"Watch your tongue, 'Teris. I am biding my time with her—"

"Yes, just as I 'bided my time' with Shara. I crafted her downfall for days while scuttling in my own shit. I plotted the perfect revenge right up to that moment when I made my valiant leap from that window."

"Shut up!"

"Mother, really . . ." he said in mock surprise. He walked up behind her and closed his hands gently over her shoulders. His chest pressed against her back, and he whispered in her ear. "Why fight me? We are not enemies. We want the same thing, and the power is at your fingertips." His hands slid down the length of her arms, touched her wrists.

She looked at the dazzling containment stone she gripped tightly against her chest. The howling voices grew louder, closer, more insistent.

"Set me free," he whispered. "And together we will destroy the upstart. Her and all the rest."

She stared out the window at the city she despised. One day, the world would be hers, but not this place. This place she would grind to blue-white dust and scatter to the winds.

"Yes," he said. "Throw the stone out the window. Shatter it. Set me free. Set us all free."

"But . . ."

Victeris's hand tightened on her wrists, clenching hard. The sensation ran into her chest, squeezed her heart. She gasped.

"Do it."

"But . . ."

"Now!"

A dull noise sounded somewhere behind her, beyond the constant roar that had engulfed them. Somebody shouted, and wood splintered in the distance.

Victeris shoved her forward, knocking her off-balance so she fell on the windowsill and leaned out over open space. He grabbed her wrists, trying to pry her hands off the containment stone. "Drop it! Set us free!"

"'Teris!" she cried, fighting him with every ounce of her strength. The distant howls crashed in on her all at once, knocking the breath from her. They were painfully loud. She couldn't hear, couldn't think.

"Issefyn!"

Someone jolted her, yanked at her hands.

"Issefyn, let go!" the deep voice demanded. "You're dreaming!"

Victeris melted away. "You were too slow," he hissed, his fading voice filled with disdain. "You have always been too slow, Mother. Just as you were with Arefaine."

Issefyn kept fighting the hands, but they were strong. They wrenched the stone from her fingers. She cried out in pain as the roaring was silenced in an instant.

The world returned in a rush. A man lay on top of her, pinning her to the windowsill. She tried to throw him off, but he was too strong. He'd taken the stone. She had to get it back.

"What do you think you're doing?!" Caleb practically yelled in her ear, his body heavy on hers.

The man's ani swirled around her, calming her, grounding her.

"Get. Off," she hissed. Her senses slowly returned to her, as did her anger. "Get off me!"

Caleb slid off her body and let her wrists go. She dove for the stone, but he snatched it away. She almost rushed after him, almost clawed it out of his hands. But the slow realization of what just happened, of what she'd almost done, closed in on her like a vise. That stone had bested her. That stone had twisted her, bent her over like a common whore.

Caleb carried the corrupted crystal across the room, wrapped it in a scarf, and set it near the broken door, shaking his hands. "Where did you get this!?"

She shuddered, rage bubbling up from her bowels, stinging her eyes. She blinked, squeezing the tears away.

"Who gave this to you? Did you steal it?"

Issefyn stared at the stone by the door. She could barely contain her anger. Her arms shook.

"By the Seasons! What possessed you, Issefyn? You could have destroyed the whole city!" He went to her, grabbed her wrist, and pulled her to her feet. "You know better than this. You can't even pass the Five Gates. What made you think you could wield black emmeria?"

"I—"

"Come on," he yanked her to her feet. "We're going to the council. You have a lot of explaining to do."

Issefyn's searing rage slowly burned itself out, turned to ice. She shook her head. "No," she murmured.

Reaching to the back of her neck, she slid the tiny blade from the butterfly clip in her hair.

Caleb turned, his hand locked on her wrist. "What?"

"I said, 'no.'"

With one quick swipe, she scratched the little knife across his cheek.

He jerked back, hand touching his face, coming away with a smear of blood.

"What are you—!" he cried, as he grabbed her other hand and tried to wrench the tiny blade from her grasp.

Then the poison hit him, and his eyes went wide.

"Issef—" he started, but was cut off with a squeak as his throat swelled shut.

Ani flared, and Caleb was a blur. His fist smashed into her chest, driving her across the room. She crashed into the wall just below the window.

Baring his teeth, he pointed his finger at her, then doubled over. His fists clenched.

"You'll have to do better than that," Issefyn murmured, sitting up.

Wind whistled out of his mouth for one long moment, then that, too, ceased. He clawed at his neck, crumpled to his knees, and curled up like a spider.

She stood up, smoothed her gown, and crossed to the doorway to pick up the beautiful, glittering containment stone. Then she sat on the bed, crossed her legs, and watched.

Caleb's face swelled horribly large, doubling in size. He spasmed, flinging himself backward, smacking his head on the floor. His heels dug into the rug, and his hands twisted inward as the scorpion venom raced through his body. One last cry whistled out of his throat. He twitched twice, then lay still.

But the skin of his cheeks continued to swell, even in death. Finally, his face burst, spraying blood across the floor.

Issefyn shuddered, savoring the moment until the thrill slowly faded. Caleb's foot feebly scuffed the rug once more.

She concentrated on her breathing until her center was restored, then slipped the blade carefully back into the hairclip. A wonderful little device, as dangerous to the user as the victim if one was not careful. But Issefyn was careful with everything, every movement of her life.

She had come across the hairclip a few days ago in Baelandra's house while convincing Faedellin that his unfortunate-looking daughter would be much better off at the Zelani school under her personal supervision.

Issefyn touched Caleb's body with her toe. Even after witnessing so many deaths, it still fascinated her how quickly the body became cool. The pathetic fool had wasted his life for a woman who never noticed him, as Shara wasted her life waiting for a man who would never return from the shadows.

Love my enemies at your peril, she thought. *This is the price.*

She glared at the exquisite stone she held in her lap. The power hummed through her as she stared into the depths of the black crystal. Someone or something lived within that infinite darkness, hiding under the guise of her dead son.

She would have to be careful. She couldn't risk setting him and his kind loose upon the world. She had no intention of letting the emmeria sully her future kingdoms.

She seethed at the idea that the emmeria had nearly thrown her, but she would break it yet. One day she would ride that beast to the ends of the earth.

"And then, my mysterious friend," she said to whatever lived within the crystal, "I will have my revenge upon you as well."

CHAPTER 9

Ossamyr awoke on a soft bed. She drew a deep breath and smiled, sliding her feet across the cool sheets. It was good to be—

Her eyes snapped open, and she sat up. Dark, wooden walls, a small window looking out at cloudy mountains near the sea. The door across the room was slightly crooked in the doorjamb. Throwing the light covers from her body, she looked at the yellow linen shift she wore. Someone had cleaned her, dressed her.

Memories flooded back. She closed her eyes and let them come. After she had told Reef everything, he had nevertheless forced her to eat his sickly-sweet leaves. She had been honest with him that first time about everything she thought was relevant. But the second time, the Islander's amber leaves had stripped her defenses away, laying her soul bare.

She had sobbed on the filthy deck of that ship's hold, whispering her most intimate details to her indifferent captor, things she had never told anyone, some things she had even managed to forget herself.

At one point in Ossamyr's life, she would rather have died than tell anyone those things. She thought she would go to her grave with them unspoken. But Reef knew everything now, and somehow she was still alive.

Sitting up, she put her feet on the cool floorboards of the little room. She expected her guilt to crush her, her shame to overwhelm her. But somehow she felt lighter, hollow and cleansed.

And Brophy was alive.

After all her unexpected crying to Reef, Ossamyr found that she had one more sob in her, but she smiled as it bubbled up, then flung herself back on the bed and looked at the low ceiling. *My beloved Brophy. You are awake. Alive.*

She lay there for a long time, worrying about him. She desperately wanted to see him, help him recover from his ordeal, but knowing he was free was enough for now.

Someone else had paid her debt. Let them bask in his radiance. Ossamyr had other things to do before she could be reunited with Brophy.

She smiled as she stood up. Her muscles ached from her torturous confinement, but they did not drag her spirit down. Instead, she felt as if she had made Ohndarien's wall run and slept for days afterward. Sore but refreshed.

What trial could compare to the hopelessness of trying to wake Brophy? Whatever came next, she knew she was equal to the task.

A simple, rough-spun dress had been laid out on the back of a wooden chair near the door. A plate of fruit and bread lay on the seat. Her belly growled, but she ignored it. She'd had enough of the Silver Islanders' drugged food. She put the dress on, though. It hung low and was far too wide through the shoulders, but it would do for now.

Ossamyr crossed to the crooked door, tested it. It opened, and she raised her eyebrows. Silently, she crept into the dark, narrow hallway. A shaft of light illuminated the steps at the far end, leading up out of the hatch. She could hear the sounds of people above, distant shouting, equipment being moved. Seabirds cried to each other.

Wary that this was another cruel torture by the Silver Islanders, Ossamyr moved forward on silent feet, ears straining. No one reached out to grab her, to imprison her again. She stopped at the base of the steps and squinted into the daylight. Clouds. Blue sky.

One step at a time, she climbed up and emerged into the fresh salt air. A sailor pushed a mop across the deck, looked up at her, and went back to his work without another glance. A second man stood at the top of the gangplank, about to start down, but he paused, hand on the rail, and watched her. She looked back at him, studied him. He was a broad man, short and stocky like all the Silver Islanders. His tattoos were disjointed where a thick scar cut across his biceps. For that brief instant, she thought the sailor was assigned to watch her, but he flicked a nervous glance to his right, then hastily turned and headed down the gangplank.

Ossamyr followed his gaze, clenched her teeth.

Reef stood alone at the prow of the ship, his huge shoulders hunched over, elbows on the rail. He wore no shirt, and his back and arms were covered with curly black hair. She couldn't see his face, but she would recognize his hulking silhouette anywhere.

Ossamyr considered jumping over the rail onto the dock and making a run for it. The deck was empty, and this might be the best opportunity she would ever have to escape.

But she paused, catching a glimpse of the harbor beyond Reef. The entire city was built on pylons extending out into the protected bay. Only a few buildings perched on the steep granite mountains that rose directly out of the water, cutting ragged points toward the sky.

Slaver's Bay. Long ago, the onetime pirate hideout had been the largest slave-trading market in the world. The city had thrived by exchanging silver for slaves, whom they worked to death mining more silver. But that was centuries ago, before the mines ran dry, before the fall of Efften. Some claimed that Efften would never have fallen if silver had kept flowing from the crags above Slaver's Bay.

Oddly compelled, Ossamyr walked up to Reef and stopped a few paces behind him. Clearing her throat, she said, "Thank you for the clothing."

He grunted, but he didn't turn, and she knew immediately that he had charted her progress across the deck without looking at her. "Politeness now, is it?"

"I wanted to acknowledge a kind gesture." Her gaze strayed to the dock. One jump. Could he stop her? But then where would she go? Run through the streets of Slaver's Bay? Try to steal a ship? Stowaway? Ossamyr was not in any condition to run from this man.

"They said I ought to kill you."

She stayed perfectly still.

"Not going to," he said, his voice as dry as a wood rasp. "I'm going soft, I know. I made the same mistake with your friend. Next thing she did was wake up the Sleeper."

"Shara?" Ossamyr asked.

Reef turned, a bear swiveling its bulk. He leaned back against the rail, once again setting his thick elbows down. His chest and arm muscles rippled as he situated himself, and his intense golden eyes considered her carefully. "I should have killed the Zelani, but there was something about her, a look in the eyes. Same as yours. Time is short, so perhaps it's time to take a different direction."

"I'm not sure what you mean."

He shook his head. "Doesn't matter. You throw the dice, and you see what comes up. You make a choice; you live with it. So does the rest of the world." He paused. "You are free to go."

Hope surged within her, mingling with hot doubt. Another trick? She calmed her breathing and spoke.

"You're just going to let me go? After everything I told you?"

Reef made a sour face. "I have heard your truth. No more damning than most. You were a child born in darkness, but you sailed beyond that horizon.

That's a feat. Not many have the strength to make that choice. It's to be admired."

At one time she would never have believed that someone could hear her list of crimes and shrug them away. This man knew things about her no one knew, no one would ever know, yet he said he admired her.

"You're still a witch," Reef continued, with a shrug. "Ignorant and arrogant, like all witches. But there is no malice in you."

Ossamyr wasn't sure about that, but she felt strangely calm, receiving his praise.

Reef pointed across the harbor to one of the ships. It had a gray stripe along the side, fading to pink. "*Silver Spear* is sailing with the tide. I've talked to her captain. He agreed to sell you passage back to the Blue City."

He meant it. He was really going to let her go. Or was this some slaver's joke? Was she hostage to the new captain the moment she stepped on board? But why dissemble? Why not just tie her up and carry her over? He'd already proven that her magic was useless against him.

"I have no money to pay," she said.

Reef gave her a wry smile. His gaze made its way down her body to her knees, then back up to her face. "I'm sure you can arrange some sort of trade." He shrugged. "Or deferred payment, if you wish. The man is a Gold Islander through and through, but he won't betray you. He'll gouge you if he can, but he's good as his word."

"Then that's it? I'm free?"

"Just one thing. A favor."

"You're asking me for a favor?"

"An exchange, if you'd rather. For your life."

"What do you want?"

"Tell the Blue City's leaders what you learned here. Tell them not to trust the Sleeper they woke. He's not what he was. And certainly don't trust the witch from Ohohhom. She doesn't care about anything but her twisted goal. She'll kill anyone who gets in her way."

Unlike Silver Islanders, of course, Ossamyr thought.

The sea breeze invigorated her, and she reached out with her magic to touch him, tried to ascertain the truth of his words. Most people could be read through their faces, but Reef was a stone wall. She needed to know. Needed to—

"Your magic won't work on me, if you use it that way," Reef said, his golden gaze on her.

She raised her chin. "I don't know what you mean."

He chuckled. "What you tried to do, just now. Do you think I'm blind?"

She clenched her jaw.

"You can't steal from me," he said calmly. "I'm protected from that brand of witchery. But if you'd ever learned to use your ani as it was intended, you'd find things very different." He shook his head. "But you won't. Your kind are all the same, so drunk on your power that you miss the small things. Problem is, the world is made up of the small things."

Her anger burned hotter with each of his words, this ignorant, barbaric soldier, but she suddenly remembered something Shara had said:

"If your anger flares so brightly at another's words, that's your body's way of fighting."

"Fighting what?" Ossamyr had asked.

"A truth it doesn't want to hear."

After a long silence, Ossamyr took a deep breath, and said softly, "Tell me."

His eyes narrowed a little as he considered her with his unsettling gaze. Finally, he said, "I could, but you won't understand."

"Try me."

He shifted out of his slouch, standing up straight, flexed a stiff hand. "Very well, you shared your truth with me. I'll share mine with you."

Ossamyr envisioned Reef confessing all of his sins, blubbering about men he had killed, broken apart with his bare hands, women he had raped, tortured.

Ossamyr waited several moments for him to say something. Finally, she raised an eyebrow. "Well?"

"Well what?"

"Tell me."

He shook his head. "Can't. Not here. Not with words."

Warnings skittered through Ossamyr's mind. "Then where?"

"The mountains." He tipped his chin at the volcanic peaks behind the city. "At night."

She found herself shaking her head. "No."

He chuckled. "'Course not. You already know everything there is to know, don't you?" He paused, and his golden eyes lost some of their intensity. He shrugged. "Good luck, then. Tell the Blue City what I said." He walked past her.

Confused, Ossamyr watched his retreating back until he went down the gangplank and off the boat. Her gaze rose, settling on the peaks behind Slaver's Bay. Shaking her head, she went in search of the captain Reef had mentioned.

❄

After all of her trials, after the bloody, life-threatening altercations with the Silver Islanders over the years, Ossamyr could hardly believe that they had let her go. She kept expecting Reef to show up with a dozen men to kill her. But here she was on the *Silver Spear*, wind picking up, ruffling her hair, and she was ready to sail with the tide. But she kept looking back at those mountains.

"Reef tell you what they do up there?" The captain's voice interrupted her thoughts. Since she had come aboard, the silver-haired, broken-nosed man had never strayed far from where she was. He'd offered her free passage if she shared his cabin during the journey. That wasn't Ossamyr's idea of "free," and she countered with an offer of twenty silver stars when they arrived in Ohndarien.

He'd accepted grudgingly, but without a real fight. His gaze had stayed on her constantly since she'd stepped aboard, but that did not bother her. If he wanted to undress her, he would have to do it with his eyes.

This captain was not Reef, nowhere close. He was a big man, broad through the shoulders, strong and fit, but he was nowhere near Reef's size. She'd tested him the first moment of their meeting. He was just a normal man, solid and very accessible. If she needed to, she could control him. She was not helpless on this ship.

"No," she replied to his question. "Do you know what they do?"

"Nope." He spat into the water. He walked up next to her, so close their shoulders almost touched. "Those Doomsayers don't talk about it. Rumor says orgies." He looked sidelong at her, a half smile on his face, hoping for something.

She stared at him steadily.

He cleared his throat, frowned, spat into the water again. "They're arrogant lunatics," he said. "As if dancing around a fire will save the world."

"That is what they do? Dance?"

"Who knows for sure? They're just rumors. But I never met anyone who actually saw. Two of my crew tried to sneak a peek once. Crept into them mountains after dark. Young. Dumb. Horny and invincible, like all young men." He shrugged. "The Doomsayers dumped their bloody heads onto my deck the next morning. They said that anyone who tried to come without an invitation would be dealt with the same." He shook his head. "None of my people have been curious since."

"Understandable," she said. Her gaze flicked to the mountains again. Reef had given her an invitation.

"Who cares what they do, anyway?" the captain said, frowning. He pointed, and her gaze followed. A long line of people carrying torches had begun a
procession up a stone path that wound up into the mountains behind the city.
"Look at 'em. Must've drunk too much water outta Slaver's Bay, you ask me.
They're just fanatics, all full of some secret purpose that don't mean nothing.
And they look down their crazy noses at everybody else just trying to make
a living. Look down their noses at us! Fools. We're making the best of the
world the way it is, not stuck three hundred years in the past, making war on
a race that has been extinct since we did for 'em during the Fall." He shook
his head.

A strong breeze came from the west, blowing Ossamyr's hair back. The
smell of the sea reminded her of fighting waves, losing her crew, all in an effort
to get past those same fanatics.

"Tide's turning," the captain said. "Be under way in an hour."

She nodded, still watching the solemn procession of torches creeping up
the side of the mountain. Following their path, she saw a faint glow in the
distance, barely seen in the twilight.

She drew a deep breath. Brophy was safe. Brophy was free.

"How often does a ship bound for Ohndarien pass through here?" she
asked, feeling almost as if someone else had spoken the words, from behind
her somewhere.

"Every couple of weeks. Once a month, maybe," the captain said.

"If I write you a letter, will you deliver it to the Zelani school in
Ohndarien?"

He smiled. "Sure I will, for a price." His smile faded then, and he frowned.
"Why don't you deliver it?"

"Because I've decided not to come with you."

❄

In another time, Ossamyr would have been fascinated by the stilt houses and
the haphazard, barely functional construction of Slaver's Bay. But the light
was failing, and she didn't know how far it was to where the Doomsayers did
whatever it was they did.

It did not take her long to cross the city. The trail leading into the mountains was easy to find in the bright light of the full moon. It almost seemed as
if the rest of the city pointed to it, existing only to be the beginning point to
this path into the mountains.

The night was warm, but there was a chill in the air as she trod the smooth path cut into the side of the mountain. Wide-leafed trees flanked the path, letting moonlight through in dappled spots. The path was obvious, but so silent that she began to feel as if she were going the wrong way. No crickets chirped. No night animals rustled in the woods. It was as if they were all holding their breath in anticipation of what would happen at the end of the road.

After an hour of climbing, sweat beaded on her forehead, and her breath was deep and quick. The breeze that had taken the *Silver Spear* out to sea still blew, cooling her as she labored to get up the mountain. Her cramped legs were weaker than she originally thought.

She was nearly at the top of the pass when she rounded a corner and instantly knew she was not alone.

Her heart leapt to her throat as she saw the figures, mere shadows blending with the darkness of the boulders alongside the path. She couldn't help thinking about severed heads tossed aboard *Silver Spear*. Reef had invited her, she reminded herself. But she had refused.

The men were burly like Reef, but they didn't make a sound. It was almost as if they had wanted her to see them, and once she had, they disappeared again, slipping into the darkness behind the boulders like wisps of black fog. They wanted her to know this was a guarded place. They wanted her to know that she continued at their sufferance.

Her heart wouldn't have been pounding so hard if she had been able to sense them with her magical sight, but like Reef, they were invisible.

Pausing in the middle of the path, she considered the lunacy of what she was doing. What if the secret ritual in these mountains was the sacrifice of one who was invited and came willingly? That would explain why he had let her go. What better way to draw her into their trap than to drop a hint about some mysterious new magic?

She stood for a long moment, waiting for the guards to reappear, waiting for some sign that she had been betrayed.

Setting her jaw, she started forward again. She crested the rise and heard distant music. A dancing orange glow emanated from the woods below. Drumming and chanting voices mingled together into an amorphous, haunting sound. It stirred her, filling her with subtle, fierce energy. She had felt this before, or almost, during her initiations with Zelani magic. It was arousing, but not the same way. This energy made her skin tingle, made her breath come faster, but it centered in her chest and belly, not in her genitals.

Making each step silent, she crept closer to the shifting light through the trees. As she drew near, her hands began vibrating with the power. Her legs were no longer tired from the climb, and she ached to break into a run, to spin, to dance. Joy spilled from her heart into every limb. She wanted to leap into the arms of someone she loved, let him hug her, spin her around.

Creeping closer, she peered into a small clearing in the trees and saw everything she desired. More than fifty Silver Islanders danced in the moonlight, weaving a chain of cavorting bodies among a dozen bonfires. They chanted, sang, beat drums. Deep male voices rumbled a throaty base note as women's voices rose above, spinning in and out of the rhythm like birds in flight.

Many of the half-naked dancers carried flutes or stones that they clapped together in time with the drums. They held each other, spun together, sweaty bodies sliding against one another, moving from one partner to the next.

Ossamyr swallowed and stared. Her hands itched to grasp, to grip. She wanted to strip off her dress and rush into that mass of flesh and flames, but she held back, moving off the path into the shadow of an evergreen.

The dance changed, and two lines of people intertwined, one line moving in one direction and the other line moving in the opposite direction, snaking through an elaborate pattern around the fires. Their movements were animalistic, yet somehow tender, sensual without being sexual. As the two lines passed each other, every person caressed each successive partner in turn, sharing a common ground for one instant, before moving to the next. Flesh slid across flesh, hands grasped and let go. The dancers traded smiles, kisses, and unabashed laughter as they traded partners down the line.

Ossamyr remained stunned, gripping a low-hanging branch as she watched, moved by the energy that flowed through her, moved by the overwhelming love she saw before her.

It wasn't long before she spotted Reef. He broke from the line of dancers and spun by himself. His huge chest, arms, and tree-trunk legs were unmistakable as he danced with the flames. The man radiated joy as he swept his head and shoulders through the towering blaze, grinning like a child being tossed into the air by his father. That sight, more than any other, made Ossamyr feel like she was in a dream, awaiting day's first light to snap her out of it.

The music grew faster, and the dancers increased their pace to match. Their breath soon came in ragged gasps. Sweat flew from their bodies and hair with every twist of their heads. Ossamyr's fingernails dug painfully into the bark of the tree limb. Her heart beat faster, as if it had become tied to the frenetic pace of the dance. She longed to join them but held herself at bay.

The song rose to a crescendo, and she opened her mouth, breathing as raggedly as the dancers below.

"Now!" Reef screamed. "Now! Now! Now!" The music suddenly ceased as the dancers tossed their instruments aside.

Reef lunged at the fire, and Ossamyr thought he would immolate himself, but he grabbed a log with both hands and tossed it away. The rest of the dancers followed, yanking the wood from each bonfire, scattering it across the dust and ash of the basin floor. In moments, the fires had been extinguished, and the entire area was a cloud of swirling cinders.

Coughing, Ossamyr peered below with watering eyes, straining to see what happened next. A steady breeze from the ocean lifted the smoke and ash, played with it, swirled it around.

A single voice keened amid the swirling smoke. Another ecstatic howl joined it, then another. All of the dancers rushed toward the center and howled, their faces turned toward the smoky sky. The voices mingled, twisted, melding into a single, endless primal roar.

Reef stood in the center of it all, a long crystal shard in one hand. The cinders swirled faster and faster, and the stone began to glow. A flicker of light sparked in its center, reddish, then purple. It changed to blue, then green, then blurred into a rainbow of colors.

The embers whipped around him, forming a swirling cone that rose up into the sky. Ossamyr realized that the wind was not natural. It didn't come from the sea but from everywhere at once.

In her magical sight, Reef exploded in a blaze of swirling colors. She gasped and turned her head away. Her head pounded at the light, and the rainbow colors in the stone shone brighter still. The primal howl dipped, faded. The swirling wind around Reef faltered, and the cinders began to settle.

The tingling in her skin, the warmth in her belly drained away, and she crumpled to the ground.

A baby cried, long and wretched, and the dancers stumbled away. One by one they fell to the dust, gaunt and exhausted. Moments ago they had been vibrant and beautiful. Now they looked like hunger-stricken Physendrian beggars. An old man dropped to his knees, put a palm flat on the ash-covered ground.

One by one, they staggered to the edges of the clearing and collapsed. Reef was the last standing. He remained upright through sheer effort of will, a lone figure presiding over a field of the dying.

But finally he, too, dropped to his knees. He clutched the stone with all the strength left in him, but his arm sagged, and he fell to the ground. The crystal shard jarred loose from his hand and rolled a short distance away in the dust. It still glowed, but the rainbow colors faded, swirling lazily.

Ossamyr struggled to stay upright as the dancers fell asleep all around her. Even the baby's cry faded to a faint whimper and finally fell silent. She crept down the path into the clearing, her knees weak, her arms heavy. Wending her way through the slumbering bodies, she reached the center where Reef lay sprawled. The crystal shard pulsed softly inches from his hand. Ossamyr marveled at it. It looked just like a tiny Heartstone.

She crouched next to it, reached out a hand—

"Don't touch it," Reef rumbled, his voice cracking.

She froze.

His golden eyes were feverish, but they cast about, finding the shard of rainbow crystal. He scrabbled for it, took it in his hand, and pulled it tight against his chest.

"What did it do to you?"

"True power," he said softly. "Has to be paid for. You can't steal it. It has to come from ..." He closed his eyes, his head moving slightly on his beefy arm.

"You created this," she murmured, realizing. "You drew it from the joy and vitality of everyone here."

He grunted. She thought that might have been a laugh. "There's more than one kind of emmeria. Efften made the black. We make the light."

His words struck her like a blow to the chest, and she sat down in the dirt next to him. "How? Why? What do you do with it?"

Reef didn't raise his head, but his golden eyes watched her through eyelids that could barely stay open. "Brophy caged the black emmeria. We kill it."

"The black emmeria is—"

"Hate," he growled. "Fear. Spite. Anger. All that and more."

"And this? This, light emmeria, is ..."

"Its opposite."

Her breath was the only sound in the clearing, and she said, "You fight fear with joy. Hate with love."

"This is my truth," he said, his words a whisper. His lips barely moved.

She put a hand over her mouth, suddenly seeing the man on the ground very differently. He was hard, uncompromising, a steel blade that would cut down his enemies, but all for this, to create this beautiful thing, to battle the impossible at such a terrible price.

"How long have you been doing this?" she whispered.

"Generations." He took a ragged breath, coughed again. When the spasm subsided, he said, "Every full moon for the past three hundred years. It's not enough. We tried, but there are so few of us who believe. So few who are willing to pay the price. And the body has limits ..." His eyelids slowly slid shut.

She reached out, pushed a sweat-soaked lock of hair back from his brow. He jerked awake, and she yanked her hand back.

"It's still not enough," he murmured, eyes closing again. "In a hundred more years, maybe. We could destroy the darkness forever. But the child is sailing, and there is no more time."

His head slumped forward again, and this time, he slept.

Ossamyr touched his sweaty cheek with one finger. Turning, she glanced up at the full moon. The two shadowy guards she'd seen earlier stood at the edge of the trees, watching her, never moving, never making a sound.

CHAPTER 10

The warm winds of the Summer Seas blew across Lawdon's face as she steered the ship. She certainly wasn't happy about her traveling companions, but she couldn't complain about the course or destination. It was good to be home, sailing the familiar waters of the Summer Seas.

Shara had politely refused to return to Ohndarien and speak to the council on Lawdon's behalf. The Zelani wanted to see the Floating Palace, and there was no changing her mind. When Lawdon asked her if she would look into Lord Vinghelt's claims of magical powers, she did nothing more than give an enigmatic smile and say, "We'll see."

Lawdon had wanted to throttle her, of course, but every time Shara was around, Lawdon's anger seemed to drift away. She couldn't help but smile at a future that seemed so bright and promising. Vinghelt was nothing but an annoying bee buzzing about.

But whenever the Zelani stepped away, the sun slipped back behind the clouds. Lawdon kept thinking the same thing over and over again: If you were harried by a shark, should you invite another shark to save you?

Lawdon watched Shara and Mikal laughing and whispering in the hammock they had strung between the masts of Shara's ship. *Shara's* ship. With help from *Shara's* crew, heading in the direction that *Shara* had told them to go. Lawdon had gone north as a captain and come back as a helmsman, and it set her teeth on edge.

It seemed like a month ago that the three of them had limped the little waterbug all the way to Port Royal. Wearing nothing but Mikal's shirt, Shara had taken the capital of Faradan by storm. Her first stop had been the shipyards, where she traded her jeweled Zelani belt for a ship three times its value. *Moon Maiden*'s builder turned the ship over to Shara for the gemstone and a story, and then, to Lawdon's slack-jawed surprise, threw in an extra sack of silver to sweeten the deal.

Shara took the money and spent every last flake on lavish, provocative clothing, strolling the day away as she visited all of the most expensive shops in Port Royal.

By sunset, every man, woman, and child in the Farad capital had noticed the visiting Zelani. On the following morning, Shara-lani and her "attendants" received an invitation to visit the king.

He wined them, dined them, flattered them all. It was as if he was entertaining the Emperor of Ohohhom. Three days later, after begging Shara to stay, King Celtigar himself led them down to the wharf to bid them good-bye. Shara glittered with rings, bracelets, and a necklace bearing a ruby the size of Lawdon's eye, all gifts from His Majesty or his smitten barons. People actually cried at the docks as Shara sailed away. By Fessa's fins, *Lawdon* had almost cried.

"Camber!" she called.

"Ho, Captain," the ever-alert sailor replied from the rigging, sliding down a rope ladder toward her. The man always seemed nervous, bursting with excess energy, which led him to do twice the work of a normal man and four times the work of your average floating crew member.

"Floating" crew always caused Lawdon's lip to curl. She had little trust for seamen who got so drunk they missed the boat they sailed in on and had to wait for another one to pick them up, but Camber and a few others they hired in Port Royal seemed competent enough. They were all anxious to work their way back home before the Floating Palace assembled.

"Take the wheel," she told the man, when he jumped off the rigging onto the deck next to her. "We're about to round the cape."

"Yes, Captain. You're off to get the wine, then?"

"No, but Mikal will jump at the chance once I tell him where we are."

Camber took the helm, and Lawdon stepped down from the afterdeck and strode to the edge of the lovers' hammock. Mikal was busy nuzzling Shara's neck. She smiled and stared up at the sky with heavy-lidded eyes as if someone were rubbing her feet.

"Seahome Bay in a quarter hour," Lawdon said.

Mikal sat up. "Truly?"

"We're rounding the cape."

He squinted at her, blinked again. "And you've no wine."

"It's in the hold."

"Ah!" He jostled the hammock as he leapt to his feet. It swung lazily, and he stepped away. "I'm dry as a dusteater's heel," he said, then stopped and cleared his throat.

> *"We're birthed from waves and born to roam*
> *The salty seas and distant shores*
> *We're kissed by sun and licked by foam*
> *But ..."*

He bowed deeply, his leg extending far back as he flattened himself almost all the way to the deck.

> *"A Waveborn's favorite port is home."*

He swiveled around, rising to his full height and stepping toward the hold in one graceful movement. The wine was important, especially to a Waveborn like Mikal. Lawdon didn't know where the tradition started, but all true Summermen quaffed a cup the first moment they saw the Floating Palace every year.

At least Mikal would be out of her hair for a few minutes. Lawdon couldn't bring herself to talk to Shara with him nibbling on her ear all the while. It was difficult enough for Lawdon to keep a straight thought in her head around the Zelani.

"Can I bother you a moment?" she asked.

"Of course." Shara swiveled and stood up, leaving the hammock swinging behind her. "Let's stand at the bow. I love looking forward at the sea."

"As you like." Lawdon shrugged, and followed Shara forward. Always following. Annoyed, Lawdon did not wait for them to reach the bow before she started talking.

"You seem bent on being ostentatious," she blurted.

The wind played with Shara's long black hair, and she ran her fingers through it, taking a deep breath and looking out over the water. "I want to be seen," she said. "I want news of my approach to travel."

"Why?"

"Because I do."

Lawdon let out a little breath, fighting the urge to nod and agree with her. "I don't know if that is the wisest course of action."

"You don't think it is safe," Shara said.

"It's not that—I mean, yes. It is that. The Summer Cities are dangerous these days."

"So you keep telling me."

"Then please listen."

"But I am. I do. You're afraid that this Lord Vinghelt of yours will hear of my coming and arrange for something foul to befall me."

Lawdon nodded.

"And he is a sorcerer?"

"That is what we suspect."

Shara shook her head. "Then I doubt he will try to harm me until he has a chance to look me in the eye."

"That doesn't matter."

"Lawdon," Shara said, putting a gentle hand on Lawdon's cheek. It felt wonderful, soothing her fear immediately. "Do you really think I would be so careless as to let a fledgling mage hurt me?"

Lawdon moved her cheek away. "Don't do that to me."

"I'm trying to help you."

Lawdon tipped her head in the direction of the ship's hold. "Like you're helping Mikal? Like you helped the owner of this ship?"

Shara drew a breath but only looked contemplative. "Meaning?"

"I don't like cheating people. Or deceiving them."

Shara laughed. "This from the girl who once tried to squeeze two hundred silver stars out of Baelandra for information about where I was being tortured?"

Lawdon firmly held on to her frown. "That was a long time ago," she said. "And it was only one hundred."

"That's not the story I heard."

Lawdon said nothing.

"Tell me, really, who have I cheated? Who have I deceived? Mikal is relaxed and happy. He is bursting with newfound potential. The man who sold us this boat was more than wealthy, and he longed to be part of my legend. He will cherish that stone and the story that goes with it long after this ship has rotted to the waterline."

"Your 'legend.' Do you hear how that sounds?"

She shrugged, and Lawdon hoped in vain for some kind of embarrassment, some hint of shame. "I am only being honest," Shara said. "The powers I wield are unique, often dazzling. I have made my mark on the world, and the man who sold us the ship will tell his children and his grandchildren that he built the ship I sailed into history."

Lawdon couldn't think of anything to say.

"You are angry with me," Shara said softly after a long moment, and

Lawdon turned to face those dark eyes. "For taking Mikal as a lover. Aren't you?"

Lawdon snorted. "If I ever wanted him, I had my chance. Plenty of them."

"I will leave him alone, if you wish." Shara murmured, laying her hand on Lawdon's forearm.

With a grimace, she wrenched herself away. "Stop it!"

"Lawdon—"

"Keep your . . . fingers out of my head," she breathed.

Shara smiled sadly and gave a little bow. "As you wish." She left the prow just as Mikal emerged from the hold.

"A vintage as fine as we may hope for," Mikal said, waving the finest bottle on the ship. "And three cups to make the toast."

"Beautiful," Shara murmured, curling into his arm.

Seahome Bay hove into view as they rounded the cape. The Floating Palace often boasted more than a hundred ships all lashed together into one vast open-air ballroom, but only thirty ships had arrived so far. They clustered together in the calm waters off Vingheld, flying colorful pennants from their masts, but none had yet been tied together. They must be waiting for the pivot ship. This year it would be Vinghelt's gaudy pleasure barge, *Glory of Summer.*

Lawdon breathed a sigh of relief. Vinghelt had not yet returned from his "duties" in Physendria, and the Floating Palace could not truly form until he arrived. She couldn't remember the last time the palace had formed around the same ship in the same place two years in a row, but things were changing on the Summer Seas.

Mikal was crestfallen.

"That's no Palace!" he said. "We can't drink to a gaggle of single ships!" With a flamboyant swing of his arm, he tossed the bottle and the three cups overboard. Lawdon opened her mouth to shout, but it was too late. The Summer Seas took the wine and goblets with four little splashes. She shook her head.

"Come, my moon maiden," he said to Shara, leading her back to the hammock. "Such a shameful sight has weakened me. Let us rest our eyes until there is something worth seeing." They tumbled backward into the hammock, almost capsizing it. It swung erratically as they settled back in, draped over one another.

Lawdon gritted her teeth and walked back to the wheel. She scanned the waiting ships as they drew nearer and spotted the welcome blue and gold pennants of *Laughing Breeze,* her lord's shiphome.

Reignholtz would make things right. He would know what to do with the shark Lawdon had brought south with her.

Lawdon adjusted her course, drew a long breath, and smiled. Mikal wasn't always the fool, she had to grudgingly admit. A Waveborn's favorite port was home.

CHAPTER 11

Moon Maiden slid alongside *Laughing Breeze*, and Lawdon gave a brief smile. Lord Reignholtz's crowd of children had already gathered at the rail. The three eldest threw lines across as soon as the ships' bumpers touched, and Shara's crew lashed them to the cleats.

Brezelle, the only child from Reignholtz's first marriage, leapt the distance before the planks had been laid down. She landed gracefully on *Moon Maiden*'s deck and ran forward, throwing her arms around Lawdon.

"Welcome home," Brezelle said softly, her neck warm against Lawdon's cheek. She held on for a long moment before letting go. "We were so worried."

"Tell me you didn't light any candles."

"Only one every night," Brezelle said, her dark green eyes looking straight into Lawdon's. She had her father's coal-black hair, but the high cheekbones, the delicate jaw, and the playful glimmer in her eyes were all from her mother. Lawdon had always envied her smooth, freckleless skin.

"I told you to stop doing that," Lawdon said.

"I told you to stop leaving."

"I was under orders," Lawdon said.

"As was I."

"Whose orders?"

Brezelle gave a flamboyant bow. "The orders of my heart, sister."

Lawdon laughed. The first time Lawdon laid eyes on Brezelle, she had been a stubborn toddler of two. Now she was a beautiful young woman, an aspiring duelist, heir to Reignheld, and a prize sought after by more than a few hungry Waveborn lads.

"Lawdon!" Rezzack yelled from behind her, sprinting across the plank before it had been tied into place. At thirteen, he was almost as tall as his father, with skinny, gangly limbs that didn't always know which way to go.

"Prepare to be boarded," Brezelle murmured, letting go of her and stepping away. "I'll see you after."

Rezzack barreled into Lawdon and tried to lift her off the ground in a bear hug, but only managed to throw them both off-balance. Lawdon stepped back, laughing and steadying herself just in time for the ten-year-old twins, Pialla and Silas, to slam into them and knock everyone to the ground.

Caretz, who'd just lost his front baby teeth, jumped onto the pile and clung to her leg. Even little Derick toddled across the plank and squirmed his way into the chaos. Evess, who was only seven and already a perfect lady, stayed back and watched the mauling with a shy look of disapproval. Everyone started shouting at once, and Silas cracked heads with Rezzack in the midst of the anarchy. Rezzack shoved him away, and Silas returned like a battering ram, knocking his older brother to the deck.

Rezzack whipped his wooden sword from the sheath and pointed it at Silas.

"Have at you!" Silas shouted, drawing his own sword, and the duel was on. The boys chased one another across *Moon Maiden*'s deck. They leapt up on the railing, halfheartedly swinging at each other as they fought to keep their balance.

The other children only watched them for a moment before turning back to Lawdon and burying her under an avalanche of questions.

Lord Reignholtz was the last to arrive, wearing a fine tunic of dark blue, with black sailor's breeches. His blue eyes glittered with secret laughter. Lawdon had seen those eyes lose their laughter only twice, and each time the intensity of that stare had stopped men in midsentence.

"My dear Captain," Reignholtz said, inclining his head. "We are glad to see you return home safely."

"Is that the royal 'we,' Dad?" Pialla asked, looking up at him and wrinkling her nose.

Reignholtz continued as if he had not heard her, though his half smile said differently. "You are most welcome here, as always, Captain Lawdon."

"It is good to be back," Lawdon said, extricating herself from the children and bowing low.

"Don't tell me you have sold our mighty *Summer's Heart* and bought yourself this sleek little vessel?"

"A swap of necessity, my lord. *Summer's Heart* is safe in Ohndarien," she said, hoping it was true.

"A safer place than the Summer Cities these days," Reignholtz said. "But it sounds like you have a story to tell."

"A story and then some."

"Good, then let us retire to—" He stopped, turned his attention to Lawdon's left. Everyone's gaze swiveled to see Shara emerge from the hold in a very short blue skirt and a low-cut blouse. Fashion on the Floating Palace had never been modest, but Shara's clothing took it to the extreme.

Rezzack paused in his fencing, his eyes going wide. Silas took the opening and smacked his brother upside the head. With a startled cry, the gangly teenager stumbled off the rail and splashed into the water.

"Moron overboard!" Pialla shouted, running to the rail. The entire herd of children thundered to the edge of the ship. Rezzack shouted for a rope, but everyone was laughing too hard to help him.

"My lord," Lawdon said solemnly, her brief joy chilled as she saw Shara fixing Reignholtz with her gaze. "May I present Shara-lani, former mistress of the Ohndarien Zelani."

❄

As she drained her third cup of wine, Lawdon finally leaned back and put her boots up on the empty chair next to her. The night was almost as warm as the day had been, and the air smelled of summer.

They had taken their dinner outside on the foredeck, and the heaping bowls of steamed mussels had never been better. The Reignholtz girls and the cook's two daughters were gathered at the far end of the table as Shara told them another story. Lawdon could hear the thumping and wooden clacking of the epic battle still raging back and forth across the main deck. Mikal was playing the villain in some elaborate sword drama the boys had concocted.

Lawdon upended her cup, found it dry, and blinked. She looked to her left for the bottle and—

Brezelle absently filled Lawdon's cup, watching Shara and listening intently to the story.

"... had taken control of my mind, you see," Shara said. "I was helpless."

"No," Evess breathed.

"It is true. All I remember is a long, terrible nightmare, repeating over and over, until I opened my eyes and saw ..."

She paused, her dark eyes watching them as she sipped her wine with agonizing slowness.

"What?" Pialla asked, leaning forward, chin in her hands. "What did you see?"

"I saw Lawdon," Shara said simply, glancing over at her.

Lawdon took a long drink from her cup as she met Shara's gaze.

"You saw Lawdon?" Evess said. "She was there?"

"She was," Shara said. "She saved my life, and she wasn't much older than Pialla here."

"I would have saved your life," Pialla said suddenly, with great conviction.

"Would you have?" Shara asked, her eyes widening slightly, her voice dropping to a dramatic whisper. "Victeris was so cruel, with bright eyes, hands like claws." She reached her hooked fingers toward Pialla. "He would have been happy to meet a pretty young girl like you ..." She suddenly turned and grabbed Evess. "And hook you forever!"

Evess shrieked, then everybody started laughing.

Brezelle leaned toward Lawdon as Shara continued the tale. "Did you really do that?" she murmured.

"I found her," Lawdon said, taking another drink. "But I didn't rescue her."

"Who did?"

"Scythe. He killed three men to do it." She didn't say anything more, and Shara continued the tale of her battle with Victeris.

"I envy you, the things you have seen," Brezelle murmured to Lawdon.

Lawdon shook her head. "Don't wish for it, Brezelle," she said. "It was brutal, and ugly. I can't believe she's even telling this story. The man was vile. What he did to her was horrific."

"But she beat him."

Lawdon slowly nodded. "She did. And almost became him in the end." *And might yet,* Lawdon thought but didn't say.

For the first time, Brezelle took her eyes off Shara and looked at Lawdon. "What do you mean?"

Lawdon waved her hand, shaking her head. "Don't listen to me. I've had too much to drink. Listen to Shara's story and thank Fessa that it's only a story now."

Reignholtz returned to the foredeck just as Shara finished with Victeris's dramatic leap from the Zelani school's tower. The Summer Prince held an immense pipe in his hand, the stem almost as tall as he was and the bowl as big as a fist. Lawdon took her feet off the chair, sat up straighter.

"I am lighting my pipe," Reignholtz announced, sitting in the chair next to Lawdon.

A collective groan of dismay arose from the children, and Lawdon smiled. Those were the words the children knew all too well. It was time for bed.

The Summer Prince settled himself in, pulling a large packet of tobacco from his vest. "A full night's sleep is a child's pleasure and duty," he announced for the entire ship to hear. "You will miss it when you are my age, and sleep does not come so easy."

"But Shara is telling stories!" Evess cried. "I want to hear one about the Sleeping Warden."

Reignholtz ignored her, stuffing the bowl of his pipe. "We must always seek the path of a sober and temperate life, lest we be left anchorless as the currents of chance sweep us away."

The children continued complaining all the way to their rooms, the oldest carrying the young ones with them. All save Brezelle.

"Is that why you drank two bottles of wine at dinner?" she asked. "To seek the sober and temperate life?"

Reignholtz raised an eyebrow at his daughter. She raised one back. With a quiet smile, he put his feet up on his little stool, setting the bowl of the fantastic pipe on the edge of his boot. Brezelle took a brand from the little brazier in the center of the table and put it delicately into the tobacco.

Reignholtz puffed his pipe for a time, and no one spoke. Lawdon sipped her wine, enjoying his presence, enjoying the simple beauty of being home. In the silence, Mikal arrived, took a chair next to Shara. He picked up a cup, searched about for the wine. Brezelle tossed the open bottle his way, and he caught it deftly in his left hand.

"So," Reignholtz said at last. "You have certainly assembled an august group of companions in your travels. Our dear young Lord Heidvell and a master of Zelanis ..." He paused. "I am sorry, my dear. Is it Zelani master or Zelani mistress?"

"It is neither, my lord. You may call me Shara, if it pleases you. Shara-lani if you must."

"Thank you, Shara. I appreciate your coming with Lawdon. As you are probably aware, she and I are anxious for any light you might shine upon our present situation."

"I am happy to do what I can."

"Excellent ..." He puffed on the pipe, still trying to get it going. "And you, young Lord Heidvell, I must apologize. Our politics on *Laughing Breeze* may not be the kind you are used to hearing. I hope we do not offend."

"Not at all, Lord Reignholtz. My mother and I have never really seen eye to eye."

"So I have heard. Tell me, does she still support Vinghelt?"

"My mother prefers to sail whichever direction the breeze is blowing."

"A sensible woman. A nasty head wind can muss the hair."

Mikal laughed. "And her hair is so very important to—"

A distant trumpet interrupted him, and they all looked to the west. A ragged cheer spread from ship to ship in the sheltered bay.

Brezelle leapt to her feet and vaulted atop the ship's rail in two quick steps.

"*Glory of Summer* has arrived," she reported, squinting into the gathering lights. "The Assembly will begin tonight." She turned. "Shall I make ready to sail, Father? We will want to be one of the earliest to tie up."

Reignholtz didn't answer his daughter for a long moment as he puffed on his pipe.

Brezelle darkened. "You can't concede the center to him. Tie up next to Vinghelt. Show the entire Summer Seas that you'll meet his lies and treachery face-to-face."

"A subtle stratagem, Brezelle, but I'm afraid we must decline to join the Floating Palace this year. I will not acknowledge his position by tying up next to him. The Floating Palace should be in Koscheld this year, with *Dancing Dolphin* as the pivot ship. Everyone knows it. Everyone seems content to ignore it. I shall not."

Brezelle opened her mouth to say something but didn't. Her green eyes flashed, and she paused on the rail. Finally, she hopped down and returned to the group.

"What exactly are you planning to do?" Shara asked, her finger circling the rim of her wineglass.

"There is injustice," Lord Reignholtz said quietly. "And it has been festering in our country for too long. The time has come for that infection to be purged."

"You mean a duel," Shara said.

"It is our way," Reignholtz replied.

"But others have challenged Vinghelt before, haven't they? This Natshea who fights for him has never lost."

"That is true."

"We think there is magic involved," Lawdon interjected.

"So we suspect," Reignholtz said. "And we hope that you, Shara, might help us understand if our suspicions are true."

"Is Lord Vinghelt so very bad? Why not let him have his way?" Shara asked.

Lawdon sat up. Reignholtz held up a hand, his smile easy and relaxed. "It is a good question, and easily answered. The glory of the Summer Cities lies in her heart, in her traditions. The hearts and minds and souls of our people are bound by a blood oath made five hundred years ago. On that day, a group of ship's captains led by Salice Mick challenged the last petty king of the Summer Seas. They denied him the right to ferry his soldiers across the water and invade the islands of his rival. To avoid a bloody conflict, Mick challenged King Ard to a duel.

"The king was a better swordsman and fatally wounded Mick, but the man's words were stronger than the king's steel. With his dying breath, Mick gave us a gift, a promise of peace, our Eternal Summer.

"Young Heidvell knows the words, why don't you speak them for us."

Mikal stared at his glass of wine, swirled it around in his glass. Finally, he spoke, barely above a whisper.

"May I be the last Waveborn with blood on his hands
May I be the last Waveborn to set foot on the land."

He took a deep draft of the wine and stood up, raising his glass to the sky. His voice rang out deep and clear in the night.

"From this day forth all talk of war shall cease
From this day forth these waves will know peace
An Eternal Summer is ours to seize
With this last drop of blood spilled upon the Summer Seas."

Mikal's words faded into the darkness. He let the silence linger for a moment, then drained the cup and tossed it overboard. Reignholtz, Brezelle, and Lawdon all did the same.

"What happened then?" Shara asked.

"Salice Mick dropped dead," Mikal said, flopping back into his seat.

"But the words he spoke resonated in the hearts of everyone there," Brezelle added, slightly annoyed at Mikal. "Ard's men tossed their king overboard and sailed back home. There has never again been a king on the Summer Seas. And there never will be."

"I see," Shara said, still twirling her finger around her wineglass. "And you believe these traditions are being trampled by this Lord Vinghelt."

Reignholtz puffed his pipe, then continued. "The man is not Waveborn. He was a drunk, a petty con man who convinced the doddering widow, Lady

Vinghelt, to marry him and claimed her title when she died. That man is no true lord. The blood of summer does not run in his veins."

"It does not run in my veins either," Shara said. "Or Lawdon's. Are we such lesser beings in your eyes?"

Lawdon tensed, hating to be cast on Shara's side against her lord.

But Reignholtz did not take her bait. He simply nodded.

"Another fair question." He tapped his boot against his pipe before continuing. "The Waveborn are different from other men, no better, no worse, just different. Our hearts are tied to the sea, where most other's hearts are tied to the land. You cannot build a wall across the ocean and claim that one side belongs to you. You cannot shepherd a school of fish and declare their lives are yours to keep. Lust for land, lust for gold, lust for power is what leads men to war. But the sea belongs to everyone."

"Perhaps, but you are lord of Reignheld, are you not? You own the farms and vineyards there, and the people who work them pay you tribute. Their hands built this boat and everything on it."

"Very true, and in return for their labors I ensure that those people, my people, can live their lives and raise their children in peace and justice. I ensure that their sons die in their beds, not on their neighbor's swords. I ensure that their daughters are not widowed and their grandchildren are not orphaned. I own all the land in Reignheld, and, therefore, no one ever need fight over it. That is why I exist, to govern. The essence of nobility is to lead others, to help them to rise above their baser natures. That is what I have always tried to do, what my children will strive to do long after I am gone."

Lawdon looked from Shara to Reignholtz. She hated to hear Shara challenge her lord so brazenly, but she had asked those questions herself, years ago. And Reignholtz had given the exact same answers.

"And what is Vinghelt after?" Shara asked.

"Physendria is the issue," Reignholtz replied. "The so-called Summer Deserts. That country is a black mark on the hearts of our people. To my disgrace, I am as much to blame as any. The Waveborn chose to seize control of our neighbor in her weak moment after the Nightmare Battle. The Physendrians had been a pack of jackals looming just off our shores for generations. We always knew they would stop fighting among themselves one day and turn their greedy eyes on us. They were a brutal people, joyless, and nakedly aggressive. If they had won the Nightmare Battle, Faradan and the Summer Cities would have fallen soon after." He paused, puffed on his pipe. "So, in our fear, we seized our chance to invade. There were no battles, very little blood was shed, but we broke our promise to ourselves, we left the sea for the land and lost our souls in the process.

"I mean to end that folly. I have long urged the Summer Princes to stop lingering in a mistake. I say we leave now. We should never have been there in the first place.

"But the other princes are afraid. Afraid to admit they were wrong. Afraid to admit defeat, afraid to lose the Physendrian gold we have come to covet so much, and afraid of the retaliation that might come after we leave. But I say we leave the jackals to themselves. We need not raise a hand unless they creep out of their desert and try to cross our sea.

"But Vinghelt has a different plan. He says that we must send more troops, not fewer. Defeat them once and for all, slaughter them if need be. In the last few years as governor, he has been squeezing the conquered Physendrians ruthlessly, practically forcing them into open rebellion. He has manufactured crisis after crisis so he may be called upon to solve them. The man's tyranny has made him rich, and he is pouring gold into the ears of our youth, selling war and calling it glory, planning an invasion and calling it a rescue mission."

"But why challenge this man to a duel if his champion is so great?" Shara asked. "Why not drive him out of office, or simply kill him?"

Lawdon saw a flicker of annoyance cross Reignholtz's face. His patience was growing thin.

"May I be the last Waveborn with blood upon my hands," he repeated the famous line. "Once we start killing each other, it will never stop. Our Eternal Summer will come crashing to an end. For five hundred years we have solved all conflict with Truth and Steel."

Brezelle cut in, determined to make Shara understand. "We do not duel to the death. We do not duel to first blood. We duel until the truth becomes undeniable, until the crowd is overwhelmed by the grace of a duelist's words and the eloquence of her sword."

Reignholtz held out a hand, asking his daughter to calm herself. Reluctantly, she sat back in her chair. "This matter must be decided by the blade. Otherwise, we destroy all we are fighting for. There is no other way."

"My lord," Mikal interjected. "If you accuse Vinghelt of these crimes, you shall have to put forth someone who can defeat Natshea. Who will stand for your cause?"

"It should not matter who stands. The sound of the truth will make a blade sing, the weight of a lie makes the sword impossible to swing. Any duelist with truth in his heart will prevail. The sun of the Summer Seas will shine on the just."

Shara raised an eyebrow.

"But," Reignholtz finished, "it will not hurt that I have enlisted Avon Leftblade as my champion."

Lawdon sat up, jostling the table. She looked at Reignholtz and his secret smile.

Mikal's eyes widened. "But I thought he retired after his injury."

"Who is Avon Leftblade?" Shara asked.

"The greatest duelist of his day," Mikal said. "Some ten years ago, every young man wanted to be him—I wanted to be him—much like every young woman wants to be Natshea today. Leftblade only dueled two years, and during that time he was never matched in verse or steel. He was very young during his run, and some said that given a little more time, he would be the greatest ever. Somehow he seemed to get better with each duel."

"How was he injured?" Shara asked.

"A jilted lover took a fish knife to his famous left hand while he slept," Lawdon said.

"Ah."

"But can he still fence?" Mikal asked, his gaze intense.

"With his left hand? No," Reignholtz said. "But he has spent the last eight years training with his right."

"Why has no one heard of this? A comeback from Leftblade would be the talk of the Floating Palace."

"Leftblade was always flamboyant," Reignholtz said. "He wanted his debut to be a particularly grand event."

"The man's verses are legendary," Mikal said, eyes glowing. "But . . ."

"But can a left-handed man ever be as good with his right?" Reignholtz finished for him.

Mikal nodded.

"I don't know," Reignholtz said. "I asked him to be my champion last year. He came to the Floating Palace in disguise to watch Natshea duel. He said he could not defeat her, not yet. Last month he sent word saying he was ready and that he was at my disposal when the time came."

Mikal was grinning now. He shook his head in wonderment. "The great Avon Leftblade." He gave Shara a sidelong glance, smacked his fist into his palm. "The look on Natshea's face will be worth a hundred gold stars when the greatest blade of our generation tosses his sword at her feet."

"Why don't you toss your sword at her feet?" Shara asked. She uncrossed her legs, then crossed them the other way.

Mikal's face darkened briefly, but his smile returned in moments. "I would dearly love to cross blades with the great Natshea," he said, patting the hilt at his waist. "But alas, I am very fond of this sword, and I would hate to drop it when she cut off my hand." He shrugged helplessly. "Perhaps I should go away and train with my left for eight years, in the hopes that it will become better than my right."

Shara rose and smiled sweetly. "Perhaps you should," she said, bowing to Reignholtz and Lawdon, then looked Mikal in the eye. "Or perhaps you should just believe in yourself." She turned and left the circle of lantern light.

"Ah ..." Mikal said softly. "Perhaps ..." He stood, and also bowed to each of them. "If you will excuse me, my lord, my lady Captain. I must think on a few things."

Reignholtz nodded, and Lawdon watched Mikal's back as he followed Shara into the darkness.

"I think I shall turn in also, Father. It will be a busy day tomorrow," Brezelle said.

"As you say, my dear. I will see you in the morning."

Brezelle leaned over and kissed Lawdon on the cheek. "It's good to have you home, sister."

"Good night," Lawdon said, as Brezelle moved off toward the girls' cabin.

Reignholtz sat puffing his pipe for a long while, and Lawdon relaxed, closing her eyes and taking a deep breath.

"That is a very unusual pair, those two," Reignholtz murmured. "Your Zelani mistress and young Lord Heidvell. He seems as lacking in conviction as ever before, and yet different somehow. And she is certainly not what I expected."

Lawdon opened her eyes, looked over at Reignholtz. He stared thoughtfully at the bowl of his pipe.

"Shara has not been herself lately," she said, wondering if she should elaborate. There really wasn't a need. Reignholtz would draw his own conclusions. "I would say she's using him if I could think of a single thing that she needs him for."

"Perhaps she needs him and doesn't know why."

Lawdon shrugged, relieved that any decisions about Shara were now up to her lord.

"So," he said after a moment of quietly puffing his pipe. "The mistress of the Zelani has come south from her walled city. The Child of Efften has left the Opal Palace for the first time, and our Eternal Summer teeters on the brink of winter. Some would call this coincidence, but I am old enough to know better. Tell me, my child, what have you seen since I saw you last?"

Lawdon drew a long breath. "Much, my lord. So very much."

"Begin at the beginning."

CHAPTER 12

Shara leapt over the ship's rail into the rowboat, landing in a crouch that barely rocked the little vessel. The Floani form thrummed through her, and she felt as if she could row to the moon and back. The Reignholtz family was obviously battening down the hatches for the night, but Shara couldn't sleep even if they tied her head to the pillow. The assembly of the Floating Palace was under way, and she wasn't going to let it pass her by.

As she untied the line, she felt Mikal's presence coming closer. A moment later, she heard the soft thump of his boots on the deck, and his head appeared over the rail.

"Going somewhere?" he asked with a grin. "I must warn you, the Summer Cities are a dangerous place these days for impressionable young ladies."

She looked over her shoulder. The music and laughter carried easily across the dark water. "So I have been told."

"Would you go into the belly of the beast without a proper escort?"

"I was hoping to meet a tall, dark stranger of impeccable virtue to defend my honor."

"I can see we think alike," he said, throwing a leg over the railing and sliding over the edge.

The little craft lurched with his heavy landing. Feigning a loss of balance, he waved his arms dramatically for a moment, then sat down next to her.

"Would you like a glass of wine?" he asked, pulling two bottles out of his pockets.

"Among other things," she murmured, looking into his eyes. His heartbeat surged, and she savored his sudden blaze of desire. He touched her knee, slid his hand slowly to the inside of her bare thigh. She let her legs drift slightly apart, and his fingers moved under her skirt.

Magic hovered like a thick cloud about her, and his lips touched the side of her neck.

"Perhaps we should wait," she murmured.

"Why is that?"

"Because the night is young," she whispered. "And so is our guest."

He stopped kissing her, turned to look up. Brezelle had just reached the rail. She peered down at them like a deer suddenly spotting a hunter.

"Good evening, young Lady Reignholtz," Mikal said. His hand retreated from under Shara's skirt, and he leaned against the side of the boat.

She cleared her throat. "Not so much younger than you, Lord Heidvell."

He laughed. "I certainly hope you don't mind our borrowing your skiff," he asked. "Did you need to go somewhere?"

"Yes," she said, effortlessly leaping over the rail. She landed next to them, rocking the small rowboat less than Mikal had. "With you," she finished.

Shara's smile widened. She had been impressed with Brezelle from the moment they met. The young woman's life light burned brightly. She was beautiful of body, with a strong mind and powerful will. Victeris would have drooled over her, once upon a time.

"As you say," Mikal replied, leaping to take the oars.

Brezelle settled herself next to Shara, taking the tiller in hand. It was a close fit on the small seat, and Brezelle's leg pressed against Shara's, her tight breeches soft against Shara's bare skin.

Shara took a deep breath as Mikal faced the two of them and began to row. The sky was full of stars, and the countless torches on the assembling ships cast broken orange streaks across the dark waters.

Brezelle steered the rowboat toward the assembly, deftly maneuvering between much larger boats jockeying for position. Each of the ships was packed with revelers in brightly colored clothing. Some wore elaborate masks or feathered costumes. Every boat seemed to have its own band, frantically trying to outplay their rivals. The separate tunes all mingled together in an energetic jumble.

At first, rowing amid so many large ships in such a small place seemed like suicide, but the Waveborn maneuvered their hulking pleasure barges as if they were a troupe of acrobats forming a pyramid. They all floated perfectly into place, missing each other by inches.

Brezelle headed between two ships that were closing together. Shara glanced at her as the boats on either side of them came closer and closer, wondering if she had made a mistake. Just before they were crushed, the towering ships on either side of them met with a soft scrape, leaving the little rowboat tucked perfectly between their curving hulls.

The crews overhead shouted to one another, and ropes flew in both directions. Planks slammed down at each of the openings in the rails, and partygoers flowed from one ship to the other.

"My lord, my lady," Brezelle said. "We are now in the heart of the Floating Palace."

"But not yet kissing her beautiful lips," Mikal said, standing up. "I'll fetch a ladder." He placed his back against one ship's hull and his hands and feet against the other. Pressing himself between the two, he began shinnying up the sides like a crab. In moments he climbed over the edge and was lost from view.

Brezelle cleared her throat. Tumultuous emotions fluttered inside her chest, belying her unruffled façade. The girl's hands rested on her knees, and Shara reached over and took one.

Brezelle looked at her, her green eyes barely visible in the deep shadows. "Can you read my mind?" she said, barely louder than a whisper.

Shara shook her head. "No. But I can feel your emotions like crashing waves. If you have a question for me, just ask."

"What if I wanted to become a Zelani?"

Shara laughed softly. Ah, such innocence. Such strength and conviction.

"That is a daring wish," she said.

"I am a daring woman."

"Are you?"

Brezelle swallowed, lifted her chin a little. The heat where the outsides of their legs touched was like a living thing, growing hotter. "I think I would be good at it."

"Perhaps you would, but not everyone can become a Zelani. You must show a certain aptitude." Shara began to match her breath to Brezelle's. The young woman felt it almost immediately, and her breathing came faster. She flipped her hand over in Shara's grip. Their fingers entwined.

"What kind of aptitude?" she breathed.

"This kind." Shara leaned over, and kissed Brezelle's neck. The young woman gasped softly, drawing away. Her eyes were wide, but her hand practically crushed Shara's. The small moment of surprise hovered between them, and Shara waited. Brezelle's dark eyebrows came together. She leaned forward and wrapped her strong, slender arms around Shara's neck, kissing her fiercely on the lips. Brezelle's fear beat frantically inside her chest but she threw herself into the kiss.

When she drew back, Shara murmured, "You are daring, but you don't need to kiss me like a man just because I am a woman. Try again . . . Try slowly."

Hesitantly, Brezelle leaned forward, touching her lips to Shara's once more. There was no rush, no urgency. Their mouths brushed lightly once, twice. Shara's tongue found Brezelle's, and a jolt of lightning coursed through them. Reignholtz's daughter gasped again, turning her head upward. Shara continued down her delicate chin, down her neck as she pressed her hand to Brezelle's breast.

When Shara's fingers brushed the cloth over Brezelle's nipple, her back arched, and Shara let the magic flood into her. With a moan, Brezelle began to tremble.

"That is a taste," Shara breathed. "Just a taste."

Brezelle's hand shook, clutching the edge of the boat. She looked at Shara with wide, wondrous eyes.

There was a slight thump next to them, as a rope dropped into the little boat. Shara looked up just as Mikal slid down, rocking the boat again as he landed.

"Couldn't find a ladder," he said. "But I'm sure such ladies as you can climb—" He paused, looking at them. "Did I miss something?"

Brezelle flushed to the roots of her hair. Shara stood up and smiled.

"Just a brief Zelani lesson."

"Ah," Mikal said. "I see. Lucky girl."

"But the night is just starting, my loves," Shara said, taking hold of the rope. "We can't spend it all at once."

❄

Shara, Mikal, and Brezelle climbed up from the shadows into the most dazzling party Shara had ever seen. The ships were ablaze with light and color. Festive pennants rained down from the rigging, fluttering among the hundreds of lanterns.

The decks were packed with endless streams of people coming and going, wearing glittering masks and costumes that showed far more flesh than cloth. But even amid that riotous crowd of color and pageantry, Shara knew that the three of them stood out.

Mikal wore tight black breeches, tall boots, and a blousy blue shirt lined with silver trim. It had open laces at the front, sleeves like billowing clouds. In Ohndarien, it would have been the blouse of an expensive prostitute. In the Summer Cities, it was the garb of a prince. The Waveborn men seemed to strut like peacocks across their floating city; the more outrageous a man's attire the better.

Shara's own blue skirt was a perfect match. Very few women wore skirts. Slender knee-high or thigh-high boots over tight breeches, like Brezelle wore, seemed to be the current fashion for women, but Shara was happy to see the boldest women seemed to be bare-legged and barefoot, just like she was.

Mikal suggested that they find something to drink, and he led them through the swirling chaos, enjoying the number of heads that turned as they passed.

They moved through the Floating Palace, ship after ship. Each one offered its own musicians and banquet tables, overflowing with everything from raw fish to roasted pig stuffed with caramelized vegetables in ginger sauce. Four colors of wine, endless spirits, and foamy ales flowed from servants' pitchers. Almost every barge had its own fool in motley spouting jaunty poems or juggling rainbow spheres. The Floating Palace was a bazaar, a circus, and a court all tied together with ropes and planks.

Shara listened to Mikal and Brezelle as they passionately debated the strengths and weaknesses of their favorite duelists. They wanted each other already, she could tell. But they wanted her more.

In Ohndarien, she'd gone to great trouble to shield herself from the thoughts and emotions of others. She'd done it out of a desire to respect others' privacy, but here she soaked it all in. She listened to the flighty emotions of a group of ladies looking forward to the masquerade this evening. She smiled as a timid young shipwright almost introduced himself to her, but swerved away at the last second. Shara even paused as if sniffing the breeze while spying on the chaotic musings of a fool who composed new poetry in his head while reciting old poetry with his mouth. The little man was either mad or brilliant, she couldn't tell which. Perhaps, in the end, there was no difference between the two.

There seemed no rhyme or reason to the frenzied movement of people around the party, and Shara was delighted to join the storm of humanity.

Mikal refilled their cups with a fruity amber wine, passing one to Brezelle and one to Shara. He drank from the bottle himself. "Hear that, over there," Mikal pointed. "The violins?"

Shara listened, trying to separate the individual sounds from the prevailing roar.

"They are the Master Strings," he said. "One of the finest troupes on the Summer Seas."

"And also decent duelists," Brezelle interjected.

Shara raised an eyebrow.

"It's true. The leader of the troupe is ranked."

Mikal winked. "A good duelist knows his opponents. Thinking of entering our little perforated brotherhood, Lady Reignholtz?"

"Only if you lead the way, Lord Heidvell," she said. Shara laughed, enjoying Brezelle's company more and more.

Mikal shrugged. "It is true that I've only fought two duels." He sketched an elaborate bow. "But I did lose them both."

"Care to come out of retirement?" she asked, half drawing her blade. "It's nearly midnight, and we've yet to see a duel. We're in danger of going down as the worst assembly in history. It is bad enough that Vinghelt has stolen the hub, but if—"

"What did you say?"

The voice rang out from the throng of people surrounding them. Brezelle turned, looking for the one who had shouted. A young man with a thick face and broad shoulders stepped out of the crowd. He wore a black and gold vest and a sword at his hip. The drunken sot had the nerve to call out again.

"Did you just impugn the greatest prince the Summer Seas have ever known?" the man asked.

Brezelle smiled as she replied, "If you think drowning simpleminded thugs in blood-flavored wine makes a great prince, then yes, I have impugned him. With relish."

The drunk spat at her feet. "This from the idiot child of a father so craven he would have us run and hide from a few desert rats."

Brezelle drew her sword in a flash. The crowd gasped as she slapped the man across the cheek with the flat of her blade. His eyes flew wide as a thin trickle of blood ran across the steel where it had broken the skin. Brezelle held her blade perfectly steady, watching him with her deep green eyes.

"If you have something to say to me, or to my family, please speak up. I would like everyone to hear."

The thick-faced thug had several friends with him, all wearing Vinghelt's colors, gold and black. Three of them moved forward slowly, hands on blades.

"Dust lover," one of them spat.

Brezelle turned her deadly gaze on the man. He hesitated.

"Draw your blade, and we'll see the truth of this matter," Brezelle said. "Make the challenge, and you will find me eager, I assure you." The man swallowed. His hand stayed glued to his sword hilt, but he did not draw.

"Brezelle," Mikal stepped forward. "Why don't we leave them to their sorry seriousness? There are other delights to be savored this night."

"I am simply giving these fine men an opportunity to test their mettle,"

Brezelle said. She searched the eyes of each man who had stepped forward. They said nothing. "But I can see that they would rather wait for another day." She snapped her sword back, stepping away in one graceful movement. She plucked a blue handkerchief from her pocket and cleaned her blade with a deft swipe, then returned it to her sheath.

"Reignholtz scum," the man spat, wiping the blood off his cheek, but he couldn't match Brezelle's icy stare. "Come on," he said to his friends. "No point in cutting this one. Nothing but sand would spill from her veins." The four men faded into the milling crowd.

The disappointed onlookers started to disperse when an earnest young man in a bright orange vest and black breeches crashed to his knees in front of Brezelle.

> *"Lady of the moons and the stars shining bright*
> *For a woman like you I would give up my sight*
> *You've taken my heart with words of soft steel*
> *I must taste the lips that bring thugs to heel."*

As though born to a stage, Brezelle took one dainty step backward and put her hand over her heart, then said:

> *"My dear thug-hating moon-loving fool*
> *Why conjure an image so bloody and cruel?*
> *There is no need to put out your eyes*
> *To taste of my lips, or even my thighs*
>
> *If you wish to sample my steely soft verse*
> *Then I suggest you start something perverse*
> *Bring yourself here, my bold bantam cock*
> *And we'll see if you can do more than just talk."*

The crowd cheered her response, and the man stood up, stunned into silence. Brezelle fell into his arms, giving him a long, deep kiss. The crowd erupted again into cheers and clapping. Boots stomped the deck as the kiss went on and on.

"You've created a monster," Mikal whispered in Shara's ear.

"No. I just set one free."

"She's a child."

"Really? Were you a child at her age? Did you go chastely to bed at sundown?"

"No, but I am a freak of nature."

"Well, so am I," Shara said softly. "And so is she. Just look at her. She is exquisite. I could make her queen of these waters within a year."

Mikal raised an eyebrow at her. "That's funny; I thought we were here to prevent that sort of thing."

❄

Shara stood on the tip of a long, narrow bowsprit looking out over the sea. A delightfully cool wind blew across her sweaty skin, raising gooseflesh. She and Mikal had been dancing, and she had lost him in the crowd. Now she was hiding from him, seeing how long it would take him to find her.

A cool draft swept across her bare legs. Shara loved the slight burn of the rum that lingered in the back of her throat. She loved the skirt she was wearing with nothing underneath. She loved the Waveborn, their Floating Palace, and their Summer Seas. This night had been everything she ever wanted as a little girl.

"Beware your step, my lady," Mikal said, coming up behind her. He walked halfway up the bowsprit and lay down facing the other direction.

Shara smiled. "I have no intention of falling."

"I am delighted to hear it, though I fear the sharks will be disappointed. It is not every day they have a chance to nibble on such exquisite legs."

"Sharks?" Shara turned lightly on one foot and nearly lost her balance. She hadn't drunk this much in years. It was delightful. "And here I thought we might go swimming later."

"I would not recommend it. The waters of the Summer Seas are perfect for swimming, but the Floating Palace creates a lot of garbage, and a lot of garbage attracts a lot of sharks."

"I thought sharks were predators, not scavengers."

"Well, the little ones patrol for food scraps. The larger ones, however . . . They wait for drunk young women to stand too close to the edge."

Shara laughed, almost slipping before she caught her balance again. A middle-aged man in an elaborate sea dragon costume paused at the ship's rail to relieve himself.

"Care to get her down for me, good sir?" Mikal called to him. "She promised to come down for a kiss, but I must admit I am afraid of heights."

"Ah, my young lord, I must decline. I was once shark food in love like the two of you." He patted his round belly. "But I fear those years have passed me by."

"Then I suppose I shall have to do it myself," Mikal said, standing up as the man tied his trousers and continued on his way. Mikal walked to the end of the bowsprit, stopping just in front of Shara.

Behind them, the party continued unabated. None seemed to notice the pair of them precariously balanced over the water, or they were so used to such things, they didn't even bother to look.

"The Eternal Summer was much colder before you arrived," Mikal said.

"If I had known how delightful the Summer Cities were, I would have come south long before now."

"And now that we have you, we must never give you cause to leave us."

"Ah." She laughed. "Keep the future where it belongs, my lover, and you shall never be sad."

Mikal frowned, staring at her as she balanced on the very tip of the bowsprit, just out of his reach.

"Kiss me," she said. "Kiss me and never stop. Kiss me until we turn to dust and float away on the summer breeze."

Shara sent her ani out to him, enveloped him. She could feel his desire like a bonfire raging between them.

Mikal raised his hand to rub his chin. "No," he said. "I don't think I will."

Shara smiled. "Are you defying me?" She let the tendrils of her magic caress him. "You know I love it when you defy me," she said, grabbing his hands, pulling herself closer until her breasts brushed against his chest. "Defy me harder," she murmured, feeling his pulse begin to race. "Defy me right here, right now, in front of everybody."

He swallowed, his hands shaking slightly. "What kind of man do you take me for?" he whispered. "I would never ravage a lady in public. . . ." A small smile broke across his lips. ". . . before midnight. How gauche."

Shara laughed and leapt into his arms. He barely caught her, slid down the bowsprit, and jumped to the deck.

Mikal surprised her more every day. Their first week together he'd followed her around like a lost puppy. She was almost ready to move on when he began to change, capturing her attention once again. It was a new experiment for her. What would happen to a man if he was flooded with limitless raw Zelani magic and left to his own devices? What would emerge?

"What about the crow's nest," Shara said, pointing with her chin. "Is that private enough for you?"

Mikal turned and glanced at the tiny platform atop the distant mast. "What about my fear of heights?"

"I'll help you get over it," she said, taking him by the hand and leading him toward the mast.

She weaved her way through the crowd, brushing against the bodies of strangers, enjoying their eyes as they followed her across the deck. A hundred people would see them climb the mast together, and she didn't care. She was already halfway up the rope ladder when a flutter of strong emotions caught her attention, and she turned.

A middle-aged woman in a rather conservative brown dress stood near the rail, waving a yellow handkerchief at them. Mikal's gaze followed Shara's, and he frowned. Pretending not to have seen the woman, he continued climbing. His conflicted emotions flowed out of him like a strong scent.

"Old friend of yours?" she asked.

Mikal sighed, knowing by now he couldn't hide anything from Shara. "You might say that. I am afraid that is the first woman I ever loved."

Shara glanced dubiously at the woman for a moment, then smiled. "That's your mother?"

"She has that privilege."

"What a pleasant surprise," Shara said, starting back down. "Come, introduce me."

He sighed. "As you wish, my love." They climbed back down to the base of the mast, where Mikal's mother was waiting.

"Oh, my dearest Mikal!" she fawned, touching his face with both hands. "I am ever so angry with you. You've been away so long, and I wouldn't have even known you returned if Lady Munkhelt hadn't told me. Last I heard you had gone north with Lady Amalitz. I did so like her, but I have been so worried about you."

"If you hadn't disinherited me, I would have had no need to be on Lady Amalitz's ship."

She tittered, flushing. "Come now, dear, there is no need to bore your friend with such things. This is a party."

Mikal returned her smile, but Shara could feel the swell of anger caged inside him.

"Well . . ." his mother said in a small voice, clearing her throat. "The least you could do is introduce me to your lovely companion that the entire Floating Palace has been talking about."

Mikal looked away briefly, the muscles in his jaw working, then he gave a half bow. "My apologies, Mother. This is Shara-lani, mistress of the Ohndarien Zelani."

"Oh my!" Mikal's mother said, acting surprised. "Why didn't you tell us we had such an august person on the Floating Palace?"

"We were having fun."

"Yes, you are very good at that," she said sweetly. "Of course you know that you must both come and stay with me on *Wavedancer*. It would do the Heidvell shiphome a great honor to have such an ... august person stay with us."

Mikal started to shake his head, but his mother raised a hand to cut him off.

"No excuse, now. I'll send a runabout and crew so you can show your friend the sights before joining me tomorrow night."

"I don't want your boat, Mother."

"But you are Lord Heidvell's son. You should travel under your father's colors."

"For all the world to see?"

She nodded. "How else, dear?"

"Especially when I'm conspicuously staying with one of the most powerful Summer Princes, who despises you and everything you stand for?"

Lady Heidvell giggled, swiped a hand gently toward Shara. "He does go on. If I didn't send a runabout for him, he would joke about that, too."

Mikal's hand curled into a fist, but Shara put a hand on his arm.

"Lady Heidvell, it was delightful to meet you," she said. "We'll be sure to come visit you as soon as we possibly can."

"Oh!" She simpered. "Thank you, my dear. How sweet." She turned to Mikal. "I do so like her. Tell her she absolutely must stay forever."

"You absolutely must stay forever," Mikal parroted in a monotone.

"There's a dear." She patted Mikal's cheek.

"I live to please my mother."

"Oh, I know that you do. Your actions speak louder than words ever could."

They were interrupted as a buzz went through the crowd. A young boy sprinted past them, clipping the back of Lady Heidvell's legs and nearly knocking her down. A little girl followed right behind him. The two children leapt from rail to rail between two ships, not bothering with the planks. The crowd surged in the same direction, packing the narrow causeways.

"What is it?" Shara asked.

Mikal grinned. "A duel, no doubt. Word travels quickly on the Floating Palace."

Mikal grabbed Shara by the hand and led her away. "Please excuse us, Mother. Shara-lani has never seen a duel."

"Of course, dear. Of course," Mikal's mother called to their retreating backs. "You go do what young people do."

"Come," Mikal said. "We don't want to miss the beginning." He grabbed her hand and led her around the crowd that was stuck at the bottleneck between the ships. "Think you can keep up with me?" he asked, breaking into a sprint and heading straight for the ship's rail.

Shara matched him stride for stride as he jumped the gap between the ships.

They landed, hand in hand, on the far side and kept right on running. Shara reveled in the freedom of her daring skirt and the feel of her bare feet on the polished decking. They dodged around loose rigging, bewildered musicians, and overloaded banquet tables across three more ships.

Mikal slowed as they neared their destination. The next ship over was packed with eager spectators. There was not a single inch of available deck space. He paused at the rail, catching his breath.

"What now?" Shara asked.

Mikal grinned, and pointed up. "I fear we shall have to make an entrance." He led her into the rigging, climbing quickly to the crow's nest, where a rope connected this ship's mast with the one next door. "Hang on to me," Mikal said, pointing at his shoulders. He drew his sword, hooked the handguard over the rope, and grabbed the pommel with both hands. The naked blade hung in front of his face as Shara wrapped her arms over his shoulders.

"Ready?" he asked.

"Always."

He kicked away from the crow's nest, and they slid the length of the rope. Three young boys were perched on a narrow ledge around the far mast with a perfect view of the two duelists already accusing each other.

Mikal shouted ahead, and the boys scattered out of the way, one tumbling halfway down a rope net to be caught by his friends. Mikal struck the mast expertly with his feet, unhooked his sword with one hand, and caught the wood with the other. He swung around the mast to kill their momentum and Shara spun into his arms. He kissed her, lingering in the dramatic pose.

Claps and whistles arose from the crowd gathered below. Mikal and Shara shared a grin before twirling into exaggerated bows, each hanging on to the mast with one hand.

"Excuse me!" a tremendously fat man in the crowd shouted. He was perched on top of a tool locker and held a pitcher of wine in each hand. "I hate to interrupt, but these noble gentlemen were about to engage in an epic struggle of life and death where that man's thunderous tide of honor was about to wash the foul stench of that man's villainy from the face of the earth!"

"My apologies," Mikal shouted back. "Please continue."

The crowd turned back to face the small open space in the center of the deck where two duelists squared off against each other. The first was short, with wispy brown hair receding from his forehead. His opponent had a long queue of blond hair, tied back with a leather thong, and was slightly taller than the first. Both of them seemed on the verge of bursting into giggles, and Shara raised an eyebrow.

"They don't look much like swordsmen."

"Ah my lady, poet duelists are unlike any swordsmen in the world."

Shara laughed. "They're fat." One of the men stumbled backward, tangling himself in his coat as he tried to whip it off with flair. "And clumsy."

Mikal chuckled. "They're drunk. And I hope their words are not as inept as their feet, or the crowd will certainly turn on them."

Shara laughed and watched the beginning of the duel. The short duelist threw his sword at the other man. It stuck, barely, in the ship's deck, wobbling back and forth at such an angle that the pommel hit the wood a couple of times. Shara winced.

"Was he supposed to do that?"

Mikal nodded. "Of course, my lady."

"Seems a poor way to treat a sword."

"Allow me to elaborate upon the unfolding events. It is, indeed, a good way to bend or even snap a blade. But it is also the first test of the prowess of the combatants."

"Ah."

The taller duelist threw his sword, which landed about four feet from his opponent at a better angle. It wobbled only a little, obviously the superior throw.

"The throwing of the blades indicates a formal challenge. Once a sword leaves a duelist's hand it can never be taken back."

"What if you hit them?"

"Sacrilege, my lady! You are booed off the ship, thrown overboard for the sharks."

"Perhaps that would be a blessing for these two."

Mikal chuckled. "Watch. They are already engaged in the traditional voicing of grievances. We'll see what sport is to be had."

"... poxy face offends the very deck upon which you stand!" the shorter duelist shouted, pointing a finger at the man with the ponytail. "Your honor is as black as the bottom of a cur's feet. Your wife rolls with baseborn dust-eaters to find the pleasure she lacks, and your children avoid you in shame. You are a vile miscreant who uses loaded dice in a fair game, and if you ever tried to drown yourself in shame, Fessa herself would spit you back from the water." He reached for his sword, realized he had already thrown it, then said, "Which I will prove now ... with my steel." He waved a hand at his nearly horizontal blade sticking out of the deck. Only a couple of halfhearted claps followed his diatribe.

Mikal winced. "This could be ugly."

"Foul, toad-nosed buffoon!" The ponytailed duelist cried in return, standing on tiptoes as he pointed downward at the shorter man. He seemed a bit steadier on his feet, but his speech slurred. "It is Fessa who denies you the luck of the Waveborn, sir, not loaded dice. The lies dribbling from your shark's smile will transform your sword arm into a sluggish swirl of flotsam. Your ugly face betrays the rot of your soul, and the seagulls throw white globs of contempt at you. A shaft of lightning should smite you for your foul lies, but my blade shall have to suffice."

Mikal looked as if he'd bitten into a lemon. "Um, he has the edge. I think ..."

"Have at you!" The short duelist yelled, charging for his sword. Ponytail lurched forward, going for his own blade. The short duelist slipped in front of his sword and bounced onto his butt. A ripple of laughter went through the crowd, but he recovered, yanked his bent sword from the deck, and spun about in time to receive Ponytail's salute.

> "To the gulls I express my sorrow
> As they taste your foul carcass on the morrow."

A few whoops went up from the crowd just as the short duelist slashed wildly at Ponytail, and shouted:

> "The sorrow to express is my own
> I think your carcass they'll leave alone."

The crowd started laughing as the two men hammered each other with a flurry of badly aimed blows.

The shorter man finally fell down, giggling too hard to get up.

"You ..." Ponytail huffed, paused, and almost laughed. A boo rose from the back of the crowd. Another echoed it. Trying to keep a straight face, Ponytail said:

> "Uh ... the seagulls will circle your bloodstained body
> Your sword work is lousy, and your verse is shoddy."

Mikal stifled a laugh, shaking his head.

"When does it stop?" Shara asked, wincing.

The short man clambered back to his feet, shouting:

> "Your gulls are for fools.
> I'll . . . carve you with my tool."

Another boo went up from the crowd, and this time was joined by many others.

"Go for a swim!" someone shouted.

"Hit him with your breath!" another joined in.

Ponytail flicked a glance at the crowd, but Short seemed oblivious. He focused his bloodshot eyes on the other man, and the two of them went at it again.

A cascade of boos drowned out the fight.

Three young men broke from the crowd, grabbing the combatants' arms. The entire circle collapsed as the spectators ran forward. The duelists were pulled away from each other, bellowing as their swords were taken away.

"I almost had him!" Short yelled, ending in a laugh.

"You hack," Ponytail shouted back. "I had the better of you from the beginning!" The duelists were raised up on shoulders and passed hand to hand to the edge of the ship, where the crowd tossed them into the water.

Mikal was beside himself with laughter. He leaned over, shaking and holding his stomach with one hand.

"That's it?" Shara asked. "That's all there is to the world-famous Summer Seas duelists?"

"That's it, my lady," Mikal managed to say through his laughter. "You've seen the ugly truth. We are not a nation of duelists with a drinking problem; we are a nation of drunks with a dueling problem."

The Waveborn dispersed, seeking other entertainment. Shara and Mikal stayed on their perch, and she watched the two combatants floundering in the water. Ponytail tried to climb back into the boat, but Short grabbed him and yanked him back.

"What about the sharks?" she asked.

"Don't worry," Mikal said. "Sharks find bad poetry as unappetizing as we do. Why eat a lousy poet when you could eat garbage?"

"I must admit I was expecting a bit more from my first duel after Lord Reignholtz described them with such religious fervor."

Mikal shrugged. "Lord Reignholtz holds the soul of the Summer Seas in his heart. And it's a good thing he does, because no one else would bother. The rest of us are much more concerned with our bellies and balls than our hearts and souls."

"So you say that Reignholtz's talk of nobility is nothing but a farce, a pleasant fable to justify his privileged position?"

"Milady!" Mikal opened his mouth in mock indignation. "Are you saying you are not a true believer? Haven't these last few days at sea washed the foul dust of land-bound cynicism from between your lovely toes?"

Shara kissed him. "You are very pretty when you're avoiding the subject, but you are still avoiding the subject. Do you support Reignholtz? Would you fight for him if it came to that?"

Mikal shrugged again. "I'm a lover, not a fighter."

"You certainly are." She started to kiss him again, but pulled away when he leaned forward to meet her. "And a fiendish avoider of questions."

He smiled. "For a woman so easy to satisfy, you are devilishly hard to please."

"Not if you give me what I want," she said, leaning in for another kiss.

He didn't take the bait this time. "Very well, once again I will give the lady what she wants. In my heart of hearts I steadfastly believe that Salice Mick was the greatest man who ever lived . . ." He paused dramatically. "Just not quite for the reasons Reignholtz chooses to believe. It's true that the glorious Captain Mick gave us the gift of the Eternal Summer, but the man was a drunken sot by all accounts, a philanderer, and a gambler down to his bones. The main reason he fought King Ard was to keep his ship from being commandeered to transport troops. I tend to believe that his glorious 'five hundred years of peace' was a bit of an afterthought, something that just popped into his mind after he'd taken his fatal wound. Nothing like imminent death to spur poetic improvisation."

"Then your Eternal Summer is nothing more than a grand mistake, a dramatic gesture from a dying drunk?"

"What rules the Summer Seas if not dramatic gestures?"

"The clever and the strong, just like any other place in the world."

Chuckling, Mikal shrugged. "Perhaps, but there is power in truth and weakness in lies, regardless of the speaker's intentions. Mick's words touched the crowd's heart that day. They still touch our hearts. Five hundred years of peace is no accident. Or, rather, it was an endless string of perfect accidents."

"What do you mean?"

"At first, the idea of charting the course of a nation based on fops spewing rhyme and swinging swords seems like madness. But there is genius hidden in that madness. Resolving conflicts by way of endearing and long-winded posturing makes it practically impossible for us to accomplish anything. And if we can't accomplish anything, we can't accomplish anything particularly unjust, tyrannical, or vile. For the past five hundred years we have just bobbed along in a state of blissful ineptitude that has made it impossible for us to war against each other, or organize ourselves sufficiently to mount a war anywhere else. Thus, the Eternal Summer continues, and we remain civilized. We do not oppress ourselves or anyone else."

"Except for the Physendrians," she said.

"Ah." He winked. "That is why Reignholtz has worked himself into a religious fervor, and why our dear Captain Lawdon's skirts are twisted into a bunch."

A trumpet sounded, and they both turned toward the sound. The crowd hushed.

"Is there always another drama to follow the previous ones?" Shara asked.

"The true festival has not even begun," Mikal said.

A tall thin man dressed smartly in black and gold stepped onto the deck of their ship and announced in a loud voice. "I present Lord Vinghelt, Prince of the Summer Seas, Master of Vingheld, Governor of the Summer Deserts, and beloved of Fessa of the Deep."

An entourage of Waveborn dressed in gold and black crossed the planks, fanning out as the Summer Prince arrived.

Vinghelt was in his late forties or early fifties with a smattering of gray in his meticulously trimmed beard. His clothes were tailored from black-and-gold silk, and he wore a blade so encrusted with jewels that it was certainly just for show. He was flanked by two swordsmen who had the easy stride and well-trained eyes of their trade. Everyone made room for the lord as he passed through the crowd, greeting all comers with a hearty handshake and magnanimous smile.

"My fellow Waveborn, I have just returned from the Summer Deserts, where our brave lads and lasses strive to bring peace. They do the goddess's work, and we should all be very proud of them."

Cheers and shouts rose from the crowd. Vinghelt smiled and nodded, then finally raised his hands. The cacophony quieted some, and he continued. "It is a blessing to return to see the loyal faces of my countrymen. The Summer Deserts are slowly walking into the light of our dear Fessa, but there is nothing like being home!"

The crowd applauded heartily, and the lord waited for it to die down before continuing.

"I would like to invite you all to share in the goddess's bounty aboard *Glory of Summer*. My humble chefs have prepared a never-ending banquet for any who would share a cup of Ardish Red with the heroes of Summer and welcome them back to the waves of their birth."

A deafening cheer rose from the crowd, and Vinghelt's supporters started a chant.

"Long live the prince!"

Vinghelt smiled tolerantly for everyone and began to greet individuals in the crowd.

"Ardish Red for all," Mikal said to Shara. "Now there's an extravagant gesture. Beware that you don't grab a bottle of Physendrian Red by mistake when you pull from Vinghelt's wine cellar."

"Physendrian Red?"

"Blood, my dulcet dear. Where do you think Vinghelt gets the gold to lavish such expensive gifts upon the Waveborn?"

"So this Vinghelt is a man who is not above using whatever resources his fingers can touch, is he?"

"Oh yes. His fingers also found their way under the skirts of a very old, very rich widow. The excitement must have been too much for the poor dear. She was dead within a month, and the next thing you know, he is Lord Vinghelt, Master of Vingheld."

"How convenient." She felt her ire rising, but she put it down. This was not her problem. At Lawdon's request, she would probe Vinghelt, but it didn't really matter to her who ruled in the Summer Cities.

"Shall we then?" she asked.

"Shall we what?"

"Join the party."

He smiled. "Yes, of course. Why not? Let us drink with the enemy."

"He's Reignholtz's enemy," Shara said. "Not mine."

"Ah ... I see. You are a lover, not a fighter?"

"Exactly."

CHAPTER 13

Shara studied Lord Vinghelt as he moved through the crowd greeting each person by name like long-lost friends. If a man like Reignholtz hated and feared the prince, Shara wanted to know why.

The man was tall and slender, with a thin neck, a chiseled jaw, and a natural smile. *Brophy could take him down with a single punch,* she thought.

She frowned and banished the Brother of Autumn from her mind.

Vinghelt's step was sure and strong, just graceful enough to be dignified. Every movement and gesture seemed to shout, "I am one of you. One of the people. A true Summerman."

His clothing was finely made, but far less outrageous than Mikal's. Vinghelt's muted attire was somewhat conspicuous in the colorful menagerie assembled on the Floating Palace. His bearing and attire projected sober restraint, but turbulent emotions leaked from him as they did from any normal person.

He paused for a moment to speak with a grossly fat man who was cloaked and cowled in a black robe. Shara could not see the man's face, but his hands were a shocking white. An albino? He struggled with almost every step, shuffling awkwardly across the deck. As he paused for a short rest, he looked up, and Shara got a glimpse of his white face and red eyes.

Her breath faltered for an instant at the contact. The fat albino smiled at her, and a rush of heat raced through her body.

She turned back to Mikal and drained her wineglass. "Shall we then?"

"Shall we what?"

"Introduce ourselves."

Mikal shrugged, and Shara led him through the crowd toward the Summer Prince.

Vinghelt was busy chatting with several people only a few yards away, but he noticed Shara out of the corner of his eye as she drew closer. At the perfect moment, as the crowd parted to create a momentary aisle between Vinghelt and Shara, he caught her gaze.

Oh, well done, she thought.

The prince strode forward flanked by his bodyguards. The two swordsmen looked everywhere but forward, but Shara knew their attention was intensely focused on Mikal and his Zelani consort.

Vinghelt stopped just in front of her and Mikal. His slender build made him seem taller at a distance. The man's nose was straight and sharp as a knife, and his smile was something you'd expect from a long-lost friend. *One day,* Shara thought, *I shall have to study the magic in a person's charisma.* If there was such a thing, Vinghelt had an ocean of it.

He bowed to her. "Shara-lani, dearest cousin of the north, you cannot know how happy it made me to hear of your arrival. You honor Fessa's waves by your presence."

"The honor is mine, Lord Vinghelt," she said, giving a curtsy as modest as her short skirt would allow. "I have heard so much about you."

"I urge you not to listen to the rumors. Some are quite exaggerated."

"Most rumors are."

"You are kind to say so." He turned to Mikal. "Lord Heidvell, you have done the Summer Seas a great service by bringing such an eminent guest to our humble Floating Palace."

"She hijacked me," he said, grinning.

"Ah." Vinghelt glanced at Shara. "I'm sure she would do the same to any of us. Only a blind man could resist such a radiant beauty. Speaking of beauty, tell me, Lord Heidvell, how is your lovely mother?"

"Going a bit senile, I'm afraid, but still utterly devoted to you."

Vinghelt only paused long enough to blink, then turned to Shara.

"Dear Shara-lani, I would consider it an honor if you and Lord Heidvell agreed to be my guests on the *Glory of Summer*. I hate to think of you lodging so far from the heart of the Floating Palace."

"What a delightful offer. I am honored."

"Excellent," Vinghelt replied. "I will be expecting you; it will give us more time to discuss our mutual passions."

"Mikal, dear, would you refresh my glass?" she asked, offering him the goblet. She gave Vinghelt her other arm. Mikal stood stunned for a moment, then snatched her cup and left.

Vinghelt led her toward the ship's rail while his bodyguards hovered discreetly behind them. "You and Mikal are an interesting pair," he said.

"He keeps me entertained."

"Yes." Vinghelt nodded, giving her a knowing smile. "I, too, enjoyed my youth. If you linger in the Summer Seas long enough, you will hear the stories. But great men live in the present."

"I heartily agree," Shara said, giving him a sly smile.

"The goddess taught me that lesson," Vinghelt continued, eating up her smile. "When she extended her hand to me, I grasped it without hesitation. All fear and doubt fled from me, never to return."

"I have heard you are a man of great faith."

"No, I am a man of great respect. Faith is a belief not based on fact. I have seen the divine with my own eyes."

"I have no doubt."

He grinned. "We are very alike, you and I. In fact, there is something in particular that we share. I too have some knowledge of the mystical."

"I had not heard that, my lord."

"Indeed. It runs strongly in my blood. I have made an extensive study of the lost arts in my travels. I have already passed through the second gate of several paths, but alas, Zelani is not a discipline I have been able to study."

"That is an unfortunate oversight, but I'm sure it could be remedied." She smiled at the prince, matching her breath to his. His emotions washed over her, desperate desires mixed with primal terror.

"Tell me," she said, leaning just close enough for the side of her breast to brush his arm. "Which of the ancient disciplines have you studied?"

He glanced around briefly before meeting her gaze with a relaxed smile that seemed impossible considering the thunderous beating of his heart. "I started along the path of the Necani, but I have branched out into Hyptani and Lowani, which I believe are where my true talents lay."

"Really, and you have passed the second gate in all three?"

"Oh, yes, I eventually hope to walk all eight paths."

"All ten, you mean?"

Shara's gaze fell upon Brezelle, who was working her way through the revelers.

"Of course I meant all ten," Vinghelt corrected himself with a smile.

"It was a pleasure meeting you, my lord," Shara said with a curtsy. "Would you please excuse me? I must visit with young Lady Reignholtz."

Vinghelt looked over his shoulder and spotted Brezelle. "Ah. Well, of course. I have duties to which I must attend, as well."

"Thank you, my lord."

"I look forward to future conversations," Vinghelt said. "As soon as possible. In fact, I would be honored if you would attend an intimate gathering I am having tomorrow night on *Glory of Summer*."

"It sounds divine, my lord. I will see you there." She gave him a winsome look and moved past him.

Leaving the prince staring at her back, she made her way through the crowd toward Brezelle. The young lady was radiant, and Shara wondered if she hadn't stolen a moment or two with the young man who'd serenaded her.

Mikal slid in smoothly next to Shara and matched her stride. "Where's your new prince?" he asked, handing her the drink she'd asked for. "Have you made him a god so soon?"

"Don't be jealous," Shara said with a smile. "It doesn't suit you."

She took a sip of the wine and continued toward Brezelle, scanning the crowd for the cowled albino. She couldn't see him anywhere.

"Are we leaving already?" Mikal asked, following her.

"No, I'm just anxious to find out how our young Queen Brezelle is enjoying her reign."

Brezelle spotted Shara, and her face lit up. She worked her way over, and the three of them created a little circle in the crush of people.

"Sorry I lost you," Brezelle said. She was quite tipsy, and her green eyes glistened as if the rum was leaking out of them. "I lost track of the time, looked up, and you were gone."

"No apologies," Shara assured her. "You were obviously chasing an inspiration. Where is your paramour now?"

"Alas," Brezelle said, "he was easily exhausted. I was forced to ..." She trailed off in midsentence as a hush crept over the crowd.

All three of them turned to see Lord Reignholtz striding across the deck, his gaze locked on his daughter. The revelers around him backed up to make room for the Summer Prince. Brezelle took a sharp breath at the sight of her father, but stood her ground as he approached.

Reignholtz drew abreast of them and spared a cool glance for Shara before addressing his daughter.

"I thought we had already discussed your attendance of tonight's festivities."

Brezelle seemed suddenly smaller. Her mouth tightened into a line, and she looked at the deck for a moment. But then she straightened, her eyes flashing. "I am Waveborn, Father. I have every right to be at the Floating Palace."

The muscles worked in Reignholtz's jaw. A score of people stood nearby, pretending not to eavesdrop. "I will not discuss this here, Brezelle," he said in a carefully modulated voice. "We will continue this conversation aboard *Laughing Breeze.*"

Brezelle and her father faced off for an agonizing moment. Finally, Brezelle opened her mouth to speak—

"My dear Lord Reignholtz," Vinghelt's rich voice interrupted them. He strode forward, and Mikal took a step back. "What a pleasant surprise. I must confess that I did not expect to see you here tonight. You should have told me if you wanted to apologize for your unseemly outbursts last season."

The crowd dropped all pretence of not listening and turned to face the two princes. Those in the back stood on tiptoes to get a better view.

Reignholtz flicked a gaze at Vinghelt, narrowed his eyes, then looked back at his daughter. "Brezelle, come with me—"

"I don't think she wants to go with you, Lord Reignholtz," Vinghelt continued. "You seem to have lost touch with a great many things, including the heart of your own daughter."

Brezelle reached for her sword, but her father motioned with his hand for her to stop.

Vinghelt sported his ready smile, but his teeth were clenched, his grin stiff. His chin elevated, and he looked down his sharp nose at Reignholtz.

Reignholtz returned the gaze. His blue eyes shone like sapphires, hard and mirthless.

"I suppose the depth of your arrogance should no longer surprise me," Reignholtz said in a dark voice. "But you've been lying to our faces and dissembling behind our backs for so long that nothing surprises me anymore."

Vinghelt snorted. "Tell me, do you still support the folly of abandoning our interests in the Summer Deserts?"

"We should never have been there in the first place, and we shouldn't be there now."

Vinghelt looked to the others around him, shrugging helplessly. "Why do the weak always hold such contempt for the strong? Why do they hate those who are fighting and dying for their liberty?"

"You have no idea what true strength is," Reignholtz hissed.

Vinghelt sneered. "I am not the traitor who cozens Physendrian terrorists who would burn every ship in the Summer Fleet to the waterline."

"A difficult feat, truly, with your boot on their necks."

"Someone must fight the difficult battles."

"While others go where the gold is."

Vinghelt began to remove his glove, but Reignholtz already had his in hand. He tossed it to the deck on top of Vinghelt's boot.

"I call you a liar, a false prince, and a traitor to the Eternal Summer," Reignholtz said. "And I call upon Fessa of the Deep to bring you to justice."

Vinghelt's eyes blazed. He ripped his glove off and threw it at Reignholtz's feet. "You'll have your duel, Reignholtz, and Fessa herself will show who the traitor is."

"Indeed she will," Reignholtz said, turned, and left. Brezelle, red with shame and rage, gave Shara a quick glance before following him.

Vinghelt turned to the crowd, projecting his voice across the now-silent revelers. "Please have some more wine. Eat! Dance! Verse and steel will illuminate the truth soon enough, but for tonight, let us enjoy the freedom that our valiant soldiers have bought us."

The crowd began departing. It was difficult to judge their mood, but the festive roar slowly returned, louder than before. Vinghelt bowed low to Shara before joining his retinue.

Shara watched Reignholtz and Brezelle until they climbed down between two ships and disappeared from view. She didn't envy Brezelle's boat trip back to *Laughing Breeze*.

Mikal sidled up next to her. His smile seemed a bit stiff. "So, you shall see a real duel after all. What did you think of our dear Prince Vinghelt?"

"I found him a bit underwhelming. Are you sure that is the man Lawdon is so worried about?"

"Oh yes. He is all but King of the Summer Seas, the spider at the center of the web."

"He looked more like the fly at the center of the web."

"What?"

"Vinghelt is impeccably polished, but there is no real power in him. If there is a plot, he is only a servant."

Mikal's brow furrowed. "You are certain?"

"Absolutely."

Mikal paused, looked through the crowd after Vinghelt, then glanced back at her. "If he is the servant, then who is the master?"

CHAPTER 14

Jesheks pressed the golden tip of his spiked pinkie sheath into his arm. A crimson pinprick welled up on his white skin. He felt the pain like a fine mist on parched skin. Just a little, just enough to whet his appetite for more.

He rested his fleshy arm upon the edge of the steaming tub so gently that the drop of blood was undisturbed, a tiny spherical ruby of adornment. The water rippled around the drooping nipples of his flabby chest.

A servant knocked on the door.

Jesheks blinked lazily, waiting. He reached outside the door with his awareness, feeling the servant's nervousness. The man didn't want to deliver the box from Physendria to Vinghelt's fearsome and repellent physician. There were rumors that some of the servants who attended the physician were never seen again.

Don't let him get behind me, the servant thought. *Keep the door open. Why isn't he answering?*

Jesheks smiled, waiting. The man knocked again.

Is he dead in there? Please let him be dead. My lord would be better off without—

"Come in," Jesheks said, his fluted voice cutting through the silence.

The servant opened the door, and Jesheks nodded that he may enter. The man looked like an emaciated pelican, overly thin, with loose flaps of skin hanging from his weak chin. His expression was blank, devoid of emotion except for a slight tightening around his eyes as he saw that Jesheks was naked in a tub of hot water.

Disgusting! Fessa of the Deep! How can he even walk by himself?

The man bowed, a box clutched in his hands.

"Close the door, please," Jesheks said.

The man's smooth demeanor faltered.

Fessa, he means to kill me.

He visibly swallowed, flicking a glance to the door.

"You've let in a chill," Jesheks said, closing his eyes as the man's fear flowed to him like a hot breeze, lifting Jesheks's spirits, touching him with little sparks of lightning.

Slowly, as if each move were painful, the servant closed the door behind him. He did not latch it, but Jesheks let that go. For a moment, he considered asking the servant to open the box, just to see his expression. Would he drop its contents onto the deck? Leap away with a shout?

But no. Jesheks was past the days of his "gentle reprimands." He'd spent a great deal of time in those years replacing servants, and such petty games were for the benighted.

Use your pain or it will use you.

He'd first heard those words when he was still a slave, eavesdropping on his former master chastising an apprentice for letting his anger and ego get the better of him. The old archmage's wisdom was lost on the hotheaded apprentice, but Jesheks listened from the shadows and listened well. After years of waiting, nurturing his anger and pain, Jesheks had stepped into the light and killed them both, apprentice and master, and became ruler of their bones and their legacy.

"You may approach," Jesheks said softly.

The servant hesitated. His head twitched as though he would look at the door, but his feet moved forward.

"Set it here," he said, indicating the towel stand next to the tub. Jesheks touched the servant's hand as he set it down, smiled as the man's heart lurched.

The man yanked his hand back. "I'm s-sorry, sir. I slipped."

Ah, the lies of the benighted.

"Of course you did." Jesheks looked into the man's eyes. They were the terrified eyes of a rabbit gazing at a cobra. And just like that rabbit, the servant paused, transfixed, his little heart thumping inside his chest. His thoughts dried up.

"You may go," Jesheks said, and the man stumbled backward as if cut from invisible strings. He lunged for the door and caught his balance as he reached it, only then remembering his dignity. He drew himself up straight, but his hand did not leave the latch.

Clearing his throat, the servant turned and asked, "Will you require anything else, sir?"

"I have everything I need."

"As you wish, sir."

"Please close the door tightly when you leave."

"Yes, sir."

The servant left, gratefully latching the door with himself on the other side.

May you die a thousand deaths, devilspawn.

It was nice to be appreciated, Jesheks thought, smiling as his pudgy fingers caressed the top of the driftwood box.

His thoughts drifted for a moment like the swirls of steam from his bath. He thought back to the previous night. Of course, it was not wholly unexpected. It had been foreseen that the Ohndarien Council might send one of their own down to the Summer Cities to see what was happening. A Child of the Seasons, most likely, a Sister of the Council, perhaps. Or even one of the vaunted Zelani. But never did Jesheks dream that Shara-lani would come herself.

He certainly thought Issefyn would have sent word if Shara was heading in his direction. Was the old woman playing games with him? He would have to talk with her about that during their next conversation. It would be something their mistress would want to know.

Despite this new development, Issefyn would no doubt have Ohndarien's locks open when the time came, just as Jesheks would have the fleet ready. If the council truly suspected what was happening, they would have sent more than one Zelani, even if that Zelani was the mistress herself.

Still . . .

It changed the playing board, and Jesheks would have to keep his attention that much more acute. Vinghelt certainly couldn't be trusted to hold a steady course. Ever since that night on the beach five years ago, when Jesheks transformed the drunken coward into a glorious tyrant, Vinghelt had proven to be a particularly difficult sheep to herd. The man certainly relished his "divine mandate," but he lacked the wit or skill to use it. Jesheks smiled at the prospect of telling the man the truth about his little meeting with his goddess before leaving the prince to choke on his new crown.

Jesheks was anxious to begin his new life on Efften, rediscovering the lost secrets of the City of Dreams. But every moment, every lesson was another opportunity to make oneself stronger. And Jesheks supposed he would think back fondly on this time in the Summer Seas, if he thought back on it at all.

Turning his gaze back to the box, he touched the corner, ran his finger along the lid. It was as dry as tinder, inlaid with gold designs. Gently, Jesheks lifted the lid and peered inside. It was filled with the twisted, translucent bodies of a half dozen dead scorpions. Frowning, Jesheks scooted their dead little limbs aside with his pointed pinkie sheath.

One of them moved lethargically, and Jesheks smiled. Good. He would have liked more of them to survive the journey from Physendria, but one was enough. One was more than enough.

A Physendrian red scorpion could kill an ordinary man within a minute. But Jesheks was no ordinary man.

He offered his hand to the little creature and watched it crawl uncertainly across his white flesh. The scorpion held its deadly stinger poised over its back as it explored its surroundings. No doubt the creature could smell the water like a heady perfume. Did such a gross amount of water repel or attract a creature so inured to the heat of the desert?

Another knock sounded at the door.

Ah, the beautiful Natshea.

He scooped his prize carefully off his hand and let it crawl back into the driftwood coffin with its fellows. *Later, my friend. We will continue our dance soon.*

"Come in," he said.

Natshea Vystholtz flung the door open. It swung wide, slowing to a stop just short of the wall. Before entering the room, she withdrew her dagger and stabbed it into the doorjamb at eye level.

"How many holes do I have in my doorjamb now?"

She closed the door and leaned against it, cocking a foot up behind her and crossing her arms. "Only one. I hit the same mark every time."

He did not doubt it. A dagger in the door had become Natshea's calling card, telling all the Summer Seas where she chose to hang her hat for the moment. If a duelist was seeking to deliver a challenge, he need not hunt for her. Everyone else was well warned to stay away. The meeting was private.

Natshea's thin, gray breeches stretched tight over her smooth hips, and thigh-high boots of soft black leather made her legs look impossibly long. A black belt trapped the billowing gold blouse about her narrow waist, and she wore black leather gauntlets at her wrists.

Tall and long-limbed, Natshea had the body that blademasters dreamed of. She was the pride of her little-known shiphome. The Vystholtzs were invited to every major event and given seats of honor because of Natshea. Her long-muscled arms had six inches of reach on most other duelists, and her reflexes were already legend. Most importantly, she had an eye for weakness. She was undefeated for the last two years running.

Most duelists were men, but since Natshea began making a name for herself five years ago, the Waveborn lords had a devil of a time keeping their daughters interested in marrying well and breeding sons.

But when Jesheks looked at Natshea, he didn't see the prodigy of the Summer Seas. Natshea was a work-in-progress, a ship half-built. He had recognized her worth when he first came to the Summer Cities, but a worth of a different sort. She had been a skittish young woman, difficult to approach. He'd arranged to be alone with her as soon as possible and confirmed his first impression.

No, he did not see a legendary poet duelist when he looked at Natshea. He saw his newly made Necani apprentice, barely a minnow in the waters of the Great Ocean. The young woman was still raw, but she had a chance to be everything that Vinghelt was not.

It had taken over a year to finally work his way into the fold of her trust, and almost another year to make her see what she really needed. And still, the battle was waged every time they talked. She resisted the difficult path, but her eyes were beginning to open. Her arms were slowly embracing him.

He had already given her three lessons in the Necani form. Her aptitude was remarkable. Not only did she have an exquisite need for his wisdom—as he had surmised from their first meeting—but she had an amazing threshold for the lessons. That was deliciously unexpected. You could never quite tell who would thrive from the lessons of Necani and who would fold. This willowy creature was no stranger to pain. She seemed equally ravenous for both the giving and receiving of the most primal form of ani.

She sketched a deep bow, and Jesheks smiled.

"I am so pleased to see you," he said.

She rose to her full height—just over six feet tall—and raised an eyebrow as she walked closer. "Yet I am the one who is getting the eyeful."

She glanced at his obese white body, and he detected no revulsion from her. Yet she hid within her little jests as a virgin behind thick layers of clothing.

"There are many different things to see."

"Indeed, and yet—"

"Take off your clothes," he said.

A flicker of a frown crossed her face, but her easy smile returned in an instant. "Really, sir." She nodded toward the door through which she'd come. "You are so forward. I have many—"

"Take them off," he said, closing his eyes and sinking deeper into the tub. A low buzzing filled his ears as he sent his awareness toward her. He did not pry into her thoughts as he had with the servant, but he listened to her body.

Her heart beat faster. Sweat oozed from the pores of her skin, prickling her scalp.

"I daresay you ought to reconsider," she said in her purring voice, still seeking refuge in her little games. She sauntered closer to put a hand on the towel stand, convinced that she was this person, this flippant, cocksure duelist who could handle everything. "If I shed my clothes, I doubt that you could resist me. We have your reputation to think of. Command me to leave instead, I beg you, before the scandal spreads from this room like wildfire."

Ah, the lies of the benighted. The might of an armada is at your fingertips, yet you insist on playing with toy boats.

"You may leave if you wish, but you will never be welcome here again. If you wish to learn what I have to teach, I suggest you unbuckle your sword and remove your clothes."

Natshea's smile faded, and she turned her head away. She stood up, licking her lips as she glanced at the door. He smelled the fear, acrid and desperate.

That's it, Jesheks thought. That was the little girl he was looking for.

Her nostrils flared, and she breathed harder. Her hand twitched. She glanced back at him, fury in her eyes. In that delicious instant, Jesheks did not know whether she would slash him with her sword or do as he had bid.

Her hands moved like lightning, attacking the belt with fervor. The long-sword dropped to the deck. Her breathing came hard as she pulled the tunic over her head, revealing small, round breasts. She pulled her boots off one at a time, gracefully standing on one leg for each. But her nostrils worked like a lathered horse as she paused, her fingers at the laces of her breeches.

Jesheks said nothing. His gaze stayed on her eyes.

"What if someone comes in?" she asked.

"Then someone does."

"I cannot—"

"There are many things that you cannot. I am ascertaining what you can."

Swallowing, she undid the laces slowly, fingers shaking. "I have . . ." she started to say, her voice raw. "There are . . ." she tried again, breathing heavily over her words as her fingers paused. "I was not prepared for this."

"I know. Continue."

With a shiver, she pushed the tight breeches down her legs and stepped out of them. She turned her head sideways, as though she were a slave offering herself for inspection.

She had the caramel skin of the Summermen, and her long limbs were perfectly shaped, the softness of youth combined with the muscles of a warrior. Jesheks let his gaze linger on every part of her. Her flat stomach was graced with the tiny nub of a protruding belly button. Below her navel, Jesheks paused. Her curly, black pubic hair shadowed the space between her legs. The insides of her thighs were covered with scars, two columns of perfect, inch-long marks stacked one above the other.

Her hands clutched the outside of her legs, as she forced herself not to hide the self-inflicted wounds the way a modest woman might long to cover her breasts.

Ah, my pretty duelist. Don't you realize why you were chosen? Pain is no stranger to you. It has been your master for many years. We will make it your servant.

"Please join me in the tub." Jesheks nodded toward the water.

Natshea's jaw muscles worked, but she did not hesitate again. She dipped one long, slender leg in the water, gracefully shifted her weight and sub-merged the other, sitting opposite him. The waterline rose up her long body to just beneath her small breasts. Inevitably, her gaze was drawn to the place between his legs.

Jesheks's belly had grown so large that he hadn't seen the remnants of his genitals in years, but he remembered that sloppy, puckered scar in exquisite detail.

She settled into the water. Her wide gaze locked on his eyes, and he studied her.

"Why are you frightened?" he asked.

"Because I don't know what's going to happen next."

He nodded, smiling. Her honesty did her honor.

"You realize," he said, "that the moment you fear, the moment you long for, is never going to happen."

Her gaze flicked to the ragged flap of skin between his legs, then back to his face. "No, of course not."

"I have no sexual feelings for you whatsoever."

"Yes, I know that," she said, and her lips pressed more firmly together.

"Yet it hurts you when I say it."

She swallowed, nodded. "Yes, it does."

Jesheks let the awkward silence fall, looking deep into her gray eyes, wait-ing for her to respond. When she didn't, he spoke.

"If you have a question, ask it."

"How did it happen to you?"

"Ah, through pain, my lovely duelist. Through the burning threshold that brings us into the world and takes us out, and governs every wisp of air in be-tween." He drew a deep breath. "My parents' identities are a mystery I've never been able to unravel," he began. "I suspect I was born in Upper Kherif shortly after the civil war, very likely a product of a soldier's brutal desire."

He paused, watching her expression, then shrugged. "Because of my unusual appearance, I was sold at birth to a traveling merchant who dealt in exotic animals. Not long after, the merchant's caravan was raided by a petty warlord who called himself the King of Upper Kherif. At that time, there were many brigands who claimed that title, and this man was no different.

"The brigand's men were horrified when they saw me, a tiny white infant with red eyes. They were ready to kill me, but the king's witch stepped forward. She claimed that I was a ghost child who could confer power over life and death and was not to be killed. She promised the king I would make a fearsome bodyguard one day. No other man could boast a ghost warrior to protect his tents."

Jesheks paused, spread his white hands along the top of the water. "So you see? I was saved by fear and superstition at the earliest moment of my life. Of course, the king was not easily convinced, but he certainly saw the effect I had on his men. Eventually, he listened to the witch's words ... along with certain other persuasions that women have used upon men since the beginning of time." Jesheks smiled.

"I have no memory of that woman. Fever took her when I was still a baby, but I was later told that she had lost her own child and that she nursed me from her own breast. Still, even after she was gone, her words lingered in the mind of the king. I was allowed to live, thrive even, in the band of raiders. I was treated no better and no worse than any other child who is raised among violent men. My duty lay in standing next to the king whenever he entertained guests, staring into the eyes of strangers until they grew frightened and looked away.

"This life ended shortly after one of the king's raids. He returned wounded, with a deep gash in his leg. Despite the care of his witches and healers, the wound began to fester. In his delirium, he threatened to kill them all if they did not find a cure. I clearly remember the king pointing an accusing finger at me, screaming that I was supposed to give him power over life and death."

Jesheks shrugged. "They were all terrified, the king was not known for making idle threats. So one of the witch women spoke a benighted lie. She said the king must take the strength of the ghost for his own. She promised that if he cut off my genitals and burned them, he could cheat death, and his wound would be healed by morning.

"The king leapt upon me, pinning my chest under his knee. He drew a dagger and cut my genitals off with three clumsy slashes."

Natshea's hand had tightened on the edge of the tub, her knuckles white.

Jesheks blinked lazily. "The king died that night, screaming in a fever, my burnt cock in his hand. His last command sealed the fate of the witch women who had counseled him. They were slain at dawn."

"And you?" Natshea asked.

"My life began again that next morning."

Jesheks looked into her eyes, seeing thoughts of her own childhood swirling there.

"What did you learn from my little story?" he asked.

"That we are very similar, you and I."

"Perhaps. Before we go any further, though, I need to know why you came back to me."

She cleared her throat and narrowed her eyes, but she didn't say anything.

"Are you in love with me?"

She didn't answer.

"You are in love with me," he said, nodding. "I hurt you, and you love me. Why is that?"

Natshea wetted her lips with her tongue, frowning as she searched for the answer. "I . . ." she started, "I've seen the power you wield. If pain is the path to greatness, I would gladly walk that path to the end."

"Why? What do you need that much power for? What do you intend to do with it?"

"I have my reasons."

"I've found that those who hoard food were once very hungry. And those who hunger for power were once helpless."

She flinched, broke gazes with him.

"Who hurt you?" he asked softly. "Where did he hurt you?"

Her jaw clenched, but she did not answer.

"Did he hurt you there?" Beneath the water, his foot shifted, and he touched her cunt with his toe.

With a violent splash, she leapt from the tub, spraying water everywhere. Momentarily blinded, Jesheks calmly blinked the droplets away. He wiped a fat finger across his eyelids and opened them. Natshea leveled her sword at his face. She stood, quivering like a drowned cat, her flesh raised with goose pimples.

"Never . . ." she whispered lethally. "Never do that."

"Who made you hate being touched there?" he asked calmly, ignoring the sword.

"I'm not going to talk about that."

"But you must. Shame. Fear. Doubt. These are all walls between you and your power. Your pain must move through you. Your anger must move through you. Don't run from them. Relish them. If you deny your pain, if you run from it rather than embracing it, you become its victim instead of its master."

She shook her head. "You lie. You're trying to own me just like ... You're trying to use me."

Jesheks looked at her kindly. "Don't you see how close you are?" he whispered. "Look at those scars on your legs." He nodded at them.

Her implacable visage softened, and her lip trembled. Her free hand went to the insides of her thighs, brushing the dozens of white, raised lines.

"How many nights have you spent with a blade? Learning. Growing. Finding your power."

Her sword drooped, the point touching the ground next to her naked toes.

"Go ahead," he urged in a conspiratorial whisper. "Make the cut. Feel it."

The blade rose between her legs, touched the inside of her thigh. She took a deep breath and let it out in a long shudder as she dragged the blade forward. Skin split. Blood wet the blade.

"You are so close, my child. So close to discovering what is on the far side of your pain."

She nodded, mesmerized by the streaks of blood crawling slowly down her leg.

"Let's take that step together and find out what's on the far side."

"What do I have to do?" she asked, her voice thick. Her shoulders curled forward slightly, relaxing.

"Look at me. Look into my eyes. There, that's right. Now climb back into the tub and tell me. Tell me everything."

She crouched and set her blade gently on the floor. Taking measured steps toward the tub, she lifted her legs and joined him once again in the hot water.

"Was it your father? Did he hurt you this way?"

"No." She shook her head.

He waited patiently for her to gather her courage. The old wounds were the hardest to reopen. The old blood was the most reluctant to flow.

"The dueling master who taught me as a small child," she finally said.

"Just tell me what happened."

"He enjoyed it. I know he enjoyed it. The punishments. The beatings. For stupidity, clumsiness, laziness. He did it with all of his students, but especially with me. Especially with me." She took a deep breath. "I gave him little reasons, little excuses, and he took them. He took every one."

She shuddered and continued with her tale.

❄

Hours later, Natshea stood at his open door, utterly exhausted but with eyes filled with love. She had shared her story with him, a tale no greater or lesser than any other, and very similar to his own. He had responded by giving her a task that would propel her into the very heart of her pain.

"Remember," he told her, as she hovered in the doorway, terrified to leave. "A slave to pain responds with hatred. A master responds to it any way she chooses. You have been given a gift, an endless well of power to draw from. You must make that pain your own. Use it. Learn to wield it like the blade you carry at your side."

She nodded slowly, lost in the darkness, doubting the light waiting before her.

"Prepare yourself. Our lord will have need of you soon, but you can leave just after your next duel. Do as I say, and you will soon find yourself in an entirely new world," he said, sending her the encouragement she sought.

She smiled, feeding on his ani. With a deft snatch, she pulled the dagger from the doorjamb and sheathed it, closing the door behind her.

Jesheks felt a twinge of sadness at her departure. The task was probably beyond her. A true Necani master was one in a million. Jesheks let out a long breath. But he would keep cracking open oysters until he found that pearl.

And yet what a delight it would be if this one actually succeeded in her task. Perhaps she would eventually try to kill him just as he had killed his own master. Wouldn't that prove interesting?

Setting the future aside, Jesheks turned back to the present moment. He carefully lifted the lid of the driftwood box and withdrew the only red scorpion that had survived. Leaning back in the cooling water, he let the creature crawl back and forth across his hands.

Necani was a difficult form of magic to master. If Jesheks was to expand his art, he had to continually push himself beyond his own limits. But it was so difficult to treat the mind to greater and greater ecstasies of pain without destroying the body in the process.

The agony caused by this scorpion's sting was legendary. By all reports, the venom caused a wound to swell so fast the skin burst, and the muscles ripped themselves off the bone.

The flush of power grew within his body, a cold sweat seeped onto his forehead. He sucked the fear back into himself and embraced it.

He picked the creature up by the tail. Its stinger twitched between his fingers, searching for something to strike.

His heart pounded, blood rushed in his veins, and Jesheks considered where to let the wriggling little creature land its strike. Perhaps the nipple?

He brought the scorpion to his chest, letting its pincers latch on to his pale skin. He began to close his eyes, then stopped.

No.

Pulling the scorpion from his chest, he opened his mouth and let it crawl inside. His body shivered. Its tiny feet skittered across his tongue.

And slowly, ever so slowly, he bit down.

CHAPTER 15

Ossamyr leaned back in the little sailboat as Reef steered across the glassy sea. For the hundredth time, she looked at the bevel-edged bottle of Siren's Blood she was supposed to drink. Multicolored lights swirled through the bottle as she held it up to the afternoon sun. The mythical wine would have made an extravagant addition to any wealthy merchant's dayroom, splashing swirling rainbows across the painted walls and exotic carpets.

"I've had Siren's Blood before," Ossamyr said. "Phandir served it at our wedding."

Reef watched her with his golden eyes. Strangely, over the last few days she had spent with him, she had become fond of that gaze. When she had first met him, his strange eyes held only menace. But considering the price this man paid for his beliefs, it was easy to see why he was so fierce with strangers. Now that she had been to the other side, his gaze made her feel safe. Reef was like a shield between you and your enemies. He would stop at nothing to protect you.

"That wasn't Siren's Blood," the Islander said, leaning on the tiller as his little ship cut through the water.

She turned a wry smile on him. "Wasn't it?"

"You had the Gold Islanders' brew." He flicked his head to the side, spitting over the side of the ship, then looked back at her. "Brewed for profit, spilled for coin. They brew their swill from a long-dead strain of Siren's Blood that lost the spark of truth years ago. The lights in their wine are extracted from unhatched songbirds. But the lights in that bottle are the souls of the fallen, the life essence of those destroyed by Efften. It is their story you will hear."

"So I'm drinking stale dead people?" She arched an eyebrow.

Reef grunted. "Your jokes are the voice of your fear."

Ossamyr snorted. "Well, you've given me every reason to be afraid, with all your veiled threats and dire predictions."

She looked back at the bottle and imagined the swirling lights floating around inside her belly, moving up her spine and into her brain where they would forever change her.

And possibly drive her mad.

"The fear is natural," Reef said, closing his eyes as he breathed in the salty air. "We will wait until you are ready."

Ossamyr had a sudden urge to crack open the bottle and pour it over his head, but she held back and let the feeling pass. She'd been the one who asked him how they created the light emmeria. If this was his way of teaching her, she'd see the lesson through to the end.

They were a couple of hours from Slaver's Bay when Reef sailed around to the back side of a tiny island that didn't look any different than a hundred others in these waters. The sun had just begun to set as they approached the jagged lump of volcanic rock with a tuft of green vegetation perched on top. Reef steered their little boat into a narrow gap between two cliffs that she never would have found without him. They sailed between black crags dripping with flowered vines of deep blues, oranges, and reds. Ossamyr couldn't stop grinning as they slipped through the narrow cleft into a sheltered lagoon with a small white sand beach. It was truly enchanting, vibrant and full of life.

If any other man had brought her here, she would have assumed he was planning a seduction. And by the Nine, it would have worked, too.

Ossamyr let her gaze linger on the hard, muscled body of the man across from her. It was a pity that Reef didn't think that way. Ever since she had the news that Brophy had awoken, Ossamyr's hunger for life had reawakened. Food tasted better. Sunsets were more beautiful than she remembered. The smiles of strangers lingered in her mind, and her own laughter came more easily. Her magic was stronger than ever, rushing through her in an overflowing fountain. She had already spent a few nights wondering what it would be like to have those massive arms wrapped around her, but Reef seemed to view sex as something that could wait until after he was done saving the world.

Reef reached the shore and leapt into the surf. He yanked the little sailboat two yards up the beach with the first tug, even farther with the second. Ossamyr followed him onto soft white sand.

She looked around at the turquoise lagoon surrounded by ragged cliffs draped in flowers. "By the Nine, this place is beautiful."

"Almost every place is, you look at it right," he said. He stumped up the beach, sat down in the sand, and put his hands out behind him. The surf rolled up the beach in tiny curls, breaking softly in a ruffle of blue and white. The coarse white sand was like nothing she had ever seen. It was made from bits of polished shell that shifted underneath Ossamyr's sandals. She slipped back a half a step for every step she took forward.

She kicked off her sandals and sat down next to Reef. He watched her calmly as she held the bottle up to the light. "What will I see?" she asked.

"The truth."

She smiled. "Is there a reason why you can't answer a simple question? Do you people take a perverse pleasure in being cryptic?"

Reef's hard features did not soften in the least. "If I gave you words to describe what would happen, your mind would simply twist those words into an expectation. Then you would try to make that expectation come to pass." He shook his head. "You'd miss any true understanding."

"And what am I supposed to understand?"

"More than you do now. Perhaps the only thing that truly matters."

She nodded sagely. "That certainly answers all my questions."

He shrugged. "You don't have to drink it," he said, closing his eyes and turning his face toward the setting sun.

Everything was so curt and final with the Silver Islanders. In Reef's mind, there was a black line right down the middle of all questions. Either you were on the right side of that line, or you weren't. She had been on the wrong side of his line once. She didn't particularly want to go back.

Ossamyr paused. The sarong she wore tickled her calves as it flapped in the breeze. "Let me rephrase my question," she said. "If I drink this, will I die? Or go insane?"

"People do not die from Siren's Blood."

"I've heard of some who did."

"Only indirectly. The drink is not poisonous, and I won't let any physical harm come to you. That is why I am here."

"You didn't address the insanity part."

He shrugged. His short-sleeved tunic was open at the throat, draw cords hanging lazily down. The breeze ruffled the black hair on his chest. "You will be changed forever, one way or another. You won't, you can't, see the world the same ever again."

"What's in it?"

"It doesn't matter."

"You can't tell me?"

"It won't answer your question. You want to know what you're getting into. There is no way to know."

"Humor me."

"Wine stock. Herbs. Fruit juice."

"And dead souls."

He nodded. "And that."

Ossamyr looked back at the bottle. She wondered, despite all of her joking, despite his calm demeanor, if he would let her leave this little island alive if she chose not to drink. How long would he wait for her to open it? The man was infernally good at waiting.

But she wasn't.

Twisting the stopper, she broke the wax seal. Reef watched her very carefully, his normally relaxed posture suddenly tense and alert.

She uncorked the bottle. A single light flew out of the neck, zipped silently around her head, then disappeared back inside. "I suppose I'm committed now," she said.

Reef nodded, held out his hand. Furrowing her brow, she started to hand the bottle to him. He shook his head. "The cork."

She handed it to him, and he flung it far out into the lagoon. "For luck," he said, staring into her eyes.

Swallowing hard, she hesitated, then brought the bottle to her lips. "To change," she murmured around the mouth of it. Tipping the bottle back, she let the liquid run into her mouth. A flood of warmth rushed through her, and she gasped. It was just like she remembered, except more.

She looked at Reef and giggled. "It's so good!" She shook her head trying to clear the buzzing in her ears. "You could make a fortune with this stuff."

Reef's gaze remained steady, his features as impassive as before. "Drink it quickly. You have a long night ahead of you."

She tipped the bottle back again, taking a long, deep gulp. Her head spun, and the ground moved underneath her. She fell back on the sand. Something warm and firm gripped her hand, and she looked over to see Reef holding her hand over the bottle.

"You almost spilled it. You must drink it all," he said. She upended the bottle, drinking and drinking and drinking until there was no more.

Her head spun, and she stared up at the blue blue sky, giggling. Clouds glowed overhead like yellow-orange candle flames soaking up the rays of the setting sun. The warmth rushed through her body in a glowing river, and she felt like she had swallowed a sunrise.

"This is the best ever!" she shouted, jumping to her feet and sprinting down the soft sand into the surf. She stopped when she was knee deep in the gentle waves and whooped for joy.

Spinning around, she looked back the way she had come. Reef sat in the same place. The air rippled around him as if he was radiating intense heat. With a laugh, she sprinted back up the beach and fell to her knees in front of him, put both of her hands on his huge forearm. "I see what you are doing. You were just waiting to get me out here all alone, weren't you?"

He watched her calmly, unmoving as an old oak with children cavorting around its roots. She leaned forward and kissed him on the mouth.

"I'm not afraid," she said. "I'm not afraid anymore."

Putting his strong hands on her shoulders, he set her gently back on her heels.

"You should be," he said, his deep oak voice thrumming through her body. "You will be."

❄

Something touched Ossamyr's face, and she shook her head, pushed it away. "No," she groaned, curling into a ball. "Leave me alone."

Reef shook her again. "Come on," his deep voice pounded on her brain. "It's time to go back."

"No," she whispered. "Let me sleep."

"You've slept for two days. It's time to go."

She opened her gummy eyes and tried to focus on the object gripped tight in her hand. She was still clutching the bottle of Siren's Blood, as dry as the sand beneath her.

Reef helped her sit up. She shook her head and looked around, the bright sun stinging her eyes. Her naked skin was a sullen red, burned by the sun and covered in scratches and scrapes packed with sand.

"Am I . . ." she said. "This is real?"

"Yes."

She nodded. "I thought I died."

"You nearly did."

Ossamyr fought to clear her head. Some memories were coming back. Others slithered away like quicksilver through her fingers. "Where are my clothes?" she croaked.

"You took them off in the ocean."

Yes . . . The swimming, under the water, looking up at the moon. It had been glorious. She'd never wanted to leave.

She lay down in the sand, but he sat her back up.

"Let me go," she groaned.

"No." He put a leather pouch to her lips and she drank deep. The cool water stung her parched throat.

"Did the spirits speak with you?" he asked.

Ossamyr grimaced as another flood of memories came fast and hard. The last of it. The last part. Her heart beat faster, and her breath came in gasps as she remembered. With an effort of will, she calmed herself, eased her breathing, and got her heart under control.

"You reached the truth," he said.

She nodded. Her mind spun with the images, the sights, the smells of agony and rage. The spirits had taken her to the beginning of time. She'd looked upon the face of Oh, shared his triumph, his deprivation, his redemption, and betrayal. She saw the birth of Efften; saw the ancient secret hiding within the glittering towers. She fell into the endless well of despair, shared a hundred screaming deaths, and felt her own heart stop beating time and time again.

"You understood what you saw?"

"How could I not?" she whispered. "I was there with them. I know what they're hiding. I know how they died."

"Then you realize that we have no choice."

She hung her head, pressing her forehead to her knees. Tears dripped from her cheeks onto the sand. She rocked her head against the hard bones underneath her skin. Life was so fragile, so easily swept away.

"The Awakened Child cannot reach Efften."

"I know. I know." Ossamyr pressed her head against her knees, hoping to drive the pounding headache away. By the Nine! She couldn't keep the images out of her head. She knew who the voice in the black emmeria was, knew exactly what would happen if he was ever set free. How could anyone live with that future bearing down on them?

The Nightmare Battle was nothing but a skirmish. The real war hadn't even started. And Arefaine was leading Brophy right into that storm. Efften's most dangerous secret still lay within her silver towers, waiting for some fool to stumble upon it and set it free.

"You'll help us kill her?" Reef asked, crushing her hand in his.

"Of course," she rasped. "Of course I will."

CHAPTER 16

M other."

Issefyn turned her head, heavy with sleep. She was so tired.

"Mother, wake up. They're coming for you."

Her mouth was painfully dry. The covers were warm and soft over her body, and there was nothing she would rather do than continue sleeping.

Her dreams shifted between the past and future, between who she had been and who she would become. Images of her unlocking the towers on Efften mixed with the thoughts of a nine-year-old girl as she returned to one of the happiest days of her childhood, the day she awoke and discovered her true self, her rightful place in the world.

Issefyn could hardly contain her excitement when her father was summoned before the king. Her slaves dressed her in her finest feathered gown for her first visit to the underground palace.

Her parents were fighting again, refusing to speak to each other as they entered the Catacombs, but Issefyn wouldn't let them ruin her perfect day. Hulking guards ushered them into a tiny room to await their royal audience. Her father kept his eyes on the ground, and his breathing came in shallow little pants like a sickly old man. He looked pleadingly once at Issefyn's mother, but she refused to meet his eyes. She stared at the wall with cold fury, her lips pressed tightly together.

The entire family was finally ushered into the king's presence. The throne room was immense. Golden carvings of The Nine glittered on the ceiling. Hundreds of Physendrian nobility fell silent when the three of them entered the room. With disapproving looks, they parted and backed up against the walls, leaving an aisle down the center of the long, narrow room on either side of a crimson carpet.

At the far end of the carpet sat the king, a young boy barely older than

Issefyn. He wore a magnificent cloak of red and gold feathers that draped over his shoulders and down the sides of his golden throne.

Issefyn's entire family knelt before the monarch just in front the plush red carpet. She was suddenly very frightened as everyone in the room looked at them with such disdain. She reached over to grab her mother's skirt, but her mother swatted Issefyn's hand away.

"You may approach the king," the steward announced. His voice echoed in the long, silent room.

Her father started to get up, but one of the Ape guards shoved him back down. Left with no choice, he began to crawl forward. Two servants began rolling up the carpet just before he reached it. Below the carpet, the floor was unpolished volcanic stone, jagged and uneven.

Her father hesitated for a moment before continuing onto the sharp stone, wincing with every step. Before he was halfway down the room, he was leaving a bloody trail behind him.

He finally reached the steps at the base of the throne. The young king leaned over and whispered something in her father's ear then waved him away. Her father mumbled an apology and began crawling back.

As he crawled back to them, an overwhelming hatred exploded in Issefyn's heart. She looked at the king, chatting with the people around him, pretending her father didn't exist. She looked at her father, hobbling forward, shrunken with shame. She could barely look at him. She despised his weakness, his incompetence.

She turned to the king, sitting on his throne of gold, and knew that she would marry him one day. She would stand at his side, share his bed, feed him delicacies from her plate. She would perfect the secrets of Efften her mother was teaching her and make them her own. She would dazzle the Physendrian nobles and make them her own. She would make this kingdom her own. She would make this world her own. And they would all crawl before her.

Issefyn tossed in her sleep, clutching the black containment stone to her chest.

"Mother."

She opened her crusty eyes, squinting in the bright light of the new day. A cloying stench filled the room, and she wrinkled her nose. Her head pounded. It was difficult to focus, but she pushed the covers from her body and sat up. Victeris stood by the window, a sardonic half smile on his face.

"They're coming for you," he said. "They are already in the school."

He was every inch the slender young man she remembered, from the coal-black hair to the way his delicate fingers rested on his arms.

Issefyn stood on wobbly legs, clutching the containment stone. Glancing down, she found the source of the awful smell. Caleb's bloated body lay sprawled on the floor. The blood from his mangled face had dried on the marble.

"How long have I been asleep?" she mumbled. Her mouth was filled with cotton.

"Mother, listen. You can hear them at the gate."

Her magic was weak, dilute, but she sent her feeble awareness outward, through the door and down the stairs outside the school. Her lip curled in a sneer. Vallia was coming, along with the other Sisters and a half dozen soldiers from the Citadel. The frightened men clutched their swords, their sweaty fingers holding tight to their courage.

They whispered to each other as they crossed the courtyard, but Issefyn could hear them clearly.

"What if the child is making up stories?" Quinn asked, upset at being here. Her head was a turbulent clash of mixed feelings. Ceysin's spell still coated her like the slick film of sex, but her own personality was reasserting itself, rising with a sense of betrayal.

"Baelandra's daughter wouldn't lie about this. If she said she saw a body in the room, she saw a body in the room," Vallia said, her rusty voice filling Issefyn with loathing.

Issefyn opened her eyes, losing the connection. The door to the room hung awkwardly on the lower hinge. The top had been torn from its moorings and dangled by a single bolt. The doorjamb was splintered.

She shook her head. How could she have slept so long?

"They are coming to kill you, Mother," Victeris said, standing by her side again. "Now is the time. I can save you. Open your heart to me."

"No," she whispered, casting about the room. She'd left other cities like this, when they finally discovered what she was doing, but she had always had advance warning through her magic. And now they were in the foyer.

Breathing hard, she tried to clear the fuzziness away, fought to think, but her attention was scattered. She heard the hunger in Victeris's voice. Had he done this? Had he kept her asleep?

She couldn't throw a glamour over herself. There were too many looking specifically for her, and those damned Sisters with their heartstones would pierce the illusion. But the heartstones no longer worked. Or did they? She couldn't remember.

Tucking the containment stone under one arm, Issefyn pushed the bed toward the door. She grunted and shoved with all her might, slamming the door at an angle, overlapping the doorjamb.

"That won't stop them," Victeris said. "Surrender to me, Mother. You were born for this." His voice seemed deeper, darker. His hunger surrounded her.

"No," she said, pushing again at the bed. "Never. You are not my son. My son is dead. All of my sons are dead."

"Perhaps," Victeris said. "But you need me more now than you ever needed your sons."

Vallia's pack of rats reached the stairs. Issefyn heard their footfalls, though they tried to move silently.

"Remember," Vallia murmured. "Do not touch the black stone. That is more important than anything. Touch the stone, and we all die."

Issefyn backed away slowly, looking frantically around the room. She stepped to the window that had been the gate to her son's death. It was too high. She would never survive that jump.

But there was a ledge, just below, a windowsill leading to Caleb's room. Breathing through her fear, she wrapped the stone in her skirt, raised it up, and held either side in her teeth. With a glance at Victeris, she climbed over the windowsill, clung to the ledge, and lowered herself. She willed herself to drop but couldn't make her fingers let go. It was forty feet to the flagstones below.

Victeris leaned his head through the window, a dagger in his hands. "Enough of these games, Mother. It's time for you to join me."

He's not real, she told herself. *He's just in the stone, just in my mind.*

Victeris stabbed her hand with the dagger, and she cried out, dropping the skirt from her mouth. The stone spilled out, and she caught it between the wall and her thighs.

He stabbed her again and again. She winced, but did not let go. *It's phantom pain,* she told herself, *just a phantom.*

The soldiers arrived at the door, pushed it, but it was wedged tight by the bed. They pushed harder, and the bed shuddered.

Issefyn stared at the narrow ledge below. Taking a deep breath, she pushed away from the wall with her toes. The stone fell, and she kicked it through the open window into Caleb's room. She heard it bounce off the desk and roll onto the carpet below.

The bed ground against the flagstones. The door cracked inward again, just as it had when Caleb came to her.

"By the Seasons, what a stench!" one of the soldiers said.

Issefyn let go.

She landed on the ledge. Her knees buckled, and she fell on her belly, half-in, half-out of the window.

With a grunt of effort, she scrambled inside as the soldiers flooded her room above.

Victeris was sitting on a chair by the door, the black stone at his feet. "This won't save you, Mother. You cannot run from that many. You must fight them. You need me to fight them."

Issefyn snatched the containment stone away from him. Its sharp edges bit into her breast.

"Enough, foul shade! I don't need you. I don't need anyone."

Muffled voices drifted from the chamber above.

"I could defeat your enemies for you. Just open your heart to me, and we'll destroy them together."

Issefyn ignored him and centered herself, breathing deep as she gathered her power. She would run for now, flee the city, and return when she'd mastered the black emmeria. This was a temporary setback, nothing more.

She sent power into her legs, into her eyes and ears. She must be ready for anything. She grabbed the door handle and sent her awareness into the stairway outside. She paused, finding something curiously delicious waiting for her.

Baelandra's daughter, Baedellin, crept up the stairway on all fours trying to see what was happening up above.

Issefyn stepped through the door and crept up behind the girl.

"Baedellin," Issefyn whispered. "Sweet child, come here. Auntie Iss has something to show you." The girl spun around, wide-eyed and trembling. She started to run, but Issefyn reached out with her ani and held her.

"Sweet child . . ." Issefyn said. "Touch this black stone for me."

The little redhead reached out a trembling hand, a slave to Issefyn's will. The girl's fingers touched the stone, and a wave of bubbling blackness swept up her arm.

"Good, very good," Issefyn cooed as she watched the girl transform, her blackened flesh contorting and elongating as she swelled to three times her former size. "Now, sweet child, there are a few people I need you to kill for me."

CHAPTER 17

G*lory of Summer* was easily twice the size of any other ship in the Floating Palace, and she still could not contain half of Vinghelt's guests. The crowd spilled onto the surrounding ships, and a small army of servants dressed in gold and black rushed around trying to please everyone.

The prince's ship was built to weather banquets, not storms. She rose four stories above the waterline, the top two decks were open to the night on all sides, and the two lower levels bled torchlight, music, and laughter through their wide-open windows. The highest deck was little more than an ostentatious balcony looking inward on the vast dance floor/dueling space on the level below. The entire ship was dripping in black and gold banners, and every square inch of her was packed with revelers.

Shara and Mikal had found a little spot of calm near the heart of the storm. They leaned against the inner rail on the uppermost deck, surveying the entire party below them.

Shara watched Vinghelt work the crowd. His entire retinue hovered around him, courtiers vying for his attention and bodyguards coolly watching for danger. One woman in particular stood out. She was tall and lean with a light brown braid hanging past her waist, and she seemed thoroughly bored. Shara caught her heavy-lidded gaze for a half second across the distance. The woman's eyes narrowed, and Shara smiled.

The woman was a panther, a stalker, and her bored gaze was all for show. Her emotions swirled with thoughts of Shara. Curiosity and jealousy. The woman knew of her.

"Who is that, and what am I eating?" Shara asked Mikal, indicating the hors d'oeuvre he had just given her.

He chuckled. "Let us answer the easy question first. This delicacy"—he held up the fish—"is fried sea trout. You can only catch them at the eastern edge of the Summer Seas, where the crystal rivers wed the dancing waves."

"But on a stick?"

"Only during formal balls, milady. For the ease of dancing and eating at once."

"I see. And how does one eat it without getting a mouthful of bones?"

"Gently, milady. Gently. If you have a delicate tongue and a light bite, you can strip the flesh without taking the bone. Like so." With a practiced motion, he slid the fish meat into his mouth, began chewing.

She tried it. It was the best fish she had ever tasted, crisp on the outside and succulent within.

"And my first question?" Shara asked.

"That stunning creature you so easily noticed is Natshea Vystholtz, the reason Lord Vinghelt has won every challenge ever issued to him."

"And what do you think of her?"

He laughed. "I think she is quite lovely."

Shara kept watching him, and he sobered for a moment, breaking gazes with her. He took a bite of fish. Then, inevitably, he turned his blue eyes back toward her, his lips twitched in a half smile. "And she is regrettably good with a blade. Very very good."

"I would guess so. She looks tightly wound."

"Natshea?" Mikal said. "The woman is liquid grace."

"That is certainly what she would have everyone believe."

"But she is . . ." Mikal trailed off, then let out a sigh. Shara followed his glance and saw Mikal's mother moving through the crowd, waving her hand-kerchief at them.

Mikal pushed away from the rail. "I shall return in a moment. In the mean-while, enjoy the fish and this idyllic spot while I conspire to prolong my own disinheritance." He headed for the lower level to intercept his mother.

Shara turned her gaze back on the crowd, feeling a cool touch on the back of her neck, a light breath of wind before a storm. She kept her eye on one specific person, a shocking blot of black and white among the colorful, strut-ting Waveborn. He was the only one who had truly piqued her curiosity.

She followed the albino's progress through the crowd as he struggled to follow Lord Vinghelt up the stairs to the highest deck. With much grunting, the albino pulled his vast bulk to the top, his chest pumping like a bellows.

Shara left the rail and started toward him. She walked past Lord Vinghelt and the small cluster of guests who were hanging on his every word.

Vinghelt spotted her and made a welcoming gesture. "Dear Shara-lani—"

he cut himself off awkwardly, hand in the air as she breezed past him and stopped in front of the black-clad albino. His ani swirled around him like a cloud. The painful exertion of his climb seemed to bolster his strength, even as it tore at his body. A small smile curved the corner of her mouth.

"Good evening," she said. "I noticed you last night, but never found a chance to meet you."

He nodded, still recovering his breath. It was difficult to tell on a man of his size, but it looked like his face was swollen. She delved deeper into his ani and discovered that he was in excruciating pain. Something raced through his body like strands of red fire, but he reveled in it, and the fog of power around him grew stronger.

"And I noticed you," he finally replied, speaking slowly and carefully. He had the voice of a child.

"You're a Necani," Shara said.

He shrugged, his red eyes like tiny fires peeking over the bulge of his cheeks. Heat spread through Shara's chest. By the Seasons, this man wore his power out in the open for anyone to see. It was a startling change from young Arefaine, who was as tight as a drum.

"And you are Shara-lani," he said.

She curtsied. "I have that pleasure."

"And many others, I suspect," he said with a slight grin.

"Are you ill? You seem to be in pain."

He nodded. "The price of power," he slurred, "is the acceptance of pain."

"Only in certain disciplines." She glanced down at his body. The high voice. The weight. Of course. He was a eunuch. "Some disciplines require pleasure."

"And is that why you have come so far south? For pleasure?"

"There is much in the world that I must see. It was a journey long overdue."

"Of course it was."

"May I have the pleasure of your name?"

"Jesheks san Rivvul."

"Kherish?"

He shrugged, and Shara noticed Vinghelt break away from his cluster of admirers. With two bodyguards in tow, he made his way toward them.

"A pleasure, Jesheks," Shara said, giving him a curtsy.

"Yes," he slurred, nodding. "It will be."

Shara turned and came nose to nose with Lord Vinghelt.

"I see you have met my personal physician," he said. Jesheks smiled politely and bowed his head. "If you are ever in need of my servant's assistance, I would be happy to send him to you."

"That is very kind of you. I'm sure your servant is a master"—she took a sip of her wine—"physician."

Vinghelt's eyes went wide, and she saw his friendly façade crack for the first time. His lip curled, and anger blossomed in his chest, but he quickly covered it up with a smile.

"This has been a lovely, intimate gathering," Shara said. "You seem to have the best friends that money can buy." She smiled and handed Vinghelt her empty wineglass.

She turned to Jesheks and nodded. "I look forward to tomorrow's duel. It will be nice to see how two great men solve their differences on the Summer Seas."

Jesheks said nothing, but his red eyes watched her as she left Vinghelt behind, holding on to her glass with a rigid hand.

She headed down the steps and met Mikal on his way up. He glanced over her shoulder at Vinghelt, then took her arm as she slipped through the crowd toward the edge of the ship.

"You seem to have made quite an impression on Lord Vinghelt," he whispered discreetly into her ear.

"Did I?"

"I thought you said he wasn't your enemy."

"He's not. I've just decided to hate the man, that is all. I don't like his smile."

CHAPTER 18

Another sunrise crept over the watery horizon. Brophy had seen three sunrises since the last time he slept. The few times he tried were brutally short, and he awoke again and again with the Fiend whispering in his mind.

Unable to sit quietly in his claustrophobic room, he spent the entire journey at the ship's prow, pacing the deck night and day.

Thoughts came and went through a haze of fatigue, but the flood of Brophy's emotions was an unending cascade of anger and desperation. He had to keep walking, had to keep ahead of the flood, or it would overwhelm him, and someone else would die.

The rising sun grew brighter, and Brophy turned his head to shield his eyes.

He stopped. That wasn't right. The sun should be behind him, to the east. Fighting to make sense of his foggy thoughts, he looked at the sails. They'd been running straight downwind for days, but now they were cutting across the wind on a broad reach. If the sun was dead off the starboard rail, that meant . . .

With a growl of frustration, Brophy stormed across the forecastle, leapt the rail, and yanked open the storm door leading belowdecks. He went directly to Arefaine's cabin and pounded on the door.

The door opened a moment later, and a line of Arefaine's six attendants filed past him, their eyes locked on the ground.

"Please come in, Brophy," Arefaine said, barely loud enough to hear.

He strode into the room and slammed the door behind him. "Why are we headed north?" he demanded.

Arefaine sat at her dressing table in a black robe. Her hair had been arranged, but her face was not yet powdered. A tub of cooling water sat in the center of the room. She rose to her feet, carefully retying her silk robe.

"We turned north during the night at the suggestion of His Eternal Wisdom. There is something on the Cinder he would like you to see."

The voices in Brophy's head surged, and his knuckles cracked as he clenched his fists. "You said you were taking me to the Opal Palace." His father's little red light took off from his shoulder and began to fly around his head.

"And we will, after a short detour."

Brophy fought the urge to lash out, smash her skull against the shiny black walls. He strode back to the door and yanked it open. "I have no desire to return to that place," he said through clenched teeth.

Arefaine nodded. She had been a constant presence since they left Ohndarien. Even when Brophy couldn't see her, he knew she was near. She continued to try to befriend him, to teach him techniques she swore would help him to sleep. But all of Brophy's energy was focused on keeping the Fiend's thoughts out of his mind. Her endless hovering just made it worse.

Arefaine followed him across the room, touching him lightly on the arm. He wanted to swat her hand away, crush her tiny hand in his fist.

"I felt the same way when the Emperor brought me back here," she said, her voice was soft, smooth. "It was part of our agreement. For many years I have wanted to accompany him to Ohndarien, but he would not agree to take me unless we journeyed to the Cinder along the way."

"Why? What is there?"

"Why don't you ask me that question?" the Emperor said from behind him.

Brophy whirled around, and two Carriers of the Opal Fire stepped between him and the Emperor. He twitched, nearly threw them backward. His arms vibrated as he held back.

"Would you join me in my chambers?" the Ohohhim leader asked, so utterly calm that Brophy wanted to rip the powdered flesh off his face. "I will answer any question you wish to ask."

Brophy breathed heavily through clenched teeth. His father hovered around his head, and Brophy snatched the little light out of the air and held it to his chest. "Good," he said, when his emotions were finally under control.

With a brief nod to Arefaine, His Eternal Wisdom began walking toward the back of the ship. His two bodyguards interposed themselves between Brophy and the Emperor as he led them down the narrow hallway. Brophy watched the Carriers of the Opal Fire with a hunter's eyes, seeing their weaknesses.

Two more Carriers stood guard at the entrance to the Emperor's chambers. They wordlessly opened the double doors. The room was nearly empty. Its unadorned wooden walls were lacquered to a mirror shine. An elegant throne stood on a dais at the back of the room, and a silver cabinet stood to one side.

The Emperor sat on his throne and folded his hands into the sleeves of his robes. "You may leave us," he said in his quiet voice to his bodyguards.

The two that had followed them into the room removed themselves. A third appeared out of the shadows of the long red draperies surrounding the thin window at the back of the room. He moved silently past Brophy and shut the door behind them.

"I would have kept them in here, if I were you," Brophy said.

"I have no reason to fear you."

"I wouldn't be so sure about that." Brophy's hand kept clenching and unclenching, aching for a sword.

"I already know the day I will die," the Emperor said. "Today is not that day."

Brophy said nothing. He suddenly longed for the cool, clear air above-deck. Despite the elegance of the room, everything seemed too small, too vulnerable.

"I am sorry for the need for secrecy," the Emperor continued. "But everything will be explained in due time."

"No," Brophy snapped. "It will be explained now!" In the back of his mind, the whispers grew louder. His father's light fluttered in his fist, unable to escape.

"There are some things I have kept from you," the Emperor said quietly. "The trip to the Cinder was one."

"What else haven't you told me?" Brophy asked in a menacing voice, trying to push back the whispers. "I don't like being kept in the dark."

The Emperor nodded. "The other secret I have kept is inside that cabinet."

Brophy stormed to the bureau and flung open the doors.

A blackened gemstone the size of a head lay nestled within, resting on a bundle of padded red silk.

"That's the Heartstone," Brophy roared.

"Yes," the Emperor confirmed. "We brought it with us from Ohndarien."

Brophy snatched up the stone and spun around. Roaring of voices flooded his thoughts, drowning out all other sounds. Brophy strode over to the Emperor, raising the stone above his head, ready to cave in the little man's skull.

Such treachery. Such deceit. He deserves to die.

Brophy paused, his clenched fingers white on the black stone. The little light of Brophy's father's soul zipped around his head, annoying and insignificant.

"Turn the ship around," Brophy rasped in a guttural voice. "We go back to Ohndarien."

The Emperor was still as a statue. "That would not be wise. Oh has shown me the future of the Fortress of Light. In a very short time, the Heartstone will no longer be safe there."

"What do you mean!"

"I am sorry, Brother of Autumn, but Ohndarien will soon fall to treachery from within. There is nothing that either one of us can do about that now."

"I don't believe you," he yelled. "It's all lies! Lies within lies!"

Crush the thief's skull. Smash the arrogance from his face.

Five Carriers of the Opal Fire burst into the room, swords drawn. The Emperor held up one hand, and they held back, waiting for his order.

Brophy teetered in indecision, his arm shaking with the desire to crush the Ohohhim's head to a bloody pulp.

End this now, and we will return to Ohndarien.

The Emperor watched him but did nothing else. "Look at yourself, Brophy," the Emperor said. "Look in your eyes."

Brophy felt his father's warmth again, frantic, insistent at the edges of his mind. Slowly, he lowered the Heartstone. Walking stiffly back to the cabinet, Brophy stared into the polished silver doors.

His eyes were pitch-black.

Lies. All lies. He wants to steal our power for himself.

Taking a shuddering breath, Brophy looked down at the Heartstone. He set it on the red silk padding and slammed the doors shut. The Fiend's voice faded.

Brophy covered his face with his hands and staggered away. He stumbled into a tall, arching beam along the wall and punched it. Wood splintered, and he sagged to his knees. The nightmare would never end. He would never be rid of the Fiend.

His Eternal Wisdom crossed the room and crouched next to him. "You have strength, Brophy," the Emperor said. "That is why you are so desperately needed. I could never have done what you just did. I know you want to protect Ohndarien. But you must help yourself before you can help anyone else. You are in need of profound healing, and that healing must begin on the Cinder."

Brophy gripped the beam with both hands. "If I go to the Cinder, you can make it stop? You can get the voices out of my head?"

"I believe so."

"And then you will take me and the Heartstone back home?"

The Emperor was quiet for a moment. Brophy looked up and saw, for the first time, a flicker of sadness cross the Emperor's powdered features. "I am afraid not, Brother of Autumn. Dangerous times are upon us and there is something you must do that is far more important than protecting a single city."

"What!" he shouted. "What more do I have to do?"

"You must teach a lost child how to love."

CHAPTER 19

Shara brushed her fingers through her long black hair and looked to the skies. It was early afternoon, but the sun was hidden behind the oppressive, gray clouds.

Lord Reignholtz sat in the middle of the runabout, as solid and grounding as a statue. He hadn't said much to her since her return to *Laughing Breeze*. He was polite enough, but every gaze he sent her told Shara that he disapproved of her liaison with his daughter.

Lawdon sat in front of her lord, staring grimly across the dark waves.

Shara could see why Lawdon had given her life to Reignholtz's service. It was a noble calling, and everyone who surrounded the prince struck Shara as being competent and worthy. Reignholtz himself played the hand dealt him and never complained.

Brezelle was the only one who seemed eager for the night's festivities. Sitting next to her father, her green eyes sparkled, though she kept herself composed.

A pair of capable servants manned the oars, and Mikal sat next to Shara at the bow.

"My lord," Mikal said. "I feel compelled to ask you something."

Reignholtz nodded.

"We row toward a duel, perhaps the greatest in many years. You mentioned the other night that Avon Leftblade is ready to stand for you, but—"

"But where is he?" Brezelle finished for him.

"That is my question," Mikal said.

Reignholtz held up his hand. "It is taken care of," he murmured, but said nothing more.

From a distance, the Floating Palace looked like a wooden island forested with a hundred masts with colorful banners for leaves. Countless little rowboats came and went from the cluster of ships like bees buzzing around a hive.

They cut through the choppy sea until the runabout bumped against the outermost ship on the Floating Palace. A subdued crowd met them at the rail. They stayed at a respectful distance, watching as Reignholtz's group climbed aboard. Everyone wore colorful cloaks in anticipation of the rain to come. Greens, reds, and blues predominated, but there was plenty of black and gold. They looked like a sea of multicolored priests, a ludicrous juxtaposition of the somber and the frivolous. As they began to walk, Shara felt a surge of emotion from Reignholtz. She looked in his direction and found his attention flick to a single man in the crowd. The man's cloak was snowy white, and his cowl was drawn. He made eye contact with Reignholtz and gave a brief nod. Underneath the cloak, his left hip bulged with the hilt of a long sword.

Mikal touched her arm, leaned close to whisper in her ear. "Leftblade. The man—"

"—in the white cloak," Shara finished for him. "I saw Reignholtz spot him. Are you sure that's him?"

"Did you see the way his left hand curled into a claw?" Mikal asked.

"No."

"It's him," he assured her, and his breath came quicker in his excitement. "Oh, what a night it will be."

Reignholtz's procession continued across the Floating Palace. Unlike that first night, most of the ships were empty. No banquets, musicians, or jugglers today. The few Waveborn they passed stopped what they were doing to watch Reignholtz's passage. Some raised flagons and nodded. Just as many scowled and turned away, but most just watched with fascination. They crossed two more ships before they reached *Glory of Summer*. By then, half the Floating Palace was following them. The other half had already gathered on Vinghelt's ship. The upper decks were packed, and spectators hung from the rigging to get a better view.

Tension hung thick in the air. Vinghelt's Natshea would duel Reignholtz's mystery man, and the crowds were vibrating with curiosity as to who it would be.

The crowd parted as they approached, leaving an open path to the dueling space in the center of the ship. Reignholtz led them into the throng, and the spectators pressed heavy at their backs once they'd passed.

Lord Vinghelt stood at the edge of the crowd, smiling expansively. Natshea towered over him to his right, her hips cocked at an angle, her arms crossed as she looked at everyone with that bored expression. Shara searched the crowd for the albino. She found Jesheks covered with his black cloak, standing in the shadows where the forecastle joined the rail. Their eyes met across the distance, and the same jolt of energy crackled between them. He smiled and gave her a slight nod.

Vinghelt stepped a few paces into the cleared arena. Cheers arose from the crowd. He gave a half bow, his charming smile seeming to target each person individually. "Thank you all for coming," he said. "It warms my heart to see that so many Waveborn patriots have come to defend our way of life. But there is one who does not appreciate those willing to lay their lives on the line for their countrymen. He does not approve of those who fight for his freedom."

Vinghelt made a graceful gesture toward Reignholtz's party.

"Last season, this man called me a traitor for pursuing our enemies to the ends of the earth, for calling the brigands to account for their crimes. He demanded we let the Physendrian killers run wild, release them to their base cruelty, to ravage our cities and rape our women as they see fit. He urged that we should leave your sons unsupported and unprotected against those foul rebels, to be slaughtered under their craven knives."

Many in the crowd cheered his words. Vinghelt let them applaud, somehow managing to look humble as he soaked up their adoration.

"But all voices are heard upon the Summer Seas," he continued, just before the crowd started to quiet. "I have called upon the Waveborn to sail forth, meet our enemies, and secure our shores once and for all." He paused for more cheers. "We must protect our Eternal Summer. We must protect the Waveborn way of life." More cheers. "If anyone disagrees, let him come forth. My truth runs from no one."

Vinghelt smiled and nodded to the crowd as they cheered and stomped their feet on the deck.

Without waiting for the sound to subside, Reignholtz stepped forward into the cleared arena. "Good people of the Summer Seas, Fessa's children, Waveborn one and all," he shouted over the crowd. "I stand before you in defense of truth, champion of the shining path that Salice Mick set before us. 'No one owns the sea.' Those words are written upon our souls, and I, for one, will live and die by them. But there is one among us who would tell us we need more than a clear heart and the wind in our sails." He pointed at Vinghelt. "I name that false prince the Herald of Winter, a greedy executioner of everything we hold dear. No true Waveborn would ask a single one of us to spill our blood upon the sand. Who among you would trade a child's life for a bag of Physendrian gold? Who among you—"

"Enough!" Natshea shouted, stepping forward to stand a foot beyond her lord. Her hand was a blur as she drew her sword and hurled it high into the air. It spun across the distance, and descended on Reignholtz. The Summer Prince clenched his jaw, but he did not move. The crowd gasped as the sword stuck in the wood between Reignholtz's feet. The hilt vibrated, swaying slightly back and forth in front of Reignholtz's chest.

A murmur of appreciation ran through the crowd. A few clapped or stomped their feet.

"No more chatter, Prince of Reignheld, unless you look to take up a sword and turn your petty words to poetry," Natshea said. "Sweet words and steel alone will end this debate. Have you a champion ready to pit his truth against mine?"

Reignholtz lifted his chin. "I do." He looked around the crowd. Shara followed his gaze, looking for the white cloak. Reignholtz had mentioned that Leftblade loved to make a dramatic entrance. Would he come swinging in from a rope? She looked to the rigging. Only spectators hung in the high nets or clung to the masts. She couldn't find the white cloak anywhere.

The seconds dripped by.

Frowning, she glanced at Mikal. He, too, searched the crowd. A long silence fell, but Avon Leftblade did not appear.

A single laugh broke the silence. All eyes turned to Lord Vinghelt as his laugh petered out to a chuckle. "Ah, dear Reignholtz. Do you have a champion or don't you?" He dabbed at the corners of his eyes with his one gloved hand. "Is there someone specific you wait for?"

Reignholtz glanced around at the surrounding crowd, but there wasn't a white cloak among them.

"Perhaps you wait for some legend of the past to appear and save you?" Vinghelt asked.

A slow flush crept into Reignholtz's bearded cheeks. He glared at Vinghelt. "Are you so vile that you would assassinate a duelist before the duel?"

"Your accusations have already been laid down, Lord Reignholtz," Natshea said. "Are these new ones?"

"How much bloody gold did you put in his pockets, Vinghelt?" Reignholtz shouted, breaking his serene composure for the first time.

"If you wish to lay any more slanders at my door, you must present a champion," Vinghelt said, then turned to the crowd. "Is that not the way of the Waveborn?" he shouted. A cheer rose in response. "Is there no one here who will stand for this man?"

The crowd noise faded into dead silence as Reignholtz stood alone in the dueling space, fists clenched, face contorted with rage. Shara flicked a glance at Mikal to find the young Waveborn's hand on his sword, leaning forward. His eyes glinted, and she smiled, began breathing in time with him. Mikal drew a breath as if to speak.

"I'll dance for truth," said a light, melodic voice beside Shara. Shara turned as Brezelle stepped forward. Her sword flashed out of its sheath and flew, sailing across the distance to stick into the deck a foot away from Vinghelt.

Quick as a snake, Lord Reignholtz grabbed Brezelle's shoulder. "Please excuse my daughter," he said to the crowd. "She spoke without thinking."

"Run back to your mother, Little Reignholtz!" someone from the crowd shouted.

"You can prick me with your pin, Brezelle!" another shouted. "If you let me prick you with mine!"

Several people in the crowd laughed uproariously at that, but Brezelle stood defiant, pretending to ignore them as a flush crept into her cheeks.

"Enough!" Natshea said, and all eyes went to her. "Step back, Lord Reignholtz, and see justice served. The sword has been thrown. No hand may take it back."

The crowd applauded.

Shara glared at Mikal, but he shrugged helplessly.

Brezelle shrugged off her father's hand and walked forward to face Natshea, who stood a full head taller. "I would rather die than take back that sword. I drew it in service of my father, my house, my lord, and my country."

A ripple of applause ran through the crowd again.

"No doubt in that order, little Reignholtz," Natshea responded, smiling for the first time.

Reignholtz spoke again, and this time the desperation was gone from his voice. "Prevail, my champion. May truth be your strength, as it is surely on our side. May your sword guide the Waveborn from these stormy seas back to our summer of endless peace."

"Let it begin," Vinghelt said.

"Let it begin," Reignholtz echoed.

Both women raced across the deck. Natshea was faster, her long legs took her to her weapon in two quick strides. She snatched up her blade and spun, lunging straight for Brezelle's chest.

Brezelle barely wrenched her sword from the wood in time to block Natshea's first thrust. Steel flashed in the dark afternoon. Natshea's blade whipped around in an arc, slicing at Brezelle's calf, but she thrust her sword down, blocking it. The desperate move buried Brezelle's sword in the deck again.

Natshea spun like a dancer, kicking high. Her boot caught Brezelle in the neck. Coughing, Reignholtz's daughter stumbled away, wrenching her sword out of the deck as she fell.

Cheers went up from the crowd. So many people stomped boots on the deck that the ship vibrated. Natshea tossed her sword over her shoulder. It sailed a dozen feet and stuck point first into the deck even as she spoke:

> "Old in the beard and blind in the eyes
> A man accuses a man
> 'Lies' he shrieks, 'Tradition' he cries
> With his head stuck deep in the sand."

Brezelle regained her feet and her composure. She tossed her sword away as Natshea had done, and spoke:

> "Words from the mouth of a long-limbed shark
> Or words from the mouth of a lord
> All add up to the same worthless sum
> When cut apart by my sword."

Appreciative cheers erupted from the crowd and both duelists sprinted for their weapons again. Brezelle was faster this time and met Natshea's charge more readily. Their blades crossed. Natshea lunged. Brezelle parried, riposted, and Natshea slammed the blade away.

Shara faded back into the throng. Those nearest gladly took her spot. Breathing consciously, she cast a mild glamour. No one gave her a second glance as she worked her way through the crowd while Brezelle and Natshea made passes at one another.

Leaving the duelists to their trade, Shara made her way to the far side of the ship. Her breathing was perfect and even. She stilled her thoughts and emptied her mind, letting her feet walk their own course as she slipped through the crowd like a wisp of silk. She reached the forecastle, turned and inched along its face, deep into the shadows. When she was close enough to Jesheks to touch him, she let the spell go.

A sudden surge of anxiety ran through the fat man's body, but he did not jump. With a smile, he turned his cowled head and nodded to her. The rest of the crowd's attention was focused forward, watching the duelists cross swords.

"Well done, Shara-lani," Jesheks said. "I have not been approached unawares in years."

"It is difficult to remain vigilant when we are so rarely challenged."

"True. It can be difficult to be a giant among dwarves." He touched his enormous belly.

"I had hoped we could continue our conversation, so quickly curtailed yesterday."

"And you also sought to test my strength."

"That also."

Standing next to the fat man, Shara glanced back at the duel as the two women completed another pass. Natshea danced back, saluted, but kept her sword as she said:

> "Yank the daggers and leave our men
> To scrabble as they may
> This is how a petty lord
> Would lie to make us sway
>
> But justice, truth and courage
> Will always win the day
> When true sons of this bright sea
> Cannot be led astray."

Again the deck shook with stomping feet, and the cheers were deafening. Brezelle made an overhead gesture with her sword, a long, graceful swoop, before she spoke:

> "Our heads are deep in sand, you say
> Your hands are deep in pockets
> Your left mouth talks of gilded truths.
> Your right speaks just to mock us
>
> Your fingers run with blood and gold
> Your touch befouls the sea
> What justice do you speak of now?
> What Vinghelt travesty?"

The cheers were the loudest yet, and applause erupted from the crowd. Natshea frowned, her eyes smoldering, and launched herself at the young woman, driving her back with superior strength and speed.

"Your pet project appears to be losing," Jesheks said.

"I think you underestimate her," Shara said, her lip curving in a smile. "She is a remarkable young woman."

"Remarkable or not ..." Jesheks adjusted his cowl as a slight drizzle started, "Natshea is the superior blade. She has more experience and a much longer reach."

Shara watched the combatants cross swords again. "Brezelle seems to be holding her own."

"Come now," Jesheks said, squinting up at her with his pink eyes. "An appealing underdog will amuse the crowd for a short time, but in the end, the mob cheers for blood. It is only a matter of time before that girl makes a mistake, and Natshea will have her."

"I have a different theory," Shara said. "Brezelle's strength runs to the bone, her confidence comes from within. Whereas Natshea is nothing more than what *you* have made her." Shara looked at him. "Some say that she is so talented it is magical."

"Do they?" Jesheks murmured.

Shara chuckled. "Tell me, how will your beloved Natshea fare if she is left to her own devices?"

Jesheks's jowls quivered, and his eyes narrowed as he smiled. "I suppose we won't know until the moment is upon us."

The man said no more, and Shara turned back to the duel, though she kept her attention upon the albino. If his ani surged, she would be there to counter it. Today, at least, the dueling on the Floating Palace would be fair.

Shara looked back as Natshea attacked, but this time Brezelle dodged the first swipe instead of parrying. She spun about with newfound energy and lashed out, clipping a piece of leather from the shoulder of Natshea's vest.

Shara turned to Jesheks. "I must admit, I am curious," she said. "You are no novice to throw your power around lightly. What is your interest in the Summer Cities? Why support a toad like Vinghelt?"

"Vinghelt is but a passing fancy," Jesheks said in his high voice. "My only true interest is in furthering my art."

"And how does war with Physendria further your art?"

Jesheks paused, and for a moment she was sure he would not answer, but then he said, "It is a small courtesy I am paying to someone who interests me."

"And why does she interest you?" Shara asked.

Jesheks smiled, and Shara knew she had guessed correctly. Reef must have been right about Arefaine pulling strings in the Summer Cities. But to what end?

"Her potential intrigues me," he said. "As I grow older, I feel the urge to pass on what I have learned. It can be so difficult to find a worthy protégé."

Shara doubted his confession was a truthful one. Arefaine certainly wouldn't stoop to being anyone's protégé. He must know that. His overconfidence might be something she could use against him.

"Why limit yourself to teaching a child," she asked. "When you could ally yourself with an equal, each sharing their knowledge openly?"

"My dear ..." Jesheks said in his childlike voice. "Are you propositioning me?"

"Perhaps."

Shara paused, but Jesheks changed the subject.

"Look." He nodded to the two combatants. "It is almost over. Natshea is getting bored with the girl."

Natshea charged Brezelle. She met the charge, but couldn't stand up to the larger woman's strength. Swords clanged and steel rang, but always Brezelle backed up a step. She tried a riposte again, but Natshea slid to the side. Brezelle's blade missed her by half an inch, but Natshea's bit deep into Brezelle's left arm. Blood wet Natshea's sword, and Brezelle gasped, jumped back, and bumped into the crowd.

Natshea laughed, but did not press the attack. It was first blood. Brezelle could now yield and leave the duel with honor. The young woman touched the blood on her arm. With a deadly gaze at Natshea, Brezelle shook her head.

Natshea nodded, then turned her back and sauntered into the center of the cleared space.

> "Your words drip from a silver tongue
> The crowd can cheer to that
> But the blood upon my steel bespeaks
> A truth quite cold and flat
>
> So come for me again, my love
> I'll dance with you all day
> And when you choose to dance at night
> I'll send my friends to pay."

Brezelle winced as she moved her shoulder, unconsciously trying to ease the wound that seeped into her beautiful blue tunic. She breathed hard, and her brow was furrowed as she stared at Natshea.

"Your ... words cannot offend
Just tossed upon the wind ..."

She winced again, and swallowed, searching for words through the pain. Shara knew immediately that it was the first time the girl had ever been hurt so badly. Reignholtz's face was grave and unmoving as he watched with glittering blue eyes.

"I'd gladly serve all those you send
If you only had some friends."

A few drunken spectators stomped their feet, but boos arose from others. The rest of the crowd stayed silent.

"I think you are mistaken," Shara murmured to the albino, still keeping her attention on his ani, making sure he was not sending any to Natshea. "I think Brezelle is just hitting her stride."

Brezelle seemed to gather herself and jumped forward, her blade a blur in the fading afternoon light. Natshea blocked, blocked, and blocked again, all the while retreating. With a snarl, she riposted violently, trying to shove the smaller woman off-balance, but Brezelle gave like a tree in the wind, allowing the riposte to miss her by inches, then slashed Natshea on the wrist.

A gasp ran through the crowd, and Natshea fell back. Shara smiled, was about to say something to Jesheks, but she stopped herself.

The lanky duelist stared at the blood on her right wrist. Brezelle paused, breathing hard, her eyes glittering. She saluted, giving a moment for Natshea to yield if she chose.

Instead, Natshea ran a finger through the line of blood, and her whole body shuddered. She looked up, a faint smile on her lips, and the light went out of her eyes.

Oh no ... Shara thought, watching what no one else could see. Power flooded into Natshea's body, a torrent of it, but it didn't come from Jesheks.

"No," Shara breathed, forgetting Jesheks, forgetting everything. Natshea leapt forward. Swords clashed again, but they were lost behind the surging bodies of the crowd. Everyone went wild, cheering madly, stomping their feet, shaking the boat.

Shara elbowed her way forward to get to Brezelle's side, but everyone wanted a look. It took Shara precious moments before she burst through to the cleared space—

Natshea's sword glimmered dully in the gloomy light. Brezelle bled from three places. Shara threw a surge of power to the girl, but it was too late. Natshea slashed viciously downward, powering through Brezelle's feeble block. Blood splattered the crowd, and Brezelle crumpled to the deck.

"No!" Reignholtz shouted, rushing forward, falling to his knees and taking his daughter's head in his lap. Brezelle twisted in her father's grip, her boots scuffing the deck as she clenched her teeth against the pain. One of Brezelle's eyes looked around wildly, but the other was bathed in blood, covered with the flap of her cheek that had been laid open to the bone.

Shara stood stunned, her heart beating fast in her chest.

A roar of approval exploded from the crowd, shaking the deck like a crack of thunder. The spectators rushed forward. Shara tried to throw a glamour over Brezelle, but she was buffeted by the crowd and lost sight of the girl.

Vinghelt and Natshea were swarmed by the crowd. Delirious supporters lifted them onto their shoulders. The prince waved to the masses as they paraded him around the ship.

Reignholtz and Brezelle were also mobbed by the crowd. Despite Lawdon's efforts to stop them, father and daughter were lifted up into the air. Reignholtz clung to his daughter as she writhed in pain. Buffeted by the crowd, they were carried hand over hand to the edge of the ship and tossed overboard.

Shara felt nauseated. She looked up to see Natshea being carried a short distance away. With a reptile's smile, the tall, lanky woman saluted Shara with her blade and licked a line of blood off her wrist. The cheers were constant now, and a chant of "Long live the prince," rose above the din.

Shara flicked her gaze to *Glory of Summer*'s forecastle. Jesheks was still there. His cowl was drawn low, and she could only see his mouth at this distance.

He held his white hands out, palms up.

Seething, Shara turned away.

CHAPTER 20

Lawdon punched the man in front of her in the kidney and yanked him out of the way as he fell to the deck. The crowd surged around her as they passed Brezelle and Reignholtz hand over hand and tossed them over the side, heedless of the bleeding girl in their arms.

Lawdon fought her way to the rail and dived in after her lord.

She spluttered to the surface and swam over to Reignholtz, who was treading water while supporting his daughter in his arms. A high, thin wail of anguish escaped Brezelle's lips though she tried valiantly to hold it in.

"It's all right, little sister," Lawdon said, forcing her voice to remain steady. "We'll get you home. It's going to be all right."

Dammit! Where the hell are Javthus and Matten?

She had told them to have the boat waiting if things went badly!

Again, a moan escaped through Brezelle's clenched teeth. "M-My face," she mumbled.

Reignholtz held the bloody mass of her cheek together, keeping pressure on the wound, his face a tight mask. Lawdon could barely keep her anger down. Natshea had been vicious, delivering three wounds in that last attack. She should have given her opponent the opportunity to yield. But that demon had sliced Brezelle in two places before giving her the spiteful gash across the face.

Red rivulets streaked down Brezelle's cheek into the water. There would be no more poetry to the beauty of Brezelle Reignholtz.

"I'm sorry, Father. I don't know what happened," she cried. "I had her. You saw. I cut her, but she was so fast."

"It's okay, little one. You fought bravely. You did all you could."

Lawdon looked at Brezelle's ashen skin. She was bleeding so much. That beautiful skin should be tan, not gray. Lawdon clenched her teeth and looked for the damn boat. Where the hell were Javthus and Matten?

Brezelle kept talking, but her words were garbled as she faded into unconsciousness.

"They're here," Lawdon said, catching sight of the rowboat as Reignholtz's men maneuvered it between the two ships. They shipped the oars and pushed against the hulls on either side to bring the runabout closer.

Lawdon hooked a heel on the edge of the rowboat and levered herself inside. With Matten's help, she lifted Brezelle into the boat, while Javthus helped Reignholtz out of the water.

"You're wounded, sir!" Javthus shouted.

Lawdon followed their gazes. High on Reignholtz's thigh, a puncture leaked blood.

"My lord!" she said, scooting forward to inspect it.

"Leave it!" Reignholtz snapped. "Man your oars and put your backs into it," Reignholtz ordered, climbing into the bottom of the boat, supporting his daughter's head and reapplying pressure to her wound. "I want her home now."

"Yes, sir," Matten replied, as they pushed the boat free and reset their oars.

"Your wound is deep," Lawdon said, taking the tiller.

"I know," Reignholtz growled. "Someone in the crowd stabbed me as we were carried away."

Lawdon remembered Reignholtz wincing as he was thrown from the *Glory of Summer*. She clenched her teeth. *Had the world gone crazy?*

The rain had finally begun. It started lightly at first, but the wind was picking up, and the droplets became heavier.

"Is the physician ready?" Lawdon asked.

"Yes, Captain," Matten said through gritted teeth, rowing as hard as he could.

"What physician?" Reignholtz asked.

"I hired one, without consulting you, my lord." Lawdon admitted. "I knew it would anger you, but ..." She took a deep breath, looking at the ruin of Brezelle's face. "I thought it would be for Avon Leftblade. In case things went badly."

"Well done," Reignholtz said, lowering his eyes to his daughter. "I should not have been so optimistic." He shook his head.

Brezelle's head rested in her father's lap. The rain made pink puddles on his cloak. Reignholtz adjusted his daughter and looked at Lawdon. "What happened? The woman was not the same fighter after Brezelle cut her."

Lawdon nodded.

"Is there some witchcraft at work here? Did your friend from Ohndarien cause this?"

Lawdon was stunned. She shook her head. "No. Shara would never do such a thing. If there was magic at work, she will be able to tell us who was behind it. I'll ask her."

"You do that. I want to know immediately. We have been more than gracious to Shara-lani. If she stood by and let this happen, I want to know."

The two stared at one another for a long moment, Reignholtz's blue eyes blazing.

"Of course, my lord ..." she said quietly.

The rain came harder, cascading down upon them. In a few minutes they wouldn't be able to see the Floating Palace anymore.

The boat suddenly jerked.

"What did we hit?" Reignholtz demanded.

Matten stopped rowing, breathing hard, and looked over the side. "I don't know, my lord. There aren't any reefs in this part of the—"

The boat shook again.

Everyone started looking over the edges, but it was difficult to see anything in the driving rain that turned the choppy water into a ruffle of impenetrable gray and white.

Lawdon's gaze fell on the front of the boat. A thin rope, barely visible in the dark, was looped around the bow.

"We're dragging a bowline!" she said, moving forward. Everyone turned to look. "Of all the times to make a stupid, dusteater mistake!"

Matten got there before her, hauled on the line, but it didn't come. He grunted, pulled hard. "We're dragging something." Putting his back into it, he hauled the line up. It jerked, and Matten dropped it. He shook his head, cursing.

"We're caught."

Javthus shipped his oar and went to help the man. Together, hand over hand, they slowly pulled the line up. "There's something ..."

A hefty beef bone emerged from the water, with chunks of raw flesh still hanging off it.

"What the—" Lawdon breathed.

Flashing teeth leapt up from the rain-pocked water. Matten dropped the bone just in time to save his hand. "Shark!" he yelled, stumbling backward into the boat.

Lawdon's blood went cold. Sabotage. She scanned the waves. With the rain, it was difficult to be sure. There could be a hundred fins out there.

"Cut that line and row!" she commanded. Javthus's dagger flashed out of its sheath, and he severed the rope. "Get us the hell out of here!" She leapt to the oars and began pulling until Matten and Javthus took her place. She hurried back to the tiller.

"When did you leave the boat?" she demanded.

Javthus didn't answer for a moment, then Matten said, "Just for a moment, Captain. To watch the duel."

"We left it tied just below us," Javthus said.

"You idiots!" Lawdon snarled.

"Enough, Captain," Reignholtz said. "The damage is done."

"They could have followed orders—" Lawdon began.

"Enough!" Reignholtz said, his voice thundering.

Lawdon raised her head, locked gazes with Reignholtz, suddenly realizing what he was thinking. No. It wasn't over. Why would someone sabotage the boat if they could simply cut the line and be done with it?

"That cut in your leg was deliberate," Lawdon breathed, not wanting the others to hear.

Reignholtz turned, searching the rain.

"Row harder," Lawdon said, wishing they'd brought more crew so they could double up on the oars.

"To port!" Matten said, pointing.

The dark prow of a ship emerged from the storm, almost on top of them.

"Row!" Lawdon yelled, yanking the tiller sideways, but the little boat barely reacted. The looming prow cut toward them.

Reignholtz grabbed his daughter and leapt into the water. Lawdon threw herself sideways as the dark ship shattered the little rowboat.

A shard of debris smacked into her head, and the hull slammed into her. She spun, her heels bouncing against wood. She pushed violently away and was tumbled in the ship's wake.

She thrashed for a moment, then came to her senses. Relaxing, she let out a few bubbles and followed them upward.

She broke the surface with a gasp, spinning around to search for the ship. Its stern could barely be seen through the rain, then it disappeared altogether.

"Reignholtz!" she screamed. There was no answer. "Reignholtz!"

She cast about, looking for anyone. Her heart hammered in her chest. There were sharks in this water. All around them.

She spotted something among the wreckage of the rowboat. A man swimming.

"Reignholtz!" she shouted, swimming after him. Her lord swam away from her, holding Brezelle limp in his arms, keeping her head out of the water. His arm across her shoulders held a naked dagger. Why didn't he answer her?

"My lord," she shouted. "We have to—"

"Get away!" he shouted.

"What—?"

"We're bleeding, Lawdon! Get away!"

She froze, sinking slightly and coughed up a mouthful of water.

"No . . ." she said, and kept swimming toward him.

"That's an order!" Reignholtz said.

"We'll tie off the wounds!" she shouted, coming closer. "We'll—"

"There is no time," Reignholtz growled. "Go!"

Lawdon hesitated, her mind desperately searching for a solution.

Brezelle screamed, suddenly awake as she was yanked downward. Her cry was cut off as she went underwater. Reignholtz fought, hauling her above the surface again, stabbing downward with his dagger, but the jerk came again, stronger than before. Brezelle's spluttering wail was cut off again as she was snatched out of Reignholtz's grip.

"NO!" Lawdon shouted, swimming toward them again.

Reignholtz cursed, water splashing as he stabbed downward again and again. With a cry, he disappeared under the waves.

"REIGNHOLTZ!"

He came up, cursing, fighting, stabbing. A shark surfaced, teeth snapping on his arm from behind. He screamed and went under. He did not resurface.

Lawdon treaded water, and the only sound was her heavy breathing and the splashing rain. He was gone. Just . . . gone.

Slowly, she began to swim backward, only a few yards from where her lord and sister had disappeared. She looked around. Javthus and Matten where nowhere to be seen, taken by the sharks already or killed in the crash.

Something brushed her back. Lawdon thrashed, spinning around. She fumbled for her dagger and drew it.

The rain came down as hard as ever, turning the ocean into a frothing mess. She looked around.

A fin cut the surface of the water. Two more were right behind it.

CHAPTER 21

The Ohohhim ship crept through the hazy darkness. Swirls of mist blew across the deck, heavy with sulfur. The scent brought Brophy back to the time when he and Shara had come this way, slipping past a line of Ohohhim warships to reach the Cinder's desolate shore. He had been a different person then, full of faith and the dream of saving Ohndarien.

He and Arefaine stood at the prow, already sweating in the heat rising from the boiling bay. The Cinder was a volcanic island that exploded eons ago, leaving the ragged edges of a vast crater poking above the ocean. The sea had rushed in to fill the crater, forming an island the shape of a crescent moon, with a bubbling bay in its center. Underwater vents created a constant torrent of steam billowing up from the center of the crescent, boiling the ocean and sending noxious gases into the air.

"Is that a dock?" Brophy asked, as they drew closer to shore. Three ships rocked gently against the stone quay. "What could they possibly need a dock for?"

"For the pilgrims who come to this place," Arefaine said.

"That's crazy," he murmured. He remembered the corrupted oxen charging out of the sea, the twisted black birds that dropped from of the sky as he, Shara, and Celinor fled with the child. "I don't want to be here."

"Neither did I when the Emperor brought me, but I looked at what he wished to show me."

The Emperor's ship slid up to the dock as they dropped the sails, and a few silent sailors leapt ashore to tie her off.

Brophy continued staring at the hated island, watching the mists swirl. No one emerged from belowdecks to go ashore.

"What's everyone waiting for?" he finally asked.

"For you." She placed her hand on his. "The Emperor suggested that you go ashore first. We'll follow a little later."

The voices in Brophy's head hovered in the distance like a storm forming on the horizon. He ignored them and said nothing.

"Don't you want to stretch your legs after so many days at sea?"

"No."

"As you wish," she said quietly, taking her hand from his. His fingers felt cold at the sudden absence.

He strode to the other side of the deck, looked into the mist away from the island. When the ship had been moving, the churning anger inside him was tolerable. It felt like his circuitous path would eventually lead him back to himself, back to Shara, back to Ohndarien. But he could not abide standing still, waiting.

Brophy still had his doubts about the Emperor's motivations. The man was utterly convinced that Arefaine must bring the Heartstone to Efften and make some critical decision that would determine the fate of the world. He practically begged Brophy to remain by her side and help her make that choice. But he wouldn't give any more details than that.

Coming from anyone else, Brophy would consider the Emperor's convictions nothing more than the ravings of a madman, a prophet of doom. But the Emperor had such a calm, bone-deep confidence that Brophy didn't know what to believe anymore.

He never mentioned the Emperor's request to Arefaine. But he asked her about the Heartstone and what she planned to do with it. The two of them ended up talking far into the night about her dreams of returning to Efften and freeing her sister's soul.

That night something had changed, and Brophy found himself pitying the girl who had been through so much. He'd asked her about the Fiend he'd faced in his nightmares. She seemed shocked at first when he'd mentioned it, but then her face became cold and unreadable again. Brophy felt he was getting to know the sorceress, but he still didn't trust her. She was hiding something, and he didn't know what.

Brophy clutched his father's spirit in his hand, drawing warmth and reassurance from the tiny light. Eventually he sighed, pushing aside his anger at the Emperor. Like it or not, Brophy was His Eternal Wisdom's guest and subject to his rule. Unless he planned on taking over the ship and killing everyone aboard, he would have to bow to the Emperor's wishes.

If his path back home led through the Cinder, there was no sense in avoiding it.

Crossing the deck, he walked down the gangplank to the stone dock. One of the sailors offered a lantern, but Brophy ignored him and headed into the darkness alone. A path led from the wharf along the island's shore, heading into the narrow canyon he had walked so many years ago. He and Shara had struggled to find the path into the crevice, but now it was paved with square stones.

He stopped, knelt. Intricate carvings graced each stone, telling miniature stories with every step. He shook his head as he rose. Who would spend so much time in a place like this?

The jagged cliffs on either side of the narrow chasm blotted out almost all of the light, but ever since waking from his nightmare, Brophy had little trouble seeing in the dark. Somehow he was stronger than before, faster and more aware, even with his lack of sleep.

The path grew steadily steeper, and he followed it for a quarter of an hour. It was nothing like he remembered. The broken stone had been cleared away. The walls had been shaped, smoothed, and the paved path was polished by the tread of many feet. Deep into the crevice, the carvings suddenly ceased, as though the artists had only been able to complete that much in the last eighteen years. Brophy continued until he reached the place where he had first met Celinor.

The narrow ledges he and Shara had used to climb out of the canyon to Celinor's cave had been expanded into steady, evenly carved steps that snaked their way into the mists above. He climbed them slowly out of the chasm and stopped on a little platform at the top, amazed by what he saw.

He stared at a vast, moonlit complex of gardens and temples. Towering monuments, little shrines, and sprawling flower beds ran from Copi's cave all the way down the hill to an enormous half-constructed dome. Ferns were planted everywhere. Flowering vines twisted around one another as they climbed the face of a vast temple built around the entrance to Copi's cave.

Sheltered alcoves had been carved into the mountainside on ether side of the cave. Little fires burned inside each of them, and two or three black-robed women worshipped at those fires. The pilgrims all held tiny, silver music boxes, each playing that haunting tune that had become so familiar to Brophy in his last days before the nightmare.

The child's tune filled the strangely hopeful landscape, but the foul mist still swirled through it all, as though it longed to wither the flowers and tear down the monuments.

Beyond the caves, scores of Ohohhim in black tunics slept in the open air atop simple woven mats. The pilgrims' gardening or stone-carving tools were stacked neatly at their feet.

The largest temple was being constructed of Ohndarien's blue-white marble. It rose from the foliage by Celinor's lookout on the edge of the cliff. Had they actually shipped that much marble from the Ohndarien quarries? That would have taken years, the work of thousands.

An Ohohhim woman turning her music box in one of the caves looked up and saw him. Her eyes widened.

"It's him. He's here," she whispered to the women around her. She descended to her knees, and bowed low, touching her forehead to the ground, still turning the handle of the music box. The women next to her cried out and did the same.

The noise alerted the others nearby, and it caught like wildfire. First the women with their music boxes, then the sleeping workers all woke and silently bowed to him. Pilgrim after pilgrim, all the way down to the unfinished temple, pressed their heads to the ground.

Brophy took a step back, his heel scuffing the edge of the stairway. He stood paralyzed for a moment, then disappeared into the fog.

❄

An hour later, he crouched at the highest point on the island, arms around his legs, chin resting on his knees. His father's spirit light floated around his head, whispering to him in words he couldn't understand.

The sulfurous mist never drifted this high, and he had a clear view of the setting moon reflecting off the distant ocean. He could see the temples, moonlight reflecting off blue-white marble half-obscured in the swirling mists. The Ohohhim were down there, still waiting on their knees for all he knew.

Arefaine had been walking up the steep slope toward him for the last fifteen minutes. He wanted to escape down the far side of the mountain, but there was nowhere to go, no way to avoid what hunted him. She took her time with the treacherous slope and wasn't even out of breath when she finally sat next to him on the craggy peak.

"All you had to do was nod," she said quietly. "And they would have gone on about their business."

"Why did you bring me here?" he asked. "Why were they kneeling?"

"They kneel because you are the Sleeping Warden. You and Copi and I are the reason they came here, to build those temples in our honor."

"Why?"

"Because the three of us are the purest embodiment of Oh's sacrifice in the last thousand years. We are almost like gods to them."

"That's insane. How did they even know who I am?"

"Not many young men with golden curls and glowing red diamonds in their chests wander onto the Cinder."

Brophy brought the fist that held his father to his mouth and bit his finger.

"They've been expecting you," Arefaine insisted. "His Eternal Wisdom knew you would someday return to these shores in need of guidance. They've been waiting for you ever since construction of this place began fifteen years ago. Many have waited years for the honor of coming here for a few months to work on your temple."

"Don't they know what I've done?"

"Yes, Brophy," she said, her voice stern for the first time since he had known her. "They know exactly what you've done, and exactly who you are. You are the only one who doesn't seem to know."

"And what have I done?" he said, louder than he intended. "Besides cut down my aunt from behind, besides slip into darkness inch by inch for the past eighteen years?"

"They came here to honor you because you followed in the footsteps of Oh—"

"I didn't—"

She touched his chin, turned his gaze down to meet hers. "Yes. You did. You walked a path that no one except the god himself has had the courage to tread."

"What do you mean?"

"What do you know about Oh? About his life as a man?"

Brophy sighed and looked up at the stars. He willed his thoughts to quiet, willed his heart to slow. "I remember some of the legends Vallia taught us when I was a child. He was the first emperor of Ohohhom. He ended all the wars and united the nation, then disappeared into his cave."

"There is much more to the story than that. Oh wasn't only the first emperor, he was the world's first and greatest magician. He and his apprentices discovered the ten paths to power and perfected each one of them."

"But I'm not a magician."

"Just listen." Arefaine put her hand on his leg. "As Oh's power grew, so did his ambitions. He longed to bring his gifts to every corner of the world. He imagined one vast nation ruled by peace, justice, and beauty, but he grew impatient with the slow progress of his dreams. He began to use his magic to push his followers harder and harder. He began to slay those who opposed him rather than taking the time to win them over to his side. An insufferable pain grew in his belly, and his hungers grew worse and worse. It was said that his eyes grew black as night, and none could bear to meet his gaze."

"He corrupted himself," Brophy said, remembering Shara in the Wet Cells.

"Yes. He succumbed to the emmeria of his own making and nearly destroyed everything he had created."

"Who stopped him?"

"He stopped himself. In a moment of clarity, Oh realized who he had become and where that path must lead. So he created a containment stone from the enormous diamond that adorned his throne and purged himself of all tainted emmeria. Then he placed that corrupted stone within a solid silver coffin and buried it in a cave. He vowed never to use magic again.

"Less than a year later he stood upon a battlefield where his magic had just laid waste the entire Vizai army. He watched as his bloodthirsty men tore down the gates of the enemy's capital and began to rape and slaughter all those within. And the Emperor began to cry.

"He knew he could never resist the allure of his power. So he marched his army back to Ohohhom, dug up the silver coffin, and climbed inside. The man's power made him a god. He could never be killed, and he could never be trusted to resist temptation for long. The allure of his power was too great. So he ordered his followers to bury him alive in a silver coffin. He willingly sacrificed his life to play eternal guardian to the sinister power he had unleashed upon the world."

Brophy nodded, seeing the connection at last.

"The Ohohhim set aside their weapons and bent their hearts and minds to the difficult task of following Oh's example. Greed and ambition became the greatest sins in their eyes. They turned their backs on power and learned to embrace duty, obedience, and self-sacrifice as the greatest of virtues."

Brophy unclenched his fist and let his father's soul fly around the two of them until it eventually landed on his shoulder.

"That is why they are building those three temples. One for me, one for Copi, and one for you. We fought a foe that Oh himself could not overcome, and we defeated it. You are the greatest of the three because you did so willingly. You knew exactly what would happen that day atop the Hall of Windows."

"I only did what the Heartstone told me—"

"Did you truly not know what you were doing?"

Brophy shook his head and looked away. "No. I knew."

"Exactly."

"But I never defeated it," he said. "I lost over and over again."

"Before you went to sleep, you held the corruption at bay for ten days on your journey back to Ohndarien. Most would have been overwhelmed in ten seconds. The Emperor himself succumbed to the corruption. No one has ever resisted it that long. Ever. I had the music box. It was that artifact, not me, that kept the black emmeria contained. Every time the music box stopped, I tried to wake. But we had to pull you from your dream, Brophy, even after the Heartstone was corrupted, even after the Zelani stopped singing. You held the emmeria with your own will, with no hope of rescue, no hope that the battle would ever end."

Brophy stayed silent.

"That's why they treat you like a god, Brophy. Because you did what only a god could do. They come here to keep fighting the battle that you started, to keep striving to reach the perfection you achieved."

"That's ridiculous."

"No more ridiculous than Donovan's dream of creating Ohndarien. The building of Efften, too, was once a flight of fancy."

Brophy picked up a rock and hurled it into the darkness. It was a very long time before it clattered down the scree slope far below.

"Fifteen years ago," Arefaine continued, "the Emperor returned to the Cinder to bury Copi's bones. As he dug her grave with his own hands, Oh spoke to him. That night, he decreed that the Cinder should be transformed. This place of pain and misery would be reclaimed by joy and life. Those modest gardens are just the beginning. He wants to remake this entire island. With the grace of Oh, generation after generation will add beauty to this place, and tend it, and keep it. It will serve as a reminder that humans can only push back the darkness with constant attention and diligent care. This monument is meant to stand as a testament to the human spirit, to our courage to stand, even flourish, in the face of evil."

Brophy scooped his father's spirit light off his shoulder and cradled it within his hands. The faint glow warmed his face. "But why this, why here? Why would they waste all this time, this effort, trying to change something that can't be changed?"

"Because it can be changed. The Emperor was once corrupted. You were nearly corrupted. I have wrestled with the darkness my entire life. And all three of us must believe that we can come back from that, that we can be whole once again."

Brophy shut his eyes as her words tugged at his heart.

"This temple is a monument to the battle we all fight in our own hearts, our own lives. You are the greatest hero in that battle. You are living proof that a single courageous soul can hold back all the evil in the world."

He blinked his eyes, looked away. "But it still has me," he said in a hoarse voice. "The Fiend crept into my bones, and I don't know how to get him out. I hear him day and night. And I want to keep hurting people. Like I hurt Bae . . . Like I hurt Shara . . ." He twitched his head, shutting out the memory.

Arefaine nodded quietly, then said, "But you never gave up, and you never will. Together, we'll get those voices out of your head. We'll get them out of your dreams."

She stopped, looked up at him again. "And we'll get them out of mine."

"Arefaine, you don't—"

She grabbed his chin fiercely.

"I know how hard it's been. You were very nearly destroyed. So was I. But we weren't. We held the darkness back."

She forced his gaze down the hill.

"You look at that, Brophy, at all of those people willing to spend their lives for only the gesture of defeating evil. Look on that, and tell me that you lost.

"If they can do that," Arefaine said softly, letting him go, "imagine what else can be done. Imagine what the two of us could do with a place like Efften."

CHAPTER 22

Lawdon pulled herself dripping from the dark waters between the boats of the Floating Palace. The rain fell steadily, dripping into her eyes. She grabbed a rope ladder with shaky hands and climbed the rungs as quietly as she could. The weight of her wet coat chafed at her armpits and elbows. Her skin was rubbed raw and inflamed from the seawater. It felt as if she'd swum the width of the Summer Seas.

Quietly recovering her breath, she checked her dagger. A surge of memories flashed through her mind, sharks frothing in the water, teeth gnashing, but she closed her eyes and clenched her teeth so hard she thought they would crack. But when she opened her eyes again and looked up, the tears had not come. She wouldn't let them. Not yet. She had one thing to do, then she didn't care what happened.

Silent as an eel, she peered over the edge of the empty ship. She was certain she would find Vinghelt's murderers waiting for her, swords in hand. But there was no one, only a quiet rail along the deck, curving into the rainy darkness. From the color of the banners she was flying, Lawdon knew the ship must belong to some minor branch of the Koscholtz family. Lord Koscholtz strongly supported Vinghelt, but Lawdon couldn't remember where his cousins stood.

She glanced quickly at the dim light from the lanterns. There were a few servants chatting on the next ship over, but none of them were looking this way. The storm had abated somewhat, cutting back to a low drizzle, and she heard the distant sounds of revelry from *Glory of Summer*.

Climbing up the last few feet of the ladder, she came aboard. She forced herself to stand tall, act naturally. At a distance, she wouldn't look any different than any other reveler who had stayed too long in the rain. She headed toward the next ship, but ducked behind a storage locker when she saw some-one coming.

Her heart thundered in her aching chest as she heard boots cross the wet deck and stop a few feet away from her. Shark teeth flashed through her mind's eye. She spun around, drawing her dagger and preparing to attack.

"Hot soup?" a voice asked.

Lawdon's face scrunched up, trying to make sense of the words.

"After that long swim, we thought you might like something warm in your belly."

"Mikal?" Lawdon said, peering at the cowled figure. He stood in the rain, a covered pot in one hand and a spare cloak in the other.

"Mind if I join you?" he asked.

She was too stunned to answer, and he hurried forward and crouched down on the wet deck next to her. "Hot soup. Warm cloak." He offered them to her.

She took the steaming pot and held it close to her chest as he wrapped the cloak around her.

"Reignholtz is dead," she said hoarsely. "And Brezelle."

Mikal closed his eyes, and he bowed his head forward. His mouth set in a tight line. "I'm sorry," he whispered. "We feared the worst."

Lawdon swallowed past the hard lump in her throat.

"How did it happen?" he asked. "Shara's been looking for you ever since you left. She found you with her magic, but couldn't locate the others. She sent me to meet you while she kept looking."

"I'm going to end this tonight," Lawdon rasped. She couldn't break down. Not now. She had business first. The mourning would have to come later.

Mikal looked at her but didn't say anything.

"That bastard is going to pay for what he did. Pay with his own life this time." She clutched the reassuring handle of her dagger.

"Lawdon." Mikal touched her shoulder. She shrugged it away.

"Don't touch me. I'm not here for sympathy."

He leaned back, his dark eyes searching her face. "Tell me what hap-pened," he said, touching her shoulder a second time. She closed her eyes and leaned her head back, fighting the tears that wanted to come.

"Sabotage," she murmured. "Brezelle's blood and . . ." Lawdon choked, then shook her head. "It doesn't matter." She set the soup down. "Tonight, Vinghelt dies. I'm going to kill him. With or without your help." She struggled to stand up, but Mikal firmly held her down.

"Calm down, Lawdon. We want Vinghelt to pay for his crimes as much as you do—"

"How dare you say that to me!" Lawdon raged, raising her voice more than she should have. She struggled to her feet and backed away from him. "This isn't some pleasure cruise. If you had the courage to draw that blade you carry, this would never have happened!"

Mikal took a long breath and sighed. "Are you done?" he asked.

Lawdon said nothing.

"Good. Then shut up and eat." He took the lid off the pot and offered her a spoonful. "I got you the shellfish in cream sauce you like so much."

Lawdon clenched her teeth. "I don't want your Fessa-be-damned soup!"

"We've already sent word to *Laughing Breeze*," Mikal interrupted. "Reignholtz kept good men about him. They'll get the children out of here, keep them safe."

Lawdon tried to calm her thundering heart. That was good thinking. There wasn't a ship in the Summer Fleet that could outrun *Laughing Breeze*, especially in a storm like this. Mikal offered the soup again. She considered kicking it into his face, but her mouth watered at the sight of it. Reluctantly, she sat back down and took a bite. It burned her raw throat going down, but warmed her belly.

"Was the blade poisoned?" Mikal asked. "Is that how Brezelle died? Vinghelt will be disgraced. We'll take it before all the Summer Princes."

"We can't. It wasn't poison," Lawdon said, between bites. "It was sharks."

"Sharks?"

She nodded. "They took him. They took Brezelle. They took Javthus and Matten." Lawdon told him of the boat that appeared out of nowhere. It was all a setup, and they had fallen for it.

"How did you survive?" Mikal asked.

"This," she said, grabbing the lapels of her soaking long coat. "This stupid thing. A few sharks approached, brushed against me, testing me the way sharks do, but none of them struck, they all turned away at the last second. There's something in the coat." She opened it and showed him the satin lining, sewed up in dozens of places, little sealed pockets.

"What is it?"

"My cabin boy, Dashiell, gave it to me. He's a superstitious boy; his mother's an herb woman from Tania. She sewed karryl leaves into the lining of the jacket." She shook her head. "Said they would keep away evil spirits of the sea. I humored him. I never thought . . ." She swallowed. "But it doesn't matter why. I shouldn't be alive, and Vinghelt will think the same."

"I see," Mikal said. "What is your plan?"

"Assassination. Quick, simple, while he thinks he's gotten away with it. There isn't time for anything else. I have to strike now, before it's too late."

"What do you plan to do about Vinghelt's men?"

"What?"

"I was followed on my way over here. And right now, the man who tailed me is chatting with a couple off-duty stewards on the boat next to us."

Lawdon peered over the locker at a small group of men standing under a rain tarp, around a smoldering deck-top fire pit.

"And Vinghelt probably has at least three more men around here someplace," Mikal continued. "If Shara can find you with her magic, then Vinghelt can find you with his. There is no element of surprise; you won't get within three ships of him."

Lawdon jumped to her feet, spilling the pot of soup across the deck. It didn't matter. She was going to kill him tonight. Kill them all if she had to! The tears had begun and she couldn't stop them.

"Come," he said, wrapping the cloak back around her. "They probably won't risk attacking us on the Floating Palace, but we can't be sure. Shara and I rented a berth nearby. We can decide what to do from there."

❋

Lawdon's tears had gone by the time Mikal led her belowdecks on a ship known to rent rooms by the hour during high summer.

A few men followed the two of them across the Palace, but Mikal had given them a wide berth and kept to well-lit and populated ships as much as possible. Vinghelt's thugs never came closer.

Mikal led her down a narrow corridor lit by a single red lantern and stepped into a room at the end of the hall.

Shara met them at the door, wearing a thin underdress. "Are you all right?" she asked, reaching out, but the look Lawdon gave stayed Shara's hand.

The Zelani stepped back, letting them into the room. The bed behind her was rumpled, the sheets and pillows tossed to the ground. Obviously the two of them had stopped to "fuel her magic" before bothering to look for anyone.

"Looks like you've been busy," Lawdon said, nodding at the bed. "It's a pity you weren't so dedicated to your art during the duel."

"It wasn't Shara who—" Mikal began, but Lawdon cut him off.

"Magic was used in that duel," she growled. "And where were you? Disappeared just like Avon Leftblade. My lord and my sister died tonight, and

where were you? Fucking in this room? Fucking on the deck? Fucking ..."
Lawdon turned away.

"I tried," Shara said. "They caught me unawares, and I was too slow to do anything about it."

"You tried?" Lawdon practically shouted. She wanted to punch Shara's pretty face.

"Easy, Lawdon—" Mikal put a hand on her arm, but she violently batted it away.

"Let me explain," Shara said softly, taking a dress from the vanity and slipping her arms through the sleeves. "You may not think so, but I did what you asked. I found the person behind Vinghelt's victories here on the Floating Palace. His name is Jesheks. He is posing as Vinghelt's physician."

"The fat albino?"

Shara nodded. "I was with him during the duel. I was convinced he was the one funneling magic into Natshea. I was ready to stop him, but I was wrong. He must have taught Natshea some of his art, for it was her power that she brought to bear. I tried to counter it, but I was too slow."

"Why? Why were you too slow?"

"I never suspected her," Shara explained, buttoning up her dress. "I scanned the woman, looked into her heart. I've never seen someone with that little confidence."

Mikal laughed. "Natshea? No confidence?"

Shara nodded. "Her bravado is an act. I never suspected someone who hated herself that much could access that kind of power. I assumed she was a puppet, just like Vinghelt."

"Then how do we kill her?" Lawdon asked.

"We're not going to kill anyone," Shara said.

Lawdon shook her head and started for the door.

"Think about what you are doing, Lawdon. Do you think you can just walk up to Vinghelt and cut his throat? That man took your lord's life. Don't let him take yours."

"What should I do? Jump off a wall and swim away from it all, is that it, Shara-*lani*?"

Shara clenched her teeth. "If you can swim away from this, then, yes, you should."

"Since when did you become a coward?" Lawdon asked.

Mikal stepped between the two women. "Hold on. Emotions are high. We've all—"

"Don't waste your life on petty revenge," Shara said, pushing Mikal aside.

"I know it's hard right now, but you will find something else that gives you joy."

"Find something else? Find something else!" Lawdon yelled. "For an all-powerful sex-sorceress, you don't know a damn thing about love, or loyalty, or family, or even common decency! What are you even doing here? What are you doing fucking Mikal all day long when the love of your life is on his way to Ohohhom?"

Shara went rigid. A flush crept into her cheeks.

Mikal reached for Shara, but she held up a hand, warning him to stay away. "Don't you talk to me about love! The man I loved gave up his life eighteen years ago. He's long gone, and there's no reason I should curl up and die alongside him."

An angry retort leapt to Lawdon's mind, but the look in Shara's eyes froze it on the tip of her tongue. The two women stared at each other for a long moment before Lawdon spoke again. "Are you going to help me kill Vinghelt or not?"

Shara sneered. "Vinghelt's blood won't mend your broken heart," she said, and breezed past Mikal, knocking his hand out of the way. "Nothing will."

She slammed the door behind her.

CHAPTER 23

Jesheks stood alone in his chambers feeling strangely dissatisfied. He considered calling a servant to fill the tub, but wasn't in the mood for a bath. He looked at the ironwood cabinet that held the tools of his craft, then turned away. No. Not that, either. He simply wasn't hungry for another routine exploration in the intricacies of his art.

The problem, he supposed, was that everything had gone exactly to plan. The end of his years in the Summer Seas had come too easily, and it left a bland taste in his mouth. He had so many contingency plans that would never be called into play. He had fingers in pots that would never be brought to a boil. He felt like a master physician who had been asked to butcher a pig.

From this point on, the outcome was in little doubt. The last significant opposition to Vinghelt's authority had been defeated. Jesheks's petty puppet would meet with the Summer Princes tomorrow, and by the end of the day they would be begging him to accept the admiralty of the Summer Fleet. Within a month they'd sail through Ohndarien and join the Opal Fleet in the Summer Seas. The combined strength of the two greatest navies in the world could overcome the fanaticism of the Silver Islanders. In eight weeks time, he and the Awakened Child would be landing on the shores of Efften, and his real work would begin. But the promise of an autumn harvest did little to ease springtime hungers.

The only lingering question in his mind was the outcome of the test he had crafted for Natshea. The child had left shortly after the duel, and Jesheks was already growing bored with her. Ever since meeting Shara, Natshea had seemed a paltry substitute for a true kindred spirit. The Zelani mistress's potential was unlimited, and Jesheks longed to unleash it, to mold it.

He took a deep breath and cycled through his disappointment. He had always savored the hunt more than the kill. There was no helping it; he would just have to keep hunting.

Unwilling to spend another night alone in his rooms, Jesheks headed abovedeck. He loathed walking, but perhaps he could find an amusing distraction amid the revelry over Vinghelt's victory.

Forcing his bulk up two narrow ladders, he emerged onto *Glory of Summer's* wet deck. It was mostly empty, just a few servants cleaning up after the celebration as the rain fell softly. Vinghelt must have moved the party elsewhere to honor the shiphomes of his staunchest supporters. The prince had always been very generous with other people's wine.

Jesheks was not interested in walking that far. He considered brewing some betony into an extra-strong sleeping draft and heading to bed, or—

Something at the bow of the ship caught his attention.

Shuffling forward, he noticed a woman perfectly balanced on the tip of the bowsprit. She stood absolutely still, legs together, arms at her sides. He extended his awareness toward her and briefly tested the turbulent ani swirling around her.

It was Shara, of course. Her power was unmistakable. But this was not the same woman who had bantered with him earlier in the day. She was distraught, deeply tormented. Jesheks smiled but kept control of the fluttering excitement in his chest.

She waited for him, no doubt probing him with her own magic as he shuffled across the deck to meet her. The few servants remaining on deck saw Jesheks coming, and all suddenly remembered important duties they must attend elsewhere.

He stopped at the prow just below Shara. Flipping his cowl down to reveal his face, he asked, "Have you been crying, child?"

"I'm not sure," she replied, still staring out at the starless night. "If I wasn't, I should have been."

Jesheks took a deep breath, careful to remain calm. Somehow, she suddenly reminded him of himself. "I did not expect you to return so soon."

"Neither did I," she replied.

With a single breath, Shara swept away her turbulent emotions. She funneled all of her ani into a surge of power and wrapped it around herself as if donning magical armor and preparing for battle. As graceful as the legendary sylph the bowsprit was carved to resemble, Shara walked heel to toe down the length of it and jumped onto the deck. "I think I might have come here to kill you."

"Really?" Jesheks enjoyed the sudden flush of fear as it rushed through his body. "Might I ask why?"

Shara smiled at him, such a sweet smile. Her lips so full, youthful. She looked barely twenty, but he knew she was older than that. Time did not move for true mages as it did for other people. Jesheks himself appeared to be in his mid-fifties, but he was half again that old.

"Consider it a favor for a friend."

"I see." Jesheks smiled. "Is your friend that pretty young woman who lost the duel today? Is she your apprentice?"

Shara shook her head. "No. My teaching days are over. Brezelle was just a canvas I was working on."

He nodded. "I understand perfectly."

"And now she is dead."

Jesheks nodded reluctantly. "I had heard. A very graceless turn of events. I assure you; I had nothing to do with that."

Shara watched him carefully, obviously searching for the truth in his words, but she kept her power to herself, not provoking a confrontation, not yet.

"And where is your canvas?" Shara asked.

Jesheks raised an eyebrow.

"Your towering young woman with the sharp tongue and eloquent blade?"

"Ah," Jesheks said. "I must admit that I have no canvases. My art is more akin to sculpture than painting. I have sent my latest piece off to the kiln to be fired."

"How long will she be gone?"

"Until she breaks," he said. "Or comes back stronger."

Jesheks watched her face; she had seemed terribly sad, almost dazed earlier, but now the wheels were turning inside her. He watched her lips for a long moment, imagining a few flecks of blood on them. Perhaps a thin cut in her chin right ... there.

"Have you decided whether or not to kill me?" he asked.

"No. But I would like to discuss our proposition."

"You would pool our knowledge? Share our experiences?"

"The idea has merit. With the archmages long dead, we are all that remains. If we do not share our knowledge, from whom will we learn?"

"What do you know about the Necani form?"

"I know you harness power from pain."

"And why haven't you sought knowledge of this before now?"

A flicker of a smile. "There are ten paths. Necani did not seem to lead where I wanted to go."

"Or you were afraid to try it?"

She paused, and he waited for the benighted lie that everyone professed at first.

"Yes," she said. "That also."

He raised an eyebrow. "I see you are not afraid of the truth."

"Magic is truth. How much of a mage could I be if I am afraid of my own art?"

"Well said." He nodded. "And what is your gut reaction to someone like me? How does it feel to stand next to a man who hurts others and himself for power?"

Energy flowed around them, their ani brushed like cloaks rippling close together in the wind, tangling, untangling. He could feel her presence all around him, sensing the same things he was sensing. Her body temperature increased, and an almost invisible sheen of sweat appeared at her temples, between her breasts and under her arms.

"It's rather unpleasant," she said.

"That is a generous answer. Most would call me horrific. An abomination. But that is simply because they do not understand. Pain is merely an intense sensation. It is only unpleasant when we resist."

"But pain is our body's way of telling us something is wrong."

"True. Pain is a message from the body, but that is the least interesting kind. There is another kind of pain that comes from much deeper. A message from the heart, the voice of the soul desperately trying to speak."

Shara paused, took a deep controlling breath. "And you strive to control that voice? Bend it to your will?"

He shook his head and felt a thrill run through him. If he were not a mage, he would never have known that this topic frightened and repulsed her. If she could control herself so well, how well could she control her surging thoughts while in the throes of real agony? She could be the one he had sought. She could be that one and more.

"Far from it," he answered. "I seek to travel the pain back to the sundered source and make it whole. One does not control pain any more than one controls an orgasm. Necani, like Zelani, is all about what happens after you lose control."

"I see."

"Not yet." He nodded, but his eyes never left hers. They drank of one another through that gaze. "But you will."

He closed his eyes, imagining Shara chained naked to his wall, rivulets of blood running down her back and around the curve of her ass. He opened his eyes, charged with the image. If she saw what he was thinking, it did not cause her to draw back. She pursed her lips ever so slightly, a glimmer in her eyes, a softness.

A cool tickle of uncertainty ran through him.

"Tell me," he said. "When was the last time you were out of control? Completely helpless in another's hands?"

The softness faded, and she withdrew into herself. Very curious.

She paused, then said, "Very recently, actually."

"Ah ..." He let silence fill the gap, then said, "I find that difficult to believe."

"Do you?"

He nodded. "Perhaps I am not making myself clear. Choosing to lose control over a strong emotion is different than what I mean. When was the last time you were helpless to make any choice?" He put one hand over another, letting the pinkie sheath rest on the back of his wrist. "When was the last time power over your pain—or pleasure—was completely in the hands of someone else?" Slowly, he pressed the pinkie sheath into his hand, letting the blood well up. "Because if you can walk away, that's not the same thing. It's not the same thing at all."

She said nothing, but her emotions were in turmoil. He could not read them, but he could feel her iron hand of control taming them, shaping them. Ah, so delicious. He shuddered at the thought of breaking this woman, rebuilding her.

"I see a pain trapped behind your eyes, Shara-lani," he said quietly, his voice almost a whisper. "Like a wild horse poorly caged. You're afraid of that animal, what would happen if it got free?"

Her chin rose, only a fraction, but he noticed it. She swallowed, and Jesheks longed to touch her, longed to put his pinkie sheath against her skin and push ...

"You came here to escape that pain, didn't you? But you will never win that race. No one can run that fast. I can show you how to embrace what you are running from, make it part of you."

She still held his gaze, but her hand went to her chest, trembling as she touched the fabric as if expecting to find something there. Her hand curled slowly in a loose fist, and she looked away.

"What are you missing?" he whispered. "Right there, between your breasts."

She yanked her hand away and shook her head.

"I can take you to the center of it, Shara-lani. I can take you to it, and through it, and you will never miss it again. You'd like that, wouldn't you?"

Her chin moved down, just a little, but she stopped herself. Ah, the control. He reached out; his thick fingers touched her collarbone and traced that delicious curve to the plunging neckline of her dress. He broke contact the moment before she pulled away, and he took her hand. He drew her closer, felt her sweet, steady breathing on his face. She closed her eyes, cycling that breath through. He felt her magic dance around them.

When she opened her eyes, she returned his gaze without flinching. He marveled at her strength. He had found the great crack in her wall, and she had mended it within two breaths.

"You are right," she said, her voice low, almost hoarse. "I am hiding something. Some . . ."

"Pain," he said.

She nodded. "A pain I cannot face."

It was all there, an ocean of power and torment, dammed up behind that wall. What a wonder she would be if she let it loose. Jesheks lost himself in the possibilities and barely noticed when her eyes focused on him again.

"But you have something hidden behind your eyes as well."

A sudden, terrifying thrill surged through him. For a panicked instant he wished he had never left his stateroom.

"You came to me," she said. "Crossed the deck to me. You have called to me since I came to the Floating Palace."

"I think you would make an amazing Necani," he answered truthfully.

She smiled, and he shifted a foot.

"It's more than that. You want something that I have," she said softly. "You want it so badly I can feel it."

Jesheks pulled his hand back and grabbed his own thigh. The spike on his finger sank through the fabric of his robe, touched his flesh. He pushed further, ready to retreat into the pain.

What was he missing? He must find the weakness. Stand in it. Gather the strength that—

He looked at her, and his image of her chained and streaked with blood was replaced. He saw her, bathed in candlelight, running a hand along his pale skin. He saw her tight, toned body sliding against his. A pain twisted in his chest. He tried to harness it, to use it, to gain that rush of power he knew so well, but it slipped from his grasp. It was a wild thing, beyond his experience.

"That may be true," he breathed, swallowing down a dry throat. "But alas, the Zelani art is quite beyond me for obvious reasons."

She reached out to him. Her long, delicate fingers touched his chest.

They were warm, soft. He quivered, wanting to draw away, but he held himself still.

"I must disagree," she said, barely a whisper.

He pulled away finally, broke gazes, and stared away in disbelief. How did this happen? He was the master here. Not her.

"My art is about pleasure, joy, and love," she said. "No blade can cut these things from you. Zelani is no more about sex than Necani is about wounds."

He closed his eyes, an emptiness yawned inside him, sudden and unexpected, hopelessly vast. He felt as if he was falling. He stepped to the side, looking for something to lean on. She took his hand, held him steady.

"If you can hurt me so badly that I will be free from my pain, then I can touch you so softly that you will feel again." She cupped his cheek and brought his face to meet her gaze. "You'd like that," she whispered. "Wouldn't you?"

Jesheks jabbed his pinkie sheath frantically into his leg, deep and hard. It poked through skin, fat, and muscle until it hit bone. He grabbed the sensation, and the power coursed through him. He forced his heart to beat slower.

"That sounds intriguing," he said, meting out his words.

"A trade?"

He nodded.

"You find my pain. I find your joy."

The fire in his leg returned his equilibrium, and the tantalizing image of her hanging in chains returned to him. He reached out, tenderly running a fingertip down a long, red wound in her back. She thrashed against her restraints, thin skin stretched tight over shuddering ribs . . .

"Exactly," he said. "It is decided then. We shall meet again under more private circumstances and see where this leads us."

She nodded. "Only one question remains."

He raised an eyebrow. The thrill of what she offered rushed through his body. He gathered his pain to himself, chasing that new, ticklish sensation that unnerved him so. "And what is that?"

"Whose path do we travel first?"

He smiled, and his anxiety faded away. Now that she had asked the question, he knew what he would answer. And so answering, he knew what her response must be.

"That is something I will let you decide, my child," he said.

Her smooth brow wrinkled ever so slightly. She had not expected that.

And when you choose what I know you must, he thought, *once you set foot upon my path, I will take you so far that you will never come back.*

CHAPTER 24

Lawdon woke with a plan.

She sat up in bed, wincing. Her back and shoulders ached from her long swim, and her skin was painfully raw and itchy. She'd fallen asleep in her salty, wet clothes. It was a stupid dusteater thing to do, but she'd been so tired last night. And she hadn't wanted to be naked around Shara, or . . . or whoever else was around.

The small, windowless room of the brothel ship was nearly black, but there was a little bit of red light coming from the crack below the door. Mikal was dozing in a chair facing the entrance, his naked blade resting on his lap. The door had been jammed shut with a triangular wooden doorstopper.

It must be nearly noon, Lawdon thought, judging by how hard and long she must have slept. Last night she had been sorely tempted to continue her plans despite Shara's and Mikal's warnings. But she slowly realized that she'd never avenge Reignholtz and Brezelle if she simply rushed off in a blind fury. If she was going to make Vinghelt pay, she'd have to be a lot smarter about it.

Quietly as she could, Lawdon climbed out of bed and pulled on her crusty boots. She removed the doorstop and slipped into the hallway.

"Where are we going?" Mikal asked. He jumped to his feet half-awake, sheathed his sword, and followed her out of the room.

Lawdon cursed under her breath but didn't answer. Keeping a hand on her dagger, she walked down the hall to the exit. She opened the hatch and was immediately blinded by the midday sun. With no other choice, she backed into the hall to wait for her eyes to adjust before risking the open deck.

"You must not have heard me," Mikal said, leaning against the wall beside her. "Where are we going?"

"*We* aren't going anywhere. Why don't you go find your pet Zelani and make some magic?"

A flash of emotion crossed his face, but he chased it off with a gallant smile. "And leave my lady undefended? Never."

"Enough with the act, Heidvell. I'm sick of it."

"Someone's got to stop you from throwing yourself upon Vinghelt's hired swords," he said, blocking her path with his leg. "Don't make me get a rope and tie you up."

Knocking his foot off the wall, she stepped past him. "I don't need a fop-pish admirer, and I don't need a high-minded babysitter. I need a steady blade at my back. If you can't do that, then get the hell out of my way."

She climbed one-handed up the ladder and onto the deck, dagger at the ready. No one was there to greet her. The ship was empty. She headed straight for *Glory of Summer*. Mikal followed her.

Lawdon's boots thumped across the decks as she crossed from one boat to the next. The sunlight danced across the waves around the Floating Palace. Her bright pennants and banners flickered in the breeze as though they were tired from last night's revelry. The Waveborn were just starting to reemerge from belowdecks. The Floating Palace was busy but not yet crowded. Law-don's eyes flicked around, looking for anything suspicious.

"I hate to ask a lady the same question three times, but where are we headed?" Mikal asked.

"Why don't you ask Shara? She's the mind reader around here."

Again, that flash of emotion. Was it anger? Worry? "I would," he said. "But she left and never came back."

"So go find her."

"I couldn't, even if I wanted to."

"Even if you wanted to? You expect me to believe you would rather be following me than her?"

"Yes."

"You actually want to help me?"

"Yes."

"You're a fool."

"A colossal fool. But I'm not going to let you do anything stupid."

"Better get a rope then, because we're almost there."

They crossed two more ships, and Lawdon could feel Mikal's tension as he realized where they were going. She led him straight to *Glory of Summer*. A small crowd in very rich dress was gathered around a heavily laden table on the main deck. Vinghelt's powerful voice could be heard as he spoke passion-ately to the attentive group.

The plank that spanned the gap between the ships was guarded by one of Vinghelt's men. Lawdon headed straight for the guard at the gap.

His hand rested on the pommel of his sword, but his gaze was turned toward the gathering behind him. At the last minute, he looked over at her. "Captain Lawdon," he acknowledged, "how good to see you. I was told that I should—"

She kneed him in the groin. He doubled over, and she leapt up to the landing. Grabbing a fistful of his hair, she swung around in a circle and flung him overboard. He caught the rail at the last minute and dangled two stories above water in the narrow space between *Glory of Summer* and *Dancing Dolphin*. Lawdon left him there and continued toward the gathering.

Guards at the three other entrances raised the alarm and rushed toward her. Vinghelt paused, and the assembled Summer Princes turned toward her.

Lawdon strode straight toward the group of stunned Waveborn. More armed men in black and gold rushed out of hatches and doorways toward her.

She made it to the table, her loose glove in hand. She swung it at Vinghelt's face with all of her strength.

A strong hand caught her wrist just before she landed the stinging slap. Her glove spun away, landing on the map-covered table. Several more guards grabbed her from behind and dragged her away.

The men tried to knock her to the ground, but she fought them, keeping herself upright through sheer force of will. The assembled princes and courtiers gave the scuffle a wide berth, creating a rough circle of cleared deck space around them.

Vinghelt watched her with amused surprise.

"My dear Captain Lawdon, have we done something to offend?"

"You know damned well what you've done!" Lawdon shouted. "And Fessa of the Deep will see you pay for it."

Mikal stood beside her, his hands held up in a placating gesture. Two of Vinghelt's men held the tips of their swords at his throat.

"I claim justice," Lawdon cried, loud enough for everyone on this boat and the next to hear. "Last night this man took the life of the greatest prince on the Summer Seas. Lord Reignholtz and his daughter were assassinated because they opposed his plans to make our people a slave to his ambition."

A murmur ran through the assembled princes.

Vinghelt's jaw clenched, but he forcibly turned it into a smile.

"Does anyone know what she is raving about?" he asked mildly, though his well-trained voice carried to everyone present. "Lord Reignholtz's daughter attempted to best my champion, but she lost." He looked at his companions. "That matter is decided. You saw it yourselves. The Test of Truth and Steel proved Lord Reignholtz's accusations hollow and false." Vinghelt held out his hands helplessly. "The prince and his daughter left here last night, and that was the last I knew of them."

"You're a liar," Lawdon said. "And an assassin. Your men cut them down last night as they fled to a physician." She spat at him. It landed on his maps.

The Summer Princes looked to one another, their expressions ranging everywhere from shock and confusion to open hostility.

"Your prince already made his challenge," Lord Koscheld, Vinghelt's strongest supporter, said in his deep voice. His voluminous burgundy clothes draped like a tent over his tremendous girth. His eyes were barely slits in his fat face. "That matter is decided, as Lord Vinghelt mentioned. He has already earned the goddess's favor and the mandate of his people." The huge man turned to the rest of the assemblage, and raised his voice. "Besides, this woman was only adopted into the Reignholtz shiphome. She was not born upon the waves and cannot issue such a challenge. Only her lord may."

Lawdon clenched her fists.

"No. No." Vinghelt held up his hands as though calming the silent crowd. His impeccable poise had returned, and the little half smile he always wore was back in place. Lawdon wished she could crack it with her fist. "I will honor this misguided grievance," he said magnanimously. "I would hate to have it said that I shrank from any challenge, no matter how baseborn its source."

Pulling off his glove one finger at a time, he stepped off the riser and approached Lawdon. With a slow swish, he brushed the glove lightly across her cheek.

"I accept your challenge."

He nodded at his men, and they released Lawdon, shoving her away from Vinghelt and standing between the two of them. She stumbled backward, wiped a hand across her mouth.

"The truth is paramount," Vinghelt said to the princes around him. "We must always strive to bring it into the light. I am happy to do whatever is necessary to bring all of the Summer Seas under a single banner of common purpose."

"No true heart would ever set sail under that banner." She pointed at the gathered nobility. "Just Summer Slaves and the Wave-bought."

Turning on her heel, she stalked away from the fuming crowd. Mikal followed, careful to avoid all of the blades still pointed at his face. They reached the gangplank and started across.

Mikal cleared his throat as they reached the next ship.

"Um, so that was your plan?" he asked.

"I am allowing verse and steel to illuminate the truth," Lawdon said tersely, pushing through a pack of curious onlookers.

"Ah, good. Tradition is a fine thing, I always say." He paused, then added, "And exactly whose steel is going to illuminate this truth?"

"I'm sure I'll find someone with a thunderous voice and steady hand willing to dance for justice."

"It will take a lot more than that to beat Natshea."

"Bury Natshea. I don't care about her."

"That's because you won't be facing her."

"I didn't go there to arrange a duel," she snapped. "One more useless duel won't solve anything." She looked around, but nobody else was within earshot. "I went there to schedule an assassination. The duel is merely a distraction."

"Oh . . ." he murmured, pondering. "I see. How long would this distraction have to last?"

"As long as possible."

"Ah-ha. Now that's a bit of a gray area isn't it."

"Yes it is."

"Wise men avoid gray areas."

"Then I had better find myself a colossal fool, hadn't I?" She kept right on walking, and he had to hurry to keep up with her.

CHAPTER 25

So, what does one wear to be tortured by a power-hungry madman ...?" Shara asked herself aloud in her little room on the brothel ship. She sifted through her new wardrobe, trying to think her statement was funny, but it didn't calm the nervousness that fluttered in her chest.

She was already late. The boat Jesheks had sent for her was waiting, but she needed to get dressed first. All of the clothes she had purchased in Faradan were on *Laughing Breeze* when it sailed with Reignholtz's children. She was left with nothing but the sapphire earrings she wore. Earlier in the day, she sold the jewels, went to the first dressmaker's barge she could find, and bought every dress they had in her size. She'd spent so much on clothes that she couldn't afford to pay for her room, and she still couldn't find a single thing she wanted to wear.

She continued to paw through her clothes, not really seeing any of them. The short green skirt? No. That was for impressing young men like Mikal. It would seem frivolous to the albino.

What the hell are you doing, she thought. Grab anything, or go naked. She snatched the short green skirt and an image of Victeris flashed through her mind. Those nights on Bloody Row, crawling incessantly across the wooden floor, her shredded knees ...

"When was the last time you were completely helpless?"

She couldn't put herself in that position again. Wouldn't.

"I see pain trapped behind your eyes, Shara-lani. I can take you to it, and through it, and you will never miss it again."

His words were a devilish mixture of wisdom and insanity, just like Victeris's had been. But what had she been before she thrust her hand into that bonfire in Faradan? Wasn't that crazy, too? Weren't all mages insane in one way or another?

She saw Victeris crushed against the rose marble of the Zelani courtyard, his brother and Gorlym rushing to his side.

Shara turned, put the green skirt away, and snatched the most sensible dress she'd bought, an ankle-length gown of blue silk with a scooped neckline crisscrossed by a network of laces.

Pulling free the knot at the back of the short skirt she wore, she slipped it over her hips and let it slide to the ground. Her fingers were at work on the buttons of her blouse when she sensed someone beyond her door.

She sent her attention through the thick wood to touch the man standing there. Mikal's life light was a tangled ball of chaotic emotions. Lawdon wasn't with him, but news of her challenge had spread across the Floating Palace. She would be safe until the duel. It would look bad if she died before it.

Shara drew a deep breath, quickly took off her blouse, and slipped the dress over her head. This was a conversation she had better be clothed for.

She crossed to the door and opened it. His neck and arms were tense, but he tried to keep the angst off his face. His jaw muscles worked as he stood there.

"Were you going to wait out there all night?" she asked.

"I've been waiting outside your door for a long time now. Another night wouldn't have mattered."

Shara sighed, turned to her mirror, and began tugging at the laces of her bodice, closing it tight. She didn't have time for this. Jesheks's men were waiting.

"You going out again?"

"Yes."

"And when can we expect you back?"

"I'm not sure."

"I see. How reassuring."

"Mikal . . ."

"What? I'd hate to ruin your sparkling social life, but it seems to me that we need you here right now. In case you haven't heard, there is a duel tomorrow, and I'd like to fare a bit better than your last set of friends."

Shara combed her dark hair to the side, glancing briefly in the mirror, and fixed it with a wooden comb. She looked back at Mikal. "I know about the duel, and I'm doing what I can."

"What exactly is that?"

When she didn't say anything, he continued. "Because it looks to me like you're leaving me behind to be Lawdon's idiot champion and personal watchdog while you've moved on to better things."

She sighed, wishing this could have taken place some other time.

"Ah, the frost queen has thawed enough to give me a sigh. I'm so honored."

She gave him a warning look.

"Don't I have a right to know where you're going?" He paused, waiting for her to answer.

Shara felt Mikal's anger like a coiled serpent. "I arranged a meeting with Jesheks," she said.

He spun around, looked like he was going to punch the wall. "I knew it! You've traded me for that bloated eunuch?"

"What are you talking about?"

He spun back around. "I'm sorry, is the poet not speaking plainly enough? I saw the way you looked at that fat man. I watched you both times. You were smiling this secret little smile that you've never given me and never will."

"It's nothing like that—"

"Don't lie to me," he hissed. "Believe me, I've been the liar often enough."

"You don't see why I have to do this," she said quietly.

"No, I don't. But I'll tell you what I do see. That disgusting albino has put you under some kind of spell."

She shook her head as he paced across the room. She thought about easing his pain, turning his anger to joy with a blissful kiss. It would only take a second, and he would be out of her hair. "It isn't that simple, Mikal."

"That's just what I told myself again and again after you took me."

"I don't have you under a spell."

"Don't you?"

"Not like you mean," she said. "No."

"Well that's what it feels like!" he shouted, smacking his fist against his chest.

She faced him, placid. "What do you want, Mikal?" she asked in an even tone. "What do you need from me?"

He grabbed her by the arm, hard. "I need your help tomorrow!" he said, shaking her. Her comb slipped, letting loose a cascade of hair. "I need you here, Shara. I love you! I love you so badly it's tearing me apart!"

She turned away from him, caught her reflection in the mirror. Calm posture, serene eyes, perhaps even a coquettish stance. Her dark eyes were alluring, whispering of promise even as she averted her gaze. Elegant, compelling, a woman of perfect control. A prize to make men salivate and fall to their knees. All of the things she had taught herself to be. She swallowed and looked away.

His hand was still on her arm, but softer now. "Don't go." His other hand closed on her shoulder, and he looked at her in the mirror. She took a deep breath. His heart was in his eyes.

"Let me inside," he said. "Let me past that door you're hiding behind."

She replaced the comb in her hair. "Believe me, Mikal, you don't want what's behind my door."

"Yes, I do," he whispered, leaning in to kiss her neck.

She turned away from him and started for the door. "I'm very late," she said. "But I'll be back as soon as I can. We'll talk about this later."

"No!" He grabbed her again, spun her around, and threw her against the wall. She let out a little breath as her back hit the wood. Mikal pressed his body against hers, pinning her arms over her head. His mouth nuzzled her neck. "Are you going to let me in," he whispered. "Or do I need to break down your door?"

Shara ripped her hands from his grasp and slapped him across the face.

"How dare you!"

He backed up, startled, and she slapped him with her other hand.

"How dare you!"

"What do you expect?" he shouted, his face twisted in anguish. "You made me this way! You did this to me! You've changed me from an abject coward into a glorious slave. Forgive me for playing the part!"

Her magic hovered around her like a haze, but she kept it at bay. "You idiot!" she said. "I did nothing to you. All I did was unlock those stupid chains you bound yourself with."

"I didn't ask you to—"

"Shut up!" she said. "You're ten times the man you think you are! All I did was fuck you hard enough for you to believe it!"

"It may have just been a fuck for you, but not for me!" he said, his voice breaking. "Can't you see that I love you?"

"You love what I've given you. Nothing more. You found your confidence with me. But it was *your* confidence. I put nothing there that didn't already exist."

"Shara—" His hand trembled, rising to touch her, but he didn't.

"You don't love me, Mikal. You lust for me. I'm that glorious rush we all get from someone who dazzles us. I care for you, Mikal, but above all else, I am a Zelani. Make no mistake about it. I do not fall in love . . ." She choked on the last word, turned away, and grabbed the door handle. "If you want love, look to Lawdon. She is the one who loves you."

"Shara, please . . ." he whispered.

She shook her head, flinging open the door. "I have to go. You have your duel to fight," she said. "And I have mine."

She slammed the door behind her.

❄

The black-clad men rowed Shara quietly across the water. Neither of them spoke. They were Vinghelt's men, of course, but she didn't care about that. Mikal's intrusion was perfectly ill-timed. Shara needed to focus tonight. She needed her emotions smooth and carefree.

She shook her head. It didn't matter. Not now. Perhaps it would all come spilling out tonight, but not here. Not in front of Vinghelt's servants.

Keeping her chin high, she breathed in the summer air as they rounded yet another outcropping of the moss-covered shores surrounding the vineyards east of Vingheld. Moonlight danced on the waves, and Shara evened her breathing.

Jesheks's personal ship hove into view, tucked into a little cove far out of sight of the Floating Palace. She suddenly realized she wasn't the only nervous one on the boat. The servants rowed hard, sweat on their brows, and she could feel their unease and disgust as they approached the black ship.

They slid up alongside and bumped the hull next to a dangling rope ladder. Neither man offered to go up first. They merely sat there.

One of them said, "The physician is the only one aboard. He's expecting you in the aft stateroom."

Shara watched his eyes flick to the rail overhead, then back to her. Finally, he lowered his gaze.

They don't think I'll be coming back, she thought, and she wondered how many people these two had rowed out here to this deserted cove for the albino's pleasure.

A shiver crept up her spine. She stood up.

"Thank you, gentlemen," she said. Neither one of them looked at her, so she turned, hooked her foot into the first sagging rung, and climbed the ladder. She hadn't even made it halfway up before they began rowing away as if ghosts were chasing them.

She moved quietly aft, her bare feet making no sound on the polished deck. The sails were furled, and the ship creaked in the wind as it slowly rocked with the waves.

Shara entered the door to the aft stateroom and found a warm and inviting cabin lit by a roaring fire. She scanned the room for signs of something unpleasant. Blades. Whips. Dried blood. There was nothing. It was as if she'd walked into Baelandra's living room.

Jesheks sat on the far side of the room in a wide wooden chair lined with thick cushions. The soft firelight playing across his pale, fleshy features.

"A fireplace aboard a ship? You are either very daring or very foolish," Shara said. She touched the edge of the door with her fingertips, hesitated. With a deep breath, she pushed it shut. The latch clicked.

"Is there a difference?" he asked. With a smile, he indicated an identical chair to his right. "Come. Sit with me. Have some wine."

She smiled slightly, crossed the room, feeling every movement in her legs, in her hands as they passed through the air. She wouldn't set Jesheks off his balance by swinging her hips, but it made her feel grounded. Pausing at the chair, she looked at the wine. "There aren't any little lights floating around in it, are there?"

He raised a pale eyebrow. "Siren's Blood? Alas no. Have you ever tasted the madmen's spirit brew?"

Shara descended into the soft and luxuriant chair, but she did not sit back. Crossing her legs, she said, "I had the opportunity once, but it was taken from me."

"Then you were closer than I have ever been," Jesheks said. "Tasting the Islander's ani wine is still on my list of things to do."

"Then I suggest that you do not raise a cup of it with Arefaine around," she said, looking past his expression to the fire, noticing something she had not before. Seven metal rods of different widths rested at the edge of the blaze, their tips buried in the coals. She swallowed, smoothing her breath to an even rhythm. She turned her gaze back on Jesheks.

"What else is on your list?" she asked.

"You."

Shara touched him gently with her magic, knowing he must be doing the same to her. He appeared calm, but inside, anticipation swirled with fear and excitement.

"I don't know who is more frightened. You or me," he said.

Shara smiled. He was straightforward, she would give him that. There was something refreshing about his brutal honesty. She expected more deception from someone like this, but Shara suddenly realized that she was the deceiver in this room, trying to seem unafraid when her heart fluttered in her chest.

"Why are you frightened?" she asked.

"You have the ability to change me, to transform me into something unknown, unrecognizable. And I have the power to do the same to you. It is a dangerous intimacy we propose. That is why it is so compelling."

She nodded. "Compelling is the perfect word. Ever since I was a child, I've been thrusting my hand into the fire to see how it feels."

"And how does it feel?" he asked.

"Like freedom."

Jesheks's red eyes flickered. "Well then, shall we set each other free?"

Shara stood up, smoothed her dress. She reached out, and Jesheks put a pale, puffy hand in hers. She helped him rise to his feet.

"Yes," she said. "Let us begin."

His thick fingers touched her temple, brushed a lock of windblown hair behind her ear. She shivered, let the sensation roll through her, and added it to her power.

"Have you decided which of us will go first?"

Fear blossomed in her chest, spreading cold tendrils through her body. She kept it, let it flow, turned it into energy. But it ached to be released. She wanted this, despite it all, she longed to see what Jesheks offered. She closed her eyes, feeling the dread seep through her limbs to her extremities, leaking out through her fingers and toes.

She opened her eyes.

"I will go first," she said.

He nodded, and Shara realized that he'd known her answer already.

"You are very brave, Shara-lani," he said softly. She felt anticipation ripple through his body.

His hand pressed lightly against her back to guide her forward, but she hesitated. He waited, fingers soft and warm through the sheer protection of her dress.

She took the first small step toward the fire, then another.

CHAPTER 26

"You remember the plan?" Lawdon asked as she watched Mikal fumble with his sword belt, his bleary eyes struggling to focus in the dim light.

"Plan? What plan?" he asked, acting surprised. He tried to flash a dashing smile, but he just looked tired. Worn thin.

Apparently Mikal and Shara had some kind of falling-out, and he'd spent the last night in a drunken rage. If Mikal's heart wasn't in the duel, Natshea would make short work of him. And if Mikal's pounding head or fickle spine weren't in the duel either, the contest would be even shorter.

The man had gotten up before her, she had to give him that. Or perhaps he hadn't gone to bed at all last night. Regardless, he returned to their rented cabin shaved, starched, and impeccably dressed for his duel. But the bright colors did nothing to hide the bags under his eyes, and the fine tailoring couldn't cover the slouch in his shoulders.

He finally conquered his buckle and sketched a flamboyant bow. "Shall we waltz to our doom?"

Lawdon nodded reluctantly. She wore new clothes as well, mostly because she needed blousy sleeves to hide her daggers. She'd also spent half the night sewing fresh karryl leaves into the lining of her new vest and boots. There was a good chance she would be swimming today, and she wanted to be prepared.

Following Mikal out of the room and onto the deck, she went over the plan one more time in her head. It was a simple plan. She'd do to Vinghelt exactly what he did to Reignholtz. As soon as the duel started, Lawdon would lose herself in the crowd and discreetly work her way as close to the false prince as possible. She'd never be noticed in the blood-hungry throng.

Despite his quips, Mikal knew his part. He was supposed to make the duel as compelling as possible, then bungle his lines and throw the match. When the crowd rushed forward to carry Vinghelt on their shoulders, Lawdon would be right there to plant her dagger in his spine. The chaos of the celebration would be the only time she could get close enough to him to assure a killing blow.

She might even be able to escape into the crowd before order could be restored.

Her only worry was Mikal. He was a reluctant ally at best. If he lost his nerve and failed to give Natshea good sport, the spectators would quickly turn on him and hardly be inspired into a victory parade.

The crowd was just as large that morning as it had been the afternoon that Brezelle Reignholtz died. The sun shone hot over the Summer Seas, and the Waveborn wore their skimpiest summer attire. The mood, however, was unusually quiet and subdued. News of Brezelle's death had spread across the Floating Palace, and last night's festivities had been the most lackluster Lawdon had ever seen. History was turning on this moment, and everyone knew it.

She couldn't help scanning the crowd, hoping that Shara would reappear. But the Zelani was nowhere to be found. As much as Lawdon distrusted what she and Mikal did together, the man could certainly use a healthy dose of whatever magic she had been feeding him.

As they drew close to the *Glory of Summer*, someone from the crowd spat at their feet.

Mikal smiled and waved at the man as if he'd just cheered. A few unconnected boos rose from the throng.

"They seem a bit hostile," Lawdon said.

"Oh some, I suppose," Mikal replied, his steps heavy, his movements slow. "But look at the many pitying gazes among the lethal stares. Not all bear me ill will."

"Pity makes you happy?"

"I am merely pointing out that some feel sad as they think of me losing."

"It doesn't matter if you lose," she whispered.

"Still, it's nice to see that my reputation precedes me." Mikal smiled as he spoke the words, but his breath shook with nervousness. "Nothing stiffens a man's resolve like the unwavering support of those he loves."

"You get us through the next hour, and I'll stiffen more than your resolve," Lawdon said, desperate for something to snap him out of his funk.

"How charitable of you," he said, feigning a rakish smile. "Nothing is quite so romantic as pillow talk from a beautiful young woman determined to get herself killed."

Lawdon looked up into his bloodshot eyes. She wasn't sure if she should slap him or start crying.

Glory of Summer was packed to overflowing just as before. Spectators filled the main deck, the viewing deck and both half-decks fore and aft. Children clung from the rigging and the masts like barnacles.

The teeming throng backed away, forming a narrow tunnel of bright clothing and somber faces leading to the empty dueling space in the center of the main deck. At the far side stood a tall, broad-shouldered gentleman leaning on his blade as if he were posing for a portrait. His right hand rested on his sword as if it were a walking stick, his other hand hung at his waist, turned aside to hide his curling fingers. Flamboyant white ruffles peeked out of the breast and cuffs of his purple surcoat. An overly large mustache curled down the sides of his mouth, trailing into waxed points on either side of his chin, and a wide-brimmed purple hat was cocked at a rakish angle on his head. An enormous white feather billowed out of his hatband. The plumage was so large Lawdon imagined a stiff breeze could carry it all the way across the Great Ocean.

"I know that hat," Mikal said, as they walked toward the man. "I never liked it."

Lawdon stopped, her rage fighting with her fear. It was Avon Leftblade. The traitor had switched sides in every way.

"Where is Natshea?" Lawdon murmured, as they entered the dueling space.

"It appears she wasn't able to make it," Mikal said.

Lawdon felt a surge of hope, but it was quickly replaced by her growing sense of dread. If Natshea wasn't here, there must be a reason. It must be to Vinghelt's advantage somehow.

Avon Leftblade pulled his sword from the deck and strode to the center of the circle, waving the blade as casually as a child with a cattail. "Thank you all for coming," he said in a rough, commanding voice. A subdued murmur rippled through the crowd.

Lawdon scowled at Vinghelt and his entourage sitting underneath the sunshade, perfectly positioned at the edge of the dueling ring. The upstart lord didn't even deign to look at her. He should be speaking in his own defense, but it would debase him to debate with the dustborn.

Leftblade continued. "Yet again, we are here to face slanders against one of our great princes. The servant of a disgraced master has brought forth vengeful accusations, but once again the truth will prevail. We shall raise a wave from the heart of the Summer Seas and wash away all of the enemies of our way of life. This man"—he pointed to Vinghelt, who did his best to look dignified and aloof—"strives to bring glory and peace to all Summermen. He does not shrink from our enemies, be they from ship or shore. He has bled with your sons on foreign sands and will pay any price to protect the very foundation of our Eternal Summer." He paused. Some cheered, and a few people stomped their feet, but this was not the same crowd that had surrounded Natshea and Brezelle's duel. They were grim and quiet, waiting for the outcome.

"Is there anyone who denies the truth of my words?" Leftblade asked, cocking his head as if he would need to hear the answer from a great distance.

Lawdon glanced at Mikal. His eyes narrowed at the purple-clad duelist. With his smirk firmly in place, Mikal drew his blade and plunked it point down, putting one hand on his waist in mimicry of Leftblade's first pose.

> "Salt and spray
> Sea and sky
> Water, wave, and Waveborn
> The very bones of the earth deny your words."

The grand master scoffed in the resounding silence. He plucked his sword from the deck and spun it round his head, just missing his hat. With a sneer, he said:

> "Your words are pretty, their sentiment amusing,
> From a brat best known for whoring and boozing
> Your jest was meant my ire to provoke
> But your life, my lord, is the true joke."

A few boots stomped the deck, and a drunken cheer burst raucously from the back of the crowd.

Mikal cocked his head to the side, as if hearing something from far away, then looked at Leftblade. "I prefer pretty words to petty ones, especially from a man whose boots spent last night under Vinghelt's bed."

A swell of murmurs ran through the crowd, and a few people cheered. "Enough words," a redheaded man shouted from the front row. "Let's see your steel!"

"Well said," Leftblade agreed, hurling his blade into the air. He feigned disinterest in his throw, looking the other way. It thunked into the deck a foot from Lawdon, who never looked at it. She kept her eyes on Mikal.

Leftblade slowly brought his gaze around to Lawdon, his eyes mere slits and his voice heavy with contempt. He pointed a stiff finger at her. "In the name of Lord Vinghelt, I name thee an enemy of the Waveborn and a Physendrian spy. Have you a champion ready to pit your truth against mine?"

Mikal turned his back on Leftblade and retreated from the circle, walking right past Lawdon. A rumble went through the crowd, but he spun just as he passed her, knocking her off-balance and dipping her backward into a long and lingering kiss. Several cheers went up at the flamboyant gesture, and the deck shook with stomping feet.

"What are you doing?" Lawdon whispered, as his lips pressed against hers.

Mikal broke the kiss, but he did not pull her up. "Stealing a kiss before I die," he whispered back, then spun her back to her feet.

"Treasonous lips could never taste so sweet," he said to the crowd.

"Save it for the bedroom," the same redhead in the front row yelled. "Show us your steel!"

Mikal swung his blade underhanded toward the heckler. The redhead's eyes went wide, but Mikal flicked his wrist at the last moment, sending the sword hurling toward Leftblade. It stuck so close to the grand master's feet that he shuffled backward. Lawdon couldn't tell whether or not the man's foot would have been skewered if he hadn't moved. A dark flush crept into Leftblade's face. The sword was supposed to have been thrown at Vinghelt, not the duelist. Lawdon had no idea what Mikal was doing, or why.

"I call that man an upstart prince," Mikal began, pointing at Vinghelt. "And cowardly murderer of his betters. He speaks of peace in a call to war. He seeks to destroy all we sail for. His lies, his greed, his hate, and his prancing hat of a champion shall not pass my blade."

Many cheers arose for Mikal's speech.

Leftblade stood calmly behind the wobbling sword. "If you dislike my hat so much, you are welcome to take it from me."

"Even a dusteater wouldn't touch that hat," Mikal called. Laughter flitted through the crowd. "But I like the feather. Perhaps I'll take that."

Leftblade removed his hat with a flourish and held it forth. "Take it then ... if you have the courage."

Mikal smiled, but he did not approach.

"I didn't think so," Leftblade said, curling the hat up his arm in a deft flip, setting it back on his head. He tugged the brim, fixing it at the same rakish angle.

Lawdon leaned close to Mikal and whispered, "What are you doing? Don't cock this up. Not now."

Mikal held up a finger to Leftblade. "One moment, please, I feel a sudden urge."

In the blink of an eye, he spun around and dipped her again, pretending to kiss her. "All is well in hand," he whispered, his lips brushing against hers. "I say we ruin Vinghelt first. Then kill him."

"No!" she hissed back. The crowd catcalled and cheered once again.

"Leftblade, doesn't Vinghelt get a kiss?" yelled a woman's voice in the crowd, and their cheers turned to laughter.

"We can't have you risking your neck," Mikal said under the cover of the crowd noise.

"I don't care about my neck."

"But I do."

He lifted her back onto her feet. "I have a weakness for freckles."

For the first time since he met Shara, Lawdon saw the old fear in Mikal's face. But it wasn't cowardice this time. It wasn't the fear of a man about to run away, but of a man about to stand still and take a hit.

"Did you come here to fight or dance?" shouted a burly man from the observation deck above.

"Dance, of course," Mikal said with a flourish, closing his eyes and sketching a few steps with a mock partner.

Lawdon was ready to kill him. The man was insane if he thought this farce would save her life. This duel was the only real chance she had at vengeance.

Mikal suddenly opened his eyes and looked surprised to be standing in the middle of a thousand people. "Oh, you're still here," he said to Leftblade. "Shall we do this then?"

"Indeed," Leftblade growled.

"Then let it begin."

"Let it begin!" Vinghelt shouted, trying to seem as if he had spoken first. His brow was furrowed in confusion.

Each man sprinted for his sword. They snatched up their weapons at exactly the same moment, turned, and lunged for one another. Steel clashed in the center of the circle. Mikal parried, riposted, and was blocked by Leftblade. The two circled, and Leftblade spoke:

> *"You fight for the servant of a disgraced lord*
> *With an idiotic kiss and a misthrown sword*
> *Your pathetic lies shall never convince*
> *True hearts to turn from their lord and prince."*

A torrent of claps arose from the crowd. Boots pounded the deck. Mikal slashed his blade at the air twice, spun the hilt around his hand, and caught it.

"I admire your logic, your ethics, your hat
Your purple coat, your tailored frills, your love of a rat
Your voluminous plume, your dedication to doom, and your sweet-smelling scat
Honestly, my friends ... Who would not follow that?"

The crowd exploded into raucous noise, half-cheering and half-booing Mikal's doggerel presented with an exaggerated cadence.

Lawdon gritted her teeth, torn between wanting to kiss him and wanting to kick him in the jewels. At least he was fighting, and she couldn't waste the time he'd given her. She backed slowly into the unruly crowd and squirmed her way toward Vinghelt's entourage.

Leftblade charged in for another exchange, and Mikal fell back under the assault, fencing with exaggerated moves, acting clumsier than he truly was. The former legend pushed him back into the crowd. Feigning complete exhaustion, Mikal stumbled into the arms of a particularly large and ugly man. The thug tossed him back into the dueling circle, and Mikal made an elaborate show of not falling down.

Leftblade stalked to the center of the dueling space before spinning and pointing an imperious finger at Mikal.

"You mock those who fight for our proud shores
You shame those who've died in our just wars
These fine people will never bend the knee.
To your dustborn trollop's shrill whimsy."

Mikal snatched a gaudy pink hat from a middle-aged woman in the crowd. He plopped it on his head backward and stood opposite his opponent, mocking his serious pose. With overblown indignation, he spouted:

"I do so love your words of peace
That ask for war and not its cease
Why not rush to this foul war?
If it brings more gold to our sweet shores?"

Again the crowd was torn between booing and cheering for Mikal's clownish poetry.

Leftblade attacked, but Mikal refused to engage him. He backed up, spun away, skipped around the open deck. Leftblade refused to chase him and stood his ground, furiously saying:

> "This pup was well-known in his time.
> A whining mongrel without a spine
> And he's still the same useless and cowardly fool
> Who was once paddled and kicked out of school
>
> He has always been a wastrel, stuck in his youth
> Who would rather make a joke than fence for the truth
> The pathetic wretch considers it the height of flair
> To run away while mocking another man's headwear."

A genuine cheer rose from the crowd. Mikal stumbled backward, pretending to be stabbed through the heart.

> "I was a very poor student, I have to admit
> Distracted and lazy, an insufferable git
> I'd a greater eye for your wife than my blade
> And rumpled your bed, when together we played.
>
> The poor girl shed light on your primary fault
> Your limp little secret that makes ladies halt
> After raising a fish knife in her frustration
> She fled back to me to be her salvation
>
> All this explains your tall hat, I surmise
> Each man should have one thing of great, swelling size
> I apologize if your grand plume I did mock
> It's surely as stiff and strong as your . . ."

Laughter erupted from the crowd as a few drunken voices shouted the missing word.

Red-faced, Leftblade chased Mikal, clashing swords in place of a rhyme. Mikal was driven back under the flurry of blows, completely on the defensive.

Lawdon hissed, wondering if Mikal's stings were enough to goad the seasoned duelist into a mistake. She continued around the crowd until she found a spot against the rail only ten feet from where Vinghelt sat.

Mikal broke from the combat and ran from Leftblade, stooping and hiding behind children in the crowd. The children shrieked in delight, making them a very difficult shield to stay behind.

Leftblade stopped his pursuit, waving his blade.

"Is this the duelist I must face
Lacking honor, wit, and grace?
A scuttling rabbit with a chicken's beak
His rhymes a sham, his sword arm weak?"

Leftblade lunged with blurring speed, slashing at Mikal and nearly hitting a child. A mother screamed, and a wave of boos rose from the crowd.

Mikal picked up the closest boy and tossed him up on his shoulders. With a laugh, the child wrapped his arms around Mikal's forehead.

Deterred by the booing crowd, Leftblade did not come after Mikal this time. He stood, seething, as Mikal's latest jest played out. Passing his sword up to the boy, Mikal said:

"The purple man's disapproval hurts me so
And now he says he wants a new foe
Perhaps this bold swordsman will give him fair game
He's a riotous fighter of most renowned name

His words are pure pain, his strikes are most cruel
He'll take this fine blade and win this foul duel
I hope lonely Leftblade will find his lost joy
But first I must ask ... what do they call you, boy?"

The crowd erupted into laughter as the boy ate up all the attention and swung the sword for all he was worth as Mikal staggered about. Leftblade watched with a frown, and said:

"How long must this farce go on?
The conclusion is long since foregone
How can you cheer for a man who throws scorn
Into the traditions that make us Waveborn?"

The boy waved the sword at Leftblade, and shouted, "You're supposed to let blood and steel decide, not blood and squeal decide."

The crowd roared in approval. Their laughter was ever-present now as Mikal won them over. He skipped around the circle, and the boy swung his sword, giggling in delight. Mikal pulled out two daggers hidden under his shirt and began juggling them.

A sudden spike of panic rushed through Lawdon. She clutched the sheath hidden in her sleeve. The blade was gone. She clutched at the other arm. Also missing. Her flood of panic boiled into rage as she realized what happened. The kisses. That traitorous thief had lifted them when he kissed her.

Fuming, she looked around the crowd for another blade she could steal. There were a few, but it wouldn't be easy. She glared back at Mikal playing the fool for the crowd. What the hell did he think he was doing?

Mikal fumbled the daggers and charged from the cleared area, and the crowd made way for him as he climbed up the forecastle steps and jumped to the railing overlooking the dueling area. He grabbed a cup of wine from a startled gentleman in a green doublet, and balanced on top of the rail. The boy on his back squealed in delight, almost dropping the sword into the crowd as Mikal wobbled on the narrow bar. Wine sloshed on the people below. Clearing his throat, Mikal began to walk the rail, arms out to steady himself as he spoke:

> "My throat is parched, my muscles sore
> As my man and I march off to war
> But I'll drink this wine, he'll drink the blood
> Of foul Physendrians facedown in mud.
>
> We'll share this salty cup with everyone
> We'll proclaim our greatness, outshine the sun
> Look how the boy loves a sword in hand
> Shall we send him to war and make him a man?"

"Shut up and duel!" A black-and-gold-clad man shouted above the cheers of the crowd. He stepped forward quickly and shoved Mikal from behind.

A woman screamed as Mikal's foot shot off the rail. With a shriek, the child dropped the sword. It clattered to the deck below. Mikal twisted in mid-air as they fell, trying to protect the child with his body. They crashed to the planks, and Mikal's head cracked on the wood.

The crowd gasped and surged forward. Lawdon fought her way through them, desperate to see what had happened. Practically crawling between their legs, she forced her way to the front.

Mikal lay stunned on the deck. The wide-eyed boy was sprawled on his legs. A frantic woman burst through the crowd and snatched the boy away.

Leftblade sauntered over to Mikal's sword, flipped it up off the deck with his boot, and snatched it out of the air with the curled fingers of his left hand. With a wry smile, he spoke:

"This chasing with swords and nasty words
Is leaning toward the rank absurd
The time has come to bow and yield
And face the awesome truth I wield."

Leftblade whipped both blades around, crossing them at a point just under Mikal's chin. A long length of blade extended past Mikal's neck on either side. One flick of the wrist, and his throat would be sliced open.

With a grunt, Mikal slowly sat up. Leftblade followed him, keeping the blades a precise inch away from his flesh.

The mirth had fled from Mikal's face. His blue eyes flashed and he spoke loudly:

"I do not yield, good sir. I will never yield
Naked, I fight with the truth as my shield."

Leftblade nodded, his blades slowly withdrew from Mikal's neck, then with a sneer and a flick of his wrist, Leftblade slashed him across the ribs with Mikal's own sword. Mikal cried out, falling back, hands at his side. Blood leaked between his fingers, flecking the deck as he rolled to his knees. Leftblade's lip curled in a sneer, and he said:

"I claim the call of first blood
Undeniable in its flood
This farce is over, the matter decided
This poor fool was lost, misguided."

The crowd stayed deadly silent as Leftblade lifted his head with a smile, waiting for applause that did not come. His smile soured. With a furrowed brow, he spoke to the crowd:

"The Waveborn heart beats ever true
Together we'll see the matter through
Together we shall rise as one
And fight until our battle's won."

Mikal rose to his feet, clenching his teeth and gripping his side. The boy who'd ridden his shoulders rushed to help him, but his mother grabbed him by the shoulder and held him back. Mikal walked forward, breathing evenly, and stood right in front of Leftblade. In a low voice that carried to the entire silent crowd, he said:

> *"Cut me again, and I will concede*
> *Cut me again, and your war proceeds*
> *Cut me again, and this matter's done*
> *Cut me again, and I'll say you've won."*

As Mikal's words trailed off, the cry of distant seabirds floated over the silent, expectant crowd. Lawdon could even hear the boats creaking and waves lapping between the ships.

Leftblade stood very still, hesitating at the deathly quiet crowd, at the intense look in Mikal's eyes.

"Give him back his sword!" someone shouted.

"Let him duel!"

"Give him back his sword!" another called, and the crowd took up the chant.

"Sword! Sword! Sword! Sword!"

Leftblade's knuckles were white on both hilts. He gave a thin smile to Mikal, then tossed the blade to him. Mikal caught it deftly with his right hand and let go of his bleeding wound.

"Enough words," Leftblade snarled. "Let's finish this thing."

Mikal said nothing. He merely saluted.

And charged.

The crowd drew back with a gasp. Leftblade withdrew, defending the flurry of blows that Mikal rained upon him. The grand master tried a riposte and almost lost his hand for it. He retreated several steps, his eyes going wide. The crowd parted behind them as the duelists fought their way across the deck.

Mikal pressed the attack, his brow furrowed, his blue eyes flashing. Leftblade tried another counterattack, and Mikal smacked his outstretched arm with the flat of his blade. Leftblade gasped, fumbled his sword, but Mikal did not cut him.

Leftblade attacked again. For an instant, he advanced a step, pushing back Mikal's onslaught, but then he gasped and stumbled back. Mikal's sword was everywhere. A strike here. A strike there, always with the flat of the blade. Murmurs ran through the crowd.

A fierce sally brought a cry from Leftblade as Mikal smacked his hand again. The legend's sword clanged on the planks. With a snarl, Mikal scissor-stepped forward and kicked his former idol full in the chest. Leftblade crashed to the deck and smacked his head against the forecastle. He sat up quickly and froze. The tip of Mikal's blade hovered an inch from his throat.

"Cut me, damn you!" Leftblade hissed. "Just cut me and end it!"

After a long, breathless moment, Mikal's deadly expression split into a smile. He took a half step back, whipped his sword around and skewered Leftblade's hat, picked it up and twirled it around the tip of his sword.

"No," Mikal said. He tossed the hat in the air and slashed at it with his sword as it fell. The white feather drifted lazily. He plucked it out of the air with his left hand and tossed his sword over his head with his right. The sword stuck into the deck at the edge of the cleared area, wobbling back and forth.

"No one else will bleed today," Mikal said.

He tucked the feather behind his ear and turned his back on Leftblade. He addressed the mesmerized crowd, his voice seemed to carry across the entire Floating Palace.

> *"You all know the next words I'll say*
> *Though they're old-fashioned and cliché*
> *They're carved upon my heart and soul*
> *They fill me up, they make me whole*
> *And if our hearts and souls agree*
> *Then speak these final words with me."*

Pressing both of his hands against the bleeding wound in his side, Mikal then raised the red palms over his head, showing them to the crowd, and cried:

> *"May I be the last Waveborn with blood on his hands"*

Several voices from the crowd took up the famous words of Salice Mick, spoken so long ago when the Summer Cities first set aside their warring ways.

> *"May I be the last Waveborn to set foot on the land"*

Mikal continued the historical lines. A thousand voices rose up to join him:

> *"From this day forth all talk of war shall cease*
> *From this day forth these waves will know peace*

An Eternal Summer is ours to seize
With this last drop of blood spilled on the Summer Seas."

The cheers were deafening, and the crowd surged forward, picking Mikal up on their shoulders. Musicians began playing, and they bore Mikal around the deck.

In a panic, Lawdon looked around for Vinghelt, but the man was gone. He must have snuck away while no one was watching.

Lawdon tried to catch Mikal's eye, but the crowd carried him away from her. She was jostled by the surging bodies for a few moments before someone recognized her, and two men lifted her up on their shoulders as well.

She and Mikal locked eyes across the flood of people. He gave her a weak smile like a small pocket of sorrow amidst a roiling sea of fierce joy.

CHAPTER 27

Jesheks clapped quietly, peering through a window of the prince's stateroom. The crowd carried Mikal from Vinghelt's ship, parading him across the entire Floating Palace. Cheers and laughter engulfed the procession, and in a few minutes, the only people left on *Glory of Summer* were those in Vinghelt's employ.

Jesheks shook his head. He had always enjoyed the Waveborn and their duels. They were quaint, like the rest of the Summer Seas, as if the entire culture grew up locked in a velvet box, protected from the rest of the world. This nation knew nothing of pain. It made them endearing in a pathetic sort of way.

Jesheks smiled, listening as Vinghelt stormed through the adjacent rooms, knocking over furniture, breaking glass.

This second duel had been unexpected, and it would make the next few days much more interesting. The outcome was still not in doubt, but the journey would certainly be more spectacular.

He could not remember being so pleased. The previous evening with Shara had been everything he had ever hoped for and more. She had truly been remarkable.

Jesheks felt Vinghelt's approach as the summer prince grabbed the door of the stateroom and yanked it open. "There you are," he spluttered. "This is all your fault!"

"I suppose it is," Jesheks replied calmly.

"If Natshea had been here, this would never have happened," Vinghelt fumed, picking up a rum decanter and smashing it against the wall.

"We have already agreed that it is my fault."

"I should bury you for this," Vinghelt hissed, stalking up to Jesheks and leaning over him.

"You could do that," Jesheks said, feeling the taller man's rum-tainted breath on his face. "But I still have so much more to teach you." He laid his white hand delicately on Vinghelt's arm, tapped his skin with the spiked golden pinkie sheath. "Perhaps we should discuss this on my ship?"

The color left Vinghelt's face. He swallowed. His mouth lay open, but no words came out.

When Jesheks first arrived at the Summer Cities, he briefly entertained the idea that Lord Vinghelt might become his apprentice. This hope was dashed after one lesson. The man crumbled before any blood had been spilled, and the memory of that moment still left the prince petrified.

As if I would ever again waste my talents on this pretentious fool, Jesheks thought as he pushed back his cowl, letting his thin, white hair fall down.

"I admit that this is a setback. The crowd was definitely with young Heidvell," Jesheks said, releasing the lord from his power.

"It's a disaster!" Vinghelt spat, backing away.

Men like this destroy themselves, Jesheks thought. They need no help from anyone else. If Jesheks ever put a crown on Vinghelt's head, the fool would lose it within a year. Even the petty warlord who had taken Jesheks's manhood was ten times the king that Vinghelt could ever be.

"Not so, my lord," Jesheks said. "Did you think I would leave our plans vulnerable to Mikal Heidvell and Reignholtz's adopted daughter?"

Vinghelt's brow furrowed. "The goddess promised me a crown. The Waveborn should be crying for Physendrian blood! They are ready to launch another Eternal Summer out there."

"True, but yesterday they were ready to turn over all their fleets to you. The mob is fickle, easily swayed. The reins of summer are still in your hands. All we must do is implement our alternative plan."

Vinghelt's face darkened. "That's just what you wanted all along."

Jesheks shrugged. "You wished to win through the duels. Or rather, you wished to bask in the glory of the duels."

"What? You dare—"

Jesheks fixed him with a stare, and Vinghelt paused, then looked away.

"You know very little of what I would dare, my lord," Jesheks said simply. "And I think you prefer it that way. Save your false dignity for your country-men. You want to become the Summer King. I want to help you. Why tempt me to change my mind?"

Vinghelt looked fiercely out the window.

"I suggested this course of action from the beginning," Jesheks continued. "But you would have none of it, and I indulged you. I was content to see if your words had wisdom. They did not. The duels are not what they once were, despite the flamboyant legends that surround them. Even with Natshea's many victories and her crushing defeat of Reignholtz's daughter, that crowd was ready to root for the young fop today. They gave him every opportunity to be their favorite. And when he won, which of them remained near your banner? Only those whom you finance. Does this sound like a people who are aligned with your purpose?"

His mouth a tight line, Vinghelt glanced briefly at Jesheks but didn't say anything.

Jesheks waved his hand, shuffling over to the table. He sat down slowly in one of the chairs, savoring the painful ache in his knees, transforming it into a brief rush of power.

"But it doesn't matter. Crowds flip one way, then another, as I said. There is no need to surrender after a single defeat. The twigs are stacked neatly, the tinder below. All we need is a spark, and it shall burn."

"It is easy for you to say. This 'alternative' plan costs you nothing."

Vinghelt would never grasp the notion that something easily won was worthless. Jesheks had given him Natshea. He had nearly given the man the Summer Fleet, and still Vinghelt wanted all rewards and no investment. "I promised to make you the Summer King," he said. "I did not say it would come without cost."

Vinghelt shifted, edging closer to the window. He put his hand on the sill. The prince couldn't stand to be in the same room with Jesheks for long. What did it say about a man that the fountain of his power was something from which he wanted to flee?

"I don't know why Fessa chose you to be my steward," Vinghelt said tightly. "But I shall have to trust her judgment. Make the arrangements for tomorrow night."

"The day after tomorrow would be better."

"Fine! Whatever." Vinghelt waved his hand, but still did not look at Jesheks. "Just leave me in peace."

Jesheks levered himself to his feet. "As my prince commands," he said, smiling. He shuffled to the door and left the prince to his weighty thoughts.

CHAPTER 28

Lawdon kept to the shadows, waiting for the wine to do its inevitable work.

She raised the annoying mermaid mask she was wearing and wiped the sweat off her face. It was an overly warm night, and she'd been running on very little sleep. She had suggested that Lady Gildheld throw a masquerade ball on her cottage ship so she and Mikal could move among the crowd unrecognized.

She and Mikal, mostly Mikal, had been the toast of the Floating Palace for the day and a half since the duel. Mikal's victory seemed to snap the Summer Princes out of a daze. Evidence was being gathered to prove Vinghelt was behind her lord's death. A fresh, sizable gouge had been found on the prow of one of Vinghelt's smaller ships. Dozens of people were coming forward with reports of his transgressions in Physendria. And the jokes were already flying about his cowardly retreat from the duel before he could be tossed overboard. Once that man's hull was breached, it started springing leaks all over the place. The Waveborn still liked to talk much more than they liked to act, but Vinghelt's ship was foundering. The man would be buried alive before the end of high summer.

Despite her grief, it raised Lawdon's spirits to see the heart of the Waveborn reassert itself. Reignholtz would eagerly have given his life to preserve the Eternal Summer. Seeing the tidal wave of change his death had caused somehow made the loss more bearable.

Lawdon was ashamed by how eager she had been to spit in the face of her lord's beliefs, stooping to the violence he abhorred. But luckily Mikal was cut from nobler cloth. For the first time, Lawdon started wondering if there was some truth to Reignholtz's faith in the blood of the Waveborn.

With the Summer Princes back in command, that left Lawdon and Mikal free to look for Shara. It had been two days since she left with Vinghelt's men. Her whereabouts were a mystery, but Lawdon knew how to find the weak link when you wanted to break a chain. And that weak link was headed right her way.

The man walked past her hiding place, headed for the privy. Lawdon paused only a moment, nostrils flaring as she looked at his gold cotton doublet, his black belt, his narrow shoulders.

With a twitch of her wrist, the dagger fell into her hand. She hurried to catch up with him, grabbed the back of his collar, and stuck the blade between his legs, tight up against his crotch.

He squeaked, dropped his wineglass, and tried to lurch away, but she spun him around and pinned him against the wall.

"Wait, please . . . !" His long mustache quivered as he craned around, trying to see her. Lawdon slid the dagger slightly forward, just enough for the tip to bite through cloth and break skin. "Oh Fessa . . ." the man whimpered.

"Cry out, and I'll trim you to match your master," she said.

"M-My master?"

"The pale one."

He craned around again, and this time Lawdon let him see her face. His mouth dropped open, and his eyes widened. "Y-You're . . ."

"Lawdon," she said. "Reignholtz's captain."

The servant's muscles tightened, readying . . .

"Don't be stupid," Lawdon said, twisting the dagger. The man gave in, breathing hard, his hands pressed against the wall. "Now calm yourself before you lose something important to you. If you help me without a fuss, you may come through this intact. I have some questions about the albino."

"But V-Vinghelt is my m-master."

"Not two nights ago he wasn't. Come on, we're going for a walk. You still need to relieve yourself." She led him along the deserted edge of Lady Gildheld's ship. It was of the new design that had a narrow companionway running all the way around the outside, which made for a perfect little alleyway for her to hide and attack a man on the way to the privy. She had waited over half an hour for the man to drink himself into a full bladder.

Together, they shuffled to the stern and down the steep ramp to the latrine barge anchored below Gildheld's ship. When they reached the bottom, Lawdon hooked her toe under the plank and flipped it into the water.

"Now, love," the man said nervously, trying to seem confident. "If you wanted some privacy, all you needed to do was ask—"

She pushed the dagger forward slightly.

"Ah! You cruel b—"

"Don't say it," she said in a lethal voice. "I've never gelded anyone before, but I can learn as I go."

His head bobbed up and down quickly. She shoved him through a curtain into one of the velvet-draped toilet stalls. He stumbled right into Mikal's waiting fist and reeled at the punch.

Mikal slugged the man in the gut, stood him up, and slugged him in the face again. He crumpled to the ground, coughing. Mikal knelt on the man's head, pressing his cheek into the wood floor.

"Just remember," Mikal said. "She's the nice one. So if you don't answer her questions, you'll be answering mine. Understand?"

The man's head shifted against the floor in a stilted nod. Mikal eased up a little, and the man blinked up at him, eyes wide. Blood trickled from a split lip.

Mikal's eyes narrowed. "Waitaminute," he murmured. "You're the ass who pushed me in the duel, aren't you?" He shoved the man's face into the floorboards again.

"All in good fun, sir!" the servant mumbled. "The summer was in m'blood!"

Mikal growled. "My footprints will be in your blood if you don't give us answers we're happy with."

"I live to serve, sir," the man said in a muffled tone, his lips mashed into the wood.

Lawdon knelt before Vinghelt's servant, put her dagger next to his nose. A single rivulet of the man's blood lingered on the blade, and she made sure he saw it.

"Where did you take Shara-lani two nights ago?"

"W-Who?" the man said, then cried out as Mikal dug a knee into his back.

"Let's try that again," Lawdon said. "Where—"

"He'll bury me, my lady. Have mercy!" the servant said. "Vinghelt is a mage. He has ways of knowing things. And the Kherish physician's eyes ..." He shuddered. "They go right through a man."

"So will my dagger. Best you worry about that first." She placed the edge very carefully against the man's eyelid.

"No! No!" he whimpered. "I took her to the physician's ship. It's no great secret."

"And where is that?" Mikal rumbled.

"Balbont's Cove, a league east along the coast."

"And what did you do to her?" Lawdon asked, keeping the knife blade where it was.

"Nothing, milady. Nothing at all. We took her there and left her, just as he ordered." He gave a little pause, looked at each of them.

Lawdon narrowed her eyes. "And?" She pushed the dagger against the top of his cheek, cutting.

"This morning!" he gasped. "We were ordered to return. We collected a bundle wrapped in a sheet."

"A bundle?" Lawdon said. "What kind of bundle?"

"Just a bundle."

"What was in it?"

"I don't know, milady. It was wrapped in a sheet."

Lawdon narrowed her eyes. "Guess. How big was it?"

"Fairly big, milady."

"Was it roughly the size and shape of a woman?" Mikal growled.

The servant swallowed, terror in his eyes. "C-Could be, milord. I didn't see anything."

"Didn't see anything?! That bastard killed her!" Mikal said, shoving his knee hard into the man's back and grabbing his hair. The servant squealed.

"No!" he gasped. "No! She moved! She was alive!"

"Enough! Stop playing games, or I take out your eyes," Lawdon said.

"There were bloodstains on the sheet, milady, but she moved, once, and . . . and she was breathing."

"Where did you take her?" Lawdon asked.

"Butcher's barge, milady."

"Son of a bitch!" Mikal growled.

"Not what you think! Not what you think!" the servant gasped, groaning under the weight of Mikal's knee. "The barge was going to the prince's ship. They loaded her on with the other meat."

"Other meat," Mikal hissed.

"Are you sure?" Lawdon asked the man.

"It was morning, milady. We couldn't just carry a bloody bundle onto the ship in bright sunlight, now could we?"

Lawdon stared at him for a long, hard moment. Mikal seethed. Finally, she said, "All right. That's it. Stick him in the hole."

"No! Don't—"

Mikal grabbed the servant by the scruff, hauled him to his feet, and up-ended him in the privy hole, headfirst. The latrine was a hand-crafted wooden stool that was open to the ocean below, and the servant hollered, spreading his legs across the rim to keep from falling all the way in.

"What are you doing?" his voice echoed up to them. "I answered all of your questions!"

"We're letting you live," Mikal said. "Which is more than you deserve. Now shut up before we change our minds."

Looking up, Lawdon grabbed one end of the decorative rope that hung above the velvet curtain in ample loops. "Get the other end," she said to Mikal. Using the rope, they tied the man's legs apart so he could not fall in.

"No! You can't leave me here!" the man called.

Lawdon pressed her dagger against his exposed crotch. "We leave you, or we kill you. Which would you rather?"

The man's whimper echoed up the privy hole.

"That's what I thought. Now shut your mouth." She inserted her dagger back into its forearm sheath.

Lawdon and Mikal left the privy stall and looked up to see a woman standing where the plank had been, looking down at them. She frowned to see them both exit together.

Lawdon smiled her best guilty smile.

"You might want to use the privy barge on the port side," Mikal called to her. Tossing her head, the woman was halfway through her turn when she stopped and turned back. She peered into the darkness. "You're Mikal Heidvell aren't you?"

Mikal shrugged. "Alas I am not he. Though many confuse us. He is a spectacularly handsome man."

The woman scowled and flounced away.

Mikal shook his head. "All my admirers are starting to get a bit annoying."

"I'm sure you'll find some way to cope," Lawdon replied, jumping to catch the rope dangling from the rail of the cottage ship. Mikal followed, and they pulled themselves aboard. They ran along the edge, quickly cutting the ropes that anchored the barge in place. She suspected that Lady Gildheld was still secretly sympathetic to Vinghelt. Lawdon didn't want word of this incident getting back to him too soon.

Mikal turned to Lawdon as the barge drifted away. "Are you sure you don't want to just kill him?"

"No point," she said. "That's a nice privy. Lady Gildheld's men will go looking for it, but I doubt they'll find it until tomorrow or the next day."

"So how do we get Shara off Vinghelt's ship?" he said tightly. "It is still his sovereign territory, and the other princes will be reluctant to violate it."

"I'll try to round up a few friends," Lawdon said. "It shouldn't be that hard these days."

"That will take time."

She could tell from his eyes that he'd rather go now.

"It would be safer, and I'd like to do this without blood, if we can," she said. "We'll hit him later tonight, just before dawn."

He paused a long moment. "Can we afford to wait that long?"

Lawdon didn't know. Despite her anger at Shara, she had no desire to see her friend dead. The Zelani had kept her promise. By luring away Vinghelt's physician, she'd made sure no magic was used in Mikal's duel. She might even have had something to do with Natshea's disappearance. But Vinghelt was on the defensive. This could easily turn into a bloodbath. "Either she's alive because they want her alive, or she's dead because they want her dead," she said tightly. "Either way, a few hours won't matter."

Mikal waited a long moment, then nodded. She was happy to see that his anger had not overcome his better judgment. He gave her a weary smile. "You must be a captain or something."

She wanted to reach out, touch his cheek, but she didn't. She managed a half smile. "We can't all be duelists."

"Lawdon ..." he started, then paused. He frowned, seemed about to say something, then looked out to sea, eyes fixed on the drifting latrine for a moment.

"What?"

He let out a little breath and looked back at her. "I'm sorry."

She shook her head. "This wasn't your fault. Shara chose to go."

"No, not that ..." he said. "I'm sorry about forgetting you," he fought for the words. "I've not been a very good man, most of my life. I see that clearly now, and I wonder how I've managed to stay blind for so many years. But with you, I mean, when I first saw Shara, she ..."

Lawdon swallowed the lump in her throat. "She didn't really give you a choice, I know."

Mikal held up a hand. "Stop. Don't make excuses for me. People have been doing that all my life. Shara gave me many choices, all along the way. And I'm not proud of all the ones that I made. I'm not as stupid as I look. I fell in love with Shara, but I'm not blind to what she's done to me. I just wanted you to know that it's all over."

"Mikal, none of that matters right now."

"Yes it does. I just wanted you to know—"

Lawdon covered his lips with her fingers, caught his gaze, and held it.

"This isn't the time. I really want to have this conversation, but let's get Shara back first."

"Lawdon—"

"That's an order," she said, standing. He stood with her, his brow furrowed.

A teenage boy stumbled toward them, looking rather green. His head jerked back and forth as he looked at the empty space where the little barge used to be.

"Where's the privy?" he asked desperately. His back shuddered, and he grabbed the rail, squeezing his eyes closed.

"This one's missing," Lawdon said. "Try the port side."

"Hey, you're Mik—" the boy started, but suddenly turned and heaved over the side. Lawdon turned her face away, but she was downwind and caught the full stench of it.

She winced and glanced up at Mikal. "Ah, the smell of home," she said. "May the summer last forever."

CHAPTER 29

Phanqui listened to the sound of his breathing, the beating of his heart. There was no light in the cell, and barely any sound. The rough rock walls sweated beads of cold water, and all he could hear was Cesshen on the other side of the cell, thrashing in his sleep. Phanqui knew exactly what the man was dreaming. He'd dreamed it himself almost every hellish night in this jail. The day would come when Vinghelt's thugs arrived to bury them all alive.

Footsteps clomped up the hall. Phanqui grimaced even as his mouth started watering. He'd never been so weak, so hungry.

Keys jangled in the door, and he backed as far away as the tiny cell would allow. Cesshen woke up and did the same.

"Hungry, maggots?" The jailer's gravelly voice floated through the crack in the door as it opened. Torchlight flickered around his dark silhouette. He had ugly bristles sticking out of his malformed jaw and looked like he shaved with a sharp piece of glass instead of a razor. With one huge eye and one squinty one, and no more than a half dozen brown teeth in his mouth, he was the very vision of despair.

Despite Phanqui's hunger, he had come to dread the moments when the jailer brought food. A bite of stale biscuit and a cup of water always came with a price.

The jailer looked particularly pleased with himself today. He set the cup of water on the floor and showed them the wooden plate with the two biscuits on it. "You two must be tired of this crappy food. Even desert dogs can't like the same old stale biscuits day after day."

Phanqui said nothing.

"How about a little something extra today?" The guard loosened the drawstring on his pants. "Can't have anyone saying I don't take good care of you." He dropped his pants around his ankles.

Phanqui cringed and turned away.

With a grin the guard picked up his testicles and rubbed them over the top of the biscuits. "How about like a little nut cheese on those biscuits, maggots." The ugly man howled at his own joke and tossed the plate onto the floor. He pulled up his pants and walked out, locking the door behind him. "Enjoy the hospitality of the Summer Seas. It's the finest in the world." The man's raspy chuckle faded as he moved on to the next cell.

Cesshen crawled over to the cup of water and took a greedy sip. He snatched up a biscuit and shoved it in his mouth. "What are they waiting for?" he said, careful to catch any crumbs in his hand. "Why don't they just kill us and get it over with?"

Phanqui crawled over to him and drank what little water Cesshen had left. With a grimace, he forced himself to take a bite of the biscuit.

"I don't know," he finally said. "I have no idea what they are planning."

He lay back on the floor and swallowed the dry lump.

It surprised him every day that he and the other rebels were still alive. Vinghelt must be waiting for something, concocting some new torture for them. Perhaps he would make them into a bloody public example. Or maybe he was just letting the pressure of impending death work on their minds. Nothing was beneath the man.

As Phanqui took another bite of the hard bread, his mind flew back to the agonizing voyage that followed their botched assassination attempt. They had sailed all the way back to the Summer Seas stuffed in barrels. The guards played with them the entire trip, filling the barrels, letting the prisoners gasp, then dumping them out only to fill them again.

Only Phanqui, Cesshen, and two others had survived the journey to this dark hellhole. He couldn't help thinking the others were the lucky ones.

He had nearly drifted off to sleep when a loud crash and a shout echoed down the hall. He and Cesshen sat up. There was a cry of pain, quickly cut off. Keys jingled.

Phanqui struggled to his feet and moved to the tiny barred window at the door. He strained his eyes to look into the hallway, but all he could see was the bobbing torchlight.

Booted footsteps thundered toward him. More than one man. Not the jailer. Phanqui backed away from the door. This was it. They were coming to kill them.

Torchlight blared through the window, and the key turned in the lock. The door was thrown open.

A Waveborn stood in the doorway, torch held high. Phanqui swallowed down his fear, held himself still. He didn't try to run. It wouldn't matter.

"You the Physendrians?" the man asked.

"Who are you?"

The man smiled. "A gift from the King of Kherif."

Phanqui's stomach clenched. He looked closer. The hook nose, the brown skin. The man was dressed like a Waveborn, but he wasn't a Summerman.

"Any friend of the fishlickers can stay here," the man said. Phanqui could hear the other cell door being opened. "The rest come with us."

Phanqui helped Cesshen to his feet and half carried him out of the cell. Hythal and Pheirdin were already in the hall with three Khers dressed as Waveborn. "Come quickly," one of them said, and led them down a long, dark hallway. They passed the guard's body lying facedown on the floor, and Phanqui snatched up his sword.

They all paused at the front door, and the leader of the Khers peered outside. "Wait here," he said. "A covered cart will be along in a moment. We'll hide you in the back." He reached into his coat and handed each of them a hard sausage. "Here. I thought you'd be hungry."

The other prisoners attacked the food, but Phanqui just held his in a limp hand. "Who sent you?" he asked. "How did you know where we were?"

"A friend of yours spent a long time and a lot of money finding out where you were."

"Who? Why?"

"He thought he owed you after running away to leave you for dead."

"The albino? He's alive? Vinghelt didn't kill him?"

The Kher smiled. "That fat man's hard to kill." He shook his head. "He sends his eternal apologies for your misfortunes. We're still trying to discover who betrayed him."

"What about Vinghelt's magic?"

The Kher laughed. "That fishlicker is no more a mage than I am. Would we be here if he was?"

Phanqui's heart surged with sudden hope. If Vinghelt was no magician, if the albino escaped, perhaps his own wife and daughter were safe as well.

"Are you taking us home?" he asked.

"We can leave tonight if you wish; Jesheks has a ship waiting for you."

The four prisoners looked at each other. "Thank the Nine," Cesshen whispered.

The Kher paused, his hand still on the door cracked open just enough to let the moonlight fall on his arm. "But," he said softly, "if you're willing to stay one day longer, we can give you the chance you missed in Physen. You can strike at the very heart of your enemies."

"What do you mean?"

"The Kherish King does not want to see the Summer Fleet in the great ocean. He sent us here to prevent that from happening. With our help, you could kill more Waveborn tonight than your countrymen have killed in the last ten years."

Phanqui's brow furrowed. He looked at the others. They were tired, frightened, physically ravaged, but anger still burned in their eyes. He could see it.

"Do you want one last chance to wet your blade with the governor's blood?" the Kher asked.

Phanqui thought of Shafyssa, thought of his little daughter. The other Physendrians said nothing, waiting on Phanqui's answer.

His lips tightening into a line, Phanqui looked up at the Kher and said just what Brophy would have said.

CHAPTER 30

Shara's eyelids flickered open. She swallowed down a dry throat, and it burned the entire way. She didn't move at all, knowing what would happen if she did. The pain was everywhere, like she had been scraped inside out.

But with the agony, with consciousness, came memory, and with memory came knowledge. The pain was hers, and she drew it into herself, bending it, using it.

"Another would be dead right now ..." She heard Jesheks's voice in her head.

She twitched, blocking the memory. Then, slowly, she let it come. He had rolled the hot iron rod across her back, searing her until she screamed.

Controlling her breath, Shara went to that spot, felt her magic growing stronger. She drew the pain out like poison from a wound, speeding the healing. Her flesh throbbed, growing red-hot, and the torment receded. Her magic grew, swelling in the quiet room.

She continued along the rest of her body, finding the weeping lacerations, the delicate, deep punctures. She visited each one, infusing it with ani, feeding her body's desperate need to heal itself.

Trembling, she remembered his thick fingers caressing her cheek.

"Fear is pain, also, my dear. Look down. See what I have done. Look and let the fear fill you. Take it. Use it."

Hanging from the scarves he had tied to her wrists, she looked down. Sweat covered her naked body. Two streaks of blood painted her sides down from her breasts, perfectly symmetrical.

"No, my sweet. Look here." She looked farther down, and saw the steel rod. Thin and glistening, it protruded from her skin, just above her hip, covered with thick, dark blood.

She shuddered, whimpering. It went through her. It went completely through her.

"Go there, my sweet. Find it. Embrace it. If you cannot harness the power, this beautiful body will be forever maimed."

The fear coursed through her, and she thrashed against the chains. "Please," she begged, "no more. No more."

"I told you, my sweet. Once we started, we could not stop."

Shara grabbed the memory and used it, swirled it into her magic.

The pain lived within her, flowing through her as strongly as any orgasm. It was not bad. It was not good. It was simply powerful, a rearing lion of energy, fierce and alive.

Shara swirled it into her magic as she went to her other wounds, the cuts on her back, the burns on her legs and feet. She went to the hole he had put through her side, filled it with energy, encouraging the flesh to knit back together.

She lay there resting, soaking in all the feverish intensity. The entire world had changed. Her eyes were opened, and she would never be the same. Her heart felt so blessedly empty that she had not even realized how clogged and tangled it had become. There was no anguish as she once knew it. No doubt. No fear. Jesheks had hurt her so badly, so incredibly badly. The pain burned everything in its path until only she remained, as clean as a baby.

The night had been nothing like she expected. Nothing at all. He had been so kind, so tender at first. He led her to the fire, and they sat together next to the warmth of the flames.

He showed her his gold pinky sheath, pricked his own palm with the sharp tip.

"The first step of a Necani is to feel your pain, really feel it, without fleeing, without taking the mind away. It all starts with the breath ..."

He pricked her finger with the point, then her palm, her wrist, and each of her thighs through her dress. Each time he breathed with her, helped her accept the sensation, embrace it. The exercise was so similar to her early Zelani training as a child that she took to it easily at first. She accepted the intensity, let it course through her.

"Ahhh ..." Jesheks murmured, shuddering. "You are radiant. Your will is iron, my sweet. Look at what you can do on your first attempt. But we will turn that iron into steel ..."

She floated on his praise, the words like a long-needed caress. She felt his magic working on her, drawing her in. She began to lean on him as he slid the golden needle deeper and deeper into her flesh. They explored these strange waters; she relaxed into his steady hands. He was not kind, but he was truthful.

Shara slowly realized that he was binding her as Victeris had bound her, as she had bound Mikal. The power swirled around her, and the pain seared as she balked.

"You're trying to take me ... Trying to make me yours," she breathed.

"I am trying to make you your own master, not a slave to pain and fear like the rest of the world. I will take you there and beyond."

He withdrew a glowing iron from the fire and she pulled back, wincing as she lost control of her breath. She should leave. She should stop, back away, take her wounds and this lesson and go, work through the Necani form on her own, at her own pace, just like she had with the other forms. This was a ruthless man, cruel and cold, his eyes delighted in the agony of others.

"Your mind will lie to you, my sweet. It will beseech and cajole, create horrors to make you flee. Anything to keep you shackled in the dark. Anything to keep you a slave. But you can be the master . . ."

A cruel man, yes, but had he ever lied to her? Hadn't he always been honest, even when it went against his own plans?

"Are you ready for more?" he asked.

Shara looked at him through half-lidded eyes. Already her mind was foggy. She should say no. She should stand and leave.

"Yes," she whispered.

"Then stand, my sweet. Take off your dress. It would be a pity to ruin it."

She rose on shaky legs.

Leave!

Slowly, methodically, she undid the laces at the bodice, tugged it apart, revealing her breasts, then pulled her arms out of the sleeves one at a time.

Run!

She worked at the sash on her waist, pulled it free. The sheer dress slumped to her waist, and she pushed it over her hips, let it fall to the floor.

As she undressed, Jesheks levered himself to his feet and shuffled to a wooden chest, withdrawing two long, silken scarves. He went to her, paused to run his hands along the smooth skin of her arms.

"You are exquisite," he said. "You will be even more magnificent before the night is done." He tied the scarves around her wrists and led her to the fireplace, ran each scarf through an iron ring bolted on opposite sides of the hearth. Tugging them tight, he tied each into a sturdy knot.

Shara's heart thundered in her chest as her arms were pulled apart. If she picked up her feet, she could hang from the scarves right in front of the roaring fire. The flames were uncomfortably hot on her thighs and belly.

"What are you going to do to me?" she asked in a breathless voice.

Jesheks stood behind her. "I'm going to take you to a place beyond your control. I'm going to break through the limitations you have placed upon yourself." He paused, ran a hand across her shoulder, across her arm to her bound wrist. A thin sheen of sweat shone on his pale arms. "I have never met one as strong as you. I will have to take you beyond your pain, to that place where you are free. I have been gentle with you to this point, but I will not coddle you further."

She nodded.

"I have been easing your path until now, but I must take away all of your crutches, even those I have given you. You must stand on your own. Do you understand?"

She nodded.

"After this point, I will not stop, no matter what you say. No matter what you do. Do you understand?"

She nodded again. Her eyelids still felt heavy.

"Now, I will release the spell I have woven."

She felt the magic around him shift, and suddenly her mind was very clear, her thoughts no longer fuzzy. She felt the fire at her breasts and thighs, hot against her skin. She jerked, pulling the scarves tight.

"No, wait," she said, trying to sound calm.

He nodded, a patient smile on his lips. "It is all right, my sweet. This is how it begins."

"No, stop." She put every ounce of command into her voice. She reached for her magic, but it was fragmented. Again, she yanked against the scarves, but they were strong, and they held her. "Jesheks, I mean it. Stop for a moment."

"That's right," he said softly. "Take the fear. Use it."

Panic exploded in her chest, and she watched in terrified silence as he knelt beside her and pulled a steel rod from the fire. Its tip glowed orange.

"Breathe . . ." he said, "and let us begin our dance."

Her heart thundering, Shara mastered herself and began an even breath. She was on the course. She would see it through. Her breath came to her, steady and powerful. She would do this. She would accept it all.

He touched the glowing rod to the underside of her arm. She lurched, wanting to gasp at the pain, but she continued her breathing.

Again, the rod touched her. Again, she yanked against her bonds, but her breathing remained steady. She pulled the pain into herself. It surged through her body, and she ran with it, riding on top of the flood. She could master this.

"Very good," he said. "Very good. So strong."

Jesheks's ani flowed around her, seeping through her wounds, swirling into her chest, warm and welcome.

"Now let's try something a little more intimate," he whispered in her ear.

He touched her again on the inside of her thigh and everything changed. The man's power exploded inside her body, engulfing her, searing her from the inside out. Shara screamed.

She opened her eyes, looking around the strange room. Black velvet drapes. No fire. Not Jesheks's room. Not that horrible, glorious room that took her beyond where she had ever thought she could go. She felt the rocking of the ship through the dull ache that hovered around her like a cloud. So much of what happened after that moment was a blur in her mind, but not the lessons. The different tortures blended together, but Jesheks's voice was always present, praising her, telling her how strong she was, how powerful, telling her she was almost there. Don't give in. Not yet. . .

She closed her eyes, feeling the deep well of calm within her. Clean. Clear. Her mind drifted back to that night.

Hanging there, bleeding, burned, vibrating with agony, the steel rod piercing her body, Shara reached a place beyond tears, beyond screams, where there was no more pain. She had not fled, but the pain did not hurt, not the way it had. It sang like music through her.

Jesheks's thick hands touched her cheeks and pushed her lolling head upward. She blinked at him. He smiled back at her.

"Can you feel that, child? You are nearly free. Washed clean. Soon your heart will be empty. You can fill it with whatever you want."

She tried to nod, but she couldn't move her head.

"We are in a place of clarity now. We can go forward in absolute honesty, or we can regress and continue this dance. Do you want to move forward?"

"Yes," she murmured.

"Are you ready for my question?"

"I ..."

"Speak, my sweet. You have the strength. You have all the strength you need and so much more. Speak."

"I want ..."

"Yes, my sweet. You know the question already, don't you?"

"I want ..."

"What do you want, my sweet? What lies in the bottom of your heart? Dig it up. Dig it out. What do you want more than anything else in the world?"

"Brophy," she sobbed. "I still want Brophy."

He smiled. "Excellent," he said. "Excellent. Now we can begin."

And he did.

Shara curled up in a ball. She was too weak to rise, and she knew it. But she must rise, and soon. Rise from this bed and begin her new life, like the day after her Zelani test, reborn. Ready to spread her fledgling wings and fly.

Jesheks had been true to his word. He had done exactly what he said he would. He had opened a searing gate, and she had stepped through, seeing these last weeks for the benighted escape they really were.

But she had a debt to pay before that new life began. As powerful as Jesheks was, he was still tortured, still fragmented. He believed he was whole, but he longed for something more, longed to be something other than a scarred and mutilated half man. His closed heart ached, and she was the only one who could open it. She could not leave him without returning the compassion he had shown her.

The albino had true strength, buried deep below the fortress of pain he had crafted for himself. She only hoped that he had the strength to reach the far side. If not, the resulting battle might be too much for both of them.

And after that debt was paid, Shara would begin her new life. Her old life. Her only life.

It didn't matter if Brophy loved her anymore. She loved him, and no amount of fear or hatred could change that. Loving him was her choice, hers alone.

She'd spent half her life fighting for that love, then gave it up simply because it could not be returned. Had she honestly thought she could love somebody only if they loved her back? Those were the thoughts of a woman still terrified of losing control. Had she honestly thought he owed her for the years she'd given him?

The sun peeked in through a slit in the black curtains, lighting the dust in the air and touching Shara's hand. Her eyelids drooped as she mingled her ani with the sunlight. Just a little bit longer and she would be ready to rise and face the day.

CHAPTER 31

The black-robed Ohohhim worked steadily and silently on their tributes to the heroes of the Cinder, and Brophy worked right alongside them. He was the Sleeping Warden, a god to the pilgrims who built these monuments, but he was content to sweat with them like a normal man.

More than that, Arefaine thought, he seemed almost at peace for the first time. It baffled her. This manual labor was a refuge to him. His tumultuous emotions grew softer the harder he worked, though they did not leave him. They would never leave. That was something she knew well.

For the past three days Brophy had thrown himself into building the monument he claimed he didn't believe in. He was stripped to the waist, a sheen of sweat on his pale skin, and she watched the muscles in his back ripple as he lifted another stone. He carried it from a dust-covered stone carver up a ramp and along some scaffolding to a pair of masons. He set the stone atop the half-built blue-white marble wall of the shrine. It was Brophy's own memorial they worked on, an exact replica of the Hall of Windows, built from marble instead of glass. A series of exquisite statues stood waiting to be placed on top of the temple at its completion. They depicted Brophy, Baelandra, Medew, and the others at the moment when Brophy closed his eyes, locking the emmeria in his dreams.

Brophy helped the masons set the stone into place and headed back to the stone carvers. He was unlike anyone she had ever known. Arefaine tried to control the emotions that welled up inside her whenever she looked at him.

Was it because he was an Ohndarien? Was it the strangeness of a foreigner she couldn't stop looking at? She had certainly felt a moment of glorious freedom with the other Ohndarien boy, Astor. It had been like running wild after a lifetime of taking tiny, measured steps. But this feeling was different.

During the first few days with him, a small thrill ran through her every time he looked at her. There was no fear in his gaze. No worship. Not even pity, the way the Emperor sometimes looked at her. To Brophy, she was just another woman. A woman like any of those Ohohhim below who labored with him. Was that what it felt like to be normal? Not a goddess, not a legend?

She had not expected this. It threw her into confusion. No matter where she went, people focused on her. Even when she was completely still and silent, her presence moved others. When she said something, it mattered. When she said nothing, it mattered.

But the only thing that seemed to matter to Brophy was moving rocks. She felt the anger seething inside of him, but he channeled it into his arms, into his legs and tirelessly continued his work. On the rare occasion he spoke at all, he spoke softly to those around him. The Ohohhim deferred to him like the god they thought he was, but Brophy treated them like brothers.

But not her. Why not her?

He was the only other person who could possibly understand what she had been through, and why she had become who she was, but he refused to claim that kinship.

Brophy returned from the monument to the benches where the stone carvers worked, but none of them were ready for him. He paused there for a moment, breathing hard, then turned to the fountain for a drink.

She kept her face a mask of calm as he approached, one hand lightly on the edge of the fountain's rim.

He stopped next to her, only glancing at her as he dipped the ladle into the water and took a drink. She could feel the heat from his body, smell his sweat.

"You look well," she said. "Temple building agrees with you."

He took another drink with closed eyes, then looked at her sideways as his breathing slowed. "It's good to be doing something useful. I haven't used my arms for anything but ..." He paused, looked down at the ladle, then took another sip. "It's nice to build something."

Arefaine wanted to reach out a hand to him, but she stopped herself. Why did she long to touch him so much? His skin tantalized her. His muscles, built during his time in the Physendrian Nine Squares two decades ago, continually drew her eye. He was tall and fair-skinned. Just like her. They were of the same people, the Great Race.

She kept her hands where they were. "Would you like to stay longer? I could talk to the Emperor—"

"No." He shook his head. "I am anxious to get on to Ohohhom."

She felt a thrill rush through her. "I thought you wanted to return to Ohndarien."

His shadowed gaze met hers for a moment. He shook his head. "I changed my mind."

"Can I ask why?"

He put the ladle down, and she feared he had somehow read her thoughts, that he would turn and leave. She felt she should say something, but she didn't, merely let him study her.

Finally, she said, "What is it?"

"Nothing." He turned away, checking to see if any of the stone carvers were finished.

"A look that long is never for nothing. What did you see?"

He cleared his throat, hesitated. For a moment she was sure he would return to his work, but he faced her again. "Sometimes you remind me of a woman I once knew."

"Shara?" Arefaine asked. Her heart thudded painfully, hopefully.

"No." He shook his head. "Another woman I knew in Physendria. We were lovers ..." He stopped, then said tersely, "It ended badly."

"I'm sorry, Brophy," she said, and reached out for his hand before she thought to stop herself.

He backed away, leaving her grasping for empty air once more. She let her hand slowly drop back to her side.

"The Emperor is trying to manipulate us," Brophy said suddenly.

She glanced up at him. Her pulse quickened. Then he saw. Of course he saw. He was of the Great Race. Such simple machinations could not slip past him, but she had been longing to hear him say it.

"Why would he do that?" she asked.

His green eyes held hers. "You tell me."

Like Shara-lani, Brophy was difficult to read when he closed his doors. She felt his crashing ocean of anger, but she could not see past it to the true meaning behind the question.

"Because we are alike, you and I," she said. "We have seen so much, know so much that the Emperor does not. Our knowledge makes us powerful, and it makes him afraid. He can't control me, so he will try to get you to control me."

"I see."

"You don't have to do what he says."

"I know." He gave her a curt nod and started downhill, headed for a stone carver who had just finished the block she was working on.

Arefaine turned away. Her hand gripped the edge of the fountain, and she tried to even her breathing. Brophy was determined to keep her at a distance, but he would come around. He would see the beauty of her vision once it began to flower. Just like Issefyn did. Just like Jesheks did. Just as the Emperor soon would.

She could wait. She had waited three hundred years already. Another few weeks or months would not matter. The Summer Fleet would sail north. The gates of Ohndarien would be thrown wide for them. The Imperial Navy would sail south to join them.

And then the two greatest fleets in the world would burn the Silver Islanders to the waterline, and Efften would rise again.

Once the Emperor was convinced, Brophy would follow. And if the man could not be convinced . . .

Well, even an emperor could be replaced.

Arefaine gathered her skirts to rise and leave when she noticed that all work around her had stopped. One by one, the Ohohhim pilgrims silently dropped to their knees and pressed their heads to the stone, all save Brophy. He continued to work as though nothing had happened.

Fighting a flutter of panic, she turned and came face-to-face with the Emperor. She was grateful for the powder that hid her sudden emotions. She couldn't help but think he had read her thoughts, though she knew he did not have such power.

Turning her gaze downward, she nodded, and said, "Your Eternal Wisdom. I did not expect to see you."

"Will you walk with me?" he asked. Two Carriers of the Opal Fire hung back, just out of earshot. She'd never known him to go anywhere with fewer than four of the Carriers nearby.

"Of course," she said, raising her gaze and reaching to pinch his sleeve. Every other time they had spoken, he had summoned her to an official audience.

He subtly shifted his sleeve away and extended his arm for her to take. She hesitated briefly, then took his arm. He'd never done that before.

Control yourself, she thought. *He has set you off-balance with barely a word.*

The Emperor nodded to the workers. They slowly rose and returned to their tasks. Brophy hoisted another block of stone on his bare shoulder and carried it toward the scaffolding. He didn't even look up.

The Emperor watched the Brother of Autumn thoughtfully as they walked, then turned to Arefaine.

"You've fallen in love with him, haven't you?" he said quietly.

Arefaine was so shocked she said nothing.

"But his heart belongs to another," the Emperor continued.

A swift pain filled her chest, and she swallowed hard. Was he trying to hurt her? She cleared her throat, and said, "People change. Feelings change. Who knows what tomorrow will bring?"

"Oh knows."

Arefaine nodded respectfully, and her equilibrium returned. For a moment, she had feared that he had seen too deeply into her plans, but he had returned to his familiar platitudes. Oh knows. It was always about what Oh knows, and Oh knew everything. "Of course," she said in a carefully moderated tone.

He led her away from the main construction to a little gazebo perched on the edge of the cliff. The monument surrounded the little shrine built by Brophy's uncle, Celinor, during his lone years of vigil on the Cinder. The man used to watch for danger hidden amid a small cluster of boulders. He had carved every available rock face with images of the city of Ohndarien and her people. This little shrine had been the Emperor's inspiration for transforming the Cinder.

"I am curious," the Emperor said, looking out over the cliff at the distant blue ocean. "Why you left that woman, Issefyn, with one of your containment stones."

A foreboding settled over her. He had looked into the case, but it didn't matter. It changed nothing. This was something she had foreseen as a possibility.

"Don't you think it is dangerous to leave a woman like that with so much power?" he asked.

The Emperor had never led a conversation so aggressively before, and it put her off her balance more than she would have thought. She couldn't tell him about the dreams of her father, of course. She'd never told anyone, and events were too precarious to confide in him now.

"It is a calculated risk," she said, careful to maintain an even tone.

"Like your alliance with the albino in the Summer Cities?"

Arefaine's breath came quicker. She felt like she was backpedaling, stumbling toward the inevitable cliff. How did he know about Jesheks? And what else did he know?

"You have strange choices in friends," he continued, again leaving little time for her to reply.

"You kept my options limited," she replied, her icy anger cooling her initial shock. Why was he confronting her now, after so many years of silence?

"I suppose I did," he said. "But that is about to change."

"What do you mean?"

"I know of your plans to lead the Opal Fleet and the Summermen against the Silver Islanders."

She found it hard to breathe. He knew. He knew everything. How? She gathered her magic, preparing for the battle if it would come. If he suspected her, why he had come himself? Why not send his Carriers?

"And you intend to stop me?" she asked.

"Certainly not. I have no desire to stop you."

Arefaine drew a quick breath and allowed herself a small smile. He'd come to join her! Would he truly join her cause?

"I wish to aid you," he continued. "You are not an enemy of the light. On the contrary, you are our last and only hope."

She favored him with a smile. His eyes sparkled, but he did not smile back. "Hope for what?" she asked.

"Completing Oh's plan. Unweaving the harm wrought by the founders of Efften."

Her heart sank, and her smile faded. Just like that, her hopes for fellowship with the Emperor faded away. The man still clung to the Ohohhim version of the history of Efften. Why couldn't he set aside his fears and embrace the possibilities? "I see," she said, trying to keep the frustration from her voice. "And what is Oh's plan?"

He led her past Celinor's shrine and stopped at the edge of the cliff that overlooked the boiling bay.

"He wants you to bring the Heartstone to Efften," he said, as though looking across the sea to the Great Isle.

"Then I agree with him."

"But you need the Opal Fleet to bring you there."

"Yes."

"And you were prepared to kill those loyal to me to get it. You were prepared to kill me?"

This time, he let the silence fall as she struggled to find the right words. She felt like a little girl suddenly, exposed and vulnerable. He knew everything.

"I had hoped it would never come to that," she said, lifting her chin.

He watched a gull float on the breeze that swept up the cliff. His curly black hair shifted. "So did I," he said softly.

Turning, he took her hands. She actually started. Was he going to try to throw her over the cliff? Instead, he looked into her eyes and for the first time, she didn't see the untouchable, unreachable Emperor. He was just a man.

"I feel I have failed you, Arefaine," he said. "I have tried to raise you as a Child of Oh. I have tried to show you the beauty of decorum, respect, and acceptance for your place in the Divine Queue. But your heart belongs to Efften. You are overwhelmed by hunger and burdened by your great ambitions."

For as long as Arefaine could remember, she had longed for this kind of tenderness from the Emperor, but not now. Not like this. She did not want a salve for her wounds and a slap for her bad behavior. It was not a crime to want to bring beauty back to the world.

"You have fallen in love with the stories of Efften's grandeur," he continued. "But you have blinded yourself to the cost of her beauty. Despite your impetuousness, you have never succumbed to the sins of your ancestors. Since coming of age, you have not made anyone a slave to your will. You have not harmed anyone in pursuit of your ambitions. Not yet."

She kept her chin high, listening to his words. This man was not her judge, no matter what the Ohohhim—or the world—thought of him. He was, in the end, just a man.

"How far would you go to fulfill your dream of re-creating the City of Sorcerers, Arefaine? Would you really have killed me to do so?"

She swallowed down a dry throat. "As I said, I had hoped it would never come to that."

He let out a breath and bowed his head for a moment, then looked up at her once more. "Very well," he said. "I have decided to remove that dangerous decision from your path. If you chose unwisely when you came to that moment, you would start down a road from which you would never return."

"What are you saying?"

He nodded once. "I have made arrangements for you to succeed me as regent of the Opal Empire upon my death. You are to have complete authority to rule as you see fit until the new Emperor is found and comes of age."

Arefaine frowned. "But only upon your death."

"Yes. But my death is only a few days away."

"What?" Her heart lurched. "No."

"Oh has shown me the time and place of my demise. It is nearly upon me."

"Then you must change it," she said quickly. "Run. Avoid it."

He smiled. "I am touched by your concern. But I do not wish to change the future. I admit that death is a very difficult thing to face with faith and decorum. But my passing is a critical turning point in Oh's struggle against the darkness."

Arefaine's eyes narrowed. "I refuse to accept that. There are a hundred paths to victory. We will find another."

The Emperor shook his head. His hands were warm on hers, and he continued to look into her eyes. "There is no victory against the darkness. All we can do is follow Oh's example, by turning our backs to temptation and giving our lives in service of the light."

Her lip trembled. "But you can't—"

The Emperor took her into his arms. "I am sorry that I raised you in such a cold and lonely home. There were so many times I wished I could hold you like this, like I would my own child. But Oh has shown me where your future lies. You will soon face a very difficult decision. And you cannot make that choice if you are afraid of being alone."

"What? What decision?" she asked, pulling back. Her throat was tight, and she felt tears welling up.

He closed his eyes and drew a deep breath. Finally, he opened them again and said, "I cannot say."

"Why not?" she said, biting her lip to keep from crying. "Why can't you just tell me what I need to know? Why didn't you just talk to me when I needed you? Why only now, when you say you're going to die?"

"Because the decision is yours to make alone. If I told you what your future would bring, you would try to avoid it, as you have just counseled me to do. You would attempt to trick fate, and this vital opportunity would be lost. Oh has shown me all possible futures. The only path that leads out of the darkness begins with my death and ends with your decision."

"What decision? What must I decide?"

"You must listen to the voice of Oh and follow the sleeve he offers you."

"Enough!" she shouted, pushing him away. "Enough of your riddles and your manipulations! Oh is nothing more than a fable told to keep your people in line. I won't follow his sleeve or any other. Throw your life way if you want, but I refuse to hide from the darkness. I will bring it back into the light where it belongs. And I will do it by myself if I have to!"

He reached for her, but she knocked his hand aside and walked away.

"No," the Emperor whispered, almost too softly for her to hear. "Brophy will be with you. Everything depends on him standing by your side."

CHAPTER 32

Lord Vinghelt stood in *Glory of Summer*'s kitchen scowling and kicking the recently delivered barrels. The prince had doubts about their plan. "It just seems such an extreme measure," he said for the third time.

Jesheks shifted his bulk, and the little stool he was perched on creaked alarmingly. He let his thoughts drift to Shara as Vinghelt went on and on, making the same points, drawing the same conclusions.

Shara-lani had slept for the last two days, drifting in and out of consciousness, but she would be awake soon. He'd been constantly monitoring her with his magic, and he could feel her thoughts drifting closer to the surface as she recovered from her wounds.

He was still astonished that she had survived. She had been the perfect clay in the hands of a master sculptor, strong yet supple enough to travel with him to the limits of his magic and back again. He had always dreamed of meeting someone who could thrive in the fires of Necani as he did, but at the same time, he had counted on her being shattered in that kiln. It was an odd feeling, to desire something and its opposite at the same time.

Now Jesheks faced a dilemma. He had his mission in the Summer Cities. Shara was the greatest danger to the mission, the only danger. Arefaine would certainly want her removed, but Jesheks would never break his word to the Zelani mistress. He had made a pact with both women and must find a way to honor both of them.

"I think we might find another way, a less dangerous way to persuade my people, that is all I am saying," Vinghelt continued, tapping an unmarked barrel with his toe.

Jesheks sighed. "People don't go to war over kitchen fires, my lord."

"I don't trust these Physendrian agents," Vinghelt said. "They could betray us."

Jesheks blinked lazily. The man was such a fool. "They are betraying us, my lord. We are counting on them to betray us. That is why we gave them the tools to set fire to the Floating Palace."

"I don't like it," Vinghelt said stubbornly.

"So you have said."

"What if someone tries to broach one of these 'wine casks'?"

"I don't imagine our dear Physendrian helpers will allow that to happen."

"But what if they are discovered ahead of time?"

"They will be posing as stewards on four different ships. The Waveborn never notice their servants. Do you remember who served you your lunch today?"

Vinghelt frowned and brushed the question away. "Are you sure they know how to handle this whale oil? Will it do the job?"

"There is nothing to handle, they simply pour the oil onto the deck, light it on fire, and run away. When the Ohndariens used this oil to repel the last Physendrian invasion, the wall of fire was over a hundred feet tall." Jesheks had already told him this story twice. "It will more than do the job."

"It just seems risky. Fire is such a random weapon."

"Exactly, that's why it inspires such strong emotions. I imagine the entire Floating Palace will be alight in a matter of minutes. That is why you must act quickly. When you hear the cry of alarm, you must light your own ship immediately. The Physendrians all have the same instructions. As soon as one fire is lit, they will all be lit."

"That is what worries me. What about those trapped belowdecks? Or those in the middle ships? Will they have time to jump to safety?"

"Vinghelt, you cannot enrage your people without something over which they may become enraged."

"Burning our ships is not enough for you?"

Jesheks waved a hand. "This is the only way, my lord. The rebels will rendezvous at a point I have designated, believing that I will then smuggle them back to Physendria. That is when we will haul them before the surviving Summer Princes and the Waveborn nobility as proof of a Physendrian sneak attack. Your people will be so outraged they will demand war, and you are the only prince fit to lead them into battle."

Vinghelt bit his lip. "It seems a great deal of death and destruction just to . . ."

"To what, my lord? To make you king? To reawaken the kingdom of the Waveborn? To change history? If we want to accomplish these great deeds, we must send your people a message written in their own blood."

Vinghelt looked away from the albino, again only able to gaze upon his voluminous bulk for a short time. Jesheks held himself still. Vinghelt had always been the weakest link of this chain.

Slowly, the prince nodded. "I suppose, if it is the only way."

"If you can manage more enthusiasm by this evening, it will go better. The moment the blaze is started, you will need to be right in the middle of it. Organizing the firefighters, rescuing children, grieving over dead bodies."

"That will not be hard," Vinghelt muttered.

"If these people are going to follow you across the world, they need to see your courage, your passion, your rage against the rebels. Arranging a small injury wouldn't hurt, either. Something that shows a lot of blood but doesn't make you look weak. Perhaps a cut to the forehead."

Vinghelt scowled, crossed to the table, and refilled his wine goblet.

"You realize you cannot trust anyone with this information. The only other people who know of the plot are those who will be buried alive for it."

Vinghelt fingered the jewels encrusted into his cup.

"And that reminds me," Jesheks said. "Do not conspicuously remove valuables from the ship, either. Take coins, jewels, anything small and easily hidden. Everything else must burn."

"Do you think I care for these things more than my own people?" He shook the goblet, spilling wine down his fingers.

Actually, Jesheks did think that, but he said, "That is why you must be strong, for the sake of your people. That is why Fessa chose you. You are the only Summer Prince who has the strength to be king."

Vinghelt shifted his gaze away again. If only Reignholtz had been corruptible. What a better man he would have been to take this mantle. Alas, that Summer Prince had fallen on the wrong side of the line.

"Greatness is never easy," Jesheks said, levering his bulk off the stool. "That is why there are so few truly great men."

Vinghelt held himself still as Jesheks approached. A trembling rabbit, wishing the predator would pass him by. Jesheks laid a hand on the prince's shoulder, whose breath became labored.

"Fessa herself chose me to be your guide," Jesheks said, drawing the point of his pinkie sheath across the man's neck. "The goddess knows what is best for her own people, and she wouldn't hesitate to sacrifice a few fish to save the whole school."

Vinghelt shuddered, slowly nodded.

"In two years' time you will be Vinghelt I, Lord of the Earth, Sea, and Sky, just as the goddess foretold."

"It is Fessa's will," Vinghelt murmured. "I am the first among the Wave-born, a people on the edge of greatness." He swallowed. "I must be bold."

"Exactly, my lord," Jesheks murmured, shuffling to the door. "Be ready, just before dawn. Remember, it will happen very quickly."

He left Vinghelt to his dreams of greatness, exiting the kitchen and taking the ladder down to a room on the lowest level of the ship. He felt his trepidation rise as he took slow painful steps along the narrow lamplit passageway. He wondered if this is what men felt like walking to their own executions. His fingers trembled slightly as he touched the handle. He waited until his hand was steady, then he opened the door.

Shara slept peacefully in his bed, a pool of midnight hair spilling across the thick pillows. She shifted in her sleep, rolling onto her stomach and stretching her slender arms above her head. The sheet covered her naked body from the waist down, like a blanket of creamy snow. His gaze lingered on the curve of her delicate shoulders, the trail of her spine, the slope of her waist, and the rise of her hips. The angry red burns across her back had become a delicate pink. Oh, she was a remarkable creature.

He touched his pinkie sheath to his leg and pushed, feeling the sweet pain. He didn't have to let her wake. He could let her die here in the fire, and she would never threaten Arefaine's plans. And . . .

He closed his eyes, swallowed deep, and opened them again.

And he would never have to fulfill his half of their bargain.

He watched Shara breathing, and realized that his interest in Arefaine's vision of an awakened Efften was slowly fading. Shara had brought something to life in him, caused him to remember something he doubted Arefaine had ever known.

The art itself was what mattered the most. *Being* a great sorcerer was not his life's quest. *Becoming* a great sorcerer was all that mattered, savoring each step of the path for the treasure that it was. Shara understood that. Did Arefaine?

Jesheks had been reborn twice in his life. First by a fevered king's blade, and second by an old Necani's red-hot irons. But the next leap forward must be of his own choosing. Jesheks was no fool. Shara's touch could rip open parts of himself long closed, long healed over. Everything he had built would cease to exist and some glorious being—or hideously broken creature—would emerge from the ruins.

Jesheks had never flinched away from blade or blaze, and if he shied away now, if he surrendered to his fear, that would be his first step into ruin. Closing this door, walking away from it, would mark the end of his ascension and begin his long, bitter fall back into the shadows.

Struggling to lower his bulk, Jesheks knelt next to the bed. He pushed a strand of hair away from Shara's face as he had done two nights ago.

Her breathing changed, and a soft sound escaped her lips. Jesheks drank the sound like sweet, rich milk. She blinked, and her hand slid down the silk sheets to cover his. Her fingers gripped his puffy flesh, warm and welcoming.

Jesheks's heart thundered. His legs twitched, and he wanted to leap to his feet, rush up the stairs, and light the oil ablaze, but he mastered his fear with his breath, cycling it back into his body.

Shara opened her eyes, looked up at him, but she didn't say anything. Instead, she pulled his hand to her lips, turned it, and kissed his palm.

A rush of heat moved up his arm, past his shoulder, and into his chest, warming his frantically pounding heart. She smiled at him, slowly. Shyly.

He cleared his throat. "How do you feel?"

"Gloriously empty," she murmured, her voice rough from sleep. "How do you feel?"

"Like I'm about to die," he said.

She gave him a mischievous smile. "But it's just a 'little death.'"

Jesheks almost laughed, but no sound came out.

"Shall we begin?" she asked.

He swallowed, looking at her slender neck, wondering if he could crush her windpipe before she could stop him.

But, no. He had chosen this path the moment he invited her to his ship.

"Yes," he said. "Let us begin."

CHAPTER 33

Shara held Jesheks's hand in hers, keeping his gaze. His muscles were stiff, but he let her touch him. How terrified he must be, she thought, a man who had never felt a loving hand. Accepting her tenderness would threaten everything he had built his life upon. She could feel him hovering within his fortress of scorn and superiority.

He wasn't just offering Shara a quick peek behind those walls. He risked their complete destruction. He risked being exposed, naked and disfigured before the world.

Tears welled in her eyes. "Your courage makes me weep," she whispered.

He flinched as if she'd shocked him. "No one has ever wept for me before," he said, clenching and unclenching his jaw.

"I wanted to thank you for the other night," she said. "You were exceptional, so patient, so tender. You took me just where I needed to go, told me just what I needed to hear."

He swallowed. "I was certain you would die. I never believed you could go that far, not in one night."

Her fingers slid up his arm a few inches, then back to his hand. "You would never have let that happen. You were an impeccable guide." Slowly, delicately, she removed his spiked pinkie sheath. His gaze went to it, and she could see the whites around his eyes. She would begin his way. He would understand that, even if he feared it. He had tied her up, made her helpless. She must take away his escape into pain. Opening a nightstand next to the bed, she put the golden spike inside and shut the drawer.

She rose naked and stood over him. "Lie down on the bed," she said, helping him to his feet. With only a moment's hesitation, he rolled onto the mattress. She crossed the room to the table, taking a thin silk robe from a chair and putting it on. Once she was covered, she brought back a pitcher of water, a basin, a towel, and a sponge.

Jesheks watched her the entire time, wanting to say something, do something, seize control of the situation.

"Lie back," she said. "Close your eyes. Just follow my lead."

One at a time, she removed his shoes, short half boots. His toes were broken and discolored. Slowly and deliberately, she began to wash his tortured feet.

"I broke them," Jesheks said. He vibrated with tension, hating her touch and loving it at the same time. "Each of them," he continued. "When I was young and still clumsy in my power. Self-maiming is a mark of vanity, the stupidity of the young. But it taught me to walk slowly, not to rush."

He's bragging, she thought, flaunting his honesty.

She bent and kissed each crooked toe individually. "I honor you for the path you have walked on these feet. What courage it must have taken, what strength and dedication."

His brow creased for a moment, then he smoothed it, but he didn't say anything.

She moved up his legs, washing delicately, only going as far as his knees. She was not truly giving him a bath. There was no need, he was spotless, obviously a man who bathed regularly in scalding water. But this wasn't about washing, it was about going slowly, about touching him in a way that his fevered mind could accept.

When Shara reached the hem of his robes, she shifted to his hands, brushing them on one side with the sponge, and on the other with her fingertips. Touching his skin was like caressing a corpse, a bloated dead thing with nothing inside it. But his heart was in there somewhere. And she would find it.

She moved from his hands to his head, wiping his lank white hair with the sponge, caressing his scalp. Fear vibrated through him, and she matched her breath to his, letting her magic permeate them both, gentle and reassuring. With every breath, she showed him how to accept the tenderness, draw it into himself, just as he had helped her accept her pain.

He followed her lead, cycling though his fears, barely keeping on top of them. He was so strong in almost any other situation, but this part of him was as weak as a baby. Yet he pressed on, trusting her as she had trusted him. He kept his eyes closed, concentrating on the breath as she stroked his forehead, his face, behind his ears, under his neck. His stoic calm began to crack. His hands twitched, tapping his pinkie into his thigh as if he could plunge the needle in.

She slowed down, reducing her touch to the faintest brushes of her finger-tips. *It's all right,* she thought. *I do not revile you. I see the strong, courageous man inside, and I will not harm him.*

His breath finally evened out, long and deep, and his hands stopped twitching. She smiled.

"Well done, my friend, well done," she said, leaning over him, letting her long hair fall softly across his face. She pressed her lips to his forehead, then drew away.

Jesheks's eyes shot open, and he pulled away from her.

"Shushhh, it's all right," she said, not reacting at all to his fear. "Embrace my words. Accept the praise. Make it part of you."

He settled back down against the pillows, finding his breath again, and Shara unbuttoned his robe and opened it. She washed his pale chest, criss-crossed with hundreds of scars. With every swipe, she sent her magic into the man, trying to find him, trying to draw him closer to the surface, always hitting those walls. But his defenses relaxed with each pass, and she continued touching him, caressing him, pulling closer.

Finally, she felt it. A distant warmth at the very heart of his being. It was still safely behind the walls, but it was there. It was a beginning.

Setting the basin aside, Shara stood up. Her fingers untied the sash at her waist. Dropping her robe, she climbed on top of him, straddling his body, sitting down on his heavy thighs. His gaze flicked quickly from her heavy-lidded eyes to her breasts to the short, trimmed hair between her legs. The bright red scars from his gelding were nearly hidden beneath the folds of his stomach. She had touched him everywhere during the bath except there. Not there. Not yet.

She leaned forward, putting two fingers over his heart, sending a gentle flow of energy into him. He jerked, and his hands trembled.

"Shhhh, close your eyes, keep breathing," she said. "Let it be. Let us be. I will not hurt you."

Imagining a golden flow of ani, she sent it through her fingers, into his body, through his body, down his torso into his legs, up through her legs and chest and back to him through her fingers.

He started trembling, but did not open his eyes.

She continued the cycle, her weight upon his legs, her skin touching his, sharing the current of golden energy again and again. In her magical sight, she saw a golden glow radiating from their bodies. They were both covered in a sheen of sweat, and his white flesh shone like the sun. He was no longer ugly, no longer a dead, empty thing. The wounded heart within was beginning to show through, transcending the pale, puffy, mutilated flesh that Jesheks was trapped in.

It's almost time, she thought. *Almost time.*

As her heart and mind opened to him, inevitably her body had followed, aroused by the strength within him. Her nipples stood erect, and her skin tingled from her scalp to her thighs, held apart by the width of his legs.

Keeping two fingers on his heart, she leaned forward, low and close. Her breasts touched his chest as she kissed him lightly on the lips. He twitched, and shivers coursed through her, one after the other.

"Open your eyes, my friend. Open your eyes and see what I see in you. See what you have done to me, to my body, without ever touching me."

His arms vibrated, and his hands started twitching again. His whole body jerked as he forced his red eyes open, saw her above him. He locked gazes with her, and he stopped breathing. She leaned in to kiss him again, and he jerked his head away.

"No," he said hoarsely. "Enough. Enough."

"Hush, my friend," she said, setting up the even breathing again. "It is all right. Look at me—"

"I said enough!" he shouted. His huge arms snapped up, grabbing her with a desperate strength.

"Jesheks—"

He threw her from the bed, and she slammed to the wooden floor. The breath shot from her body, and stars burst in her vision. She looked up in time to see him descending on her, moving like an enraged bear. He grabbed her by the arm and threw her onto her feet again. She stumbled backward, hitting the wall, and he was on her, shoving his great bulk against her, pinning her against the wood.

Gasping, she controlled her breathing, her head pressed sideways by his hand.

"Enough, you bitch!" he roared. Spittle flecked her face. "You cheap, conniving whore! I'll crush you where you stand! I'll rip you apart!"

Shara took the pain of his grip, the weight of his body against her, and added it to her magic, just as he had shown her, all the while breathing steadily, sending gentle tendrils back to him.

His heart thumped out of control, hammering against his rib cage. She had pushed him too far, too fast.

"You'll never touch me again! Never!" Yanking her back, he slammed her into the wall again. "The other night was a joke," he snarled. "You know nothing of the pain I could give you. Nothing!"

With a growl, he shambled backward and dragged her by the neck, threw her onto the bed.

"You can't do this to me," he growled. His chest heaved with his quick, desperate breaths. "I won't let you." His meaty hands grappled at her neck, squeezing.

Staring up into his contorted face, she sent a steady stream of serenity into the flood of rage coursing through him.

"I could kill you now," he hissed. "I could make you love me when I do it."

Without fighting his fierce grip on her throat, she reached up and touched his chest with two fingers, sending her ani into his body.

I know you could, she said directly into his mind. *But you won't. You won't hurt me. I trust you.*

His grip eased up enough for her to draw a breath. She forced herself to make it match his panting, then to slow it down, bringing him with her.

He sneered. "That won't work, child," he said, changing his breathing away from hers. He gritted his teeth and squeezed harder.

We've danced with pain together, but you won't hurt me. Not now. Not tonight. You won't hurt me, and you won't hurt yourself.

The whites of his eyes became smaller, and his grip eased. Panting like a woman in labor, he shook his head, let go of her completely. Droplets of sweat flecked the bed and Shara's bare skin. "I . . ."

"Don't," she murmured, kept time with his panting, always looking him in the eye. "It is difficult. So so difficult. I am amazed that you have come this far."

His gaze flicked to the bed, back to her, to his hands.

"You can go just a little further, can't you?" she asked. "Just a little bit further."

His heavy breathing slowed, and he blinked. With soft hands, she guided him backward, pushed him back onto the bed.

"Lie down, my love. Lie back down, and we'll go back to the feet. We'll start again with the feet."

CHAPTER 34

Natshea returned under the cover of the stars and the thin moon. Mooring her boat at an unused tie-up on the northern edge of the Floating Palace, she flew up the frayed rope ladder and landed lightly on the deck, her boots barely thumping.

The palace was particularly festive tonight, perhaps due to the recent duel Leftblade had botched. She looked forward to rectifying that error, but Heidvell could wait. First things first.

She flipped her cowl up, covering her telltale braid. Normally she loved to be seen, stared at, adored, but not tonight. Tonight was a celebration for her greatest victory, and all she wanted to do was get to the one person in the world who could appreciate it.

Natshea had never felt so powerful, so beautiful, so fierce and deadly. She saw possibilities that had never been there before. Reaching inside her cloak, she drew her dagger and cut a quick line across her forearm. She gasped as the surge of power washed over her. She'd had a breakthrough during her mission and now, if she concentrated hard, she could spy on other people's emotions, could feel their pain, their pleasure.

Sending her awareness before her, she scanned the crowd. She felt the sadness and isolation of a pathetic little lordling watching his latest fancy in the arms of another man. She felt the anger of the chief steward at an incompetent newcomer who had been hired at the last moment.

Practically skipping across the deck, she made her way through the late revelers and the ever-vigilant crew of the Floating Palace. She passed a pair of young lovers necking in the lee of a cabin, hidden from the soft torchlight, and she thought of that first moment when her old dueling master had touched her, so full of wretched guilt and false bravado as he pushed up her skirt. She thought of his final whimpers as he lay bleeding on the bed, the light fading from his eyes. Her former teacher's eyes had actually turned pitch black by the time she was through with him. It was some delicious side effect of the Necani that she would have to ask Jesheks about.

With a grin stamped on her face, she paused at the bow of Lord Ardholtz's ship and looked north into the vast darkness. She could hardly contain her joy at her liberation and there was still so much to learn, decades' worth of knowledge to explore, one crimson drop at a time. She couldn't imagine the intensity.

The best part was that she finally had a teacher, a man with a fearless, unwavering hand who would never lie to her, never run from her in fear of her gifts like the dead blade master had, calling her dirty, a freakish, broken thing.

Who is broken now, teacher? she thought, remembering his skin flayed open on the silken sheets. She'd actually seen his heart beating beneath his exposed ribs before the end.

With a flip of her head, she continued on to *Glory of Summer,* wending her way through a near riot on Munkholtz's ship. They had run out of wine, and Munkholtz's emaciated steward apologized repeatedly to the rowdy crowd.

Such frivolous people, she thought, living out their frivolous lives. But Jesheks was never frivolous. They would travel from country to country, growing stronger together. He would hurt her—she drew a delicious breath at the thought—and someday she would be ready to hurt him in return. He could not ignore her strength now.

One of Vinghelt's guards, Farlan, blocked her path as she tried to cross the plank.

"The lord's not to be disturbed tonight," he said.

"I'm here to see the physician."

The man shook his head. "Not tonight."

"He'll see me," she assured him, hopping from the plank to the rail and leaping across the gap. "If you want to stop me, draw that sword of yours and see how you fare."

He protested, but she ignored him and jumped through the open hatch, grabbing the ladder on the way down to break her fall. Skipping down the first flight of steps, she passed the galley, turned the corner, and slid down the final ladder to the lowest level of the ship. She stopped in front of Jesheks's door, so familiar. How had she ever been afraid to pass through it that first time?

Plucking her dagger from its sheath, she flipped it, caught it, and prepared to stab it into the doorjamb. How happy would Jesheks be to hear that sound, never expecting her to succeed so quickly? He could probably already sense her joy through the door.

She stopped, the dagger hovering over her shoulder.

Smiling wide, she sheathed the blade. Of course.

No doubt he had tracked her with his magic. She would do the same with hers, show him what she had learned.

Putting light fingertips on the door, Natshea sent her awareness into the room—

Her eyes shot open, and she stumbled backward. Her smile vanished. It couldn't be!

Forcing herself to send her awareness out again, she reached into the room like a child reaching into a hole full of spiders. Her master was ...

Natshea couldn't breathe. The world tilted, and she almost fell, grabbing a doorjamb across the hall to hold herself upright. That woman, Shara, was giving him pleasure. Sexual pleasure.

She closed her eyes and panted in the dark, but she could still feel the trembling of that whore in there, could feel the tingling in her body, and in Jesheks's body, too.

She fled, staggering along the corridor and up the ladder. Boots thumped in the hall behind her, and she ducked into the ship's galley. The boots followed, and she dived into a storeroom, slamming the door behind her. Her heavy breathing filled the dark room, and she tried to get her emotions under control. What was he doing? He had told her, had shown her ...

"You realize, the moment you fear, the moment you long for, is never going to happen."

His high-pitched voice reverberated in her head, pouring acid on what she had just seen.

Slumping down between two wine barrels, Natshea slammed her head back against the bulkhead. The pain blossomed, and she drank it in, slammed her head against the wall again.

How could he do it? He'd told her. He'd promised her. Was it all a lie? Everything he'd said? Everything she'd done?

"Bastard!" she screamed, leaping to her feet. She kicked over a wine cask, and it skidded across the room. She knocked over shelves, tore apart a sack of flour, shattered a butter churn.

Screaming, she leapt upon a wine barrel, driving the heel of her boot through the wooden staves. The barrel spilt open and its contents sloshed onto the floor.

The pantry door was flung open. Lanternlight blared into the dark little storeroom, and Vinghelt's silhouette filled the doorway.

"By the tides, what are you—" he shouted, then recognized her. His eyes widened, then narrowed again. "What are you doing here? Are you crazy—"

Natshea drew her sword and lunged, slashing Vinghelt across the face, laying his cheek open to the bone. He shrieked, hands grappling at torn flesh as he backpedaled. He slipped and fell backward. She advanced, towering over the summer prince. The sight of his blood calmed her somehow. She turned her panting into long, even breaths.

Vinghelt rose to his knees, staring wide-eyed at his bloody hands. He pushed frantically at his cheek, trying to hold it in place. "My face!" he wailed. "My face!" He stared up at her, one eye almost pushed shut by the damage. "Are you insane?"

She raised her sword with a snarl on her lips. Vinghelt held one pathetic hand in front of himself as if he could block her blade with his arm. She drew her blade back to finish him, but she stopped, her face crinkled in disgust.

What was that horrible smell? Natshea looked at her boots. A puddle of yellow sludge crept around her heels, soaking into the wood.

Oil.

Natshea leveled her sword on Vinghelt again, but he scrabbled away, stumbling as he fled. She didn't chase him.

Oil. Why was there whale oil on this boat? She turned, looking at the wine cask she had ruined. She watched as the dregs of the yellowish liquid dripped from the broken barrel. It crept across the floor and through the hatch to the lower level, seeping deeper into the ship. Slowly, she smiled.

"I have no sexual feelings for you whatsoever."

Liar.

She looked at the lantern hanging overhead, fuzzy with dust and grease. Jumping atop the butcher block, she unhooked the lantern and crouched. With a flick of her wrist, she tossed the lantern into the storeroom. It shattered, and the oil ignited. She narrowed her eyes and turned her head away as a wave of heat whooshed out. Flames swept across the floor, following the oil out the doorway.

The air seared her, and she soaked it in, feeling the skin on her unprotected forearms and face bubble. She tried to master it, cycle it into her magic, make herself stronger, but it was too much.

Leaping from the table, she cleared half the room in one jump, landing on the burning floor just before the doorway. She slid on the slick wood through the doorway and leapt to the ladder. The flames surrounded her, but she flew up the rungs to the main deck in moments. She emerged in a plume of smoke, coughing and nearly blinded. Her clothes burned in a couple of places, and her oil-covered boots were still on fire. She shook the burning oil off, savoring the pain as it rushed through her, threatening to overwhelm her. A pillar of flame erupted from the main hatch, and the rigging was already starting to catch fire.

Burn, she thought. *You and your whore will burn for your lies.*

CHAPTER 35

Astor leapt from the skiff, stepping in the boiling surf as they dragged the boat onto the rocky shore. Without being told, his companions all helped lift the little craft and carried it up the beach. Running through the foggy darkness, they joined the others behind a clump of boulders. They stashed the boat out of sight, and Astor peered through the mists at the grim faces of his fellow Lightning Swords and the handful of Zelani who had joined them. No one looked forward to this night's work, but each knew that it had to be done. The Heartstone belonged in Ohndarien. One could not continue without the other.

"Is that everyone?" Bendrick whispered, as Astor joined him in the darkness.

"I was the last," Astor said, gritting his teeth against the pain from dunking his boots in the boiling bay.

Astor certainly had his doubts when they first saw the cursed island. He could not believe the Emperor would take the Heartstone here of all places, but the corrupted half snake had led them true. It had been a moment of agonizing decision when he realized that the serpent was taking them north, away from Ohohhom. But he'd made his call and stayed the course. Following the snake, they found the Emperor's ships hidden by the mists within the boiling bay. Staying out of sight, they left their ship unattended around the far side of the island and approached quietly from the north as soon as night fell. If anyone found the boat, they might never leave this place.

"The Emperor is still aboard his ship," Wasley-lani said, his eyes closed. "And . . . seventeen others."

"Carriers?" Bendrick asked.

"Certainly, though exactly how many I cannot say. At least eight."

"Arefaine?" Astor asked.

The Zelani paused, and his brow wrinkled. "No. She's not there. Or she is hidden from my probing."

Astor took a deep breath, kept his voice controlled. There was only one person whose location he really needed. "And Brophy?"

Wasley-lani stayed silent, then turned his face toward the island. "Not on the boat." He pointed. "There. Atop those cliffs. He is not alone. There are many, many others up there, over a hundred."

Bendrick hissed. "We have no hope against that many."

"Then we'll have to strike quick," Astor said. "Before the alarm can be raised."

"What about the Heartstone?" Bendrick asked. The other Lightning Swords stayed quiet, waiting for their orders.

"It's there," Wasley-lani said. He shuddered. "I can feel it seething with black emmeria. The Heartstone and two others. There's so much of it."

"Astor?" Bendrick turned to him.

"You lead the attack," Astor said. "Strike hard. Strike fast. If they see reason, spare them. But don't waste time with talk. Don't hesitate if anyone stands in our way. No one would have stolen that foul magic without a black purpose in mind."

Everyone nodded, their eyes sparkling. Leather creaked, and metal shifted. This was the moment they had waited for.

"Remember," Bendrick told everyone. "Leave the stones to the Zelani. Nobody else touches them. You know what will happen to you."

The Lightning Swords nodded.

"What about you?" Bendrick asked Astor.

"I will hold the canyon and cover our exit. If Brophy or any of the others farther inland come to the Emperor's aid, I will delay them long enough for you to escape."

"At least take a few swords with you," Bendrick insisted.

Astor shook his head. "That canyon is too narrow, we would just get in each other's way."

"How do you know?"

"I was raised on stories of this place. That canyon is barely four feet wide, and the only way to get from the bay to the cliffs above."

"But one man is surely not enough—"

"We need all our strength at the point of attack. I'll be fine, I'm the strongest blade, and I have this." He patted the Sword of Autumn.

Bendrick had his doubts. Astor hated lying to his friend, but there was more that had to be done on this island than recovering the Heartstone.

"Go," Astor said. "Be swift. Once you get the Heartstone, take everyone you can and get back to the ship. Don't wait for stragglers."

Bendrick nodded and led the others into the darkness. The Emperor's ships were only a half mile farther along the shore. Astor waited until they were just out of sight, then turned his gaze toward the dark cleft in the mountain obscured by swirling mists.

"I'm coming for you," he whispered. "It's time to pay for what you've done."

Silent as a breeze, he crept toward the dark canyon.

❄

The stone path was steep and narrow. Astor rushed through the darkness, guiding himself by running a hand along the side of the steep chasm. Astor plunged forward, worried that he would run into an Ohohhim headed back to the ships late. They would never see each other in the swirling mists.

He almost missed the staircase in the dark. Hewn out of the living rock, it had been shaped and polished perfectly. Astor took the steps two at a time, breathing hard after only a few moments.

As he neared the top, he slowed. Strange, tinkling music floated down from the summit, drifting lazily like the mist. He crept forward—crawling up the last few steps—and peered over the rise. He was stunned by the sight before him.

Sulfurous fog swirled across a verdant garden. Ferns surrounded bubbling fountains. Three half-completed stone buildings rose above the gardens, shining in the moonlight. The music came from women kneeling in sheltered alcoves, turning music boxes. They swayed in time with the music, moving like underwater corpses with pale faces and jet-black hair. Dozens of other bodies lay in perfect rows along the paved walkways. Astor couldn't tell if they were dead or sleeping.

The entire place looked like a twisted temple to some foul religion the Ohohhim were hiding from the rest of the world. *Is this why they had stolen the Heartstone and brought it to this wicked place?*

Astor moved like a shadow among the mists, keeping behind whatever cover he could find. No one saw him, and he watched them, looking, searching . . .

Finding.

His heart hammered in his chest as he saw a tiny red glow in the distance. There was only one thing that red glow could be. He looked down at the

Sword of Autumn where he'd covered the shining pommel stone with a scrap of black cloth.

Creeping closer, Astor saw a tangle of golden, curly hair fluttering behind a stack of building stones. The mist obscured his view for a second, then blew away. Yes . . .

He could see the faint red glow from Brophy's heartstone as he lay sleeping on the floor of an unfinished dome. He appeared to be by himself, far away from the rest of the Ohohhim.

Astor crept closer, keeping the short wall between him and his quarry, hand on the hilt of the Sword of Autumn. His lip curled in a sneer. Astor paused. A pale light emanated from Brophy's closed fist, lighting his young face with a faint glow. Asleep, Brophy seemed younger than Astor. His yellow curls made him seem almost like a child.

But that child had killed his mother.

Slowly, quietly, Astor drew the Sword of Autumn, muffling the steel as it emerged. He circled around on silent feet, putting the pile of stones between himself and the sleeping man.

As Astor neared, he slowed. He placed each foot carefully, staying out of Brophy's line of sight. He had to be quick. Brophy had caught him unawares last time. But Astor had been overwrought, not heeding any of his sword lessons. This time all the advantages were on his side. He had the higher ground, the superior weapon, and the element of surprise.

And he would not waste honor on this man. This was an execution.

Moving around the edge of the stacked stones, Astor strained his ears, making sure each footstep was silent. Brophy's golden head came into view again.

His lip twitching, Astor raised the sword high.

"I'm so sorry it has to be like this," Brophy said.

Astor chopped. Brophy spun out of the way, and the sword sparked against the stone where he'd been. Astor swung again, chasing him. With a grunt, Brophy jumped backward over the loose stones. A pale light shot from his hand and whipped around his head like a shooting star.

"If someone else had killed her, I'd do the exact same thing," he said.

"Shut up!" Astor yelled, charging around the stones, knocking several to the ground. Brophy backed away, hands extended out in front of himself. His green eyes shone in the dark.

Astor swung again, desperate to strike him down before the alarm was raised. He could not believe the speed of the unarmed man.

Brophy retreated behind a blue-white marble sculpture of a wounded swordsman. Astor feinted to the left, followed with a spinning strike. Brophy twisted sideways, slipped behind the statue. Chips of stone flew, and steel sparked as the stone swordsman blocked the strike. Astor followed, but Brophy kept the figure between them.

Three pasty-faced Ohohhim rushed out of the mist toward the noise. Brophy held up a hand and shook his head, a fierce look in his eyes. The Ohohhim stopped, but they didn't leave. Others rushed up to join them.

Astor stabbed left, spinning along the statue and coming around right, flushing Brophy into the open. Astor's heart leapt, and he charged, stabbing the sword through cloth. Brophy's tunic ripped, but the sword didn't pierce flesh.

Astor stumbled, catching his balance on another sculpture. He glanced at it and was suddenly struck by what he saw. It was his mother. Young, slender, tired but still beautiful, cradling her broken wrists to her chest. He looked around. There was Shara-lani, kneeling, with Brophy's head in her lap. And Scythe on the verge of death. Mother Medew cradling a crying baby. What was this place?

Brophy backed away, keeping his hands between them. "I loved her, too, Astor."

"You cut her down from behind!" Astor yelled. "You slaughtered her like a pig!"

Astor snarled and rushed at him. Brophy caught his wrist and twisted. With a cry, Astor stumbled, falling to his knees. He turned to slash at Brophy's legs, but his cousin stomped on the blade. Pain fired through Astor's fingers and jolted into his shoulder. The Sword of Autumn clanged across the rock floor.

Astor leapt for the blade, but Brophy snatched up the sword and tossed it into the mists. It clanging to the ground far away.

Astor charged, driving his shoulder into Brophy's belly. They tumbled to the ground.

"Astor," Brophy said in a hoarse voice. Astor punched him in the jaw, slamming his head to the side. Pinning one of Brophy's arms under a knee, Astor hit him again with all of his strength. And again. And again. Jolts of pain shot up his forearms with each blow.

"Monster!" he spat, grabbing Brophy's other arm and pinning it. He groped for one of the scattered stones, raised it over his head, and brought it down in a crushing blow.

Brophy yanked a hand from under Astor's knee. The rock smacked against his forearm, deflected away. Brophy's heartstone flashed and, one-handed, he twisted the rock from Astor's grasp.

"No!" Astor smashed a fist into Brophy's face. Brophy's head snapped sideways, and Astor hit him the other way, hit him again, and again. One fist, then the other, then the other.

"Why," Astor yelled. "Why did you kill her!"

Brophy's left eye was cut and bleeding. His nose was broken, his lip split. His breath whistled through mashed nostrils. "I'm so sorry," he slurred softly, spitting blood with each word. "I'm so . . . so sorry."

Astor kept hitting him, and Brophy let him. Why? Why didn't he fight back? Finally, Astor collapsed forward onto one hand, staring at the ruin of Brophy's face. There was blood everywhere. Brophy's golden curls were drenched in it.

Brophy reached up, wrapped an arm around Astor. Astor batted him away, slammed a fist into Brophy's bloody face. "Why!" he screamed. "Why did you do it?"

Brophy pulled him down into a fierce embrace. Astor shuddered against his cousin's chest. Through cut lips, Brophy mumbled. "I'm sorry. I am so sorry. Hit me as much as you want. Hit me as much as you need."

CHAPTER 36

W e got trouble."

Lawdon hopped off the bed and hurried over to the curtained window Mikal was peering through.

"That's her," Mikal said. "Natshea."

Lawdon ducked below him and put her eye to the gap in the curtains. Someone in a dark cloak skipped past a guard on the closest gangplank of the adjacent ship. She headed for an open hatch in the center of the ship. "Are you sure?" she asked.

"Yup. I can tell by the way she walks."

"That's the last thing we need."

"One more won't make a difference."

Lawdon had to agree. Four of the Summer Princes had agreed to join her raid on *Glory of Summer*. To her surprise, they had even agreed to arrest Vinghelt himself. Each prince was sending twenty men to make sure there wouldn't be a struggle, or if there was, it would be a short one. With the handful of Reignholtz's men that Lawdon had been able to gather, that was almost a hundred swords against the four men guarding Vinghelt's gangplanks and the eight more playing dice in the forward compartment. A hundred against twelve. And Natshea. And a fat magician. Lawdon liked those odds.

She and Mikal had kept an eye on Vinghelt's ship all day, making sure nobody, especially nobody carrying suspicious bloody bundles, left the ship. She had two men on the other side doing the same thing, and ten more wandering the decks in shifts.

The four princes would send their men just before dawn. In a few hours, this would all be over.

"She's gone belowdecks," Mikal said.

"Good. Let's hope she stays there."

Mikal had become such a solid presence in the last few days. Quiet, re-served, intense. But he still managed to come up with a joke, usually at his own expense, exactly when she seemed to need one. She had to admit, she liked him a lot better when Shara wasn't around.

Lawdon heard a faint sound coming from *Glory of Summer*. "Did you hear that?" she asked.

Mikal nodded. "It sounded like a scream."

He headed for the door. "No, wait," Lawdon said, but he was already through the door and down the hall. She followed him onto the deck of *Dancing Dolphin*.

The guard on the closest gangplank was looking toward the center of the ship. The eight men in the forward compartment rushed onto the deck.

"What was that?" one of them shouted.

"Don't know," the man at the gangplank shouted back. "Go look."

Before the men could respond, a deep "whump" shook the deck. Half the portside windows shattered, and tongues of flame shot up between the ships.

"Fessa's tail!" Lawdon hissed, flinching away from the flying glass.

Mikal rushed forward. A figure emerged from the central hatch, just ahead of a column of flames that shot up into the rigging.

"Go ring the fire bell!" Mikal shouted, running toward the other ship. "Go!"

"What about Shara?" she called running after him.

"I'll get her. You ring that bell. This whole place could go up!" He followed the gangplank guard onto the ship.

Lawdon whipped around, looking for *Dancing Dolphin*'s fire bell. She couldn't see one, but there was a huge silver one on *Glory of Summer*'s aft deck, reflecting the shifting flames.

She sprinted in that direction.

❄

Natshea shook the last of the flames off her boots and looked at her blackened and blistered hands. Her vision wavered as the pain rushed through her. She drank it up like wine poured straight down her throat.

A man in black and gold ran up to her, put his hand on her shoulder. "Are you all right?" he asked.

She whipped her sword out of its sheath and sliced his hand off. He screamed and fell to his knees, collapsing against her legs. Her knee snapped up under his jaw, and he flew three feet backward. "Don't you touch me!" she screamed, the sound strangely muffled as voices howled in her head.

Natshea's gaze snapped up as another man ran toward her, a naked blade in his hand.

"What are you doing?" he yelled, and she recognized him immediately. The new champion had arrived to rescue his whore.

Natshea raised an eyebrow and spun her sword around. "Is that a challenge?"

"What?" Young Heidvell shook his head and moved toward the burning hatch, shielding his eyes. "How many people are still below?"

She slipped into her dueling stance and said:

> "As naked steel cuts naked soul
> I reclaim the title that you stole
> We'll dance until my name is sung
> And know who—

"Shut up, you crazy bitch! People are dying in there!"

The voices in Natshea's head howled, and she scissor-stepped forward, lunging for Mikal's heart, but he was already moving. Spinning, he blocked her strike and moved to the side, knees bent, feet stepping lightly.

"Are you mad?" he cried.

She struck at him again. Sword clanged off sword. Mikal matched her, his teeth clenched in rage as he narrowly countered each strike.

Natshea spoke again as she fenced:

> "Death is more than she deserves
> And the foul master that she serves
> They'll feast on flesh and flame tonight
> As I'll wash them clean from my sight."

Pain surged through her burned skin and blistered hands as she drove the upstart back. He would pay for what he'd done. They would all pay.

❄

Shara shuddered, but held herself in check. The haze of overwhelming pleasure hovered around them like mist, but she didn't embrace it. Not yet.

She lay atop Jesheks, one hand splayed on his chest, one tucked between her feverish thighs. They looked into one another, eyes open. Skin on skin. Hearts so close.

The ani swirling around them could have enthralled an army, but Jesheks still resisted, and Shara would not surrender to the cresting wave without him. Every sensation that rippled through her body she funneled into his chest, into his heart.

Faltering in his breathing, Jesheks clenched his eyes shut and turned his head away.

"Keep them open, my love. Keep them open," Shara gasped, feeling as if the waves of pleasure would rip her apart, but she held them, rode the crest of that wave. He was close, so very close. When he finally let go, she would give it all to him, but not a moment before. The man's defenses were crumbling, shivering with every bit of energy she gave him, but his walls were still bound to the core of his being.

"Show me what you see," she whispered breathlessly, sliding against him. "Show me."

Forcing his head back up, he opened his eyes and gave it all to her, let it flow freely. Her breath came suddenly, and she entered his mind.

The cabin swirled away. Time slipped away, and Shara was back in Jesheks's room with the crackling fire. She looked down the length of her arms, tied again to the iron loops above the fireplace, but this time with thick links of chain. The flames were searing hot on her face, breasts, and belly. Sweat dribbled down her naked body.

A cool hand touched her shoulder, and the smoke from the fire stung her eyes. She blinked and turned.

Jesheks stood behind her, but not the Jesheks she knew. He was slim and muscled, with broad shoulders and skin that shone like ivory. His ridged stomach glistened, stacked squares in stark relief in the flickering light. A silver river of hair cascaded down his back, spilling over shoulders and arms that were smooth and unscarred.

He grabbed her waist in powerful hands and lifted her off the floor.

"Yes," she whispered. "Yes ..."

His muscled stomach pushed against her butt. With a grunt, he slid his ivory cock into her.

She gasped, shuddering as it filled her, stretching her to the brink of joy and agony.

"Yes," she cried as her control slipped. "But let me face you. Let me look at you."

Her chains dissolved, and she pulled away, the loss of connection heartrending. She slipped around in his embrace, slick with sweat. His hands were frantic, bestial. He picked her up, spread her legs, and shoved himself inside her again.

The power rocked her, and she shuddered. Not yet! Not yet! Her back bent, and she grappled with his neck, wound his silver hair in her fist. He slammed into her again, and again.

"Not yet," she moaned, to herself or to Jesheks, it didn't matter. "Not yet. I want you. I want you. The real you."

Using a thin fraction of the power that surged through the room, Shara changed the dream, slowly. Oh so slowly.

The silver hair became lank and white. The perfect man thrusting into her became round, soft, covered with scars.

In the distance, a bell rang.

Jesheks continued moving inside her, every thrust jolting her entire body.

The bell rang again, urgently.

"All the way," Shara said. "All the way."

His cock disappeared, but her hand continued to move between her legs.

"Like this," she whispered. "Like this."

The vision faded altogether. Shara still lay atop Jesheks, her legs squeezing him. He stared at her with eyes wide-open, astonished. Their sweat mingled, and his breath came in little gasps.

"What ..." he huffed. "What is this? What are you doing?"

Shara grinned.

"That feeling? What is ..."

"Rush into it," she said. "Rush into it, my love. You are close. So close." She leaned into him, and he did not flinch away. "Look at me." He gazed into her eyes, and her heart welled over. "Look at me."

Her fingers moved faster, harder, in time with the distant bell. The smoke continued to sting her eyes, and a tear fell from her face, splashed on his cheek.

Let me see you. Let me love you. All the way—

A loud bang jolted her. Her breath faltered. Jesheks turned away.

Another bang reverberated through the room.

Someone was shouting. "Get out here! Get out here and save us!"

Disoriented, Shara turned to look at the door. She could hardly see through the smoke in the room.

Another loud bang and a crunch this time. The door flew open, rebounding against the wall.

Vinghelt stumbled through, an axe in his hand. A bloody wound marred his face, and smoke billowed in after him.

"Jesheks! Get us out! Get us out! We're trap—" He stopped in his tracks when he saw them, his jaw hanging open. His face curdled like sour milk. "Fessa of the Deep!" he cried in revulsion.

Jesheks threw her to the other side of the bed and leapt to his feet, his whole body quivering in rage.

"That's disgusting!" Vinghelt gasped, his nose wrinkled high.

With a roar, Jesheks launched himself at the Summer Prince.

❄

Lawdon slammed the hilts of her daggers against the fire bell, one after the other. It seemed a lifetime before she heard the resounding answer to the aft, then to port and starboard. She continued hammering at it until the entire Floating Palace was a cacophony of bells.

She turned to the madness on the deck below. Mikal was fighting furiously with Natshea as the rigging burned above them. The woman was insane! What could she possibly be trying to do?

Cocking back a hand, Lawdon threw a dagger. She barely missed, just behind Natshea's back. Her blade tumbled across the deck and disappeared over the side. She drew back to throw the other one, but Natshea shifted, moving so Mikal was between them.

Lawdon turned, ready to run and help him when another gout of flame spurted skyward from Lord Munkholtz's ship, three over.

"What—" she murmured, squinting. Another flicker erupted to the north. Lawdon spun. And another to the west.

What was it? Some kind of attack? For an excruciating moment, Lawdon stood paralyzed. How could they fight off that much fire? How could...

She could hear Reignholtz's voice in the back of her mind.

"Keep focused. Only a fool tries to sail the entire ocean. One wave at a time. You ride a storm one wave at a time."

Flames soared out of the open hatch and through the open windows on the lower decks. How in the world could it be burning so fast? She had never seen a fire like this before. If she didn't do something, the entire Floating Palace would go up. Mikal would have to fend for himself. She'd have to trust that he could take care of himself long enough for her to put out this fire.

"You!" she shouted at the stunned guards on Vinghelt's deck. "Find buckets! Get help! Start a chain!" She ran to starboard, shouting at the small group of spectators standing on the next ship over, mesmerized by the flames. "You, start cutting lines! Separate this ship!" She paused, looked around. "No, wait, separate all of the ships. All of them! Do you hear me? Spread the word! Free the Floating Palace!"

The twelve of them just stood there, staring dumbly at her.

"Now, you morons! Get axes! Go! Go!"

A gray-haired woman was the first to move, and the rest followed right after her.

Lawdon paused, gazing at the roaring flames. Too fast. The fire was moving too fast. Buckets weren't going to do it. They needed more water. An entire sea of water.

Running to the rail, she looked down at the dark waves below. They had all the water in the world, but how did she get it up where it was needed?

The "thunk" of an axe sounded, and she glanced along the rail to see one of Vinghelt's men cutting lines. She squinted behind her. Natshea and Mikal's battle had moved beyond her sight, obscured by people and smoke.

She turned back to the task at hand, thinking hard. They could breach the hull, let in the water that way. If they had enough axes. If they could rig a sling to lower someone along the hull. She squinted back at the blaze, roaring skyward.

No. It had to be something else. Something now. Ram it with another ship?

No time. Not enough time! She couldn't possibly separate the ships and bring any of them back at speed soon enough.

They needed a storm, a wave to heel the ship on its side, swamp the ridiculous windows on this hulking pleasure barge.

She stopped, stared up at the rigging. If they could set the sails, catch a cross gust . . .

The sky was clear overhead. Stars blinked back at her through the haze of smoke. No storm. No wind at all. She growled in frustration, staring at the mainmast. If it were a toy boat, maybe she could . . .

Wait!

She spun around, her gaze flicking toward *Dancing Dolphin* to the starboard, then back to Vinghelt's mainmast, staring up the long pole.

Yes, she thought. It might just work. It would have to work. There was nothing else. She just hoped that Vinghelt had bought good rope.

Very, very good rope.

❄

Natshea followed Heidvell across the smoky deck, reveling in the moment. He reached the forecastle and spun around to face her. Mikal shuffled sideways, desperate for an escape route. The scowling idiot didn't seem to realize that he was completely outclassed. He hadn't made a single attack that had come close to touching her, but he was proving infernally hard to hit. She lunged, going for a thigh, but he danced aside, his sword sliding between them just in time.

He ducked around the corner of the cabin and backed up a set of stairs leading to the second deck. She tried to follow, but he was using the height and constriction of the stairs to his advantage.

Smiling, she said:

> *"I expected a better show from you*
> *Surely you know a rhyme or two*
> *I heard you were once quite clever*
> *When Leftblade's right you did sever."*

She launched a flurry of blows, driving him backward up the steps. With a sudden twist, he tossed his sword from right to left and slipped out of her reach, racing into open space again.

Natshea followed slowly, drinking in her pain, feeling stronger and stronger with every step. The voices sang to her like a crowd chanting her name.

Mikal gathered himself, his sword held back in a defensive position. She stopped just in front of him, lowered her guard, and shrugged. "What?" she asked.

He didn't reply, and she continued:

> *"From this day forth all talk shall cease*
> *From this day forth your tongue will know peace*
> *Then your golden reputation is mine to seize*
> *With your last drop of silence spilled on the Summer Seas"*

Despite himself, Heidvell smiled and gave a little snort. He rose to his full height, and he finally spoke.

> *"I cannot imagine where you lost your mind*
> *Or what by this duel you hope to find*
> *If you persist, it is to your shame*
> *But since you insist, I'll give you game.*

I fear that steel is on your side
But the truth does not with you reside
And we all know the inevitable fate
That waits for hearts soaked in hate."

Her anger flared, and she attacked again. He met her blade with cowardly blocks, constantly backing up. *If the bastard would face me like a real duelist, try a cut, a riposte, leave himself open just once, I could end this farce!*

She pressed her advantage, breathing harder than she ever had in a duel. They traded blows through the swirling smoke, and he finally tried an attack. She stepped forward at the last second, blocking his blade with her left forearm. His sword cut deep into her arm, glancing off the bone, and she drove her knee toward his crotch.

He barely spun out of the way, and she caught him hard on the inner thigh, throwing him off-balance. He stumbled to his knees, barely hanging on to his sword.

Natshea held back, waiting for him to recover. She shuddered with the delicious pain in her arm. A flap of skin dangled just above her wrist, and a steady stream of blood poured off her elbow. She hissed and drew the power into herself. Her entire body felt like it was growing larger, faster, more powerful. A few more wounds, and she would be invincible.

She was going to enjoy Heidvell's death, enjoy it immensely.

❄

Vinghelt shrieked and rushed into the hall, with Jesheks right behind him.

Shara leapt from the bed, following. Turning the corner, she saw Jesheks grab Vinghelt and throw him bodily against the burning ladder. The wood snapped, and Vinghelt tumbled behind it to the far side.

"How dare you disturb me!" Jesheks shouted.

"Has everyone gone mad!?" Vinghelt shrieked. "We're trapped!"

Jesheks stopped and, for the first time, seemed to realize that they were in the middle of an inferno. He stared at the broken ladder. A steady stream of burning oil poured through the opening from the deck above them. The flames above were blistering—there was no way they could go up that way.

Shara rushed to Jesheks's side, trying to send her magic to him, trying to calm him.

He spun around, clubbed her with his fat arm. "Stay away from me!"

She stumbled back, reeling. His red eyes were feral, and he jerked his head around, looking for a way out. The man she had touched in the bed just a few moments before was utterly gone. He didn't even look like himself anymore. She had lost him and would never get him back.

Vinghelt stammered, shying away from the flames still pouring through the hatch. "I've got an axe!" He cringed against the wall, as far away from Jesheks as he could get. "We could chop out through the hull."

"The hull's a foot thick, you idiot!" Jesheks snarled, snatching the axe out of his hand. "You've killed us! We're all going to die in here! Burned alive!"

❄

Lawdon raced into the rigging, avoiding the flames as best she could. Fire bells were ringing all around her. The Floating Palace had been alerted, but there were fires everywhere. The nearby Waveborn had begun a small bucket brigade, but it was like spitting on a bonfire. Too little, too late, and that blaze was spreading with a mind of its own.

"Listen! We need this ship cut free!" Lawdon shouted down to the crowd below. "Cut her free. Cut every last line. Now!"

Pulling the loop of rope from her shoulder, she wrapped it around the mainmast and cinched it tight with a reef knot. When it was set, she looked down.

"Get everyone to the starboard side! Get onto the next ship over!" she yelled, throwing the line to the deck below. The crowd milled hesitantly. "Do it!" she screamed. "There are people in there. We need to get them out!"

They moved to the starboard side, many leaping the gap to *Dancing Dolphin*.

"You there!" She pointed. "Run the line to the windlass on that ship. You with the axe, cut the shrouds." The man with the axe in his hands hesitated.

"Now, sailor!" she shouted. He jumped to work, chopping through the lines that steadied the mast on the starboard side.

"Tie it to another line. Tie it tight. The strongest knot you can make," she shouted. "And then run it to the windlass over there." She pointed to the other windlass to *Dolphin*'s aft.

"We're going to tip it! Swamp it!" she shouted at the gawking sheep. "Everyone grab a line and pull to starboard. We'll dip the lower deck underwater and flood the ship." Finally comprehending her plan, one of them jumped to grab a line and started pulling.

"Everyone!" she shouted. "Quickly! Let's go! Let's go! There are people dying in there!" The rest grabbed ahold of whatever lines they could and heaved together. The ship creaked.

With renewed urgency, Lawdon spun around and slid down a rope, thumping onto the deck. She sprinted to the rail and leapt to the adjacent ship, where everyone was heaving on the lines. Grabbing hold of the nearest line, she added her strength.

With each pull, the men at the windlass took up the slack and tightened it. The rope held, and they pulled again.

❄

Natshea laughed, pointing her sword at Mikal. He scrambled to his feet and ran from her. She nearly caught him, but he bolted up another flight of steps from the forecastle to the observation deck. She shouted after him:

> *"Turn 'round and fight, you feckless cur*
> *I've seen your love and who's fucking her*
> *I heard that vile eunuch make her grunt*
> *With his pasty fingers jammed in her cunt."*

Heidvell slowed and turned around. She devoured the anguish written across his face. For a moment she thought he would launch himself down the stairs at her, but he held himself back. Smiling, she said:

> *"She left you for a bloated thing,*
> *What lovely image that does bring?*
> *Her precious thighs did unlock*
> *For a lying bastard with no cock."*

She sauntered up the stairs toward him, stumbling slightly as the deck moved under her. Mikal took a deep breath, and the cocksure grin returned to his lips:

> *"A woman's charms are hers to share*
> *With whom she chooses, foul or fair*
> *But I'm guessing that she pricked your ire*
> *Enough to make you light this fire."*

Natshea sneered and rushed him again. The deck continued tilting, growing steeper and steeper under their feet. People were shouting below, but Natshea didn't take her eyes off Heidvell's blade. She compensated for the tilting deck and continued forward, driving him toward the rail at the stern of the ship.

"Why yes I lit this lovely blaze
To trap them in their lovers' haze
I think their lust will surely sour
When they wake in a burning bower."

She slashed at him, repeatedly working his off-sword side, taking advantage of the awkward footing. Each time, he barely got his block up and retreated another step. A few more feet, and he would have nowhere left to go. She saw the sweat on his brow as he strove to keep himself alive, but somehow the bastard was smiling.

"Could it be that ghostly man
Holds your heart in his fat hand?
With a cruel thrust, you've been shoved
From the albino's nest, alone, unloved."

With a roar, she charged forward, but she kept bumping into the rail. She couldn't stand up straight. Heidvell fell back, barely parrying her blows. He shifted his stance, putting one foot on the deck, one on the rail and crab walking backward.

"You're just a lonely, crippled thing
With a bitter sword and broken wing
If this sad, ugly tale is true
Then, poor child, I pity you."

"Pity! Pity!" she screamed. "I'll flay you open! I'll peel your flesh away and make you love it. Make you love me."

Natshea could barely breathe. Her heart beat out of control, and shooting pains lanced down her left arm. She fell to the right, leaning on the rail. The world was falling, shifting under her feet. And there was pity in his eyes! Pity!

Her heart limped in her chest, not beating the way it should. Her left arm hung limp at her side.

The night began to grow blacker, she could barely stand, barely see.

"I'm so sorry," Mikal said. "So, so, sorry about what they've done to you."

She screamed and rushed him, swinging her sword high overhead.

With blurring quickness, he shifted to the side. Her blade sank into the railing, a hairbreadth from his flesh. He slammed both fists into her hand, throwing his full weight into the blow. The blade sprang from her grip, and she stumbled backward. Her sword clattered through the railing, falling out of sight. Mikal's sword flashed up, the tip tucked under her chin.

"That's it," he said. "It's over. There's been enough blood spilled tonight."

Natshea laughed, did the fool actually think he was being noble? She grabbed his weapon with her bare hands.

"It's not over, I'm not done with you yet." She yanked on the blade, but he danced back, wrenching the steel from her grip. Screaming at the pain, she leapt on top of him, bloody hands closing around his throat. Mikal rolled backward, snapping his knee up and lifting her off the ground. He planted a boot firmly on her belly and launched her over his head. She clung to his neck as she fell, but the railing struck her in the left thigh, and she spun around, losing her grip.

She tumbled through the air, blinded by the smoke, and screamed just as she struck the water.

❄

"All together!" Lawdon shouted. "Heave! Heave!"

The two ships creaked as if they were being torn apart. The windlass crew took up the slack, then everyone else heaved again. The ships creaked louder, protesting. The lines quivered, and Lawdon prayed they wouldn't snap. They were not made for so much strain.

"Again!" she called, and everyone pulled. Vinghelt's ship leaned a little more. "Again!"

The windlass crew turned the spool, locked it in place.

"How close are we?" Lawdon shouted. Three kids stood at the rail, staring down at the gap between the ships. "One more foot!" one of them shouted.

"One last big pull!" Lawdon shouted again. She looked down the line of panting, sweating Waveborn. "One more. On my mark. Ready! Set! Heave!" The ships groaned, the Waveborn grunted, and the ship dipped the farthest yet.

"They're in!" the boy yelled. "They're in!"

"Hold!" Lawdon shouted. "Hold!" Her feet slipped on the deck, and she clenched her teeth. Mikal startled her by coming up behind her, grabbing the line, and helping steady it.

She turned, flooded with relief. "What happened to Natshea?"

"Poor girl's too enamored of the sight of blood. Especially her own, as it turns out." He closed his eyes, shook his head. "There was nothing I could do."

"Sounds like a story," she said. "Tell me, if we live through this."

He gave a quick nod.

Planting her boots, she held firm to the quivering line. Mikal grimaced and strained beside her, his knuckles white.

"She's flooding!" the boy yelled just as a plume of steam rose from the crack between the ships. The kids squealed and scampered away from the edge. The straining lines from the mainmast stopped vibrating, then went slack as Vinghelt's ship began to sink.

❄

"What's happening? What's happening?" Vinghelt shouted, as the ship tilted. The whites showed around his eyes, and his fingers scrabbled down the wall as he slid backward. The fire roared above them, flaming oil dripping into the hallway.

Shara ducked low on the tilting floor, looking for sweeter air. The blaze was almost upon them.

Jesheks attacked the wall with Vinghelt's axe. His ani blazed around him, keeping him alive with little air.

Her heart twisted as she looked at the roaring inferno above her. She started to gather her power, preparing the Floani form, hoping her new Necani abilities would carry her through the flames. She didn't want to die like this so far from home, so far from Brophy.

The ship lurched and tilted farther.

"What's happening?" Vinghelt babbled.

We're about to be burned alive, she thought. *That's what's happening.*

A hissing sound rose beyond the snapping and crackling of the fire. Shara stopped, suddenly realizing what was happening.

"Someone's thinking up there," she said. "They're swamping the boat."

"What!" Vinghelt shrieked.

Jesheks stopped swinging the axe and turned around.

"They're swamping the boat! They're putting out the fire!" She shouted, moving forward, "Quick, take hold of—"

A gush of water blasted through the hole in the ceiling, extinguishing the flames, plunging them into darkness.

The water rushed into the narrow hallway, flooding the trough where the wall met the floor. Shara rose to her feet, fighting the torrent.

"Jesheks!" she shouted, lunging forward, but the wall of water surged between them. She couldn't keep her footing on the slick wood. She fell, and the water swept her back, smashing her against the end of the corridor. She was tossed in the darkness, spun around as the deluge tried to drown her.

Gulping a deep breath, she fought the surge, but it crushed her against the bulkhead for an interminable minute.

Slowly, the weight decreased, then disappeared. She floated underwater, but she couldn't see anything in the darkness. She swam forward, brushing the wall with one hand to remind her where she was.

Her lungs burned, throwing her into memories of the Wet Cells. She swam down the hallway, feeling for the exit. Her fingers closed over the edges of the hatch where the fire had been. The burned wood was still hot, even underwater. She pulled herself through and continued on, feeling her way through the labyrinth of a ship she barely knew.

She took as much time as she dared, willing herself to keep her wits about her. *Go slow*, she told herself, half-crawling, half-swimming up the stairway until she saw a flickering red light ahead.

She kicked upward, abandoning caution as she saw fire dancing in the water above. Where there was fire, there was air.

The walls of the ship passed beyond her, and she was suddenly in the open water. She wanted to check behind her, wanted to save Jesheks at least, but she had no air left. Kicking for the surface, she broke the waterline and gasped the hot, smoky air.

Flames roared all around. The upended stern of Vinghelt's sinking ship was still visible in the midst of the other burning boats. The Floating Palace was afire all around her.

With a cry, Shara peered desperately through the haze and flame, looking for Jesheks. She called for him, but if he was there, he did not answer. She reached out with her magic and was instantly overwhelmed by the cacophony of desperate emotions. She would never find him amid all that rage and fear.

Slapping the water, Shara screamed frustration. She'd lost him. He'd been so close, and she'd lost him forever.

CHAPTER 37

Astor sobbed in Brophy's arms. The boy shook, and Brophy bowed his head. The muscles in his arms were tense, stiff in their embrace. The black emmeria still thrashed inside him, feeding on Astor's rage, the pain on his face. He ached to crush the boy crying in his arms, and Brophy hated himself for it.

But he locked that feeling away. He was tired of running. Tired of fleeing from what he'd done and who he might become. If he could not escape this battle, then so be it. He would see it to the end.

Footsteps thumped in the distance, heavy boots slapping on stone. Brophy raised his head. The crowd of Ohohhim parted and three Carriers of the Opal Fire burst through the mists. Their swords were naked in the moonlight, one of them covered with blood. They fanned out in an attack formation.

"No!" Brophy said, wiping a hand across his mangled face. It came away bloody. "Stay back. I'm all right."

Astor brought his head up. His red-rimmed eyes flicked from one Carrier to the other. He reached to his belt for the Sword of Autumn, but it was long gone.

"No, it's okay," Brophy assured him. He let go of the boy, stood up, and put his hands out in a pacifying gesture.

"Are you injured, Warden?" a Carrier asked. "Do you require aid?"

Brophy shook his head. "I'm all right," he said, then murmured in a lower voice, "I'm better than I have been in a long time."

The Carriers kept their swords out. Slowly, they closed on Astor.

"Please don't hurt him," Brophy said, as they took Astor's arms. He didn't resist, turned to Brophy with a dazed look.

"The Empress Regent has already given orders that the survivors are not to be harmed."

"Empress Regent?"

The Carrier gave a quick, terse bow of the head. "His Eternal Wisdom's sleeve has passed beyond our grasp. He has taken his final steps into the welcoming darkness of Oh's cave."

"What?" Brophy whispered, looking quickly at Astor. The boy's gaze focused on the stone floor.

Brophy sprinted for the steps.

❄

Brophy's feet barely touched the ground all the way back to the quay. The walls of the canyon flew by in a blur. He charged through the sulfur mists of the boiling bay and up the ramp onto the Emperor's flagship.

For a moment, he thought he was back in the nightmare. Bodies littered the deck, both Ohohhim and Ohndarien. Blood stained the wood in patches.

"By the Seasons . . ."

A half dozen Ohndarien Lightning Swords lay facedown on the far side of the ship, trussed up hand and foot. A wounded Carrier stood guard over them. Arefaine's handmaidens were arranging the corpses in an orderly row. Several Zelani were among the dead. Three other Carriers stood protectively over a small figure hunched over one of the bodies, lying separate from the others. The Carriers ignored him, their eyes stoically fixed on nothing.

"No," Brophy murmured, moving closer.

Arefaine looked over her shoulder at him. Tears painted tracks in the white powder of her face. The Emperor's head lay in her lap.

He knelt beside her, and she followed him with her eyes.

"He knew," she whispered, looking back down at the Emperor's placid, unmoving face. "He told me this would happen. He could have stopped them. He could have left at any time."

Brophy wrapped his arm around her shoulder, squeezed. "I know."

"I don't understand. He said he did it for me, but why? How could this possibly make a difference?"

Brophy looked into her pale blue eyes. She searched his face desperately. He leaned toward her, and she threw herself into his arms, hugging him tightly as she cried.

Brophy had a guess why the Emperor had done it, but he couldn't tell her. Not now. Not yet.

CHAPTER 38

Lawdon stood at the stern of her ship, *Moon Maiden*. It actually belonged to Shara, but the uncharacteristically quiet Zelani had waved her off when Lawdon mentioned it.

"What need do I have of a ship?" she asked, still looking north across the sea spotted with islands.

Lawdon stared at the charred wreckage that lay upon the shifting Summer Seas. What remained of the Floating Palace bumped against her hull as she slid through the morning waters.

To the east, Jesheks's ship flew Vinghelt's colors. The bodies of three Physendrians dangled from the bowsprit, the lower halves of their bodies chewed away by the sharks.

A mighty host had gathered in Seahome Bay. They had come from all over. Gildheld, Munkheld, Ardheld, Koscheld, and even some from Reignheld. Every Waveborn and peasant patriot had emerged in the last two days, and more were sailing north to join Vinghelt's host.

The entire Summer Fleet was gathering for the first time in five hundred years. More ships arrived every hour, packed with eager recruits drunk on revenge and the free ale gushing through Vinghelt's fingers.

Lord Vinghelt had emerged from the wreckage of his ship like the reincarnation of Salice Mick. His men had barely dragged him out of the water before he started barking orders, leading the hopeless fight against the flames that consumed the Floating Palace.

The prince's aquiline face had been torn open by the blade of one of the Physendrian saboteurs, or so Vinghelt claimed. No one doubted the prince's story about the Physendrian saboteurs once he produced their bodies. Hundreds of witnesses had seen them posing as wine stewards, and the blaze had obviously started with wine casks filled with whale oil.

Natshea had admitted to lighting the blaze on the *Glory of Summer,* so Vinghelt must have been behind the attack somehow. It had certainly played right into his hands. But why would he allow himself to be trapped in his own ship? None of it made any sense, but no one wanted to listen to Lawdon's doubts and concerns. The Summermen wanted blood, and they intended to get it.

Vinghelt's albino physician probably knew the truth, but he had drowned or burned to death in the conflagration. The only other possible witness was the single Physendrian who had escaped. But half the Waveborn young men had rushed off, vowing to return with his head. Lawdon held little hope that his story would ever be heard.

She glanced at Shara, whose black hair was blowing in the light breeze. Her oversized white peasant shirt billowed back like a sail. There was a story surrounding that shirt. It was not Shara's style, and it didn't particularly suit her. But when Lawdon asked her about it, she only smiled a little and shook her head.

Lawdon and Mikal had spent a day and a half searching the wreckage for Shara's body, and had nearly given her up for dead when the Zelani showed up in bright daylight the very next morning, wearing the man's shirt and a brown dress.

"I thought it would be better if I stayed out of sight until Vinghelt was looking the other way," she had said. Lawdon didn't know what had happened to Shara in those two days with the albino, but she suddenly seemed like the woman Lawdon had known many years ago, at ease with herself, quietly confident, not showy without a purpose.

Lawdon's gaze lingered on Shara's back. No, it was more than that. Shara had never seemed so at peace as she did now, so clear. She seemed like a woman who knew what must be done and exactly how she planned to do it. The cocksure daring that had marked her arrival at the Floating Palace was gone. Somehow, Shara suddenly didn't have a thing to prove to anyone.

Turning away, Lawdon looked back at Vinghelt's new ship. Shouts and whistles erupted for a moment, then faded away. Vinghelt was giving another speech. The man had been giving speeches every hour for three days. There were always new recruits, and he was always willing to fill their heads with his vision.

Lawdon frowned and spat into the water. Watching the man spin lies into gold was even worse than knowing that her idea had saved his miserable life. Still, how could she be bitter? She had also saved Shara. The Waveborn got Vinghelt, and Lawdon got Shara.

When hearing the news of Vinghelt's ascension, Shara had shaken her head, brushed Lawdon's hair back from her face, and looked at her like a mother might look at a dirt-smeared child. "The game is not over yet," she said, then went to the portside rail and watched the northern horizon, waiting patiently until *Moon Maiden* was ready to sail. Lawdon had a horrible time try-ing to find a crew to man the ship. She finally located a handful of Reignholtz's men who were willing to join them. It wasn't a full crew, but Lawdon could handle the *Maiden* shorthanded if she needed to.

Despite what Shara said, the bitter gall of Vinghelt's call to war stung the back of Lawdon's throat. The man's victory was complete. Everything that Reignholtz had fought and died for was lost.

Shara suggested that they make immediately for Ohndarien. There was still hope that they could convince the council to bar the gates and send the Summer Fleet away. Without the resources or experience to lay siege to Ohndarien, the Summermen would eventually lose interest and go home.

Lawdon bit her lip. She wished she had more faith in the Ohndariens, but every time she allowed herself to believe in Shara's plan, she felt Suvian's fingers in her mind, felt his fingers sliding over her stomach and down her breeches.

Mikal moved up alongside her, leaning his palms on the rail. He stared at the host of ships, listened to the shouting and cheering, and didn't say anything.

She liked that about him. Before Shara, before they returned to the Sum-mer Cities, Mikal felt the need to fill every silence, but the duel with Leftblade had changed him. In many ways he was back to his old self. He had resumed flirting with her, and from time to time he spouted his bad verse to anyone who would listen and many who wouldn't. But this time, there was a core of steel beneath his foppish veneer.

"Shara and I are over," he said suddenly, still watching Vinghelt's ship.

"Let me guess. She caught you humping the maid," Lawdon said.

The side of Mikal's lip curled, and the corners of his eyes grew crow's-feet. "Well, it wasn't just that."

"You humped someone else?"

Mikal drew a deep breath and gave her a brittle smile. "She's in love. Al-ways has been. Who knew?"

"Only the entire civilized world, and probably most of the uncivilized world. Have you never heard the epic poem 'The Ward of Autumn'?"

"In other words, everyone but me."

"So it would seem."

"Some fellow named Brophy. The way she talks about him, you'd think he saved the world."

She chuckled, but Mikal didn't laugh, and she sobered.

"I'm sorry," Lawdon said. "That must be difficult for you."

He shrugged. "It's for the best. If I didn't let her go, I'd probably have to fight him eventually, and I wouldn't want someone Shara cared about to die."

She raised an eyebrow, looked at him. "Brophy won the Nine Squares, you know."

"Oh, I meant me. The dying part, that is. Very sad for Shara. Want to spare her that."

She laughed.

They both watched Vinghelt's boat for a while. The cheering quieted, and you could almost hear the Summer Prince's words as his voice carried across the wreckage-strewn waters.

"So now what?" Lawdon asked. "It's back to maid-humping?"

He smiled again. "Oh, I think I've acquired a taste for love, Fessa help me."

She swallowed. "So what are you saying? That a man like you can now be tied down by one woman?"

"I'd let the right woman tie me up." He smirked.

"I said down, not up."

"Up, down, back, forth. It's all the same on a ship."

She shook her head. "Why come north, then?" She tipped her head at Shara, still staring to the west, peasant shirt billowing out behind her. "Why torture yourself?"

"Would you prefer I join the glorious warriors of truth over there? Make myself a necklace from dusteaters' big toes?"

"That's not what I meant. There is much you could do here. What about all of the lonely women?"

He looked over at her for the first time. Distant cheers rose again from Vinghelt's ship.

"Think of all the betrothed, intended, and even married lasses that are being left behind," Lawdon said. "Someone must comfort them."

"Sad, but true," he said, "but I think I've had my fill of lonely women."

"Have you moved on to lonely men, then? Lonely little boys?"

"Your tongue is wicked enough to make you a duelist. You wouldn't even need the sword."

"I believe I've had enough of poet duels," she said.

"Indeed," he said, nodding, then interjected, "No, I think I shall be celibate for a time."

She laughed. "Now that I would like to see."

He gave her a sidelong glance. "Careful what you wish for, my love, you may get it."

She found she could not form a snappy reply. Licking her lips, she turned away from Vinghelt's ship and faced the cool sea breeze. She cleared her throat and called out an order. The sailors in the rigging reset the sails. She spun the wheel around and set a course for the edge of the bay.

Mikal shifted his position also, turning and leaning back on the rail with his elbows.

"Time for a new tack?" he asked.

Lawdon wished she didn't blush so easily. "I guess so," she said crisply.

"Let's make it a good one."

The ship slid free of the dark debris of the Floating Palace, heading north toward Ohndarien.

EPILOGUE

Ossamyr took a deep breath and opened her eyes. The cabin was still dark, but she could feel the approach of dawn. Sunrise would bring the end of one voyage and the beginning of another.

Untwining her fingers from Reef's hand, she lifted the Islander's arm out of her way and crawled from their bed. The cabin floor was cold on her bare feet as she crossed the chilly room and crawled into her fur-lined robe.

Cracking the door, she slipped into the corridor. She paused before shutting the door, looking back into the room. A stripe of lanternlight cut across Reef's enormous body as he slept in their bed. Once again, the two of them had made love through most of the night, storing as much light emmeria as they could before they had to part ways.

The Islander was like no other lover Ossamyr had known. His sheer size, his brute strength, had frightened her at first. She felt like a doll next to him, something that could be crushed in an instant. The first time they tried to make love, they couldn't even finish the act. It hurt too much. But Ossamyr had learned to adapt on their long voyage to the Opal Empire. Now she adored the long, passionate nights she spent with him, filling her chest with light emmeria. He held her so fiercely, so tenderly, making love not for himself or even for her, but for the entire world.

She'd even told him she loved him one night. And he said the same to her. It was as simple as that, a pair of quiet truths, honestly given and honestly received.

Ossamyr had never told Brophy those words. Though she still felt them as fiercely as the ones she'd shared with Reef. As much as she cared for the Silver Islander, Ossamyr sometimes still wished it was Brophy in her bed. She couldn't imagine Reef laughing while he was inside her or playfully pinching her butt while she tried to get dressed.

The two of them together would be the perfect lover, the man and the boy, honor and joy, the prince and the pirate.

She imagined all three of them in bed at the same time and smiled. That was a little dream that would certainly never come true.

With a soft heart, she closed the door and walked up on deck. The night was cold and drizzly, and she huddled into her cloak. She had never been this far north before. At first she hated the cold weather. It felt like an unwarranted personal attack, as if nature herself had become suddenly hostile. Now she didn't mind it so much.

Heavy clouds hung low over the rocky coastline of Ohohhom, and a misty rain obscured the rocky peaks in the distance. The rain never stopped in this place, and everything grew tall and green. Moss covered every rock, the base of every tree. Towering evergreens covered every inch of ground from the mountaintops to the sea. It was green everywhere, greener than anything she had ever seen. For the first time in years she missed Physendria and looked forward to returning there someday, during happier times.

She walked to the rail and let the cold rain fall on her bare head. The rainbow magic swirled within her stomach, keeping her warm. The night before she and Reef left the Silver Islands, they traveled back into the mountains with his followers. The entire community showed up to lend their life force to the ritual that would make her one of their own. They danced, drummed, and sang through the night, imbuing a tiny crystal flake with a flood of light emmeria. When it was over, she knelt before Reef as he placed the swirling rainbow flake on the tip of her tongue.

Ossamyr's magic was completely transformed. From the moment she swallowed that flake, she felt a searing pain whenever she used her Zelani in the wrong way. If she used her magic to gain power over someone rather than make power with someone, it filled her with agony. But she didn't miss the old ways, and the Zelani she used to fuel her and Reef's lovemaking was like nothing she had ever experienced before. He was no longer invisible to her magical sight. The crystal he carried in his own belly only hid him from those who meant him harm. Just as her own shard would give her some protection from the sorceress she had vowed to kill.

She had practiced all the arts of the Opal Empire: powdering her face, the tiny steps, keeping her eyes locked on the ground. She could pass for an Ohohhim if she had to. And she had to. Everything depended upon it.

Ossamyr thought of the task ahead of her. Her old self would have felt the crushing burden of her mission. She would have slipped into anger or arrogance to armor herself against the dangers on the horizon.

But now she was at peace.

Ever since she drank the Siren's Blood, ever since she'd seen the truth that left the world teetering on the brink, her heart had been light.

Somehow only the present moment mattered.

And this particular moment was a very, very good one.

THE END

THE ULTIMATE DICTIONARY
of SPORTS QUOTATIONS

THE ULTIMATE DICTIONARY
of SPORTS QUOTATIONS

CARLO DE VITO

Facts On File, Inc.

The Ultimate Dictionary of Sports Quotations

Copyright © 2001 by Carlo De Vito

Checkmark Books
An imprint of Facts On File, Inc.
11 Penn Plaza
New York, NY 10001

Library of Congress Cataloging-in-Publication Data

The ultimate dictionary of sports quotations / [compiled by] Carlo De Vito.
    p. cm.
  Includes index.
  ISBN 0-8160-3980-1 (hard)—ISBN 0-8160-3981-x (pbk.)
    1. Sports—Quotations, maxims, etc. 2. Sports personnel—Quotations.
  I. De Vito, Carlo.
GV707.U47 2001
796—dc21   99-059375

Checkmark Books are available at special discounts when purchased in bulk quantities for businesses, associations, institutions or sales promotions. Please call our Special Sales Department in New York at (212) 967-8800 or (800) 322-8755.

You can find Facts On File on the World Wide Web at
http://www.factsonfile.com

Text design by Joan M. Toro
Cover design by Cathy Rincon

Printed in the United States of America

MP Hermitage 10 9 8 7 6 5 4 3 2 1
      (pbk) 10 9 8 7 6 5 4 3 2 1

This book is printed on acid-free paper.

Contents

Acknowledgments

First and foremost, I would like to thank my brother, Eugene T. Venanzi II, for his help and encouragement, whether it be a simple conversation during a game of catch or a meal, or a loan of some of his highly prized first editions; he was both critical and generous to a fault.

To the staff of the Monmouth County Library, Symmes Road, who suffered my many greedy borrowings with both amusement, humor, and horror.

To Buz Teacher, for his acquiesence, approval, and friendly advice.

And to a whole round of friends and family who offered suggestions and pointers, including Scott Liell, Gil King, Rob McMahon, Ken Samuelson, Chris Terry, and Rick Wolff.

Thank you.

Thanks to Bert Holtje, who found a home for this project, and was shepherd to it like no one else.

Special thanks to my kind, patient, and prodding editor, James Chambers. His persistence and demanding standards made this a better book than the author could have provided. Also, thanks to copy editor Jerry Kappes.

Introduction

Games lubricate the body and the mind.
—*Benjamin Franklin*

The term *sports* can be defined as any activity or experience that gives enjoyment or recreation. Sports are also referred to as pastimes or diversions. Many dictionaries follow exactly such a line. By defining our editorial content to "athletic sports" we keep a truer course to the spirit of the book, and what we naturally assume when we refer to the term *sports*. The word *athlete* is of Greek extraction and in classical times meant one who competed for prizes in the public games. The sports mentioned herein are restricted to those sports calling for some measurable degree of physical skill or prowess, and the quotations are confined to just that.

However, they are not without their human element. The following pages feature quotes from such notable sports figures as John Wooden, Arthur Ashe, and Vince Lombardi, as well as from gregarious individuals like Casey Stengel, Yogi Berra, and Charles Barkley. Their words are funny, inspirational, honest, stupid, truly thought-provoking, and incredibly hilarious. From U.S. presidents to outrageous fans, from Roman historians to taxi drivers, sports in all cultures have been held up for inspection as a metaphor for life.

Sports have been a popular form of recreation and entertainment since the Egyptians, Greeks, and Romans ruled the world. Sports such as footraces and swimming contests, wrestling and boxing, feats of strength and skill, have forever given to those who observed them the opportunity to comment and debate. Many games in the earliest times were in fact conditioning and training for combat and warfare or for hunting,

trapping, or herding. Sometimes contests were held near religious shrines either in conjunction with funeral rites or as offerings to a particular god or group of gods. Despite such serious intent, most of the earliest organized games were almost always festive and purely recreational.

The Olympic Games are of course the most famous of all organized sporting events. In 776 B.C. the first champions of these games were recorded, and this tradition continued for 382 years, or until 394 B.C. The games were not revived for more than 2,000 years. In those times many smaller towns also held public games. The most popular sports featured footraces, broad jumping, spear throwing, discus, and chariot racing. In Rome public games were referred to as *ludi publici,* and included gymnastics and forms of mock combat. The first gladiatorial combats were not recorded until 264 B.C.

Horse racing, while not an Olympic sport, was incredibly popular from the fifth century A.D. onward in Western civilization. Many Asian countries had such events, largely predating the Christian era, and it was reported by Homer as a popular event among the Greeks during the Trojan War.

The Middle Ages saw a reduction in the role of sports in everyday life. In the Middle Ages self-denial and preparation for the afterlife were of paramount importance. Various forms of combat sports, racing, and throwing were practiced, though almost entirely military in nature. Jousting on horseback was the most popular of these events, which were greeted enthusiastically throughout Europe. These events spawned the word *tournament*. Favored by nobility, these contests were first recorded in the year of the Norman Conquest, 1066 A.D., and ended sometime around the 16th century. Archery enjoyed widespread popularity in the Middle Ages among both nobles and commoners, although also encouraged largely by the military, as were fencing and other types of swordplay.

From the Middle Ages to the Renaissance, sports were at the mercy of the fancies and whimsies of the nobility. For example, football was banned in England by Henry II (1154–1189) and by James I (1603–1625), who both considered it an excuse for public brawling. The Puritan era, especially in England, in the 17th century, saw the temporary end of sports.

But the 1700s and the 1800s saw a return to sports. By 1743 the London Prize Ring rules had been established by James Boughton. These were the rough-and-tumble days of the bare-knuckle fighters. Not until 1867 was the contest divided into rounds and contestants provided with gloves (however slight). These changes were termed the Marquis of Queensbury rules.

Rugby as we know it today was established at the Rugby School in England in 1823. Originally a form of soccer, the Rugby School provided that any player, not just the goalie, could pick up the ball and run with it. Football (soccer in the U.S.) aficionados began forming organizations around this time to keep out Rugby School type teams. Rowing, golf, lawn tennis, and track and field all enjoyed rejuvenation in the 1800s throughout Europe.

Sports were not so popular in America during the 1700s as they were in Europe. Americans were consumed with building a new country. The Dutch at New Amsterdam were most notable for their interest in bowling, skating, sleighing, and various forms of ball playing. Generally however, America was so lacking in athletics that even Charles Dickens and Anthony Trollope remarked on how serious Americans were. In fact, it was not until after the Civil War that spectator sports began to experience a rise in interest. With the reintroduction of the Olympic Games in 1876, track and field gained in popularity in America, as did rowing.

American football became one of the more popular sports. In 1875 Harvard played McGill, which played rugby. Harvard liked the game so much it prevailed on friendly schools such as Yale, Princeton, Columbia, and Rutgers to follow suit. Thus American football was born, a game in which a back would run up into the line.

Baseball was also extremely popular at this time. A version of rounders, this game was played from the time of the Civil War on. In fact, the 90-foot base paths date from 1845. By 1890 many colleges and universities had baseball teams. In addition, many professional teams and leagues were soon formed.

With baseball we see the real beginnings of professional sport. Famous boxers and jockeys were also more plentiful around this time, and so was born the professional athlete. The years after World War I produced an ever growing number of professionals as the popularity of other sports began to emerge. Tennis, golf, swimming, polo, hockey, and basketball gave rise to a whole culture. As more and more Americans wanted to see these events, more and more arenas were built, as were golf courses with larger gallery areas. These large gates provided more cash prizes, and the skill level of participants grew ever more boundlessly. Ever since sports have been a chance for many to advance themselves, not only as individuals but also for their race. While sports have provided opportunities since Roman times for the disadvantaged to improve their standing in society, never was it so evident or important as when Jesse Owens beat the athletes of Hitler's Germany, or as when Jackie Robinson broke the color barrier in America's preeminent sport of baseball in 1946. Standouts such as Wilma Rudolph not only made strides for African Americans

but also for the physically disadvantaged when she won an Olympic gold medal. Such people help raise sports from games or entertainment to life lessons for the ages.

Even today, when sports may seem like a training ground for the broadcasters and actors of tomorrow, we must remember that those who strive for excellence, who pursue greatness of skill or effort personify the values we find worthwhile in celebrating sports. The effortless smoothness of Ted Williams or Willie Mays's swing, the artfulness of Michael Jordan's gliding drives to the basket, the careful pirouette of Lynn Swann or Del Shoffner catching a football in midair, the quick-wittedness of John McEnroe, the grace of Bill Tilden, the swiftness and balletic form of Peggy Fleming, the imposing presence of Alberto Tomba navigating a mountain, these are the qualities we watch in awe, understanding that we are capable of so much as human beings. To see others will themselves to do what seems effortless or impossible is to understand what the human body is capable of achieving and finally to see what a glorious thing being a human is. The artfulness of any one of the above-mentioned athletes or of so many in other sports is what we celebrate in these pages.

Sports teach about dedication, single-mindedness of purpose, knowledge, understanding, the importance of practice, and, most important, teamwork and a sense of fair play. These qualities are the classroom for life. The great coaches throughout time, the Vince Lombardis and the John Woodens, and the unsung coaches of the world teach the value of hard work, patience, practice, rules, skill, and understanding. These hard-learned lessons are what make sports invaluable to society and why sports are so celebrated.

While individuals are often singled out for their achievements or abilities, teamwork is probably one of the most important lessons that sports teach. The receiver in football cannot catch a pass if the lineman does not protect the passer; the left fielder must hit the cutoff man in baseball; the center in basketball cannot post-up if the guard does not set up the play and make the assist; the soccer player cannot score if no one passes. The list of cause and effect goes on and on. In short, it teaches that everyone's job is valuable. And more important, everyone must do his or her job if the team is to be successful. In the end, sports teaches about competition and fair play, about achievement and striving for excellence, and that we are all in the game together.

★ ★ ★

The quotes in this book not only celebrate sports, they are also a mirror of our world, and so I have included quotes ranging from the themes

that celebrate our athlete culture to those that decry it. As we find in newspaper sports pages, I have also shown sport's foibles, whether it be ego, greed, sex, or drugs. Whatever are our darker sides, they appear here as well. Especially in the more prominent sports, i.e. baseball, football, basketball, soccer, each has had its share of heroes won and lost, as well as tales of sadness and disappointment in human faults.

At the risk of being morbid, I was most surprised at the section on death. Obviously, sports are meant to be fun; that's why we enjoy them so much. However, some sports are fun but dangerous, and it usually takes a tragedy to remind us that some sports, while not well covered by the media, can lead to a very mortal end. Mountain climbing is always perilous, but then so is sailing. Some of the most dramatic moments in sports come from scenes too horrible to imagine—and help us to remember the beauty of life.

Even truer is that this collection as a whole shows what all athletes have in common. There is not a section that doesn't reflect what unites all athletes in the same cause—drive, effort, pain, success, failure—all these are common experiences in each athlete's life. What also struck me as I emptied out my local library's shelves was that most of the athletes we celebrate are winners, or people we perceive as winners. But most athletes lose more than they win. Great athletes use losses to spur themselves on. Many athletes are remembered for a pinnacle, but there are also many losses on the path to victory. We often forget that. How many playoffs did Michael Jordan lose? How many tournaments ended in despair for Pelé? How many Super Bowls did John Elway lose? We usually consider winning as everything.

Vince Lombardi was the well-known coach of the Green Bay Packers, a championship dynasty. The quote he was most famous for is a reflection of what I was just talking about—"Winning isn't everything—it's the only thing."

People are still awed by the sheer power of that remark. *The only thing.* We have taken it to heart and forgotten what is best about sports—sportsmanship, the true teacher, why sports helps us to grow as human beings.

Vince Lombardi was a good man, and he believed in playing hard. He was one of the Seven Blocks of Granite as an underclassman at Fordham University. In the end it deeply offended him that people so misunderstood the quote. He was horrified that people turned it just slightly from what he meant to an ultimatum to win at all costs. He later said, "I wish to hell I'd never said the damn thing. I meant the effort . . . I meant having a goal. I sure as hell didn't mean for people to crush human values and morality."

Vince Lombardi celebrated what is best about the athlete, which is to say that the sportsmanlike athlete personifies the goals to which we should all aspire. To understand ourselves, what we are like under duress, what we are like *in the moment,* we should celebrate that understanding and the fun involved, no matter who wins or loses. Sports is the most enjoyable and best learning experience there is, and it's about our favorite subject—ourselves.

Notes on This Collection

I have tried to avoid separating out personalities as their own entries. I have saved this "honor" for those athletes whose feats or celebrity have both outgrown their particular field of endeavor as well as that of sport itself. Athletes who have transcended sport and whose names have become part of the everyday language have been broken out, i.e., Babe Ruth, Michael Jordan, Wayne Gretzky, Pelé, Ali, etc. These people have soared above the arenas and stadiums of the world to occupy a more iconic realm.

The idea is to keep quotes within their respective sport or fit them into a category more universal to the athlete. Whether athlete, coach, or fan, one can look up themes that stretch across all fields of endeavor, i.e., focus, training, effort, etc., and find it therefore a much more useful volume.

THE ULTIMATE DICTIONARY
of SPORTS QUOTATIONS

Aaron, Henry "Hank"

(b. Feb. 5, 1934) *Hall of Fame baseball player; holder of the all-time home run record of 755, all-time RBI record of 2,297, played in 24 All-Star Games*

Babe Ruth may have died twenty-five years ago but his ample ghost has been with us all summer and he seems to grow more insistently alive every time Henry Aaron hits a baseball over a fence.

Red Smith, sportswriter

Trying to sneak a fastball past Hank Aaron is like trying to sneak sunrise past a rooster.

Curt Simmons, professional baseball player

Abdul-Jabar, Kareem

(b. Lew Alcindor April 16, 1947) *Hall of Fame basketball player; won three NCAA basketball championships; won six NBA titles; league MVP six times*

He scored 40 points against me on Mother's Day . . . and my own mother called me to complain.

Darryl Dawkins, professional basketball player

One of the smallest men I ever met.

Joe Falls, sportswriter, "Farewell, Alcindorella," after Jabar was rude to a group of sportswriters in Detroit

Ability

He could only jump over the Thursday newspaper.

Darryl Dawkins, professional basketball player, about Wes Unseld, professional basketball player

I've seen him make chicken salad out of chicken feathers many times.

John Brockington, professional football player, about Walter Payton

Academics

I play football. I'm not trying to be a professor. The tests don't seem to make sense to me, measuring your brain on stuff I haven't been through in school.

Clemson University football recruit Ray Forsythe, ineligible because of academic requirements

1

Son, looks to me like you're spending too much time on one subject.
Shelby Metcalf, basketball coach at Texas A&M, to a player who received four F's and one D

Achievement

Achievement is difficult. It requires enormous effort. Those who can work through the struggle are the ones who are going to be successful.
Jackie Joyner-Kersee, Olympic track and field gold medalist

In the NBA, you're a piece of meat. That's it, bottom line. Well, if I'm a piece of meat, I want to be the best piece. I don't want to be hamburger.
Doc Rivers, National Basketball Association player and coach

Back when I came up, baseball was about establishing yourself. You wanted to get into a position to break the records of the players you grew up watching.
Tony Gwynn, Major League Baseball player, perennial batting champion and All-Star

At eight I decided that I wanted to be the best tennis player in the world. From then on, it was always in the back of my mind.
Tracy Austin, tennis champion, from her autobiography, Beyond Center Court

Adversity

Adversity teaches a man about himself.
Alonzo Mourning, professional basketball player and All-Star

African Americans

Being a Black heavyweight champion in the second half of the twentieth century was now not unlike being Jack Johnson, Malcom X, and Frank Costello all in one.
Norman Mailer, Pulitzer Prize–winning writer from his essay "King of the Hill"

Proportionately, the black athlete has been more successful than any other group in any other endeavor in American life. And he and she did it despite legal and social discrimination that would have dampened the ardor of most participants.
Arthur Ashe, champion professional tennis player, writer

The path to fame and wealth for all but a few black athletes has been "A Hard Road to Glory."
Arthur Ashe, champion professional tennis player, writer

Agassi, Andre

(b. Apr. 29, 1970) *Tennis champion—won Wimbledon; U.S. Open; Australian Open; French Open*

If he was ranked two-hundred-and-fifty and he dressed like that, people would make fun of him.
Andrea Temesvari, professional tennis player

Age

Age is like a bulldozer. It's gonna push you out of the way once you stop moving.
Archie Moore, champion boxer

All the rookies call me Mr. Long and I can't recognize any of the music they listen to.
Howie Long, professional football player, Hall of Famer, and broadcaster

Back in the good old days, I was what you might call a "poor man's Bruce Jenner."
Bob Mathias, two-time gold medalist decathlon competitor, politician, and actor

Contrary to popular opinion, I have not worn that uniform before.
Jackie Slater, professional football player, one of the oldest players in the National Football League, commenting on a reproduction of a Rams uniform from the 1950s

He's twenty. In ten years he'll have a chance to be thirty.
Casey Stengel, Hall of Fame baseball player and manager

He thinks when I was born I was already sixty years old and had a wooden leg and came here to manage.
Casey Stengel, Hall of Fame baseball player and manager, referring to Mickey Mantle

He wanted to block, dodge, or pick off punches as used to be his custom, and strike with lightning speed and with savage finality, but he never quite could do it. He didn't have the coordination, that irreplaceable element so necessary to boxing which vanishes so rapidly as you grow old.
James P. Dawson, sportswriter, about Joe Louis's last fight

He won on points, but I proved my point.
George Foreman, champion boxer, who at 40 years of age, lasted fifteen rounds with Evander Holyfield, heavyweight boxing champion

I am not the pigtailed girl anymore, but I hold her dear to my heart.
Olga Korbut, Olympic gold medalist gymnast

I feel two hundred years old. All they got to do is lay me down and close the box.
Bill Russell, Hall of Fame basketball player referring to his last year in the National Basketball Association

If I get tired now, it's not because of my surgery. It's because I'm old.
Joe Torre, professional baseball player and manager

I just started to feel the fatigue, mentally and physically, that I've never felt before.
Wayne Gretzky, Hall of Fame hockey player

It's like suddenly they say, "Give me your skates, you're done."
Wayne Gretzky, Hall of Fame hockey player

I'll never make the mistake of being seventy again.
Casey Stengel, Hall of Fame baseball player and manager

I'm sort of like a late model car that rattles a lot. It's a lot of little things.
Tim Green, National Football League player & broadcaster

I'm still Reggie, but not as often.
Reggie Jackson, Hall of Fame baseball player

I swing just as hard, but I walk slower and get to my ball quicker.
Sam Snead, champion professional golfer, when asked if age had affected his golf game

It ain't what it was, but then what the hell is?
Dizzy Dean, Hall of Fame baseball player,
speaking about his arm and aging

I've lost a step, I can't leap like I used to, and the rim looks a little hazy from the three-point line. But I can still take you to the hole on one leg. And I may have to.
Rick Telander, sportswriter

I was raised, but I never did grow up.
Pete Rose, professional baseball player
and all-time hits leader

No, but I used to be.
Frank Shorter, champion marathoner, when asked
by a fan if he was Frank Shorter

No, Jackie, this isn't a coach-athlete thing. This is your husband telling you it's time for you to go.
Bob Kersee, track and field coach to Jackie
Joyner-Kersee, Olympic gold medalist track
and field competitor, asking her to retire

One of those guys who hangs on and on, telling himself that he can still be competitive when he knows good and well he can't.
Ambrose "Rowdy" Gaines IV, Olympic
champion swimmer, commentary
on his own retirement

Sometimes I wonder if the years that slip
   beyond recall
Are marked upon the Book of Time as
   weekends after all?
We hit the line with unchecked youth—
   and as a vision gleams
We find that we are gray and old along the
   road of dreams.
Grantland Rice, sportswriter

Sooner or later, God takes it away from all of them—all of them.
Bill Parcells, professional football coach

The older I get, the better I used to be.
Connie Hawkins, professional basketball player
and playground legend

The only thing old on me is this bald spot, and I'll have that fixed the next time we're in L.A.
John Lucas, professional basketball player
and coach, when he was still playing
as one of the oldest players in the
National Basketball Association

The sadness of the end of a career of an older athlete, with the betrayal of his body, is mirrored in the rest of us. Consciously or not, we know: There, soon, go I.
Ira Berkow, sportswriter

They got to lower the roof or raise the floor. 'Cause the Hawk don't soar no more.
Connie Hawkins, professional basketball
player and playground legend

We looked young.
Larry Brown, professional basketball coach,
after a lopsided losing effort

Who's this guy? He's too old for our games. Is he supposed to be good?
Joe Hammond, college basketball player, to a
teammate before a one-on-one with Herman
"The Helicopter" Knowings, street player
legend of Harlem

My mind's right there. Tells me just what to do. But my legs ain't with it. In their own

world. I send the message and by the time they move, it's too late.

John Edgar Wideman, award-winning novelist, college basketball player, from Philadelphia Fire

They tell you things change at 40. But they don't tell you how much.

Johnny Unitas, Hall of Fame quarterback, who spent his last few years on the bench and unhappy

Agents

From drugs to prostitutes, to vacations, cars, and envelopes of cash, some agents will give whatever it takes. When the player's contract is ultimately signed, the agent of course deducts the cost of these predraft perks directly from the player's signing bonus. What appear to be lavish gifts of friendship turn out to be merely unsecured loans for vices and luxuries.

Tim Green, professional football player, broadcaster, and writer

He sees all the devious ways you can rip people off.

Unidentified baseball executive about sports agent Scott Boras

I swear those agents could sell swampland in Manhattan.

John Feinstein, writer, from Hard Courts

I want to be remembered for making rich people richer.

Hughes Norton, sports agent

Kids have agents now before they even make it into their teens.

Mary Lou Retton, Olympic gold medal gymnast

My opinion has always been that I would rather work for the star than work for the movie house. The star is always going to be pursued.

Scott Boras, sports agent

Sports agents have become a virus in sports.

Mike Lupica, sportswriter

We got sick and tired of being put in the position of constantly having to call people and make excuses for our clients, which, often as not, we knew weren't true and they knew weren't true.

Ivan Blumberg, sports agent

AIDS

I could name close to thirty people in skating who have died from AIDS. A lot of skaters aren't admitting that we've lost skaters to AIDS. Hell, it's a disease that people are dying from.

Randy Gardner, Olympic pairs skater

I know what it's like to learn that you are HIV-positive, to face your own mortality.

Greg Louganis, Olympic gold medal diver

We all say things we don't mean. We mean things we don't say. When a very close personal friend is afflicted, you begin to realize the depth of this whole thing, and you think, "Holy smokes, this is not a joke anymore."

Bill Toomey, Olympic track and field medalist about Dr. Tom Waddell, who was dying of AIDS

Alcohol

Football players go together with beer like wine goes with cheese.

Tim Green, professional football player, broadcaster, and writer

I always assumed no one knew about my drinking because, in my mind, I was perfectly normal when I drank. In reality everyone knew. The girls on the tour would smell alcohol on my breath at eight in the morning, then roll their eyes and go about their business.

Laura Baugh, professional golfer, and recovering alcoholic

The pitfalls are drink. And at his age, women—and then believing what other people tell him, other people than us. If he believes what we tell him, he'll go a long way—but if he believes people outside the game saying he's the best thing on earth, he'll come unstuck.

Brian Flynn, soccer manager, speaking of Johnathan Cross, professional soccer player

Ali, Muhammad

(b. Cassius Clay, b. Jan. 17, 1942) *World Heavyweight Champion; won the title on three different occasions; Olympic gold medal boxer (1960)*

Astute, double-hearted, irresistible.

Toni Morrison, Pulitzer Prize–winning author

He worked apparently on the premise that there was something obscene about being hit.

Norman Mailer, Pulitzer Prize–winning author about Ali's early career

The bluegrass bard from Louisville.

Red Smith, sportswriter

Alternative Lifestyles

From the very beginning the worlds of athletics and homosexuality have intersected more often than many people realize . . . The root word for gymnasium—*gymnos*—has nothing to do with athletics; it means nude.

Dan Woog, writer

Gay athletes and coaches are nowhere near as visible as say, gay actors, musicians, or even student government leaders. The reason has less to do with percentages than it does reality. The sports world does not exactly high-five them or grasp them with a winner's hug.

Dan Woog, author

I was welcomed as an openly gay athlete. It was a real thrill for me, and that experience made me realize how important it is for athletes to feel welcomed for who they are.

Greg Louganis, Olympic gold medalist diver

There was so much camaraderie. There was this whole crowd of guys just like me—people with real jobs, who didn't abuse their bodies. And to top it off, it was extremely competitive, too.

Gene Dermondy, wrestling coach, about the Gay Games

What matters to me is setting an example so that other gay and lesbian athletes don't feel compelled to hide. I had hoped that my example would quickly change things . . . that hasn't been the case, and it's taught me a valuable lesson. Deciding to be openly gay or

lesbian is a very personal decision, and it's one I can't make for someone else.

Rudy Galindo, champion figure skater

Welcome to the Games. It's great to be out and proud!

Greg Louganis, Olympic gold medalist diver, at the opening of the Gay Games

Amateurs

Amateurism, after all, must be the backbone of all sport.

Richard S. Tufts, writer

In love as in sport, the amateur status must be strictly maintained.

Robert Graves, writer and poet

It has always been a source of pride for me that I competed in a sport that, by and large, was purely amateur.

Dan Jansen, Olympic gold medalist speed skater

It is a rare bird who can hustle a living in today's going and still have time to excel as an amateur.

Grantland Rice, sportswriter

It is no secret that in any pure sense, no world class skier is an amateur. There is no way racers could have lived the lives we did without money.

Jean-Claude Killy, Olympic gold medalist skier

I was lucky. I don't mean in the competition, but in the fact that I had a wife who made decent money and who was just as committed to seeing me win the gold medal as I was. In this country, unless an amateur athlete has a working wife or a wealthy family or a very

tolerant boss, the odds are that he's never going to get the chance to try for a gold medal.

Bruce Jenner, gold medalist decathlon competitor

Let's be honest. The proper definition of an amateur today is one who accepts cash, not checks.

Jack Kelly Jr., Sports Illustrated

There are no longer true amateurs in track.

Adrian Paulen, International Amateur Athletics Foundation president

The Russians are no more professional than the Americans, who give their athletes free college educations.

Avery Brudage, International Olympic Committee president

Trust funds are not necessary anymore. They give the public a false impression that the athletes somehow are still amateur.

Carl Lewis, gold medalist track and field competitor

We're all professionals, rules don't mean anything.

Frank Shorter, champion runner, testifying before the President's Commission on Olympic Sports

Andretti, Mario

(b. Feb. 28, 1940) *Champion race car driver; won Daytona 500, Indianapolis 500, World Formula 1 title*

Mario Andretti was a hell of a race car driver, but he looked like a little girl dribbling the ball.

Bob Netolicky, professional basketball player, referring to a charity game once played between the Indianapolis 500 drivers and the press corps

Angling

Angling is extremely time consuming. That's sort of the whole point.

Thomas McGuane, writer

Anglers are living proof that fish is not brain food.

Randy Voorhees, fisherman and writer

God never did make a more calm, quiet, innocent recreation than angling.

Izaak Walton, writer

The fish is the hunter; the angler is the hunted.

Richard Waddington, Catching Salmon

Soon after I embraced the sport of angling I became convinced that I should never be able to enjoy it if I had to rely on the cooperation of fish.

Spars Grey Hackle, fisherman and writer

There is certainly something in angling that tends to produce a gentleness of spirit and a pure serenity of mind.

Washington Irving, writer

Appearance

I have to believe it was all in the hair.

Michael Douglas, actor, director, producer, to Pat Riley, professional basketball coach, referring to the coach's hair style that Douglas copied for his Academy Award–winning performance in Wall Street

Archery

A bow is a very personal piece of equipment.

Mike Brodeur, champion archer

Every good bow is a work of love.

Saxton Pope, bow hunter and writer

What a glorious weapon the long bow is.

Maurice Thompson, archer and writer

Yew wood was a gift from God to the bowmaker.

Earl Ullrich, attributed by John Strunk, archer

When you pick up a bow to shoot your first arrow, you are partaking in an activity dating back at least 20,000 years. The bow and arrow are pictured in drawings . . . on a cave wall in Spain's Valltorta Gorge.

K. M. Haywood and C. F. Lewis, archers

Arrests

I'd like to refer to this whole thing from start to finish as a real Mickey Mouse operation, but that would be an insult to Mickey Mouse.

Bobby Knight, three-time champion college basketball coach, after being arrested and arguing with police

Art

LeRoy, you're improving.

Weeb Ewbank, Hall of Fame football coach, to artist LeRoy Neiman, after stepping on one of Leroy's paintings during a practice session with a muddy boot

Athletes

All I am is a basketball player. That's who I am and what I am. And when I realized that, it made me feel relieved and happy.

Michael Jordan, professional basketball player & future Hall of Famer

Don't think of him as a dumb jock. Think of him as a smart guy who can kick your butt.
from an ad for Men's Health Magazine

I have the greatest job in the world.
Derek Jeter, professional baseball player

People train much harder than they did before . . . Is there a limit? Athletes don't think that way.
Bill Rogers, marathoner

Players today are faster, stronger and better. This is a different game.
Jason Williams, professional basketball player

The athlete knows he controls what happens to him. He blames no one but himself when things go wrong.
George Sheehan, runner and writer

We're not poets, philosophers, or statesmen. I shoot a ball through a hoop for a living.
Grant Hill, all-star professional basketball player

Attitude

A bad attitude is worse than a bad swing.
Payne Stewart, champion professional golfer

Allus I do is what I please and nobody stops me.
Gorgeous George, professional wrestler

Attention to detail instills pride and discipline.
D. Wayne Lukas, thoroughbred horse trainer

Humor was everywhere—in the good stories one heard, in the quick ripostes and the one-liners, the constant joshing and put-downs,

invariably bawdy and raucous—all of it a hedge against the boredom and regimen.
George Plimpton, sportswriter, writer, and editor

I am not a victim. I am a survivor.
Lance Armstrong, champion cyclist; won Tour de France after surviving his bout with cancer

I like my boys agile, mobile, and hostile.
Alonzo Jake Gaines, college football coach

I feel great!
Pat Croce, professional training guru, National Basketball Association executive and owner

It ain't over 'til the fat lady sings.
Dick Motta, champion professional basketball coach. When his team was down in the finals and it looked as if they might lose, Motta referred to opera, meaning the game wasn't over until the big finish at the end, usually sung by a diva.

It's not whether you get knocked down, it's whether you get up.
Vince Lombardi, professional football player and coach

I learned that if you want to make it bad enough, no matter how bad it is, you can make it.
Gale Sayers, Hall of Fame football player

My motto was always to keep swinging. Whether I was in a slump or feeling badly or having trouble off the field, the only thing to do was keep swinging.
Hank Aaron, Hall of Fame baseball player

The principle is competing against yourself. It's about self-improvement, about being better than you were the day before.
Steve Young, champion football player

When someone tells me there is only one way to do things, it always lights a fire under my butt. My instant reaction is, "I'm gonna prove you wrong."

Picabo Street, Olympic gold medalist skier

You have no control over what the other guy does. You only have control over what you do.

A. J. Kitt, Olympic gold medalist skier

I always thought I was better . . . Anybody who doesn't think that shouldn't be out on the course.

Sam Snead, champion professional golfer

If beating someone as badly and as quickly as I could is having a killer instinct, then, okay, you can call it that.

Don Budge, professional tennis champion

I come to play. I come to beat you. I come to kill you.

Leo Durocher, professional baseball player and manager

I could play with anybody.

Jack Kramer, professional tennis champion, asked how he would do against today's stars

I feel like I came down here as much to get out of the cold weather and to see my friends as anything else. Let's face it, that's not a great attitude to start the year with.

Pam Shriver, professional tennis player

I think human beings that have difficult times think different things at different times. What I had to look at was what was bad in my performance and move forward. I think that's something I have to do from now on.

Hideki Irabu, professional baseball player

I won't let you take advantage of me. I'll kill you before I ever let you take advantage of me.

Kevin Garnett, professional basketball player

My philosophy is you better do it the way you drive your race car: 110 percent.

Max Papis, race car driver

Never go to bed a loser.

George Halas, Hall of Fame owner and coach

No one can throw a fastball past me. God could come down from Heaven, and He couldn't throw it past me.

Ted Williams, Hall of Fame baseball player

Not me. I'm not riding in a white Rolls-Royce.

Leon Hess, sports owner, industrialist and known for being very down to earth, when offered a ride in a white limo at an owners' meeting

People thought I was ruthless, which I was. I didn't give a darn who was on the other side of the net. I'd knock you down if you got in the way.

Althea Gibson, professional tennis champion

What's to worry about? These L.A. goofballs are positively guaranteed to screw up and lose it.

Red Auerbach, National Basketball Association executive, referring to the Los Angeles Lakers in a championship games versus his team, the Boston Celtics (who won)

You didn't beat me. You merely finished in front of me.

Hal Higdon, writer and runner

You can't treat it as any game. Do that and you have a short season. Every game is

important, and you always like to start off with a win after all that training.

Gayle Sayers, Hall of Fame football player

You have to be persistent and you have to be dedicated. You have to be hardworking. I've never run into the guy who could win at the top level in anything today and didn't have the right attitude, didn't give it everything he had, at least while he was doing it; wasn't prepared and didn't have the whole program worked out.

Ted Turner, champion yachtsman and baseball owner

You have to strap it on and go get them.

Roger Clemens, profesional baseball player

Audibles

Four set! . . . uh, red, right . . . uh, 22 . . . Ah, shit, son-of-a-bitch, time-out.

Don Meredith, broadcaster and professional football player, during a televised game as the quarterback of the Dallas Cowboys

Auerbach, Red

(b. Sept. 20, 1917) *Champion National Basketball Association coach and executive of the Boston Celtics; won nine NBA titles as coach; won seven more as General Manager*

Fan and foe alike have always agreed on one point—Red Auerbach is undoubtedly the genius of basketball.

Lawrence F. O'Brien, National Basketball Association Commissioner

I've never known anybody who played for him that didn't like him. Of course, I've never known anybody who played against him who did like him!

Bill Russell, Hall of Fame basketball player and coach

Red Auerbach will never be known as a gracious winner.

Freddie Schaus, professional basketball coach of the rival Los Angeles Lakers, a frequent victim in the finals

Autographs

I can't sign it, dear. League rules. Where are you going to be after the game?

Ted Williams, Hall of Fame baseball player to an adoring female fan

I get people knocking me down for an autograph every day.

Tiger Woods, champion professional golfer

Auto Racing

A race car driver's résumé needs to say only one thing—winner.

Benny Parsons, race driver

As a sometime rally driver I have often wondered, in times of great stress or impending accident, just what makes the rally driver tick.

Graham Gauld, writer and racer

The best way to make a small fortune in racing is to start with a big one.

Junior Johnson, champion driver

Driving a race car is like dancing with a buzz saw.

Cale Yarborough, champion driver

Experience is more important than muscle in this business.

Lee Petty, champion race car driver

Everyone loves a Ferrari, even if they hate old man Enzo.

Denis Jenkinson, author and race car journalist

I enjoy racing at high speeds. I am happy when I am running 180 . . . It's my fun as well as my business.

Lee Roy Yarbrough, champion race car driver

In Grand Prix you have to drive ten-tenths most of the time. Nine-tenths isn't good enough.

Graham Hill, champion race car driver

I never felt scared of racing. If I did, I'd quit.

Richard Petty, champion race car driver

In the cutaway cockpit he was clearly visible, arms tensed against the kicking steering wheel, teeth clenched with the sheer effort of controlling this turbulent machine. And you knew as you watched that this was something beyond the reach of ordinary men. This, to me, was motor racing.

F. Wilson McComb, writer

If I can pass someone, I'll do it; I don't care if he is in my other car or if he's Christ Almighty himself. When I am in a race car, I've got one thing in mind: passing *everybody.*

A. J. Foyt, champion race car driver

One thing about great champions in Winston Cup is that the truly great champions are the ones who have won more than one championship.

Jeff Gordon, champion race car driver

On the whole, the Peking-to-Paris race has proved conclusively that the motor-car is a much stronger and more resistant machine than has so far been thought.

Luigi Barzini, Sr., writer, participant in the winning car with driver Prince Borghese, which took 60 days in 1907 (it has not been run since)

People refuse to believe that a man who is wrestling 700 screaming horses, pushing himself up to and beyond the limits of his skill, and betting his life on every turn of the wheel isn't running a lot of profound thoughts through his head.

Mario Andretti, champion race car driver

Sometimes as I sit in the cockpit just before taking off, I wonder just what in the hell am I doing there.

Craig Breedlove, former land speed record holder

Stock car racing is two ends of the world. You win and you're at the very top . . . You blow an engine, you blow a tire, strip a gear, hit a wall, or do one of a thousand freakish things that can keep you from victory and you're a nobody.

David Pearson, champion race car driver

The crashes people remember, but drivers remember the near misses.

Mario Andretti, champion race car driver

The early morning shift is the worst and later with the sun in your eyes. It's the time at LeMans they wreck all the cars. The drivers are tired and the cars start to reach the breaking point.

A. J. Foyt, champion race car driver

The only philosophy that pays off in racing is that you go fast enough to win and slow enough to finish.

Ken Miles, champion race car driver

There's no fifth or tenth. Racing is about winning. That is why I got involved.

Greg Ray, race car driver

There's no secret. You just press the accelerator to the floor and steer left.

Bill Vukovich, champion driver

They really don't make drivers like they used to. That's a fact.

A. J. Foyt, champion race car driver

Until ten years ago nobody made any money in stock car racing. Compared to other professional athletes, drivers didn't make that much money. Owners didn't, promoters didn't.

Humpy Wheeler, racing promoter

What are we going to do, just keep trying to beat each other until we kill ourselves?

Art Arfons, former land speed record holder, to Craig Breedlove, also a former record holder

We didn't have no tickets, no safety equipment, no fences, no nothing. Just a bunch of these bootleggers who'd been arguing all week about who had the fastest car would get together and prove it.

Junior Johnson, champion race car driver

We're not really race drivers because we don't drive in traffic, vary speeds, pass other drivers in traffic, go around corners, but we need all the tools of a good driver—determination and courage and quick reflexes.

Dan "Big Daddy" Garlitz, drag and funny car racer

Backups

It's like you're doing a good job at work and the other guy keeps getting the raise.

Allan Bester, professional hockey player

He's the third-string catcher—when is he going to play?

Don Zimmer, professional baseball player and manager, about bullpen catcher Mike Figga, when asked by beat reporters if Figga would get any time on the field

It was like being retired. I'd get eighteen, maybe twenty minutes against the backup center. It was hardly playing.

Bill Cartwright, champion professional basketball player

Bad Day

If you see a defense with dirt and mud on their backs they've had a bad day.

John Madden, champion football coach and Emmy Award–winning broadcaster

I hit the rough, the bunkers, the trees, the gallery, the water . . . You can't make a living doing that.

Tiger Woods, professional golfer, after finishing 11 over par and in last place

I only arrived two days ago, and now I'm going home tomorrow.

Pete Sampras, professional tennis player, ranked #1 in the world, on losing in the opening round of the Swiss Indoors Championship

I should re-enlist in the Army I was so lousy tonight.

Billy Conn, champion professional boxer

When 15 Giants plays netted 1 yard, the suspicion grew on the Giant's bench that something drastic would have to be done to resurrect the team's offense.

Bill Pennington, New York Times, *on the worst offense in the National Football League*

Badminton

Badminton is an attacking game.

Jake Downey, champion badminton player

Badminton is my soul.
*Motto painted on Jakarta's largest badminton
training center*

Every morning I think, God, I'm lucky. The Bureau liked me playing badminton, and my wife loved to play, too. I haven't a complaint in the world.
*Joe Alston, champion badminton player and
Federal Bureau of Investigation agent*

Explosive muscle power is an asset . . . but it is often overshadowed by exceptional reaction time, endurance, recovery of balance, and overall qualities of movement within a small court area.
Barry C. Pelton, writer

In badminton rallies there is constant planning, constant searching for an opening, constant probing for weaknesses.
Frank J. Devlin, champion badminton player

Matches are won or lost on service. It is the one shot that can be practised alone, but sadly there is little evidence of it.
*Judy Devlin Hashman, champion badminton
player, and C. M. Jones, writer and editor*

Suprinto can send a shuttlecock screaming at 200 miles per hour, which makes him a ringer in most any backyard barbecue match.
*Steve Rushin, sportswriter, writing about one of
the world's best badminton players*

The serve in badminton—unlike all other racket games—is essentially a defensive shot.
Frank J. Devlin, champion badminton player

The shuttle is a Prima Donna.
Pat Davis, badminton champion

Top-level badminton is to the game we play at family picnics what the NBA is to H-O-R-S-E in the driveway.
Barry Large, sportswriter

Ballet

In all my years of watching football I can honestly say that I have never once confused football with ballet.
*Joan Tisch, wife of Bob Tisch, owner
professional football team*

The difference between sports and ballet is that in sports you root for somebody. Nobody yells at one of the ballerinas, "Break a bleepin' leg, ya bum."
Mike Littwin, sportswriter

This is sports as ballet, something utterly new and modern, its roots African American, ballet as contested sport. No one, after all, ever guarded Baryshnikov.
*David Halberstam, bestselling author
of* Playing for Keeps, *speaking of
Michael Jordan and basketball*

What's the idea of that dance out there. The ballet's downtown, not here.
*Leo Durocher, baseball player and manager, to
Willie Mays, Hall of Fame baseball player*

Barkley, Charles

(b. Feb. 20, 1963) *All-star National Basketball Association player; Olympic gold medalist; league MVP 1993*

What has he done? Nothing but spit on kids, throw people through windows and talk

racist when he has a white wife, and talk crazy about black people. He's nobody.

Allen Iverson, professional basketball player

Baseball

A boy's game, with no more possibilities than a boy can master, a game bounded by walls which kept out novelty or danger, change or adventure.

F. Scott Fitzgerald, writer, from a eulogy for his friend Ring Lardner

Alex, my seven-year-old, had the Mark McGwire card I'd bought him in the souvenir shop, holding onto it like it was a winning lottery ticket.

Mike Lupica, sportswriter

Baseball gives every American boy a chance to excel. Not just to be as good as everyone else, but to be better. This is the nature of man, and this is the name of the game.

Ted Williams, Hall of Fame baseball player

Baseball has changed so much from the days when we played that I am fast becoming a stranger to the game.

Bob Gibson, Hall of Fame baseball player

Baseball is a crazy game. Anything can happen.

Fernando Tatis, professional baseball player

Baseball is almost the only orderly thing in a very unorderly world. If you get three strikes, even the best lawyer in the world can't get you off.

Bill Veeck, baseball owner and racetrack operator

Baseball is an 1890 game. It's a peaceful afternoon in the country. What baseball needs to compete is more violence.

Bill Veeck, baseball owner and racetrack operator

Baseball is an allegorical play about America, a poetic, complex, and subtle play of courage, fear, good luck, mistakes, patience about fate, and sober self-esteem . . . It is impossible to understand America without a thorough knowledge of baseball.

Saul Steinberg, writer

Baseball is a worrying thing.

Stan Coveleshi, writer

Baseball is more than just a game. It has eternal value. Through it, one learns the beautiful and noble spirit of Japan.

Suishu Tobita, professional baseball player and manager

Baseball is not a life-or-death situation, and in the big picture, this game is just a small part of our lives. The important thing is to use baseball to help other people.

Ken Griffey, Jr., professional baseball player

Baseball is not the sport of the wealthy, it is the sport of the wage earner.

Bill Veeck, baseball owner and racetrack operator

Baseball is pieces of minutiae that need belaboring.

Bill Scheft, writer

Baseball is so ingrained in Cuba that it has thrived as the "national sport" through 40 years of bitterly anti-American revolution.

Roberto Gonzalez Echevarria, writer

Baseball is the very symbol, the outward and visible expression of the drive and push and rush and struggle of the raging, tearing, booming nineteenth century.

Mark Twain, writer and humorist

Baseball's grip on Japan's collective psyche is due, ultimately, to the fact that it suits the national character . . . baseball provided the Japanese with an opportunity to express their renowned group proclivities on an athletic field . . . Over the years—and despite Oh's home runs—it has been the team aspects of the game, the sacrifice bunt, the squeeze, the hit-and-run, that have come to characterize Japanese baseball.

Robert Whiting, writer, from You Gotta Have Wa

Baseball's summer of '98 provided authentic moments of poetry and passion, the kind of stuff that shines through the crassness and nonsense, to remind us why we still care.

Bob Costas, broadcaster

Baseball's 90% mental. The other half is physical.

Yogi Berra, Hall of Fame baseball player

Baseball was played since the beginning of the nation, hence it was part of the nation.

Roberto Gonzalez Echevarria, writer, referring to the nation of Cuba

Cut me and I'll bleed Dodger blue.

Tom Lasorda, baseball manager

During my lifetime, two events clearly stand out above all others as milestones in the history of batting in baseball: Joe DiMaggio's fifty-six-game hitting streak, and Ted Williams's seasonal batting average of .406. Unfortunately, I missed them both because I

was busy gestating during the season of their joint occurrence in 1941.

Stephen Jay Gould, eminent scientist and baseball enthusiast

Every great hitter works on the theory that the pitcher is more afraid of him than he is of the pitcher.

Ty Cobb, Hall of Fame baseball player

Fanaticism? No. Writing is exciting and baseball is like writing.

You can never tell with either
   how it will go
or what you will do?

Marianne Moore, poet and baseball fan

For the first hundred years of its existence, baseball had the press of this nation in its pocket. The true story of baseball was never told.

James Michener, Pulitzer Prize–winning author

He's not Mr. October, he's Mr. May.

George Steinbrenner, baseball owner, about Dave Winfield when asked by sportswriters to compare him with Reggie Jackson

I'd walk through hell in a gasoline suit to keep playing baseball.

Pete Rose, professional baseball player and coach

Some kids dream of joining the circus, others of becoming a major league baseball player. I have been doubly blessed. As a member of the New York Yankees, I have gotten to do both.

Graig Nettles, professional baseball player

Hello, Joe? It's Frank. Giants three, Dodgers nothing.

Franklin D. Roosevelt, president of the United States, in a telephone call to Joseph Stalin, dictator, Soviet Union

High school baseball is an education of the heart, the ground is a classroom of purity, a gymnasium of morality; that is its essential meaning.

Suishu Tobita, professional baseball player and manager

If not for baseball, he'd be a bum.

Al Martin, friend of Jason Kendall, professional baseball player

I gave up a lot to play ball. I gave up human relationships. Baseball was my relationship.

Maury Wills, professional baseball player, broadcaster, and manager

I guess I just couldn't believe it. But it's true all right. The flags are down, the lights in the temple are out, and the Harlem River flows lonely to the seas.

Roger Kahn, writer, about the closing of Ebbets Field, after the Dodgers left Brooklyn

I see great things in baseball. It is our game. The American game. It will repair our losses and be a blessing to us.

Walt Whitman, poet

Last year, more Americans went to symphonies than went to baseball games. This may be viewed as an alarming statistic, but I think that both baseball and the country will endure.

John F. Kennedy, president of the United States

Lots of good fans are losing interest in the big leagues because it's a great game but it's being played lousy.

Whitey Herzog, professional baseball player, manager, and executive

Never trust a baserunner with a limp. Comes a base hit and you'll think he just got back from Lourdes.

Joe Garagiola, professional baseball player and broadcaster

Ninety feet between the bases is the nearest thing to perfection that man has yet achieved.

Red Smith, sportswriter

Oh, somewhere in the favored land the sun
    is shining bright;
The band is playing somewhere, and some-
    where hearts are light,
And somewhere men are laughing, and
    somewhere children shout;
But there is no joy in Mudville—mighty
    Casey has struck out.

Ernest Lawrence Thayer, writer, from "Casey at the Bat"

One of the strongest points of baseball is that it has room for its critics and those who do not toe the party line. There's a little room for the heretic in the game.

Keith Olbermann, broadcaster

Tell the gentlemen I am glad to know of their coming, but they'll have to wait a few minutes till I make another base hit.

Attributed to Abraham Lincoln, speaking of a group of men coming to convince him to run for the Senate

The strongest thing that baseball has going for it today are its yesterdays.

Lawrence Ritter, writer

The Yankees are baseball.

Joe Torre, professional baseball player and manager, on the Yankees record-winning season

There was ease in Casey's manner as he
stepped into his place;
There was pride in Casey's bearing, and a
smile on Casey's face.
And when, responding to the cheers, he
lightly doffed his hat,
No stranger in the crowd could doubt 'twas
Casey at the bat.

Ernest Lawrence Thayer, writer,
from "Casey at the Bat"

The romance between intellectuals and the
game of baseball is, for the most part, one-
sided to the point of absurdity. A large percentage of intelligent Americans evaluate the
four hundred men who play major league
baseball as demigods. A large percentage of
the muscular four hundred rate intellectuals
several notches below umpires.

Roger Kahn, writer

Well, that kind of puts the damper on even a
Yankee win.

Phil Rizzuto, US sports commentator, remark
during a Yankee baseball game, on hearing that
Pope Paul VI had died

Well, this year I'm told that the team did well
because one pitcher had a fine curve ball. I
understand that a curve ball is thrown with a
deliberate attempt to deceive. Surely that is not
an ability we should want to foster at Harvard.

Charles William Eliot, president of
Harvard, 1869–1909, reply when asked
why he wished to drop baseball as a
college sport.

What's important is that kids discover that
baseball is fun—and that it gets to be more
fun as you get better at it.

Mickey Mantle, Hall of Fame baseball player

When I began playing the game, baseball
was about as gentlemanly as a kick in the
crotch.

Ty Cobb, Hall of Fame baseball player

Whenever I decided to release a guy, I always
had his room checked first for a gun. You
couldn't take chances with some of those birds.

Casey Stengel, Hall of Fame baseball manager

Baseball is a game of race, creed and color.
The race is to first base. The creed is the rules
of the game. The color? Well, the home team
wears white uniforms, and the visiting team
wears gray.

Joe Garagiola, professional baseball player
and announcer, from his book Baseball Is a
Funny Game

Whoever wants to know the heart and mind
of America had better learn baseball.

Jacques Barzun, writer

Mexican baseball is exactly like American
baseball, except for the extraneous embel-
lishments. They work the hit and run and
turn the double-play ball, but they don't sell
the hot dog.

Peter Golenboch, sportswriter

Only boring people find baseball boring.

Peter Golenboch, sportswriter

Other sports are just sports, baseball is a love.

Bryant Gumbel, broadcaster

Professional baseball, like any other business,
grants no favors. There's more money for the
winners, and the way to win is to learn your
opponent's weaknesses and play to them.

Carol Hughes, sportswriter

When a poor American boy dreamed of escaping his grim life, his fantasy probably involved becoming a professional baseball player. It was not so much the national sport as the binding national myth.

David Halberstam, writer

You spend a good piece of your life gripping a baseball and in the end it turns out that it was the other way around all the time.

Jim Bouton, professional baseball player and writer

You've gotta have a lotta little boy in you to play this game.

Roy Campanella, All-star professional baseball player

You've gotta have b★lls to make it in this league.

Pam Postema, female umpire

Basketball

Any American boy can be a basketball star if he grows up, up, up.

Bill Vaughn, writer

Basketball embodies everything our culture now craves: excitement, speed, dynamic personalities, up-close relationship with stars, the exciting physical nature of the contest, and, of course, the incredible suspense that is possible with each game.

Bill Walton, professional basketball player and broadcaster

Boys are playing basketball around a telephone pole with a backboard nailed to it. Legs, shouts. The scrap and snap of Keds on loose alley pebbles seems to catapult their voices high into the moist March air blue above the wires.

John Updike, award-winning novelist

When it's played the way is spozed to be played, basketball happens in the air; flying, floating, elevated above the floor, levitating the way oppressed peoples of this earth imagine themselves in their dreams....

John Edgar Wideman, award-winning novelist

Basketball for me has always been a celebration of all the elements in life: the joy of teamwork, the pride of skill development, the enthusiams of the crowd, the running and jumping and cheering and yelling at the refs.

Bill Walton, professional basketball player and broadcaster

Basketball is the city game.

Pete Axthelm, sportswriter

Basketball is the MTV of sports.

Sara Levinson, National Football League executive

Guards win games, but forwards win championships.

ÎAnonymous

I couldn't imagine not playing basketball. To me, basketball is what life is all about.

Bill Walton, college and professional basketball player and broadcaster

It's a fact that the city game is played when and where it was designed not to be played: outdoors, in the sweltering heat, when the gentler games of summer—baseball, tennis, golf, swimming—should rule.

Rick Telander, sportswriter

I haven't been able to slam-dunk the basketball for the past five years. Or, for the thirty-eight years before that, either.

Dave Barry, writer

I love the game because I think it's the one sport where the personal expression of the individual ballplayer comes across the best.

Woody Allen, writer, director, actor

In New York, you can always search and find a player better than you are, to push you to greater things. It is an entire sub-culture built on competition.

Al McGuire, college basketball coach and broadcaster

It's just a game played with a little round ball.

Hot Rod Hundley, professional basketball player

It will be surprising to many to know how little the game has really changed throughout the years. People often believe that much of basketball is completely new, whereas in reality, the things that have been considered of recent development were embodied in the game almost from the very conception.

Dr. James Naismith, the inventor of basketball

Life in basketball has a lot of suffering in it.

Pat Riley, professional basketball player and coach

One thing about the top players in Harlem is that even a 30-point pick-up game is a serious thing. You don't just play the game for the hell of it.

Sonny Johnson, street player, Harlem

Sometimes this game comes down to makes and misses.

Jeff Van Gundy, professional basketball coach

The Game itself is about skills, problems, answers, unselfishness, rotations . . . it all comes back around.

Spike Lee, writer, actor, director

The Good Samaritan . . . was a basketball player who kept throwing passes when he was only two feet from the goddamn basket. You know what God did? He cut him for overpassing.

Bobby Knight, champion basketball coach, to one of his players

There is absolutely no way the best team in the NCAA could even dream of beating the worst team in the NBA . . . You're talking about men vs. boys.

Bill Walton, college and professional basketball player and broadcaster

There's only one way to think about this game and one way to play it. That's all out, foot to the floor, pushing myself as hard as I can for as long as I can. I love playing basketball.

Ervin "Magic" Johnson, Hall of Fame basketball player

This basketball bounces a certain way every time . . . Your behavior must be like a bouncing basketball. I have to be able to predict success based on your behavior and your behavior must be the same every time I call on you.

John Chaney, college basketball coach

This is, above all, a game of movement, of accuracy, of flow.

Harvey Araton, sportswriter

Nobody is going to pay to come out and watch your players run up and down the court in their underwear.

Jerry Adelman, ticket broker, speaking to a National Basketball Association executive in 1960

What is so fascinating about sitting around watching a bunch of pituitary cases stuff a ball through a hoop?

Woody Allen, writer, from Annie Hall

When I get to the NBA, first thing I'm going to do, I'm gonna see my Momma. I'm gonna buy her a house. Gonna get my Dad a Cadillac . . . so he can cruise to the games.

Arthur Agee, age 14, from Hoop Dreams

When Kentucky was upset by Texas Western, with the tenacious defense, disciplined play, and marvelously named players like Big Daddy Lattin and Willie Cager, we were all stunned . . . Maybe I was wrong about the capabilities of black basketball players . . . About a lot of things.

Frank Fitzpatrick, writer, about Texas Western upsetting Kentucky for the national championship. There was not a single player of color on Kentucky. Western Texas started five African Americans, the first team to do so and win a national championship.

When you have played basketball for a while, you don't need to look at a basket when you are in this close. You develop a sense of where you are.

Bill Bradley, basketball player and U.S. senator

Winning in the NBA more often has to do with the psychological qualities than the physical ones.

David Halberstam, wruter

You begin by bouncing a ball—in the house, on the driveway, along the sidewalk, at the playground. Then you start shooting: legs bent, eyes on the rim, elbows under the ball . . . No equipment is needed beyond a ball, a rim, and imagination.

Bill Bradley, U.S. senator, champion professional basketball player, and writer

You know what you learn in the NBA? You learn how to play basketball. That's it. The only other thing I learned in my career with the Celtics was how to follow tall men through airports.

Kevin McHale, professional basketball player and executive

You play against other great players and see if you can make things you see out there part of your game. If a new wrinkle works, you use it. A basketball player's game is always under reconstruction.

Ray Haskins, college basketball coach

You smell yourself if you've been playing . . . in the cluster of men lounging around the bench in the middle of the court's open side. Mostly players around the bench, men who've just finished playing the last game of the evening, each one relaxing in his own funk, cooling out, talking the game, beginning to turn it into stories.

John Edgar Wideman, award-winning novelist, college basketball player, from Philadelphia Fire

Batboy

Butch was here before you came, and Butch will be here after you're gone.

Mort Cooper, professional baseball player, to an unidentified rookie, who was needlessly criticizing St. Louis Cardinals' batboy Butch Yatkeman

You're on thin ice. We better win soon or you'll be gone.

Derek Jeter (and other teammates), All-Star professional baseball player, to the batboy during a losing streak, ribbing him that he was bad luck

Becker, Boris

(b. Nov. 22, 1967) *Tennis champion; won Wimbledon, U.S. Open, and Australian Open*

Boris is the kid who, if you tell him not to put his hand in the fire because it's hot, he'll stick his hand right in the fire.

Ian Tiriac, tennis coach

Belmont Stakes

The extra 550 yards could make a big difference.

Elliott Walden, champion thoroughbred trainer

The longest, toughest test of stamina a 3-year-old colt and his trainer can face.

Jerry Izenberg, sportswriter

You don't run this distance but once in a horse's life. There's no telling what will happen.

D. Wayne Lukas, champion thoroughbred trainer

Berra, Yogi

(b. May 12, 1925) *Hall of Fame baseball catcher; played on 10 championship teams, won pennants with both the Yankees and the Mets; three-time American League Most Valuable Player*

He talks OK up there with a bat in his hands. A college education don't do you no good up there.

Casey Stengel, Hall of Fame baseball player and manager

That boy is too clumsy and too slow.

Branch Rickey, baseball executive, on unknown prospect Yogi Berra

Bird, Larry

(b. Dec. 7, 1956) *Hall of Fame National Basketball Association player; 1980 Rookie of the Year; won three NBA championships; 1998 Coach of the Year*

Bird was one of the few white guys who could play what people call the "Black Game."

Dennis Rodman, professional basketball player

He will cut your heart out to win.

Matt Goukas, professional basketball coach, about Larry Bird

He can dominate a game without even taking a shot. He is truly a guy who can make other players better.

Ervin "Magic" Johnson, Hall of Fame basketball player

He will take your heart out, stomp on it, and walk off the court with a sly grin on his face. He won't stop until he whips your ass!

Pat Riley, professional basketball player and coach, to his team before a National Basketball Association finals game

Birdie

I deny the allegations by Bob Hope that during my last game I hit an eagle, a birdie, an elk and a moose.

Gerald Ford, president of the United States

One time at Chattanoga, I hit a real pretty tee shot to the green, and danged if my ball didn't hit a bobwhite in the air and knock it dead. My ball stopped about a foot from the cup and I tapped it in. Only time I ever made two birdies in one hole.

> *Sam Snead, champion golfer*

Blocking

Somewhere in the player's contract, maybe in the fine print, it says, "You're supposed to block."

> *John McKay, college and professional football coach*

The secret is watching the center and going with the snap

> *Nate Allen, professional football player, about blocking punts and field goals*

Blunders

I thought it was a no-brainer.

> *Chuck Knoblauch, who argued with an umpire about an infraction by a base runner instead of fielding a ground ball, which resulted in a run scoring and the Yankees losing a playoff game*

Boats

A boat is a boat, I guess—nothing more than boards and paint and memories. Boards and paint are destined to rot away, but memories are priceless with age.

> *Larry Dablemont, writer*

A small sailing craft is not only beautiful, it is seductive and full of strange promise and a hint of trouble.

> *E. B. White, writer*

Ben Lexcen came up with the greatest innovation in 12-meter yacht design in decades. He deserves all the credit he got and more.

> *Dennis Conner, businessman and champion yachtsman*

Big sea, little boat, out to sea I go.

> *Molly Mulhern Gross, outdoorswoman, editor, and journalist*

Every well-built canoe, yacht or ship, has some individuality, some peculiar trait of its own.

> *George W. Sears, outdoorsman and journalist*

For a vessel to sail easily, steadily, and rapidly, the displacement of water must be nearly uniform along her lines.

> *George Steers, yacht architect, and builder of* America, *the racing yacht for which the America's Cup is named*

Good-bye old girl. God only knows when I shall tread your decks again.

> *Ben Butler, sailor, politician, and entrepreneur, speaking to* America, *the racing yacht for which the America's Cup is named*

Health, south wind, books, old trees, a boat, a friend.

> *Ralph Waldo Emerson, writer*

Her maker had warned me that he would not warrant her for an hour. "She may go to pieces like an eggshell," he said. He builded better than he knew.

> *George W. Sears, outdoorsman and journalist, about the* Sairy Gamp, *a canoe that traveled thousands of miles in the Adirondacks, built by J. Henry Rushton*

It has a picture of a tomato on the front, a mean vicious tomato with blood running from its fangs. It has green vines for hands and they are wrapped around the lighthouse at Cape Hatteras.

Hans Meijer, sailor, who previously had bad luck sailing off of Cape Hatteras

I ought to desist from crusty sailing man's thoughts about "stinkpots." I should try and see such craft not as gas-guzzling noisemakers but as potential nice guys who someday may pull me off a shoal to tow me into harbor when my mast falls down.

Anthony Bailey, writer and sailing enthusiast, about motorboats

It's those dishonest little things, skinned-out hulls to save weight, that can't take it . . . Designers have to change the emphasis from speed to safety.

Ted Turner, yachtsman, baseball owner, about yacht design after the 1979 Fastnet Race

Men who own the biggest boats are always thinking about records.

Roger Vaughn, sailor and writer

Sailing people who live in houses often envy those who live on boats. But those who dwell afloat all year round miss one great thing: the annual pleasure of throwing off a land-based existence in exchange (however briefly) for a seagoing life that will rock them with different demand and buoy them up with different delights.

Anthony Bailey, writer and sailing enthusiast

The lowly skiff might well be called the universal boat.

Edwin Monk, sailor, boat builder, and writer

There is a certain fascination about boat building, in watching a boat gradually take shape, and this particularly so when the results are your own efforts.

Edwin Monk, sailor, boat builder, and writer

There is nothing—absolutely nothing—half so much worth doing as simply messing around in boats.

Kenneth Grahame, writer

The old working craft in which modern sailing craft have their origins have virtually disappeared from the ports of the developed nations.

Bob Bond, sailor, instructor, and writer

Tracing the lines of boats is like tracing the lines of songs. It's a matter of influence. A sheer line or bow profile is transposed, and transformed, personalized and made original.

Douglas Whiynott, writer and sailor

You build someone a boat, and the people who own it become your friends, and they often remain friends for years. You take that away and boatbuilding can be a kind of joyless thing.

Eric Dow, boat builder

Bob Hope

(b. May 29, 1903) *Comedian, movie star*

Never before has anyone swung with so much for so little.

attributed to Winston Churchill about Bob Hope's golf swing, during a charity golf event during World War II

Bodybuilding

Don't get sand kicked in your face.

Charles Atlas (also known as Angelo Siciliano),
bodybuilder, from an ad for his
bodybuilding regimens.

Form is very important. Anyone can go into the gym and lift a weight. The trick is using the proper form to make your muscles give you the results you want.

Sharon Bruneau, champion bodybuilder

I built my American dream one rep at a time.

Bob Paris, champion bodybuilder

Nice business, isn't it, professional bodybuilding? More pimps and whores than Hollywood.

Steve Machalik, world champion bodybuilder

Physically I don't finish a set until I literally can't work the fatigued muscle any longer. I more or less continue until the barbell actually drops from my momentarily paralyzed fingers.

Tom Platz, world champion bodybuilder

Sport or not, bodybuilding as an art, as a science, as a lifestyle, and as a form of entertainment is here to stay.

Fredrick C. Hatfield, writer

The guiding axiom in competitive bodybuilding is "no pain, no gain." As a result, elite bodybuilders frequently joke about being participants in "the sport of masochists."

Bill Reynolds, weightlifting editor and writer

Whatever else I do, I want to always be a kind of ambassador, a preacher for bodybuilding.

Arnold Schwarzenegger, champion
bodybuilder and actor

Whatever it is you do in life, you can never grow in self-esteem unless you get good and pumped first and stay that way. Any time you spend without a pump is time you can never get back again.

Franco Columbo, champion bodybuilder

World governed by a savage force that swallowed me whole from a bookstore in New York City, and did not relent until it had chewed me up and spit me out 80 pounds heavier and 3,000 miles later on a posing dais in Burbank, California. I was swabbed in posing oil and competition color, flexing with all my might, when I came to, a sadder and wiser man.

Samuel Wilson Fussell, bodybuilder

You just haven't lived until you try doing 4 to 6 sets of 100 reps in various quadriceps and hamstring excercises.

Diana Dennis, champion bodybuilder

Books

A major distinction between the athlete of today and those of yesteryear is that the old jocks rarely read books. Today, some even write them.

Howard Cosell, broadcaster

First things first: I can read my own book.

Dexter Manley, professional football player

I haven't read it yet.

Johnny Unitas, Hall of Fame football
player, on his biography

It is all true. But I wish he had come to me. I would tell him so much more.

Primo Carnera, referring to Budd Schulberg's
roman à clef The Harder They Fall, *a novel*
based on Carnera's life

I should've read it.

Charles Barkley, professional basketball player, All-Star, author

I've dug ditches, lubed jackhammers and manned the graveyard shift at a 7-Eleven. But the worst job I ever had was writing Wayne Gretzky's autobiography.

Rick Reilly, sportswriter, commenting on Gretzky's reluctance to talk about himself

Three years ago I couldn't spell author. Now I are one.

Don Cherry, professional hockey player

Bowling

One of the advantages bowling has over golf is that you seldom lose a bowling ball.

Don Carter, champion bowler

I'm just tickled to death to get out of the house.

Carl Koch, 100-year-old bowler who bowled a 199

Good bowling involves repetition.

Mike Aubrey, champion professional bowler

This is the secret of bowling strikes! SQUEEZE the ball at the point of explosion.

Dawson Taylor, champion professional and amateur bowler

Bowls

There's plenty of time to win this game, and to thrash the Spaniards too.

Sir Francis Drake, admiral and navigator, who insisted he finish his game of bowls before fighting the Spanish navy

Boxers

A boxer knocked down is the loneliest guy in the world.

Gene Tunney, champion boxer

A boxer requires a *nob* as well as a statesman does a *head*, coolness and calculation being essential to his second efforts.

Heywood Broun, writer

Boxers, bullfighters and soldiers contract syphilis for the same reasons that make them choose their professions. In boxing most sudden reversals of form, the majority of cases of what is called punch drunkness, of "walking on the heels," are products of syphilis. You cannot name the individuals in a book because it is libelous, but any one in the profession will tell you of a dozen recent cases.

Ernest Hemingway, Nobel Prize–winninng author

But one thing remains. Jeffries must emerge from his alfalfa farm and remove that smile from Johnson's face. Jeff, it's up to you!

Jack London, rooting for Jim Jeffries, former heavyweight champion and commonly known "then" as the "Great White Hope," who lost to Jack Johnson, the champion. Afterward, London wrote: "Once again has Johnson sent down to defeat the chosen representative of the white race. . . ."

Dempsey was alone and Tunney could never explain himself and Sharkey could never believe himself nor Schmeling nor Braddock, and Carnera was sad and Baer an indecipherable clown; great heavyweights like Louis had the loneliness of the ages in their silence, and men like Marciano were mysti-

fied by a power which seemed to have been granted them.

Norman Mailer, Pulitzer Prize–winning writer

Durante in boxing shorts.

Jim Murray, sportswriter and writer,
about Luis Rodriguez, boxer

Hardly a blow had been struck when I knew I was Jeff's Master.

Jack Johnson, champion boxer, about the famous
Jack Johnson vs. Jim Jeffries match

He was gauche and inaccurate, but terribly persistent.

Heywood Broun, writer, about a
forgettable match

He works in the daytime at odd jobs, but what he wants is to walk down the street in the slum where he lives and have the people on the stoops and the guys on the corner recognize him as a man who is a prize fighter. He walks by them sharp in his zoot suit, the satchel in his hand, and they say, "There goes the fighter," and that is his reward.

Jimmy Cannon, sportswriter

I am a fighter who walks, talks, and thinks fighting, but I try not to look like it.

Marvelous Marvin Hagler, champion boxer

I don't want to knock my opponent out. I want to hit him, step away, and watch him hurt.

Joe Frazier, champion boxer

I can't be a poet. I can't tell stories.

Barry McGuigan, professional boxer, when asked
why he was a boxer

I haven't got long to go, and I want my family to be around me, happy, on one more Christmas. I won't be here for another. Please, Jack, I want to fight.

Billy Miske, professional boxer, to a boxing
promoter; the dying boxer was begging for
a fight so that he could buy presents for his family

If fighting is your business, fight!

Grantland Rice, sportswriter

I got into this business, because I got tired of beating up people for free.

Larry Holmes, world champion boxer

I know a good thing when I see it. Fighting is a good thing. It is like gold in that it is found in a nugget cluster of baser metals often buried in the mud.

Budd Schulberg, writer and screenwriter

I'm not boxing anymore. I'm going back to fighting the old-school way. I'm going to walk through guys and destroy them.

Oscar De La Hoya, champion boxer

I was never knocked out. I've been unconscious, but it's always been on my feet.

Floyd Patterson, champion boxer

I was one of the those hungry fighters. You could have hit me on the chin with a sledgehammer for five dollars. When you haven't eaten for two days you'll understand.

Jack Dempsey, champion boxer

Like a dancer, a boxer "is" his body, and is totally identified with it.

Joyce Carol Oates, writer and boxing aficionado

Old fighters react to training the way beautiful women react to scrubbing floors.

Norman Mailer, Pulitzer Prize–winning writer

Prizefighters often are a rough, surly group of men. They use boxing to release rage.

Seth Abraham, HBO executive

So far as the boxing game is concerned the contest next Monday is well named "the fight of the century." These two men, in a class by themselves so far as other fighters go, yet so radically different from each other as to have no salient characteristics in common.

Jack London, author and outdoorsman, writing about the Jack Johnson and Jim Jeffries fight

Someday they're gonna write a blues song just for fighters. It'll be for slow guitar, soft trumpet and a bell.

Sonny Liston, world champion boxer

The closer a heavyweight somes to the championship, the more natural it is for him to be a little bit insane, secretly insane, for the heavyweight champion of the world is either the toughest man in the world or he is not, but there is a great deal of possibility he is. It is like being the big toe of God.

Norman Mailer, Pulitzer Prize–winning writer

Theirs is a lonely sport, at time ugly, brutal, naked. You have to get inside a ring to appreciate how small it is. You wonder how men can ever escape.

Howard Cosell, broadcaster

The uninitiated, the cultivated, the educated don't accept that boxing has existed since pre-Hellenic Greece, and possibly since the time of the pharoahs, because it concedes one musky truth about masculinity: hitting a man is sometimes the most satisfying response to *being* a man. Disturbing, maybe, but there it is.

J. R. Moehringer, sportswriter

The most symbolic battles are no longer, as in the old days of Jack Johnson, Joe Louis, and Ray Robinson, white versus black, nor, as in the sixties and seventies with Muhammad Ali, Joe Frazier, and Ken Norton, black versus black, but rather black versus Latin. No fight could have more appropriately opened the era of the eighties in boxing than the first Sugar Ray Leonard versus Roberto Duran bout.

Gerald Early, sportswriter

They all have their entourages. Every lawyer, every accountant, every hustler is hanging around.

Lou Duva, Hall of Fame boxing trainer

What do you know about prize-fighting, for Christ's sweet sake?

Ernest Hemingway, writer and outdoorsman, to Budd Schulberg, writer and screenwriter, both boxing aficionados

When I see blood, I become a bull.

Marvelous Marvin Hagler, champion boxer

Boxing

After a round of dancing and jabbing, he was hit in the face with a wet sponge. He was rubbed, patted, squeezed and kneaded. Cold water was poured into his trunks. He was harangued, he was reprimanded, and he listened to nothing at all.

Leonard Gardner, novelist, from Fat City

As a younger fighter I was just a boxer. But now my main strength is starting to come. I can tell when I hit someone.
Ricardo Williams, Jr., professional boxer

Benny's an awful smart boxer. All the time he's in there, he's thinking. All the time he's thinking, I was hitting him.
Jack Britton, champion boxer, replying to a question how he beat his opponent Benny Leonard

Boxing is the sport to which all other sports aspire.
George Foreman, champion boxer

Boxing gave Liston an opportunity to meet bigtime hoodlums instead of small time ones.
Attributed to a police officer by Jimmy Cannon, sportswriter

'Cause the referee counted 11.
Gene Fullmer, professional boxer, recounting what his manager replied when he asked why his fight with Sugar Ray Robinson had been stopped; he had been knocked out

Did you keep your chin down?
Cus D'Amato, Hall of Fame boxing trainer, to Jose Torres, champion boxer, who called the trainer after he had been arrested for a street fight

Each boxing match is a story—a unique and highly condensed drama without words.
Joyce Carol Oates, writer

Every talent must unfold itself in fighting.
Friedrich Nietzsche, philosopher

Fighting is the only racket where you're almost guaranteed to end up as a bum.
Rocky Graziano, champion boxer

Float like a butterfly, sting like a bee.
Muhammad Ali, champion boxer

I just knocked him down and that ended the boxing for the night.
Hugh Casey, professional baseball player, about Ernest Hemingway, author and sportsman, during a sparring match

I'll moider da bum.
Tony Galento, heavyweight boxer, when asked what he thought of William Shakespeare

The hardest thing about Prize Fighting is picking up your teeth with a boxing glove on.
Kin Hubbard, humorist and author

The heavyweight championship is, after all, a fairly squalid office.
Murray Kempton, writer

He hits you in the belly and it's like someone stuck you with a hot poker, and left it there.
Billy Soose, professional boxer, about Tony Zale

Honey, I forgot to duck.
Jack Dempsey, champion boxer, to his wife, after losing to Gene Tunney

Hurting people is my business.
Sugar Ray Robinson, champion boxer

It's a terrible sport, but it's a sport . . . the fight for survival is the fight.
Rocky Graziano, champion boxer

It's more important to be a fighter than a sideshow.

Lou DiBella, HBO boxing promoter

I wanted to hit him one more time in the nose so that bone could go right up into his brain.

Mike Tyson, champion boxer, speaking about his fight with Jesse Ferguson

I zigged when I should have zagged.

Jack Ropes, professional boxer

Looking at a fighter who can't punch is like kissing your mother-in-law.

Jack Hurley, boxing promoter

Man, this is a fight, not a rumble.

*Evander Holyfield, champion boxer,
to Mike Tyson, champion boxer, after
the latter bit off part of the former's ear*

My toughest fight was with my first wife.

Muhammad Ali, champion boxer

Nobody's marketing minivans to boxing moms, not yet, but it does seem that the sport has become a little more suburban than we remember it.

Richard Hoffer, sportswriter

No dentist ever advised his patient to have his teeth removed by force. So you're not allowed to go into the ring without a mouthpiece. Of course, you become toothless with a mouthpiece, but you usually lose them one at a time.

Jimmy Cannon, sportswriter

Only in boxing do you have that ritual, of two men, nearly naked, exhausted, the smell and taste of each other, after such serious battle, the strange intimacy of that.

Gay Talese, writer

The air was a stink of blueness, sharp with the heat of bodies, and with the weight of puddle beer drying into boards that never knew soap and water, and soured with tobacco spit. Black and gray they huddled on the benches, the sportsmen, with their faces red in rows, regular as match heads, one behind the other, every mouth wide, every eye wild, and there voices mixed in a thickness of sound, an untidiness of raw tone without good thought or sense.

*Richard Llewellyn, novelist,
from* How Green Was My Valley

The bigger they come the harder they fall.

Bob Fitzsimmons, boxer

Boxing has been infested with corruption and gangsterism from the day it began, yet it engages our basic emotions like no other athletic activity.

Howard Cosell, broadcaster

The English scribes were rather indelicate in their descriptions of the contest, implying that both fights were as rehearsed as a Shakespearean play.

*Jack Sher referring to two fights between Primo
Carnera and Young Stribling*

A fight, a piece of writing, a painting or a passage of music is nothing without emotion.

*W.C. Heinz, sportswriter, to Floyd Patterson,
champion boxer*

Sorry? Are you kidding? Boxers are never sorry.

Carmen Basilio, professional boxer

There is a quality about boxing that attaches to no other sport. Well, maybe not boxing; maybe the men who fight, rather than the science itself. They are the most interesting of all athletes, for they seem to have the deepest feelings about life.

Howard Cosell, broadcaster

They are the time-killers, the guys fighting as you come down the aisle to your seat. They are only half seen in their small moments of triumph, and their disgraces are vaguely remembered, like a joke told very late at night when everyone is drunk.

Jimmy Cannon, sportswriter

Bradley, Bill

(b. July 28, 1942) *Olympic Gold Medalist; won two National Basketball Association titles; former U.S. senator*

He dislikes flamboyance, and unlike some of basketball's greatest stars, has apparently never made a move merely to attract attention. While some players are eccentric in their shooting, his shots, with only occasional exceptions, are straightforward and unexaggerated.

John McFee, writer

British Open

Well, you know what they say. The opera is generally not finished until the large woman begins singing.

misquote of Jack Nicklaus at the 1984 British Open, in a statement released by British Open officials

Broadcasters

Like Odysseus at sea, I was drawn by a voice, and I sail in direction of that voice. In other words, I go with Tim McCarver.

Bill Scheft, writer

One of the joys of baseball is the comfort of seeing a familiar face in the booth, and the smugness of feeling superior to that guy.

Bill Scheft, writer

The federal government in all its majesty is worried that sports broadcasters do sinister things, like rooting for the home team.

George Will, writer and part owner of the Chicago Cubs

He could go all the way!

Chris Berman, broadcaster, his signature call, which is an homage to the late Howard Cosell

Let's go to the videotape!

Warner Wolf, sports broadcaster

You could be a thief, a murderer, a gangster, you could run over your wife with your car in the driveway, but you carry around a briefcase and that stock portfolio, and the announcers can't do anything but swoon over you and sing your praises.

Art "Fatso" Donovan, Hall of Fame football player

Broadcasting

The beauty of radio was that you could add color to the game, and be dramatic, and sometimes be over dramatic and build it

up . . .You could put all the drama you cared to into a no-hitter, Brock stealing a base, or whatever.

Jack Buck, broadcaster

All you're going to do on radio is talk.

Julius Israel, father of Mel Allen, broadcaster, who was against his son becoming a broadcaster

I don't understand what kind of damn radio that can be if you can't get a score of a ball game on it.

Harry Caray, broadcaster, to a taxi driver who only had a dispatch radio in his cab

If I was this big an asshole when I was playing, shoot me right now.

Jimmy Connors, tennis champion and broadcaster, trying to get interviews at a tennis match

I got nothing better to do that pays me so much.

Don Meredith, professional football player and broadcaster

I like radio better than television because if you make a mistake on radio, they don't know. You can make up anything on the radio.

Phil Rizzuto, professional baseball player and broadcaster

I never understood the value to your broadcasts because I never got to listen, but now I've got to tell you that the one thing that keeps me going is hearing your broadcast.

Lou Gehrig, Hall of Fame baseball player, to Mel Allen, broadcaster, after Gehrig had taken ill and retired from baseball

If I knew what was going through Jack Nicklaus' head, I would have won this tournament.

Tom Weiskopf, champion professional golfer, after being asked on national television what Nicklaus was thinking as he prepared to tee off on the 16th fairway in the final round, as he was driving to win his sixth green jacket at the Masters in 1986; Weiskopf was a runner-up

I think I'll take another bite of my coffee.

Frank Gifford, Hall of Fame football player, broadcaster, while announcing the famous Ice Bowl game

Goooal!

Andres Cantor, broadcaster

People ask me, do you like broadcasting games? And I say, "Yeah, but it's not as good as playing. It's like methadone to a heroin addict."

Tim Green, National Football League player turned broadcaster and writer

You're the professional announcer. I'm just a washed-up, out-of-shape ex-fighter.

Rocky Marciano, world champion boxer, to Howard Cosell, broadcaster

Brushbacks

If the on-deck batter is standing too close to home plate, you brush him back.

Brent Kemnitz, coach of Witchita State, who was suspended for the rest of the season, after one of his pitchers ended the career of an on-deck batter after beaning him

I wouldn't throw at her, but I might brush her back.

Johnny Allen, professional baseball player (pitcher) to Doc Cramer, who said to Allen that he would throw at his own mother

When I came to, I didn't remember anything. After Jeffcoat hit me in the face doctors examined me and said, "What have you got in there?"

Don Zimmer, professional baseball player and manager, about being beaned

Within that unwritten brushback and beanball code, there is a vague by-law: an opposing pitcher cannot be allowed to constantly hit your guys, intentional or not, without being answered; an opposing pitcher should always be held to a high standard of care when projecting a baseball, lest he injure one of your guys.

Buster Olney, sportswriter

Bullfighting

Bullfighting is the only art in which the artist is in much danger of death and in which the degree of brilliance in the performance is left to the fighter's honor.

Ernest Hemingway, Nobel Prize–winning author

The bull is stronger, but the matador is smarter.

Muhammad Ali, world champion boxer

It is a decadent art in every way and like most decadent things it reaches its fullest flower at its rottenest point.

Ernest Hemingway, Nobel Prize–winning author

I've never seen a corrida where I didn't feel the need to cheer the death of the bull. There's relief on behalf of the matador—that the guy hasn't had his innards unzipped—and you feel an intensely visceral release from a spectacle that combines athletics with blood, blades and mortal danger.

Tony Hendra, writer and humorist

The sexuality of the bullring isn't something aficionados talk about much, perhaps because, from Homer to Hemingway, bulls have tended to be a guy thing. There are few more potent symbols of machismo than a fellow in spangled tights facing down what Tom Lehrer once called "a half-ton of angry pot roast"—and it's a very serious business.

Tony Hendra, writer and humorist

Business

Baseball is too much of a sport to be called a business, and too much of a business to be called a sport.

Philip K. Wrigley, baseball owner

I'd just like to say hello to my attorney, my business partner, my ancillary adviser, my theatrical agent and my publisher. Hi, boys. We're doing fine.

Steve Cady, sportswriter, proposing what athletes panned by the camera on the sidelines should say instead of "Hi, Mom!"

I don't look on football as a career, It's a stepping stone. I know too many ballplayers who were lost when opportunity didn't knock on their door.

Frenchy Fuqua, professional football player

If I could make more money running a supermarket, I'd run a supermarket. My best thing is driving cars . . . It's a business, like any other business.

Richard Petty, champion race car driver

In my time, it was the army generals running Brazil who tried to pick the team. Today, it's the sponsors, the businessmen, the media moguls. The World Cup Finals is the world's biggest TV show.

Carlos Alberto Perreira, champion
soccer manager

It's what it aims to be. It's a show. The pros are in the entertainment business.

Red Blaik, champion college football coach

Our main goal is to get people to spend their disposable income with properties associated with the company, whether they're our theme parks, videos, movies or our sports teams. If you've got a dollar, we want it.

Tony Tavares, executive at Disney, which owns
several sports franchises

Murdoch and Fox changed the economics of sports when they took football away from CBS.

Robert M. Gutkowski, sports marketing
executive

The Champagne has been chilling so long it has frostbite.

Timothy W. Smith, New York Times writer,
commenting on the length of negotiations between
Evander Holyfield and Lenox Lewis for a
unification bout of the heavyweight division

The sports hero must always be on top. If he goes down, he becomes a loser. I quit when I was on top, and the business opportunities came.

Jean-Claude Killy, world champion skier

This is an obit, which is short for obituary. An obit tells of a person who has died, how he lived, and of those who lived after him. This is the obit on the Brooklyn Dodgers.

Dick Young, sportswriter

I'm for sale!

Martina Hingis, women's tennis player, on
reaching superstardom and cashing in

These days you have to be a utility player: if you do only one thing, you're not sellable; you have to be able to sing *and* dance.

Joe Favorito, Women's Tennis Association
executive

We're still trying to develop a product for him. What we like is that he's a positive role model, reflects a positive image. He's unique.

Michael Jordan, professional basketball player,
referring to signing Derek Jeter,
professional baseball player, to an
Nike Air Jordan contract

When you look at Michael Jordan the business man, you see someone who has cultivated relationships with companies over a long period of time. He has met with their chairmen and has golfed with them, socialized with them and has spent time with them. And he has learned a lot.

Pat Riley, professional basketball
player and coach

You can be sold, traded or released at will. You are carried on the books as a depreciable capital asset and exist like a piece of chattal.

Rick Sortun, professional football player

I don't think anyone, unless they're very peculiar, has a relationship with a toothpaste brand. You tell someone to come for a pint

and a pie and talk about their team, and they'll knock your door down.

> *Peter Draper, group marketing director for Manchester United, comparing brand loyalty to sports loyalties*

"Meet me in the garage and take what you want for yourselves," I said to the workmen. They were astonished at what they found there: big piles of bats, balls, gloves, caps, jogging suits, sportswear, tennis rackets, shoes . . . The men looked a little overwhelmed; I guessed they'd never read about this sort of thing in the sports pages.

> *Cyndy Garvey, ex-wife of professional baseball player Steve Garvey*

Prices are touching the stars!

> *Vittorio Cecchi Gori, president, Fiorentina professional soccer club*

Butterflies

Anyone here have butterflies?

> *Ralph Branca, professional baseball player, to Pee Wee Reese and Jackie Robinson, after being brought in to pitch against Bobby Thompson in the bottom of the ninth, for the pennant*

As a professional competitor, I believe that you should have some butterflies and healthy tension before you go out to the mound. You may risk staleness or flatness in your pitching if the adrenaline is not flowing.

> *Tom Seaver, Hall of Fame baseball player*

I get a few butterflies right when they are introducing our names, but when they throw the ball up, I'm out there playing, and it doesn't matter who it's against.

> *Jason Williams, professional basketball player*

I think we all get butterflies before we race. I know I did before each of the 176 Grand Prix I competed in.

> *Graham Hill, champion race car driver*

I was a little nervous out there. It was like any opening day. I don't care how long you played—you always get a little nervous.

> *Yogi Berra, Hall of Fame baseball player and manager*

Karas always has been ready on Sundays, keyed up so intensely that he vomits just before kickoff time.

> *Myron Cope, sportswriter*

No matter how long you have been playing, you still get butterflies before the big ones.

> *Pee Wee Reese, Hall of Fame baseball player*

Some of us shake on the outside, some of us on the inside.

> *Roberto Clemente, Hall of Fame baseball player*

Tighter than a bullfighter's pants.

> *Tommy Holmes, sportswriter, writing about Duke Snider in his first World Series appearance*

What's bigger than butterflies? A buzzard? I had a buzzard in my stomach.

> *Allen Iverson, professional basketball player*

Button, Dick

(b. July 18, 1929) *Two-time Olympic gold medalist figure skater; five-time World Champion; award-winning broadcaster*

Dick Button introduced real athletics in the form of "barrier" high jumps into skating. The strength and virility of his performance simply crashed into the sober circles of the ice world and staged for a moment their conventional ideals . . . He gave to skating its own *raison d'être.*

Nigel Brown, writer and ice skating historian

C

Camping

Thank Heaven there are a few green spots on this green earth that it does not pay to "improve," but they are remote.

George W. Sears, outdoorsman and journalist

The blessed calm of lonely places, where the bright-eyed, wary wood folk come almost to your feet as you sit quietly . . . where the arch rascal man does not intrude; where one may camp for months without seeing a human face or hearing the buzz of civilized racket.

George W. Sears, outdoorsman and journalist

There is a sort of freemasonry among woodsmen that only woodsmen know.

George W. Sears, outdoorsman and journalist

Canoeing

A paddle is a very personal tool.

Robert Kimber, outdoorsman and writer

Canoe races and high-powered whitewater paddling are all well and good. But for me, what canoeing is really all about is getting out into the big, wild country with a fly rod and some good friends along for the company.

Robert Kimber, outdoorsman and writer

I hope at no distant day to meet independent canoeists, with canoes weighing twenty pounds or less, at every turn in the wilderness, and with no more duffle than is absolutely necessary.

George W. Sears, outdoorsman and journalist

Some people buy these boats and never put them in the water, just keep them in the living room like a work of art.

Mike Faunce, maker of Old Town Canoes

They hardly knew which to admire more, the little craft or the reckless (!) woodsman who would risk his life in such an eggshell.

J. Henry Rushton, canoe builder, about George W. Sears and the canoe he built him, the Sairy Gamp

Toward the end of every long carry, a canoeist strains to spot the glint of water or

the thinning of the canopy that marks the end of the trail.
Christine Jerome, outdoorswoman and journalist

Waterproof bags tend to either be dependable and awkward to use or undependable and easy to use.
Cliff Jacobson, outdoorsman and writer

Career

Having a long NFL career is an accomplishment in itself.
Joe Montana, Hall of Fame professional football player

I guess if I had to describe my career, I'd have to say it's been one of turmoil and happiness.
Richard Neal, professional football player

I wanted to play shortstop for the Yankees. When I would say that in class, teachers would tell my dad that maybe I should think about other careers as well. But it's worked out OK.
Derek Jeter, professional baseball player

It wasn't a career. What it was, was joy and pain, thunder and sunbursts, mountains to climb, rivers to cross and odds to defy.
Jerry Izenberg, sportswriter, about Julie Krone, jockey

Mr. Rodgers, why don't you concentrate more on your vocation rather than your avocation.
the school principal, to Bill Rodgers, champion marathoner, at the school where Rodgers taught for a living

The frightening thing about playing professional football is that it gives you a sense of security. The trouble is that a player enters football when he's about twenty-one. Barring an injury which obviously puts him out earlier, he has a career of ten to fifteen years during which he advances his education only in football.
John Gordy, professional football player

Catcher

A good catcher is the quarterback, the carburetor, the lead dog, the pulse taker, the traffic cop, and sometimes a lot of unprintable things. But no team gets very far without one.
Miller Huggins, champion professional baseball coach

Cell Phones

Using one is disrespectful to other players. Any time you get a chance to talk, you should be talking to other players about baseball.
James Baldwin, professional baseball player, about the banning of cell phones in the White Sox clubhouse

Challenge

Don't catch me after one night.
Pete Rose, professional baseball player, to Tony Gwynn, professional baseball player, both of whom got more than 3,000 hits, after Gwynn got his first major league hit

Hit Sign, Win Suit
Abe Stark, tailor, businessman, politician, from a sign he installed in right field at Ebbetts Field at the base of the scoreboard

I like the challenge. I like the idea of being on more or less even footing with the game. Against my advantages of better eyesight, a rifle, and—I hope—a better mind, the deer match their superior senses of smell and hearing, their intimate knowledge of the cover, and their wonderful alertness.

Ted Trueblood, outdoorsman, editor, and writer

I've never really turned away from a challenge in my career. You can't ever be afraid to do something.

Mike Piazza, All-Star professional baseball player

The idea of such a big challenge intrigued me.

Tom Landry, Hall of Fame football coach, speaking about starting the Dallas Cowboys from scratch in the well-established National Football League

Champions

A champion is one who gets up when he can't see.

Jack Dempsey, champion boxer

A champion is someone who can't settle for second best.

Warren Spahn, Hall of Fame baseball player

A winner never whines.

Paul Brown, champion professional football coach

He's got to improve himself, just like anybody else.

Joe DiMaggio, Hall of Fame baseball player

If you're going to be a champion, you must be willing to pay a greater price than your opponent.

Bud Wilkinson, coach

It's a cockiness really. To be a champion you got to believe so much in yourself you're cocky. You're always trying to play it down, trying not to let your cockiness show, but sometimes it'll show.

Bill White, professional baseball player and American League president

It sounds trite, but I think one must have a reason for being a champion. With most people the reason is a hunger—a hunger for financial gain or a hunger for glory.

Vince Lombardi, Hall of Fame football coach

I would rather be number one and not making any money than number four and making millions.

Pauline Betz, professional tennis champion

Keep your head up; act like a champion.

Paul "Bear" Bryant, Hall of Fame college football coach

Look like a winner and act like a champ all the time. If you win, be gracious. Keep your head on.

James Francis "Jumbo" Elliott, champion track and field coach

Meet the new champ.

Eddie Arcaro, Hall of Fame jockey, introducing rookie jockey Willie Shoemaker, Hall of Fame jockey

My Triple Crown season would have meant nothing, it would have been a waste, unless we got the world championship back.

Mickey Mantle, Hall of Fame baseball player

No team wins the championship holding its breath.

Harvey Araton, sportswriter

Several times I have been threatened with overthrow by phenomenals. On one or two occasions it has been whispered around in such a way as to reach my ears, that importations have been made and it was good-bye to Shrubb. These importations have once or twice materialized. Like deer they would run for a distance and keep me guessing. All of a sudden they would disappear and I, smilingly relieved, would trudge on alone.

Alfred Shrubb, champion runner

Skill alone does not make the champion.

John Devaney, sportswriter, What Makes a Champion?

If you are going to be a champion, you must be willing to pay a greater price than your opponent.

Bud Wilkinson, professional football coach

If you win a championship, you got to go out there next year and prove you're still a champion.

Sam Huff, Hall of Fame football player

I remember when we got our rings . . . I flew out to California after that season and gave it to my father. I didn't need it to prove anything anymore.

Bud Harrelson, professional baseball player

One day we were the laughingstock of baseball, and the next we were champions.

Ed Kranepool, professional baseball player, referring to the 1969 Miracle Mets

There is only a half step difference between the champions and those who finish on the bottom. And much of that half step is mental.

Tom Landry, Hall of Fame football coach

What creates champions is, first, the decision to stay in the sport and work hard. Perhaps nothing more heroic may be involved in this decision than habit, boredom or commitments to friends.

Daniel F. Chambliss, swimming coach and writer

Winning back-to-back championships is tougher than anything because you've got to sustain, and stave off complacency.

Michael Jordan, All-Star professional basketball player

Winning the NBA title is about will, luck, and understanding the *other* guy's game.

Spike Lee, writer, actor, director

You don't get there on natural ability alone. A lot of people are born with natural ability, but few of them become champions.

Chuck McKinley, tennis champion

Championships

After twenty-one years in the major leagues, I still can't recall a game won in extra innings on a botched squeeze play that'd be replayed more times than the Zapruder film.

Durwood Merrill, umpire, after the 1997 American League Championship Series between Cleveland and Baltimore

Every championship, by definition, is historic.

George Vecsey, sportswriter

Finals are about winning or losing; any entertainment that ensues is a welcome side-product which cannot be guaranteed.

David Lacey, sportswriter

I'm not going to tell you what it is that allows you to win at this level. You're going to have to learn it yourself.

Ervin "Magic" Johnson, Hall of Fame basketball player, to Isiah Thomas, professional basketball player, executive, and coach

I played the tour in 1967 and told jokes and nobody laughed. Then I won the Open the next year, told the same jokes, and everybody laughed like hell.

Lee Trevino, champion professional golfer

One gold medal in a championship is ordinary. I wanted to get two golds and be a little different.

Haile Gebreselassie, world champion runner

This is a division championship game. The players will play. You know it's not like there's a dance after the game that we're waiting for, and if there is, I don't have anybody to take. Maybe I'll call Kathleen Turner.

Bill Parcells, professional football coach, responding to a reporter's question about which players would play

To win a championship you've got to do it throughout the whole year.

Jeff Gordon, champion race car driver

When you have a championship team, you have things built into your arsenal to deal with problems.

Greg Ray, race car driver

Winning a championship, even for the stars, is like a stamp of approval. It gives them the feeling that, "Now, I have done it."

Doug Collins, professional basketball coach

Winning the world championship catapulted me to the top. Not only did I make headlines but I was even mentioned in the United States.

Greg LeMond, champion cyclist

You cannot take a seven and win—anytime—during seventy-two holes of title play.

Gene Sarazen, champion golfer

Character

The Battle of Waterloo was won on the playing fields of Eton.

Duke of Wellington, British general and prime minister

As Duke Ellington once said, the Battle of Waterloo was won on the playing fields of Elkton.

Babe Ruth, Hall of Fame baseball player, misquoting the Duke of Wellington

Football doesn't build character. It eliminates the weak ones.

Darrell Royal, National Football League player

My father always told me in the midst of adversity, in the midst of a struggle, "It builds character. Stay strong, be positive, look ahead, don't look back."

Bruce Smith, All-Pro professional football player

Our struggles against aggressors throughout our history have been won on the play-

grounds and corner lots and fields of America.

John Fitzgerald Kennedy, president of the
United States

Sport develops not character, but characters.

James A. Michener,
Pulitzer Prize–winning author

Sport: If you want to build character, then try something else.

Thomas Tutko, writer

There will never be a day when we won't need dedication, discipline, energy and the feeling that we can change things for the better.

George Sheehan, runner and writer

You don't build character without somebody slapping you around.

Vince Lombardi, Hall of Fame football coach

You have to suck it up, do what you have to do for the team to win.

Patrick Ewing, professional
basketball player, about playing hurt

Charisma

Charisma is winning major championships.

Tom Watson, champion professional golfer

Chatter

Mr. Durocher just told me not to talk to you.

Willie Mays, Hall of Fame baseball player, to
Roy Campanella, Hall of Fame baseball player,
in Mays's rookie year, because Campanella's
chatter interfered with Mays's concentration

Cheap Shots

They'll only warn you the first time.

Jack Dempsey, champion boxer, speaking about
how you can throw one or two in a fight without
being disqualified or losing points

Cheating

Cheating in baseball is just like hot dogs, french fries, and cold Cokes.

Billy Martin, professional baseball player and
manager

It's in the mindset of players and managers to cheat whenever they get a chance. They believe it is the equivalent of their First Amendment right in baseball to cheat.

Durwood Merrill, umpire

Chemistry

Chemistry is bullshit. I'll tell you what gives you good chemistry: winning. Losing gives you bad chemistry.

Mike Piazza, professional baseball player

Climbing

A climb is the most human relationship possible with a mountain face.

Harold Drasdo, mountain climber

A couple of years ago I had met a rather unsavory character . . . As our acquaintance dragged on, I discovered that we had much in common. For one thing we were both rather lazy . . . an important quality of the serious climber.

Warren Harding, mountain climber

A day well spent in the Alps is like some great symphony.

George Leigh Mallory, alpinist

A slip was not to be thought of; steadiness was essential.

R.L.G. Irving, mountain climber

A tendency to indulgence, whether in food, mountains, or liquor has, happily, always been a feature of the members of our Club.

Malcolm Slesser, mountain climber

Because it is there.

George Leigh Mallory, alpinist, answering the question, "Why do you climb Everest?"

Because I'm grumpy when I'm *not* climbing.

Doug Scott, climber, when asked why he climbed

Bonatti removed any chances of glory for anyone when he walked all over it by himself in one weekend.

Mick Burke, mountain climber, referring to the feat of climbing Mt. Blanc solo in one weekend by Walter Bonatti, alpinist

Climbers spend money and accept trouble to climb the mountain. They go home and five months later they are thinking about it again. This is the sickness of the alpinist.

Cesar Morales Arnao, climber

Climbing above 8,000 meters . . . any mistake is amplified in rarified air . . . a swallow of hot tea from a Thermos is the difference between life and death.

Anatoli Boukreev, climber and guide

Climbing is a drug, and I need a fix.

Dick Shockley, mountain climber

Climbing is all about facing problems; the better the problems, the more memorable the climb.

Anthony Greenbank, climber and writer

Climbing is more an art than it is a sport.

William A. Read, climber

Climbing would be a great, truly wonderful thing if it weren't for all that damn climbing.

John Ohrenschall, mountain climber

Climb the mountains and enjoy their good tidings. Nature's peace will flow into you as sunshine into flowers. Streams will bring you their freshness and storms their energy, and cares will fall off like autumn leaves.

John Muir, outdoorsman and philosopher

Everest was not mine alone, the highest point on earth, unattainable, foreign to all experience, was there for many boys and grown men to aspire toward.

Thomas F. Hornbein, mountain climber

Every man must seek the pleasures of mountaineering in his own way.

R.L.G. Irving, mountain climber

Even if Mallory and Irvine touched the summit, they didn't make it—that's like swimming to the middle of the ocean.

Ed Viestreo, climber, who did summit Everest

Fear is something that all climbers feel at some time. Without it there would be no caution.

Joe Brown, sportswriter

Forget the hype about the new "extreme" sports; mountaineering has been around for

centuries and is clearly the most extreme of all.

Men's Journal

From my deepest and oldest memories, I was always fascinated with the mountains. They had a magical quality about them and climbing was a part of that . . . In climbing you can have a very intense, sometimes spiritual, highly emotional adventure and you can turn around and have another one.

William A. Read, climber

Guiding and climbing are mutually exclusive. I've never been hurt climbing, but when you're guiding, there's always a chance that the client will make a mistake.

Jack Tackle, climber and guide

How free and exultant is the true mountaineer, when he exchanges the warmly glowing atmosphere of the south for the cold and invigorating blasts of the mountain; when he leaves behind him the gentle beauty of the lakes and glories in the savage grandeur of riven rock and contorted glacier.

Edward Shirely Kennedy, alpinist

Hungry! Cold!

Stefano Longhi, alpinist, his last words before he froze to death on an exposed ledge

I always thought anyone who fell off a mountain simply blacked out or died of fright or by some other means was delivered from consciously suffering such a disagreeable fate. This belief persisted . . . until I fell . . . and proved it wrong.

Peter Potterfield, climber

I awoke to strangely mixed feelings of discomfort and anticipation . . . Suddenly my

mind cleared, and I remembered that this was the most important day of all, for it was our turn to start on the long slow upward grind that might, with luck, end on the summit of Everest.

Sir Edmund Hillary, mountain climber, first man to reach the top of Everest

I can do no more.

Toni Kurz, alpinist, his last words, died of exposure, suspended in midair as his ropes knotted up

I closed my eyes and let the sickness spin me away from the bitter realities into unconsciousness. That night the tent became a frozen coffin. We tossed and turned and rolled onto each other through the long, long night.

Jonathan Waterman, climber and writer

I could climb for a million years and still not know why I do it.

Chuck Pratt, mountain climber

I don't expect this climb to make everything right. It'll just feel real good.

Jeff Lowe, climber, talking about how climbing will not solve life's problems

If anything goes wrong it will be a fight to the end. If your training is good enough survival is there; if not nature claims forfeit.

Dougal Haston, mountain climber

I felt very quiet, very tired. I sat there for more than a half an hour. I took some photographs and I had no fear about getting down. It was very peaceful.

Reinhold Messner, climber, referring to what he did as the only man to climb Everest alone

I found that climbing was the only thing in life that gave more than momentary satisfaction.

Dougal Haston, mountain climber, when asked "Why do you climb?"

I live not in myself, but I become
Portion of that around me; and to me
High mountains are a feeling, but the hum
Of human cities torture.

Lord Byron, poet

I move like a snail with my home on my back going slowly from place to place, going steadily but always going.

Reinhold Messner, climber, during his climb on Everest alone

I never left a mountain unfinished.

Cesare Maetri, climber

In the United States, great alpinists remain as obscure as chess champions.

David Roberts, outdoor journalist

I think it is not so necessary that a guide chat good, but that he can climb good.

Anatoli Boukreev, climber and guide, was a guide during the Everest disaster of 1996

I think that people that have experiences that are on the edge of life and death want to tell people about them and people want to read about them. Climbing is a real ultimate activity.

Arlene Blum, climber

It is lamentable that whenever a serious accident occurs . . . there is generally an outburst of ignorant and foolish criticism. The public are warned against the folly of mountaineering; they are informed that we witfully run unnecessary risks; that we climb almost impossible peaks from a pure spirit of bravado, from a desire to brag of our exploits, or from some other motive of equal silliness and stupidity.

C. E. Matthews, mountain climber

It is not important for me to just climb Everest, but it is a much greater achievement to climb the mountain without using oxygen. I can sit in my home in Italy and know I can climb Everest with a can of oxygen . . . Man can reach the moon with the aid of technology, but it is a philosophical question to reach the top of Everest without it.

Reinhold Messner, climber

It is not the role of grand alpinism to face peril, but it is one of the tests one must undergo to deserve the joy of rising for an instant above the state of crawling grubs.

Lionel Terray, mountain climber

It seems to me that the contemplative side of mountaineering can only have an interpretive value, and that the ecstasy of creation can come from action alone.

Giusto Gervasutti, alpinist

It was impossible that a mountain that far away could take up so much of the sky.

David Roberts, climber and writer

K2 has earned over the years a reputation as a killer.

Peter Potterfield, climber and writer

Ms. Pittman was known in certain elevated circles more as a social climber than mountain climber.

Joanne Kaufman, journalist, about Sandy Pittman, who was one of the surviving party during the fatal 1996 Everest climb

Mountaineering was a discovery. There were men, of course, right back through history, who were attracted by individual hills, and went—or tried to go—up them. Just as there were men in Newton's day who watched apples falling, and ate them.

Geoffrey Winthrop Young,
mountain climber

People have climbed from the earliest times . . . but these early venturers went no higher than it was necessary for hunting game or perhaps crystals. The alpine passes were routes for trade or invasion, but the peaks were places of fearsome mystery, the abodes of the gods, devils or dragons.

Chris Bonington, mountain climber

Perhaps we had become a little arrogant with our . . . age of easy mechanical conquest. We had forgotten that the mountain still holds the master card, that it will grant success only in its own good time. Why else does mountaineering retain its deep fascination?

Eric Shipton, mountain climber

Something besides courage and determination is needed to climb a mountain like this. Forgive me if I call it intelligence.

Robert Dunn, climber and writer

Superclimbers are, on the whole, uncheerful about hiking, impatient with the weather, insensitive to the subtleties of landscape.

David Roberts, mountain climber

The age of discovery and conquest has given way to a new period of personal and creative mountaineering.

Robert W. Craig, mountain climber
and writer

The mountain doesn't play games. It sits there unmoved.

Bruce Barcott, climber and writer

The transient population that ends up on the glacier includes serious expedition climbers and raw neophytes on guided climbs, adventurers, dopers, drinkers, and marginally socialized eccentrics looking for an extreme experience.

Peter Potterfield, climber and writer,
about Mt. Everest

The true mountaineer is a wanderer . . . a man who loves to be where no human being has been before, who delights in gripping rocks that have previously never felt the touch of human fingers.

Alfred Mummery, alpinist

There are still a great many walls of rock and ice and a diminishing number of high summits that haven't been touched, but these are going to talented young climbers from every part of the world seeking the untried or that which has not been done. What is creative about these routes and ascents is the style in which they are done.

Robert W. Craig, mountain climber and writer

This time we were without guides, for we had learnt the great truth that those who wish to really enjoy the pleasures of mountaineering must roam the upper snows trusting exclusively to their own skill and knowledge.

Alfred Mummery, alpinist

Today's climber doesn't want to cut himself off from the possibility of retreat; he carries his courage in his rucksack, in the form of bolts and equipment . . . Retreat has become

dishonorable, because everyone knows now that a combination of bolts and single-mindedness will get you up anything, even the most repulsive-looking direttissima.

Reinhold Messner, mountain climber

Well, we knocked the bastard off!

Sir Edmund Hillary, mountain climber, to George Lowe, expedition leader, after Hillary became the first man ever to reach the top of Everest

We made it.

Reinhold Messner, climber, after making it to the top of Everest without the aid of compressed oxygen, along with Peter Habeler

"What is the use of going up mountains?" is a question often put. To such I would say: go up a good-sized mountain, and you will know.

Edward Whymper, mountain climber

You find something that is larger than your life and you can take from that and put it into your life. There is such a bonding with people—trusting, sharing, and communicating . . . It makes your life much richer.

Alison Osius, climber

You think of the huge crowds that show up to watch a football game, massive crowds that just go crazy watching a sport, where at the very worst a team is going to gain less points than another. Then you think about some horrendous solo climb where a guy has trained his mind for years and there is nobody at all. If I solo . . . I don't want anybody to watch, because it's absolutely a personal thing.

Todd Skinner, climber

Coaches

Coaches do what works for them, what their personality is.

Jeff Van Gundy, professional basketball coach

Coaches have to watch for what they don't want to see and listen to what they don't want to hear.

John Madden, champion football coach and Emmy Award–winning broadcaster

His peers betray their torment, wincing, grimacing, politicking, intriguing, job-hopping, balding, graying, gaining weight until they flop into the off season like beached whales.

Mark Heisler, sportswriter, about Pat Riley, professional basketball coach

It is much more difficult for coaches now than it ever was. The off season is gone. You're constantly on the job. The pressure to win is constant.

Rich McKay, general manager

Phil Jackson always seems to have a little smirk on his face, as if to say, "I know something the rest of you don't."

David DuPree, sportswriter

There are two kinds of coaches. The kind that have just been fired and the kind that are going to get fired.

Bum Phillips, professional football coach

Coaching

A coach can't hide behind the fact that some players didn't play as well as they could have because that's his job.

Scotty Bowman, champion professional hockey coach

A great manager has a knack for making ballplayers think they are better than they really are.

Reggie Jackson, Hall of Fame baseball player

All I do is take the bows. These are the guys who do all the work.

James Francis "Jumbo" Elliott, champion track and field coach, referring to his two longtime assistants Jim Tuppeny and Jack Pyrah

Barney, what did you do? That's the steal sign!

Leo Durocher, professional baseball player and manager, to Barney Kremenko, sportswriter, after Durocher used the sportswriter to send in signs during a game Durocher had been thrown out of. At one point, Kremenko inadvertently scratched his nose, and a runner was thrown out attempting to steal second.

Behind every half-decent baseball man, there's a better one who took the risk of writing his name in the lineup for the first time.

Whitey Herzog, professional baseball player, executive, and manager

Be reasonable: Do it my way.

sign on desk of John Calipari, college and professional basketball coach

Coaching is easy. Winning is the hard part.

Elgin Baylor, Hall of Fame basketball player

Coaching is teaching. Some coaches try to make what they do sound mysterious and complicated when it's not. . . . to be a good coach, you have to be a good teacher.

John Madden, champion professional football coach, writer, and award-winning broadcaster

Could I be a good coach and lose? To me, that's like asking if a guy can be a good doctor even though his patients keep dying.

Red Auerbach, Hall of Fame basketball coach and executive

He's going to come back and coach for me someday.

Caroll Rosenbloom, owner, about Don Shula, professional football player and coach, whom he would hire and then fire after Rosenbloom's Colts would lose to the Jets

I am going to make a distinction between a coach and a teacher. A teacher or instructor shows you how to do a figure or a particular skating movement. A coach, on the other hand, not only helps you to improve your figure but advises you about your diet, keeps your family away from you when they become bothersome, makes sure you have the right pair of skates, and sees that you get up at the right time for a competition.

Carlo Fassi, figure skating coach

I don't think it's proper to talk about a job or speculate or meet with somebody about a job if the job is filled . . . I wouldn't say it's an unwritten rule in the coaching fraternity because the coaching fraternity doesn't have a lot of rules. But among good people, though, that's the rule.

Dick Harter, professional basketball coach

I'd rather be a football coach. That way you only lose 11 games a year.

Abe Lemons, coach

I don't tell opposing coaches who's starting the second quarter. Why tell them who's

starting the first quarter until right before the game starts.

Danny Ainge, professional basketball player and coach

If I had one wish, it would be for Jackie Robinson to be here to see this moment.

Frank Robinson, professional baseball player and first African-American major league manager

If you're losing sleep and you have a knot in your stomach, that means you're probably doing your job.

Bill Walsh, professional football coach

I had the idea that the team could be run by committee, but it's like a business. You need a strong man.

Leon Hess, sports owner

I probably couldn't play for me. I wouldn't like my attitude.

John Thompson, basketball coach

I'm a people coach. People play the game, not X's and O's.

Leeman Bennett, professional football coach

I'm not much of a golfer. I don't have any friends. And, all I like to do the day of a game is go home and be alone and worry about ways not to lose.

Paul "Bear" Bryant, college football coach

I told my coaches, "If the backs don't start running like Chuck Foreman, you're fired."

Dick Vermeil, professional football coach

It's a lot tougher to be a football coach than a President. You've got four years as Presi-

dent, and they guard you. A coach doesn't have anyone to protect him when things go wrong.

Harry Truman, president of the United States

I've heard of managers coming back as part of the grounds crew, or sitting in the front row giving signs, or sitting in the bleachers with binoculars, or standing behind a photographer or a cameraman.

Bobby Valentine, professional baseball player and manager, after being thrown out of a game as a manager, referring to his fine for appearing near the bench after his ejection, disguised in sunglasses and a greasepaint mustache

I want them to use the court to express themselves. But on the other hand, I don't want them to be flip. I don't want to be good old Riley to the players, the guy they could treat as an old shoe.

Pat Riley, professional basketball player and coach

Listen, if you start worrying about the people in the stands, before too long you're up in the stands with them.

Tom Lasorda, baseball manager

Of all the mistakes a coach can make, I think one of the worst is to fall in love with the sound of his own voice. When I see a coach waving his clip board, furiously drawing diagrams, I see a coach who's selling himself to the TV cameras, selling himself to the crowd, when what he should be doing is selling his team.

Red Auerbach, Hall of Fame basketball coach and executive

On most teams the coach worries about where the players are at night. Our players worried about the coach.

> *Art Rooney, owner, about Johnny Blood,*
> *professional football player and coach, about*
> *Blood's infamous lifestyle*

On this team we are all united in a common goal: to keep my job.

> *Lou Holtz, college and professional football coach*

People keep saying that Woody Hayes is a great football coach who overstayed his time. This implies that there was a time when slugging a member of the opposing team was proper coachly deportment.

> *Red Smith, sportswriter*

Some coaches pray for wisdom. I pray for 260-pound tackles. They'll give me plenty of wisdom.

> *Chuck Mills, football coach*

That's a coach's dream, to be able to put our guys against your guys—real gladiator stuff.

> *Erik Howard, professional football player*

The difference is that as a player, you come in, put in your two hours and leave. As a coach, you never really leave; at least your mind doesn't. One of the things I've learned is to keep a pad of paper near the bed so I can write down ideas that come to me in the middle of the night.

> *Kurt Rambis, professional basketball*
> *player and coach*

The job of coaching, rather than yelling at "unruly" kids and constantly pointing out their faults, is to provide an environment in which the racers can learn once and for all that their success depends on disciplining themselves . . .

And if a racer is incapable of disciplining himself, he doesn't belong on the team.

> *Billy Kidd, Olympic silver medalist downhiller*

The players win the matches. Coaches get too much credit and too much blame. I think we deserve credit for an assist.

> *Tom Gullikson, professional tennis*
> *player and coach*

The more you lose, the more positive you have to become. When you're winning, you can ride them harder because their self-esteem is high. If you are losing and you try to be tough, you're asking for dissension.

> *Rick Pitino, college and professional*
> *basketball coach*

The pro game is like being a step-parent: you have the responsibility without the authority.

> *Rick Majerus, college and professional*
> *basketball coach, about the differences*
> *between coaching college and pro*

They can't fire me because my family buys too many tickets.

> *LaVell Edwards, Brigham Young University*
> *football coach and one of 14 children*

To train a champion a coach must be willing to adapt and adjust his or her methods to each skater. That is the key to good coaching.

> *Carlo Fassi, figure skating coach*

I can be out of town in 20 minutes, 30, if I have stuff at the cleaners.

> *Tom McVie, National Hockey League coach*

I can only show you the way. It's up to you to go there.

> *Larry Ellis, track and field coach, to Bob*
> *Beamon, Olympic gold medalist long jumper*

If I was half the coach on the bench that I was in the stands, we'll have no problems.
Bob Plager, professional hockey coach

I've got to coach a guy who won't answer roll, who won't say anything . . . He played well, but it was a bad situation. It was totally against everything that I believed in.
Dan Reeves, professional football player and coach, as an assistant coach, about Calvin Hill's yearlong silence

He can take his'n and beat your'n, or he can take your'n and beat his'n.
Bum Phillips, National Football League head coach commenting on fellow National Football League head coach Don Shula

Have you ever seen a Fellini movie? My life is like a Fellini movie.
George Karl, professional basketball coach

I didn't feel I was properly coaching unless I was butting their heads, pushing them off the line, blocking them on their rears. Football is a show me game, not a preach to me game.
Chuck Knox, professional football coach

If the man tells you there's cheese on the mountain, then you best bring crackers.
Keith Byars, National Football League player on head coach Bill Parcells

If you become paralyzed by the thought that you may be criticized for doing something, you're never going to be the risk taker you need to be as a good coach. Risk taking is part of it. If it doesn't work out, you've got to accept the responsibility for it not working out.
Jeff Van Gundy, professional basketball coach

It takes some time to realize that you are, in fact, World Champion. "World" is such a big word, but when it does begin to sink in you begin to realize what a terrific responsibility you owe to your sport, the people who put you there, and to everybody around you.
Graham Hill, champion race car driver

I teach them how to grab the guy's shirt and step on their toes.
Bob Zawoluk, assistant Lehman College coach

I taught him everything he knows. I didn't teach him everything I know.
Charlie Whittingham, thoroughbred horse trainer, about someone who had worked under him and now was a competing trainer

I was never a rah-rah guy. I was never one of those guys that went around and rah-rahed . . . Rah-rah don't get it done.
Sparky Anderson, professional baseball player and manager

Old coaches never die. They start selling insurance or get promoted to high school principal. Or they ride off to the golf course.
Durwood Merrill, umpire

The greatest horror of coaching is losing.
Joe Schmidt, professional football coach

The player can walk away from losing, but the coach—well, then he should be out . . . he's in the wrong profession.
Joe Schmidt, professional football coach

There is nothing, absolutely nothing, like the feeling of being the coach of a Grand Slam champion.
Nick Bolletieri, professional tennis coach

They forgot to introduce me. Guys were looking at me and saying, "Is this guy a player? Manager? What is he?"

Jeff Van Gundy, professional basketball coach, on his first day as an assistant in the National Basketball Association

To hell with you. I'll see you out begging on the street.

Enrique Soto, coach, in the Dominican Republic minor league to his young players

When a kid has given you the best he has to give, and you have to tell him it wasn't good enough, that's when you ache inside and think maybe there's a better way to make a living.

Vince Lombardi, Hall of Fame coach

When we win, I have no idea why we win. When we lose, I have no idea why we lose. I'm totally confused.

George Karl, professional basketball coach

There's about a foot difference between a halo and a noose.

Bobby Bowden, champion college football coach

You don't get a vote here, son. If you want to get back to the free world, take your things with you.

Vince Lombardi, Hall of Fame professional football coach

Your mother wants you to improve. Your father wants to see you improve. But I just don't give a good goddamn.

Frank Cunningham, crewing coach

You've got ten million dollars worth of players here, so sit down.

Charles Barkley, professional basketball player, to Chuck Daly, coach, at the Olympics during the first Dream Team

College

A school without football is in danger of deteriorating into a medieval study hall.

Vince Lombardi, professional football player and coach

Behind the scenes, millions of dollars flow from booster to assistant coach to player, everyone knows it, everyone's a pimp or a whore.

Kevin Mackey, college and minor league basketball coach

College football is an ugly business.

Mike Tomco, college football player

College football would be more interesting if the faculty played instead of the students—there would be a great increase in broken arms, legs and necks.

H. L. Mencken, humorist and author

College is the fountain of life. You have to drink from it.

John Chaney, college basketball coach

If you find the right junior college kid, he's going to be so thrilled to have a chance to play . . . that he might come in here with a better attitude than the freshman. A junior college kid is older, he's been kicked around a little. He may be a little tougher.

Bobby Knight, champion basketball coach

I hated college football with a passion. I wouldn't walk across the street to see a col-

lege game—all those poor guys out there killing themselves for nothing.

Alex Karras, Hall of Fame football player, actor,
and broadcaster

It was just the fact that I enjoyed not going to class. That last period of every day had to be taken up with the sport you were participating in, so I ended up going out for every sport throughout the school year. That's how in reality I became involved in so many sports.

Chuck Howley, professional football player,
who lettered in five sports in college

I will not permit thirty men to travel four hundred miles to agitate a bag of wind.

Andrew Dickson White, president of Cornell
University, who would not allow his football
team to travel to play Michigan

I will tour the world for four years, playing tennis for the University of Miami. Then after four years of publicizing your university, you will give me a diploma.

attributed to Bobby Riggs, professional tennis
champion and legendary hustler, by Gardnar
Mulloy, professional tennis champion, to Dr. Ash,
president of University of Miami. Being turned
down, Riggs turned professional shortly after.

Jimmy Taylor, the great fullback of the Green Bay Packers, spent four years in college and emerged unscarred by education.

Dick Schaap, sportswriter, best-selling
writer, talk show host

My job is to win football games. I've got to put people in the stadium, make money for the university, keep the alumni happy, and give the school a winning reputation. If I don't win, I'm gone.

Frank Kush, college football coach

Otis Sistrunk, from the University of Mars

Alex Karras, professional football player,
broadcaster, and actor, during a Monday Night
Football game, when asked what college he went
to (real answer was none)

Scottsdale Community College Steams are called the "The Fighting Artichokes." That smarty pants name, like the cheerleader in an artichoke costume, is drollery intended to de-emphasize athletics.

George Will, writer and baseball enthusiast

Student athlete is a term susceptible to various definitions. It can mean a biochemistry major who participates in sports, or a Heisman Trophy candidate who is not necessarily a candidate for a bachelor's degree. Some student athletes are more studious than athletic, and vice versa.

Red Smith, sportswriter

Comebacks

I feel like a pussycat off the tee and a gorilla around the greens. I'm not quite there, but I'm not that far away.

Jack Nicklaus, champion professional golfer

I thought I could live off of reputation, and The Game proved me wrong. The Game taught me a lesson.

Michael Jordan, professional basketball player,
regarding his first season back in basketball
after leaving baseball

It's hard to get rid of the reputation of being a "sore-armer," but you feel in your heart you can make it back to the majors.

Bill Rives, sportswriter, referring to
Johnny Beazley, who never made it
back to the major leagues

I might say that no one at ringside tried to break my fall.

> *Jack Dempsey, champion boxer, referring to being knocked clear out of the ring by Luis Firpo, whom he knocked out in the next round*

It's like Todd has been frozen for a year-and-a-half. He's thawing out, but it takes time.

> *Rick Dempsey, professional baseball player and coach, about Todd Hundley*

I've had things handed to me and always been able to come through my career pretty quick. But this time I couldn't just come back nonchalant, I had to find the depths of myself to get back.

> *Chris Antley, professional jockey, and recovering substance addict*

The fact that I was in uniform, out there competing, it made the fans see another side of me and allowed them to learn something about recovering from cancer that maybe they'd never see or learn. A man or a woman can come back from cancer and not just exist, but produce at the same level—at a higher level.

> *Eric Davis, professional baseball player, on coming back from cancer*

The mark of the great player is his ability to come back. The great champions all have come back from defeat.

> *Sam Snead, champion professional golfer*

This is something I've waited for for almost two years. I was getting a lot of ribbing from the guys before practice, guys asking me if I remembered how to get into my stance. And that felt great, too, because I felt a part of the team again.

> *Brian Williams, professional football player, who took two years to recover from an eye injury*

When is the last time I contended? Heck, I don't think I could have contended for my club championship the last couple of years.

> *Paul Azinger, champion golfer, coming back from cancer*

You have no choice about how you lose, but you do have a choice about how you come back and prepare to win again.

> *Pat Riley, professional basketball player and coach*

Commissioner

I always dreaded this day would come and the day is here.

> *Gary Bettman, National Hockey League commissioner, speaking of the retirement of Wayne Gretzky*

Oh-h-h, my yes, I would love to be the hockey commissioner. But I don't know if I have the qualifications. You see, I can't skate.

> *Tiny Tim, musician, sports fan, when asked by a reporter if he would like to be the National Hockey League commissioner*

Competition

A competitor will find a way to win. Competitors take bad breaks and use them to drive themselves just that much harder. Quitters take bad breaks and use them as reasons to give up. It's all a matter of pride.

> *Nancy Lopez, champion professional golfer*

After eight years in the NFL, I'm convinced that the only thing that separates chumps from champions is the individual's competitive drive.

> *Joe Montana, Hall of Fame professional football player*

Compete against yourself, not others.
Peggy Fleming, Olympic gold medalist skater and broadcaster

Competing in athletics helps you face problems. In sports, you have to fight for everything you get. Nobody is going to hand you anything.
Betty Meade, champion squash player

Competitive sports teach and reaffirm for the players all the positive values of life.
Harvey S. Wiener, writer and swimmer

Hole it. I'm giving you nothing but hell today.
Gene Sarazen, champion golfer, to Walter Hagen, champion golfer, at the Professional Golfers Association championship

I am really happiest playing golf, playing tennis, playing a game, being in competition, doing something—I really come alive. That kind of life is fulfilling for me. I get a kick out of that.
Bobby Riggs, professional tennis champion and legendary hustler

I could not shrink from a challenge. If the chance was there and if—no matter how difficult it appeared—it meant winning. I was going to take it. It was the sweetness of the risk that I remembered, and not its dangers. You must play boldly to win.
Arnold Palmer, champion professional golfer

I know quite a few players who have the ability to do more. I have worked hard to be where I am. They need to work harder.
Steffi Graff, champion professional tennis player

I'm telling you, you cannot one-up this girl.
Debbie Thomas, Olympic silver medalist figure skater, about Katarina Witt, Olympic gold medalist figure skater

I'm very competitive. I want to be the best player in the world. To be that, you have to beat the best.
Annika Sorenstam, professional golfer

In golf, I'd rather Bobby Jones beat me eight and seven than for me to beat some duffer nine and eight. I've never got any fun out of beating second-rate opponents.
Dev Milburn, college football player, one of the Four Horsemen

I started racing before I ever had my driver's license. I'd be out there racing kids my age, and their dads would be out their tuning up their engines trying to make the cars run faster, and my dad was usually racing with the stock cars. I wasn't competing with the other kids, but with their dads.
Alan Kulwicki, race car driver

It is the battle, the contest, that counts, not the score. If two meet, one must win and one must lose. But they can both have a great afternoon!
Dev Milburn, college football player, one of the Four Horsemen

I've always felt that competition, stripped to its essence, is a battle of will. Skills, conditions, even luck may vary. Only one thing remains constant: break an opponent's will and you'll beat him every time.
Jim Brown, Hall of Fame football player

I would just say that we have a need to compete. It's as natural as sleeping or eating. We have a need to excel.

Ted Turner, champion yachtsman and baseball owner

Look, if my mother put on a helmet and shoulder pads and a uniform that wasn't the same as the one I was wearing, I'd run over *her* if she was in my way.

Bo Jackson, professional baseball and football player

Ski racing chose me—I was thrown into it because it was all around me. And because I discovered I had a strong, competitive spirit, I stayed with it.

Jean-Claude Killy, Olympic gold medalist skier

There's no denying the pleasure of kicking your compadres' collective butts.

Fred Matheny, cyclist and writer

We Americans are a competitive race. We bet on anything. We love to win.

George S. Patton, U.S. general

We knew if we weren't in awe of them we could play them.

Kevin Ault, college basketball player

What, me help another discus thrower? I would make recommendations that would be very difficult for him to follow—have him concentrate on something that had absolutely no relation to his problems.

Al Oerter, Olympic champion discus thrower

When you step on that field, you cannot concede a thing.

Gayle Sayers, Hall of Fame football player

When we're on the road, they are like my family. But when qualifying starts, they are the opposition.

Dario Franchetti, automobile racer, about some of his friend/competitors

You are never really playing an opponent. You are playing yourself, your own highest standards, and when you reach your limits, that is real joy.

Arthur Ashe, champion tennis player and writer

Composure

The ballplayer who loses his head, who can't keep his cool, is worse than no ballplayer at all.

Lou Gehrig, Hall of Fame baseball player

People have said it's going to be a boxing match, a rumble in the jungle. It's hard to play body to body and not get into a skirmish. But a cool head has to prevail.

Chris Childs, professional basketball player

Concentration

Concentration is the ability to think about absolutely nothing when it is absolutely necessary.

Ray Knight, professional baseball player and manager

I never hit a careless shot in my life. I bet only a quarter but I play each shot as if it were for a championship. I concentrate as hard for a quarter as I do for a championship.

Walter J. Travis, professional golfer

The secret of shooting is concentration.
Bill Bradley, basketball player and U.S. senator

You think of the ball *first,* and *then* what's coming for you down the field. Reverse the order, and you've got yourself a fumble.
Tommy Watkins, professional football player

Confidence

All of a sudden, I lacked that confidence and that energy it takes to be any athlete.
Julie Krone, professional jockey

Coach, after all the shit we've been through, there is no way we lose tonight.
Michael Jordan, professional basketball player, to Bobby Knight, college coach, a note taped to Knight's blackboard before the Gold Medal game in the 1980 Olympics

Confidence is a lot of this game or any game. If you don't think you can win, you won't.
Jerry West, Hall of Fame basketball player and executive

Confidence is everything. From there, it's a small step to winning.
Craig Stadler, champion professional golfer

I always thought I could play pro ball. I had confidence in my ability. You have to. If you don't, who will?
Johnny Unitas, Hall of Fame football player

I don't consider myself a lesser known. . . . When I'm playing with Norman or Fred Couples, I feel I'm as good as them. If you don't, you don't belong out here.
Scott McCarren, professional golfer

I knew I was going to be a champ when I was ten.
John Newcombe, champion tennis player

I really lack the words to compliment myself today.
Alberto Tomba, Olympic gold medalist skier

No one can guard me one-on-one. I'm not afraid of anyone in this league.
Allen Iverson, professional basketball player

What you're thinking, what shape your mind is in, is what makes the biggest difference of all.
Willie Mays, Hall of Fame baseball player

Whenever he was able to impart his confidence, that part of the game just sparkled.
Frank Clarke, football player, about Tom Landry, Hall of Fame coach

I knew I wasn't going to be average.
Chamique Holdsclaw, basketball player

The ones who believed in themselves the most were the ones who won.
Florence Griffith-Joyner, Olympic medalist track and field competitor

Without confidence a golfer is little more than a hacker.
Bobby Jones, champion golfer

Confrontation

He can run, but he can't hide.
Joe Louis, champion boxer, about Billy Conn, before a title bout

Consistency

My dad taught me about the importance of consistency. He told me if you're consistent, you can last longer.

Ken Griffey, Jr., professional baseball player

This game is like the N.C.A.A. tournament. Coaches rise up and win one now and then, but there's only one John Wooden. I think I have proved I can sustain that high level of excellence, and I believe we're going to be this good for a long time.

D. Wayne Lukas, thoroughbred horse trainer

Consolation Game

Consolation affairs attract all the attention of a bunion at a nudist colony.

Blackie Sherrod, sportswriter

Control

Control the elements, control what's inside of you.

John Chaney, college basketball coach

To me the game is a question of control: control yourself, control your emotions, control of your opponent.

Fred Perry, professional tennis champion

Corbett, Gentleman Jim

(b. Sept. 1, 1866; d. Feb. 18, 1933) *World Heavyweight Champion, 1892–1897*

I honestly think he is better than Benny Leonard. He's the greatest thing I have ever seen in the ring. I learned plenty.

Gene Tunney, champion boxer, speaking after an exhibition match with the aging, ex-champion Corbett (Leonard was a then top-ranked contender)

Cosell, Howard

(b. Mar. 25, 1920; d. Apr. 23, 1995) *Broadcaster of* Monday Night Football *and* Wide World of Sports

Everything you've ever heard about Howard Cosell, good and bad, is true. But it's probably understated.

Roy Firestone, broadcaster

Arrogant, pompous, obnoxious, vain, cruel, verbose, a show off. I have been called all of these. Of course, I am.

Howard Cosell, broadcaster

A voice that had all the resonance of a clogged Dristan bottle.

1973 Year Book, Encyclopedia Brittanica

Get that nigger-loving Jew bastard off the air. Football is an American game.

Anonymous letter received by ABC during the first year of Monday Night Football *about Howard Cosell*

If Howard Cosell was a sport, it would be Roller Derby.

Jimmy Cannon, sportswriter

I tell it like it is. Howard Cosell tells it like Roone Arledge wants it told.

Harry Caray, broadcaster

Courage

The miracle isn't that I finished . . . The miracle is that I had the courage to start.

John Bingham, runner and writer

To uncover your true potential you must first find your own limits and then you have to have the courage to blow past them.

Picabo Street, Olympic medalist skier

Crenshaw, Ben

(b. Jan. 11, 1952) *Champion golfer; won two Masters*

He can't keep his ball in the fairway. I've told him that he might have a tan like mine if he didn't spend so much time in the trees.

Lee Trevino, champion professional golfer

Crew Chief

As crew chief, I have one philosophy—to be everyone's friend. I like to be one of the guys, but at the same time I have to be the boss too. I like to treat them like I wanted to be treated when I was doing their job.

Andy Petree, crew chief

Cricket

April: This is the time of year when the sentimental cricketer withdraws his bat tenderly from its winter bed and croons over it, as if it were a Stradivarius or a shoulder of mutton.

R. C. Robertson-Glasgow, sportswriter

Athletics, unlike cricket, is a sport in which individual brilliance can be measured, regardless of the quality of the competition.

Peter Lovesey, writer

Call me sad, but like a substantial minority of other Scots, I actually enjoy cricket.

Neil Robertson, sportswriter, columnist

Cricket is the only game where you are playing eleven of the other side and ten of your own.

G. H. Hardy, mathematician

For a cricket fan America is a sporting Sarah.

Tunku Varadarajan, writer

Half the charm of cricket is its ever changing patterns.

T. Baily, Championship Cricket

I couldn't bat for the length of time required to score 500. I'd get bored and fall over.

Dennis Compton, writer

England lacked—why do I use the past tense, let us say it lacks—gumption, guts, class, technique, battle, ability, panache, sinew, courage, pride, passion, determination, vim and depth. The team is a mournful gaggle of trundlers and plodders, which will be blown away, game after game. . . .

Tunku Varadarajan, professor of law and sportswriter, speaking of the England team before an international test match

I do love cricket—it's so very English.

Sarah Bernhardt, actress

I have always looked upon cricket as organized loafing.

William Temple, Archbishop of Canterbury

I tend to believe that cricket is the greatest thing that God ever created on earth . . . certainly greater than sex, although sex isn't too bad either.

Harold Pinter, playwright

It's a funny kind of month, October. For the really keen cricket fan, it's when you realize your wife left you in May.

Dennis Norden, comedian

It's as exciting as mailing letters.
Pat Hayden, professional football player and
Rhodes scholar

Like the British Constitution, cricket was not made; it has "grown."
Neville Cardus, English Cricket

Is there life after cricket?
Marvin Cohen, The Time Factor

Cricket is a team game of individual encounter.
J. M. Kilburn, cricketer

A fast bowler who doesn't get results has no future.
John Snow, cricketer

On the day I can't play cricket anymore, I'll do as them Romans did—I'll get into a 'ot bath and cut my ruddy throat!
Cecil Parkin, cricketer

The bowler's Holding, the batman's Willey.
attributed to a BBC broadcaster by Steve
Rushin, sportswriter, referring to a match
wherein the opposing players were Michael
Holding and Peter Willey

The new woman is taking up cricket evidently with the same energy which has characterized her other and more important spheres of life.
Cricket magazine, in 1895

There is no such thing as a crisis in cricket, only the next ball.
W. R. Grace, cricketer

There's no use hitting me there, there's nothing in it.
Derek Randall, cricketer, after being hit on the
head by a bouncer from Dennis Lillee

They came to see me bat not to see you bowl.
W. G. Grace, cricketer, at a famous match in
which he was bowled first ball

Polite baseball.
K. A. Auty, cricketer and writer

Croquet

Depend upon it, croquet is the game of the future. It wants writing, though.
George Eliot, novelist

He has the true croquet spirit. He trusts no one but himself; never concedes—no matter far behind he may be—and hates his opponents with an all-enduring hate.
Moss Hart, playwright and screenwriter, on
Darryl Zanuck, movie producer

In some people's minds croquet is a quaint and literally gentle Victorian game in which good sportsmanship and polite manners carry the day. Yet to anyone who has played the game often, the inaccuracy of this image is as close at hand as your favorite mallet.
Christopher R. Reaske, writer and
croquet player

I would rather see our youth playing football with the danger of an occasional broken collarbone than to see them dedicated to croquet.
John Cavanaugh, president
Notre Dame University

Kahn's course was flat and as smooth as a billiard table.
Harpo Marx, actor, speaking about
Otto Kahn's croquet lawn

Keep your temper and remember when your turn comes.

A. Rover, writer and croquet player

Recently a Connecticut couple married thirty-three years, got a legal separation, the man explaining "his wife was not aggressive enough in croquet mixed-doubles."

Dynamic Maturity, *1974*

Rutherford B. Hayes also liked to play croquet on the White House lawn, but even there the Democrats would not let him alone. They charged he had squandered six dollars of taxpayers' money for a set of fancy boxwood croquet balls.

Roger Butterfield, historian

Talbott's estate was particularly prized for its glass-smooth croquet court. One evening in the late 1920's, in a scene worthy of Gatsby, several of the Round Table's diehard croquet fanatics fought off the falling darkness by driving their cars through the shrubbery to the perimeter of the course. In the cross-hatch of beams their headlights threw on the lawn, they played all night.

James R. Gaines, writer, referring to the wits of the Algonquin Round Table

The ingenuity of man has never conceived of anything better calculated to bring out all the evil passions of humanity than the so-called game of croquet . . . Our forefathers early recognized the insidious wickedness of the game and rooted it out.

Living Age *magazine, in 1898*

The ladies will very much oblige all their associates in croquet by avoiding long dresses, which are continually dragging the balls about over the ground greatly to the annoyance of the players and disturbance of the game.

A. Rover, writer and croquet player

There are really two great moments for a croquet player, aside from winning the game. The first is when he is introduced to croquet. The second is when he feels he is good enough to order his own mallet with his initials on top of the handle.

Peter Maas, writer

The workmen have come out . . . to mow the lawn into perfect smoothness, and make it as even as we trust the paths of the players may be through life.

Harper's Weekly, *in 1871*

When staying with Sir Edward Cassel he was often pitted against the Duchess of Sermoneta, who was not only extremely pretty but also a very bad player so that a game with her always put him in a good mood.

Christopher Hibbert, historian, referring to King Edward VII, of England

Crying

I remember sitting in the corner of the locker room, crying my head off.

Dave Meggyesy, professional football player and political activist, addressing a loss and the question of whether athletes cry

Curling

It is the broom that wins the battle.

Rev. John Kerr, curler

Cycling

A lot of Americans regard European racing with too much reverence.

Kent Gordis, American cyclist

An Army from Mars could invade France, the government could fall, and even the recipe for sauce Bernaise be lost, but if it happened during the Tour de France nobody would notice.

Red Smith, sportswriter

As I get into the countryside, I have the feeling that nobody else exists. The world is there for me, and as I cycle on, everything happening around me seems specially put there by nature for my personal enjoyment.

Jean-Claude Killy, Olympic gold medalist skier

Cycling is necessarily a constant series of descents.

H. G. Wells, writer

Everybody says how hard a marathon is, but twenty-five thousand people show up for one in New York. Only two hundred people can enter the Tour de France, and it takes years to get there because you can't just sign yourself up for it.

Greg LeMond, champion cyclist

Fix a man's bike and he'll ride for a day,
Teach a man to fix his bike and he'll ride
      forever.
      Attributed to anonymous by Allen St. John,
      cyclist and writer

Get a bicycle. You will never regret it if you live.

Mark Twain, writer and humorist

Hurrah, hurrah, for the merry wheel,
With tires of rubber and spokes of steel;
We seem to fly on the airy steeds
With eagle's flight in silent speed.
      Wheelman, a turn of the century cycling journal

I have always struggled to achieve excellence. One thing that cycling has taught me is that if you can achieve something without a struggle it's not going to be satisfying.

Greg LeMond, cyclist

If I had never had cancer, I would never have won the Tour de France. I'm convinced of that. I wouldn't want to do it all over again, but I wouldn't want to change a thing.

Lance Armstrong, champion cyclist, winner of
Tour de France, cancer survivor

I'll tell you what racing's about. It's about suffering. It's about pain—racing hurts.

Andrew Juskaitis, cyclist and writer

It's professional cycling and the killer instinct comes out after 170 miles.

Jackie Simes, U.S. cycling team director

It would not be at all strange if history came to the conclusion that the perfection of the bicycle was the greatest incident of the nineteenth century.

Detroit Tribune, *in 1896*

Look at it closely and you'll see that a bicycle frame has more triangles than a *Dynasty* rerun.

Allen St. John, cyclist and writer

Many a woman is riding to the suffrage on a bicycle.

Elizabeth Cady Stanton, suffrage leader

Most people underperform because their training lacks purpose. They don't have a plan, so they ride too hard or too easy.

Massimo Testa, champion cyclist

My job was to work for Hinault. He was the only rider on our team with a shot at the win

and we had to make sure he had minimum effort throughout the race. That meant bringing back break aways and making sure that at the end of the race we kept up a good pace.

Johnathan Boyer, cyclist

My job is to help the team. We're here to protect the yellow jersey, and I'm here to protect it.

Frankie Andreu, professional champion cyclist

Nowadays, if there is an elopement, a stagnation in the peanut market, a glut in smoking tobacco, or a small attendance at the theaters, everyone who is a loser points to that bicycle and says, "You did it."

Bicycle World, *in 1898*

Quite a number of our young men, who formerly were addicted to stupid habits, and seeking of nonsensical distractions and vulgar pleasures, are now vigorous, healthy, energetic, and for the sake of this extraordinary machine submit themselves to an ascetic rule of life, and, induced by taste and passion, acquire habits of temperance, the imperative desire of quiet and regular living, and most important of all, the steady exercise of self-control.

Henri Desgranges, founder of the Tour de France, in 1895

Ride lots.

Eddy Merckx, cyclist

Sprinting is a function of three elements—fast pedaling, the power to turn the big gear and your position in the group.

Fred Matheny, writer and cyclist

The fellow who is ambitious to ride a century every Sunday belongs in the category

with the prize pie eater and the one who enters gorging and guzzling contests.

The New York Herald, *1890s*

There is something uncanny in the noiseless rush of the cyclist, as he comes into view, passes by, and disappears.

Popular Science, *in 1891*

The notion of transforming this recreation into a mode of mass transit is PC looniness of legendary proportion.

Brock Yates, cyclist

The Tour de France may be finished, but it feels as though no one told my body.

Frankie Andreu, cyclist and writer

This is the home of the yellow jersey.

Stuart O'Grady, champion cyclist, his home answering machine message

Thoughtful people . . . believe that the bicycle will accomplish more for women's sensible dress than all the reform movements that have ever been waged.

Demerarest's Family Magazine, *in 1895*

Threadless streeters, sleeveless jerseys, clipless pedals. Why does the bike biz have this penchant for naming things after things they aren't?

Don Cuerdon, cyclist and writer

What do you call a cyclist who doesn't wear a helmet? An organ donor.

David Perry, cyclist and writer

Wheelies looked impressive when you were 12, and they still look cool today. But even if you're on a circus-clown career track, wheelies

are more than just flashy stuff—they're mighty useful besides.

Andrew Juskaitis, cyclist and writer

When you're out peddling, you smell the blossoms blooming, feel your heart pumping, and remind yourself that life is good.

Shair Karin, cyclist

Your legs will turn to rubber after three days. You'll get the worst case of crotch rot you can possibly imagine. And some lonesome lumberjack is gonna see you ride by in those tight black shorts and those purple shoes, and he's gonna chase you down, and make you squeal like a pig.

Bike shop manager to David Nolan,
outdoor journalist, when the latter
told the former he was going to be
biking through the Canadian wilderness

Darts

You don't have to be a beer drinker to play darts, but it helps.

Anonymous

Dawkins, Darryl

(b. Jan. 11, 1957) *National Basketball Association All-Star; famous for shattering backboards during NBA games*

Everyone knows he used to call himself "Chocolate Thunder." But on the nights he didn't play well we used to call him "Chocolate Blunder."

Michael Ray Richardson, professional basketball player, teammate

Daytona 500

It's the largest picnic in the world.

Peter Golenboch, sportswriter

Death

As a traveling sportswriter, Death has been a constant companion on the road. This can be vexing, especially when Death gets the aisle seat on airplanes.

Steve Rushin, sportswriter

Can you believe it, Joy? Can you believe this shit?

Brian Piccolo, professional football player, to his wife, Joy, as he lay dying of cancer. He was dead three hours later.

Crikey—he's the heir to the throne . . . If he crashes, I'll be the heir to the bloody Tower.

Graham Hill, champion race car driver, trailing his own Formula 2 car being driven by Prince Charles, at over 160 mph

Death? I give it a quick, glancing thought.

Juan Manuel Fangio, champion race car driver

Everybody wants to go to heaven, but nobody wants to die.

Joe Louis, champion professional boxer

Every good hunter is uneasy when faced with the death he is about to inflict.

José Ortega y Gasset, philosopher

I don't want to find out I've lost my reflexes when I'm in a race car. I want to be ahead of that.

Arie Luyendyk, race car driver

If I close my eyes and meditate, I can still see them.

Jimmy Murphy, assistant soccer manager, about eight soccer players from the 1958 Manchester United team who died in a snowy plane crash at Munich Airport

It is so pleasant to sit and do nothing—and therefore so dangerous. Death through exhaustion is—like death through freezing—a pleasant one.

Reinhold Messner, mountain climber

It hurts when you lose friends. But, this is our business. Death and injury are part of the sport.

A. J. Foyt, champion race car driver

I love you. Sleep well, my sweetheart. Please don't worry too much.

Rob Hall, mountain climber and guide, his last words via radio and satellite to his wife, as he froze to death on the side of Everest

It's been a good 'un.

Don Meredith, professional football player and broadcaster, to a fellow passenger when it was thought his flight was going to crash

Mummy—a plane has crashed in fog at Arkley golf course on its way from Marseilles to Elstree . . . They think Daddy's dead.

Damon Hill, son of Graham Hill, champion race car driver; the child reported it to his mother during a dinner party. He had seen it on television.

Now you will not swell the rout
Of lads that wore their honors out,
Runners whom renown outran
And the name died before the man.

A. E. Housman, poet

The casualty rate is three or four times higher than any other sport. Last year, we had nine deaths, quite a few broken backs, and quite a few paralyzed.

Eddie Arroyo, jockey

The championships were canceled due to the death of the entire American team in a plane crash at Brussels.

United States Figure Skating Association Press Guide, entry for the 1961 champion, in its list of champions

The plain truth is that I knew better but went to Everest anyway. And in doing so I was a party to the death of a good many people, which is something that is apt to remain on my conscience for a very long time.

Jon Krakauer, outdoorsman, mountain climber, journalist

The others are all dead—I am too weak to push the button on the radio any longer—this is my last transmission—goodbye.

Elvira Shataeva, mountain climber, who was the last of eight Russian women climbers lost during the ascent of the High Pamirs

Well, this should be interesting.

Dr. Tom Waddell, Olympic decathlon competitor and gay rights activist, died of AIDS, his last words

When I can't play tennis anymore, I'll die.

Bill Tilden, professional tennis champion, who played the day before he died

When men take up a dangerous sport some must expect to die.

> Yachting World *magazine, referring to the 1979 Fastnet Race*

You always feel bad when your fellow yachtsmen drown. But you never can really be completely prepared for what nature has in store.

> *Ted Turner, champion yachtsman and baseball owner*

You just have to treat death like any other part of life.

> *Tom Sneva, champion race car driver*

You know the risks, you accept them. If a man can't look at danger and still go on, man has stopped living. If the worst ever happens—then it means simply that I've been asked to pay the bill for the happiness of my life—without a moment's regret.

> *Graham Hill, champion race car driver, the last words of his autobiography, which he was writing when he was killed in an airplane accident*

Decisions

Like throwing the ball out of bounds. All the crowd knows is that the ball was thrown out of bounds. A quarterback knows that his receiver was covered.

> *Y. A. Tittle, Hall of Fame quarterback*

Dedication

Most of my time was spent racing, so I did miss out on some of the things the other kids did. But I never have regretted it.

> *Jeff Gordon, champion race car driver*

Defeat

Defeat creates orphaned thoughts.

> *Madeleine Blais, writer*

Losing is no disgrace if you've given your best.

> *Jim Palmer, baseball player*

The taste of defeat has a richness of experience all its own.

> *Bill Bradley, Hall of Fame basketball player and U.S. senator*

You never really lose until you stop trying.

> *Mike Ditka, football player and coach*

Defense

Any time your defense gives up more points than a basketball team, you're in trouble.

> *Lou Holtz, college and professional football coach*

The art of defense is really an art based on hard work.

> *Bill Russell, Hall of Fame basketball player and coach*

Tonight we played defense like the Washington Generals trying out for the next Harlem Globetrotters game.

> *Rick Pitino, professional basketball coach and collegiate champion coach, remarking on a poor showing by his Boston Celtics after being blown out by the mediocre New Jersey Nets*

Dempsey, Jack

(b. June 24, 1895; d. May 31, 1983) *World Heavyweight Champion 1919–1926*

His complete intent was an opponent's destruction. He was a fighter—one who used every trick to wreck the other fighter. Yet outside the ring, Jack is one of the gentlest men I know.

> *Grantland Rice, sportswriter*

I don't know why I did that. I guess it was just instinct. But later, I thought to myself, "My God, they could have shot or stabbed me."

> *Jack Dempsey, world champion boxer, discussing how he knocked out two muggers with his bare hands when he himself was already a senior citizen*

I'll take on Dempsey any time in any street he wants to name. I'll knock him out for nothing.

> *Harry Willis, a.k.a. the Brown Panther, the black boxing champion whose shot at Dempsey and the championship was blocked by racism*

More than any other individual, Jack Dempsey created big-time sports in America.

> *Roger Kahn, best-selling writer*

The public suddenly saw him in a new light, the two-handed fighter who stormed forward, a flame of pure fire in the ring, strong and native, affable, easy of speech, close to the people in word and deed and feeling.

> *John Lardner, writer*

Whenever I hear the name, Jack Dempsey, I think of an America that was one big roaring camp of miners, drifters, bunkhouse hands, con men, hard cases, men who lived by their fists and by their shooting irons and by the cards they drew.

> *Jim Murray, sportswriter*

Designated Hitter

I'll soften my answer by just saying that it's appalling.

> *A. Bartlett Giamatti, Major League Baseball comissioner*

It relieves the manager of all responsibility except to post the lineup card on the dugout wall and make sure everybody gets to the airport on time.

> *Red Smith, sportswriter*

Desire

Ever to be the best and to surpass others.

> *Achilles in* The Odyssey, *by Homer*

I have got to make it here. I just can't go back to Louisiana and Arkansas. I've been there and I know what's there.

> *Lou Brock, Hall of Fame baseball player, about making the major leagues*

I haven't run as fast as I can, I haven't spoken as well as I can, and I haven't written as well as I can. If you take any less than that view, you're finished.

> *George Sheehan, runner and writer*

It doesn't matter about your coach so much if you have the desire to win. You got to have it. It's not boring if you're winning.

> *Hank Kashiwa, downhiller, U.S. ski team*

Somebody asked me, "Does this place owe you one?" I don't believe in things getting owed to you. I think you go out there and you play well enough to get them yourself.

> *Greg Norman, champion golfer*

There is no way you will ever be a great player unless *you* want it.

> *Bobby Knight, champion college*
> *basketball coach*

Who wants to play in a game that means nothing?

> *Roberto Clemente, Hall of Fame*
> *baseball player*

You can make a man hustle by fining him. But you can't teach him desire. It's there or it isn't.

> *Johnny Keane, professional baseball manager*

You would have to take a stun gun or whatever and shoot him to get him off that court. He's going to leave it all out there.

> *Jeff Van Gundy, professional basketball coach,*
> *about Patrick Ewing, who played an*
> *entire game with a torn Achilles tendon in the*
> *playoffs and out-scored and out-rebounded the*
> *opposing player to lead the team to a win*

Determination

If desire is what we want and dedication is the price we pay to get what we want, then determination is what keeps us there.

> *Dennis Green, professional football coach*

It's not whether you get knocked down, it's whether you get up.

> *Vince Lombardi, Hall of Fame professional*
> *football coach*

They're going to beat me, a good fake has got to beat me, but the thing is not to give up.

> *Night Train Lane, professional football player*

DiMaggio, Joe

(b. Nov. 25, 1914; d. Mar. 8, 1999) *Hall of Fame baseball player; won 10 World Championships; holds all-time record for hitting safely in a game—56 games*

Joe, put on a uniform—they can use you.

> *Henry Kissinger, U.S. secretary of state to*
> *DiMaggio after a Yankee playoff loss in the*
> *1990s*

Where have you gone Joe DiMaggio
A lonely nation turns its eyes to you.

> *Paul Simon, singer and songwriter,*
> *from the song "Mrs. Robinson"*

DiMaggio even looks good striking out.

> *Ted Williams, Hall of Fame baseball player*
> *and champion fisherman*

DiMaggio's streak is the most extraordinary thing that ever happened in American sports.

> *Stephen Jay Gould, writer*

He was the perfect Hemingway hero . . . His grace and skill were always on display, his emotions always concealed.

> *David Halberstam, writer*

It was so wonderful, Joe. You've never heard such cheering.

> *Marilyn Monroe to her then husband, Joe*
> *DiMaggio, after appearing in front of troops in*
> *Korea. DiMaggio replied simply: "Yes I have."*

I would like to take the great DiMaggio fishing. They say his father was a fisherman.

> *Ernest Hemingway,* The Old Man and the Sea

This son of Italian immigrants gave every American something to believe in. He

became the very symbol of American grace, power and skill.

William Jefferson Clinton,
president of the United States

Diving

Hockey players get hit in the face with a puck and they get fifty stitches and then come out and play the rest of the game. You only have four stitches, and you only have to do two dives.

Ron O'Brien, U.S. Olympic
diving coach, to Greg Louganis

The irony about divers is that, like dancers, we were never the healthiest lot.

Greg Louganis, Olympic gold medalist diver

Doctors

I'd like to find me a plastic surgeon and have my face redone. I'd play a year in college, get drafted number two overall in the NFL draft, take the league's money, put it in the bank, and then have the plastic surgeon restore my original face.

Dexter Manley, professional football player, who
was banned for life by the National Football
League for substance abuse

If the doctors had told me that I might die playing football, I'd have asked them what the chances were—"Give me the odds, Doc"—that's how much I wanted to play.

Jack Youngblood, professional football player

I have two good doctors—my right leg and my left.

Anonymous

Get your ass out of my office, Dr. Dayton. You've got ten minutes to clean your shit out of my locker room and ten more minutes to get off campus. I'll mail your last check.

Paul "Bear" Bryant, Hall of Fame college
football coach, to the team doctor of the Texas
A&M, whom he felt was too protective of players

Medicine is just about life and death. Sports is more important than that.

Andrew Edgar, philosopher

The joker got funny and said he found urine in my whiskey. I fired him.

Ty Cobb, Hall of Fame baseball player

Dog Shows

How many other times a year do you get to see dogs with better haircuts than their owners?

Linda Stasi, journalist

I am struck by an irony central to the lot of a purebred dog: As it attains the hallmarks of its breed, it seems to simultaneously relinquish its basic dogginess, until it is less a dog . . .

Jean Hanff Korelitz, journalist

I took her to a show in New Jersey when she was 6 months and 3 days old to get her used to shows—the car, the throwing up, the night in the motel—and she hated it. Every time we picked her up she peed on us. Then we took her to Maine, and she liked it a little better. . . .

Nonie Reynders, owner-handler
of Norwich terriers

She's never shown better. People say she's better the second time around. She's the Tina Turner of Dogs.

Michael Canalizo, handler of Afghan hound Ch. Tryst of Grandeur, commenting that she was one of the favorites to win the show after not being on the dog show circuit for two years

She's not getting married or anything. She's a showgirl so she's going to have a string of affairs.

Fran Sunseri, owner of Salilyn 'N Erin's Shameless (a.k.a. Samantha), a Springer spaniel, winner of the 2000 Westminster Kennel Club Dog Show, when asked what the dog was going to do, as she was being retired from the ring

The bitch is back! After two years of male domination, the venerable Westminster Kennel Club awarded its top award last night to a Norwich terrier bitch. . . .

Gersh Kuntzman, writer

The participants are extremely competitive people. That dog out there is an extension of your ego. There's a lot of backbiting—"That dog's had plastic surgery," which is illegal, or "That judge is fixed." You don't see many good losers.

Michael Stern, writer

This is a dog show, after all.

Roger Caras, announcer, writer, humane activist, after a German shorthair pointer relieved itself in the ring during the Westminster Kennel Club Dog Show

TV is going to the dogs tonight: USA is televising the "Westminster Dog Show," while Fox is presenting yet another blood-and-mayhem sweeps special.

David Bianculli, media critic and columnist

Welcome to the . . . Westminster Kennel Club Dog Show, where the dogs don't act

like dogs, the people sometimes fight like them.

Rick Hampson, journalist

Double Plays

These are the saddest words—
Tinker to Evers to Chance.
Picking forever our gonfalon bubble,
Causing a Giant to hit into a double,
Words that are heavy with nothing but
    trouble,
Tinker to Evers to Chance.

Frank Adams, sportswriter

Draft (the)

In pro football the college draft is what makes good teams great, as the youngsters imbue a team with their youth and enthusiasm, pushing the veterans to play harder, and sometimes pushing them out.

Peter Golenboch, sportswriter

It's sure different. I don't want to make a habit of it.

Jerry Krause, team executive, after being in the National Basketball Association lottery for the first time, a season after winning the championship six out of the previous eight years

I was a very late draft choice of the Mittendorf Funeral Home Panthers. Our color was black.

George Will, author and baseball enthusiast, about his Little League draft

We avoided guys who could play the piano.

Paul Brown, football coach and team owner

We don't take underclassmen.
Red Auerbach, basketball executive, on why the Celtics passed on Julius Erving

We would have moved up to take a sexier player, but we were very cautious about doing something just to be sexy.
George Seifert, professional football coach

Whenever you draft, your chances of being wrong are much greater than being right. Every time you take a player, you leave behind six hundred or so others, and chances are that some of them will turn out to be better than the guy you took. No matter how you slice it, the numbers are against you.
Bill Tobin, team executive

Drinking

Colonel Jacob Ruppert makes millions of gallons of beer and Ruth is of the opinion that he can drink it faster than the Colonel and his large corps of brewmasters can make it. Well, you can't! Nobody can!
"Gentleman" Jimmy Walker, mayor of New York, speaking at a banquet honoring Babe Ruth, where he admonished him for his drinking, whereupon Ruth swore not to abuse alcohol anymore, and went on to have one of his best seasons

Drugs

A guy strung out on cocaine cares about setting an example for kids? He cares about stuffing his nose with cocaine. Period.
Jim Brown, Hall of Fame football player

All I really need to know about drugs is that you can't take them and play golf.
Nancy Lopez, champion professional golfer

America discovered cocaine for the first time in the mid-70s. Back then cocaine was the drug you heard about. It was Donna Summer and Barry White and disco music and limousines and *Hollywooooood.*
Thomas "Hollywood" Henderson, professional football player and recovery counselor

Being responsible for yourself, about knowing why you get high an' why you don't need to get high. You know what I'm sayin'? Some guys don't know that they don't need to get high.
Dirk Minnefield, professional basketball player

Drugs are very much on the scene in professional sports today, but when you think about it, golf is the only sport where the players aren't penalized for playing on grass.
Bob Hope, comedian and actor

How many great athletes need to die or have their careers ruined before they get the message? I don't respect anyone who uses drugs. It's so obvious that drugs do nothing but debilitate your mind and your body and, no matter who you are or how old you are, drugs will destroy you sooner or later.
Larry Bird, Hall of Fame basketball player and coach, from a statement issued after the death of Len Bias

I'd always tried to be the best at anything I did . . . I was the best drug addict going. I took great pride in doing it right.
Maury Wills, professional baseball player, broadcaster, and manager

I don't know. I never smoked Astroturf.
Tug McGraw, professional baseball player, when asked if he preferred grass or Astroturf

If I don't make it to the NBA, I'm gonna be a drug dealer. Somehow I gotta get me a Lexus. Whatever it takes.
Booger Smith, high school basketball player, the opening line of the documentary Soul in the Hole

If track is serious about ridding the sport of illegal drugs, then a separate organization is needed, whose only duty is to catch cheaters, regardless of the potential media impact.
Steve Holman, Olympic runner

I got caught in Seoul, lost my gold medal, and I'm here to tell people in this country it's wrong to cheat, not to take it, and it's bad for your health. I started taking steroids when I was nineteen years old because most of the world-class athletes were taking drugs.
Ben Johnson, champion track and field competitor, who was stripped of an Olympic gold medal for testing positive for steroid use

I had good results without doping, but pressure from the sponsors forced me to jump the gun. It was a personal decision . . . I have made a mistake.
Alex Zulle, champion cyclist

In the quest for the winning edge, the advantage over one's opponent, many athletes have opted to dig deeper into their pharmaceutical grab bag.
Fredrick C. Hatfield, writer

It's terrible for the sport but in a strange way it may be good for the sport. This tells all the riders that no matter how much of a star you are,

no matter what race you are leading, you can be caught and punished if you are using drugs.
Bernard Thevenet, champion cyclist and broadcaster, about the drug crackdowns in the European tours

I've got enough problems keeping myself under control without putting some shit in my body that's supposed to make me wild. I do all right on that without any help.
Dennis Rodman, professional basketball player

My high comes from victory. Sports are my drugs.
Jean-Claude Killy, Olympic gold medalist skier

Never has a urine sample been given with such enthusiasm.
Dan Jansen, Olympic gold medalist speed skater, after "holding it in" so that he could deal with a throng of reporters after his last Olympic gold medal

The poor horse got to his feet and galloped for ten miles away from the course; a lucky thing for the trainer, because the horse was not found in time to be given a saliva test.
Dick Francis, champion jockey and novelist, referring to a horse that fell and then ran off a track and away after being given a dose of performance-enhancing drugs

What you had was a thirty-nine-year-old male, 6-foot-5, in excess of 300 pounds, a healthy individual, took one shot of heroin and basically dropped dead as a result.
Bruce Glassrock, Plano, Texas, police chief, on the death of Mark Tuinei

I am a rich man. Just look at my arms. All of my money is in my veins.
Earl Manigault, Harlem playground basketball legend and ex-convict

We won it at the fitba and cocaine's the fitba player's drug. It doesnae stey in the system for long so ye can beat the random tests. So it has to be charlie. It's only appropriate that the money should stay in the game.

Irvine Welsh, Scottish novelist, from Trainspotting

Dunks

From this day on you shall refer to that historic tribute to interplanetary strength as "Chocolate Thunder Flying, Robinzine Crying, Teeth Shaking, Glass Breaking, Rump Roasting, Bun Toasting, Wham Bam, Glass Breaker I Am Jam." Hopefully, that will satisfy everyone who has been bugging me to put a name on that dunk.

Darryl Dawkins, professional basketball player

He stays up so long he has to file a flight plan with the FAA when he dunks.

Darryl Dawkins, professional basketball player, referring to Michael Jordan

The 360-windmill was just the warm-up act, a perfect score that put Carter in catch-me-if-you-can mode. For the rest of them playing the Washington General Dunks to Carter's Globetrotters, it was enough to just sit back and hope for a miss that just didn't happen.

Chris Young, sportswriter, referring to the 2000 National Basketball Association All-Star Slam-Dunk Contest

When Darryl broke that backboard, it was one of the greatest things I ever saw happen in sports history.

Joe Namath, Hall of Fame football player, referring to Darryl Dawkins, professional basketball player

When Darryl jammed that dunk, he didn't just break the rim off the backboard—that backboard exploded.

Neil Funk, sportswriter

Durocher, Leo

(b. Jul. 27, 1905; d. Oct. 7, 1991) *Major League Baseball manager; won one World Series and three pennants*

Durocher played people, not colors.

Bill White, baseball player and league executive

He's no Boy Scout, but he understands people. You'll get no special favors from him, but neither will anybody else.

Monte Irvin, professional baseball player

Earnhardt, Dale

(b. Apr. 29, 1952; d. Feb. 18, 2001) *Champion race car driver; won NASCAR seven times; won Daytona 500*

Dale was a lot of fun to race against because he had a cockiness about him. He was full of himself, but there was a funness about him. He enjoyed driving race cars, had a good time doing it.

Jeff Hammond, crew chief

Eating

There are two opposing schools about breakfast. If you knew you were not going to be into fish for two or three hours, a good big breakfast would be the thing. Maybe it is a good thing anyway but I do not want to trust it, so drink a glass of vichy, a glass of cold milk and eat a piece of Cuban bread, read the papers and walk down to the boat. I have hooked them on a full stomach in that sun and I do not want to hook any more that way.

Ernest Hemingway, Nobel Prize–winning writer

Edge (the)

If somebody wants to get an edge on me, they'll have to search for the cracks themselves. They will have to find that advantage themselves. I'm not going to give it to them.

Chuck Knox, professional football coach

There's the guy who says, "Even if I go Oh for three, when I get home I'm just Dad." It sounds to me like they're taking too many Oh for threes. I guess I'm a little afraid of losing that edge.

Mike Piazza, professional baseball player

Effort

Because there might be somebody out there who's never seen me play before.

Joe DiMaggio, Hall of Fame baseball player, to Jimmy Cannon, sportswriter, after Cannon asked him why he played so hard in games after the pennant had already been won

Cinderella never worked this hard.

Rick Pitino, college and professional basketball coach, responding to how it felt to be a "Cinderella" team

Doing your best is more important than being the best.

Shannon Miller, Olympic gold medal–winning gymnast

Don't let anyone outwork you.

Attributed to Derek Jeter's father, by Derek Jeter, professional baseball player

He looked like a big, fat pussy toad out there.

George Steinbrenner, baseball owner, about Hideki Irabu, pitcher

If I do something, it must be 100 percent. There can be no 99.9.

Dominik Hasek, professional hockey player

I just can't sit there and expect the ball to come to me because that makes me easy prey for defenders.

Ronaldo, professional soccer player

I like to see people work . . . Whatever you do, do well. You should be the best you can.

William Talbert, professional tennis champion

I'm just a ball player with one ambition, and that is to give all I've got to help my ball club win. I've never played any other way.

Joe DiMaggio, Hall of Fame baseball player

Industry is not the expenditure of shoe leather. It is having ideas—ideas about the job you hold, how to improve it and yourself.

Branch Rickey, baseball executive

It's not about the market, it's about winning and playing good, you know, that's all that counts.

Latrell Sprewell, professional basketball player

I wish to hell I'd never said the damn thing. I meant the effort . . . I meant having a goal. I sure as hell didn't mean for people to crush human values and morality.

Vince Lombardi, Hall of Fame football coach, referring to his famous quote: "Winning isn't everything, it's the only thing."

My father always told me if I trained hard and took it seriously, my time would come.

Ricardo Williams, Jr., professional boxer

No ballplayer gives 100 percent on every play. He can't. But if you don't on a crucial play, one that loses you a game, oh, geez, it tears you up inside.

Rick Casares, professional football player

No, you grunted. When you grunt you made an effort, and it counts.

Sam Snead, champion professional golfer

People come out to see you perform and you've got to give them the best you have within you.

Jesse Owens, Olympic gold medal–winning runner

When your nose is bleeding and your eyes are black and you are so tired you wish your opponent would crack you on the jaw and put you to sleep, fight one more round remembering that the man who fights one more round is never whipped.

"Gentleman" Jim Corbett, champion professional boxer

You big, dumb son-of-a-bitch, why don't you go in and take that uniform off and go home, for chrissake? You're out here screwing around, with an eleven-run lead . . . You're gonna lose the game, at least you're not gonna get credit for the win, somebody else is on the Dodger team, so why don't you just take that uniform off, because you're not pitching.

Jackie Robinson, Hall of Fame baseball player, to Don Newcombe, when Newcombe was admittedly "experimenting" with a few pitches with a comfortable lead and suddenly loaded up the bases with Ralph Kiner in the box

You should learn a lesson from this smaller guy. He was determined and he really tried hard.

Jesse Owens, Olympic gold medalist track and field competitor, to a group of youngsters, referring to a pint-sized Carl Lewis, Olympic gold medalist track and field competitor, at the Jesse Owens meet

Ego

It is the great word of the twentieth century. If there is a single word our century has added to the potentiality of language it is ego. . . . Muhammad Ali begins with the most unsettling ego of all.

Norman Mailer, Pulitzer Prize–winning writer

The only players I hurt with my words are ones with inflated opinions of their ability.

Bill Parcells, National Football League head coach

Elliott, James Francis "Jumbo"

(b. 1915; d. 1981) *National Collegiate Athletic Association champion track coach*

He holds the all-time record for attendance at weddings and funerals.

Jim Tuppeny, track and field coach, at the legendary track coach's own funeral

There is an old saying, "There are no irreplaceable men on this earth." To me, that is not quite true. Ask the hundreds who knew and loved him.

Jack O'Reilly, stadium announcer, broadcaster, and track and field historian

Emotion

Emotion only stays with you a short period. What you want is a sustained effort of performance.

John Chaney, college basketball coach

Endorsements

American Express. Don't steal home without it.

Wesley Snipes, actor in Major League

I'd rather get Gatorade poured on me than bust my butt selling it.

Bill Parcells, professional football coach

I want to take some time off and do more endorsements.

Oscar De La Hoya, champion boxer

Of the many accolades in sports the right to design your own athletic shoe for the world's top sneaker company is pretty special.

Leigh Gallagher, journalist

Endurance

Believe you can do it. Think no other way but "Yes you can." The human body is capa-

ble of considerably more physical endurance than most of us realize.

Paul Reese, Cross USA runner

My strength is being the last man standing.

Robyn Benincasa, extreme athlete,
adventure racer

Enthusiasm

If your work is not fired with enthusiasm, you will be fired with enthusiasm.

John Mazur, professional football coach

Equestrian

Clearly it helps to have some gypsy blood, as I must have, in order to enjoy moving around the globe with six horses, two trucks, a trailer, an assortment of motorcycles, bicycles, and better than one hundred pieces of "luggage." Logic, common sense, and practicality must not be essential, for they seem to be missing from my repertoire, else I long since would have stayed home.

Deidre Pirie, champion team driver

Dressage may not strike the uninitiated as a very dramatic sport, but like so many of the really good things in life, it can easily become an acquired taste.

Sandy Pflueger, champion equestrian

Every little boy has a dream. Some dream of pitching in a World Series, some of playing in the Super Bowl. My dream was to ride in the Olympic Games.

Greg Best, Olympic silver medalist

He's everything a horse should be. He's just waiting for me to deliver the ride.

Alice Debany, show jumper, about The Natural,
a horse she was riding

He wanted to be a good horse. And now he's a winner, and there aren't a lot of horses that want to win the way he does.

Lisa Jaquin, Olympic equestrian, speaking about
her horse For The Moment, who went to win the
grand prix of the Los Angeles International

I had to realize that if you didn't win a ribbon in the finals, it didn't mean you aren't a good rider, and if you do win a ribbon it doesn't mean you're going on to greatness.

Kate Chope, show jumper

I love my horses. I love to ride. And I love to win.

Debbie Dolan, show jumper

We have heard the allegations regarding the alleged acts of violence to horses for insurance purposes . . . The well-being of horses at the Winter Equestrian Festival, and of horses everywhere, is our primary concern. We offer our total cooperation with the police and the FBI in any investigation they may choose to conduct and should there be any truth to these allegations, we hope the investigations will lead to the arrest of anyone involved.

Gene Misch, chairman of the Winter Equestrian
Festival, regarding the famous equestrian
insurance fraud case

Whenever anyone asks them what I did, they say, "Oh, she plays around with horses."

Lisa Jaquin, Olympic equestrian, speaking
of her family

Winning at Devon is different from winning every place else. Even placing well here is better than winning at other shows.

David W. Hollis, rider and journalist

Equipment

At one time, I had sixteen different rackets with my name on them . . . A computer goes to work. No racket had won so many major tournaments.

Jack Kramer, professional tennis champion, on the best-selling tennis rackets of all time, the Jack Kramer model

The old glove is dead. The Richie Ashburn model for left-handers, veteran of 10,000 baseballs, has expired at the age of 23.

Ray Fitzgerald, sportswriter, in a column when the glove was taken out of production

What you need is a suit of armor. I haven't got none of those around.

Friday Mcklem, equipment manager Detroit Lions, to George Plimpton, writer posing as a free agent quarterback

Era

There will never be another period like those Twenties . . . There were a lot of first-rate competitors . . . there were millionaire sportsmen around who had interest in all sports. If you thought you could make your point, those were the days to prove it.

Gene Tunney, champion boxer

Equipment Managers

We're the mothers of the organization. We do every thankless task. We pack for them, we clean up after them. If we didn't, they'd show up with two left shoes.

Mick McCord, equipment manager, football

Excuses

No excuse in the world counts for squat.

Mark Schubert, U.S. Olympic swimming coach

Execution

I think it's a good idea.

John McKay, college and professional football coach, responding to a question as to what he thought of his team's execution

Executives

An ability to see beyond the obvious is vital for a general manager.

Mike Wise, sportswriter

A real executive goes around with a worried look on his assistants.

Vince Lombardi, Hall of Fame football coach and executive

Coaches get fired everyday, but a GM can be dumb and last forever.

Doug Moe, professional basketball player and coach

I'm not going to beg anyone to coach this team.

Dave Checketts, franchise executive, after Pat Riley had left the New York Knicks

It's never one loss or a losing streak. That's not how you make the decision.

Dave Checketts, franchise executive, about firing other executives or coaches

In order to run an efficient organization there has to be a Dictator.

Al Advise, owner, football

I've never wanted to sit in a fancy luxury box. I'm in the same seat every game, right in the midst of the crowd. And I'm there because I want to be there.

Red Auerbach, Hall of Fame basketball coach and executive

Front office brilliance in baseball is rarer than a triple play.

Roger Angell, writer

No athletic director holds office longer than two unsuccessful football coaches.

Bob Zuppke, Illinois University football coach

The problem is, they have so many selfish, egotistical people in upper management who think they know more about baseball than Branch Rickey.

Attributed to unknown/former Baltimore Orioles executive

Exercise

Any kind of exercise, is generally better than no exercise at all. Walking is better for you than sitting in front of a television set and playing a sport is better for your health than just being a spectator.

Arnold Schwarzenegger, champion bodybuilder and actor

Exercise has always been my form of meditation. I draw great strength from it, physically as well as emotionally and intellectually.

Dr. Tom Waddell, Olympic decathlon competitor and gay rights activist

Exercise is bunk. If you're healthy, you don't need it; if you are sick, you should take it.

Henry Ford, United States industrialist

Exercise is king. Nutrition is queen. Put the two of them together and you have a kingdom.

Jack Lalanne, fitness guru

I have never taken any exercise . . . and never intend to take any.

Mark Twain, writer

What time does the dissipation of energy begin?

Lord Kelvin, physicist

Expectations

Problems begin when expectations exceed ability.

Johnathan Beverly, runner and writer

Most of us find something frightening about surpassing our own or another's expectations, and this fear usually keeps us from doing it.

Timothy Galloway, writer

The expectation I feel here has risen and rightfully so because we have won. And that's the way it should be. I don't ever want to be a part of any organization that doesn't have high expectations.

Pat Riley, professional basketball player and coach

When I came up, Casey told the writers that I was going to be the next Babe Ruth, Lou Gehrig and Joe DiMaggio all rolled into one. Casey kept bragging on me and the newspa-

pers kept writing it, of course, and I wasn't what Casey said I was. I don't mind admitting that there was incredible pressure on me because of what Casey was saying, and the fans were expecting so much, which I wasn't able to deliver.

Mickey Mantle, Hall of Fame baseball player

You have to expect things of yourself before you can do them.

Michael Jordan, champion professional basketball player

Experience

I value every single game I ever coached. Based on my experience over thirty years in the league, eighteen as a coach, you value every game. And if you don't value it, the players won't value it.

Pat Riley, professional basketball player and coach

Extreme Sports

A harmless and enjoyable walk across England.

Alfred Wainwright, Cross UK walker

Extreme athletes are the sporting industry's answer to our insatiable hunger for anything anti-establishment.

Joanne Chen, writer

Few people have reached the top in the sport of triathalon. Fewer still have been able to maintain that position.

Scott Tinley, champion triathlete

I encourage all of you . . . triathletes to reach for your goals, whether they be to win or just to try. The trying is everything.

Dave Scott, champion triathlete

I felt so good when I crossed the finish line. People who saw me on TV thought I was spaced out . . . All I did was go beyond [my previous] limit.

Julie Moss, champion triathlete, after the 1982 Ironman triathlon

I saw the Ironman for the first time on television in 1982, when Julie Moss fell and crawled across the finish line . . . People were crying and cheering. I thought, "This is incredible."

Mark Allen, champion triathlete

I like to sit on top of my BASE objects for a while, just to look at all those creatures walking to work and stressing.

Thor Alex Kappfjell, BASE jumper

It's no secret that triathlons would be much larger if they didn't have that swim part.

Terry Laughlin, triathlete

I was never the "sweat when no one sees you" kind of person, but I really wanted to test my limits.

Tammy Street, competitive deep freediver

Many dedicated endurance athletes don't need to be told what to do—they need to be told what not to do

Scott Tinely, champion triathlete

Race day is harvest time—that's when you reap the benefits.

Mark Allen, triathlete

Technically, these guys did not run entirely from coast to coast contiguously, because they crossed the Hudson River and Mississippi River by ferry.

Paul Reese, Cross USA runner, who covered both rivers by running across bridges and ran the

entire United States at age 73, speaking of early runs

The feeling I get at the starting line is that it's over—all the hard work and training are over: The race is the fun part.

Julie Moss, champion triathlete

There are a lot of guys that have more jumps than I have, but when I do jump, I make a point of jumping from special objects in special places.

Thor Alex Kappfjell, BASE jumper

The X Games is about performing at the very highest standards of the modern mixed-climbing game. Not stewing in a tent, freez-ing your hands at 20,000 feet, or living on freeze-dried yak droppings.

Will Gadd, extreme mixed-climber

My favorite BASE jump is always the last one I've done.

Marta Empinotti, BASE jumper

When all is said and done, the only pressure you have is what you generate for yourself.

Paula Newby-Fraser, eight-time Ironman champion

When it's good, it's really good. And when it's bad, it's still pretty good.

Scott Tinely, champion triathlete, comparing sex and pizza to the Ironman triathlon

Failure

Every athlete has to deal with his past failures.

Dan Jansen, Olympic gold medalist speed skater

I can accept failure, but I can't accept not trying.

Michael Jordan, professional basketball player

For every Michael Jordan, there's an Earl Manigault. We can't all make it. Somebody has to fail.

Earl Manigault, Harlem playground basketball legend, and ex-convict

I have figured out that part of the reason I do the things I do, and cannot seem to conquer that one word—myself—is because . . . is because . . . I am a coward.

Floyd Patterson, champion boxer, on why he insisted on leaving arenas in disguise after losses

Fame

Celebrity is a privilege. It is not a right.

Grant Hill, professional basketball player

Great stars that knew their days in fame's bright sun. I heard them trampling to oblivion.

Grantland Rice, sportswriter

I had pro offers from the Detroit Lions and the Green Bay Packers, who were pretty hard up for linemen in those days. If I had gone into professional football, the name Jerry Ford might have been a household word today.

Gerald R. Ford, president of the United States, former center for the University of Michigan

I walk out in the morning, and the UPS guy tells me to go get 'em or something. It's fine, but . . . there's definitely something to be said for anonymity.

Mike Piazza, professional baseball player

I . . . went to the ESPYs, the ESPN sports awards . . . and was simply amazed when famous athletes asked me for *my* autograph. That just doesn't happen to speed skaters.

Dan Jansen, Olympic gold medal speed skater

Mama raised us never to think we're better than anybody else. All the publicity doesn't make you a better person because it's only there for a short time.

Lee Roy Selmon, professional football player

No longer four sous, but one. What a solemn lesson lay in the fall of price! Fate conveys her pronouncements even through the cries of street vendors. Our popularity had fallen seventy-five percent in two hours.

Luigi Barzini, Sr., writer, participant in the Peking-to-Paris race, where he rode in the winning car with Prince Borghese, driver

Oh my gosh, I can't believe I did that. They probably think I'm a real dingbat.

Shannon Miller, Olympic gold medalist gymnast, after mistaking warning motorists as adoring fans and driving the wrong way down a one-way street

Smart lad, to slip betimes away
From fields where glory does not stay
And early though the laurel grows
It withers faster than the rose.

A. E. Housman, poet

There are always thousands of kids around the village, and they all want autographs. After signing a few hundred books, it's easy to brush the kids off or break the monotony by signing yourself as "Bing Crosby" or "Satchel Paige," but if you're square with the small fry . . . you'll discover they'll open doors for you that make your Olympic trip twice as interesting.

Bob Mathias, gold medalist decathlon competitor, politician, and actor

This is the toll of fame: it is always there—always demanding.

Bill Furlong, sportswriter

Family

I got two daughters, one 4 months and one 17 months. It's so much easier to be playing football than taking care of them. Now that's a real job. People ask if I change diapers. I say, "Are you kidding me? I'm the diaper man."

Jesse Armstead, professional football player

I guess we've been Cup crazy the last few years.

Steve Yzerman, professional hockey player, whose wife bore him two children during the playoffs in consecutive years

I had never been there for Bump—or for many of my children. I wasn't home when he was born. I wasn't home to watch him play ball or graduate from school or celebrate his birthday. I was always playing ball.

Maury Wills, professional baseball player, broadcaster, and manager

I love hopping in that car and being home in about two hours. It's the most exciting thing in my life right now. I'm getting back to being a son to my mother, and that's a bond you can't replace with all the money and fame in the world.

Kerry Collins, professional football player

My family is the most important thing to me. I love basketball, but I need my family around me.

Karl Malone, professional basketball player

My life is strange (it has always been strange!), but I feel a lovely calm these days, and a great deal of that comes from being with you and Mom—and watching you grow.

Dr. Tom Waddell, Olympic decathlon competitor and gay rights activist, who wrote this in his journal for his young daughter before he died of AIDS

The kids like to call to hear their father's voice.

Jeannie Fischer, wife of Scott Fischer, mountain climber, who had died a year earlier on Mt. Everest, and whose voice was still on the family's answering machine

My sister's expecting a baby, and I don't know if I'm going to be an uncle or an aunt.

Chuck Nevitt, North Carolina State basketball player, explaining to his coach why he appeared nervous at practice

The prudent climber will recollect what he owes to his family and his friends.

C. E. Matthews, mountain climber

They can't understand why I can't stay home with them all the time. Why just the other day Bobby Jr., told my wife, Joanne, to take my suitcase away from me.

Bobby Hull, Hall of Fame hockey player

Fans

All that a spectator gets out of the game is fresh air, the comical articles in his program, the sight of twenty-two young men rushing about in mysterious formations, and whatever he brought in his flask.

Robert Benchley, humorist, writer and screenwriter

Anyone at the stadium can lose his life. Take the match that Mexico lost to Peru, two-one. An embittered Mexican fan shouted in an ironic tone, "Viva Mexico!" A moment later he was dead, massacred by the crowd.

Ryszard Kapuscinski, journalist

As a people, we count on going to the ballpark or the arena hungry. For three hours we sit there, gorging ourselves like ancient Romans.

Wells Twombly, sportswriter

Fans are the only ones who care. There are no free-agent fans who say, "Get me out of here. I want to play for a winner."

Dick Young, sportswriter

Fifteen Years of Lousy Football.

A banner on a plane that flew over Giants Stadium, in New Jersey

For the real fan, sports are life—and death.

Mike Littwin, sportswriter

Having to watch the Yankees 42 games in one year is the Red Sox fan's equivalent of the Witness Protection Program: it's no way to live, and if you're lucky, no one will find you.

Bill Scheft, writer, a Boston Red Sox fan who lived in New York City

In most European countries, football-related violence is currently a predominantly internal problem, with the majority of incidents occurring at club-level matches, while supporters of the national team abroad are generally better-behaved. The English are an obvious exception to this rule.

Executive Summary, Fan Violence report, Social Issues Research Centre, Oxford, UK

I apologize to the spectators that it was over so quickly. But if it continues like this at the French Open, I'll be happy.

Martina Hingis, professional tennis player, referring to a match she won in 42 minutes, sweeping her opponent 6-1, 6-0

I don't think about a big home run or a big play in the field. I think about warming up in left field and looking out behind the stadium and seeing thousands of people rushing into the ballpark for the first pitch.

Art Shamsky, professional baseball player

I'm beginning to see that the real source of the madness is the unconsciousness of the crowds. I mean, I've been trying to blame the players, the coach, the owners, and the Commissioner for the ugliness, but really WIN OR BE KILLED is a thing in a culture. These fans today were murder.

Arnold J. Mandell, sports psychiatrist

In ancient Rome, citizens befuddled by the complexities of the waning empire found in battles waged by the gladiators precisely the simplistic relief from the government problems of their day.

James Michener, Pulitzer Prize–winning author

In each home, team affiliation was passed on from father to child, with the crucial moments in a team's history repeated like the liturgy of a church service.

Doris Kearns Goodwin, writer and historian

If I have a bad game and they boo me, that's fine. I make the big money. I'll take the blame. But if I take a shot and it doesn't go in, and they boo me? It's ridiculous.

Antoine Walker, professional basketball player

If you make plays and the team wins, the fans will be fine. I don't worry about the fans.

Donovan McNabb, professional football player

If you're a Cleveland Indians fan, that's how it goes: no justice, only irony.

Scott Raab, sportswriter

I'm standing there in the gift shop trying to buy a magazine when this woman starts screaming my name. I didn't even turn around. It was so annoying and embarrassing. There were 15 people in the store staring at me.

Lindsay Davenport, tennis player

It's the kind of place where you can be a successful neurosurgeon, but if you were a lousy football player, people still look at you funny.

Geno DeMarco, Geneva College football coach on local fans

Insufferable ass loses for Reds!

Jimmy Powers, sportswriter, suggesting a headline after a fan leaned over and interfered with a ball in fair play, which the umpire ruled an automatic home run

I owe the public nothing . . . I refuse to be nice to the kiddies.

Bill Russell, Hall of Fame basketball player and coach

I've never been to Maracana, and there is no way you could ever get me to go there. Just to think of all those stinky, sweaty men shouting curse words, fighting and pouring beer and urine all over each other makes me nervous.

Leticia Carvalho de Almeida, Brazilian female soccer fan

The fans finally got what they wanted. They got Allie Sherman fired and they got it with the power of song, with "Good-bye, Allie" serenade that had become a lynch chant wherever the Giants played and lost.

Gene Roswell, sportswriter

The fans have had their hearts broke too often. Come through for them one day, that's

nice. Blow it the next, and you're a bum all over again.

Marty Barrett, professional baseball player

Maury, we just wanted you to know that our last name is Wills and we named our little boy Maury, after you. We want to thank you, Maury.

Attributed to unknown fans at Dodger Stadium, by Maury Wills, professional baseball player, broadcaster, and manager

New Yorkers are fanatical fans. Even with the harshest New York fans, though, they're pretty forgiving.

Al Leiter, professional baseball player

Nowhere else in the country do people spit at you, throw bottles at you, throw quarters at you, throw batteries at you and say, "Hey, I did your mother last night—she's a whore."

John Rocker, controversial professional baseball player, about New York fans

On the morning of the start, it seems incredible to relate, there must have been two thousand people on the dock (which I thought would collapse into the seas). This enormous crowd of well-wishers and the merely curious walked back and forth . . . The people came to see this strange breed of men about to set off on a great adventure, the first part of which would keep them at sea for almost two months.

Hal Roth, yachtsman

Parisians like tennis, but they love *la cuisine* more.

Yannick Noah, champion professional tennis player

Please, please get a hit. If you get a hit now, I will make my bed every day for a week.

Doris Kearns Goodwin, writer and historian

Professional sports add something to the spirit and vitality of a city . . . A winning team can bring a city together, and even a losing team can provide a bond of common misery.

Bill Veeck, baseball owner and racetrack operator

Quite a few of them start with, "you big ass-hole."

Joe Schmidt, professional football coach, quoting his fan mail

Roger has stolen my fans.

Mickey Mantle, Hall of Fame baseball player, about Roger Maris, after Maris was booed

Sports owners have always been scum. Players have always been greedy. The average fan has always been treated like crap.

Mike Lupica, sportswriter

The dream is not for the player. It is for the fan, the worshipper without whom there would be no professional game at all. It is for the lover of the game who doesn't really know what it's like out there on the field, and never *will* know.

Danny Blanchfowler, professional soccer player

The old Dodger fans were the kind of people who picket. The old Giant fans would be embarrassed to do anything so conspicuous, but they were the kind of people who refuse to cross picket lines. Yankee fans are the kind of people who think they own the company the picket line is thrown around.

Murray Kempton, Back at the Polo Grounds

The real stars of the Cubs were the fans. The players change, but the fans stay.

*Stuart Gordon, theater and film
director and producer*

There's a new television show called *thirtysomething, Cowboysnothing.*

*Anonymous, reported by
Peter Golenbock, sportswriter*

These frenzied spectators literally overwhelmed him, swarming round, shouting, yelling, dancing and jumping about like madmen. Those who got near him slapped and banged him on the back, yelling as they did so, "Good!" "Splendid!" "Glorious!" Thus they continued until all the little remaining breath in George's body was well-nigh beaten out of him.

*account from an unnamed newspaper about
Walter Goodall George's victory in a running
event with William Cummings
in England in 1886*

The Yankees were the "Bronx Bombers," whose pinstriped uniforms signified their elite status, supported by the rich and successful, by Wall Street brokers and haughty business men. The Dodgers were "dem Bums," the "daffiness boys," the unpretentious clowns, whose fans were seen as scruffy blue collar workers who spoke with bad diction. The Giants, owned since 1919 by the same family, the Stonehams, were the conservative team whose followers consisted of small business men who watched calmly from the stands, dressed in shirts and ties, their identity somewhat blurred, caught, as they were, between the Yankee "haves" and the Dodger "have-nots."

Doris Kearns Goodwin, writer and historian

They booed Holzman, DeBusschre and Reed. I guess I'm in good company.

Al Bianchi, Knicks executive

This community doesn't want academic excellence. It wants a gladiatorial spectacle on a Friday night.

*Dorothy Fowler, high school teacher,
in Odessa, Texas*

We are here for the purpose to win for the fans. That is who we work for.

Roberto Clemente, Hall of Fame baseball player

We had the opening-day upper-deck brawl to end all brawls—a brawl so spectacular, a brawl that went on so long, a brawl that spilled over so many rows of blue seats, it actually brought the baseball game to a brawl-gaping halt.

*Jayson Stark, sportswriter, referring to a fight in
the stands that actually stopped the game, in an
opening day game between the Phillies and
Braves in Philadelphia*

We're not looking for trouble. It's all in fun. But these people take it personal. It's the fifth inning and we're already in our third section.

*Bobby Kline, Mets fan, who along with his
rowdy buddies went to Veterans Stadium to root
for his team loudly amidst the Philly faithful*

We've got an undertaker with us from Utica, so you don't have to worry, you can hit him as hard as you like.

*Anonymous fan to Rocky Graziano,
before a championship bout*

When fans come to the ballpark, damn it, every last one of 'em is a manager.

*Whitey Herzog, professional baseball player,
executive, and manager*

When we were on the bench, we would look up into the stands and count the people.
Larry Grantham, professional football player on the terrible New York Titans, whose games went largely unattended

When we were uptown we got a lot of fat broads who, when they got tired of beating up their husbands, came to the Garden looking for a fight. Or we got West Side hookers on the make.
Anonymous New York Knickerbockers executive

You can't compare Brooklyn fans with any other . . . It was OK if they wanted to holler against their own. But they didn't want strangers to do it.
Gil Hodges, professional baseball player and manager

We were in Dallas together in 1960 when [Landry] coached the Cowboys and I coached the Texans. We got along very well. But there was a lot of confusion because of the teams' names, and I used to get a lot of his mail, and he would get a lot of mine. If I got a letter and it was someone saying something negative about the Cowboys, I would seal it back up and send it to him. The ones that said good things about the Cowboys, he never saw.
Hank Stram, Hall of Fame football coach and broadcaster

Without Tittle the Giants couldn't go from Grand Central to Times Square on the subway.
Irwin Shaw, best-selling author, attributed to his next-door neighbor

You wolves been howling for blood all year. Maybe this'll shut you up.

John King, professional baseball player, pitcher, as he threw fifty chunks of meat into the stands

Fatigue

Fatigue makes cowards of us all.
Vince Lombardi, Hall of Fame football coach

Fats, Minnesota

(b. Jan. 19, 1913; d. Jan. 18, 1996) *Infamous and brash pool player and trick shot artist; portrayed in the motion picture* The Hustler *by Jackie Gleason (who was taught by Fats's arch nemesis Willie Mosconi)*

He starts playing for two dollars a game, and pretty soon the butcher and baker are playing for a hundred bucks a game and they never saw a pool table before that.
Anonymous pool hustler about Minnesota Fats, legendary pool player

"Hustler" is another word for "thief," and "Minnesota Fats" is another word for "phony."
Willie Mosconi, world champion pool player

He's probably never been to Minnesota.
Willie Mosconi, world champion pool player

Fear

Correct form is the forerunner to good performance, and the early cure of fear.
Branch Rickey, baseball executive

Do I have fear? I've asked myself that question a million times and come up with a million answers.
Shanny Shanholtzer, downhiller, U.S. ski team

Fear? A downhiller with fear? If I had fear, I wouldn't race.

Karl Schranz, champion downhiller

Fear is your best friend or your worst enemy. It's like fire. If you can control it, it can cook for you; it can heat your house. If you can't control it, it will burn everything around you and destroy you.

Cus D'Amato, boxing trainer

Fear of failure, especially in our success-oriented society, is a common malady that afflicts us all in one degree or another. The thing to do is simply recognize it for what it is, then treat its symptoms. Fear of failure manifests itself as tension.

Eric Evans, Olympic kayaker and outdoorsman

He was kind of staring . . . It was as if he knew something bad was about to happen.

Ed "Too Tall" Jones, professional football player, about Craig Morton in a Super Bowl loss

I always ran through fear—of being beaten. It brought out the best in me, being terrified of being beaten.

Shirley Strickland De La Hunty, Olympic medalist track and field competitor

I'd love to play baseball, even now, but I have this one great fear, you see: I'm afraid of the ball.

Tiny Tim, musician, sports fan

I guess I'm more afraid of being afraid than actually being afraid.

Ted Turner, yachtsman and baseball owner

In a sense, fear became a friend—I hated it at the time but it added spice to the challenge and satisfaction to the conquest.

Sir Edmund Hillary, mountain climber

It is never possible to conquer fear, but it can be subdued for a time. Watch the great athlete work at his craft and you see someone who has known fear before and will know fear again, but who goes about his job fearlessly. This is the courage of an athlete and it is towering to behold.

Roger Kahn, sportswriter

Those moments when I went from calmness to curiosity to worry to panic (I have always feared drowning) . . . Why seek them? Perhaps not only to have stories to tell, but also to make sense of the stories we already know.

Andrea Barrett, sailor and kayaker

To taste fear . . . and choke it down is a continuing act of bravery.

Roger Kahn, sportswriter, referring to the constant brushback pitches thrown at Gil Hodges, and his ability to stand at the plate

When everything is working perfectly, I'm no more afraid than I am driving the family car on a highway. When something goes wrong, it scares the hell out of me.

Fireball Roberts, champion race car driver

Fencing

Dueling at the drop of a hat was as European as truffles and as American as mom's apple pie.

Barbara Holland, writer

Fencing came to me out of the blue, one of those quirks of fate. But it must have been a pretty strong quirk. I came to the sport not so much by choice as by pure necessity.

Ralph Faulkner, fencer

For as long as I have known, the throwing of bouts has been going on in fencing.
Lev Rossochick, sportswriter

For the screen, in order to be well photographed and also grasped by the audience, all swordplay should be so telegraphed with emphasis that the audience will see what is coming. All movements—instead of being as small as possible, as in competitive fencing—must be large.
Fred Cravens, competitive fencer and stunt coordinator, attributed by Nick Evangelista, fencing instructor

In fencing you lose a lot. We tell them "Stop crying; life is going to be this way."
Peter Westbrook, Olympic bronze medal fencer and fencing coach

It is customary for profligates to learn the art of fencing.
London edict, 1286 A.D.

It is the fencing master's strict moral duty toward his artistic ancestors to see to it that centuries-old traditions are respected, honored and enforced.
Aldo Nadi, fencer

It's not necessarily who's hitting first, but who is hitting correctly.
Eric Perret, writer

The entire secret of arms consists of only two things: to give, and not to receive.
Molière, Le Bourgeois Gentilhomme

The sabre is a cavalry weapon, so your target is a mounted man from the waist up; and it's an edged weapon, so you're not limited to poking—you get to wing the thing. It leaves welts. Foil and epee fencers say it's for barbarians.
Eric Perret, writer

World Cup bouts are for sale, and an unscrupulous few go that route.
Don Lane, Canadian fencing team

You can't go nowhere, you can't fight with anybody, unless you have good footwork. It's impossible. You can't do nothing without good footwork.
Peter Westbrook, Olympic bronze medal fencer and fencing coach

Field Goals

It was a good game . . . if you like field goals.
Don Meredith, professional football player and broadcaster

Twenty-two straining giants in perfect condition fight for fifty-nine minutes. Then some European runs onto the field, kicks a fifteen-yard field goal, wins the game, and shouts, "Hooray!"
Alex Karras, professional football player, broadcaster, and actor

Field Hockey

Field hockey is preeminently a game of swift and fluid movement . . . more a passing game than a dribbling and dodging game.
Wendy Lee Martin, field hockey coach and player

It's not too much to say that the character of the playing surface determines the level of play possible in this game—just as it does in baseball or billiards.
Wendy Lee Martin, field hockey coach and player

The true elegance of field hockey is the team passing game. Unfortunately, many players are remembered for their dribbling skills instead of their passing skills because it appears to be more spectacular.

Elizabeth Anders, Olympic field hockey player and college field hockey coach

Fielding

Although he is a very poor fielder, he is also a very poor hitter.

Ring Lardner, sportswriter

Don't let it hit you on the coconut, Maxie!

Dick Groat, baseball player and manager, warning second baseman Maxvill not to botch an easy pop-fly hung up in midair

Etten's glove fields better without Etten in it.

Joe Trimble, sportswriter, about Nick Etten, professional baseball player

I fought the wall, and the wall won.

Dmitri Young, professional baseball player, after dropping a fly ball when he ran into the outfield wall

Fights

Here I am, come out and get me.

Tommy Lasorda, professional baseball player and manager, to Hank Bauer and Billy Martin, from the mound, as a Kansas City pitcher, after knocking down three batters in a row

If they took away our sticks and gave us brooms, we'd still fight.

Phil Esposito, former professional player and executive

If you see European hockey, there are no fights, and it's boring.

Eddie Johnston

I have never liked it when guys on my team have gone out and fought somebody after I got hit.

Steve Yzerman, professional hockey player

I'll kill you. You remember that, I'll kick your ass! You've got a good team and you don't need that edge! That's why I told my kid to knock your f****** kid in the mouth!

John Chaney, college basketball coach, to John Calipari, college coach, after an altercation between the two

I'm low on sticks, and I didn't want to lose one on his head.

Mike Richter, on not swinging at Tie Domi, who was fighting with one of his teammates

Sometimes people ask, "Are hockey fights for real?" And I say, "If they weren't, I'd get in more of them."

Wayne Gretzky, Hall of Fame professional hockey player

They key is to be fast with your dukes. First, you get him with a good shot. The gloves come off right away—that's automatic—then you get him with the first punch.

John Ferguson, professional hockey player

We don't want anybody to be fighting for no reason. We don't want anybody to get kicked out because that's not professional. But, if that's what we have to do, then we're going to have to do it.

Antonio Davis, professional basketball player

We're the last of the gladiator teams.
Isiah Thomas, professional basketball player,
executive and coach, about being part of the
Detroit Pistons

Finley, Charles O.

(b. Feb. 22, 1918; d. Feb. 19, 1997) *Major*
League Baseball owner (won three World Series);
also owned National Hockey League and Ameri-
can Basketball Association teams

Charles O. Finley is as vulgar as spit. I think
he's beautiful.
Charles McCabe, sportswriter

A combination of Machiavelli and Billy
Graham.
Charles McCabe, sportswriter

Firings (coaches)

It's like a marriage. You're not going to fight
with your lover when you're having sex and
having a good time. But as the marriage goes
on and goes on and you get used to each
other, you get set in your ways and this and
that.
Michael Cooper, professional basketball player,
referring to the departure of Pat Riley,
professional basketball player and coach

Try to exercise, eat better, try to do some fun
things with my wife.
Tom Davis, college basketball coach, on what he
was going to do after he was fired

You've taken my team away from me.
Tom Landry, Hall of Fame professional football
coach, after coaching the Dallas Cowboys to 20
straight seasons with a winning record,
on the day he was fired

Fishing

Abating in his flurry, the whale once more
rolled out into view; surging from side to side;
spasmodically dilating and contracting his
spout-hole, with sharp, cracking, agonizing
respirations. At last, gush after gush of clotted
red gore, as if it had been of purple lees of red
wine, shot into the frightened air; and falling
back again, ran dripping down his motionless
flanks into the sea. His heart had burst!
Herman Melville, novelist, from Moby-Dick

After toiling and watching and creeping
about for the greater part of a day, with
scarcely any success, in spite of all our
admirable apparatus, a lubberly country
urchin came down from the hills with a rod
made from a branch of a tree, a few yards of
twine, and, as Heaven shall help me! I believe
a crooked pin for a hook, baited with a vile
earthworm—and in half an hour caught
more fish than we had nibbles throughout
the day.
Washington Irving, writer

All great fishermen go to bed early.
Ted Williams, Hall of Fame baseball player and
world-class fisherman

All men are equal before trout.
Herbert Hoover, president of the United States

Although the thrill of fishing is catching the
fish, the greatest challenges any captain faces
are often keeping the crew focused, making
sure the vessel remains mechanically sound,
and returning safely to port.
Linda Greenlaw, swordfish boat captain

Angling is somewhat like poetry, men are to
be born so.
Izaak Walton, writer

Angling may be said to be so like the mathematics, that it can never be fully learnt.

Izaak Walton, writer

As a big game fisherman, I never saw a sailfish that didn't look better in the ocean than on somebody's line—or wall.

Grantland Rice, sportswriter

At the outset, the fact should be recognized that the community of fishermen constitute a separate class or subrace among the inhabitants of the earth.

Grover Cleveland, president of the United States

Casual observers are apt to think that people who scrinch along brooks swatting mosquitoes and getting their seats wet are just trying to escape these tension–producing atomic days; nothing could be further from the truth. The creep'n'crawl society is dedicated to the proposition that small streams operate on the short–term payment plan.

A. J. McClane, outdoorsman and writer

Cruelty disguised as a sport! Fishing is the vice of the shirker and the rummy. No-works, ashamed of their laziness, cover it up by doing their loafing with a fishing line in their hands.

Jimmy Cannon, sportswriter

Fishing, if a fisher may protest,
Of pleasures is the sweetest, of sports the best,
Of exercises the most excellent,
Of recreations the most innocent,
But now the sport is marred, and wott ye why?
Fishes decrease, and fishers multiply

Thomas Bastard, writer (1598)

Fish in the water are always larger than fish out of the water.

Randy Voorhees, fisherman and writer

Fishing is a test of character, but it's a test you can take over and over as many times as you want.

John Gierach, fisherman and writer

Every healthy boy, every right-minded man, and every uncaged woman, feels at one time or another, and maybe at all times, the impulse to go 'a fishing.

Eugene McCarthy, writer, politician

Fishing is a jerk at one end of the line waiting for a jerk at the other end.

Mark Twain, writer

Fishing is an Art, or at least, it is an Art to catch fish.

Izaak Walton, writer

Going all over the world doesn't make you a top fisherman, it makes you a top traveler.

Lee Wulff, outdoorsman and writer

Good fishing never stops. There are only times when in some places it is better than in others.

George Fichter, fisherman and writer

How capricious is the memory of anglers! I cannot remember the name of my first dog, my first schoolteacher, or the first girl I kissed . . . but I can remember the correct name of the first trout stream I ever fished.

M. R. Montgomery, outdoorsman and writer

I do it because it won't be done much longer. I fish with my hands, well, jus' 'cause I can.

Patrick Mire, grappler (or hand fisherman)

I have done a little research with waitresses, bellhops, and bartenders. The waitresses say that fishermen abuse them most and tip with a miser's caution.

Jimmy Cannon, sportswriter

I have found repeatedly, of late years, that I cannot fish without falling a little in self-respect. I have tried it again and again. I have skill at it, and, like many of my fellows, a certain instinct for it, which revives from time to time, but always when I have done I feel that it would have been better if I had not fished.

Henry David Thoreau, philosopher and writer

I have had a marlin sound four hundred yards straight down, all the rod under water over the side, bent double with that weight going down, down, down, watching the line go, putting on all pressure possible on the reel to check him, him going down and down until you are sure every inch of line will go. Suddenly he stops and you straighten up, get onto your feet, get the butt in the socket and work him up slowly, finally you have a double line on the reel and think he is coming to gaff and then the line begins to rip out as he hooks up and heads off to sea just under the surface to come out in ten long, clean jumps.

*Ernest Hemingway,
Nobel Prize–winning author*

I have never caught a fish on a first cast, nor have I ever made a first cast without thinking I would catch a fish.

Ellington White, writer

I have to admit that those golden trout sure are small. But then I ask, How big exactly

does a nugget of true gold have to get before it is of true value?

Thomas McIntyre, outdoorsman and writer

If Satch and I were pitching on the same team, we'd cinch the pennant by July 4, and go fishing until World Series time.

*Dizzy Dean, Hall of Fame baseball player,
referring to Satchel Paige,
Hall of Fame baseball player*

I spent a season in my new craft fishing on the coast, only to find I did not have the cunning to bait a hook.

*Joshua Slocum, sailor, first modern sailor
to sail around the world alone*

It is impossible to avoid the conclusion that the fishing habit, by promoting close association with nature, by teaching patience and by generating or stimulating useful contemplation, tends directly to the increase of the intellectual power of its votaries and through them to the improvement of our national character.

Grover Cleveland, president of the United States

Just sort of estimate 'em, son. For some inscrutable reason, the Lord made fish light and women heavy.

*Havilah Babcock, outdoorsman and writer,
attributed to his father about never
weighing a fish*

Most trout fisherman I know, in these later days of greatly heightened fishing pressure on streams, where the anglers appear to outnumber fish, approach their sport with the attitude of the gambler who, on being told that the roulette wheel was crooked, said: "I know, but what can I do? It's the only wheel in town?"

Arnold Gingrich, outdoorsman and writer

No fish is more humbling than a big tailer who ventures into glass-calm shallows—a mere presence that dares you to make the first move.

A. J. McClane, outdoorsman and writer

No misanthrope, I must nevertheless confess that I like and frequently prefer to fish alone. Of course in a sense all dedicated fishermen must fish alone; the pursuit is essentially a solitary one; but sometimes I not only like to fish out of actual sight and sound of my fellow addicts, but alone in the relaxing sense that I need not consider the convenience or foibles or state of hangover of my companions....

Robert Traver, outdoorsman and writer

Nothing quite properly prepares you for the look of your first California golden trout you take from a creek and hold in your hand ... What he most looks like as he flutters in your hand is a terrible drink or a goddamned Technicolor sunset!

Thomas McIntyre, outdoorsman and writer

One of the attractions of wading into a stream is that you become a part of the world of the trout, salmon, or steelhead that you seek.

*Joan Salvato Wulff, outdoorswoman,
broadcaster, and writer*

People may fish in different ways, for different species, and for different reasons, but we all connect as anglers. The language of fishing cuts across all differences.

*Jim Brown, fly-fisherman and collector of
antiquary fishing equipment*

Rainbow trout fishing is as different from brook trout fishing as prizefighting is from boxing.

*Ernest Hemingway,
Nobel Prize–winning author*

Salmon, male and female, are called cocks and hens, I learn from my books. The salmon appears to be a very odd fish.

*William Humphrey,
outdoorsman and journalist*

Somehow I feel that all the elements and all life, whether human or otherwise, are directly related, so much so that anyone who is sincerely enraptured by the wonders of nature stands very close to the great beyond. To such souls fishing is an outlet to the feelings, a surcease from life's trials.

Edward C. Janes, fisherman and writer

Sometimes, after staying in a village parlor till the family had all retired, I have returned to the woods, and, partly with a view to the next day's dinner, spent the hours of midnight fishing from a boat by moonlight, serenaded by owls and foxes, and hearing from time to time, the creaking note of some unknown bird close at hand.

Henry David Thoreau, philosopher and writer

Sometimes you think you've got the fish caught and cleaned, and he slips back into the water.

Charlie Whittingham, thoroughbred horse trainer

The gods do not deduct from man's
allotted span the hours spent in fishing.

Babylonian proverb

The minds of anglers are usually as crammed as their fishing vests although not necessarily with information that will enlighten non-anglers.

M. R. Montgomery, outdoorsman and writer

The minnow was thrown as a fly several times, and, owing to my peculiar, and hith-

erto unpublished, methods of fly throwing, nearly six pennyworth of the triangles came off, either in my coat-collar, or my thumb, or the back of my hand. Fly fishing is a very gory amusement.

Rudyard Kipling, Nobel Prize–winning author

The real angler knows his sport transcends every limitation of economics, class and culture. In my own hometown, fishing was the only place the doctor, the alcohol welder, the priest, the barber, and the town bum could meet on equal footing.

Thomas McGuane, writer

The real lessons of fishing are the ones that come after you've caught the fish. They have to do with solitude, gratitude, patience, perspective, humor, and the sublime coffee break.

John Gierach, fisherman and writer

The red tide now poured from all sides of the monster like brooks down a hill. His tormented body rolled not in brine, but in blood, which bubbled and seethed for furlongs behind in their wake. The slanting sun playing upon this crimson pond in the sea, sent back its reflection into every face, so that they all glowed to each other like red men.

Herman Melville, writer

The rest of the world's trout may be taken in summer, to the sounds of birds and the pleasant hum of insects, but the steelhead—the big, sea-going rainbow of the Northwest coasts—is winter's child.

Paul O'Neil, outdoorsman and writer

These are my tarpon, but you may play with them.

Jake Jordan, fisherman

The true sportsmen among anglers is the trout fisherman, who wades right into the fish's territory and battles it out hand to hand, taking an honest man's chance of being swept down the rapids and bashed against the rocks.

Red Smith, sportswriter

The whole madness of Opening Day fever is quite beyond me: it deserves the complexities of a Jung or a Kafka, for it is archetypal and rampant with ambiguity. And still you would not have it.

Nick Lyons, outdoorsman, writer, and publisher

There are a dozen justifications for fishing. Among them is the importance to the political world. No political aspirant can qualify for election unless he demonstrates he is a fisherman, there being twenty-five million persons who pay annually for a license to fish.

Herbert Hoover, president of the United States

There certainly is something in angling, if we could forget, which anglers are apt to do, the cruelties and tortures inflicted on worms and insects, that tends to produce a gentleness of spirit, and a pure serenity of mind.

Washington Irving, writer

There is no use in walking 5 miles to fish when you can depend on being just as unsuccessful near home.

Mark Twain, humorist and writer

This is where they painted spots on him and taught him to swim.

Meade Schaeffer, angler and artist, commenting on a fishing village, Roscoe, New York

Throw your bread upon the water and a carp will beat you to it.

Hugh E. Keogh, sportswriter

To capture the fish is not all of fishing. Yet there are circumstances which make this philosophy hard to accept.

Zane Grey, writer

To celebrate Opening Day on the Beaverkill is a little like observing Christmas in Bethlehem.

Red Smith, sportswriter

Upon finishing his residency in tropical medicine, he got married, went on a fishing honeymoon to Ireland, returned to London, where he set his wife up in a flat in South Kensington, and shipped out to Nairobi. There he spent the next twenty-five years, returning home on three months' leave every year to fish, and to see his wife.

William Humphrey, outdoorsman and journalist, referring to a fishing companion

Your three- or four-pound sophomores smack resoundingly. But your real fish, your juggernauts, your deans and full professors sort of roll ponderously and engulf your lure.

Havilah Babcock, outdoorsman and writer

You will search far to find a fisherman to admit that a taste for fishing, like a taste for liquor, must be governed lest it come to possess its possessor.

Sparse Grey Hackle, writer

Fixing

I'm forever blowing ball games . . .

Ring Lardner, writer, (sung to the tune of "I'm Forever Blowing Bubbles"), about Claude Williams, one of the conspirators in throwing the 1919 World Series

This series is fixed. You can have it—I'm going to the race track.

Champ Pickens, event promoter, speaking about the 1919 World Series

Fly-fishing

Anyone can tie a fly and name it after himself, but the trick is to create one that will be used consistently by other fishermen.

Nelson Bryant, writer

Down in Maine, when they say "fly-fishing only" they mean fly-fishing only the way a gentleman would fish, for fish only a gentleman would fish for. In other words, casting dry flies to trout or salmon and—if one must, wets, too, though the latter act is regarded as questionable at best, somewhat akin to picking up chicken wings with one's fingers.

Ted Williams, Hall of Fame baseball player and world–class fisherman

Fly-fishing is easy to learn, like calculus or the golf swing.

Randy Voorhees, fisherman and writer

Fly-fishing is probably the final refinement in angling. In no other fishing is the balance of tackle so vital. This is the system that really lets you test the limits of your equipment and skill.

Ray Bergman, fisherman and writer

Fly-fishing takes you to spectacular places and gives you a reason for being there that is far more compelling than just looking at the scenery. You become a participant rather than a spectator, the creatures of the water world become an extension of those things you

care about . . . It is difficult to feel lonely when you are "out fishin'."

Joan Salvato Wulff, outdoorswoman, broadcaster, and writer

Fly-fishing. There was a small stream up behind our house, with brook trout. I taught myself how to fly-fish—learned practicing on the brook trout—and got to be pretty good at it.

Greg LeMond, champion cyclist, when asked what he did when he wasn't racing

Fly rods are like women; they won't play if they're maltreated.

Charles Ritz, writer and sportsman

For years my fly-casting technique has compared, rather banally I might add, to an old lady fighting off a bee with a broom handle.

Patrick F. McManus, outdoorsman and writer

In August the multitudes run to the beaches by hordes, the politicians return to their conventions and their drums and flags and slogans, most of the sporting magazines turn to hunting, the city turns deathly gray and dry and hot and anxious, and I begin to hear the last chords of the fly-fisherman's year.

Nick Lyons, outdoorsman, writer, and publisher

In our family there was no clear line between fly-fishing and religion.

Norman Maclean, A River Runs Through It

It's funny how we always expect that, in the wilderness, innocent fish will pounce greedily on any fly. It does happen, of course, but in my experience there have been just as many occasions when I had to eat humble pie.

A. J. McClane, outdoorsman and writer

No pursuit on earth is so burdened by arcane lore as fly-fishing, beside which brain surgery and particle physics are simple backyard pastimes.

Charles Kuralt, broadcaster and writer

Presenting a fly to a fish moving through the water is like shooting game birds; you must lead the target to make the interception.

Joan Salvato Wulff, outdoorswoman, broadcaster, and writer

The angler can have no cold nor discomfort nor anger, unless he be the cause himself. For he can lose at the most only a line or hook, of which he can have a plentiful supply of his own making.

Dame Juliana Berners, Treatise of Fishing With an Angle, *written in 1496*

Until man is redeemed, he will always take a fly rod too far back.

Norman Maclean, writer

When I first started fly-fishing it was largely because of casting, that incredible suspension of the line overhead, the sweeping curve following, in a delayed reaction, the motion of the rod. The point of all other fishing was to bring home meat, but with a fly line the process itself was the purpose. The elegance of casting justified the endeavor, regardless of the catch.

Wayne Fields, outdoorsman and writer

While it is true that flowing rivers create difficulties for the fly-caster, these are trivial compared to the problems faced by the trout.

M. R. Montgomery, outdoorsman and writer

101

Focus

I just went out and tried to do my best because I wanted to do my best, not because I was focused the whole time on winning. If you focus on winning, you have to focus on other people. I would focus solely on doing my best.

Greg Louganis, Olympic gold medalist diver

I'm just focused on what I have to do, not why I was brought here.

Latrell Sprewell, professional basketball player

I'm not going to relax. Now is the time to be even more focused, more positive, more serious, to make sure things go in the right direction.

Corey Pavin, champion professional golfer

I try not to get too caught up in thinking about the task ahead. I just do what has to be done. I have the belief in myself that what I'm doing is right. Then I let the rest happen.

Eamonn Coghlan, world champion miler

None of us can relax until we get to the final, lift the cup and take it back to Brazil.

Ronaldo, professional soccer player

Too many golfers get concerned about what others do and forget to do what they have to do to play the game.

Sam Snead, champion golfer

With a chance to win, Durocher was hardly fit to live with. He could only see one thing—the pennant. He wouldn't settle for anything less, wasn't interested in anything less, and wouldn't talk about anything less.

Russ Hodges, broadcaster

The conventions of the ring demand that a fighter in training become a monk. For months at a time, he hardens his body on roadwork and beefsteak, and practices an enforced loneliness—even (tradition has it) sexual loneliness—better to focus the mind on war.

David Remnick, writer

My plans are all Dempsey.

Gene Tunney, champion boxer, who shunned a few lesser, easy fights, because he wanted to become champion

When you're riding, only the race in which you're riding is important.

Bill Shoemaker, Hall of Fame jockey

You've got 45 minutes left in your dream. If you don't use this time wisely you're going to go home and be sad about it.

Tony DiCicco, soccer coach, U.S. women's World Cup team

Food

Carrots may be good for my eyes, but they won't straighten out the curve ball.

Carl Furillo, professional baseball player

I eat what I eat and I weigh what I weigh.

George Foreman, champion boxer

If we're not willing to settle for junk living, we certainly shouldn't settle for junk food.

Sally Edwards, Ironman triathlete and writer

Most of the top runners I know feel the same way about diet. They're skeptical about nutrition being the prime element in racing success, but they like to check each other's grocery lists. Just in case.

Don Kardong, runner and writer

Some days you want broccoli, other days Hostess Ding Dongs. Don't ask why.

Scott Tinely, champion triathlete

Sometimes I wonder whether I run high mileage so I can eat like this, or do I eat like this so I can run high mileage?

Bill Rodgers, champion runner, speaking of his favorite snack of mayonnaise and chocolate chip cookies

Take me out to the ball game,
   take me out to the crowd.
Buy me some peanuts and Cracker Jack,
I don't care if I ever get back.

lyrics from "The Old Ball Game"

Take away the hot-dog and all its attendant comestibles, such as peanuts, popcorn, Cracker Jacks and egg salad sandwiches, and you'd have a different country.

Wells Twombly, sportswriter

Together they are capable of devouring any two Chinese restaurants east of Shanghai on the same night. That they have not yet succeeded is not for lack of trying.

Jerry Izenberg, sportswriter, on professional football players and roommates Erik Howard and John "Jumbo" Elliott

Football

As a reflection of American life, the most popular sport in America is professional football: brutal, precise, competitive, and highly standardized. In football, as in much of American society, the competitor is The Enemy, and the all-consuming passion is to win, often at any cost.

Dr. Ross Thomas Runfola, sportswriter

At the base of it was the urge, if you wanted to play football, to knock someone down, that was what the sport was all about, the will to win closely linked with contact.

George Plimpton, writer and editor

You go outdoors to play football. You go in the house to get warm.

Bud Grant, professional football coach

Football is a game designed to keep coal-miners off the streets.

Jimmy Breslin, journalist

Football is unique and good. Where else in life do you see dedication and teamwork and spirit? People enjoy it because it is reassuring to them to see good things.

Woody Hayes, college football coach

Football is not a game but a religion, a meta-physical island of fundamental truth in a highly verbalized, disguised society, a throw-back of 30,000 generations of anthropological time.

Dr. Arnold Mandell, sports psychologist

Football players, like prostitutes, are in the business of ruining their bodies for the pleasure of strangers.

Merle Kessler, writer

Forget touchdowns, I played football for the chance to hit another man as hard as I could—to fuck him up, to move through him like wind through a door. Anybody who tells you different is a liar.

Elwood Reid, writer

Due to its ingredients . . . courage, mental and physical condition, spirit and its terrific body contact which tends to sort the men from

the boys . . . football remains one of the great games of all time.

Grantland Rice, sportswriter

I do believe that my best hits border on felonious assault.

Jack Tatum, professional football player

In a universal sense, football is so insignificant, it's ridiculous.

Pat Hayden, professional football player

I never realized what it meant to take a team from a warm climate into the ice-box area of the Midwest. To my sorrow, I found out twice in three years.

George Allen, professional football coach, reply on losing his second cold weather Conference championship.

If their IQ's were lower, they would be geraniums.

Russ Francis, professional football player, on defensive linemen

If you've never been tackled by L.T. [Lawrence Taylor], don't feel bad about it. Believe me, there are better things you can do with your time.

Eric Dickerson, professional football player

Is it normal to wake up in the morning in a cold sweat because you can't wait to beat another human's guts out?

Joe Kapp, professional football player

It's not the fact that men love football that makes modern woman want to scream . . . It's the assumption that she is incapable of loving it too.

Sally Jenkins, writer

It would be a real misfortune to lose so manly and vigorous a game as football.

Theodore Roosevelt, president of the United States

Let's face it, you have to have a slightly recessive gene that has a little something to do with the brain to go out on the football field and beat your head against other human beings on a daily basis.

Tim Green, professional football player, broadcaster, and writer

Football is a game played down in the dirt, and always will be.

Steve Owen, champion professional football coach

Football is the closest thing we have to the Christians and the lions.

Dan Jenkins, best-selling author

Men are clinging to football on a level we aren't even aware of. For centuries, we ruled everything, and now, in the last ten minutes, there are all these incursions by women. It's our Alamo.

Tony Kornheiser, writer

Monday Night Football.

Camille Paglia, writer and feminist, when asked what was her favorite television show

Professional football is no longer a game. It is a war. And it brings out the same primitive instincts that go back thousands of years.

Malcolm Allison, writer

Pro football is like nuclear warfare. There are no winners, only survivors.

Frank Gifford, professional football player

The prevalent nature of the professional football player is that of soldier of fortune. He's trained and willing to bust people up.
Jim Brown, Hall of Fame football player

We're basically a save-the-whales-team; we can't turn down big people who can play.
George Young, professional football executive

When it comes to football, God is prejudiced—toward big, fast kids.
Chuck Mills, professional football player

Football is, after all, a wonderful way to get rid of your aggressions without going to jail for it.
Heywood Hale Broun, writer

Football is the quintessential American sport: lots of violence punctuated by committee meetings.
George Will, political analyst and baseball aficionado

Football isn't a contact sport, it's a collision sport. Dancing is a contact sport.
Vince Lombardi, National Football League Hall of Fame coach

The best thing in football was to really pop someone. One of the great joys of my life was to get a bead on a guy and really put him out.
John Gordy, professional football player

The head coach can be considered the general, and his assistants the butt-kicking drill instructors, along with the whole coterie of trainer-medics, physicians, waterboys and office helpers. In addition the President can come to the war zone and see how his boys are doing.
Rick Sortun, professional football player

A boy who doesn't like contact shouldn't play football, because he isn't going to change.
Red Blaik, former college football coach

Some guys might play pro football for the money alone, but after two years they're gone. This is just too punishing a sport to play just for money.
Rick Casares, professional football player

To me, no football player is too young, no football player is over the hill, no football player is dumb. They are all smart enough, all champions—if I and my coaches are good enough to teach them.
Chuck Knox, professional football coach

Western supremacy in football is a triumph of the middle-class over the rich.
Knute Rockne, Hall of Fame college football coach

When I played football I was turning people onto violence, competition and greed.
Chip Oliver, professional football player

Women get pleasure and empowerment from subverting and making fun of football. In part because it's clear to them that it's an all-male institution that celebrates exclusively male values, such as brutality and aggression.
Dr. Margaret Carlisle-Duncan, human kineticist

You'll know, because you'll be looking out of your ear hole.
Ronnie Barnes, trainer, to David Meggett, professional football player, referring to what in the National Football League is called an "Official NFL hit"

You've got to be a son-of-a-bitch to play this game right.

> *Carl Brettschnieder, professional football player*

Ford, Gerald

(b. Jul. 14, 1914) *president of the United States; played football at University of Michigan; avid golfer*

Be careful, Jerry! You're going to hit a Democrat.

> *Tip O'Neill, speaker of the House (Democrat),*
> *to President Ford (Republican)*
> *at a celebrity golf tournament*

There are forty-two golf courses in the Palm Springs area and nobody knows which one Ford is playing until after he hits his tee shot.

> *Bob Hope, comedian and actor, on the former*
> *president*

It's not hard to follow Jerry Ford on the golf course, you just follow the wounded!

> *Bob Hope, comedian and actor,*
> *on the former president*

Four Horsemen

Outlined against the blue-gray October sky, the Four Horsemen rode again. In dramatic lore they are know as Famine, Pestilence, Destruction and Death. These are only aliases. Their real names are Stuhldreher, Miller, Crowley and Layden.

> *Grantland Rice, sportswriter, writing about the*
> *famed starting Notre Dame football backfield*

Fox Hunting

A chance-bred hound is like a chance-bred race horse; he may be very good at his work, but he is worthless for breeding. Not being carefully bred himself, the faults of his progenitors are certain to be reproduced in the offspring.

> *Lord Willoughby de Broke, master of the*
> *Warwickshire Hunt*

Hounds that run forward and frequently examine the discoveries of others when they are casting about and hunting have no confidence in themselves, while those who will not let their cleverer mates go forward, but fuss and keep them back, are confident to a fault.

> *Xenophon, philosopher, pupil of Plato*

Hunting literature has never, or so it seems to me, dwelt sufficiently on the charm of foxhounds. Their purely professional qualities are extolled—nose, tongue, speed, endurance—but nothing is said for their social gifts. Or, for example, the charm of the reception that, in their own domain, the bitch-pack will accord to a friend.

> *Edith Oenone Somerville,*
> *master of Foxhounds, West-Carbery*

If hunting were based on exclusiveness it would have perished long ago.

> *William Bromley-Davenport,*
> *sportsman and politician*

In that word 'unting what a ramification of knowledge is compressed.

> *R. S. Surtees, writer and foxhunter*

It's not that I loves the fox less, it's that I loves the 'ound more.

> *R. S. Surtees, writer and foxhunter*

Just before she sank, a few horses and hounds got loose and jumped over board, and one of the hounds, seeing a horse swimming near it,

managed to scramble onto its back, apparently immediately recognizing it as a friend. The hound was rescued.

Philip K. Crowe, environmentalist, outdoorsman, and writer, referring to the sinking of a ship that was transporting horses and hounds for hunting to India, when the ship sank

Never had the fox or hare the honor of being chased to death by so accomplished a huntsman; never was a huntsman's table graced by such urbanity and wit. He could bag a fox in Greek, find a hare in Latin, inspect his kennels in Italian and direct the economies of his stables in French.

Peter Beckford, hunter and writer, about William Somerville, hunter

Subscription packs are productive of more energy and less cavailling than private packs; every man feels his interest at stake both summer and winter and will look to things all the year round, instead of lounging carelessly out during the season, leaving the breeding and protection of foxes, the propitiation of farmers and other etceteras to the private owners of the hounds, who in all probability leaves it to the huntsman . . . A subscription pack makes every man put his shoulder to the wheel, not only to keep down expense, but to promote sport.

R. S. Surtees, writer and foxhunter

The ducks flew up from the Morton Pond
The fox looked up at their tailing strings,
He wished (perhaps) that a fox had wings. . . .

G. D. Armour, poet, from Reynard the Fox

The English country gentleman galloping after a fox—the unspeakable in full pursuit of the uneatable.

Oscar Wilde, writer

There can be no more important kind of information than the exact knowledge of a man's own country; for this as well as for more general reasons of pleasure and advantage, hunting with hounds and other kinds of sport should be pursued by the young.

Plato, philosopher

They're not dogs, they're hounds. And they don't bark, they tongue.

Evelyne Hoover, field master, Pickering Hunt, to a person who complained about barking dogs

When hounds come out of cover and dwell on the line of the fox, it always appears to me that they are, so to speak, timing and making sure that the scent of the fox is really that of a fox. If all foxes smelt the same, why should they dwell? . . . I have seen hares . . . hunted by staunch foxhounds who themselves would never dream of hunting hare if they knew what they were doing.

M. F. Berry, journalist and foxhunter

When men seek in cover for a fox and the hounds happen to find him, then the hunter rejoicest for the exploit of his hounds . . . If the hounds put up a fox while drawing for hare, a warning must be blown that there is a thief in the wood.

Edward, Duke of York, grandson of Edward III, master of hounds

A fox has . . . a large amount of reasoning faculty in his beautiful head, the very expression of his eye tells it, and it is further proved by the impossibility of the stuffer or preserver of beasts and birds to give the specimen its crafty and observant expression; it is also beyond the power of the painter.

Grantly Berkley, Member of Parliament, author, and foxhunter

My life divides into three parts. In the first I was wretched; in the second ill at ease; in the third hunting.

Roger Scrunton, media personality, writer, foxhunter

Of all the things in this world, Fox-hunting is the most difficult to explain to those who know nothing about it.

Lord Willoughby de Broke, outspoken foxhunter

When you're on a horse, hunting foxes, you're back in time, like you're in the 1700's or 1800's. You're not thinking about the real world. You don't have cell phones.

Shepherd Ellenberg, real estate investor and foxhunter

The upland and copses, which at the end of August had still been green islands among the black fields plowed ready for winter corn, and the stubble had become golden and lurid red islands in a sea of bright green autumn crops. The gray hare had already changed half its coat, the foxes' cubs were beginning to leave their parents, and the young wolves were bigger than dogs. It was the best time of year for the chase.

Leo Tolstoy, novelist, from War and Peace

Freshmen

Freshmen get nothing but abuse . . . but plenty of that.

Knute Rockne, college football coach

Fumbles

I told Ricky to forget about the fumbles. What was I going to do, jump on him?

Mack Brown, Texas A&M coach, speaking about Rick Williams's fumble after breaking all-time rushing and all-time all-purpose yards college career marks and rushing for 250 yards in his final game

The only time I would ever get the ball is when there is a mistake. So the less I get the ball the happier I am.

Tom Mack, professional football player, offensive lineman

Future

OK, so we don't intend to win this year, maybe not even next year. It's the future we're concerned with.

Chuck Knox, professional football coach, after having traded away four star players

The future is now.

George Allen, professional football coach

Gaijin

The old isolationist thinking is still prevalent here. Gaijin are useful as scapegoats when things go wrong. But they are not really welcomed by the baseball establishment.

Takenori Emoto, writer

We're mercenaries, pure and simple. Our job is to do well and let the Japanese players have the glory and take the blame when things go bad.

Leon Lee, professional baseball player

You're an outcast no matter what you do. You go 5-for-5 and you're ignored. You go 0-for-5 and it's, "Fuck you, Yankee go home."

Warren Cromartie, professional baseball player

Gambling

A fool and his money are soon parted, usually before they run by the second half of the daily double.

Kelso Sturgeon, Guide to Sports Betting

A gambler is nothing but a man who makes his living out of hope.

William Bolitho, writer

But there, right there, the beast quit. Quit dead, do you hear? Two other horses went S-W-O-O-S-H and passed him at the finish. I was down to a bus ticket.

Tiny Tim, musician, sports fan

Everybody loves a gambler, until he loses.

Vince Lombardi, Hall of Fame football coach

For sure the best poker player will be my utility infielder and he'll be taking money off my All-Star shortstop. It always works like that.

Joe McCarthy, professional baseball player and manager

I believe it is more moral for government to legalize gambling than it is to force people to gamble in the unregulated and ruthless domain of organized crime.

Howard Samuels, first OTB (Off-Track Betting) head

I bet on a horse at ten-to-one. It didn't come in until half-past five.

Henny Youngman, comedian

I can't stand to look at a team that hasn't beaten the spread and thinks it's won.

Pete Axthelm, writer and broadcaster

I didn't necessarily know about horses more than the next guy, but I might have known a little more about playing. I never was afraid to bet.

Art Rooney, owner, Pittsburgh Steelers, who won approximately $200,000–$300,000 in one day at Saratoga

Information, sound information, is what you need at a racetrack.

Arnold Rothstein, gambler, fixer of the 1919 World Series

It matters not who wins or loses, but how you cover your points.

Steve Cady, sportswriter

I went to bed Charles Barkley and I woke up Pete Rose.

Charles Barkley, professional basketball player, after being fined $5,000 by the National Basketball Association for making a side bet with Mark Jackson (then of the Knicks) about who would win the game

Money won is twice as sweet as money earned.

Paul Newman in The Color of Money

Organized baseball has a phobia about gambling. The parks are policed to prevent it, the clubhouse bulletin boards have placards that shout in bold print the penalties meted out to players and club employees caught at it, and the most witless jockeys of the dugout know better than to joke about fixing games.

Lee Allen, sportswriter

The better the gambler, the worse the man.

Publius Syrus, Roman historian

The horseplayer doesn't consider himself a horseplayer. He thinks he can break the habit anytime he wants to. The shylocks know he's hooked forever.

Jimmy Cannon, sportswriter

The horseplayer who insists on wagering large amounts of money on the sure things must live and die broke.

Kelso Sturgeon, Guide to Sports Betting

Of all the human emotions none is so productive of evil and immorality as gambling.

Charles-Maurice de Talleyrand, statesman and writer

The urge to gamble is so universal and its practice is so pleasurable, that I assume it must be evil.

Heywood Broun, sportswriter

The best thing in the world is to win at the racetrack. The second best thing is to lose at the racetrack.

Old racetrack aphorism, attributed by William Murray, writer

There was, shall we say, a bookie element in Boston, and I thought everyone who asked me about my health was a gambler. Men would call up and say they were taking their sons to the games so they wanted to make sure I was okay. They were just checking.

Bill Russell, Hall of Fame basketball player

What you did was gamble. In those early days . . . I guess we all gambled.

Chandler Harper, golfer

You beat someone gambling, you don't have to feel sorry for him. He wouldn't be gambling if he didn't know what the hell he was doing, you understand, or thinks he knows what he's doing.

> *Minnesota Fats, legendary pool player*

You don't need a lot of money at the track, you need winners.

> *Gerry Okuneff, professional handicapper*

It was a complete oversight on my side.

> *Hansie Cronje, South Africa cricket team captain and star, who took payoffs from bookmakers, after admitting to the government that he had taken an additional $100,000 he had not admitted to earlier*

He is called Hot Horse Herbie because he can always tell you about a horse that is so hot it is practically on fire, a hot horse being a horse that is all readied up to win a race, although sometimes Herbie's hot horses turn out to be so cold they freeze everybody within fifty miles of them.

> *Damon Runyon, writer*

You're blind! You're a crook! You're robbing me!

> *Walter Matthau, actor, to the different umpires and referees who appeared on as many as fifteen televisions in his home, during his many gambling binges*

Garagiola, Joe

(b. 1926) *professional baseball player; broadcaster*

When Joe was playing baseball, he could never hit a curve. Well, he can now. His slices are majestic.

> *Bob Hope, comedian and actor, about Joe Garagiola*

Gehrig, Lou

(b. June 19, 1903; d. June 2, 1941) *Won six World Series; second all-time games played (2,130); two-time League MVP*

Don't feel badly, Lou. It took twenty-one hundred thirty games to get you out, and sometimes it only takes fifteen minutes to get me out of a game.

> *Lefty Gomez, professional baseball player (pitcher), to Gehrig, after he took himself out of a game for the first time*

They better get Gehrig out of there before somebody kills him. I pitched him inside, across the letters today—just once! If Gehrig saw that ball he couldn't move away from it. The ball went through his arms . . . not over or under 'em, but through his arms!

> *Jo Krakaukas, professional baseball player, speaking of Gehrig's final at-bats*

Gibson, Bob

(b. Nov. 9, 1935) *Hall of Fame baseball pitcher; two-time Cy Young Award winner; won two World Series*

Gibson pitches as though he's double parked.

> *Vin Scully, broadcaster*

He'd knock you down just for having bad breath.

> *Joe Garagiola, professional baseball player and broadcaster*

Gibson, Josh

(b. Dec. 21, 1911; d. Jan. 20, 1947) *Hall of Fame baseball player; played in Negro Leagues; called the "Babe Ruth of the Negro Leagues"*

If they had ever let him play in a small place like Ebbets Field or the old Fenway Park,

Josh Gibson would have forced baseball to rewrite the rules. He was, at the minimum, two Yogi Berras.

Bill Veeck, baseball owner and thoroughbred racetrack operator

Gipp, George

(b. Feb. 8, 1895; d. Dec. 14, 1920) *All-American college football player*

Gipp is no football player. He's a runaway son-of-a-bitch!

John J. McEwan, college football coach

Rock, I know I'm going . . . but I'd like one last request . . . Someday, Rock, sometime— when the going isn't so easy, when the odds are against us, ask Notre Dame to win a game for me—for the Gipper. I don't know where I'll be then, Rock, but I'll know about it and I'll be happy.

attributed to George Gipp, a dying college football player, by Knute Rockne, college football coach, and recounted by Rockne for the legendary 1928 Notre Dame–Army football game

Gleason, Jackie

(b. Feb. 26, 1916; d. June 24, 1987) *Comedian, actor, sportsman, and avid golfer*

He has the only cart with a bartender.

Bob Hope, comedian, actor

When he gets into a sand trap, the sand has to get out.

Bob Hope, comedian, actor

Goalie

Being goalie is a much bigger responsibility than anyone else on a team, but it's something I really like about this job. I've always liked responsibility.

Dominik Hasek, professional hockey player

Guys strike out all the time in baseball, but if a goalie misses one, the world is over.

Murray Bannerman, professional hockey player

Right now he feels like he's stopping a basketball and right now we feel like we're shooting at a lacrosse net.

Wayne Gretzky, Hall of Fame hockey player, on Dominik Hasek, hockey goalie

What goaltenders are afraid of is being scored on.

Lorne Worsley, professional hockey goalie

You're the last line of defense. Any way you can, no matter what part of your body you use, you keep the ball out of the net.

Mark Morris, professional soccer player

Goals

It's so special to score goals—it's the home run.

Ron Coron, hockey executive

You have to have stepping-stone goals that are within reach. Once you keep getting up those stepping-stones, you'll reach the pinnacle of your goals and your dreams.

Dominique Dawes, Olympic gold medalist gymnast

Golf

A controlled shot to a closely guarded green is the surest test of any man's golf.

A. W. Tillinghast, writer

All my life I've been trying to make a hole in one. The closest I ever came was a bogey.
Lou Holtz, college football coach

First you teach a golfer to hook the ball by using his hands and arms properly. Then you teach him how to take the hook away by using his body and legs properly.
Harvey Pennick, professional golf instructor and coach

Getting in a water hazard is like being in a plane crash—the result is final. Landing in a bunker is similar to an automobile accident—there is a chance of recovery.
Bobby Jones, champion professional golfer

Give me the fresh air, a beautiful partner, and a nice round of golf, and you can keep the fresh air and the round of golf.
Jack Benny, comedian and actor

Golf and sex are the only things you can enjoy without being good at.
Jimmy Demaret, champion golfer

Golf: a game in which you claim the privileges of age, and retain the playthings of childhood.
Samuel Johnson, writer

Golf combines two favorite American pastimes: taking long walks and hitting things with a stick.
P. J. O'Rourke, writer and journalist

Golf gives you an insight into human nature, your own as well as your opponent's.
Grantland Rice, sportswriter

Golf is a game that has drawn . . . together and created a special fraternity among the celebrities of show business, sports, and politics.
Bob Hope, comedian, actor

Golf is a good walk spoiled.
Mark Twain, humorist and author

Golf is in the interest of good health and good manners. It promotes self-restraint and affords a chance to play the man and act the gentleman.
William Howard Taft, president of the United States

Golf is the most fun you can have without taking your clothes off.
Chi Chi Rodriguez, champion professioal golfer

Golf is the reason for being. We work so that we may live, and we live so that we may play the game.
E. Parker Yutzler, Jr., amateur golfer

Golf is twenty percent mechanics and technique. The other eighty percent is philosophy, humor, tragedy, romance, melodrama, companionship, camaraderie, sussedness, and conversation.
Grantland Rice, sportswriter

Golf is played almost entirely between your ears.
Seve Ballesteros, champion professioal golfer

Golf may be played on Sunday, not being a game within view of the law, but being a form of moral effort.
Stephen Leacock, humorist

Golf seems to me an arduous way to go for a walk. I prefer to take the dogs out.
Princess Anne of Great Britain

Grip it, and rip it!
John Daly, champion professioial golfer

Humiliations are the essence of the game.
Alistair Cooke, writer and historian

I am happy to learn that half the people taking up golf today are women. I shudder to imagine the bad advice those women are getting from husbands and fathers and boyfriends, most of whom should keep their minds on their own vexations of their own game.
Harvey Pennick, golf coach and writer

I am the captive of my slice
I am the servant of my score.
Grantland Rice, sportswriter

If you wish to hide your character, do not play golf.
Percey Boomer, teaching pro

I don't say my golf game is bad, but if I grew tomatoes, they'd come up sliced.
Miller Barber, champion professional golfer

I look at a golf course as a huge waste of pastureland.
Karl Malone, professional basketball player

In the fell clutch of grip and stance
I've often winced and cursed aloud.
Grantland Rice, sportswriter

I regard golf as an expensive way of playing marbles.
G. K. Chesterton, writer

I still enjoy the ooh's and aah's when I hit my drives. But I'm getting pretty tired of the aw's and uh's when I miss the putts.
John Daly, champion professional golfer

If you are caught on a golf course during a storm and are afraid of lightning, hold up a 1-iron. Not even God can hit a 1-iron.
Lee Trevino, champion professional golfer (thrice hit by lightning himself)

The income tax has made liars out of more Americans than golf.
Will Rogers, entertainer and humorist

In golf, you don't lose to another guy. You lose to the golf course, or you lose to yourself.
Glenn Laydendecker, professional tennis player

It is nothing new or original to say that golf is played one stroke at a time. But it took me many years to realize it.
Bobby Jones, champion professional golfer

The peculiar thing about this game—any game really, but this game far more than most—is, the more you fight it, the more it eludes you.
Braxton Dodson, to his son, James Dodson, writer

This game, you never lick it.
Harold Sanderson, professional golfer

It is the fashion these days to speak of golf as a kind of religious experience, a doorway to the spiritual side of man, an egress to the eternal. My father was a man of faith, but I don't think he viewed the golf course as a path to God. He thought golf was a way to celebrate the divinity of life, the here and now, and simply the best way to play.
James Dodson, writer

In good company there is no such thing as a bad golf course.

James Dodson, writer

No game designed to be played with the aid of personal servants by right-handed men who can't even bring along their dogs can be entirely good for the soul.

Bruce McCall, writer

One of the nice things about the Senior Tour is that we can take a cart and a cooler. If your game is not going well, you can always have a picnic.

Lee Trevino, champion professional golfer

Rail-splitting produced an immortal president in Lincoln, but golf hasn't produced even a good A-1 congressman.

Will Rogers, entertainer and humorist

Republican religion. That's why so many men worship it on Sunday morning.

attributed to Kristen Cress by James Dodson in Final Rounds

The golf swing is like a suitcase into which we are trying to pack one too many things.

John Updike, novelist and critic

The mystery of golf is that nobody can master it. You can shoot a good score today, but can you do it tomorrow?

Curtis Strange, champion professional golfer

There are only two things in the world you gotta do with your head down—golf and praying.

Lee Trevino, champion professional golfer

There are two things that made golf appealing to the average man . . . Arnold Palmer and the invention of the mulligan.

Bob Hope, comedian and actor

There is the fantasy, indulged by every hacker on his pillow, of playing with Nicklaus or Palmer.

Alistair Cooke, writer and historian

The spice of golf, as of life, lies in variety.

Robert Hunter, writer and golfer

The very summer in which I at last, acting on an old suggestion of my genial publisher, settle to the task of collecting my scattered pieces about golf turned out to be an unhappy one for my game.

John Updike, novelist and critic

The woods are full of long drivers.

Harvey Pennick, golfing instructor and philosopher

Through golf you get to know the inside of people.

Willie Turnesa, golfer

What golf develops best is masochism.

Bruce McCall, writer

What other people may find in poetry, I find in the flight of a good drive.

Arnold Palmer, champion professional golfer

You can talk to a fade, but a hook won't listen.

Lee Trevino, champion professional golfer

Golf Clubs

A good driver is a hellava lot harder to find than a good wife.

Lee Trevino, championship professional golfer, married three times

Actually, the only time I ever took out a one-iron was to kill a tarantula. And it took a seven to do that.

Jim Murray, sportswriter

Damn the car. My golf clubs are in the trunk. The best set I ever had.

Lawrence Taylor, Hall of Fame
professional football player,
responding to the news of
his car being reported stolen

When I first got to playing, the clubs I used were made out of coat hangers.

Walter Stewart, golfer

When practicing, use the club that gives you the most trouble, not the one that gives you the most satisfaction.

Harry Vardon, professional golfer

Golf Courses

Every hole should be a demanding par and a comfortable bogey.

Robert Trent Jones, Jr.,
golf course architect

Putting greens are to courses what faces are to portraits.

Charles Blair McDonald,
golfer and writer

The ardent golfer would play Mount Everest if somebody put a flagstick on top.

Pete Dye, golf course designer

The strategy of a golf course is the soul of the game.

Robert Trent Jones, Jr.,
golf course architect

Gordon, Jeff

(b. Aug. 4, 1971) *Won Daytona 500; NASCAR Rookie of the Year; three-time Winston Cup champion*

He's not just the driver of the future. He's the driver of the *immediate* future.

Dale Janett, writer

Graduation

I'm going to graduate on time, no matter how long it takes.

Senior basketball player at the
University of Pittsburgh

Grand Slams (tennis)

If ever there was a first family of Wimbledon it is the Sterry-Cooper alliance. Since the early days of 1894 there has always been a Sterry or Cooper in the All England Club. They are as ubiquitous as strawberries and cream.

Gwen Robyns, writer

Like clockwork, their sorority meets once a year, every year, on the red clay of Paris, in springtime. For the past decade, Steffi Graff, Monica Seles, and Arantxa Sanchez Vicario have exerted a virtually monopoly on the French Open. The older they get, the nicer it is to slide along on the clay and let the surface do their walking for them.

Robin Finn, sportswriter

The All England Lawn Tennis and Croquet Club's Championship at Wimbledon is the greatest show on earth. It is an anachronism . . . it is a bland mixture of English gar-

den party atmosphere with hard–core professional organization.

Gwen Robyns, writer

The first day of a Grand Slam . . . is a renewal: friendship and flings may begin or spring up again; someone new on the tour may turn some heads. At the very least, gossip will crop up in the locker rooms and in every corner of the players' lounge.

John Feinstein, writer, Hard Courts

The U.S. Open is tennis at its most gladiatorial. The spectators are an amalgam of the knowledgeable and ignorant, the drunk and the sober, the crude, rude and reserved.

H. A. Branham, writer

To be the U.S. Open champion is the greatest feeling you could have. And to try and do it again is what you live for. If these guys aren't living for that, something is wrong.

Pete Sampras, professional tennis champion

When you look back on the greatest tennis players of all time, you look at the number of Grand Slam tournaments they have won; the ranking is something everyone just takes for granted. In my mind the major titles are the most important thing.

Pete Sampras, professional tennis champion

Grange, Red

(b. June 13, 1903; d. Jan. 28, 1991) *Hall of Fame football player; All-American college football player*

On the field, he's the equal of three men and a horse.

Damon Runyon, writer

Grass Courts (tennis)

It is not the speed of grass that does guys in, but the unpredictability.

Arthur Ashe, tennis Hall of Famer

Greatness

A truly great player makes the worst player on the team good.

Oscar Robertson, Hall of Fame basketball player

He's taking his stubbornness and turning it into a positive. He's not too old . . . He's just stubborn and competitive, because that's what great players are made of.

Allan Houston, All-Star basketball player, referring to teammate Patrick Ewing

I am still the greatest player in the world. I just didn't perform well that night.

Ronaldo, professional soccer player, after a loss in the World Cup

Jordan's swagger, Gretzky's grace and Elway's determination were not dulled by age or eroded by exposure.

Richard Hoffer, sportswriter

I don't know anything about greatness. That's for others to decide.

Richard Petty, champion race car driver

There won't be another Jordan. There won't be another Gretzky.

Jaromir Jagr, professional hockey player

We were of the same era. We were the two top players of our league. In my heart I have always felt that I was the better hitter than Joe, which was always my first consideration,

but I have to say that he was the greatest baseball player of our time.

Ted Williams, Hall of Fame baseball player

When I watch myself on film, sometimes I don't even believe some of the things I do.

Walter Payton, Hall of Fame football player

When you're as great as I am, it's hard to be humble.

Muhammad Ali, champion boxer

You have to win everywhere to be a great player.

Gary Player, champion professional golfer

Gretzky, Wayne

(b. Jan. 26, 1961) *Hall of Fame hockey player; won four Stanley Cups; 10-time National Hockey League scoring champion; holds 61 National Hockey League records*

He played hockey like a chess master, several steps ahead of everyone else.

E. M. Swift, sportswriter

He was able to turn on a dime like no one else.

Mario Lemieux, Hall of Fame hockey player

He was the greatest [player] in the history of his sport, perhaps the single most innovative North American athlete since Babe Ruth. He changed his game.

George Vecsey, sportswriter

He was the kind of guy who got to know the clubhouse people, the stickboys. With older people it was always Mister.

Scotty Bowman, professional hockey coach

His passion to be the best player in the world is what drove him. He never had a game where afterward you would say, "Wayne looked a little flat tonight."

Mike Keenan, professional hockey coach

I heard people say he was the Michael Jordan of hockey. Horsepuck. Jordan was the Gretzky of basketball.

Rick Reilly, sportswriter

No person in sports has done as much for their sports as you have done for yours.

Gary Bettman, National Hockey League Commissioner, to Wayne Gretzky

The Edmonton Oilers without Wayne Gretzky is like *Wheel of Fortune* without Vanna White.

Attributed by Joel Stein (sportswriter) to Canadian House leader

Wayne Gretzky was a hockey artist in a sport often stereotyped for brute force and violent intimidation, using his stick as a paintbrush and his skates as dance slippers.

Joe Lapointe, sportswriter

Gymnastics

Competing is my favorite part of gymnastics. I just love being out there. I love the challenge.

Shannon Miller, Olympic gold medalist gymnast

Everyone is focusing on "You're an Olympic champion," but it's a lot more than that. We are representing our sport. We have a larger role to play.

Kerri Strug, Olympic gold medalist gymnast

Gymnastics is an expression of my innermost emotions, my response to love and care with which I have always been surrounded in my life.

Olga Korbut, Olympic gold medalist gymnast

Gymnastics makes me feel good about myself—knowing I can set goals and accomplish them, organize my time, and please lots of people.

Shannon Miller, Olympic gold medalist gymnast

Gymnastics taught me how to be focused and disciplined, which helped me prepare for life.

Kerri Strug, Olympic gold medalist gymnast

I don't want to be responsible one day for any young woman coming up to me and saying, "You robbed me of my childhood."

Al Fong, gymnastics coach

In gymnastics, one "off" movement and you're ruined.

Kerri Strug, Olympic gold medalist gymnast

I've never been very strong in the vault, which is probably why I didn't like it. But I've worked on it and I've got it under control. But even if you do it a million times, once you get into a competition situation, anything can happen.

Amanda Borden, Olympic gymnast

I'm mad on the platform. I want myself to be violent. Otherwise, I wouldn't be competitive.

Nelli Kim, Olympic gold medalist gymnast

I was never thinking of the score. You can't . . . You must do the exercise, because the score will come.

Nadia Comaneci, Olympic gold medalist gymnast

I weighed ninety-eight pounds and I was being called an overstuffed Christmas turkey. I was told I was never going to make it in life because I was going to be fat. I mean, *in life.*

Kristie Phillips, Olympic gymnast

Ninety percent of gymnastics is the mental ability to perform when the time comes.

Kurt Thomas, Olympic gymnast

The four-inch-wide apparatus requires nerves of steel and unwavering dedication.

Susan Vinella, journalist

There is an instant after you have released your grip on the apparatus when you are in the air, free. There is no feeling like it.

Yuri Titov, world champion gymnast

These girls are like little scorpions. You put them all in a bottle and one little scorpion will come out alive. That scorpion will be a champion.

Bela Karolyi, Olympic gymnastics coach

This isn't golf.

Bela Karolyi, Olympic gymnastics coach, referring to the seeming age limit there is on gymnastic careers

We rarely ask what becomes of Olympic gymnasts when they disappear from view. We don't want to see them parade past us with their broken bodies and mangled spirits.

Joan Ryan, writer

H

Hall of Fame

A man never gets to this station in life without being helped, aided, shoved and prodded to do better. I want to be honest with you; the players I played with and the coaches I had . . . they are directly responsible for my being here.

Johnny Unitas, Hall of Fame professional quarterback

Whitey and Mick both made the Hall of Fame and I didn't. I wasn't a bad influence on them, they were a bad influence on me.

Billy Martin, professional baseball player and manager

Handball

Anybody involved with handball has a childish mind.

Morris Levitsky, handball aficionado

Handballers share a camaraderie unique to the handball community.

George J. Zafferano, handballer and writer

Human hands are to the handball player as the racket is to the tennis player.

Wayne McFarland and Philip Smith, authors

It is the only game in which you *dive* head-first on concrete.

Michael Disend, writer

The one-wall game originated along the beaches of New York, where bathers found hitting a tennis ball against the open walls of the bath houses with their hands an excellent game . . . New York City is considered the stronghold of the one-wall game.

Michael Yessis, writer

The origin of throwing or striking a ball against a wall and chasing after its crazy rebound is rather obscure and lost in antiquity.

George J. Zafferano, handballer and writer

The time to start using the off hand is sooner rather than later.

Wayne McFarland and Philip Smith, writers

121

Hazing

It's good for them. It embarrasses a little, but relieves them a lot. Makes them part of the group.

Vince Lombardi, Hall of Fame coach, talking about rookie hazing in pro football

Heart

Holyfield's biggest asset, or course, was his ticker. He doesn't know how to quit . . . Without a doubt, he has the biggest heart I've ever encountered in this business, which is why he's such a great champion.

Mills Lane, district court judge and boxing referee

Heroes

Each of our idols are [*sic*] unique; yet each of them experienced life in ways that illuminate the history and culture of their times. Although not all of them came up swinging or dribbling from the slums, their stories suggest how sports empowers not only individuals, but whole classes, races, and generations of people—even those, perhaps especially those, who have been denied the full opportunities of American life. . . . Because their lives helped shape our values, our habits, the content of our character, no full understanding of America is possible without an understanding of its sports idols.

Robert Lipsyte and Peter Levine, from their book Idols of the Game

Every athlete is a role model, whether they want to be or not. You have to recognize that position.

Dale Earnhardt, champion race car driver

Heroes and cowards feel exactly the same fear. Heroes just react to it differently.

Cus D'Amato, Hall of Fame boxing trainer

My dad was my biggest hero, but they haven't made a poster of him yet.

Derek Jeter, professional baseball player

One sign of a hero is if you feel enhanced simply when talking about him—recounting his feats, recalling a time when your own little life was touched by his.

Roger Rosenblatt, sportswriter

We could hear what the ballplayers said to one another as they ran onto the field and could watch their individual gestures and mannerisms as they loosened up in the on deck circle. There come to earth, were the heroes of my imagination, Snider and Robinson and the powerful-looking Don Newcombe.

Doris Kearns Goodwin, writer and historian

High School

Life really wouldn't be worth livin' if you didn't have a high school team to support.

Bob Rutherford, realtor and fan

Today, more civic loyalty centers around [*sic*] high school basketball than around any other one thing. No distinctions divide the crowds which pack the school gymnasium for home games, and which in every kind of machine crowd the roads for out-of-town games, North Side and South Side, Catholic and Kluxer, banker and machinist—their one shout is 'eat 'em, beat 'em Bearcats.

Robert and Helen Lynd, sociologists

Hiking

The only thing predictable about bears is that they are unpredictable.

Craig Medred, writer and camper/hiker

Hope and the future for me are not in lawns and cultivated fields, not in towns and cities, but in the impervious and quaking swamps.

Henry David Thoreau, philosopher and writer

One should always have a definite objective, in a walk as in a life—it is so much more satisfying to reach a target by personal effort than to wander aimlessly.

Alfred Wainwright, Cross UK walker

Puny man pitted against the elements. A flyspeck of humanity out there alone, somewhere in an endless waste of ice and water, snow and gale, staving off death hour after hour—or waiting for it numb and half frozen, with cold begotten resignation.

Ben East, sportswriter

The necessity of relying on one's own skill and judgment for comfort and safety is one of the many attractions of wilderness travel of all kinds.

Raymond Bridge, outdoorsman and journalist

You can't see anything from a car; you've got to get out of the goddamn contraption and walk, better yet crawl, on hands and knees, over the sandstone and through the thornbrush and cactus. When traces of blood begin to mark your trail, you'll see something, maybe.

Edward Abbey, naturalist and writer

Hitting

But you don't have to go up in the stands and play your foul balls. I do.

Sam Snead, champion golfer, to Ted Williams, Hall of Fame baseball player and fisherman, arguing which was more difficult, to hit a moving baseball or a stationary golf ball

Every time he hits the ball, it's like he waits to break it. I'm pulling for him. He's the man.

Mark McGwire, professional baseball player, commenting on Sammy Sosa

Frank caught the ball and was trying to get across the field when Chuck Bednarik nailed him. Chuck weighed about 240 pounds and hung Frank out on his arm, just clotheslined him and smacked him on the chin . . . They took him to the lockeroom on a stretcher, and I remember going back to the huddle and everybody saying, "It's all over for Frank, no way he can survive that hit."

Sam Huff, Hall of Fame professional football player, referring to the play in which Chuck Bednarik almost ended Frank Gifford's career. Gifford came back a year later

I don't need to hit a home run anymore. I only have to hit a single. I do everything for the team. I just want to win.

Sammy Sosa, professional baseball player

If you want to be a great hitter, don't go to the movies. It ruins your eyes.

Rogers Hornsby, Hall of Fame baseball player

Get it in the air.

Ted Williams, Hall of Fame baseball player and world class fisherman, was famous for telling hitters to make sure their swing was on an upward slant against the pitcher's downward velocity

Here comes Jim Brown through a hole and I'm right there to meet him. I hit that big sucker head-on and my gear came down and cut my nose and my teeth hit together so hard the enamel popped off. He broke my nose, broke my teeth, and knocked me cold.

Sam Huff, Hall of Fame professional football player, about Jim Brown, Hall of Fame running back

Hit 'em like you live—hard and in the alleys.

Reggie Smith, professional baseball player and coach

Hit the ball carrier harder than he hits you.

Ray Nitschke, Hall of Fame football player

In America the big thing is that you want to hit something. I used to walk around in my tennis clothes with a racket all the time and ask everyone, "Do you want to hit?"

Fred Perry, professional tennis champion

It's a lot easier hitting a quarterback than a little white ball.

Bubba Smith, professional football player, on why he preferred football to golf

It took me seventeen years to get three thousand hits in baseball. I did it in one afternoon on the golf course.

Hank Aaron, Hall of Fame baseball player

Keep your eye on the ball and hit them where they ain't.

Wee Willie Keeler, professional baseball player

Once my swing starts, I can't change or pull up. It's all or nothing at all.

Babe Ruth, Hall of Fame baseball player

Say you get four at bats; that's twelve strikes a game. If you can't hit four hard, you're not in the right business.

Mike Piazza, professional baseball player

Stand your ground and take your lumps.

Yogi Berra, Hall of Fame baseball player and manager

That guy can hit me in the middle of the night, blindfolded and with two broken feet to boot.

Don Newcombe, professional baseball player, about Tommy Heinrich

The more hitters we have in this game, the better it is for the game. Listen, when you're coming towards the park and you're two blocks away, and you hear a tremendous cheer, that isn't because someone has thrown a strike. That's because someone has hit the ball.

Ted Williams, Hall of Fame baseball player

With old-timers, whether it be baseball players or fighters, the ability to hit goes last.

Grantland Rice, sportswriter

When he hits you, he buries you.

Walt Michaels, professional football coach, about Greg Buttle, professional football player

When I hit a guy, I'll hit him in the throat—he doesn't have pads on there.

Conrad Dobler, professional football player

You don't think and hit at the same time.

Yogi Berra, Hall of Fame baseball player and manager

You can eliminate a guy with a big hit. Some guys, if you get them with a big pancake hit, they disappear the rest of the game.

Brian Burke, Vancouver Canucks
general manager

Hockey

By the age of 18, the average American has witnessed 200,000 acts of violence on television, most of them occurring during Game 1 of the NHL playoff series.

Steve Rushin, sportswriter

I just loved the game. It gave me so much. All I ever wanted to do was be a hockey player, and then give something back when I retired.

Willie O'Ree, professional hockey player, first
African-American hockey player

He who lives by the cheap shot dies by the cross-check.

Stan Fischler, hockey commentator and historian

Hockey belongs to the Cartoon Network, where a person can be pancaked by an ACME anvil, then expanded—accordion-style—back to full stature, without any lasting side effect.

Steve Rushin, sportswriter

Fighting has been part of hockey for 50 years. It'll be with us another 50. Count on it.

John Ferguson, professional hockey player

It's hard to believe . . . that hockey methodically set out to make the games more physical, more damaging to players, more breathtaking to the increasing number of warm-climate fans who did not grow up skating on ice and appreciating finesse. Yet the high sticking and the league's relentless merchandising of thumping checks feels something like a trend.

Robert Lipsyte, writer

It would be a better game if it were played in the mud.

Jimmy Cannon, sportswriter

I went to a fight the other night and a hockey game broke out.

Rodney Dangerfield, comedian and actor

No other team sport in recorded history accepts fighting as such a crucial aspect of the game.

Dr. Ross Thomas Runfola

People talk about skating, puck handling and shooting, but the whole sport is angles and caroms, forgetting the straight direction the puck is going, calculating where it will be diverted, factoring in all the interruptions.

Wayne Gretzky, Hall of Fame hockey player

The problem with hockey is that there's too much hockey and not enough fighting.

Ira Berkow, sportswriter, sarcastically discussing
the physical play of the Philadelphia Flyers

There aren't any black hockey players; they play football or baseball.

Jackie Robinson, Hall of Fame baseball player
and first African-American major league baseball
player, to William O'Ree, first African-American
National Hockey League player

We get nose jobs all the time in the NHL, and we don't even have to go to the hospital.

Brad Park, professional hockey player

We're not the smartest group of guys, but we are the most down-to-earth group of guys.

> *Dixon Ward, professional hockey player*

We take the most direct route to the puck and we arrive in ill humor.

> *Bobby Clarke, professional hockey player and team executive*

You could have a house party with two hundred people and have more room than you have in the crease.

> *Grant Fuhr, professional hockey player*

I can sympathize with Canadians whose noses are out of joint. How would Americans feel if the baseball commissioner was Japanese?

> *Bob McKenzie, columnist, writing about the Americanization of hockey, which Canadians feel is their national sport*

Hogan, Ben
(b. Aug. 13, 1912; d. July 25, 1977) *Champion golfer; won four U.S. Opens, two Masters, two PGAs, and one British Open*

He was as grim as a rattlesnake.

> *Gene Sarazn, champion golfer*

I don't say Ben's the greatest golfer in the world or the greatest swinger of a golf club, but nobody ever worked like him.

> *Babe Didrickson Zaharias, champion professional golfer*

Hollywood
I broke into Hollywood the old-fashioned way: I knew somebody.

> *Jim Brown, Hall of Fame football player*

I empathized with the plight of the man/monster who didn't want to hurt anybody and just wanted to be left alone to live his life. I understood his anger and reveled in his power and strength and the way that his tormentors would ultimately bow down before him when he eventually lost his temper.

> *Lou Ferrigno, champion bodybuilder, professional football player, and actor, star of* The Incredible Hulk *TV series*

I just can't stand the thought of her kissing another man, let alone being in bed with someone, even though I know it's only for the cameras.

> *Ronaldo, professional soccer player, about his girlfriend Suzanna Werner, who has made several movies and television cameos*

I love acting . . . All you do is look in the camera, smile, and lie with charm. I learned how to do that watching Don King promote fights.

> *Tex Cobb, professional boxer and actor*

My wife's been trying to talk me into doing movies once baseball is over, but I've seen what it's like, long 14- 15-hour days. I think this job's probably more fun.

> *Matt Williams, professional baseball player*

Home (games)
I don't think home court means a lot until it gets to a deciding game. In a deciding game, I think it's a huge factor.

> *Jeff Van Gundy, professional basketball coach*

Home Run Heard Round the World

I jumped and skipped around the bases like I was half nuts. Gee whiz, I kept saying, gee whiz! I guess you could call me an "accidental hero."

Bobby Thompson, professional baseb all player, who hit the Home Run Heard Round the World

I literally went berserk when he hit the homer. I threw the cards in the air, kicked the table, and kept yelling, "He did it! He did it!"

George Plimpton, writer and editor

Now it is done. Now the story ends . . . the art of fiction is dead. Reality has strangled invention.

Red Smith, sportswriter

Safe prediction: the home run that Bobby Thompson of the New York Giants hit off Ralph Branca of the Brooklyn Dodgers on October 3, 1951, will forever remain the quintessential moment in baseball history.

David Lehman, writer and historian

Seldom does the stuff of myth, of fact and of interborough history come together more exactly.

David Lehman, writer and historian

That was the single greatest moment probably in sports in my lifetime.

Woody Allen, writer, director, actor

The Giants win the pennant, the Giants win the pennant, the Giants win the pennant! I don't believe it, I don't believe it, I don't believe it!

Russ Hodges, broadcaster

Home Runs

I just felt if I got a strike to hit, I would hit it out . . . it really wasn't one of my greatest.

Hank Aaron, Hall of Fame baseball player, on his 715th home run, breaking Babe Ruth's all-time record

I just wish I could have enjoyed it as much as Sammy Sosa and Mark McGwire enjoyed it last year.

Hank Aaron, Hall of Famer, speaking about chasing Babe Ruth's record and the hate mail that interfered with enjoying the pursuit

I must admit when Reggie Jackson hit that third home run and I was sure nobody was listening, I applauded into my glove.

Steve Garvey, Hall of Fame baseball player, who played on the losing side

That ball got out of here in a hurry. Anything going that fast better have a damn stewardess on it—don't you think?

Kevin Costner, actor, in Bull Durham

The ball sailed so high that when it came down it was coated with ice.

Bill McGeehan, sportswriter, writing about one of Babe Ruth's home runs

There is nothing harder to do in all of sports than hitting a home run.

Ted Williams, Hall of Fame baseball player and champion fisherman

Nothing

Ted Williams, Hall of Fame baseball player, when asked what he was thinking about during his last at-bat, when he hit a home run

Honesty

Honesty is as important in fishing as it is in golf.

Randy Voorhees, fisherman and writer

Hope

If you have hope, there's a light at the end of the tunnel. Hope makes you better. The air in the locker room is different when you have hope.

Dixon Ward, professional hockey player

I'm a football fan, and we're still in the first quarter. Let's keep going awhile and we'll see where we are around halftime.

Jimmy Vasser, automobile racer

It ain't over 'til it's over.

Yogi Berra, Hall of Fame baseball player and manager

It's just a matter of hoping nobody comes and gets you. There's no use looking back.

Chris Antley, professional jockey, on being ahead in the homestretch

When the astronauts walked on the moon I figured we had a chance to win. Nothing seemed impossible after that.

Tug McGraw, professional baseball player

You gotta believe.

Tug McGraw, professional baseball player

Horseback Riding

The horse is such a beautiful animal. When you're on him, in control of him, moving with him as one, it is a beautiful feeling. The best is when you're almost getting him to know what you want to do.

Steve Cauthen, jockey

It doesn't matter what you do in the bedroom as long as you don't do it in the street and frighten the horses.

Daphne Fielding, playwright, The Duchess of Jermyn Street

It takes a good deal of physical courage to ride a horse. This, however, I have. I get it at about forty cents a flask, and I take it as required.

Stephen Leacock, journalist

Horses

A horse may have the look of eagles, but I've never seen yet an eagle who could run.

Charlie Whittingham, thoroughbred horse trainer

Anyone who's not happy with the job I'm doing can pick up their horses and leave tomorrow.

Woody Stephens, thoroughbred horse trainer

A race horse must be judged in three directions—speed, stamina and time—the time he lasts.

Grantland Rice, sportswriter

Did any other horses besides Charisma ever get left out in the middle of the night in a strange field in a lightning storm during a horse competition?

Susan Cox, U.S. district attorney, during the trial of Marion Hulick and George Lindemann, Jr. for the murder of Charisma and insurance fraud. The horse was murdered that night.

Don't say anything bad about a horse until it's been dead ten years.
Charlie Whittingham, thoroughbred horse trainer

Get yourself a good horse, son, and you'll dine with kings.
Charlie Whittingham, thoroughbred horse trainer

He's about as much as it costs to run my airplane for a while.
Jimmy Stone, businessman and thoroughbred owner, about his horse, Menifee

Horses are like people. Some kids don't mature until college.
Arthur Hancock III, owner, speaking of how sometimes you discover what a horse has in big races

Horses are more important to me than most people.
Mary Bacon, jockey

Horses can certainly race every two weeks, and in some cases even more than that. The velocity is going to be higher among horses of talent. They're running on the edge.
Dr. Larry Bramlage, veterinarian

I feel as a horse must feel when the beautiful cup is given to the jockey.
Edgar Degas, painter, after seeing one of his paintings sold at auction

I never saw Man o' War but I'd bet my money on Citation if they ever hooked up. Right now, if they blow the bugle where he's buried, Citation would break out of the grave and beat what's around.
Jimmy Cannon, sportswriter

It's not the money. It's not some genius on a computer figuring marriages made in heaven. It's the horse. You've got to have the horse.
D. Wayne Lukas, thoroughbred horse trainer

I've talked to thousands of horses . . . but not in their tongue apparently.
Grantland Rice, sportswriter

Men are generally more careful of the breed of their horses and dogs than of their children.
William Penn, preacher & founder of Pennsylvania (1644–1718)

Nothing brings out the prick in a man faster than his first good horse.
Francis Dunne, professional steward

Power is in controlling the blood, not the money.
Steve Crist, sportswriter, about the power of breeders

That was one big horse. I had to get a stepladder to attach the wire to his ear.
Tom "The Sandman" Burns, professional horse assassin, referring to the electrocution of show horse Belgium Waffle, owned by Tammie Bylenga Glaspie, who was convicted of mail fraud for collecting the insurance money

The mistake everyone was making was breeding those classic distance mares to a classic distance horse.
D. Wayne Lukas, thoroughbred horse trainer, referring to the lack of speed in the equation

There's no blue book on horses.
Richard Baily, supposed horse trainer, murdered Helen Brach, and con man who duped would-be horse owners

They have an unusual relationship. They're buddies. They have a window between their stalls, and they stand there and look at each other. They like each other. And both have a shot to win.

Bob Baffert, thoroughbred horse trainer, on two fillies he entered in the Preakness Stakes

We all buy our feed at the same place, and use the same veterinarians. It's all the horses. All we can do is screw up.

David Whitely, thoroughbred horse trainer

We thought a few times, maybe we ought to quit paying the bills for this horse.

Bob Lewis, owner of thoroughbred Charismatic, surprise Kentucky Derby winner

When a horse doesn't run his race, there's a reason.

Seth Hancock, owner and breeder

You can lead a horse to water
But you can't make him drink.

Anonymous proverb

You can't mourn the horse that got away.

Richard Mandella, trainer

You may have my husband, but not my horse. My husband won't need emasculating, and my horse I won't have you meddle with.

D. H. Lawrence, writer, from his novel St. Mawr

Horse Racing

A horse is worth $50 and what the traffic will bear.

John Nerud, thoroughbred trainer and owner

By the end of the year he'll be running in Omaha.

D. Wayne Lukas, thoroughbred horse trainer, about a horse that did not measure up

Claiming horses is like trying to make a living by going through people's garbage cans.

Lefty Nickerson, thoroughbred horse trainer

Did you ever notice, old pal, in the race track's dizzy spin
There are ninety ways a horse can lose—but only one way to win?

Grantland Rice, sportswriter

Don't tell me who a horse is by. Tell me who he can run by. Unless a foal is born with two heads or three legs, there's no way of knowing that he's a no-account when the farm turns him over to the trainer.

John Nerud, thoroughbred horse trainer and owner

The first question I was always asked—invariably, everywhere—was how I found horse racing compared to baseball. My answer—invariably, everywhere—was that, fans excluded, you meet a nicer brand of human being in racing.

Bill Veeck, baseball owner, racetrack operator

Hell, I'm not a horseman.

Bob Lewis, thoroughbred owner, whose horses won two Kentucky Derbys

Horses don't know the odds.

Nick Zito, thoroughbred horse trainer

If he had his way, he'd enter the Budweiser Clydesdales in a race.

Jerry Berger, about friend Bob Lewis, thoroughbred owner, who made his fortune in the beer business with Budweiser

If he runs on the lead, he'll finish at Kennedy Airport.

Alfredo Callejas, thoroughbred horse trainer

If I believed in reincarnation, I'd come back as a second guesser.

Carl Nafzger, thoroughbred horse trainer

It's time to be quiet and let the horse run.

Elliot Walden, thoroughbred horse trainer

The horses were ready to run, but track officials said there was nothing for them to run for.

Fred S. Buck, Horse Race Betting. Referring to New York racetrack official who had absconded with association bankroll

If you want a friend on the race track, buy a dog.

Jerry Izenberg, sportswriter

I knew it for a "dog," a horse which hated racing.

Dick Francis, champion jockey and novelist

It's a quick way for a rich man to get his name in the newspapers. It's like buying a baseball team. There's always going to be someone with too much money who we can get interested in horse racing.

John Nerud, thoroughbred horse trainer

It's not how many races you win that counts, but that you win the good ones.

Charlie Whittingham, thoroughbred horse trainer

I want to destroy the two myths about racing that I think have kept ninety percent of the public from ever attending. First, that racing is an elite sport dominated by fourth-generation snobs who think fans are an intrusion.

Second, that racing is a sport that attracts unemployed degenerates and creepy old men who have nothing better to do with their time.

Robert Brennan, racetrack owner

Some horses have extraordinarily strong preferences for one or two tracks, or for left-handed or right-handed courses only, or for hard or soft going, or for sun on their backs, and a wise trainer does not try to lay down an opposite law. Put a horse on a track he likes, on going he likes, with a jockey he likes, and he will be worth a stone and ten lengths by the finish.

Dick Francis, champion jockey and novelist

Stupid horses . . . are exasperating. They will not put themselves right before a fence, and they resist their jockey's efforts to do it for them.

Dick Francis, champion jockey and novelist

The farm wasn't for me. It was too laid-back and too slow. It was the racetrack I loved. I loved getting the *Racing Form* and handicapping the racing. I wanted to be where the action was—around the track, on the go and with the horses.

Elliott Walden, thoroughbred horse trainer

The horses and their keepers sleep through the night, awaiting the early dawn of a new day with its quota of hope, of promise, of providing for every hard knocker in the world a possible pot at the end of a glorious rainbow.

William Murray, writer

The losing jockey blames the owner, trainer, track, and horse while the trainer indicts the jock, owner, program seller, and stewards and

the owner views the business as a Communist plot.

Phil Jackman, sportswriter

This business has always been about dreams.

D. Wayne Lukas, thoroughbred horse trainer

This is a sport where the horses tend to sound alike and the jockeys, for all their courage and skill, are existentially cast in supporting roles.

Harvey Araton, sportswriter

This sport features the highest of the highs and the lowest of the lows.

Al Michaels, broadcaster

When it comes to busting for that opening it's all largely instinct. You've got a split second to decide. You are right or you are wrong. You can't wait.

Eddie Arcaro, jockey

While all of racing is a bet, each race is a sport.

Frank Deford, sportswriter

Year in and year out, the *Racing Form* has maintained a special status in American journalism. Besides being the most expensive U.S. daily, it is also one of the oldest.

Fredrick C. Klein, writer

One after another the fresh horses for the coming race made their appearance, for the most part English racers, wearing horsecloths, and looking with their drawn up bellies like strange, huge birds.

Leo Tolstoy, novelist

It was a glorious sight, and the come and go of the quick little hoofs, and the incessant salutations of ponies that had met before on other polo grounds and racecourses were enough to drive a four-footed thing wild.

Rudyard Kipling, novelist

The changing room for jockeys was warm and gay like a busy little nursery. Jockey's valets, with the air of slightly derelict family butlers, had been ironing in their shirtsleeves since seven in the morning.

Enid Bagnold, novelist, from National Velvet

Howe, Gordie

(b. Mar. 31, 1928) *Hall of Fame hockey player; played in five decades; number two on all-time goals (801) and points (1,850)*

Mr. Howe, before I die, please tell me how you can skate so gracefully down the ice, with three or four hockey players in front of you, and still manage the puck so magnificently. Tell me, Mr. Howe, how are you able to stick control the puck so beautifully in that kind of situation?

Tiny Tim, musician, sports fan, to Johnny Carson when asked who he would want at his deathbed

Hull, Bobby

(b. Jan. 3, 1939) *Hall of Fame hockey player; All-Star; prodigious scorer*

He's so powerful that defensemen don't want a piece of him—they don't want to take him head on.

Glenn Hall, professional hockey player

Hull dominates all thought about the game; he changes its traditions and shapes its rules.

Bill Furlong, sportswriter, The Price of Fame for Bobby Hull

Humor

There is no room in baseball for a clown.

Chuck Dressen, professional baseball manager, to Bob Uecker, player and later broadcaster

Hunting

A bird-eating dog is worse than an egg-sucking hound or a stump-sucking mule. Whatever the seven deadly sins of dogdom are, bird-eating is deadliest.

Havilah Babcock, outdoorsman and writer

A brash young shooting guest informed me over her second drink that preserve shooting was as artificial as patronizing a brothel. She hadn't shot on a preserve and I have never visited a brothel so neither of us were too well qualified to discuss it.

George Bird Evans, hunter, outdoorsman, and writer

Africa is flesh and blood, and the hunt is ever a love affair.

Isak Dinesen, novelist

All hunters should be nature lovers.

Theodore Roosevelt, president of the United States

As hunting tools, the bow and arrow are enjoying something of a renaissance these days, though Robin Hood and Hiawatha, were they around, would hardly recognize the instruments for all of their twentieth-century refinements.

John G. Mitchell, writer

Bracing against the predawn chill in a duck blind with my father was one of the most vivid memories of growing up in Eastern Arkansas. Similar mental snapshots have been created across our nation for centuries as parents have introduced their children to the beauty of our wildlife through hunting and fishing.

Blanche Lambert, U.S. congresswoman

Each autumn when the nights grow longer than the days and the aspens turn to gold on the hillsides, I am faced by an annual dilemma: Should we explore some new area or should we hunt once more in the old, familiar spot?

Ted Trueblood, outdoorsman, editor, and writer

Even a dog of general purpose breed cannot be expected to work properly unless he is correctly trained.

Michael Brander, sportsman and writer

Except for the early years of my childhood, I can't remember a time when the handling of fly rods and shotguns has not made for magic moments in my life.

Richard Wentz, outdoorsman and writer

Far from the truth lay the antique assumption that man had fathered the weapon. The weapon, instead, fathered the man.

Robert Ardery, scholar

For a man who's bred to hunting
  Must forever be that way.

Archibald Rutledge, poet

For many people throughout history, the most seductive voice of Mother nature at special times of the year has been the invitation to join the hunt.

James A. Swan, environmentalist, outdoorsman, and writer

133

He could train a dog with less exertion, and with less expense to the English language, than any other man I have ever known. I verily believe he could take a full-blooded July hound and turn out a passable bird dog in six weeks.

Havilah Babcock, outdoorsman and writer

He hunted big game all throughout the United States and Canada, water fowl on the Chesapeake Bay, and rabbits in the Catskill Mountains of New York. His true love, however, was on party boats, where the camaraderie meant as much as the full cooler.

Vincent T. Sparano, sportsman, about
George H. Hass, sportsman,
editor, and writer

Hounds and houndsmen are not like you and me. A hound is not made for bringing you the Sunday paper, honoring a point, or retrieving a gadwall. He is made for trailing and running larger mammals, treeing them, or baying them on the ground and catching them, to hold for the hunter. Houndmen, if they are true houndmen, would rather run their dogs in the woods than spend an all-expense-paid weekend in Paris, France.

Thomas McIntyre,
outdoorsman and writer

Hunting can become almost an obsession, as evidenced by garages filled with boats and decoys, gun cabinets, engraved shotguns, hunting dogs, trophies on the walls, stacks of sporting magazines, wildlife paintings and carvings, stacked bales of hay in backyards for archery practice—camouflage for water fowl, wild turkey, and archery deer seasons, and bright orange for hunting big game with a rifle.

James A. Swan, environmentalist,
outdoorsman, and writer

Hunting is a complex affair with roots too deep to be pulled up and examined. If a hunter is asked to explain his sport, he can no more rationalize hunting than he can describe emotion.

John Madson and Ed Kozicky, writers

Hunting is a glorious sort of vice working its narcotic with all the efficacy of the ubiquitous poppy.

Colonel Charles Atkins, outdoorsman

Hunting is almost anything the hunter wants to make of it—including not pulling the trigger at the last minute.

Roger Caras, broadcaster,
animal rights advocate, and writer

Hunting is the oldest, and by all odds the most diversified, sport known to man. The chase began long before the dawn of recorded history. It is the only sport, born of grim necessity, which now continues as a recreation enjoyed by millions.

The New Hunter's Encyclopedia

Hunting is what an animal does to take possession, dead or alive, of some other being that belongs to a species that is basically inferior to its own. Vice versa, if there is to be a hunt, this superiority of the hunter over the prey cannot be absolute.

José Ortega y Gasset, philosopher

I am a hunter, too, but slowly the hunting has become more important than the shooting . . . I was raised in the hunting tradition, but even in me something has begun to happen; there is a voice of warning of coming scarcities, there is an apprehension for the future; there is a fear of the

unknown qualities of majorities soon to govern the land.

Dayton O. Hyde, writer

I am truly moved at these moments. I really don't understand them completely. I know I am participating in life.

Ted Nugent, musician,
outdoorsman, and hunter

I am very fond of hunting and there are few sensations I prefer to that of galloping over these rolling, limitless prairies, rifle in hand, or winding my way among the barren, fantastic and grimly picturesque deserts of the so-called Bad Lands.

Theodore Roosevelt, president of the United
States, conservationist, and outdoorsman

I can take a good deal, but I won't have my dog called down.

E. Annie Proulx, writer

If I could shoot a game bird and still not hurt it, the way I can take a fly trout on a fly and release it, I doubt if I would kill another one. This is a strange statement coming from a man whose life is dedicated to shooting and gun dogs.

George Bird Evans, hunter,
outdoorsman, and writer

I have observed that the more bungling and inept a hunter is, the more likely he is to find fault with a dog.

Ted Trueblood, outdoorsman,
editor, and writer

In conversation I have never heard anybody call a woodcock anything but a "woodcock," although sometimes, when we're hunting woodcock exclusively and don't expect to flush grouse, we might refer to them simply as "birds." When we miss them, we usually call them sonsofbitches.

William G. Tapply, outdoorsman,
sportsman, and writer

In some strange way the birds we kill fly on forever. Perhaps its the broken arc, the interrupted parabola, the high zig through the alders that never quite made it to zag—all those incompletions crying out to be consummated. But something there is that keeps them airborne if only in our hearts, their wings forever roaring at the base of our trigger fingers.

Robert F. Jones,
outdoorsman and writer

In the act of hunting, a man becomes, however briefly, part of nature again. He returns to the natural state, becomes one with the animal, and is freed of the existential split: to be part of nature and to transcend it by virtue of his consciousness.

Erich Fromm, psychologist

I shot him nine times with a .220 Swift. . . . One time I hit him in the face and took away his lower jaw and still he didn't die. He just bled and began to snap fruitlessly with half a face at his own dragging guts.

Robert Ruark, writer, about using
enough gun to kill your prey

It is not essential to the hunt that it be successful.

José Ortega y Gasset, philosopher

I was never successful in outwitting antelope on the several occasions when I pitted my craft and skill against their wariness and keen

sense, always either failing to get within range or else missing them.

Theodore Roosevelt, president of the United States, conservationist, and outdoorsman

Man and dog have articulated in each other their own styles of hunting, and this represents the height of hunting.

José Ortega y Gasset, philosopher

Neither in body nor in mind do we inhabit the world of those hunting races of the Paleolithic era, to whose lives and life way we nevertheless owe the very form of our bodies and structures of our minds. Memories of their animal envoys still must sleep, somehow, within us; for they wake a little and stir when we venture into wilderness.

Joseph Campbell, philosopher and historian

No sportsman can ever feel much keener pleasure and self-satisfaction than when, after a successful stalk and good shot, he walks up to a grand elk lying . . . in the cool shade of the great evergreens, and looks at the massive and yet finely molded form.

Theodore Roosevelt, president of the United States, conservationist, and outdoorsman

Only good shots—or gentlemen—should hunt together. Learn leisureliness alone. The beginner must work out his own salvation, and the fewer spectators present to witness the infamy and psychoanalyze his failures the better.

Havilah Babcock, outdoorsman and writer

On rare occasions, novice hunters have stalked another hunter who is gobbling. There is no need for that kind of nonsense.

Experienced hunters know that it is almost impossible to stalk a wild tom successfully.

Nelson Bryant, outdoor writer

Over the centuries man and his dog have hunted together and, though the shotgun and the rifle have replaced the bow and the spear, few of the basic methods of hunting have altered.

Michael Brander, sportsman and writer

Storytelling began with Stone Age hunters sitting around the campfire recounting their deeds.

Stephen E. Ambrose, historian

The big-game rifle is the weapon of romance and, when a man picks one up, he becomes for the moment a pioneer, an explorer, a wilderness hunter, a present-day Daniel Boone.

Jack O'Connor, sportsman, outdoorsman, and writer

The chase is among the best of all national pastimes; it cultivates that vigorous manliness for the lack of which in a nation, as an individual, the possession of no other qualities can possibly atone.

Theodore Roosevelt, president of the United States, conservationist, and outdoorsman

The chase is the thing. The game in the hand is not much more than a reminder of the pleasurable efforts expended on its taking.

Larry Koller, outdoorsman, editor, and writer

The difference between mere killing and a glorious sport is the manner in which you do it—over thrilling dogs, in magnificent country and with a reverence for the game.

George Bird Evans, hunter, outdoorsman, and writer

The hunter, beset too long by the moralizer, will point to the slaughterhouse with an enigmatic look. Of course, he has a point. A great many well-hunted deer and quail die better in this country, at least, than cows, sheep, pigs, chickens, ducks, turkeys, and horses do.

Roger Caras, broadcaster, animal rights advocate, writer

The hunter's life, with its adventures and dangers, must have been of tremendous importance for the evolution of man. It was a touchstone of intelligence, courage and skill.

G. H. R. von Konigswald, scholar

The hunter's vision is itself a part of nature . . . His eye roves across a landscape which is itself living. The hunter in man lives an eventful life, a present, sound filled pulse which collectively is the dynamic, oral, traditional society, where the poet is historian and men are bound in myth and music to a generous and religious existence.

Paul Shephard, environmentalist and outdoorsman

The kill matters. And the manner of the kill matters. All else is trivial, for nothing else is final.

Robert Elman, outdoorsman and writer

The licensed hunter kills only a tiny fraction of the game in Africa. In fact, the fees he pays are in most cases the sole revenue the government can rely on to pay the warden. The poachers and the advance of agriculture are the real enemies of wildlife.

Philip K. Crowe, environmentalist, outdoorsman, and writer

The mere size of the bag indicates little as to a man's prowess as a hunter and almost nothing as to the interest or value of his achievement.

Theodore Roosevelt, president of the United States, conservationist, and outdoorsman

The only reason I played golf was so I could afford to hunt and fish.

Sam Snead, champion professional golfer

The pursuer cannot pursue if he does not integrate his vision with that of the pursued. That is to say, *hunting is an imitation of the animal.*

José Ortega y Gasset, philosopher and hunter

The pointing dog is a refinement, unlike any other canine. Only the hunting dog has so strong a tie with the hunter, a partnership through thousands of years. When the chukar calls are silenced by the hunter's nearness and their exact location is unknown, the dog is no mere possession or servant but a full-fledged partner and collaborator.

Charles F. Waterman, outdoorsman and writer

The reward is in the hunt.

Ted Trueblood, outdoorsman, editor, and writer

The wonderful, silent ease with which hunting elephants negotiate jungle has always been a source of wonder to me . . . I had already loaded my rifle and now swung the barrel around ready for action. The bull had winded us, however, and even though I saw his head, and a great head it was, the angle was not right, and before the elephant could be maneuvered into a better position, he made off down the mountain.

Philip K. Crowe, environmentalist, outdoorsman, and writer

Twenty pockets is an adequate number for an evening out. For hunting, on the other hand, I need a lot more.

Patrick F. McManus, sportsman and writer

Upland shooting is at its highest level when the bird-dog-gun triad is balanced by a gun and a dog worthy of the bird.

George Bird Evans, hunter, outdoorsman, and writer

When I go hunting with him, he does that as hard as he plays football.

Bud Holmes, attorney, about Walter Payton, Hall of Fame football player

When some of my friends have asked me anxiously about their boys, whether they should let them hunt, I have answered, yes—remembering that it was one of the best parts of my education—make them hunters, though sportsmen only at first, if possible, mighty hunters last, so that they shall not find game large enough for them in this or any vegetable wilderness—hunters as well as fishers of men.

Henry David Thoreau, writer and philosopher

Winter is a greater hunter than man will ever be.

Thomas McIntyre, outdoorsman and writer

You can practice calling with a record, and pick up calling tips from authorities, but it is the wild turkey himself, ultimately, who teaches you really how to call.

Thomas McIntyre, outdoorsman and writer

Any fool, without encountering the smallest modicum of risk, can murder a bull elephant at 200 yards with a lung shot. This is not elephant hunting, but elephant killing.

Peter Hathaway Capstick, big game hunter and writer

Hunting big, dangerous game is an excellent method of cultivating one's own fatalism. People die from the slightest error, while others survive without a scratch the most mind-boggling acts of idiocy.

Peter Hathaway Capstick, big game hunter and writer

Hustle

Good things happen to those who hustle.

Chuck Noll, professional football coach

Hype

As in a Super Bowl, there can be more hype than substance in the Subway Series, more newsprint and bluster than worthiness.

Buster Olney, sportswriter

The hype is there, but the game is all the same.

Greg Maddux, professional baseball player

Who knows? Amid world beating hearts
The Tumult and the Shouting starts.

Grantland Rice, sportswriter

You could say that he's been underpromoted, but you would be tragically understating the case.

Cedric Kushner, boxing promoter, about Sugar Shane Mosley

Indianapolis 500

A man can be a splendid race driver, but if he doesn't compete at Indianapolis, he is nothing. If he doesn't win at least once at Indianapolis, well, there always is the insinuation that maybe something was lacking.

Mario Andretti, champion driver

This is the Indianapolis 500, a gigantic, grimy lawn party, a monstrous holiday compounded of dust and danger and noise, the world's biggest carnival. . . .

Red Smith, sportswriter

Iditarod

It's a bad place to get lost. From here to anywhere is a long, long way, and help is hard to find.

Craig Mildred, sportswriter

Those who live in dog country dissect the Iditarod's entry list like the Yankees batting order on Opening Day.

Brian Patrick O'Donoghue, political columnist and sled racer

Individuals

I got fed up with team sports, which I played as a kid—football-soccer and cricket—I was an individual.

Fred Perry, professional tennis champion

Society loves conformists. I'm not a conformist. I'm a big believer in individuality, in freedom.

Pam Postema, female umpire

Injuries

All right, no limping. If you have to limp, don't scrimmage. If you want to scrimmage, don't limp.

Red Blaik, college football coach

A piece of scenery fell on me. I'm a stagehand at the Metropolitan Opera. You can't make a living as a referee.

Arthur Mercante, Jr., referee, replying to a question about his injured hand

A thigh. A neck. A leg. Is it an anatomy class? A butcher's inventory? It's the National Football League's injury report!

Ira Berkow, sportswriter

Being apart from the team. That may have been the toughest part.

Brian Williams, professional football player, commenting on being out of football for two years due to an injury to his eye

Chris Childs spit a tooth into his hand and fixed a menacing stare on Dikembe Motombo, who trotted away innocently.

Selena Roberts, sportswriter, referring to Chris Childs, professional basketball player, after being elbowed by Motombo, a sharp-elbowed center

I didn't do this operation for golf. I did it for quality of life, so that my wife, Barbara, didn't have to put up with me having my hip dominating my life.

Jack Nicklaus, champion professional golfer

I don't feel like "the man." I feel like less than a man.

Chris Childs, professional basketball player, on being injured during the playoffs

I'm a good candidate for a knee replacement.

Steve Williams, a.k.a. Stone Cold Steve Austin, professional wrestler

I'm going to become a ventriloquist. I'll get a little football player and put him up on my knee.

Dan Dierdorf, professional football player and broadcaster, through clenched teeth after his jaw had been broken

I'm more likely to get hurt bumping into things around the house.

Walter Payton, Hall of Fame football player

It collapsed like a folding chair.

Rebecca Lobo, professional basketball player, about injuring her knee

It is Monday morning, and all over the land the bill is being presented to some large, tough men for playing so fearlessly with the equation of mass times velocity; only the backup quarterback bullets out of bed on recovery day.

Mark Kram, sportswriter

It's from all those people kissing your ass.

Pete Sheehy, clubhouse manager, to Joe DiMaggio, after he asked Sheehy if he had injured his butt

It looked like a piece of sausage.

Mitch Libonati, hotel employee, who found the remains of Holyfield's ear

I've added a scar on my knee. That's all.

Jason Seahorn, professional football player

I've busted up my body and scarred myself and gotten burned—I've got scars I'll carry to the grave—just to make some money.

A. J. Foyt, champion race car driver

I was doing a floater, and I came down sort of awkward on my heel. I hit it hard enough to break my fibula and tibia. If it weren't for my board, I would have drowned. I was in that much pain.

Jason Buttenshaw, surfer

My back is sore, my knee is sore, my hand is sore, and I have bruises on both my feet.

Erik Howard, professional football player

My catcher, Mr. Berra, is wearing a lemon on his thumb.

Casey Stengel, Hall of Fame baseball player and manager, referring to a lemon Yogi's mother insisted he wear on his injured thumb for three days, contrary to Yankee physician's orders to treat it otherwise

Nobody is hurt. Hurt is in the mind. If you can walk, you can run.

Vince Lombardi, professional football player and coach

One of the things that happens is you watch the team and suddenly you're saying "they" instead of "we" because in the middle of it all, you feel invisible again.

Joe Morris, professional football player

Progressively and inexorably, as I moved through high school, college and pro leagues, my body was dismantled. Piece by piece . . . as the organization and competition increased, the injuries came faster and harder.

John McMurtry, professional football player

Sometimes it's so hard for me to move, it feels like I'm standing in cement.

Rik Smits, professional basketball player, after trying to play through a broken toe

This is a human body, and we don't always expect 100 percent.

Lornah Kiplagal, marathoner, after being forced to withdraw after a bout of bronchitis

To a new life where knees do not throb and tendons do not ache at dawn and the ghostly potential for permanent disability no longer

rides just an errant hoofbeat off your right shoulder.

Jerry Izenberg, sportswriter

Two long half-moon scars ran down either side of his knee, which no longer had the outlines of a kneecap, but seemed as shapeless and large in his leg as if two or three handfuls of socks had been sewn in there.

George Plimpton, writer, referring to the knees of Gil Main, professional football player

Young lady, try my left arm—I think you'll find I'm still alive.

Tex Hughson, professional baseball player, to a nurse trying to take his pulse on one of his arms where the muscles had grown so big they were choking off the blood supply

Years of training. Hours of dreaming. And knowing it all came down to an unfortunate, untimely, unbelievable stroke of bad luck.

Don Kardong, runner and writer, speaking about the Olympics and injuries

You were supposed to depersonalize your body, it wasn't your leg, it was "the leg."

Rick Sortun, professional football player

You don't worry about injuries this time of year. We're in a pennant race. If you can walk, you can play.

Davey Johnson, champion baseball manager, to Wally Backman, player, and team doctor, when the doctor told him that Backman might have a broken leg and it should be x-rayed

You should sue your legs for non-support.

Dan Reeves, professional football head coach and player, to Dandy Don Meredith, professional football player, referring to the latter's bad knees

Inspiration

Ability may get you to the top, but it takes character to keep you there.

John Wooden, basketball coach

Ain't no man can avoid being born average, but ain't no man got to be common.

Satchel Paige, Hall of Fame baseball player

He who is not courageous enough to take risks will accomplish nothing in life.

Muhammad Ali, boxer

Keep Mendoza in the bullpen.

Don Zimmer, professional baseball player and manager, speaking words of encouragement to starting pitcher Hideki Irabu, about Mendoza, whom he'd forced from the rotation

Talent is God-given, be humble; fame is man-given, be thankful; conceit is self-given, be careful.

Anonymous (quoted often by John Wooden)

The big thing is not what happens to us in life, but what we do about what happens to us.

George Allen, professional football coach

You always have to focus in life on what you want to achieve.

Michael Jordan, basketball player

Intelligence

Nobody in football should be called a genius. A genius is a guy like Norman Einstein.

Joe Theismann, football commentator and former player

Why would anyone expect him to come out smarter? He went to prison for three years, not Princeton.

Dan Duva, boxing promoter, on Mike Tyson hooking up again with promoter Don King

I told him, "Son, what is it with you? Is it ignorance or apathy?" He said, "Coach, I don't know and I don't care."

Frank Layden, Utah Jazz president, on a former player

We weren't the tallest, fastest, or best jumpers. We were just the most intelligent team I've ever seen.

Walt "Clyde" Frazier, Hall of Fame basketball player and broadcaster, talking about the championship New York Knicks teams of the late 60s and early 70s

Interpreters

There's only one thing wrong with my interpreter. He can't speak English.

Attributed to an American baseball player in Japan, by Robert Whiting, writer

Irving, Julius (Dr. J)

(b. Feb. 22, 1950) *Hall of Fame basketball player; won two championships (one ABA and two NBA); All-Star; one of only three players to score more than 30,000 career points; broadcaster*

My coach said to me, "Marvin, stop watching the gut . . . stop idolizing him."

Marvin Barnes, professional basketball player

Jackson, Shoeless Joe

(b. July 16, 1889; d. Dec. 5, 1951) *Major League Baseball player; lifetime .356 batting average; banned from the game as one of the Chicago "Black Sox" who threw the 1919 World Series*

I copied my swing after Joe Jackson's. His is the perfectest.
> *Babe Ruth, Hall of Fame baseball player*

Say it ain't so, Joe!
> *Attributed to a little boy after Jackson was accused of conspiring to throw the 1919 World Series*

Jackson, Reggie

(b. May 18, 1946) *Hall of Fame baseball player; won five World Series*

There isn't enough mustard in the world to cover Reggie Jackson.
> *Darold Knowles, professional baseball player*

When you unwrap a Reggie bar, it tells you how good it is.
> *Catfish Hunter, professional baseball player*

Jockeys

A bad rider can't do what you tell him and a good one won't listen to you anyway.
> *Charlie Whittingham, thoroughbred horse trainer*

Every steeplechase jockey has two ambitions. One is to ride more winners than anyone else in one season, and become Champion Jockey for that year. The other is to win the Grand National at Aintree.
> *Dick Francis, champion jockey and novelist*

G-Man, give me a shot.
> *Chris Antley, jockey, to Gary Stevens, jockey, during the Preakness, where Antley was trapped on the inside with Charismatic by Stevens's Stephen Got Even, to which Stevens replied, "Go ahead, little buddy." Charismatic won the race.*

He was hungry. He had a passion to get back into it. He's always been a great rider—a great finisher that fit that horse.
> *D. Wayne Lukas, thoroughbred horse trainer, about Chris Antley, jockey*

If I did not enjoy riding horses that do not win I could not be a jockey. No one could. It is a hard life in some ways, but the pleasures of riding by far outweigh the knocks; and every jockey thinks the same, for if he did not, he would change to another job.

Dick Francis, champion jockey and novelist

If it is possible to inherit so vague a quality as a wish to be a jockey, I did so. My father was a jockey, and his father also.

Dick Francis, champion jockey and novelist

No secret is so close as that between horse and rider.

William Shakespeare, playwright and poet

Lady jockeys? Well, they do more for the silks than the boys do.

Bill Veeck, baseball owner and racetrack operator

She was all jockey and no lady until after the race was won.

Jerry Izenberg, sportswriter, about Julie Krone, jockey

There is no quicker way for a jockey to go out of business. He must either find a way to live with his fear or quit.

Roger Kahn, sportswriter

You've got to make sure the horse thinks you're a part of him.

Eddie Arcaro, Hall of Fame jockey

Johnson, Jack

(b. Mar. 31, 1878; d. June 10, 1946) *Heavyweight Champion of the World 1908–1915; first African-American boxing champion*

I grew to love the Jack Johnson image. I wanted to be the rough, tough, arrogant, the nigger white folks didn't like.

Muhammad Ali, champion boxer

Johnson was magnificently defiant, and defiantly magnificent.

David Remnick, writer and editor

Jordan, Michael

(b. Feb. 17, 1963) *Won six National Basketball Association championships; six-time National Basketball Association Finals MVP; Rookie of the Year*

He painted his own masterpiece on the ceiling of basketball's Sistine Chapel, and he didn't need a scaffold to lift him there. Michael Jordan can fly.

Ray Sons, sportswriter, after Jordan scored 63 points in an All-Star game

He's the simplest, purest player who plays the game.

Jerry West, Hall of Fame basketball player and team executive

In my prime I could have handled Michael Jordan. Of course, he would be only 12 years old.

Jerry Sloan, professional basketball player and coach

Jesus in Nikes.

Jason Williams, professional basketball player

Jordan has created a kind of fame that exceeds sports; he is both athlete and entertainer. He plays in the age of the satellite to an audience vastly larger than was possible in

the past and is thus the first great athlete of the wired age.

David Halberstam, writer

Michael Jordan is in Paris. That's better than the Pope. It's God in person.

France-Soir, *French newspaper*

Michael Jordan is one of the greatest athletes in any sport in any era, and all of us are fortunate that we saw him play, because the greats are like that—spectacularly individual. Singular in approach. There will never be another one truly like him.

Spike Lee, writer, actor, director

That was God disguised as Michael Jordan.

Larry Bird, Hall of Fame basketball player and coach

The only thing I thought—Michael Jordan left too early. I've got kids who idolize him. I wish he was still playing.

Wayne Gretzky, Hall of Fame hockey player, about Michael Jordan's retirement

You don't bring your wife and children to the game when he comes to town 'cause he'll embarrass you.

Mark Jackson, professional basketball player, on Michael Jordan

Kayaking

A kayaker needs to know and become familiar with all the idiosyncrasies of water on the move.

Jay Evans, Olympic kayaker
and outdoorsman

I know how to spell the word relax, but it's not something I do very often. When I get in a sea kayak and leave the shore, it's one of the few times that I can really enjoy the ultimate escape—away from faxes, phones, voice mail, and time commitments.

Deb Shapiro, kayaker

Loose hips save ships.

Attributed to anonymous by Shelly Johnson,
kayaker and journalist

Sea kayaking gives a person the opportunity to venture on to a wild, unpredictable expanse in a craft that moves solely by the strength of their arm, directed by their experience and knowledge.

Derek C. Hutchinson, canoeist, kayaker, and
journalist

The correct hip-flick makes the roll almost effortless.

Raymond Bridge, outdoorsman
and journalist

The kayak . . . cuts no groove and leaves no scar. The same stretch of water can be paddled every day but the surface may never be the same twice.

Derek C. Hutchinson, canoeist,
kayaker, and journalist

The kayaker relies on his or her paddle as much as on the boat.

Raymond Bridge, outdoorsman and
journalist

There was nothing else to be done except lash the two kayaks together side by side, stiffen them with snowshoes under the straps, and place the sledges athwart them, one before, one behind.

Fridtjof Nansen, kayaker, speaking
about his legendary experience with
Hjalmer Johansen, on the
Arctic Ocean

This is a sport that requires technique. Women tend to be better listeners, so they develop better technique.

Judy Harrison, publisher of
Canoe and Kayak Magazine

Thoreau was right: rivers are a constant lure to the adventurous instinct in mankind. If Henry were alive today, he would pursue that lure with the modern recreational kayak.

Jay Evans, Olympic kayaker
and outdoorsman

When you sit in the cockpit of your boat, you are at eye-level with the world around you: a curious harbor seal, a magnificent sea cliff of forbidding granite, a horizon line as the sun breaks free for the day. This vantage point is breathtaking in its intimacy.

Shelly Johnson, kayaker and journalist

Kentucky Derby

Churchill Downs crackles with the anticipation of what will be over in a few minutes. It is not so much the prospect of a good horse race that the Derby crowd looks forward to, as to that of instant history.

Steve Crist, sportswriter

Horses seem to thrive in Kentucky in the springtime.

Nick Zito, thoroughbred horse trainer

I don't care if she never wins another race or if she never starts another race. She has won the greatest race in America and I am satisfied.

Harry Payne Whitney, owner of Regret,
winner of the 1915 Kentucky Derby

The stretch looked like a cavalry charge.

Joseph Durso, sportswriter

When you win the Derby, everybody goes over there to Pimlico to beat the Derby winner. But to the guys crying about the size of the field, I'd say, "Don't enter."

D. Wayne Lukas, thoroughbred horse trainer

Kickers

How many guys we got in this league— 1500? Well, that means there are 1,495 guys he can't lick.

Bill Parcells, professional football coach, referring
to his kicker, who had told the media he wanted
to get in some hits during an upcoming game

I am a kicker, but I'm tough. On kickoffs, I'll barrel through there and knock those runners right on my fanny.

Errol Mann, professional football player

I was flabbergasted. I thought he meant my punting. But he clarified it. He said, "Why are the Giants so terrible?"

Dave Jennings, professional football player and
broadcaster, when asked "Why are you so
terrible?" on a radio talk show

Kicking

That young 'un can't be doing that all by himself. He's got to be getting some dang help from somewhere. Let's get us some of them balls to take back home.

Bum Phillips, professional football coach, who
accused Oakland of filling Ray Guy's football
with helium, because his kicks went
so high and so deep

King, Billie Jean

(b. Nov. 22, 1943) *Tennis champion; won six Wimbledons, four U.S. Opens*

King gave the women's game credibility, not by winning the Grand Slam singles titles but by beating Bobby Riggs in the infamous "Battle of the Sexes" match.

John Feinstein, writer

On the court, she's an evil, merciless bastard. Totally ruthless. She'll do everything and anything within the rules to win.

Frank Hammond, tennis referee

King, Don

(b. Aug. 31, 1931) *Famous boxing promoter*

Looks black, lives white, and thinks green.

Larry Holmes, world champion boxer

Knight, Bobby

(b. Oct. 25, 1940) *Champion college basketball coach; won three NCAA basketball titles; Olympic gold medalist basketball coach (1984)*

Bob Knight is unique. In another time, he would have been a superb general. He never made it past private in the Army, but he has proved himself to be a fantastic leader throughout his career. He may well be the last of the coaching dictators.

Al McGuire, champion college basketball coach and broadcaster

You know, there were times, when if I had a gun, I think I would have shot him. And there were other times when I wanted to put my arms around him, and hug him, and tell him that I loved him.

Isiah Thomas, professional basketball player

Knockouts

I knew it was all over then. I saw his cheekbone cave in.

Jack Dempsey, champion boxer, speaking of an opponent

Krone, Julie

(b. July 24, 1963) *All-time winningest female jockey; won Belmont Stakes*

She is a jock in both senses of the word—a jock as in an athlete, with agility and courage and a consuming need to beat your brains in regardless of the game we're playing, and a jock as in shorthand for jockey, rider of four-footed things that weigh a dozen times her hundred pounds.

Bill Lyon, sportswriter

Lacrosse

In a sport like lacrosse there is continuous movement, a flow that exhilarates the player and arouses the spectator.

Mike Keenan, champion
hockey coach

It is a beautiful game—above all, for the skill of stick handlers in throwing and catching either long, looping passes or balletlike shorter ones.

Bob Scott, champion college coach

Lacrosse may be called a madman's game, so wild it is.

New York Herald Tribune

When I play lacrosse it makes me feel like I am playing the game with all of my ancestors. It also makes me proud that it was our people who gave lacrosse to the world. For these reasons, lacrosse is more than just a game.

Chief Irving Powless, Jr.,
Onondaga Nation

Landry, Tom

(b. Sept. 11, 1924; d. Feb. 13, 2000) *Hall of Fame professional football coach; All-Pro defensive back; won two of five Super Bowl appearances; third all-time winningest coach (270)*

He was known as Ol' Stone Face, and on the sideline it was easy to see why. However well or poorly the Dallas Cowboys were playing, Coach Tom Landry's expression under his snap-brim fedora never changed. But that's the way he wanted it.

Dave Anderson, sportswriter and writer

He helped build one of America's premier sports organizations, but I think that as a coach—both offensively and defensively—he was an incredible innovator. He was ahead of the learning curve on both sides of the ball.

Calvin Hill, All-Pro professional football player

He's the man that pretty much molded me into the man I am today.

Tony Dorsett, Hall of Fame professional
football player

151

He shaped my philosophy on everything. I followed his philosophy on football and how he handled himself on and off the field. He was a tremendous influence on me.

Dan Reeves, professional football coach, who took two different teams to a total of four Super Bowls, professional football player

He wasn't just about building football teams. It was about building men of character. Many of the things he did were to teach us important lessons about our success in life after football.

Drew Pearson, All-Pro professional football player

He was so stable, so consistent. He never got excited. He never got down. Tom was just stable. He didn't show great emotions when things were going right and he didn't show great dejection when things were going wrong. I think that made him a great leader.

Lee Roy Jordan, Hall of Fame football player

He will be remembered for many special reasons, including his record as a coach, the innovations he brought to our game, and the personal integrity he displayed.

Paul Tagliabue, National Football League commissioner

It was always difficult playing against him because he did things differently. We always had to go against the 4–3 flex defense. I don't think any coach ever figured out how to contain that flex defense. It was a tremendous defense. It still surprises me that nobody plays the flex today.

Ron Jaworski, All-Pro quarterback and broadcaster

Ours is a land that prides itself on sports' achievement, but never in the history of sports in this state has there been anything larger and more captivating than the mighty reign of Landry and the Cowboys.

Randy Galloway, sportswriter and writer

There was somewhat of a shyness about him, but he was always there when you needed him. I don't know anyone who didn't have respect for him as a person. As a human being, coach Landry is right there among the very best. There's nothing phony about him.

Roger Staubach, Hall of Fame quarterback

They were different than anybody else we played, and it took a lot of preparation to play them. They had good players in their scheme, but their defensive scheme was always so much different than anybody else. It took a while to get the players to know what they were doing.

Chuck Noll, Hall of Fame football coach, won four Super Bowl titles

The thing I remember about Tom is how completely confident he was without being cocky. I remember one time when Tom presented the defensive game plan for that particular week, and Sam Huff asked what if they do something other than you just described, and Tom said, "Sam they won't."

Wellington Mara, National Football League owner

When you played for him, he's the boss. When I coached for him, he was the boss, too, but when you played for him there was a fear in there.

Mike Ditka, Hall of Fame professional football player and Super Bowl–winning coach

A reporter asked me once if I'd ever seen Tom Landry laugh. 'No,' I answered, 'I only played nine years."

Jerry Glanville, professional football player and head coach

Lanier, Bob

(b. Sept. 10, 1948) *Hall of fame basketball player; eight-time All-Star; coach*

Lanier played defense in his sleep. I call him Mr. Sweet Hands. The referee could look right at him holding you, and he wouldn't see it.

Darryl Dawkins, professional basketball player

Lardner, Ring

(b. Mar. 6, 1885; d. Sept. 25, 1933) *Newspaper columnist, humorist, and novelist*

Over the years the sports page has been hyped as a literary showcase. Its first writing star was Ring Lardner.

Benjamin DeMott, writer

Ring was closer to being a genius than anyone I've ever known. He had a sense of humor that was sometimes beyond this world. He was tall, dark and slender and was never what you'd call loquacious.

Grantland Rice, sportswriter

Last Place

Actually, I don't ever recall them not being in last place.

Bob Wolff, Hall of Fame broadcaster, referring to the Washington Senators

Leadership

"Leadership is a matter of having people look at you and gain confidence, seeing how you react," he once said, alluding to his Cowboys players. "If you're in control, they're in control."

Tom Landry, Hall of Fame football coach and all-pro football player

A lot of parents think kids ought to learn responsibility from work, and I've always said, "Baloney." Kids learn leadership and organization from games, from having fun.

John Madden, professional football coach and commentator

I believe in leadership. And I definitely believe I am a leader. But I believe I lead by example.

Mike Piazza, baseball player

If they were Indians back in the early days of this country, Lawrence would be the emotional war counselor who leads the braves into battle. But Banks would be the tribal chief. When you have two personalities like that in one linebacking corps, it's a coach's dream.

Bill Parcells, professional football coach, about Lawrence Taylor, Hall of Fame football coach, and Carl Banks, professional football player

I guess I don't talk much, but I think a man can set an example for his team by his actions on the field.

Harmon Killebrew, professional baseball player

Leaders have a different look from followers. They get it sometime while being potty-trained or tumbling around a kindergarten playroom. . . . People who don't get it early never do.

Harvey Manning, mountain climber

Leadership is getting people to do something they shouldn't be able to do.

> Al Roberts, college football player

Listen, I'm a leader. If anyone gives me trouble in a huddle—I don't care who they are—I'm going to sting them.

> Terry Bradshaw, Hall of Fame football player

You lead by example.

> Alvin Dark, professional baseball player

Lee, Spike

(b. Mar. 20, 1957) *Comedian, writer, actor, director, sports fan*

Sometimes he opens his mouth a little too much and gets the *other* guys going.

> Reggie Miller, professional basketball player

Le Mans

Le Mans has to be the most dangerous race in the world. It is one long accident looking for a place to happen.

> Mario Andretti, champion driver

Liebling, A. J.

(b. May 31, 1904; d. Dec. 29, 1963) *Columnist, sportswriter, humorist*

The problem for Liebling and for the *New Yorker* must have been how to sell a blood sport like boxing to a genteel, affluent readership to whom the idea of men fighting for their lives would have been deeply offensive; how to suggest boxing's drama while skirting boxing's tragedy. It is a problem, that for all his verbal cleverness, Liebling never entirely solves.

> Joyce Carol Oates, writer

Life

A life is not important, but for the impact it has on other's lives.

> Jackie Robinson, Hall of Fame baseball player

Desperate situations are not necessarily our proudest moments, and are difficult to describe truthfully.

> B. M. Annette, mountain climber

Each of us has to discover his own path—of that I am sure. Some paths will be spectacular and others will be peaceful and quiet—who is to say which is the most important?

> Sir Edmund Hillary, mountain climber, first to scale Everest

Golf is golf and life is life, and blurring the line between the two can be disastrous.

> Laura Baugh, professional golfer, recovering alcoholic

I might have had a tough break, but I have an awful lot to live for.

> Lou Gehrig, Hall of Fame baseball player, who was afflicted during his playing days with amyotrophic lateral sclerosis, an incurable disease

I'm old, I'm bald, and I'm short not only in stature but also in patience with those unwilling to give their best effort. . . . Life's nothing but one continual battle from start to finish. We come into it kicking, and if we've got an ounce of gumption, we go out the same damned way.

> Mills Lane, district court judge and boxing referee

I'm not going to turn around and be a golfer again just because I had hip surgery. I've got other things to do.

Jack Nicklaus, champion professional golfer

In life, not just basketball, the key is to be able to control the little things. No human being is capable of overcoming all the big things in life, the things that aren't in your control. . . . A person is an idiot if he doesn't manage the things he can't manage.

John Chaney, college basketball coach

I swing big with everything I've got. I hit big or I miss big. I like to live as big as I can.

Babe Ruth, Hall of Fame baseball player

I know that I'm never as good or bad as any single performance. I've never believed my critics or my worshippers, and I've always been able to leave the game at the arena.

Charles Barkley, professional basketball player

Life is like boxing. You've only got so many punches to throw, and you can only take so many.

George Foreman, champion boxer

Life hangs by a very thin thread and the cancer of time is complacency. If you are going to do something, do it now. Tomorrow is too late.

Pete Goss, champion solo sailor and writer

Life is truly a balancing act. In one hand you hold your running, and in the other, you hold your job, your family and other tasks and challenges that you face on a daily basis. For all the things that are important in your life, you have to find that balance.

Joan Benoit Samuelson, marathoner

The people who I know who BASE jump all love life, and because they do they're pretty reflective about it. When you put yourself in such dangerous situations, where one mistake will kill you, it makes you think.

Thor Alex Kappfjell, BASE jumper

The solution to any problem—work, love, money, whatever—is to go fishing, and the worst problem, the longer the trip should be.

John Gierach, fisherman and writer

"There's nothing left to do!" is a common cry you hear from all sorts of young people and it's sad in a way because you know the speaker must be closing his eyes to the adventurous opportunities that still abound. The world is full of interesting projects—if you have the imagination and resourcefulness to seek them out. Finding new adventures has never been a problem in my life—the big difficulty is finding the time to do them.

Sir Edmund Hillary, mountain climber,
first to scale Everest

Trying to achieve goals in life shouldn't prevent you from enjoying life.

Max Papis, automobile racer

We do have choices, we do have control, but in the end we are going to have only one life unfold. In that sense you have to know when to relax and stop worrying about it.

Eammon Coghlan, champion runner

Limits

Know your limits and listen to your body. Find your own rhythm and stick to it.

Bobby Julich, cyclist

Lineman

Usually for linemen the only recognition you get is from your mother and your wife.

Korey Stringer, defensive lineman, football

Locker Room

If you are not a player, but some peripheral member of the tennis establishment—a promoter a writer or a pretty girl or even just some hanger-on, or a friend of a friend—it is easy to get into the Player's Tea Room. Either you give the old guard at the bottom of the stairs a pound or two the first day or you can climb over a little fence from the press balcony.

Arthur Ashe, Hall of Fame tennis champion and writer

If you go into rooms where athletes change their clothes as much as I do you would be disgusted by the way the place smells. The customary odor of the locker room is a healthy one and is dominated by liniments, sweat, soap melting in the hot waters of the showers.

Jimmy Cannon, sportswriter

Locker rooms that wrestlers use are very different from any other—dingy and small and dirty, and always with this distinctive smell, a body smell that's worse than anything you find in places where football players and baseball players have been. I don't know why.

Alex Karras, Hall of Fame football player and professional wrestler

That's so when I forget how to spell my name, I can still find my #%@# clothes.

Karas Grimson, Chicago Blackhawks left wing, who kept a color photo of himself above his locker.

Sometimes all I get is a large closet. Sometimes I dress in the first-aid room.

Barbara Jo Rubin, jockey, referring to the fact that most tracks didn't have separate locker rooms for male and female riders in the beginning

The competitors' lounge at the All England Club is the meat market of the world of tennis.

Gwen Robyns, writer

There were rats in pretty nearly every building, including our locker room. The rats would chew on the leather shoulder pads at night, and we'd come back the next day and find their teeth marks.

Don McIlhenny, professional football player

The philosophy of the locker room . . . physical strength and the ability to withstand pain are the most positive virtues. Women are things. Bookish people and little people are suspect.

Rick Sortun, professional football player

Years ago the competitors' lounge at Wimbledon had, in theory, been the sacrosanct preserve of players and their guests. But, in practice, it had always been a throbbing hive of hustlers, racquet dealers, clothing reps, agents, tournament directors, assorted groupies, gofers, and camp followers.

Michael Mewshaw, writer

Lombardi, Vince

(b. June 11, 1913; d. Sept 3, 1970) *professional football player and coach*

He went from warm to red hot. You could hear him laughing or shouting for five blocks.

Wellington Mara, National Football League Hall of Fame owner

Vince fears high winds make every forward pass a gamble. To Vincent T. Lombardi gambling on a football field is a crime against nature.

Red Smith, sportswriter

Losing

As soon as I was in front I started praying for someone to pass me. It was a horrible realization . . . Instead of running it out of them, I was running it out of me.

Eamon Coghlan, champion runner, about losing in the Olympics

Athletes seem to have a much healthier attitude. There's a difference between a good loser and learning how to lose. I was never a good loser, but losing teaches you something.

Betty Meade, champion squash player, amputee

Every time you win, you're reborn; when you lose, you die a little.

George Allen, professional football coach

I despise losing and would do anything to avoid it.

Michael Jordan, professional basketball player

I didn't have to run that extra mile, didn't have to spar that day, I could have stayed up that night in camp and watched the late show . . . I could have fought tonight in no condition.

Floyd Patterson, champion boxer, his thoughts after the second Patterson–Liston fight, which he lost

I'd lost to him the first four times. I was beating him 7-5, 3-0 and he walked off the court. He didn't even give the satisfaction of beating him.

John McEnroe, professional tennis champion, about Jimmy Connors

I hate to lose. Hate, hate, hate to lose.

George Steinbrenner, owner, New York Yankees

I never learned how to lose.

Jim Ryun, track athlete

I slept like a baby—I woke up and cried every two hours.

Fred Taylor, professional football player, after a loss

I used very, very poor judgment and I'm man enough to admit that.

John A. Kelly, champion marathoner, after pressing too early in a race, wearing himself out and losing the race to Ellison Brown, who eventually beat him with an unexceptional time

I was overconfident. I overestimated my powers at the time, and I underestimated hers. Now, when you do that in any competitive event, it is a big mistake.

Bobby Riggs, professional tennis champion and legendary hustler, about losing to Billie Jean King in the "Battle of the Sexes" match

With the Red Sox, the past is always the present. If it's not Babe Ruth's departure, it's Bucky Dent's home run.

Dave Anderson, New York Times, regarding historical playoff losses by the Boston Red Sox

Washington: First in war, first in peace, last in the American League.

Anonymous, regarding losing franchise, the Washington Senators

The hardest part of losing is knowing you have failed those who are depending on you.
> *Johnny Roach, professional football player*

Let's call the whole thing off.
> *Dr. A. Harry Kleinman, ringside physician to the referee, at the Jerry Quarry–Joe Frazier heavyweight bout. Quarry lost.*

Losing is the great American sin.
> *Jerome Holtzman, writer*

Sometimes when you go out on the court, you have a feeling of being useless and you know everything is doomed.
> *Rosie Casals, champion tennis player*

We couldn't make a basket, we couldn't rebound, and we didn't play defense. You might say we put it all together.
> *Bill Fitch, professional basketball coach*

My baseball career spanned almost five decades—from 1925 to 1973, count them—and in all that time I never had a boss call me upstairs so that he could congratulate me for losing like a gentleman. When you're playing for money, winning is the only thing that matters. Show me a good loser in professional sports, and I'll show you an idiot. Show me a sportsman, and I'll show you a player I'm looking to trade.
> *Leo Durocher, professional baseball player and manager*

Nice guys finish last.
> *Leo Durocher, professional baseball player and manager*

The minute you start talking about what you're going to do if you lose, you've lost.
> *George Schultz, secretary of state*

They just made us look lousy.
> *Ron Greschner, professional hockey player, referring to the Montreal Canadiens defeating the New York Rangers*

Wait 'til next year.
> *Anonymous, attributed as Brooklyn Dodger fan lament*

We wuz robbed—we should have stood in bed.
> *Joe Jacobs, boxing trainer, after his fighter, Max Schmeling, lost to Jack Sharkey*

When you're not winning any matches since two months, it feels like you'll lose forever.
> *Yevgeny Kafelnikov, professional tennis player*

Winning is one thing. They don't remember their victories as much as their losses. Losing is a more powerful energy for them.
> *Vic Braden, tennis commentator, on John McEnroe and Jimmy Connors*

You either get a good trip or a bad trip. Today we got the nightmare trip.
> *Gary Stevens, professional jockey*

Louis, Joe

(b. May 13, 1914; d. Apr. 12, 1981) *World Heavyweight Champion 1937–1949; longest continuous reign by any world champion*

Everybody loved Joe. From black folks to redneck Mississippi crackers, they loved him.
> *Muhammad Ali, champion boxer*

He was a credit to his race—the human race.
Jimmy Cannon, sportswriter

He carried in a sense so many of our hopes, maybe even our dreams of vengeance.
Maya Angelou, poet

His name was Joe Louis and he was black and he was simply the greatest heavyweight fighter who ever lived. He could fend like Johnson and jab harder than Tunney and punch like Dempsey at Toledo.
Budd Schulburg, writer and screenwriter

I remember Joe Louis as a kid. Every time he was in a fight the whole family gathered around the radio. . . . When Joe Louis fought, the whole black neighborhood came to a standstill.
Maury Wills, professional baseball player, broadcaster, and manager

Louis was the anti–Jack Johnson. His talent was so undeniable and his behavior was deferential that in time he won over even the Southern press. . . . Unlike Johnson, Louis knew his place. He offended no one.
David Remnick, writer and editor

Nobody trained like Joe Louis. He always wore white knit trunks with a white tank top and black boxing shoes with white socks. He was all business.
Lou Duva, Hall of Fame trainer

Save me, Joe Louis. Save me, Joe Louis. Save me, Joe Louis.
Last words of a prisoner condemned to die in a gas chamber, reported by Martin Luther King, as the pellets were being dropped in

Love (of the game)

Do it because you love it. Don't do it because you want to make a lot of money at it. If you do it because you love it . . . everything else will fall into place.
Wayne Gretzky, Hall of Fame hockey player

I'm a firm believer that people only do their best at things they truly enjoy. It's difficult to excel at something you don't enjoy.
Jack Nicklaus, golfer

The reasons I was playing the game have always been the same. The game was all I cared about; it never felt like a job.
Dennis Rodman, professional basketball player

There's a love of the game in this city that is very difficult to put into words. You start off when you're very young and you never get it out of your system. You might get married to a woman, but basketball is still your first love.
Willie Hall, street basketball player, Harlem

You've got to love what you're doing. If you love it, you can overcome any handicap or the soreness or all the aches and pains, and continue to play for a long, long time.
Gordie Howe, hockey player

Luck

Dame Fortune is a cock-eyed wench, as
   someone's said before,
And yet the old Dame plays her part in any
   winning score.
Take all the credit you deserve, heads-up in
   winning pride,
But don't forget that Lady Luck was riding
   at your side.
Grantland Rice, sportswriter

Everything in a game happens by chance, so what you're doing is trying to make your own breaks.

Nate Allen, professional football player

First you've got to be good, but then you've got to be lucky.

"Lighthorse Harry" Cooper, golfer

Good luck is what is left over after intelligence and effort have combined at their best.

Branch Rickey, baseball executive

If I knew what it was, I'd take it with me every week.

Meg Mallon, professional golfer, when asked why she had been so lucky

If you don't get lucky, you just sit there like a big dork.

Don Nelson, professional basketball coach, speaking of the National Basketball Association lottery

Luck is the residue of design.

Branch Rickey, Hall of Fame baseball executive

Luck means a lot in football. Not having a quarterback is bad luck.

Don Shula, professional football coach

Smart is better than lucky.

Alvin Clarence Thomas, from Titanic Thompson

Sometimes you have to have good breaks.

Jose Maria Ozabal, champion golfer

You can play very well and lose, or play very badly and win. Things can happen. And you know what? That's just the way it goes.

Carl Eller, professional football player

Lukas, D. Wayne

(b. Sept. 2, 1935) *Champion thoroughbred horse trainer; won Preakness five times, Kentucky Derby four times and Belmont four times*

He's a coach and he pushes his athletes—and that's the nature of the game. The thing about him is he's got energy and goals.

Carl Nafzger, thoroughbred horse trainer

He's got his opinions and they come out quick. He wants you to hear them and listen to them. But I believe he has earned that right for all he's done for the game.

John Nerud, thoroughbred horse trainer

Madden, John

(b. Apr. 10, 1936) *Professional football coach; won Super Bowl; award-winning broadcaster*

John is a dominating personality. He can get people to stay with a bad game longer than anyone.

Barry Frank, agent

McEnroe, John

(b. Feb. 16, 1959) *Tennis champion; won U.S. Open four times, won three Wimbledon titles*

The guy is an artist. There's no one in the game quite like him.

Gerry Armstrong, professional tennis umpire

Majors, The (golf)

Most distressing to those who love the game of golf is the applauding and cheering of misplays or misfortunes of a player. Such occurrences have been rare at the Masters but we must eliminate them entirely if our patrons are to continue to merit their reputation as the most knowledgeable in the world.

Bobby Jones, champion golfer, note printed on the back of every Masters ticket since the 1930s.

Most of the time, professional golfers are playing for money. It is how they are measured by the end of the year. But four times a year, the money becomes completely irrelevant. They are playing for history.

John Feinstein, writer

Only one player will prevail, and considering the caliber of names at the top, the magnitude of the event and the difficulty of the course, the winner will have to overcome one of the greatest challenges of his career. But then, isn't that what a major is supposed to be about?

Clifton Brown, sportswriter

Playing in the U.S. Open is like tippy-toeing through hell.

Jerry McGee, golfer

The Masters doesn't begin until the back nine on Sunday.

John Feinstein, writer

The week of a major just has a different feel to it than other weeks. There's more tension during the practice rounds. You pay more attention to the golf course and the greens than to whatever bets you may have going.

Tom Watson, champion golfer

Management

It's like a child doing something bad at the dinner table. You send him to bed without dinner, but he's back down for breakfast in the morning.

George Steinbrenner, baseball owner, on rehiring Gene Michael, executive

Risk is something general managers live with every day.

Selena Roberts, sportswriter

Managing

A manager's job is simple. For 162 games you try not to screw up all that smart stuff your organization did last December.

Earl Weaver, baseball manager

I don't happen to think that a manager is a significant influence in major-league baseball. For the most part managing a team is a farce. One wearies of their studied idiosyncrasies, the spitting of the tobacco, the hitching of the belt, all the rest of the nonsense that goes with conducting a game that's juvenile enough to be totally understood by eight-year-olds in Little Leagues.

Howard Cosell, broadcaster

Managing is getting paid for home runs that somebody else hits.

Casey Stengel, baseball manager

Managing is like holding a dove in your hand. Squeeze too hard and you kill it; not hard enough and it flies away.

Tom Lasorda, baseball manager

Once there was a theory that devising strategy, dictating and alternating tactics, matching wits with the licensed genius across the way were part of the manager's job and that his degree of success in these areas accounted for his ranking in his profession.

Red Smith, sportswriter

Mantle, Mickey

(b. Oct. 20, 1931; d. Aug. 13, 1995) *Hall of Fame baseball player; won 7 of 12 World Series; won Triple Crown batting title; three-time league MVP*

He is the only baseball player I know who is a bigger hero to his teammates than he is to the fans.

Clete Boyer, professional baseball player

Mickey Mantle had those dual qualities so seldom seen, exuding dynamism and excitement but at the same time touching your heart—flawed, wounded. We knew there was something poignant about Mickey Mantle before we knew what poignant meant.

Bob Costas, broadcaster

Mickey Mantle just was everything. At my bar mitzvah I had an Oklahoma accent. And I think I once told my parents, "Play me or trade me."

Billy Crystal, comedian

Mickey was like Marilyn Monroe. He didn't have to be the greatest ballplayer. He had that charisma.

Hank Aaron, Hall of Fame baseball player, about Mickey Mantle, Hall of Fame baseball player

Shoot, if he'da told me, I'da give him first base.

Satchel Paige, Hall of Fame pitcher, telling sportswriters after the game what he thought of Mickey Mantle bunting to try to get on base

There were days when Mickey Mantle was so darn good that we kids would bet that even God would want his autograph.

Bob Costas, broadcaster

Maradona, Diego

(b. Oct. 30, 1960) *Champion soccer player; led team to two World Cup finals; won 1986 World Cup*

He was the most naturally talented player ever—a cheat, a drug-user, but on his best playing days, a magician with a ball.

Jimmy Burns, author

Pele had almost everything; Maradona has everything. He works harder, does more and is more skillful. Trouble is that he'll be remembered for another reason. He bends the rules to suit himself.

Sir Alf Ramsey, soccer executive

Sadly, you can't keep a good man down, nor Diego.

Terry Badoo, CNN soccer analyst and writer

Marathons

After every experience, it's natural to reflect that you might have done better. Only after a marathon can I say I have given everything.

Kenny Moore, champion marathoner

I wanted to try a marathon.

Grete Waitz, champion marathoner, when asked why she had come to her first New York City Marathon

Often, the enjoyment is the training before and the memory after.

Doug Kurtis, marathoner

Rejoice. We conquer!

attributed to the Athenian runner who ran from the plains of Marathon all the way to Athens to announce the Greek victory over the Persians, and then died

The marathon is the ultimate endurance test. Oh, sure, people sometimes go longer than that. But 26 miles 385 yards is where racing ends and where ludicrous extremes begin.

Joe Henderson, runner and writer

The winners run at speeds equaled or surpassed by no more than a handful of runners ever in the world. As important for me was the fact that more than fifteen thousand people from sixty-eight countries compete in our race.

Fred Lebow, organizer of the New York City Marathon

To succeed in the marathon at a very high level of competition you have to live in a very stable environment. You need people to support you and help you out. If you don't have this kind of backing, you're not going to make it.

Bill Rodgers, champion marathoner

Too many runners attempt the marathon much too early in their careers and then become ex-runners.

Robert Eshich, college running coach

To understand the marathon is to run it a lot . . . You really can't know it until you've felt the other side of it. That's the only way it's possible.

Bill Rodgers, champion marathoner

Marketing

If you're not the way the NBA wants you to be, you pay the price. If you look at the players they market, they have that nice, goody-two-shoes image. If you don't have it, you fall by the wayside.

Rod Strickland, National Basketball Association player

Marching Band

The critics agreed the Yale band was two steps faster than Harvard's.

Red Smith, sportswriter

The majorettes, their black-and-white costumes falling just below their buttocks, twirled and beckoned as the band—fifty-four clarinetists, fifty-one flutists, thirty-six coronetists, twenty-six trombonists, twenty-five percussionists, eighteen saxophonists, fourteen French Horn players, nine baritone players and nine tubaists—belted out "Boogie Woogie Bugle Boy." The color guard waved its flags to "Barbara Ann."

H. G. Bissinger, author

The marching band, brassy and brisk whether or nor it was led by an amazing baton-twirler of either sex, is an essential feature of a major college football. Its pregame entrance and half-time maneuvers represent a distinctive, indigenous American pop art form.

Leonard Koppett, writer,
The Avant-Gardes of 'Music'

The players tried to take the field,
   the marching band refused to yield,
do you remember what was the deal,
   the day, the music died?
Don McLean, musician, "American Pie"

Marriage

I fought Sugar Ray six times; I only beat him once. This is my sixth marriage and I ain't won one yet—so I figure I'm due.

Jake LaMotta, world champion boxer

I guess to be honest you just get use to them not being part of your life. You just have to build a life around yourself and then when they come back . . . there are sometimes a bit of an adjustment, depending on how long they've been away for. But overall it just sort of happens, you just slot back into good old routines.

Kylie Wetzell, partner of Adrian Cashmore, New Zealand rugby player

Look down at the field, and there was Steve at first base. How many games, how many years had she been sitting there? When Steve had waved to me in the crowd, was it really me he was waving at?

Cindy Garvey, ex-wife of professional baseball player Steve Garvey, upon seeing her husband's mistress for the first time

When he didn't remember our anniversary, I knew he was OK.

Lisa McCaffrey, wife of Ed McCaffrey, professional football player, referring to a concussion

When you divorce baseball, someone once said, baseball divorces you.

Danielle Gagnon Torrez, ex-wife of professional baseball player Mike Torrez

You've got to time your babies for the off-season and get married in the off-season and get divorced in the off-season. Baseball always comes first.

Liz Mitchell, wife of professional baseball player Paul Mitchell

Masculinity

He treats us like men. He lets us wear earrings.

Torrin Polk, University of Houston receiver, on his coach John Jenkins

To me being tough includes going into corners without phoning ahead to see who's there.

Ted Lindsay, professional hockey player

Masters, The

Something magical happens to every writer who goes to the Masters for the first time, some sort of emotional experience that results in a search party having to be sent out to recover his typewriter from a clump of azaleas.

Dan Jenkins, writer

Maturity

A lot of players don't really mature until their early 30's, or mid-30's and at that point they really break out.

Jim Furyk, professional golfer

Even though I think I'm mature on the football field, I'm still a kid. If there's a good play, I'll jump up and down on the sidelines.

Gary Parris, professional football player

Every player goes through a maturation period where they develop and improve.

Alonzo Mourning, professional basketball player

I made some mistakes—my immaturity is the one thing that sticks out—but I've learned a lot. Sometimes that takes time.

Kerry Collins, professional football player

Mays, Willie

(b. May 6, 1931) *Hall of Fame baseball player; played in 24 All-Star games; also known as "The Say Hey Kid"*

There have been only two geniuses in the world. Willie Mays and Willie Shakespeare.

Tallulah Bankhead, actress

This game was invented for Willie Mays a hundred years ago.

Ray Sedecki, professional baseball player

When you watched Willie Mays play baseball, it wasn't like watching anyone else play baseball. That was a style that was sensational, and he was so electrifying. Every time he came up, every time he was on base, every time a ball was hit to the outfield, there was a moment when you waited for him to do

something, and so many times he did it. It's so hard to do that in baseball.

Woody Allen, writer, actor, director

Media (the)

Good. You won't be able to put my picture in the media guide.

Leon Hess, sports owner, when told by his public relations staff that they could find no pictures of him anywhere in the organization

I forgot some appointment twelve years ago and *Sport* magazine hasn't let up on me since.

Ted Williams, Hall of Fame baseball player to Ed Linn, sportswriter

If you're famous in America the media will exploit you. The media is also America's safeguard. A lot of them are bastards, but I'd rather have those bastards than no media at all.

Jim Brown, Hall of Fame football player

I'm rapidly getting to the point now where I don't care about the interviews or anything anymore. I guess from a business point of view every bit of publicity you can get is good, but it's just not worth it to me. You get sick about talking about the same thing over and over again.

Alberto Salazar, champion marathoner

I think playing my first match was great. But the media is really sort of out of control.

Jennifer Capriati, professional tennis player, after her first professional tour match

I thought they were a sport magazine, not the *National Enquirer*.

Jim Pierce, father of Mary Pierce, professional tennis player, after a scathing article about him appeared in the magazine

I told him, "Don't buy the papers tomorrow. You're not going to like what you read."

Bill Parcells, professional football coach, about Phil Simms after a bad game

It would be impossible to overstate the degree to which sports-talk radio is shadowed by the homosexual panic implicit in the fact that it consists almost entirely of out-of-shape white men sitting around talking about black men's buff bodies.

David Shields, writer

Maybe this isn't a good time to have you doing undercover surveillance work.

Attributed to Federal Bureau of Investigation managers, by Joe Alston, champion badminton player, after the undercover surveillance FBI agent was featured on the cover of Sports Illustrated

That box over there, you know, people pass judgment on players, athletes, and people in general by what they see on TV.

Alonzo Mourning, professional basketball player

Too bad, America, but you missed one of the greatest basketball shows on Earth.

Attributed by Michael Berg, writer, to Sports Illustrated, *about the American Basketball Association's last championship series, which was not televised*

You have to show the winner pass the finish line, and then cut to the jubilation, but when there was the developing story as soon as the race was over . . . then all you can do is cover it.

Curt Gowdy, Jr., television producer, about Charismatic's dramatic loss in the Belmont Stakes and subsequent injury

Mental

Certainly the difference between winning and losing, between the winner and the runner-up, is always a mental one.

Peter Thompson, professional golfer

If you don't sharpen up your minds at a young age, you'll never be sharp at all. If you don't spend quality time doing what you're supposed to be doing now, you can't look forward to doing what you think you should be doing later on.

John Chaney, college basketball coach

I learned a long time ago, you can't let outside forces get inside your head and affect how you play.

Allan Houston, professional basketball player

I'm about five inches from being an outstanding golfer. That's the distance between my left ear and my right.

Ben Crenshaw, champion professional golfer

In order to be eligible to play, it was necessary for him to keep up his studies, a very difficult matter, for while he was not dumber than an ox, he was not any smarter.

James Thurber, writer, cartoonist, about an offensive lineman from Ohio State University

Ninety percent of the game is half mental.

Yogi Berra, Hall of Fame baseball player and manager

Raw power was giving way, at least a little, to cunning. More than ever, headwork won ballgames.

Burt Solomon, writer

Success is 90% physical and 10% mental. But never underestimate the power of that 10%.

Tom Fleming, runner and writer

The good Lord was good to me. He gave me a strong body, a good right arm and a weak mind.

Dizzy Dean, Hall of Fame baseball player and broadcaster

The simpler I keep things, the better I play.

Nancy Lopez, champion professional golfer

The key is being able to endure psychologically.

Greg LeMond, champion cyclist

The mind is the limit. As long as the mind can envision the fact that you can do something, you can do it—as long as you really believe 100 percent.

Arnold Schwarzenegger, champion bodybuilder and actor

You've got fast feet. But there are millions of people who have fast feet. The people who win races are the ones with fast brains.

Ross Kitt, father of A. J. Kitt, champion downhiller, to Kitt before a big race

Minor Leagues

The CBA has been a proving ground for players, coaches, and referees. The CBA has been instrumental in the development of many of the people you see in prominent positions all over the NBA.

Rod Thorn, National Basketball Association league executive speaking of the Continental Basketball Association

The CBA is only a bounce away from the NBA.

Kevin Mackey, college and minor league basketball coach, favorite recruiting and motivating line for players in the Continental Basketball Association

If you're playing here for money you're playing for the wrong reason. You could be further on in your career if you're out there working at something else.

Gerald Oliver, assistant coach, Continental Basketball Association

The NBA is sirloin, medium rare; the CBA is a double cheeseburger, ketchup only. The NBA is a best-selling novel; the CBA is a feature in the *National Enquirer*. The NBA is fantasy; the CBA is reality.

Bob Ryan, sportswriter, comparing National Basketball Association to Continental Basketball Association

You know in high school, how your parents came to the games and your girlfriend and friends? In pro ball, those people aren't around anymore. In Fort Myers, you look up in the stands and there's 200 or 300 people, and you don't know any of them. You're alone and you're fighting for a job that only 5 percent of the people get.

Shane Gunderson, minor league baseball player

Don't worry kid, you'll be back.

George Steinbrenner, owner, New York Yankees, to Bernie Williams, All-Star Major League Baseball player, early in Williams's career

Mistakes

Be quick, but never hurry.

John Wooden, basketball coach

Can't afford to miss, or you get beat.

Ben Hogan, champion golfer

His right name was Frank X. Farrell, and I guess the X. stood for "Excuse me." Because he never pulled a play, good or bad, on or off the field, without apologizing for it.

Ring Lardner, sportswriter and novelist, from Alibi Ike

I accept the fact that I am going to miss it sometimes. I just hope I miss it where I can find it.

Fuzzy Zoeller, champion professional golfer

If you make a mistake, you die.

Todd Skinner, mountain climber

I sometimes think about what we're doing out here and how hard some people work at it and then when it isn't happening, some player will say to me, "I'm sorry, coach, but I'm trying," and I'll tell him exactly what my father told me: you don't get any medals for trying.

Bill Parcells, professional football coach

Joe Frazier did not come out smokin'. Jerry Quarry did. It was Quarry's mistake.

Roy McHugh, sportswriter, referring to Quarry's loss in the fight

Most coaches hate preventable mistakes as much as I did. Somebody asked Don Shula if it wasn't a waste of time to correct a small flaw. "What's a small flaw?" Don wanted to know.

John Madden, professional football coach and commentator

Oh my God! I'm on the ice! What am I doing down here?

Michelle Kwan, medal-winning Olympic skater, after falling on the ice during the 1997 U.S. National Championships

She didn't win; I gave it to her. I hit so many errors. It was absolutely absurd.

Serena Williams, professional tennis player, speaking of a loss to Martina Hingis

The man who complains about the way the ball bounces is likely to be the one who dropped it.

Lou Holtz, professional football coach

We did something we should never do. We took it for granted.

Jenni Meno, pairs skater (with Todd Sand), after losing at the National Championships in which they were heavy favorites

When all is said and done, as a rule, more is said than done.

Lou Holtz, college football coach

When you make a mistake, there are only three things you should ever do about it; 1) admit it; 2) learn from it; 3) don't repeat it.

Paul "Bear" Bryant, professional football coach

Money

Good stockbrokers are a dime a dozen, but good shortstops are hard to find.

Charles O. Finley, baseball owner

I don't like money, but it quiets my nerves.

Joe Louis, champion boxer

I'd rather play for pay than run for fun.

Mel Gray, professional football player

I really don't like to talk about money. All I can say is that the Good Lord must have wanted me to have it.

Larry Bird, Hall of Fame basketball player and coach

I'm sick of people talking about money, money, money all the time.

Shaquille O'Neal, professional basketball player

Money isn't everything, but it's way ahead of whatever is in second place.

attributed to unknown by Mario Andretti, champion race car driver

People make too big a deal about the money. Some guy was complaining to me, and I told him, "Hey, if you don't like it, take your kids to see *Riverdance*."

Mike Piazza, professional baseball player

The beauty of money is that money can buy what the farm can't grow.

William C. Rhoden, sportswriter

The difference in Namath and me is that when you make the money he makes, they say you're ruggedly handsome. When you make the money I make, they say you have a big nose.

Jim Valvano, college basketball coach

The only reason I'd go to the NBA is if someone throws funny money—players' money—at me.

Jim Calhoun, college basketball coach

The pressures that are generated these days are not confined to jumping clear rounds, producing a brilliant extension or going fast. These days, we have pressures from sponsors, owners, and organizers that were unheard of a few years ago. The reason is simple—money.

Jane C. Wofford, champion equestrian show jumper

The winner gets $100,000 and the loser goes home and sits on his ass and does nothing.

Bobby Riggs, professional tennis champion

They both knew how to spend the green stuff but neither knew anything about conserving it.

Grantland Rice, sportswriter, speaking of Bill Tilden and Babe Ruth

This is terribly embarrassing for me to admit, but money makes me happy ... But maybe if you never had money you're more inclined to use it just to remind yourself that you've got some.

Arthur Ashe, Hall of Fame tennis champion and writer

Those boys playing football get their $2 or $3 million up front, and if they don't have a good day, they are not out anything. They still get paid on Monday. If we don't win, we don't get paid on Monday.

Richard Petty, champion race car driver

We have the highest-paid orange juice squeezer in the world.

Frank Graham, Jr., baseball executive, pointing out Roy Campanella, National League Most Valuable Player, who sat at nights in spring training with the kitchen staff, squeezing oranges

We took ALL the money.

Woody Stephens, horseracing trainer, his favorite saying

When I read the sports pages these days I think I'm reading the *Wall Street Journal*.

Dan Jansen, Olympic gold medalist speed skater, referring to player's salaries and other sports business dollars

When they say it's not about money, it's always about money.

George Young, football team executive

When you're fighting, you're fighting for one thing: money.

Jack Dempsey, champion boxer

When you spend what we've spent on talent, to be a .500 team is unacceptable. Period.

Dave Checketts, franchise executive, about the New York Knicks, one of the highest-salaried teams in history

Yes, it is forever about the money. Sports teaches you that eight days a week, making virtues of greed and lust, littering its fields with the currency of betrayal.

Ian O'Connor, sportswriter

You go between horses for money, not for fun.

Eddie Arcaro, jockey

You wasted your money.

Bill Russell, Hall of Fame basketball player and coach, responding to Seattle Supersonics owners, who pleaded with him ("But Bill, we paid a million dollars for him") not to release Jim McDaniels.

Motherhood

I left my babies to go compete against girls half my age.

Laura Baugh, professional golfer and recovering alcoholic, referring to times in her life when golf was all she had

Motivation

I like praise. But if I'm doing bad, I want to hear about it. That's what drives you.

Kobe Bryant, professional basketball player

It was a violent game. I don't mean there were any fights—but they were desperate and they were committed and they were more motivated than we were.

Pat Riley, professional basketball player and coach, referring to the Kentucky vs. Texas Western championship game. Riley played for Adolph Rupp at Kentucky. Texas Western was the first team to start five African Americans and win a national championship.

True motivation is not getting people to play their potential. True motivating is getting people to play beyond their potential.

Rick Pitino, college and professional basketball coach

You can only whip the mule so much before the mule turns around and says I've had it.

Kurt Rambis, professional basketball player and coach

Moving

We didn't care if the team moved here from Hartford, we don't care if they win or lose while they're here, and we don't care when or where they'll go if they pack up and leave.

Dennis Rogers, columnist, about the Hurricanes playing in Raleigh, North Carolina, after they had moved from Hartford

Nagurski, Bronco

(b. Nov. 3, 1908; d. Jan. 7, 1990) *Hall of Fame football player; All-American college football player*

I believe that 11 Nagurskis could beat 11 Granges or 11 Thorpes.

Grantland Rice, sportswriter

Namath, Joe

(b. May 31, 1943) *Hall of Fame football quarterback; won Super Bowl III; club owner; actor*

The Joe Namaths of the world are meaningless. They come and go, fleeting figures of passing glamour. You'll find them in the sports tomes but not in the history books.

Howard Cosell, broadcaster

A saloon keeper, from Beaver Falls, Pennsylvania.

Red Smith, sportswriter

National Association for Stock Car Auto Racing

Bloody black magic.

Alan Jones, champion Formula 1 racer, commenting on stock car racing

There is no way growing up in the thirties and thinking in the nineties this is where we are going to be.

Junior Johnson, champion stock car racer

The very words "stock car" are an acute bit of merchandising con, a deadpan form of mislabeling.

John S. Radosta, sportswriter

Negotiations

He was waiting to sign his new deal and he needed something to drive, so I took care of him. I told him before he brought it back to clean and service it.

Alonzo Mourning, professional basketball player, talking about fellow player Mark Strickland

I'd walk into the owner's office to talk contract and I'd say, "Hi ya, partner."

Joe DiMaggio, Hall of Fame baseball player, asked what he might be worth in today's free agent market

If you believed my side, I'm worth $2 million. If you believed theirs, I should be back in pee-wee hockey.

Ken Wregget, professional hockey player

I never tried to be bigger than the organization. I sacrificed my chance for free agency from time to time to help them with contract extensions that gave them salary cap room. This time, I had an idea what I deserved, and they met me halfway.

Jesse Armstead, professional football player

He wants Texas back.

Tommy Lasorda, Dodger manager, when asked what terms Mexican-born pitcher Fernando Valenzuela wanted in his upcoming contract negotiations

If our first pick was a contract holdout for 20 minutes, that would be too long.

Al Lerner, owner, speaking of how the Cleveland Browns got first-round draft choice Tim Couch to sign before their time on the draft clock was up

I got a million dollars worth of free advice and a very small raise.

Ed Stanky, professional baseball player

KISS MY ASS.

Auggie Busch, baseball owner, sent this telegram to Frank Lane, general manager, who was holding out for contract extension

Loyalty is a one-way street. They got to want you. You got to want to stay.

Tony Gwynn, professional baseball player

Maybe Hiromitsu can bleach his hair blonde and put on blue contact lenses. Then maybe he'll get the salary he deserves.

Wife of Hiromitsu Ochai, professional baseball player, who won Japan's Triple Crown, but still made less than half of what American players were paid

On the basis of what they're offering, I could play four or five games.

John Riggins, professional football player

That boy in there has a lawyer with him and he doesn't need one.

Unidentified basketball executive, referring to negotiations with then rookie Bill Bradley

Then Mr. Gehrig is a badly underpaid player.

Joe DiMaggio, Hall of Fame baseball player, to Ed Barrow, general manager, when Barrow remarked that Gehrig in his peak years didn't make as much money as what DiMaggio was negotiating for

We're just kind of dancing, but we haven't kissed yet.

Isiah Thomas, professional basketball player, coach, executive, and broadcaster, about his negotiations with the Washington Wizards basketball team

Negro Leagues

As the eighth commissioner of baseball . . . I apologize for the injustice you were subjected to. Every thinking person in this country agrees. Your contribution to baseball was the finest because it was unselfish.

Fay Vincent, Major League Baseball commissioner, addressing the Negro League reunion at the Baseball Hall of Fame

I have played against a Negro All-Star team that was so good, we didn't think we had an even chance against them.

Dizzy Dean, Hall of Fame baseball player

Nicklaus, Jack
(b. Jan. 12, 1940) *Champion golfer; won six Masters; four U.S. Opens; three British Opens*

He's been on a 30-year lucky streak.

Frank Beard, professional golfer on Jack Nicklaus

If Nicklaus tells you an ant can pull a bale of hay, don't ask any questions, just hook him up.

Lee Trevino, champion golfer

Nicknames
That's better, anyway you look at it, than someone calling you a shoeshine boy.

Sal "The Barber" Maglie, professional baseball player, who was asked what he thought of the nickname he'd been given by opposing teams, referring to the constant brushback pitches he threw

Night Clubs
Nobody ever goes there anymore—it's too crowded.

Yogi Berra, Hall of Fame baseball player and manager

No-Hitter
A million-to-one shot came in. Hell froze over. A month of Sundays hit the calendar. Don Larsen today pitched a no-hit, no-run, no-man-reach-first game in a World Series.

Shirley Povich, sportswriter

Notre Dame
RUM + VODKA + IRISH = FIGHT

Red Smith, sportswriter

Half the world loves Notre Dame and the other half seems to hate us. . . . I couldn't begin to tell you where it all started but I can tell you that there aren't many people unemotional and objective about us.

Richard W. Conklin, associate vice president, University of Notre Dame

Offense

I got used to getting touches and cutting and creating and anticipating what I could do next to get easier shots. Here, I'm not allowed to do that. I'm not used to an offense that's focused on one individual. The biggest adjustment has been standing out there, waiting to catch and shoot threes. That's not my style.

Scottie Pippin, professional basketball player

Those big tough guys on defense want to play our strength against their strength. I'd rather play our strength against their weakness.

Bob McKittrick, professional football coach

What's creative about throwing the ball into some big bruiser and watching him bull his way to the basket?

Don Nelson, professional basketball coach

Officials

A bald, mumbly judge from Reno.

David Remnick, writer, describing fight referee Mills Lane

Boo the players, but leave the referees alone. They're doing a difficult job well and they don't need 5,000 assistants.

Scotty Morrison, referee-in-chief, National Hockey League

Go out through your dugout. I don't want you crossing the field and showboating in front of the crowd.

Ed Hurley, umpire, to Dan Dressen, baseball coach, after throwing him out of a game

I did the first Frazier–Ali fight. Twenty-eight years later my son does another heavyweight championship. It's like two bookends.

Arthur Mercante, Sr., Hall of Fame referee

Imagine the job description: you're to run around in the mud on a Saturday afternoon and accept the malicious abuse of up to 40,000 people for ninety minutes plus injury time. Pay negligible.

Nicholas Royle, writer

Judges are supposed to be unbiased, and if you believe that I have a bridge to sell you.

Debbie Thomas, Olympic medalist figure skater

177

The trouble with referees is that they just don't care which side wins.

Tom Canterbury, college basketball player

There are good judges and there are judges who you will feel are not as capable; in the long run of a career, they seem to balance out.

Carlo Fassi, figure skating coach

The referee won't stop the clock now unless they draw blood.

Doug Collins, professional basketball player and broadcaster

This here official, JoJo Guerra, should be put in jail.

Pat Petronelli, Marvin Hagler's co-manager, referring to the judge who scored the Hagler–Leonard fight 10-2 in favor of Leonard

To me, sports is a rental business and it's an entertainment business.

Wayne Huizenga, baseball and football owner

With the introduction of the referee the crudeness of "The Noble Art" passes over into the relative sophistication of boxing.

Joyce Carol Oates, writer

You wanna know the chief quality a ref has gotta have in the NBA? That's a pair of elephant balls.

Jason Williams, professional basketball player

Officiating

As the referee, you've got to reside over this licensed wrath while keeping a tight rein on order. That's the job, keeping up with the pounding action, slipping in and out of that specter of unmitigated furor and confusion, prying apart hundreds of pounds of frustration, rage and fury.

Mills Lane, district court judge and boxing referee

If the referee's not going to take care of it, you got to take care of it.

Tim Harding, professional basketball player

I thought about it and I thought about it, and I decided it was the right thing to do. Let the chips fall where they may.

Mills Lane, boxing referee, who disqualified Mike Tyson for biting off a piece of Evander Holyfield's ear

I'm not allowed to comment on lousy officiating.

Jim Finks, New Orleans Saints general manager

It's all right, but what we need in Yorkshire–Lancashire matches is no umpires—and fair cheating all around.

Maurice Leyland, cricketer

Mother, may I slug the umpire,
May I slug him right away?
So he cannot be here, Mother,
When the clubs begin to play?

attributed to anonymous by Bill Mazer, broadcaster

There were 2,200 calls last weekend, and how many are we talking about?

Dick Hantak, head of officiating, National Football League

The greatest accolade is silence.

Dolly Stark, basketball official

The officials could see it better than I could. I was too busy fighting.

Floyd Patterson, champion boxer, after losing his first fight on points

What does it take to be a good referee? Beats the hell out of me. No one thinks any referee is good.

Richie Powers, basketball official

What you learn about the job, though, is that you can never predict what will happen. The most innocuous, innocent match can blow up at any time, anywhere. You always have to concentrate totally because you never know where a problem is going to come from.

Gerry Armstrong, tennis umpire

When the bell rang to end the twelfth round, both of them continued slugging it out. And when I stepped in to break it up, Bowe nailed me with a solid shot to the back of the head. I'm getting too old for that shit.

Mills Lane, district court judge and boxing referee

Why did you wait until the second half?

attributed to South American soccer fans, when a referee was kicked to death by irate fans of the home team, which was losing the match

You're a rookie official. I don't talk to rookie officials.

Norm "The Dutchman" Van Broklin, Hall of Fame professional football player and professional football head coach, to a league official during a game. He did not talk to the official the entire game.

Olympics

Citius, altius, fortius. . . . swifter, higher, stronger.

Olympic motto

First time I ever slept on my back. Had to, or that medal would have cut my chest.

Muhammad Ali, world champion boxer, gold medalist

"Going for the gold" is a good expression. It's not caution. It's abandonment.

Frank Carroll, figure skating coach

Hitler was there every day, watching. He looked like Charlie Chaplin sitting up there, him and the fat guy, Goering.

John A. Kelly, champion marathoner and Olympic runner

I'm absolutely positive that it does work if you're wining and dining judges and bringing them in, buying them dinners and stuff. But it's up to the individual judges to spot if they're being played for suckers or if it's genuine.

Alex McGowan, Olympic figure skating coach

I'm glad they were able to continue the games. What they're about is peace and sportsmanship.

Shannon Miller, Olympic gold medalist gymnast, after the bombing in Atlanta during the Olympics

I really just hoped to make the finals. Winning the medal was just . . . extra.

Amy Chow, Olympic gymnast

It was a lifetime of training for just 10 seconds.

Jesse Owens, Olympic gold medalist track and field competitor

I wish there were two gold medals, but it wouldn't mean as much if there were two gold medals.

Michelle Kwan, Olympic medalist figure skater, after losing to Tara Lipinski in the Olympics

I would say that going to the Olympics and winning a gold medal is a far greater challenge than defending the America's Cup, because, first of all, there's a lot more people you're competing against. There was a total of, I think, only seven boats in the entire America's Cup, whereas in the Finn class at the Olympics there are probably five to six hundred sailors who try for a slot.

Ted Turner, champion yachtsman
and baseball owner

The great global festival of sinew and sweat.
Red Smith, sportswriter

The most important thing about the Olympic Games is not winning, but taking part.

Pierre de Coubertin, sportsman and educator

The Olympics are a dinosaur, running out of cities . . . If you use the politics of a nation to judge whether or not you compete with that nation, you might as well say that international sport is dead.

Sebastian Coe, champion runner

Medals are more important than times. Medals stay forever. Times change.

Rosa Mota, Olympic gold medalist marathoner

No athlete wins Olympic medals based entirely on the coach's direction. I believe that the coach contributes only 30 percent of what it takes to become a champion. The other 70 percent is the skater's will, determination, intelligence, and ability to compete.

Carlo Fassi, figure skating coach

Nobody ever beats the decathlon. You might set a record and kick the hell out of it one day, but you know it will always be there, waiting for you to try again, telling you, "Okay you son of a gun, try and get me this time."

Bruce Jenner, Olympic gold medalist
decathlon competitor

No one can ever imagine what it's like to stand on the podium and be called one of the world's greatest athletes. What I do in football, I just do it, but nothing will compare to that.

Bob Hayes, champion Olympic sprinter and
professional football player

Olympic Village was under siege. Two men lay murdered and eight others were held at gunpoint in imminent peril of their lives. Still the games went on.

Red Smith, sportswriter

Once the gun goes off, there isn't a lot of thinking, just instinct.
Bonnie Blair, Olympic gold medalist speed skater

The Olympic year is a very trying period, and most athletes have problems afterwards, sometimes as long as a year or two. It just knocks you off track.

Ekaterina Gordeeva, Olympic gold medalist pairs
skater

The self-appointed, self-perpetuating kangaroo court that calls itself the International Olympic Committee.

Red Smith, sportswriter

These Olympics, probably more than any before, are showing a lot of little girls it's okay to sweat, it's okay to play hard, and it's okay to be an athlete.

Lindsay Davenport, champion tennis player,
about the 1996 Olympics

The sport is bigger than the man. Any man. Nobody ever shaped the decathlon in his own image.

Bruce Jenner, Olympic gold medalist decathlon competitor

Winter Olympians are the hibernating animals of sport. Every few years we stick our noses out of our caves, venture into the cold to skate, ski, luge, or knock a hockey puck around, then disappear again, into the forest or the North Pole or wherever it is we go until another Olympics roll around again.

Dan Jansen, Olympic gold medalist speed skater

Part of the charm of the Winter Olympics is that ice skating and all the rest of those Olympic sports completely disappear for four years at a time.

Dan Jenkins, writer and best-selling author

On the Road

You just can't sit in your room at the hotel watching CNN.

Monica Seles, champion professional tennis player

Opportunity

We're the only ones who have a chance.

Jim Valvano, champion college basketball coach, when asked if he thought his team had a chance in the championship game against the heavily favored University of Houston Cougars, during an improbable run through the NCAA Men's Basketball Tournament in which his team won

Owners

Charles Comisky was not only the meanest skinflint in baseball, but a man who could cruelly flaunt his wealth, while treating those who brought it to him as peons.

Stephen Jay Gould, scientist and baseball enthusiast

Getting money out of those people—track owners—is like trying to squeeze a lemon dry.

Eddie Arroyo, jockey

I admit he's the greatest ticket seller in the history of sports, but I'm not going to pay him $4 million a year. I'm just not going to do it.

Jerry Reinsdorf, basketball and baseball owner, about Michael Jordan, for whom he eventually paid much more

I don't earn as much as a utility infielder, but baseball is my game and I can't let one or two high-priced players drive me out of it.

Bill Veeck, baseball owner and racetrack operator

I have owners who don't mind spending the $25,000 it costs to fly a horse across the country for a big race. They know they'll usually make more money than that by running.

D. Wayne Lukas, thoroughbred horse trainer

I'm going to write a book, *How To Make A Small Fortune In Baseball*—you start with a large fortune.

Ruly Carpenter, baseball owner

Irsay had been dealing with San Diego and the Raiders, and he'd gotten mad at them. You want John Elway? . . . You're going to get John Elway—twice a year on another team. I'm just thankful we got him 16 times a year—on our side.

Dan Reeves, professional football coach

I say to our trainers, "I won't try to tell you how to train horses, just don't tell me how to sell beer."

Bob Lewis, thoroughbred horse owner, winner of two Kentucky Derbys

Just a fad—passing fancy.

Philip Wrigley, baseball owner, on baseball played after dark under the lights

Make no mistake. This decision was not easy.

Robert Kraft, on moving the New England Patriots from Foxboro, Massachusetts to Hartford, Connecticut and taking a sweetheart deal

Maybe all the owners should do like Charlie—run the team on the phone from Chicago and make the decisions after consulting cab drivers and the guys in the barbershop.

Bill Cutler, baseball executive, talking about Charles O. Finley, Major League Baseball owner

My, God. I've heard the story of all that sweat and sacrifice of how he made his money, five hundred times.

Bill Dauer, about Charles O. Finley, Major League Baseball owner

Running a two-car team was my main preoccupation in 1975 and I recommend it as a surefire way of getting ulcers.

Graham Hill, champion race car driver

Those first few years my brother used to go to school—at Fordham Prep—with a handful of tickets to give away, and I'd give them away at grammar school.

Wellington Mara, Hall of Fame football owner

Owning the Yankees is like owning the Mona Lisa.

George Steinbrenner, owner

Remember, half the lies they tell about the Dodgers aren't true.

Walter O'Malley, baseball owner

The ironic thing is that I've never seen [Al Davis] and Darth Vader in the same place.

Howie Long, professional football owner, about Al Davis

The most beautiful thing in the world is a ballpark filled with people.

Bill Veeck, baseball owner and racetrack operator

This is the ultimate ego play for a wealthy New York investor.

Marc Ganis, a sports consultant, on the prospect of buying the New York Jets

We can't hopscotch franchises around the country. We have built this business in the trust of the fans. If we treat them as if it doesn't count, it isn't going to wash.

Art Modell, football owner, speaking out against the proposed move of the Rams from Los Angeles to St. Louis. Modell would also later move his franchise from Cleveland to Baltimore, despite sellout crowds for his team.

Wellington Mara . . . cloaks himself in the piety of Saint Patrick's and behaves as if his ownership derives from the Vatican.

Howard Cosell, broadcaster

When you come right down to it, the baseball owners are really little boys with big wallets.

Harold Parrott, writer

You could make more money investing in government bonds. But football is more fun.

Clint Murchison,
football owner

You like being with the Yankees? We'll, let me give you two tips. You wear your hat like a Yankee and you call me sir.

George Steinbrenner, owner, New York Yankees,
to Shane Spencer, rookie

Pain

If you're gymnast something is always hurting, but you still train. You just have to learn to live with discomfort.

Mary Lou Retton, gymnast and
Olympic gold medalist

I hate to say it, but it's true—I only like it better when pain comes.

Frank Fletcher, professional boxer

I knew at the time I was damaging myself, but I made a decision. I said, "Look, you are going to have arthritis and you are going to have pain—what do you want to do? Do you want to stop now and have the pain, or can you live it?"

Dr. Tom Waddell, Olympic decathlon competitor
and gay rights activist

I know how the pain of cycling can be terrible: in your legs, your chest, everywhere. You go into oxygen debt and fall apart. Not many people outside cycling understand that.

Greg LeMond, cyclist

It is an aspect of training, but a subtle aspect. I don't think about it much.

Jim Ryun, track athlete

Pain is a given. I don't try to fight the pain or pretend it's not there. In fact, I give into it. But only for a little while.

Ric Munoz, marathoner,
HIV-positive for 12 years

Races always evoke some dread about pain that will come. But we can't escape the fact that the more discomfort we can accept in a race, the faster we will run. Successful racing means *courting the pain.*

John Elliott, runner

The man who can drive himself further once the effort gets painful is the man who will win.

Roger Bannister, runner

There has never been a great athlete who died not knowing what pain is.

Bill Bradley, professional basketball player
and U.S. senator

This is the best feeling there is.
Pat Fischer, professional football player

Thrust against pain, pain is the purifier.
Percy Cerutty, Australian Olympic coach

We train through the winter in deep snow and ice. Our slogan is "Pain is good, more pain is even better."
Matt Carpenter, mountain runner

When you win, nothing hurts.
Joe Namath, Hall of Fame football player

Palmer, Arnold

(b. Sept. 10, 1929) *Champion golfer; won four Masters, two British Opens, and one U.S. Open*

There are dozens on the pro tour who would be as good as Palmer if they had his outlook. But you can't put something into a man that isn't there.

Ed Furgol, professional golfer

Parents

As a footballer, I wasn't even his shadow. At the most, he inherited my passion for soccer. His class? . . . That's the divine gift.
Nelio, father of Ronaldo, professional soccer player

He has taught me to follow in his footsteps as a boxer, and to learn from his mistakes in life.
Floyd Mayweather, Jr., professional boxer, whose father was once a number one contender and then went to jail later on for drugs

I could beat on other kids and steal their lunch money and buy myself something to eat. But I couldn't steal a father. I couldn't steal a father's hug when I needed one.
Bo Jackson, professional baseball and football player

I don't reckon I regret it. When he wins, he can have it, but he ain't gonna have it given to him.
Lee Petty, champion race car driver, who had his son's win in a race nullified, because he hadn't fulfilled the requisite number of laps. The victory instead went to himself.

I'm so sorry I ever heard of tennis because it cost me my family. I spent years grooming her. Now she's got $4 million in the bank and I don't have enough to fill up my tank at the gas station.
Jim Pierce, father of Mary Pierce, professional tennis player, who has a restraining order against her father

It's amazing. I thought I knew my father really well. But there were things in the book about him—what he felt about the game—that I never knew.
Cal Ripken, Jr., professional baseball player, who read his father's posthumously published book

It was like one of those karate pictures when the pupil has to fight the master. He was strong. He got tired and quit, but I learned a lot and respected him even more afterward.
Ricardo Williams, Jr., professional boxer, referring to a boxing match he had at the age of fourteen with his father, retired boxer, Ricardo Williams, Sr.

My Daddy was a race car driver, so I became a race car driver. If he'd been a grocer, I might have been a grocer . . . But he was a race car driver, so here I am.
Richard Petty, champion race car driver

Oh, what a feeling! I'll never forget this as long as I'll live. I want to thank my mother for buying me my first pair of skates.

Harry Sinden, hockey coach, after his Philadelphia Flyers won the Stanley Cup

The cops won't take you; the fire department won't take you. The only thing you'll be able to do is drive a cab.

Matty Ferrigno, father of Lou Ferrigno, champion bodybuilder, professional football player, and actor

There's a lot of people in this sport that live through their kids. We'll never do that.

Jack Lipinski, father of Olympic gold medalist figure skater Tara Lipinski

When it would rain, we'd go under the boardwalk and I'd throw to him. In the apartment we rented, I'd move the furniture out and he would hit Wiffle Balls.

Vince Piazza, father of Mike Piazza, professional baseball player

When I go home to visit my parents these days, both of them still perky into their eighties with a social calendar more advanced than my own, it doesn't take my dad long to get started about the modern game. I'm old enough now to realize that we've had almost the same conversation for close on thirty-five years.

Steve Grant, writer

Passing

I like to throw the ball. To me, the pro game *is* throwing. I may be wrong, but putting the ball in the air is the way to win.

Y. A. Tittle, Hall of Fame quarterback

It doesn't matter how simple or fancy a pass is. The only good pass is one that is caught by its target.

Red Auerbach, Hall of Fame basketball coach and executive

Passing is the most important fundamental in lacrosse.

Jim Hinkson, champion lacrosse coach

Ten years from now, they won't even talk about my goal scoring; it'll just be my passing.

Wayne Gretzky, Hall of Fame hockey player

Wendell [Ladner] was the only guy I ever met who could throw a bad pass to himself. He'd throw it and go get it, throw it and go get it.

Steve Jones, professional basketball player

Passion

Maybe it's wasn't talent the Lord gave me. Maybe it was the passion.

Wayne Gretzky, Hall of Fame hockey player

As long as it's still fun, which it still is, as long as I'm still passionate, which I still am, and as long as I am still competitive, which I hope to be, then I'll be around.

Lance Armstrong, champion cyclist, winner of Tour de France, and cancer survivor

Patience

Bob Knight was many things: brilliant, driven, compassionate—but not patient.

John Feinstein, writer

As long as my pitchers throw strikes, I'll have patience. But when they start walking people and getting behind—I don't need that.

> *Lou Pinella, professional baseball player and manager*

Today, I just told myself, "You have 64 more holes to get it back." I'm going to be patient in this tournament.

> *Tiger Woods, champion golfer*

Payroll

As Phil Rizzuto and Whitey Ford raised the World Championship banner, Shepard proudly announced, "The flag we are about to raise is a symbol of courage, conviction and everlasting truth." He forgot to mention the 1999 Yankees' $86 million payroll, the highest in baseball.

> *William C. Rhoden, sportswriter*

Pelé (Edson Arantes do Nascimento)

(b. Oct. 23, 1940) *Soccer player; won three World Cups*

Brazilians who travel report that they are asked about Pele by people who would not know where to find Brazil on a map.

> *Janet Lever, sociologist and writer*

His name and tales of his talents have spread throughout the world . . . Barely civilized African tribes that play soccer with human skulls supposedly shout "Pele!" as they play.

> *Chuck Casscio, writer*

Pele's ability when receiving a high-cross is particularly fascinating to watch. He lets it ride off his chest, pivots, and takes a thunderous shot at the goal. Or the next time, he may deflect the ball behind the oncoming defender and follow up at top speed to create a split-second opening for himself.

> *Hubert Vogelsinger, writer*

Pele's fame is of global proportions. He has visited eighty-eight countries, met two popes, five emperors, ten kings, seventy presidents, and forty other chiefs of state. Biographies of Pele have been translated into more than 100 languages.

> *Janet Lever, sociologist*

Pele is the greatest sportsman of all time in all sports.

> *Ian Woosnam, North American Soccer League commissioner*

Pele won't finish the World Cup. It's amazing he hasn't gone mad.

> *attributed to a French journalist, by the* Sunday Times History of the World Cup, *after Pelé was brutally cut down by a Bulgarian midfielder named Zhechev*

The wonderful thing about watching Pele is that he represents soccer in its purest form, soccer as it should be played. All the facets of the game are there, embodied in one man, all of them beautifully balanced to produce soccer perfection.

> *Paul Gardner, sportswriter*

To me you are still a little boy, but everyone else seems to think you're grown up. Maybe I am wrong. Maybe I shouldn't stand in your way if this is really a chance for you.

> *Pelé's mother, saying goodbye when he went to play professional soccer in Brazil at the age of fifteen*

When you talk about Pele you break out a box labeled "Superlatives" and roll out all the

euphemisms. When Pele plays he makes straight news coverage obsolete. Pele never jumps, he always soars; he never runs, he always darts; he never outhustles his opponent, he victimizes them; he never kicks, he always blasts; he is never led, he always leads.

Chuck Cassio, writer

Penalties

You're going to get it whether you return it or not, so you might as well hack somebody once in a while.

Steve Yzerman, professional hockey player

Performance

Don't try to perform beyond your abilities—but never perform below them.

Frank Robinson, baseball player and manager

What do I think of his performance?! That's a helluva question!

Tommy Lasorda, professional baseball manager, being asked about Dave Kingman's performance against his team, after he had eight RBIs in one night

Physically Impaired Athletes

Have a dream, make a plan, go for it. You'll get there, I promise.

Zoe Koplowitz, marathoner, afflicted with multiple sclerosis

Running on an artificial leg at full speed is like driving backward at 55 miles per hour, using only your rearview mirror to guide you.

Thomas Bourgeois, champion runner, below-the-knee amputee

When I am running, I feel everything is in sync. Even my mechanical leg becomes a part of me.

Sarah Reinersten, marathoner, above-the-knee amputee

Pitching

Anyone can light it up for one or two starts. To do it over the course of a year, you have to be a superstar.

Joe Torre, champion professional baseball player and manager, referring to Roger Clemens's drive for a record number of wins without a loss

A perfect pitcher is an impossible concept, as long as major league hitters remain capable of hitting perfect pitches.

Bob Gibson, Hall of Fame baseball pitcher

A pitcher will take any little advantage he can today, and I don't blame him. I'd pitch in front of the rubber when I had a chance. I never used a cut ball much, but I wasn't to proud to.

Preacher Roe, professional baseball player

As a rule, pitchers can't bunt, can't hit, can't field, can't run and can't slide. The only thing they can do is throw the ball longer and harder than anyone else.

Maury Wills, professional baseball player, broadcaster, and manager

Baseball's roadside is littered with the careers of terrific rookie pitchers who quickly dissolved into rusty, dented mediocrities.

Daniel Okrent, sportswriter

Every hitter likes fastballs, just like everybody likes ice cream. But you don't like it when

someone's stuffing it into you by the gallon. That's what it feels like when Nolan Ryan's thrown balls by you.

> *Reggie Jackson, Hall of Fame baseball player and executive*

Every pitcher has to be a little in love with death.

> *Bill Lee, professional baseball player*

Good pitching will always stop good hitting and vice-versa.

> *Bob Veale, professional baseball player*

He calls it his Hall of Fame pitch because it puts some pitchers in Cooperstown before their time.

> *Ken Griffey, Sr., professional baseball player and coach, about Durwood Merrill, umpire*

He talks too much. He talks like he's Bob Gibson. I'm the only guy who can't hit him.

> *Charlie Hayes, professional baseball player, about pitcher Todd Stottlemyre*

His arm has been scanned and prodded and manipulated and sliced.

> *Buster Olney, sportswriter, about David Cone's arm*

I'm gonna send every one of those sons-of-bitches on their backs . . . there was always that lousy talk about me choking up and never being able to win the big ones. But I never had a teammate of mine tell me that I couldn't protect him with that baseball when it was time for somebody to be sent right on his ass.

> *Don Newcombe, professional baseball player*

I never throwed an illegal pitch . . . Just once in a while I used to toss one that ain't never been seen by this generation.

> *Satchel Paige, Hall of Fame baseball pitcher*

In the politically correct, number-crunched, no-salt-added modern facsimile of baseball, there is no place for an older pitcher to whom the game, any game, was a war.

> *Lonnie Wheeler, writer*

It's lonely out there.

> *Rick Cerone, professional baseball player, catcher, after fulfilling a childhood fantasy and pitching one inning in a real game at Yankee Stadium*

It's not just the one he throws out there that just falls off the table. It's the sounds. There's the grunt of the fastball, and then there's the sound of that fastball away.

> *Bobby Valentine, professional baseball player and manager, talking about the pitching of Roger Clemens*

I've never heard a crowd boo a homer, but I've heard plenty of boos after a strikeout.

> *Babe Ruth, Hall of Fame baseball player*

Just a bit outside.

> *Bob Uecker, professional baseball player, announcer, and actor, in Major League, describing a wild pitch*

Nothing. No movement, no jerk, no reach . . . That kind of thing isn't always appreciated, but it makes or breaks a pitcher.

> *Tim Belcher, professional baseball player, pitcher, speaking about good catchers*

Stand on the rubber and read the writing on the mitt. Total focus. Shut the world out.

> *Jan Reid, sportswriter*

Strikeouts are boring—besides that, they're fascist. Throw some ground balls. More democratic.

> *Kevin Costner, actor, to his pitcher,*
> *in Bull Durham*

That last one sounded a little low.

> *Lefty Gomez, professional*
> *baseball player, to an umpire on*
> *a third called strike*
> *by Bob Feller, pitcher*

There is nothing quite like the feeling of expectation on the morning of the day or night that you are scheduled to pitch.

> *Tom Seaver, Hall of Fame*
> *baseball player*

The mound is my personal zone. During those moments on the pitching rubber, when you have every pitch at your command working to its highest potential, you are your own universe.

> *Bill Lee, professional*
> *baseball player*

The Tigers might be hurt, but I'll tell ya one thing, the pitchers all over the league will improve.

> *Casey Stengel, Hall of Fame baseball manager,*
> *commenting on Detroit's big slugger*
> *Harvey Kuenn, being called up in*
> *front of the draft board*

Pitino, Rick

(b. Sept. 18, 1952) *NCAA, NBA basketball coach*

This guy is not a real person, he's a rattlesnake.

> *Peter Vecsey, sportswriter*

Playbook

My college playbook was like a Dr. Seuss book. With the 49ers, it's like a cookbook.

> *Terrell Owens, wide receiver, professional*
> *football player*

Play Calling

Baby, no one sends in plays for Francis.

> *Fran Tarkington, Hall of Fame football player,*
> *when asked who called his team's plays*

I think you can hit Warfield on a down-and-in pattern.

> *Richard M. Nixon, president of the*
> *United States, to Don Shula, Hall of Fame*
> *football coach*

No, we ain't gonna play that. We're gonna kick their butts.

> *Lee Roy Jordan, Hall of Fame football*
> *player, waving off a defense called*
> *in from the sidelines*

Playing Time

The two most important things to athletes: playing time and money.

> *John Paxson, champion professional*
> *basketball player*

Playoffs

In the playoffs, there are no lay-ups, so when guys get in the paint they're usually getting hacked.

> *Latrell Sprewell, professional basketball player*

It was what I expected. Challenging, nerve-racking at times, exhilarating at times. Just

like every playoff game I've ever been a part of.

Kurt Rambis, professional basketball player and coach

The team I was with last year is home watching us right now, and I'm in the playoffs. I'm having fun.

Marcus Camby, professional basketball player

We can't think about the playoffs. We would not even accept a bowl bid at this time.

Dan Henning, professional football coach

Where else would you want to be in October, except here?

Derek Jeter, professional baseball player

You need to be a little bit lucky in the playoffs.

Yanic Perreault, professional hockey player

Politics

Beyond the happy rhetoric, our hockey triumph didn't validate our system any more than defeats in other years had undermined our way of life.

Pete Axthelm, author, referring to the 1980 victory of the U.S. Olympic hockey team over the Olympic team from the U.S.S.R.

Durwood, you might not realize this, but you just hung up on Marlin Fitzwater.

George W. Bush, politician and baseball owner (later, 43rd U.S. president), to Durwood Merrill, umpire, after the latter hung up the phone on the press secretary to George H. W. Bush, U.S. president, thinking it was a prank phone call. President Bush wanted a real umpire's windbreaker to throw out the first pitch at a Texas Rangers game, his son's team

Glad to meet ya, Mr. Vice Prez. Love ya, but didn't vote for ya.

Don Meredith, football player and broadcaster, to Vice President Spiro T. Agnew

I did all I could to make Coolidge president.

Ring Lardner, sportswriter, to Warren G. Harding, U.S. president, after accidentally knocking down a tree limb that fell on the then president

I made a technical critique, one that I still deeply believe. This left has really gone all the way. But let's get real—with the country in the condition it's in, does it seem serious to transform a soccer critique into a state affair?

Silvio Berlusconi, former Italian prime minister and opposition leader, media magnate and owner of AC Milan, referring to criticisms he made of Dino Zoff, champion goalie and coach of the Italy 200 team, just after Italy's heartbreaking loss to France in the 2000 European championship. Zoff immediately resigned after Berlusconi's criticisms and the constitutional government criticized Berlusconi for trying to use the loss to advance his own political gain.

In our political system that is sometimes impossible, unless you're willing to sell your soul. It's like playing football with eleven men on your team and thirty-three on the other. You're forever running into a stone wall.

Bob Mathias, gold medalist decathlon competitor, politician, and actor

It's better than "Pomp and Circumstance."

Joe Torre, professional baseball player and manager, to Bill Clinton, U.S. president, and Hillary Clinton, first lady, at a ceremony honoring the World Champions, as Torre approached the podium and the band played "Hail to the Chief"

The box score always adds up—politics never does.

James Reston, journalist and author

The White House needs a little less Vince Lombardi and a little more Abraham Lincoln.

Dave Meggyesy, professional football player and political activist

This is sport. More important things are waiting for us off the court.

Vlade Divac, professional basketball player, a citizen of the former Yugoslavia, whose family and friends were caught up in the war in Bosnia

Well, I don't think he'd enforce a rigorous curfew.

George Will, political columnist and baseball aficionado, to Roy Firestone, television interviewer, after he was asked what kind of baseball manager Senator Ted Kennedy would be

Whether in sports or politics, competition in and of itself is good.

Bill Bradley, Hall of Fame basketball player and U.S. senator

You travel around Texas with me, and everyone wants to talk about Nolan Ryan.

George W. Bush, governor of Texas and baseball owner

You've got to stick your butt out more, Mr. President.

Sam Snead, champion professional golfer, to Dwight D. Eisenhower, U.S. president, giving the president a lesson.

Polo

The sport of kings.

Anonymous

Man is a ball tossed onto the field of existence, driven hither and thither by the chaugan-stick of destiny, wielded by the hand of Providence.

Persian proverb

No sport, save possibly steeplechasing and football, is so good a school . . . as polo.

George S. Patton, U.S. general

Polo irritates people in a way that other sports don't. One reason my be the subtle sense emanated of a private game in which spectators are not so much welcomed as endured.

Frank Milburn, writer

Polo Grounds

The return of the Polo Grounds to the National League was like the raising of a sunken cathedral.

Murray Kempton, sportswriter, about the 1962 New York Mets debuting of Polo Grounds after the Giants moved to San Francisco

Pool

By rights it should be a reasonably easy game. . . . No one is allowed to block or tackle you to prevent you from getting to the ball. No one can move the balls to make them harder to hit.

Steve Mizerak, champion pool player and beer pitchman

If you know a good player who is tempted by pool hustling, introduce him at once to a career guidance counselor, a psychotherapist or a surgeon who does lobotomies.

Robert Byrne, champion pool player and writer

It is a game of infinite variables. . . . True excellence is rare and vanities are punished.
Jim Harrison, novelist, from Just Before Dark

It is impossible to imagine Goethe or Beethoven being good at billiards or golf.
H. L. Mencken, critic, humorist, author

Let us to billiards.
William Shakespeare, from Antony and Cleopatra

Petty thievery is a more profitable job than pool hustling.
Robert Byrne, champion pool player, columnist, and writer

Sex after ninety is like trying to shoot pool with a rope.
George Burns, comedian, actor

Some people meditate, others paint. I shoot pool.
Laura Shepard, champion pool player

The human race divides itself neatly into two different groups—those who love pool and those who don't. Neither understands the other and often doesn't care to.
Mike Shamos, champion pool player

The trouble with shooting pool is that it's no good if you don't win.
Paul Newman, in The Color of Money *(written by Walter Tevis)*

There are 350 varieties of shark, not counting loan or pool.
L. M. Boyd, writer

When I realized that what I had turned out to be was a lousy, two-bit pool hustler and drunk, I wasn't depressed at all. I was glad to have a profession.
Danny McGoorty, champion pool player and hustler

You can put two eight-year-olds on a pool table and go to Europe for a week. Those kids will still be at the table playing pool.
Minnesota Fats, legendary pool player, hustler, trick shot artist

To play billiards well was a sign of an ill-spent youth.
Herbert Spencer, philosopher

Post Season

In the post season, teams play for forty minutes.
Tyrone Grant, college basketball player

Potential

I just want to realize my potential. That would be a victory in itself.
Steve Bartkowski, professional football player

Practical Jokes

How could you do that to that poor little animal!
Art "Fatso" Donovan, professional football player, finding a dead groundhog in his bed after sneaking in late from breaking curfew

I knew he would have killed me if he caught me.
Cale Yarborough, champion race car driver, about Little Joe Weatherly, after he put a live, defanged rattlesnake in Weatherly's lap while he was getting ready to race.

My God, what is it?
> *Adolph Rupp, college basketball coach, upon smelling a dead skunk underneath his chair during a game against South Eastern Conference rival Mississippi State.*

Practice

A football player has certain responsibilities. Practice is one of them. You'd have no kind of team if the players didn't report to practice.
> *Joe Schmidt, professional football player*

An hour of hard practice is worth five hours of foot-dragging.
> *Pancho Segura, professional tennis player*

Concentration is why some athletes are better than others. You develop that concentration in training. You can't be lackadaisical in training and concentrate in a meet.
> *Edwin Moses, medal-winning track star*

For the best part of eighteen years I've averaged a round a day. That's three hundred and sixty rounds of golf times eighteen, or six thousand, five hundred and seventy rounds . . . a lot of walking . . . a lot of shots. I've worked . . . I've worked like hell.
> *Babe Didrickson Zaharias, Olympian and champion golfer*

It's not necessarily the amount of time you spend at practice that counts; it's what you put into the practice.
> *Eric Lindros, professional hockey player*

The more I practice, the luckier I get.
> *Gary Player, champion professional golfer*

There aren't any tricks. It's hard work and pain and loneliness. But you can come back. That's what I want everybody to know—you can come back.
> *Gale Sayers, professional football player*

There's no such thing as natural touch. Touch is something you create by hitting millions of golf balls.
> *Lee Trevino, champion professional golfer*

To so many players, practice is like a pause between their cell-phone conversations.
> *Marty Conlon, professional basketball player*

You play the way you practice
> *Pop Warner, professional football coach*

You hit home runs not by chance, but by preparation.
> *Roger Maris, professional baseball player*

For every pass I ever caught in a game, I caught a thousand in practice.
> *Don Hutson, National Football League player*

Practice, practice, practice.
> *Paul Hornung, Hall of Fame football player, response to a question asking how he could play so well despite being notorious for breaking late-night curfews*

Practice wasn't a right but a privilege.
> *John Vargas, coach, U.S. national water polo team*

Rock used to load us down with extra-heavy practice gear. On Saturday, when we climbed into game suits we felt like four Lady Godi-

vas. Actually we were four pounds lighter on Saturday than on weekends.

> *Elmer Layden, college football player,*
> *one of the Four Horsemen, speaking of*
> *Knute Rockne, coach*

I won't do it on Thursdays because I don't get paid to do it on Thursdays.

> *Alex Karras, Hall of Fame football player,*
> *discussing his practice habits*

You can learn twice as much about the tune of your boat in two hours of practice sailing as you can for the same time on the race course, with its tactical distractions.

> *Mike Fletcher, sailor and journalist*

Predictions

I guarantee it.

> *Joe Namath, Hall of Fame football player,*
> *regarding a Jets victory over the Baltimore*
> *Colts in Super Bowl III*

This team has a chance of going all the way. So did the *Titanic*.

> *Jim Murray, sportswriter*

We're going to turn this team around 360 degrees.

> *Jason Kidd, upon his drafting to*
> *the Dallas Mavericks*

Prefontaine, Steve "Pre"

(b. Jan. 25, 1951; d. June 1, 1975) *All-American track and field runner; National Collegiate Athletic Association champion*

Pre inspired a whole generation of American distance runners to excel. He made running cool.

> *Alberto Salazar, marathon runner*

Preparation

Hours of running stadium steps, hours of rowing on ergometers, hours of lifting weights and work in the tanks had come down to a few minutes of racing.

> *Devin Mahony, coxswain*

How many successful people have you ever heard say, "I just make it up as I go along?" I can't think of one.

> *Mike Ditka, professional football coach*

Everyone wants to win on game day. Every coach and player walks on the field fired up and raring to go. But if they have not put in the time to prepare during the week, they will fall flat on their faces.

> *Joe Gibbs, professional football coach*

In football and in business preparation precedes performance.

> *Bill Walsh, professional football coach*

The will to win is grossly overrated. The will to prepare is far more important.

> *Bobby Knight, champion college basketball coach*

The will to win means nothing without the will to prepare.

> *Juma Ikangaa, champion marathoner*

When you start the Daytona 500, that car doesn't know when it was built. As long as you've done it right and on the line, that's all that counts. But the earlier you build it and

the more time you take with it, the more you test it, the greater the odds you are going to get it right.

Alan Kulwicki, race car driver

Press (the)

I've never known a football writer who ever had to stand up to a blitz.

Joe Namath, Hall of Fame football player

We don't turn on the TV anymore. We unplugged it. We don't buy any New York newspapers.

Chuck Knoblauch, professional baseball player, after an error cost the Yankees a playoff game in 1998

Pressure

Make or miss, win or lose? Not many people can say they've been in that situation, and now I have.

Allan Houston, professional basketball player, who scored the game-winning basket in the playoffs to win a first-round series, with a last second shot

There's always pressure to perform.

Scott Brosius, professional baseball player

To me the pressure is game to game, inning to inning, batter to batter, pitch to pitch, and it's that way May, June, September—any month.

Roberto Clemente, Hall of Fame baseball player

When you face an elimination game, you can go one of two ways. You can start looking for scapegoats or you can rally behind each other.

Brendan Shanahan, professional hockey player

When you play in a World Series, you either accept the challenge and do better than you normally do, or the pressure gets to you and you fall beneath your normal level.

Red Rolf, professional baseball player

Pride

The proudest day of my life wasn't the day I won the 500 or when I won my first USAC title or the Daytona 500 or Sebring. It was April 15, 1964—the day I became an American citizen. More than most people, I understand the meaning of the words "Only in America."

Mario Andretti, champion race car driver

You've got to look at it like when you were back in high school, when you had the pride, you were glad and proud to put on the jersey, you were a Brave, or whatever you were.

John Starks, professional basketball player

Prizes or Prize Money

I may buy the Alamo and give it back to Mexico.

Lee Trevino, champion golfer, replying to a question regarding how he'd spend the prize money after winning the U.S. Open

When someone offers you two million dollars you don't spit in their face.

Ivan Lendl, champion tennis player, referring to accepting an invitation to the Grand Slam Cup

When you get $180,000 to win a race, how can you be disappointed in time?

Laz Barrera, jockey

Professionals

Being a professional athlete is just being a big kid.

Larry Csonka, Hall of Fame football player and broadcaster

I found out pretty quickly that pro football ideals are in the gutter. These men are supposed to be the best, but I found they were pretty hung up on money, booze, and sex.

Chip Oliver, professional football player

Now, how would you define a track athlete who spends all of his or her time training and competing, is paid to appear in meets, paid bonuses for good performances, paid to wear certain shoes, paid to say good things about corporate sponsors? Unless you are totally naive and incredibly ignorant, or unless you have reason to twist the truth, "professional" would have to be your answer.

Carl Lewis, Olympic gold medalist track and field competitor

Professional football is a damn tough way to make a living. And when it's all said and done, that's precisely what the game is—a job.

Johnny Sample, professional football player

The guy who says he'd give it all up to play this game for free? I'm like, "Yeah, go right ahead." The fact is, this game is just too hard. You can't do it for nothing.

Phil Simms, professional football player and broadcaster

We ought to pay attention to the world of professional sports. What happens at the elite levels makes its way into our culture.

Lucy Danziger, sports magazine editor

You have to perform at a consistently higher level than others. That's the mark of a true professional.

Joe Paterno, college football coach

Promoters

It ain't the number of seats you got, it's the number of asses in 'em.

George Gainford, boxing manager

Prostitutes

This is the baddest cat in the world, and I'm with your husband and five hookers!

Muhammad Ali, world champion boxer, to Nancy Seaver, wife of Tom Seaver, Hall of Fame baseball player

When they saw it was Edwin, I think they felt, "This is a nice fish to fry."

Gordin Baskin, manager of Edwin Moses, after he was arrested for soliciting for prostitution

Where's the good stuff? I want it all.

Darryl Strawberry, professional baseball player, to an undercover policewoman posing as a prostitute

Putting

A bad putter is like a bad apple in a barrel. First it turns your chipping game sour. Then it begins to eat into your irons. And finally, it just eats the head off your driver.

Sam Snead, champion professional golfer

A good putter is a match for anyone. A bad putter is a match for no one.

Harvey Pennick, golf teacher

I don't know anyone else who putts with a swizzle stick.

> *Bob Hope, comedian and actor, referring to Jackie Gleason*

It wasn't a misread, it was a bad putt.

> *Annika Sorenstam, professional golfer*

I was the world's worst putter.

> *William "Wild Bill" Melhorn, professional golfer*

I've played with some of the best players in the world . . . and the difference between their game and my game is about four putts a round. Nothing else. But it's everything.

> *Dana Quigley, champion golfer*

The mistake I made was becoming a wrist putter.

> *Sam Snead, champion golfer*

There are very few truths about putting. You get the ball in the hole, and it doesn't matter how.

> *Arnold Palmer, champion professional golfer*

When a player holes a crucial short putt, or rolls one in from sixty feet, it is on the green—on the "dance floor," as golfers like to say—where he punches the air and does a little jig of celebration.

> *Al Barkow, writer*

You can always recover from a bad drive, but there's no recovering from a bad putt. It's missing those 6-inchers that causes guys to break up their sticks.

> *Jimmy Demaret, champion professional golfer*

Quarterbacks

A quarterback doesn't come into his own until he can tell the coach to go to hell.

Johnny Unitas, Hall of Fame football player

Get more open—I'm getting old.

Dan Marino, quarterback, to Lamar Thomas, professional football player (receiver)

If a survey was taken, I think you'd find more injuries happen to a quarterback while standing in the pocket than by taking off with a ball.

Steve Grogan, professional football player

One day I throw the ball like Roger Staubach, one day like Roger Rabbit.

Mike Winchell, college football player

There was no mistaking a professional quarterback's throw—one had the sense, seeing it come, of a projectile rather than a football.

George Plimpton, writer

Quitting

I learned, one, you shouldn't ever quit. And I learned, two, you'll never be able to explain it to anybody.

Jim Ryun, track athlete

No más, no más. No more box.

Roberto Duran, champion boxer, refusing to continue fighting Sugar Ray Leonard, champion boxer

The Jets haven't been worth the aggravation, but I'd be damned if I ever quit. I'll never sell.

Leon Hess, owner of the perennial American Football Conference East doormat New York Jets

The first time you quit, it's hard. The second time, it gets easier. The third time, you don't even have to think.

Paul "Bear" Bryant, Hall of Fame college football coach

Race Walking

Thirty-seven soft-shoe shufflers in their underwear crowded up to the starting line for the 20,000 meter walk—a sprint of about twelve and a half miles.

Red Smith, sportswriter

Racism

Are you crazy, man? You can get electrocuted for that! A Jew looking at a white girl in Kentucky?

*Muhammad Ali, world champion boxer,
to Dick Schaap, sportswriter, regarding a
comment by Schaap about a pretty woman
on a street corner in Louisville, Kentucky*

As a kid, I carried the sousaphone in my school marching band. Believe me, I'm used to being noticed.

*Thurl Bailey, professional basketball player, who
is an African American and Mormon*

As a black youngster I would say to myself, "Josh Gibson was just as good—if not supe-

rior to—Yankee Bill Dickey . . . Satch Paige is just as good as the Yankee Red Ruffing . . . then why can't they play in the big leagues?"

Art Rust, Jr., sportswriter

Baseball is America's sport and has to reflect what is going on in America.

*Dave Winfield, professional baseball player,
referring to African Americans not getting
managerial and front office positions*

Hey, Jewboy, you aren't going to win any gold medals!

*Unnamed U.S. Olympic swimmer to
Mark Spitz, Olympic gold medal swimmer*

I don't give a damn about the color of a man's skin. I'm only interested in how well or how badly he plays this game.

*Leo Durocher, professional baseball
player and manager*

I don't have any regrets about not playing in the majors. At that time the doors were not open only in baseball, but in other avenues that we couldn't enter. They say I was born

too soon; I say the doors were opened up too late.

James Bell, Hall of Fame baseball player and Negro Leagues star

I don't want to be the best black golfer ever. I want to be the best golfer ever.

Tiger Woods, champion professional golfer

If it had not been for the wind in my face, I wouldn't be able to fly at all.

Arthur Ashe, champion tennis player and writer

It can now be honestly doubted that the boys from the Hookworm Belt will have the nerve to foist their quaint sectional folklore on the rest of the country.

Stanley Woodward, sportswriter, speaking of a strike contemplated by some professional baseball players upon the introduction of Jackie Robinson into the major leagues

Little boy's playing great out there. Just tell him next year not to serve fried chicken at the dinner. Or collard greens or whatever the hell it is they serve.

Fuzzy Zoeller, champion golfer, about Tiger Woods, for which he later apologized

The argument that blacks are physically superior to whites is merely a racist ideology camouflaged to appeal to the ignorant, the unthinking and the unaware.

Harry Edwards, sociologist and motivator

The hate mail won't be thrown away yet. We still have hatred in the country and we need to be reminded.

Hank Aaron, Hall of Fame baseball player, speaking about the hate mail he got when he broke Babe Ruth's all-time home run record

This is the United States of America and one citizen has as much right to play as another. The National League will go down the line with Robinson whatever the consequences.

Ford Frick, National League president

This isn't revolution, it's evolution. The need for better players at all positions has overtaken the need to preserve the myth of white dominance and heroism embodied by the quarterback.

William C. Rhoden, sportswriter, about the first draft in which three African-American quarterbacks were taken in the first round

Hemus, that's a goddamn cheap Jew hit and you're a goddamn Jew hitter!

Attributed by Solly Hemus, professional baseball player, to Warren Spahn or Lew Burdette regarding a "cheap single" during a regular season game

Hey, no Mexicans allowed on this course!

Chi Chi Rodriguez, champion golfer, to Lee Trevino, champion golfer—both are Hispanic

How can it be the great American game if blacks can't play? Hell, we sell beer to everyone.

Auggie Busch, baseball owner

I ain't got no dog-proof ass!

Sonny Liston, champion boxer, responding to comments about his not participating in civil rights marches

If I were black, I'd be just another center who plays well. . . . I want to be judged for my play, not my color. I don't deserve any medals for my color.

Bill Walton, Hall of Fame basketball player

If I weren't earning more than $3 million a year to dunk a basketball, most people on the street would turn and run in the other direction if they saw me coming.

Charles Barkley, professional basketball player

If you're a basketball player, a movie star, or an entertainer, it's more acceptable for you to cross racial boundaries. If you're just a normal, everyday person, people look at you like you're doing something wrong.

Dennis Rodman, professional basketball player

I have seen many Negro players who should be in the major leagues. There is no room in baseball for discrimination. It is our national pastime and a game for all.

Lou Gehrig, Hall of Fame baseball player

I've seen hate mail in a lot of situations. I've never seen anything like that, never. It was tragically unfair and just plain wrong.

Bud Selig, baseball owner and commissioner, speaking about the hate mail Hank Aaron received as he was about to break Babe Ruth's all-time home run record

It's hard being black. You ever been black? I was black once—when I was poor.

Larry Holmes, champion boxer

No one can say how many Negro champions were barred from practically all fields.

Grantland Rice, sportswriter

No one questions the color of a run.

Bobby Bragan, baseball executive

The South African government considered me too activist, a latent troublemaker. The fact that I had once made a flip offhand remark to the effect that an H-bomb should be dropped on Johannesburg may have caused the government to arrive at this conclusion.

Arthur Ashe, Hall of Fame tennis champion and writer

We played in a time when black people were supposed to stick together, so I asked Gibby one time why he always threw at the brothers. He said, "Because they're the ones who are gonna beat me if I don't."

Dick Allen, professional baseball player

When I began to sound off, I was portrayed as a wise-guy, uppity nigger.

Jackie Robinson, professional baseball player and first African-American major-league player

When you talk about racism in basketball, the whole thing is simple: a black player knows he can go out on a court and kick a white player's ass.

Dennis Rodman, professional basketball player

Racquetball

You are in control of your racquetball destiny when you are serving because the serve is the only shot in racquetball that you initiate and control.

Ed Turner, writer, and Marty Hogan, champion racquetball player

Rankings

If you win Wimbledon and the Open you've won the two biggest tournaments of the year. I think that makes you No. 1, no matter what the computer says.

Martina Navratilova, champion tennis player

There really isn't a number one tennis player, as such. At any given time there's maybe five or six top players who are interchangeable in the top spot. I'm good, but I'm not an unequivocal number one. Things change too fast to make that kind of judgment.

John Newcombe, champion
tennis player

Being No. 1 puts a lot of pressure on you. Everybody is always gunning for you. Every time you go out to play a match you feel as if you have to protect something. Even so, it's better than being No. 2.

Rod Laver, champion tennis player

Reality

Ten of you guys, out of two hundred, will play varsity basketball in high school. If you're lucky, one of your guys might play division one college basketball. Those are the odds—maybe even less than that.

Grant Hill, professional basketball player,
warning kids to study and make
something of themselves through
academics

There are so many guys I know who had the intelligence to do almost anything, but all they thought about was basketball. And then when basketball didn't work out, they had nothing to turn to.

Charles Barkley, professional
basketball player

Things are never quite as good as they seem. Things are never quite as bad as they seem. In between falls reality.

John Calipari, college and professional
basketball coach

Rebounds

Every time a shot goes up, I believe that the rebound is mine. I really believe it. I go after every ball because I believe it belongs to me.

Moses Malone, professional basketball player

I don't believe in boxing out. My idea about rebounding is just to go get the damned ball.

Charles Barkley, professional basketball player

I never thought I'd lead the NBA in rebounding, but I got a lot of help from my teammates—they did a lot of missing.

Moses Malone, professional basketball player

I never want to score. Never. I want to rebound.

Dennis Rodman, professional basketball player

What's rebounding? A dog can go after a ball. If that's what they want me to do, I'll do that.

Jason Williams, professional basketball player

Receiving

A wide receiver just has to be flexible and give the quarterback a break.

Sammy White, professional football player

I can throw the ball 100 yards, and one of these days I'm going to throw the ball all the way back down the field.

Harold Carmichael, professional football player

It's like a gunfight: When you draw, you don't have time to look, only to react.

Bobby Hammond, professional football player,
about receiving punts and kickoffs

People talk about big targets but what the passer wants is an open target.

Harold Jackson, professional football player

Records

He could break all the records before he's through.

Gil Hodges, professional baseball player and manager, speaking about rookie Nolan Ryan

How do you run a world record? You compress all your baser urges into one minute and forty-two seconds of running.

Peter Coe, father of Sebastian Coe, champion runner

I can't believe I did it. Seventy home runs. It's absolutely amazing—I am in awe of myself right now.

Mark McGwire, professional baseball player, after setting the new mark for most home runs in one season

My feeling is that as long as the record stands, fine, I'm happy . . . But it won't last forever. Some young guy will come along and he won't be one bit impressed.

Bruce Jenner, gold medalist decathlon competitor

Perhaps there is no such thing as an unbeatable performance but for a reasonable facsimile thereof, Beamon's leap of 29 feet $2^1/_2$ inches at the Mexico City Olympics October 1968, does nicely.

Red Smith, sportswriter, about Bob Beamon's all-time record broad jump

Records are made to be broken.

Fred Lieb, sportswriter, quoting the old saying

Records don't drive me. I'm going to do whatever I can to help the team, plain and simple. It doesn't matter what numbers you put up, the most important ones are in the won-lost column.

Ken Griffey, Jr., professional baseball player

These records are only borrowed, precious aspects of the sport, temporarily in one's keeping.

Sebastian Coe, champion runner

There's no such thing as a "presumed" record. It's either a record or it's not.

Seymour Siwoff, statistician, Elias Sports Bureau

We never try to put ceilings on anyone. Years ago certain records were unattainable, but it happens. In any given situation in any given time, anything can happen.

Sue Humphrey, track and field coach

Whenever that goal comes, it will be special, but I want it to be in a winning cause.

Mia Hamm, soccer player, on scoring the goal that would make her the world's highest-scoring soccer player

You couldn't play on my Amazing Mets without having held some kind of record, like one fella held the world's international all-time record for a pitcher getting hit on the ankles.

Casey Stengel, Hall of Fame baseball manager

Marciano couldn't carry my jockstrap.

Larry Holmes, champion professional boxer, after he lost his title, when he was questioned about falling one victory short of equaling Rocky Marciano's record for consecutive undefeated title defenses

Recruiting

Recruiting is like shaving. Do it every day or you will look like a bum.

Anonymous

I was promised money, credit cards, apartments, come home on weekends when I wanted to. Everybody was promising something. It was just who was promising me the most.

Derric Evans, high school football player

Just once I'd like to see a picture of one of these guys with the caption "He's a dog" underneath it. "Ate up $8,000 worth of groceries in four years and can't play worth a lick."

Abe Lemons, Texas University basketball coach

I have the job I want. I am not looking for a job. What I'm looking for is a tall player that can play.

Mike Jarvis, college basketball coach

I'm looking for guys you toss meat to and they'll go wild.

Harold Ballard, National Hockey League executive

Religion

A rooster crows only when he sees the light. Put him in the dark and he'll never crow. I have seen the light and I am crowing.

Muhammad Ali, champion boxer, on finding the Muslim religion

God gets you to the plate, but once you're there you're on your own.

Ted Williams, Hall of Fame baseball player

Fate? Synchonistic destinies? I prefer to think it was a guiding hand, the One who looks after fools, drunks, and sailors in distress.

Tristan Jones, sailor and writer

I find that prayers work best when you have big players.

Knute Rockne, Hall of Fame college football coach

I never pray on a golf course. Actually, the Lord answers my prayers everywhere except on the course.

Lee Trevino, champion golfer

It's easy to see golf not as a game at all but as some whey-faced, nineteenth-century Presbyterian minister's fever dream of exorcism achieved through ritual and self-mortification.

Bruce McCall, writer

I understand that yesterday the daily double windows were kept open longer than usual and when they closed there were still lines waiting and 150 people were turned away. If any of those people are here this morning, we will cheerfully accept those bets, in the collection basket.

Priest at St. Peter's Parish, Saratoga

The biggest fallacy is people's perceptions of Christianity and their belief that you can't be a Christian and still be competitive . . . When you read the Bible, you'll find many places where it definitely says you don't have to live your life without being competitive.

Dan Reeves, professional football player and coach

There are 108 beads in a rosary and 108 stitches in a baseball. When I found that out, I gave Jesus a chance.

Susan Sarandon, as Annie Savoy, in Bull Durham

When I come back, I want to be re-incarnated as a dolphin—or as an F-16.

Bo Jackson, professional baseball and football player, speaking on reincarnation

Responsibility

Never shirk responsibility.

Althea Gibson, profession tennis champion

Reputation

If one's reputation is a possession, then of all of my possessions, my reputation means the most to me.

Arthur Ashe, Days of Grace

Retirement

When an athlete doesn't—or can't—envision the end, it comes as a shock.

Pat Riley, professional basketball player and coach, commenting on the end of his own playing days

Each is the last to learn from fate
That his story is finished—and out of date.

Grantland Rice, sportswriter

For the big horse, it's all fun now.

Red Smith, sportswriter, regarding the retirement of champion thoroughbred Secretariat, who was already scheduled to stud

He's all through as a racehorse; we expect him to be fine as a stallion.

Dr. Larry Bramlage, veterinarian, referring to the career-ending injury to failed Triple Crown hopeful Charismatic

Hey, I'm not dropping off the face of the earth, you know.

John Shimooka, surfer

I'd like to play long enough so that when I'm finished, I won't have to go out and dig ditches or punch time clocks.

Bobby Hull, Hall of Fame hockey player

If a player, any player, feels he doesn't want to play, there's nothing a coach can do.

Bob Brett, tennis coach

I feel like I just got rid of a 2,000-pound load.

John Elway, professional football player, after telling owner Pat Bowlen he was going to retire

If the graceful exit were easy, it would have been executed more often by great athletes.

Richard Hoffer, sportswriter

If you don't want me, I'll retire.

Ted Williams, Hall of Fame baseball player, to management

I guess that time has come to stop thinking about what comes next and start acting on it. It's hard to look in the mirror and say it, but at twenty-eight I'm a lot closer to the end than I am to the beginning.

Pam Shriver, professional tennis player

I'm also going to spend a little time just sitting on the grass and looking at the sky. I think I'm going to like that.

Julie Krone, jockey

I'm definitely glad it's over, but I think I'm satisfied as I am because I went out on top. The seven gold medals count, of course, but what is more important to me is that I did the best I could, and when I finished I was on top.

Mark Spitz, Olympic gold medal swimmer

I miss football so much—heck, I even miss the interceptions.

Archie Manning, professional football player and broadcaster

I'm not Joe DiMaggio anymore.

Joe DiMaggio, Hall of Fame baseball player

I went back to my room and cried for hours. I swam my last race. That was it.

Ambrose "Rowdy" Gaines IV, Olympic champion swimmer, during one of his several "retirements"

No shooting man wants to be aware of when he shot that final shell, but when he does, let it be in the gun he loves most, at the bird he loves most.

George Bird Evans, hunter, outdoorsman, and writer

Sometimes you go to funerals and sometimes you go to weddings. And to me, this is a party.

Wayne Gretzky, Hall of Fame hockey player, at his retirement press conference

There will come a day when some of these fellows draw that pension money years from now and they will probably have completely forgotten how they earned it. They got it because a lot of guys stuck out their necks.

Tim McCarver, professional baseball player and broadcaster

This guy looks really interested.

Wayne Gretzky, Hall of Fame hockey player, referring to his son during the announcement of his retirement. His son was practically asleep.

This has been an incredible love for me. To even think about walking away from it, that's very painful.

Jerry West, Hall of Fame basketball player and basketball executive

Today, I consider myself the luckiest man in the world.

Lou Gehrig, New York Yankees, Hall of Famer, as he retired

I been all over the world. I fought maybe three, four hundred fights and everyone of them was a pleasure. If I just had me a little change in my pocket I'd get along fine.

Sam Langford, professional boxer

I could upset everything—tell 'em I'm making a comeback.

Stan Musial, Hall of Fame baseball player moments before his retirement ceremony

I was concerned that normal life would be a letdown after the excitement of football life, but I have found that there is a lot to life beyond football. I get excited about going to announce big games as I did in one, but I also am excited going to act in a segment of my series.

Merlin Olsen, professional football player, broadcaster, actor

So many great days, so much excitement. Then all of a sudden when most guys are just hitting their peak in business, you're through.

Sam Huff, Hall of Fame professional football player

The drum beats for everyone. It's important for every pro athlete to realize that. No matter who you are, there's going to come a time your career is over and you'd better be ready for it.

> *Doug Williams, professional football player; first African-American quarterback to win a Super Bowl; Super Bowl MVP*

This will be my last decathlon. You can't keep this up forever.

> *Bob Mathias, gold medalist decathlon competitor, politician, and actor, after winning his second decathlon in as many Olympics, at 21 years old*

Well, boys, better take a good look around you, because most of us won't be here next year.

> *George Metkovich, professional baseball player, played during the last year of the war, to his then teammates before the "real" major leaguers came back from World War II*

We walked through the parking lot. Neither of us said anything. We thought the world had ended.

> *Anne Ryun, wife of Jim Ryun, track athlete*

What would I do if I retired? Go into the middle of town, where nobody knows me and nobody talks about horses?

> *Woody Stephens, trainer*

When it ceased to be fun, she had the good sense to know when to leave.

> *Jerry Izenberg, sportswriter, about Julie Krone, jockey*

When you stop playing the game, it's like dying.

> *Tim Green, National Football League player*

Yesterday I drove by the track at San Jose State, where I did a lot of training. I looked out the window at the rest of those guys and I felt sorry for them. And right then, I knew I'd made the right decision to quit when I did.

> *Bruce Jenner, gold medalist decathlon competitor*

You know how I realized when I was through with football? It was during the Cincinnati game. I didn't want to hurt anybody.

> *Chip Oliver, professional football player*

Rice, Grantland

(b. Nov. 1, 1880; d. July 13, 1954) *Sportswriter; coined "The Four Horsemen," Notre Dame backfield and Red Grange as "The Galloping Ghost"*

Nothing can be said of him that he didn't say better of someone else.

> *Red Smith, sportswriter*

Rickey, Branch

(b. Dec. 20, 1881; d. Dec. 9, 1965) *Baseball general manager; instituted farm system in Major League Baseball; first GM to integrate Major League Baseball by calling up Jackie Robinson*

A hypocritical preacher.

> *Judge Kenesaw Mountain Landis, baseball commissioner, speaking about Branch Rickey*

Branch Rickey, who supposedly is the finest scout in baseball history, chose Robinson with wisdom, that borders on clairvoyance, to right a single wrong.

> *Roger Kahn, writer*

Next to Abraham Lincoln, the biggest white benefactor of the Negro has been Branch Rickey.

Grantland Rice, sportswriter

Riley, Pat

(b. May 20, 1945) *National Basketball Association player; NBA coach; won four out of six appearances in the NBA finals; all-time NBA playoff wins*

He vowed a crown, but he wanted a throne.

Mark Kriegel, sportswriter

Ten years ago, Pat carried the bags of West and Goodrich. In 1982, he's the coach of the West. The way he's going, in ten years he'll probably be the president of the United States.

Bill Fitch, professional basketball coach

Paramount Communications had not given us a basketball coach but some sort of a Warren Beatty facsimile.

Mark Kriegel, sportswriter

Rivalries

Gentlemen, you are about to play football for Yale. Never again in your lives will you do anything so important.

Tad Jones, college football coach

Damn, Alzado, another draw.

Art Shell, Hall of Fame football player, to Lyle Alzado, an opposing lineman, who battled each other regularly for many years

Defeat-less Army and victory-less Navy, crashing head-on, slugged it out toe to toe, march for march, touchdown for touchdown, and point for point in a 21-to-21 tie that left their categories undisturbed and 102,581 spectators limp with excitement.

Jesse Abramson, sportswriter

Here were two teams that had made a career of failure and had enjoyed staggering success at it. One had lost four games, the other three. Neither had beaten anyone of importance.

Red Smith, sportswriter, referring to the 1947 Yale–Harvard game

I always had only male friends in the tennis world. The rivalry among women tennis players is overwhelming.

Steffi Graff, professional tennis player

I know there is a lot of animosity between the two teams. You have to be aggressive, but show poise too. You have to know when to back off.

Latrell Sprewell, professional basketball player

I would rather beat the Bruins than the Russians.

Ted Newland, college water polo coach

The Army–Navy game, dear reader, is a joke. An awful anachronism. As out of touch with the times as a plodding brontosaurus.

Jim Hawkins, sportswriter, The Awful Anachronism

The New York of the Giants, Dodgers and Yankees was an annual re-evocation of the War between the States. The Yankees were the North, if you could conceive a North grinding along with wealth and weight without the excuse of Lincoln. The Giants and Dodgers were the Confederacy, often under-

manned and underequipped and running then because it could not hit.

Murray Kempton, Back at the Polo Grounds

Rizzuto, Phil
(b. Sept. 25, 1918) *Hall of Fame baseball player; longtime Yankee broadcaster*

Come on, admit it. You loved Phil. Come on, because he was always there, and because *you* knew who was on deck, a better recipe for red sauce and a quicker route to the bridge.

Bill Scheft, writer

Robinson, Jackie
(b. Jan. 31, 1919; d. Oct. 24, 1972) *Hall of Fame baseball player; first African American in the major leagues; Rookie of the Year (1947); league MVP; won one World Series*

He could have done anything he set out to do. It didn't have to be baseball. He was articulate and sharp—and when he started to speak out, easy to dislike. But he taught me a lot more than I ever taught him.

Pee Wee Reese, professional baseball player

There are certain people in American sports who are now valid figures in the nation's history books. Jackie Robinson is one.

Howard Cosell, broadcaster

Rockne, Knute
(b. Mar. 4, 1888; d. Mar. 31, 1931) *Hall of Fame college football coach; won three national championships; highest-winning percentage of all time (.881)*

Whenever Rock opened his kisser, the throng became as silent as a tomb.

Harry Grayson, sportswriter

Rocker, John
(b. Oct. 17, 1974) *Professional baseball player, controversial relief pitcher of the Atlanta Braves, who made racist statements in his interview with* Sports Illustrated

No one is defending Rocker's statements, although the Ku Klux Klan has yet to weigh in.

Stan Savran, sportswriter

We've got Hispanics in this band, Italians in this band, people who are Polish and Russian. We're all immigrants, all foreigners—quote unquote—and this is our way of saying his comments were not acceptable.

Jay Jay French, guitarist and cofounder of heavy metal rock band Twisted Sister, who asked that the Atlanta Braves no longer play one of their songs each time Rocker made an entrance

Imagine having to take the 7 train to [Shea Stadium] looking like you're [in] Beirut next to some kid with purple hair, next to some queer with AIDS, right next to some dude who got out of jail for the fourth time, right next to some 20-year-old mom with four kids. It's depressing.

John Rocker, controversial baseball player, from an interview with Sports Illustrated

The biggest thing I don't like about New York are the foreigners. You can walk an entire block in Times Square and not hear anybody speaking English. Asians and Koreans and Vietnamese and Indians and Russians

213

and Spanish people and everything up there. How the hell did they get in this country?

John Rocker, controversial baseball player, from an interview with Sports Illustrated

Rodman, Dennis

(b. May 13, 1961) *Controversial All-Star professional basketball player, has won five National Basketball Association championships; two-time Defensive Player of the Year; changes hair color often*

And even if the birth certificate isn't lying, Dennis Rodman has absolutely nothing in common with the blankness, tumbleweeds and football loons of Texas, who tend to associate drag with cigarettes and hot rods.

Jay Mariotti, sportswriter

In the real world, people have to show up on time, listen to the boss, take care of their kids and try to be a decent role model. Anyone who hires Rodman on Rodman's terms is an insult to people who pay their hard-earned money to buy tickets.

Terry Pluto, sportswriter and best-selling writer

Role Models

The ability to run and dunk or to hit 40 homers or rush for 1,000 yards doesn't make you God Almighty. And secondly, they shouldn't look up to someone they can't be . . . They should be looking up to their parents.

Charles Barkley, professional basketball player

Mr. Rickey, I'm no pioneer, I'm just a ballplayer.

Roy Campanella, professional baseball player, to Branch Rickey, when discussing if he would be the first African-American baseball player in the major leagues

Professional athletes should not be role models. Hell, I know drug dealers who can dunk. Can drug dealers be role models?

Charles Barkley, professional basketball player

Some athletes today do not believe they should be considered role models, but I believe you don't really have a choice if you are a "celebrity," so I try to set the best example I can.

Shannon Miller, Olympic gold medalist gymnast

The problem I have with the idea of being a role model is that I like to skate . . . And just because I won a medal doing what I love to do, why should that make me a role model? I don't belong on a pedestal, not for winning a medal.

Rudy Galindo, champion figure skater

You become a role model whether you like it or not. People admire your talent and they see your character. I don't think of it as a burden; it is very satisfying to set a good example.

Hakeem Olajuwon, professional basketball player

Rookies

Being a rookie . . . meant you had to carry the rock. The rookie rock was a big, flat rock that was kept at a hotel in Switzerland, where the guys often stay in between races . . . The only way to get rid of it was to ski Kitzbuhel.

Mike Wilson, writer

He doesn't look like a rookie to me. He's a good kid and he knows how to put his foot on the gas.

Jimmy Vasser, automobile racer, about teammate Juan Montoya

In games he'll test the newcomers with an extra shove, a needless elbow, a protruding hip. To Russell all rookies on trial have the same name: "Boy!"

Fred Katz, sportswriter

The refs won't even call rookies by their names.

Jason Williams, professional basketball player

Where the hell do you suppose they dredge up these rookies from?

Terry Barr, professional football player, referring to George Plimpton, writer, who was posing as a rookie

Roosevelt, Theodore

(b. Oct. 27, 1858; d. Jan. 6, 1919) *President of the United States; Nobel Peace Prize winner; proponent of "the active life"; naturalist, author, sportsman*

He came down hard on market hunters or anyone who killed for sport. Virtually all the game he killed ended up in the pot, to be eaten around the campfire. He was one of America's first conservationists, and he is still her greatest, because of what he was able to do through the Boone & Crockett Club and as president of the United States.

Stephen E. Ambrose, historian

The charm about this ranch man as author is that he is every inch a gentleman–sportsman.

the British Spectator, *reviewing* Trips of a Ranchman

The overwhelming impression left after reading *Trips of a Ranchman* is that of love for, and identity with, all living things.

Edmund Morris, writer

Rose, Pete

(b. Apr. 14, 1941) *Professional baseball player; all-time record for most hits (4,256); won three World Series; League MVP; known as "Charlie Hustle"; banned for life from baseball by Baseball Commissioner A. Bartlett Giamatti for betting on baseball*

Just so nothing improper would take place, I had him sign balls in my office for each player. I put each ball in the player's locker the day after Pete was gone.

Bruce Keiter, owner, minor league baseball team, who was questioned by Major League Baseball for possibly violating the ban on Pete Rose

Rothstein, Arnold

(b. Jan. 17, 1882; d. Nov. 6, 1928) *Sportsman; big-time gambler; person responsible for fixing the 1919 World Series; was the prototype for F. Scott Fitzgerald's character Meyer Wolfsheim in* The Great Gatsby, *"the man who fixed the World's Series back in 1919."*

Arnold Rothstein is a man who waits in doorways . . . a mouse waiting in the doorway for his cheese.

William J. Fallon, lawyer for Abe Atell, former champion boxer, and associate of Arnold Rothstein. Atell was a go-between for Rothstein in the Black Sox scandal.

He had a deep love for the racetrack and a deeper loathing for the stock market.

Grantland Rice, sportswriter

Rowing

Always remember, there's more to life than rowing—but not much.

Donald Beer, Olympic medal-winning oarsman

Coxing is like sitting in a racing car with electric probes stuck to your ego.

Devin Mahony, coxswain

Down this narrow stretch we . . . race, graceful engines of pain, sinews and bones straining in the most powerful fluid of motions—the unison swing of the oars propelling the shells along until one of us overpowered the other, reaching the finish line first, proving once and for all which crew was the best.

Devin Mahony, coxswain

Form is for gymnastics and figure skating and diving, not rowing . . . Rowing is about winning. If you win, then everyone says your form is good anyway.

Tiff Wood, Olympic oarsman

It was in its way a very macho world. The egos were immense—they had to be for so demanding a sport. Men of lesser will and ambition simply did not stay around.

David Halberstam, writer

The noblest of sports. In rowing, everyone is part of the effort.

Anita DeFrantz, Olympic silver medalist oarswoman

The sophomores are good, but they haven't learned the humility of crew yet.

John Biglow, Olympic oarsman

Rugby

Both chess player and rugby player operate under stringent demands for speed of decision.

Jim Greenwood, rugby coach and writer

Breaking the line and setting up the outside or setting someone up for a try, I always find that an awesome feeling when I can break the defense line and really put someone away and see them score a try, it really gets me up and focused on the game.

Pita Alatini, New Zealand rugby player

From personal experience I can tell you there is nothing more frightening than to see eight All Blacks bearing down on you with malice aforethought.

Don Rutherford, professional rugby player

I could write a whole book on scrums and most of it would be junk.

Derek Robinson, journalist

If they do their job at scrum and lineout, get around the field and form the core of the rucks and mauls and push and work, they are fine players. If from time to time they can run with the ball and even score—that's a bonus. But we aren't interested in the bonus if it's at the expense of the rest.

Wilson Whineray, professional rugby player, referring to his front five

In rugby, there's active ignorance, passive ignorance, and cock-eyed ignorance.

Derek Robinson, journalist

In the amateur past, touring was regarded as a welcome break from the daily grind of normal work, however, for professional players, these visits are now strictly busmen's holidays.

Neil Robertson, sportswriter

It's no use criticizing our tackling. Tell us how to catch them first, then we'll tackle them all right.

Graham Wiliams, professional rugby player

More players have nervous breakdowns trying to understand the off-side law, than get kicked to death by green canaries.

Derek Robinson, journalist

The knowledge that others are relying on you and that you are relying on them is the very essence of the game of rugby.

J. J. Stewart, professional rugby coach and writer

The only thing I know about rugby is that there is more than one way to play it.

Neil McPhail, professional rugby coach

The blood-bin ruling was introduced because of obvious health concerns but the whole situation needs to be tightened up in the wake of serious abuses of the system such as this. The only way to do so would be to have an independent medical adviser on the touchline to ensure that there are sufficient grounds for a blood replacement, otherwise, we may as well go the whole hog and introduce rolling substitutes.

Neil Robertson, sportswriter

The way I want to play it, I want to be a No. 8 that gets the forward pack going forward. I want to be able to make yards for the team and be able to cut guys in half on defense.

Ron Cribb, New Zealand soccer player

There are times in your career when you get frustrated or you get disappointed, and things like that. I suppose that's when I did sit down and ask why I did want to play rugby. I just wanted to get out and enjoy it, and try and think about the results later. Just get out and enjoy your rugby! There's no difference between now and when I was a kid, I still enjoy the game and like getting out there with all my mates and having a lot of fun.

Todd Blackadder, New Zealand rugby player

What absurdity is this? You don't mean to say that those fifty or sixty boys, many of them quite small, are going to play that huge mass opposite.

Thomas Hughes, novelist, in Tom Brown's School Days

Your opponent may get you—but he must never get the ball.

Jim Greenwood, rugby coach and writer

Rules

Cheating is as much a part of the game as scorecards and hot dogs.

Billy Martin, professional baseball player and manager

Football has one glaring weakness. The game is built largely on constant rule breaking such as holding, off-side, backs illegally in motion, pass interference and other factors that play a big if illegal part in the results.

Grantland Rice, sportswriter

I am disgusted by any player who feels he doesn't have to play by the rules. The game is violent in nature, but if we accept players trying to hurt one another it will become something ugly and dangerous.

Merlin Olsen, professional football player

I believe in rules. Sure I do. If there weren't any rules, how could you break them?

Leo Durocher, professional baseball player and manager

One of the things unique about sailing is that it's one of the few sports where rules are enforced by the competitors themselves. We don't have referees out there calling the shots, or players trying to get away with anything they can. We have a system where conscience still counts and the way you play counts as much as the final outcome.

David Dallenbaugh, yachtsman

[The Raiders] are responsible for many rules changes. There's the no-clothesline rule. The no-spearing rule. The no-hitting out of bounds rule. No fumbling in the last two minutes of the game. No throwing helmets. The no stikum rule . . . So you see, we're not all that bad.

Ted Hendricks, professional football player

The rules of sport are founded upon fair play.

Hugh E. Keogh, sportswriter

Running

A lot of people run a race to see who's fastest. I run a race to see who has the most guts.

Steve Prefontaine, Olympic medalist track and field competitor and champion runner

Certainly the personal aspect of long-distance running, where success rests with the individual rather than the team, is similar to boxing. Perhaps the violence of boxing, directed at another individual, is sublimated in running, becoming a different kind of aggression. Both sports definitely require coming to terms with personal suffering in pursuit of success.

Don Kardong, runner and writer

Don't let anybody kid you. Runners make runners. Coaches like to take all the credit, but day after day, the upper classmen show the younger fellows how to run, how to train, how to take care of themselves.

James Francis "Jumbo" Elliott, champion track coach

Everyone knows about the bear. He's that invisible animal that waits for you about a hundred yards from the finish line. He jumps on your back and starts clawing and scratching and he seems so heavy that you want to stop running so that he'll get off and leave you alone.

Bruce Jenner, Olympic gold medalist decathlon competitor

Great running is an art so intensely personal, no two men do it quite alike. When a cat makes a beautiful run, it's poetry and jazz . . . Great runners are works of God.

Jim Brown, Hall of Fame football player

I always cringe inside when people say running comes naturally to me, that training is an uplifting joy. That's not why I race well. I'm competitive.

Eamon Coghlan, champion runner

I became a runner because it suited my personality. It suited me as an individualist.

Bill Rodgers, champion marathoner

I could run very fast. After all, in Alabama, all we kids had to do was run, so we ran.

Jesse Owens, Olympic gold medalist, track and field

If you have ever been around a runner who has just broken a barrier—say suddenly being able to run a 10-, 9-, 8-, or 7-minute mile—then you understand the magic.

Jeff Galloway, runner and writer

I have a good time. I let my mind go blank.
Jim Ryun, track athlete, about running

I was filled with relief that I hadn't been chewed over by the pack in the third lap. From then on I was just running for the tape.
Sebastian Coe, champion runner

I like it, the way I live, but I can't explain the satisfaction to people who do not run. . . . Once you know international racing, you can't just ease off a bit. It has to be one or the other, as hard as you can, or just for fun.
Grete Waitz, champion marathoner

I love to buy running shoes. I don't mean that I just enjoy the process of trying on new shoes. I mean I love buying running shoes.
John Bingham, runner and writer

I love testing myself more than I feared being beaten, and front running is the ultimate test. You need a total, irrevocable commitment to see the race through to the end or it cannot justify your effort.
Ron Clarke, champion runner

I run. I am a runner. I am an athlete.
Joan Benoit Samuelson, marathoner

It is not necessary for me that you are running. But if you don't run, I'm sure you'll be sorry for it later on.
Husband of Fanny Blankers-Koen, Olympic gold medalist in track and field, when she asked her husband if they could leave the 1948 London Olympics to see their children, including their six-month old daughter. She won four gold medals at those games.

It's something in me, deep down, that makes me different in a race.
Eammon Coghlan, champion runner

I've been running a lot of open races against Kenyans and they like to blow it out hard in the beginning . . . It's a little scary doing that because you can just die out there doing that.
Mike Mykytok, champion runner

I've learned that it's what you do with your miles, rather than how many you've run.
Rod DeHaven, runner

I like people to make people stop and say "I've never seen anyone run like that before!" It's more than just a race, it's style. It's doing something better than anyone else.
Steve Prefontaine, Olympic medalist track and field competitor and champion runner

I was born to run. I simply love to run. It's almost like the faster I go, the easier it becomes.
Mary Decker Slaney, champion runner

I was not very talented. My basic speed was low. Only with will power was I able to reach this world-best standard in long-distance running.
Emil Zatopek, Olympic gold medalist runner

I was now running for the tape, the mental agony of knowing I had hit my limit, of not knowing what was happening behind me. I was not to know they were fading, too. The anxiety over the last 20 meters was unbearable, it showed in my face as I crossed the line.
Sebastian Coe, champion runner

Jogging is what people do when they're so out of shape they can't do anything else. Running is what athletes do in training.

attributed by A. J. Poulin,
comedian and writer, to his girlfriend

Me thinks that the moment my legs begin to move, my thoughts begin to flow.

Henry David Thoreau, writer and philosopher

My thoughts before a big race are usually pretty simple. I tell myself: Get out of the blocks, run your race, stay relaxed. If you run your race, you'll win.

Carl Lewis, Olympic gold medalist track and
field competitor

Nobody running at full speed has either a head or a body.

William Butler Yeats, poet

Of all athletic forms running is perhaps the most taxing and the most exciting; that is, when carried to the extreme.

Alfred Shrubb, champion runner

Pain, like time, is a backdrop to running.

Sally Pont, writer and runner

People seem to think that running is much easier than it is. So I tell them that it's harder than they think, and that it'll take longer than they want it to take.

Dr. John Peters, cardiologist and runner

Running is a way of life for me, just like brushing my teeth. If I don't run for a few days, I feel as if something's been stolen from me.

John A. Kelly, champion marathoner

Running is for me. There's no coach telling me what to do. It's up to me whether or not to run each day.

Kerri Strug, Olympic gold medal–winning
gymnast

Running is my meditation, mind flush, cosmic telephone, mood elevator, and spiritual communion.

Lorraine Moller, Olympic bronze medalist
marathoner

Running is the greatest metaphor for life because you get out of it what you put into it.

Oprah Winfrey, actress and talk show host

Running well is a matter of having the patience to persevere when you are tired and not expecting instant results. The only secret is that it is consistent, often monotonous, boring, hard work. And it's tiring.

Robert de Castella, runner and writer

Set aside a time solely for running. Running is more fun if you don't have to rush through it.

Jim Fixx, runner

Start slowly and taper off fast.

slogan of the Dolphin Running Club,
San Francisco

That journalistic cliché "The Mile of the Century" has been applied to scores of races, each with claims to excellence, and it is an absorbing, if futile occupation to argue the merits of this mile and that as being the most sublime athletic event of the twentieth century.

Peter Lovesey, writer

There is no finish line.

Nike ad

The camera's eye
Does not lie,
But it cannot show
The life within,
The life of a runner.

W. H. Auden, poet

The custom of greeting every runner who passes, just because he or she happens to run, has become obsolete.

Joe Henderson, runner and writer,
mourning the lack of civility in the sport

The difference between a jogger and a runner is an entry blank.

George Sheehan, runner and writer

The social aspects of running are not to be underestimated.

Bill Rodgers, champion marathoner

The difference between walking and running isn't speed or biomechanics. It's determination.

Amby Burfoot, runner, writer, and editor

There can be nothing superior to cross-country running for either pleasure or health. The sport itself is ideal, whether a race be contested in fine or muddy weather.

Alfred Shrubb, champion runner

There is an itch in runners.

Arnold Hano, sportswriter

Track is a hobby, but it is a life too.

Jim Ryun, track athlete

Whatever moves the other runners made, I knew I could respond . . . I felt like if I had to, I could fly.

Grete Waitz, champion marathoner

When testing the limits of your potential, racing can be harder mentally than physically. After all, your body is in pretty substantial distress, and your mind's main task seems to be to figure out how to better the situation as soon as possible.

Bill Rodgers, champion marathoner

Where you finish doesn't matter. The tragedy is when you have to walk in.

Dr. George Sheehan, runner

With victory in hand, running at maximum effort becomes very difficult. Without some company in the difficult miles, the body's mission becomes lonely and dark.

Frank Shorter, champion runner

You may run that fast again, but then again, you may not.

Ron Hill, champion runner, to Frank Shorter,
champion marathoner

Ruth, Babe

(b. Feb. 5, 1895; d. Aug. 16, 1948) *Hall of Fame baseball player; second all-time home run record with 714 (that record stood for many years); prodigious home run hitter, who hit 54 or more runs four times in his career; two-time 20-game winner; may have single-handedly saved baseball after Black Sox scandal; known for the larger-than-life aspects of his athletic feats, as well of his personality and his appetites; Baby Ruth candy bar was allegedly named after him*

Born? Hell, Babe Ruth wasn't born. He fell from a tree.

Joe Dugan, professional baseball player

I know, but I had a better year.

Reply when a club official objected that
the salary he was demanding was
greater than the U.S. president's.

In his time, George Herman Ruth was a holy sinner. He was a man of measureless lust, selfishness, and appetites, but he was also a man undyingly faithful, in a manner, to both his public and his game.

Roger Kahn, sportswriter

Ruth must have admired records because he created so many of them.

Red Smith, sportswriter

I swing big, with everything I've got. I hit big or I miss big. I like to live as big as I can.

Babe Ruth, Hall of Fame baseball player

That last one sounded kind of high to me.

Babe Ruth, questioning the umpire about three fast pitches that he had not seen

The day I can use him in the outfield and take advantage of his bat every day—well, they'll have to build the parks bigger, just for Ruth.

Ed Barrow, professional baseball coach and Red Sox manager

Ryan, Buddy

(b. Feb. 6, 1934) *Professional football coach; defensive guru was defensive coordinator for two Super Bowl champion teams (1969, 1986); head coach known for aggressive teams*

Buddy Ryan is a Neanderthal and he attracts Neanderthal players. Neanderthals can win certain kinds of wars, but they lose some they should win if you can find a way to make them make enough choices.

Bill Parcells, professional football coach

Sacks

Rushing the passer is grueling work. It requires a great outlay of speed, strength, energy, and determination. A man must drive himself if he is going to break through on every pass play.

Stanley Woodward, sportswriter

Sacking the quarterback is why I'm here. It's the only glamour there is on the defensive line. Everything else is pretty dull.

Cedrick Hardman, professional football player and actor

Sailing

A long voyage refreshes rather than tires me. Every healthy person ought to try it and see how it tones the skin and sharpens the sense.

Philip S. Weld, champion solo yachtsman and writer, winner of the OSTAR solo race from England to the United States

Although we go afloat for independence and solitude, we now and then crave talk with other people. Sometimes we're lucky enough to come across friends . . . but more often we strike up conversations with strangers who may own similar boats or be anchored close by. This has always been the way among seafarers.

Anthony Bailey, writer

A man in jail has more room, better food, and commonly better company.

Samuel Johnson, writer, referring to sailing voyages

Anyone can hold the helm when the sea is calm.

Publius Syrus, writer, first century B.C.

Circumstance, not choice, places one in the middle of . . . a maelstrom. . . . Therefore when it happens, there can be no recriminations, no regrets. One must respond the best one can to the test, and only enjoy the rare opportunity— the privilege, in fact—that brings vessel, gear, and crew close to an outer limit of strength, resourcefulness, and endurance.

attributed to Roger Vaughn "Fingers," sailor and racer, after the 1979 Fastnet Race

For hours I slice up my grand fish . . . Finally I slice these into sticks which I hang on strings to dry, like dozens of fat fingers, delicious fat fingers. I write in my log that this is a strange prison in which I am slowly starved but occasionally thrown a 20-lb. filet mignon.

Steve Callahan, sailor, lost 76 days at sea after his sloop sank in a race

Here was a sport in which enlarging experience could offset diminishing vigor. I found out, eighteen years later, that a 4,000-mile race at sixty-four tired me out less than a 3,000-mile race at fifty-six because I'd become wiser in choice of boat and gear and in the husbanding of my energies.

Philip S. Weld, champion solo yachtsmen

I am the closest to having dreadlocks as I will ever be. A week without shampoo, three days without brushing my hair, and salt water is all it takes.

Renee Mehel, sailor, in her journal during the Whitbread Around-the-World race

I turned my face eastward, and there, apparently at the end of the bowsprit, was the smiling first moon rising out of the sea . . . "Good evening, sir," I cried. "I am glad to see you." Many a long talk since then I have had with the man in the moon; he had my confidence on the voyage.

Joshua Slocum, first modern sailor to sail around the world alone

I was aware that no other vessel has sailed in this manner around the globe, but would have been loath to say another could not do it . . . I was greatly amused, therefore, by the flat assertions of an expert that it could not be done.

Joshua Slocum, first modern sailor to sail around the world alone

Frankly I would rather have my name on their trophies than on their membership list.

John B. Kilroy, yacht sailing skipper, when asked why he had not joined the New York Yacht Club

If you just did go to the 7-Eleven, then why the hell did you come back?

Deborah Scaling Kiley, sailor and writer, to a deranged sailing teammate after they had been lost at sea in a raft for weeks

In sailing there is a term called *lift,* which is both technical and poetic at once. It describes the moment of acceleration in a sailboat, the moment when the sails harden against the wind and the boat begins to slide forward faster and faster until you can feel what William Buckley meant by the title of his sailing book, *Airborne.* How something moving so slowly, about the pace of a moderate jogger, can impart something so exhilarating at this moment, is probably unanswerable.

Tony Chamberlin, sportswriter

Life at sea is fearfully demanding, and that is why its measured joys are so distinctive. But these pleasures—the obliging winds, the beneficent sky, the sweetly composed set of sail, the fleet speed—are building blocks for the supreme pleasure of camaraderie. I have always thought it impossible, and if possible abominable, to harbor it all to oneself.

William F. Buckley, writer, editor, yachtsman

The challenge of sailing 1,000 miles is something I've got to do. It's been a dream for some time.

Hans Meijer, sailor

Obstacles are obscured by the dark. Massive ships become skeletons of running lights floating through the night on an invisible horizon. Everything disappears in the dark....

Dawn Riley, champion yachtswoman

One of the greatest moments in the history of mankind must have been when man first discovered that he could move in water either by swimming himself or by riding along on a log.

Jay Evans, Olympic kayaker and outdoorsman

People go sailing for different reasons. Some just seek peace and quiet, an escape from life's everyday sound and fury. Some sail for the challenge, physical and mental, of battling with the elements. Others cannot be enticed onto the water unless there is someone else out there to race against.

Mike Fletcher, sailor and journalist

Sailing a boat on a full-out plane is the essence of sensuality. The harder the wind blows, the steeper the seas, the faster the boat goes in its mad, futile attempt to become airborne, the closer it brings the crew to delirium, an edge that is unmistakably orgasmic.

Roger Vaughn, yachtsman and writer

Sailing is a wonderful and unique thing, and the sensation of being noiselessly and smoothly propelled without the cost of fuel is one of the most satisfactory pleasures known, but when you add to the fact that the sailboat itself is one of the most interesting things which God has let man make, well, then you get a combination which is almost too sacred.

L. Francis Herrshoff, sailor and writer

Sailboat racing is the thing I like to do most in my life and I get a great deal of personal pleasure out of it.

Dennis Conner, businessman and champion yachtsman

Take with a grain of salt anything told to you by anyone who claimed he or she was an expert celestial navigator, at least on yachts. On such unstable platforms as such small craft underway, celestial navigation, using a sextant, was never any easy task, and neither was the result often accurate.

Tristan Jones, sailor and writer

The man at the wheel was said to feel
  contempt for the wildest blow,
but it often appeared when the gale had
  cleared
that he'd been in his bunk below.

John Masefield, poet

To be able to face it all and come through it is exhilarating. Sailing in rough weather is what the sport is all about.

Ted Turner, yachtsman and baseball owner

The bottom line is, every job on the boat has its own specific requirements. If you look at both men and women, you have a perfect combination—power, agility, finesse and knowledge. Together, on a team, they can become very efficient.

Dawn Riley, champion yachtswoman

There are no old, bold sailors.

Tim Hebden, sailor and captain

The winning sailor consistently does everything just a little bit better than the competition. He anticipates windshifts more accurately than the rest of the fleet, plays his

sails with more finesse, handles his boat more effectively, knows his competition better, and has a sounder practice routine. His racing edge is a composite advantage, built from all the different phases of sailboat racing.

Ted Turner, champion yachtsmen and baseball owner

They that go down to the Sea in Ships, that do business in great waters, these see the works of the Lord, and His wonders in the deep.

Psalm 107

This crew has already mutinied once. Be careful.

Barry McKay to Dawn Riley, champion yachtswoman, about a boat she was taking over in midrace

When you look toward shore from miles out, you see what appears to be the skyline of a built-up city. But as you get closer, it is really ocean swells coming together, and the waves break right up into the air.

Michael Worrell, sailor

With these winds alone, and with the bounding seas which follow fast, the modern clipper, without auxiliary power, has accomplished a greater distance in a day than any seas steamer has ever been known to reach.

Matthew Fontaine Maury, oceanographer, who mapped wind patterns in 1853

Salaries

People always tell me to my face that I'm overpaid, but they're always drunk.

Brett Hull, National Hockey League player

Salary Cap

I think a lot of the NBA teams use the salary cap as an excuse. When a team wants to do something, it always seems able to do it.

Dennis Rodman, professional basketball player

Scalpers

I could sell drugs for a living because I'm a hustler. But why sell drugs and go to prison when I can sell tickets and make money?

Cleveland Chris, scalper

You get called a lot of things out here, a lot of cracks about your heritage and all that, but I just tell 'em, "Hey, buddy, I got the tickets and you don't."

Keylon, a scalper at Tennessee Vols games, as told to Tim Layden

Scoreboard Watching

You know you've come a long way when you look at the out-of-town scoreboards and there are no scores.

Wayne Gretzky, Hall of Fame hockey player, on looking at the scoreboard in the finals

Scoring

An average of twenty points in basketball is comparable to baseball's criterion for outstanding pitchers, whose immortality seems to be predicated on their winning twenty games a year.

John McFee, writer

There is no better tonic for an injured hockey player than scoring a goal.

Bobby Hull, Hall of Fame hockey player

This year we plan to run and shoot. Next year we hope to run and score.

Billy Tubbs, college basketball coach

Was Wayne Gretzky sick?

Larry Robinson, professional hockey player, upon the announcement he had won the National Hockey League Player of the Week Award

We had a game out in Denver and, oh, my God, Les Savage took 30 three–point shots . . . Not only was the other . . . team trying to block his shot, we were blocking it so we could touch the ball.

Steve Chubin, professional basketball player

When I was 12. The next year I got down to a plus three.

Jack Nicklaus, champion professional golfer, when asked after hip-replacement surgery when was the last time he had a handicap

The ball goes through the net, the team gets two points. A player hardly ever scores by himself.

Ervin "Magic" Johnson, Hall of Fame professional basketball player

Scouting

At the Asian games I saw more major league scouts than Asian scouts.

Acey Kohrogi, baseball executive

Half the time the scouts have their heads down making notes and don't even see which way the ball is hit.

Tom Greenwade, legendary professional baseball scout

Season (the)

Face it, people, this is the Black Hole on the sports calendar. The endless, meaningless hockey season trickles on, drawing slightly more attention than the endless, meaningless NBA season.

Jack Todd, sportswriter, referring to the time between the Super Bowl and baseball's spring training

The sports department usually goes into deep-sleep mode after the Super Bowl until pitchers and catchers report to their camps in Florida and Arizona. The minihibernation is disturbed only by the midseason plodding of the NBA and NHL, still months from their interminable playoffs.

Bill Conlin, sportswriter

In this season, I played on five continents, made 129 airplane trips, slept in 71 different beds and traveled 165,000 miles.

Arthur Ashe, Hall of Fame tennis champion and writer, from one Wimbledon to the next in 1975

Professional tennis has no real season, no linear progression from start to finish. Instead, the tour is cyclical and it leads to a condition rather than a destination.

Michael Mewshaw, writer

There isn't a single professional sports season now that doesn't go on at least a month too long. Baseball starts in football weather, and football in baseball weather, and basketball overlaps them both.

James Reston, writer

There's only one difference between a game in May and a game in September. You lose in September, there's less time to get it back.

Roberto Clemente, Hall of Fame baseball player

227

Second Place

I didn't come here to finish second. Rivalries are probably good for hype, and good for the sport. But nobody remembers who finishes second.

Pat Day, jockey

In this country, when you finish second, no one knows your name.

Frank McGuire, basketball coach

In this country, you either finish first or last, there is no second place.

Buddy Werner, writer

I was choked with tears . . . Was that it, the return for all the years of frenzied study, self-mastery, struggle, unyielding self-sacrifice? A silver disk on a colored ribbon?

Yuri Vlasov, Olympic weightlifter

When she didn't hug me on the podium, it was honest. She was just upset. And I can relate to that.

Katarina Witt, Olympic gold medalist figure skater, about Debbie Thomas, silver medalist

Secretariat

(foaled 1971; d. 1989) *Triple Crown winner— 1973; first since Citation in 1948; set track record at Belmont with 31-length Belmont Stakes win in a time of 2:24; took first 16 times; second three times; third once (finished fourth once—first race)*

He hasn't run, he hasn't worked, and he hasn't won, so he doesn't know why he's in the winner's circle.

Penny Cherney, owner of Secretariat, during his final farewell tour

I thought I was going to win, and win big. Then I see this thing coming up on the outside of me and it just went, whoosh. I couldn't believe it.

Laffit Pincay, Jr., jockey, about Secretariat, while he was aboard Sham in the Kentucky Derby

90% of the farm's visitors, even among clients who come to do business involving other horses, ask about Secretariat and want to have one look at the horse they can still remember seeing win the Belmont Stakes by 31 lengths.

Steve Crist, sportswriter

Sex

Fifty percent of life in the NBA is sex. The other fifty percent is money.

Dennis Rodman, professional basketball player

Going to bed with a woman never hurt a ballplayer. It's staying up all night looking for them that does you in.

Casey Stengel, baseball manager

I believe that skiing and sex have a special affinity.

Jean-Claude Killy, Olympic gold medalist skier

It has often occurred to me that sport, like sex, is an activity that should either be performed or watched—but not written about.

Paul Gardner, sportswriter

The other night someone asked Dr. Ruth what she thought about sex and sports. She said it was fine to make love the night before a game, because it releases tension. But you

shouldn't do it with someone new, someone you've just met, because then you might stay up all night and end up exhausted!

Bob Gansler, professional soccer coach

There are a lot of weird relationships on the tour. A girl gets lonely or in the mood, and she meets a man and goes with him. But she can't be sure it's love. It may be the situation, the isolation of the circuit.

Andrea Temesvari, professional tennis player

The satisfaction of running downhill and the satisfaction of making love to someone I really care about are probably pretty similar . . . A lot of it is instinct. But to explain the physical sensations of downhill is really, you know, how do you explain sex to a virgin?

Shanny Shanholtzer, downhiller, U.S. ski team

Sheehan, George

(b. Nov. 11, 1918; d. Oct. 27, 1993) *Marathon runner; promoter; philosopher; best-selling author of* Running & Being

George's mind always outran us. More than anyone, he widened running's moral purpose, which was not to live longer but to live better, to have more energy and self-worth and clarify for all the more important things to do in life than run.

Robert Lipsyte, writer

The "guru" and "philosopher king" of running.

William Jefferson Clinton, president of the United States

Shoemaker, Willie

(b. Aug. 31, 1931) *Professional jockey; all-time wins record of 8,833; five-time Belmont Stakes winner; won Kentucky Derby four times and the Preakness twice*

He had such good hands. He was so easy on them, but they ran for the devil like him anyway. As small as he was, he could still make a big horse do whatever he pleased.

Charlie Whittingham, thoroughbred horse trainer

Ice water runs through his veins. He is never excited or bothered.

Eddie Arcaro, jockey

Shooting

And I left my gun
Forever standing in the hall.

Archibald Routledge, poet

I myself am not, and never will be, more than an ordinary shot.

Theodore Roosevelt, president of the United States, conservationist and outdoorsman

I've dreamed elaborate dreams about shooting, but that I would someday own a Purdey was not one of them. I had shot my Fox for thirty-four years, and while no love affair lasts that long without a crisis, after the restocking job we were closer than ever and I had intended to continue shooting it as long as the two of us lasted.

George Bird Evans, hunter, outdoorsman, and writer

Shooting friendships—probably residual from tribal hunting—are at their best when sharing the failures as well as the successes.

George Bird Evans, hunter, outdoorsman, and writer

Some games Chinaglia took more shots than the entire opposing team.

Gerald Eskenazi, sportswriter, referring to Giorgio Chinaglia, professional soccer player

Some of the three-pointers I took were bad shots . . . I was just trying to do too much. Instead of helping us, I was hurting us.

Allen Iverson, professional basketball player

The fascination of shooting as a sport depends almost wholly on whether you are at the right or wrong end of a gun.

P. G. Wodehouse, writer

We're shooting 100 percent—60 percent from the field and 40 percent from the free-throw line.

Norm Stewart, college basketball coach

Shor, Toots

(b. May 6, 1903; d. Jan. 23, 1977) *Restaurateur; saloon keeper; sportsman; raconteur; well-known friend of athletes, sportsmen, and entertainers*

Celebrating 40 years of Toots Shor is like celebrating a broken hip.

Red Smith, sportswriter

When I was a busher in Milwaukee, he was just as obnoxious to me as when I had world champions. He's a foul-weather friend, which is the worst kind.

Bill Veeck, baseball owner and racetrack operator

Showboating

I barely raise my arms when I score. I don't want people mad at me for making them look stupid. I don't want them looking for me.

Brett Hull, professional hockey player

Sifford, Charles

(b. June 2, 1922) *First African American to play on the PGA tour 1960; first African American to win a tour event; turned pro 1948; won two tour events (1967, 1969); won the 1975 PGA Seniors Championship*

I have always had a great deal of admiration for Charlie Sifford . . . he has made himself a symbol that has inspired young black golfers in this country and the world—past, present and future. Probably more than any other single individual, Charlie paved the way and made life in professional golf so much easier for others of his race who have followed and will follow him.

Arnold Palmer, champion professional golfer

The pain and suffering and sacrifice experienced by Mr. Sifford in being a lonely pioneer for black golfers on the PGA Tour will never be forgotten.

Tiger Woods, champion professional golfer

When any black man is making his mark in a sport or profession, black people are aware of it. Charlie stands out. He was . . . a hero to blacks.

Willie McCovey, professional baseball player

Simpson, O. J.

(b. July 9, 1947) *Hall of Fame football player; Heisman Trophy winner 1968; first to rush for*

more than 2,000 yards in a season; broadcaster; actor; accused of murdering his ex-wife, Nicole Simpson, and her friend Ron Goldman in 1994; acquitted in a criminal trial; lost civil suit

The best of Jimmy Brown and Gale Sayers all rolled into one.

Art Hunter, professional football player

Skating

As soon as it's a woman's body, it's over. When they have lovely little figures like the girl on the street, they're probably too heavy. The older you get trying to do children's athletics, the thinner you must be.

Evy Scotvold, Olympic figure skating coach

Choreography is something very personal, and every individual skater should have some little trademark that separates him or her from the others.

Carlo Fassi, Olympic figure skating coach

Even now, people come up and say, "You should have won," and I'm like, "Come on, what competition were you watching?"

Debbie Thomas, Olympic silver medal figure skater

Good grief! What have we wrought the world? Oh my!

Dick Button, two-time Olympic gold medal figure skater and broadcaster, about Tara Lipinski, Olympic gold medalist

How do you expect to be taken seriously as a sport if you keep on having public relations blunders like this?

Jere Longman, sportswriter, to U.S. skating officials, they announced that Michael Weiss's

controversial quadruple toe loop was being withdrawn from the record books

I always felt a special connection with my audience. It's a bond I share with them that makes performing the thing I love the most.

Scott Hamilton, Olympic gold medal figure skater, broadcaster

I always say to them, "You never see a fat ballerina at the ballet."

Alex McGowan, Olympic figure skating coach

I have seen some Officers of the British Army, at Boston, and some of the Army at Cambridge, skait [sic] with perfect Elegence.

John Adams, president of the United States and patriot, in a letter to his son in 1780

I love to skate, skate, skate.

Rudy Galindo, champion figure skater

In my grief, I feared I had lost myself. To find myself again I did the only thing I could think of, the thing I knew best, the thing I'd been trained to do since I was four years old. I skated.

Ekaterina Gordeeva, champion pairs skater, referring to the death of her partner and husband, Sergei Grinkov

In skating, the thing that wins you the medal is your Long Program . . . You practice it until it is all you think throughout the day and then you dream of it all night. You practice until everything comes together naturally as breathing, and you hope you get it right when it counts.

Peggy Fleming, Olympic gold medalist, figure skating, broadcaster

I've never seen a little girl so determined to skate, with the ability to do it with so much sparkle and verve.

> *Oscar Holte, figure skating coach,*
> *about Sonja Henie*

Jump every jump like it's the last in your life.

> *Alexi Mishin, legendary Russian*
> *figure skating coach*

Kerrigan and Baiul staged a battle at the 1994 Olympic Games that defined the two central aspects of skating. Kerrigan's magnificent athleticism was matched against Baiul's timeless artistry . . . it was not political.

> *Christine Brennan, writer*

Long before Tonya Harding and her associates crash-landed into the sport, women gunned for other women in practice sessions. They trashed their rivals—gossiping about nose jobs and stage mothers and bank accounts—for as long as there have been rivals to trash.

> *Christine Brennan, writer*

Next thing you know, she'll make me kill someone on the ice.

> *Sergei Grinkov, Olympic gold medal–winning*
> *pairs skater, about his coach, who*
> *wanted him to "act" more on the ice*

On the ice, my father was like a thoroughbred. I'm more like a train. I chug.

> *Brett Hull, professional hockey player,*
> *speaking of his father, Bobby Hull,*
> *Hall of Fame hockey player*

Picking a winner in figure skating is more like choosing a sorority sister than crowning a sports champion.

> *Christine Brennan, writer*

Seven minutes on the ice. Give or take a few seconds that's all a figure skater gets at the Olympic Games. After ten or fifteen years of training, after giving up school and families and any semblance of normalcy, it's all over in seven minutes.

> *Christine Brennan, writer*

She went out there and flopped around like a dying walrus.

> *Evy Scotvold, Olympic figure skating coach*

Skating is a sport and a form of artistic expression.

> *Carlo Fassi, Olympic figure skating coach*

Skating was about flying, about feeling the wind in their faces, about interpreting beautiful music, about skimming across the frictionless ice below their feet.

> *Christine Brennan, writer*

Skating was the only thing I did that really gave me confidence.

> *Tonya Harding, world champion skater,*
> *bizarre sports personality*

The anonymity of our sport in the off-Olympic years virtually guarantees that Olympic experiences are all we have to deal with.

> *Dan Jansen, Olympic gold medal*
> *speed skater*

The one thing I want to be able to do after it's all over is say, "That was my best." It's better to lose that way than to win with something less than that. But it's fun to win, isn't it?

> *Tenley Albright, Olympic gold medalist,*
> *figure skating*

The skater must develop the ability to interpret the music with feeling. This will make the difference between a great champion and a mediocre skater.

Carlo Fassi, Olympic figure skating coach

This is the corniest thing I've ever done.

Nancy Kerrigan, Olympic silver medal figure skater, during a parade in her honor at Disney World, for which she was a spokesperson

This sport is so unforgiving. Finish second and all of a sudden you're a has-been.

Jurina Ribbens, ABC Sports, referring to international ice-skating competitions

Two years ago people would say, "Gee, she really jumps." Now, people don't mention her jumps and spins anymore. They say, "That was gorgeous, that was beautiful."

Frank Carroll, figure skating coach, about Michelle Kwan

Where first in my life, it being a great frost, did see people sliding with their skeetes [sic], which is a very pretty art.

Samuel Pepys, writer

Why me? Why me?

Nancy Kerrigan, Olympic silver medal figure skater, after having her knee hit with a tire iron by friends of competitor Tonya Harding

You can either skate to . . . music or you can express it.

Katerina Witt, Olympic gold medalist, figure skating

You seduce with your fingers. Your body's worth twenty kopecks, but your fingers are worth gold.

Galina Zmievskaia, figure skating coach

Skiing

Downhill is fast, sexy, perilous. Downhill racers go like hell from the top of the mountain to the bottom, sometimes at eighty miles an hour, frequently out of control.

Mike Wilson, writer

Every time I launch myself off 120-meter ramp . . . I don't feel like I'm moving. I can't hear anything. I'm just flying.

Lindsey Van, ski jump champion

I am going to kick your ass.

A. J. Kitt, champion downhiller, speaking to the mountains at Kitzbuhel

I am often asked, was there not one special moment when I decided to be a ski racer. No, it was more that a series of experiences throughout my early life cast the mold for me. Ski racing had to become my world.

Jean-Claude Killy, Olympic gold medalist skier

I'm standing in the slalom gates and I'm thinking of my classmates and some of them I know make twelve hundred dollars a month already and what am I doing here?

Spider Sabich, Olympic and professional skier, contemplating turning pro

In a sport full of daredevils and smart-asses, Tomba was the most outrageous character. Off the snow, he was a notorious egomaniac and lecher . . . Even so, he was a genius on the hill, arguably the most powerful technical racer who ever lived.

Mike Wilson, writer

It is unbecoming for a cardinal to ski *badly*.

Pope John Paul II, asked if he thought as a cardinal he should be skiing

Just say no to slalom.
Tim LaMarche, coach, U.S. ski team

Of all the myriad dangers inherent in a journey by ski and dogsled across a frozen ocean, perhaps the most worrisome is the possibility of falling through the ice. During spring—the only period when this journey is feasible—the frozen surface of the sea is constantly shifting, cracking, opening up, and refreezing.
David Nolan, outdoor journalist

Racing is an art form . . . I'm not there to hear the crowd yelling or to achieve glory or to earn money. I'm there to ski a perfect race.
Jean-Claude Killy, Olympic gold medalist skier

Real expert skiing has been called "classic skiing." It's functional, not faddish.
Lito Tejaela-Flores, champion skier and instructor

Skiing combines outdoor fun with knocking down trees with your face.
Dave Barry, writer and humorist

Ski racing is unique. It is a dangerous, lonely sport, where each individual is racing against the clock and himself. It is a technical sport that demands precision and split-second reactions that are developed over years of training and constant practice; a ski racer can lose his timing after three weeks of being off his skis.
Peter Miller, writer

Ski wild and loose; ski over your head a bit.
Dick Duckworth, skiing coach, U.S. ski team

Speed hangs like an opium cloud over the start corral at a downhill.
Paul Hochman, writer

Summer vacations? Bah, humbug!
Herb Gordon, outdoorsman, skier, and writer

Telemark skiing was counter-cultural. It was a response to the alpine scene.
Paul Parker, telemark (or free heel) skier

That's all I've gotten this year—a bronze medal from an airline.
Steve Porino, downhiller, U.S. ski team

The American racer has never felt at home in Europe. There is a psychological barrier to crack, for he is competing in the opposition's front parlor. For some reason many Americans develop an inferiority complex when they cross the Atlantic.
Peter Miller, writer

The international race circuit is not all glamour and excitement. You might think this is what it's like for racers traveling from one glamorous resort to another. But ski racing for much of the time is hard work and drudgery.
Billy Kidd, Olympic silver medalist downhiller

The real fathers of the sport were not the men who made a few halfhearted experiments with skis and then abandoned the fickle boards in despair, but those who first proved by solid achievement the wonderful possibilities of the ski.
Arnold Lynn, telemark (or open heel) skier

There's nothing like flying down a mountain so fast that the run literally opens up before your eyes. I love to rock'n'roll right out of the gate.
Picabo Street, Olympic medalist skier

There was something very appealing about these American skiers. They wear Levi's and sleep in trucks and eat hamburgers, but they show up on the slopes with the best equipment they can buy. They'll join the ski patrol or wash dishes or do anything around a ski area that will keep them alive and let them go skiing because that is what they love to do.

Jean-Claude Killy, Olympic gold medalist skier

To me, skiing has always been more than just running gates. I wanted to do more on the snow than simply go fast.

Jean-Claude Killy, Olympic gold medalist skier

The mountain is skiing me, I'm not skiing the mountain.

Jeff Olsen, downhiller, U.S. ski team

We do everything to extremes. We work hard, we play hard, we train hard, and we ski hard.

Jeff Olsen, downhiller, U.S. ski team

When reduced to its basic elements, snow is piddling, uncomplicated stuff: water, dust, and air.

Peter Oliver, skier and writer

You haven't truly felt your heart ballooning in your throat until you've flown over a knife-edged mountain ridge in a helicopter . . . Imagine standing atop the world's tallest building and looking down to discern that the floor is gone. That's what it's like.

Peter Oliver, skier and writer

You need guts to run downhill and not everyone has it.

Karl Schranz, champion downhiller

Skill
Producing while making it look easy was the epitome of skill.

Spike Lee, writer, actor, director, basketball fan

Slumps
Hey, I went 0-for-24 once. And I turned out OK, didn't I?

Yogi Berra, Hall of Fame baseball player and manager

I never got down. I remained positive. I was swinging the bat well. It was bad luck here or there.

Nomar Garciaparra, professional baseball player, who broke out of a homerless slump with a three home run, 10 RBI night

The hardest part of any slump is looking up at the scoreboard and seeing your stats in huge numbers.

Jason Giambi, professional baseball player

Most slumps are like the common cold. They last two weeks no matter what you do.

Terry Kennedy, professional baseball player

Sneakers
Is it the shoes, Money? Is it the shoes?

Spike Lee, alias Mars Blackmon, to Michael Jordan, about the new Air Jordans

There is something about a new pair of sneakers that makes a boy feel he can run faster and jump higher.

Spike Lee, writer, actor, director

Snowboarding

Cliff jumps look spontaneous in videos and in movies. That's because all you usually see is the edited version of the film. You rarely get to see all the scouting and planning . . . or the terrifying crashes.

Matt Goodwill, champion snowboarder

Just concentrate on being the board.

Master Fwap, Buddhist monk

Last night's storm has blanketed the mountain in knee deep powder. Snow boarder's nirvana.

Jeff Bennett, snowboarder

Skiing was too social for me; it lacked the pure intensity and grace of standing atop of a four-and-a-half-foot long fiberglass board while plummeting straight down mountains of snow.

Dr. Fredrick Lenz, snowboarder

When you're riding fast on a flat base you're in *no-man's-land*—a place where either edge can take control without warning.

David Sher, snowboarding champion

Snider, Duke

(b. Sep. 26, 1926) *Hall of Fame baseball player; known as "The Duke of Flatbush"; hit forty or more home runs five seasons consecutively; played in six World Series, won two*

A King of Kings, the Lord my God, the Duke himself.

Philip Roth, writer

Soccer

Am I so round with you as you with me
That like a football you spurn thus?

You spurn me here and you spurn me hither;
If I last in this service you must case me in leather.

William Shakespeare, Comedy of Errors

Chinaglia is one of those players who must have the ball. But when Pele is on your team you do not get the ball so often.

Gerald Eskenazi, sportswriter, about Giorgio Chinaglia and Pelé playing for the New York Cosmos

Concerning football playing, I protest to you it may rather be called a friendly kind of fighting, than recreation. For, does not everyone lie in wait for his adversary, though it be on hard stones, in ditch or dale, or whatsoever place it may be he cares not, as long as it has him down.

Unknown, translated from Old English

England has never exactly been an El Dorado for soccer players.

Paul Gardner, sportswriter

Fifty million Brazilians await your victory!

Mayor of Rio de Janeiro, to the Brazilian national soccer team, which later lost to Uruguay

Football is a suitable game for girls, but it is hardly suitable for delicate boys.

Oscar Wilde, humorist

Football is my work, my life. I didn't cry because of second place, but because the referee had not the right to blow that penalty against us.

Diego Maradona, professional soccer player

Football, it seemed to me, is not really played for the pleasure of kicking a ball about, but is a species of fighting.

George Orwell, writer

Football reflects the nationality, it mirrors the nation. Without football, we Brazilians do not exist—just as one would not conceive of Spain without the bullfight.

Betty Milan, writer

For as sundry complaints are made that several persons have received hurt by boys and young men playing football in the streets. . . .

notice posted by Boston town authorities in 1657

Gentlemen, if the Czechs play fair, we'll play fair. That's the most important thing. But if they want to play dirty, then we Italians must play dirtier.

Benito Mussolini, dictator

Good pay, good lodging, and a decent burial.

job listing in the United States for soccer referees in South America

I can teach things to players, things only I can do.

Diego Maradona, professional soccer player

I don't know how it can be done, General, but Italy must win the World Cup.

Benito Mussolini, dictator, to General Giorgio Vaccaro, president of the Italian Olympic Committee

If you're attacking, you don't get as tired as when you're chasing.

Kyle Rote, Jr., professional soccer player

I have been an avid football fan ever since my youth in Furth, a soccer-mad city in southern Germany. My father despaired of a son who preferred to stand for two hours—there were very few seats—watching a football game rather than go to the opera or visit a museum.

Henry Kissinger, secretary of state and author

In Latin America the border between soccer and politics is vague. There is a long list of governments that have fallen or been overthrown after the defeat of the national team.

Luis Suarez, journalist

It is an exciting experience to see young boys and even grown men . . . responding to the beauties of soccer.

Pelé, professional soccer player

It's a game of athleticism, a game of power and competition and strength. Anybody who thinks football is just a game of deftness of touch without those other things *wouldn't win.*

Bobby Robson, professional soccer manager

On the field, when you beat a player, you've always got to be looking for the next option.

Mia Hamm, champion soccer player

Other countries have their history. Uruguay has its football.

Ondino Viera, professional soccer manager

Soccer is not about justice. It's a drama—and criminally wrong decisions against you are part and parcel of that.

Pete Davies, writer

Soccer sells products all over the world. All this is due to my work.

Joao Havelange, Federation of International Football Associations executive, who brought in big-name sponsors and called them official partners and marketing sponsors

Some people say soccer's a matter of life or death, but it isn't. It's much more important than that.

> *Bill Shankly, professional soccer*
> *player and manager*

The Argentine team was not cowardly. It was not the penalty that caused our defeat . . . You can say that Argentina did not perform well, but do not say that it was afraid, because that would be slanderous.

> *El Grafico, Argentine magazine,*
> *about the World Cup loss to Uruguay*

"The Black Diamond" took his foot out of his shoe and kicked the ball with all his might to tie the game.

> *Diego Lucero, journalist, describing*
> *Leonidas Da Silva's famous*
> *"Stocking Goal," Brazil 6, Poland 5*

The culmination of a work of art. The most beautiful goal ever scored.

> *Andres Cantor, broadcaster, about Diego*
> *Maradona's second goal against England*
> *in 1986, generally considered as one of*
> *the all-time great goals*

The goal was scored a little bit by the hand of God, another bit by the head of Maradona.

> *Diego Maradona, professional soccer player,*
> *questioned after an illegal goal was*
> *allowed to stand*

The military right wing can be assured of at least five more years of peaceful rule.

> *Luis Suarez, journalist, referring to a Brazilian*
> *team that had won the World Cup*

The problem was a misunderstanding between our forwards and their defenders.

Their defenders weren't standing where our forwards had told them to.

> *Franz Beckenbauer, professional soccer*
> *player and manager*

The roots of our Soccer Tribe lie deep in our primeval past.

> *Desmond Morris, writer*

This is why I love soccer. Soccer is all about mistakes. I thought about my friendships on this team and I thought about the crowd.

> *Brandi Christain, soccer player, U.S. women's*
> *World Cup, referring to a miscue where she*
> *accidentally put the ball in her own net,*
> *but helped the team to overcome the*
> *mistake and win*

Today was just not a football match between two countries. This was one of the best matches ever played in my life.

> *Juergen Klinnsman, professional soccer player,*
> *after the West Germans beat the Netherlands*
> *2-1 in 1990 to win the World Cup*

To say these men paid their shillings to watch twenty-two hirelings kick a ball is merely to say that a violin is wood and catgut, that *Hamlet* is so much paper and ink.

> *J. B. Priestley, writer*

To the aesthete it is an art form, an athletic ballet. To the spiritually inclined it is a religion.

> *Paul Gardner, sportswriter*

Soccer is already the major sport of the rest of the world; it only remains for America to join the fray.

> *Rick Telander, sportswriter*

Soccer is like traditional jazz in that the players know the tune that is to be played, know

there are an infinite number of varieties as to how to strike a note or chord—or a play.

Gordon Bradley and Clive Toye, writers

Unfortunately women's soccer still doesn't even have a chance in Brazil. The best woman player in Brazil will never be as popular as the worst male player, and the main reason is that women have been idolized as delicate objects of desire, incapable of playing a physical-contact, body-to-body sport.

Armondo Nogueira, broadcaster

Whenever the ball flew toward our goal and a score seemed inevitable, Jesus reached his foot out and cleared the ball.

Jornal dos Sports, Rio de Janeiro sports newspaper (one of the largest newspapers in South America), referring to a game between Brazil and England

While football has changed remarkably in terms of pace, competitiveness and anxiety for reward, it is still controlled on the field, where it matters most, from the ranks of the clerks and shopkeepers and foremen.

Arthur Hopcraft, writer, referring to the main occupation of referees

While soccer may have other hallowed matches—Barcelona–Real Madrid, Boca Juniors–River Plate in Buenos Aires, Roma–Lazio in Rome, Flamengo–Fluminese in Rio—none come close to matching Celtic–Rangers for a purity of hatred that involves politics, class and, above all, religion.

Grant Wahl, sportswriter

Women can now be doctors, lawyers, politicians—and even soccer players.

Mia Hamm, champion soccer player

You can tell the world, soccer has finally come to America.

Pelé (Edson Arantes do Nascimento), champion soccer player

Your mission is part of the confrontation between Iraq and the Forces of Evil embodied by the U.S. and its allies.

Al-Qadissiya, Iraqi newspaper, to the Iraqi national soccer team

Chelsea lose two-nil to Portsmouth, and you want to go home and bury an axe in your face.

M. John Harrison, novelist

Football is played at a series of levels, from Premiere League to where it's barely worth wearing a kit or marking out pitches. What separates serious professionals from those they leave behind—to scatter their dreams across council playing fields up and down the country—is not so much talent as a crucial difference in temperament.

Tim Pears, novelist

I set myself one goal when I started as national coach. That was winning the European championship. I failed, I have to take the consequences, and it's time now for a new coach.

Frank Rijkaard, coach of the Dutch national soccer team, resigning after the Dutch lost to the Italians in a shoot out 2-1, in the Euro 2000

It's a white world, soccer: the board members, the journalists, the referees. When I am in a stadium, I always look around the stands, and I hardly see black faces in them.

Humberto Tan, professional soccer player

239

These bouts of lunch-time football made going to work something to look forward to rather than dread. After playing, especially is the weather was fine, we were reluctant to return to the warehouse, and sat against the graffiti-mottled wall, the sun dazzling our eyes, gulping down water and chewing mouthfuls of bread and tomato, the minutes ticking by until, begrudgingly, like troops returning to the front, we tramped back . . . to work.

Geoff Dyer, writer

The spirit of soccer is no longer containable in the allotted ninety minutes.

Rob Hughes, sportswriter, after the Euro 2000 semifinals and final were all decided in overtime or shoot outs

The zigzags suddenly disappeared to reveal a cannonball of a football player burst out of a huddle of adversaries, to kick a blur of a football into a perfect arc that went between the outstretched arms of a vaulting goalkeeper and into the top right-hand corner of the net. And I couldn't help it. It rose up in a warm and intoxicating wave from my deepest inner recesses without my willing or understanding it.

Maureen Freely, columnist and novelist

Playing soccer is more fun than sitting around talking about soccer.

Vincenzo Sarno, 12-year-old Italian soccer prodigy on the set of CBS's Early Show

Speed
Act quickly, but never in a hurry.

John Wooden, champion college basketball coach

I never had the speed I used to have but I get the job done.

Tommy Heinrich, professional baseball player

The art of self-defense—100 yards in 10 seconds.

Hugh E. Keogh, sportswriter

The race isn't to the swift, but that is where to look.

Hugh E. Keogh, sportswriter

Speed makes him seven feet tall.

Eddie Robinson, college football coach, to George Young, football executive, about David Meggett, professional football player, after Young had commented that Meggett looked too small to play professional football

Team speed, team speed. Just give me some big c★★★★★★★★ who can hit the ball out of the park.

Earl Weaver, professional baseball manager

Spending
There was nobody in the ballpark. And as soon as Mr. Piazza showed up, things picked up. You've got to put a nickel in to get a nickel out.

Nelson Doubleday, baseball owner, referring to Mike Piazza, professional baseball player

They need the money, baseball executives said . . . Those dreadful players have held them up so much that they must recoup their losses any way they can.

George Vecsey, sportswriter

Sports

A little over a century ago athletics was almost wholly a professional sport; some schoolboys and undergraduates competed as amateurs, while amateur oarsmen or gymnasts sporadically arranged diverting afternoons on the track.

Peter Lovesey, writer

A man described as a "sportsman" is generally a bookmaker who takes an actress to nightclubs.

Jimmy Cannon, sportswriter

Athletic competition clearly defines the unique power of our attitude.

Bart Starr, Hall of Fame football player

Athletics are all I care for. I sleep them, eat them, talk them, and I try my level best to do them as they should be done. You must feel that way.

Babe Didrickson Zaharias, champion golfer and Olympian track and field competitor

At three, four, five and even six years the childish nature will require sports; now is the time to get rid of self-will in him, punishing him, but not so as to disgrace him.

Plato, philosopher

Baseball is what we were. Football is what we have become.

Mary McGrory, journalist

Beyond the undeniable romance and sweet sentimentalities of fishing and wing shooting, beyond the elegance of fly rods and rising trout, the aesthetics of fine guns and noble gun dogs, beyond the esteemed history and venerable traditions of Sport, with a capital S, lies something that our spouses, especially if they themselves are non-hunters and non-fishpersons, have suspected all along: we're just great big kids.

Jim Fergus, outdoorsman, writer, and author

Every sport pretends to a literature, but people don't believe it of any other sport but their own.

Alistair Cooke, writer and historian

Football is easy if you're crazy as hell. Baseball is easy if you've got patience. They'd be easier for me if I was a little crazier—and a little more patient.

Bo Jackson, professional baseball and football player

Forget love and Esperanto: The only two international gauges are music and sports.

Steve Rushin, sportswriter

Games are the last resort of those who do not know how to idle.

Robert Lynd, writer

Games lubricate the body and the mind.

Benjamin Franklin, U.S. patriot and inventor

I am delighted to view any sport that may be safely engaged in.

Charles Dickens, novelist

I believe sport is a natural, wholesome, enjoyable form of human expression comparable to the arts.

Dr. Roger Bannister, champion runner and first man to run a mile in less than four minutes

If all the year were playing holidays,
To sport would be as tedious as to work.

William Shakespeare, playwright and poet

If you can keep your head when all about
   you
  Are losing theirs and blaming you;
If you can fill the unforgiving minute
  With sixty-seconds worth of distant run,
Yours is the earth and everything that's in it,
  And—which is more—you'll be a man,
   my son.

Rudyard Kipling, writer and poet

In defending athletics I would not for one moment be understood as excusing that perversion of athletics that would make it the end of life instead of merely a means in life.

Theodore Roosevelt, president of the United States, conservationist, and outdoorsman

In those days, a sportsman meant a rich man with a passion for hunting, fishing, and horse racing, a man who would shoot at the best lodges in the nation and fish distant waters for giant billfish, but who rarely knew about baseball, which was essentially a blue-collar sport.

David Halberstam, writer

I owe sport a great deal. Not only has it enabled me to earn a comfortable living; it helped me to grow up.

Grantland Rice, sportswriter

It is in games that men discover their paradise.

Robert Lynd, writer

I turn to the front pages of my newspaper to read about men's failures. I turn to the sports pages to read about their triumphs.

attributed to Oliver Wendell Holmes, U.S. Supreme Court justice, and to Tonto Coleman, executive of the Southeastern Conference

Literature and sports are not mutually exclusive, though at times one may despair of finding their common ground.

Garth Baptista, writer, publisher, and runner

Looking back, it would be *impossible* to overstate the impact of sports in my life.

Spike Lee, writer, actor, director

Observing team sports, teams of adult men, one sees how men are children in the most felicitous sense of the word.

Joyce Carol Oates, writer

Play is where life lives.

George Sheehan, runner and writer

Sports are too much with us. Late and soon, sitting and watching—mostly watching on television—we lay waste our powers of identification and enthusiasm and, in time, attention as more and more closing rallies and crucial putts and late field goals and final playoffs and sudden deaths and world records and world championships unreel themselves ceaselessly before our half-lidded eyes.

Roger Angell, writer

Sports and games have always been an inherent part of man's physical involvement in life. Play, properly perceived, is an essential element in life.

Barry C. Pelton, writer

Serious sports has nothing to do with fair play. It is bound up with hatred, jealousy, boastfulness, disregard of all rules and sadistic pleasure in witnessing violence: in other words it is war minus the shooting.

George Orwell, writer

Sports cut across racial, language, cultural, and national boundaries. It is what countries should use to compete instead of war.
Hakeem Olajuwon, professional basketball player

Sports gives us all the ability to test ourselves mentally, physically and emotionally in a way that no other aspect of life can.
Dan O'Brien, Olympic gold medalist decathlon competitor

Sport is a powerful tool that our society needs to understand better and utilize better.
Anita DeFrantz, Olympic silver medalist oarswoman

Sport is a right of the people.
Fidel Castro, president of Cuba

Sports do not build character. They reveal it.
Heywood Broun, writer

Sports has expanded the boundaries of bad behavior and violence.
Robert Lipsyte, writer

Sports is a lot of damn nonsense.
Harry S. Truman, president of the United States

Sports is human life in microcosm.
Howard Cosell, broadcaster

Sports is the toy department of human life.
Howard Cosell, broadcaster

The art of activity.
Sir Francis Bacon, artist

The essence of sports is that while you're doing it, nothing else matters, but after you stop, there is a place, generally not very important, where you would put it.
Dr. Roger Bannister, champion runner and first man to run a mile in less than four minutes

The lead-in drive, the fresh new feel of underfoot gravel going against the iron muscles of my legs.
Allan Sillitoe, writer and runner

The literature of athletics is rich in histories and technical manuals, but the historian of athletics is overwhelmed and embarrassed by the sheer mass of material on each branch of the sport.
Peter Lovesey, writer

There is no doubt that basic weekendmanship should contain some reference to Important Person Play.
Stephen Potter, writer

The rich soup that is the environment of the fan of team sports, with its franchises and divisions, its superstars and their agents, is very different from the sporting world occupied by the solitary angler on a woodland stream.
Thomas McGuane, writer

The sixties were a time for grunts or screams . . . The sports that fitted those times were football, hockey and mugging.
Bill Veeck, baseball owner and racetrack operator

The world of sports provides that first early test where a man meets obstacles and dangers and pressures. It is where a man begins to excel.
Arnold Hano, sportswriter

Those who seek to compete in sports do so because they have a specific need to be met. Somewhere there is a hole that needs to be

filled; their involvement is a race, a game or match gives them an arena in which to seek their goal.

Scott Tinely, champion triathlete

We do not want our children to become a generation of spectators. Rather, we want each of them to become participants in the vigorous life.

John Fitzgerald Kennedy, president of the United States

When you're ten, eleven, and twelve, the most important lesson you can have in sports is to have fun.

Grant Hill, professional basketball player

Which game do I like better? I like baseball better in the spring. I like football better in the fall.

Bo Jackson, professional baseball and football player

Sportsmanship

Be strong in body, clean in mind, lofty in ideals.

Dr. James Naismith, inventor of basketball

Brutality and foul play should receive the same summary punishment given to a man who cheats at cards.

Theodore Roosevelt, president of the United States

For when the Great Scorer comes
  To write against your name,
He marks—not that you won or lost—
  But how you played the game.

Grantland Rice, sportswriter

Friendships born on the field of athletic strife are the real gold of competition. Awards become corroded, friends gather no dust.

Jesse Owens, Olympic champion, track and field

Good sportsmanship and reasonable standards of conduct are important.

Ted Turner, champion yachtsman and baseball owner

If you want to know the truth, I never liked the . . . players I butted helmets with. Not even when the game had ended.

Dick Butkus, National Football League Hall of Famer

In the ring, it was always for money; if you don't take him out, he'll take you out. But outside the ring I was always nice to everybody; it costs you nothing.

Jack Dempsey, world champion boxer

It's better to be a good person than to be good-looking or a good tennis player. Being a good person is for always.

Gabriella Sabatini, champion professional tennis player

It's how you get there, the work you do, the players you work with, how you live your life and help others to live theirs. Winning . . . winning isn't really that important to me.

Ted Newland, college water polo coach

I would like to be thought of as an athlete who enjoyed the sport, rather than any controversy he could create surrounding the sport. I would like people to feel I had done something to enhance not only myself, but the game itself.

John Havlicek, professional basketball player

One man practicing sportsmanship is better than a hundred teaching it.

> *Knute Rockne, college football coach*

Sportsmanship should be the very mortar of an athlete but never an entity in itself for conscious display.

> *Grantland Rice, sportswriter*

Take me to him. I want to shake his hand.

> *Jack Dempsey, champion boxer, temporarily blinded after being badly beaten by Gene Tunney*

The tradition of professional baseball always has been free of chivalry. The rule is: "Do anything you can get away with."

> *Heywood Broun, sportswriter*

Well, Ralph, it certainly is a pleasure to meet you. Now, my name is Cy Young. And these fellas over here are Zack Wheat and Ty Cobb.

> *Cy Young, Hall of Fame baseball player, to Ralph Terry, who unwittingly introduced himself as a major leaguer to three old men in the stands*

What is really happening in American sports is that sportsmanship and fun and fair play have disappeared in favor of violence and winning and selfishness.

> *Maury Allen, sportswriter*

You can't overestimate the importance of a high level of sportsmanship, because of the intensity and closeness of the players on the court. During a match you're at such a pace and your reaction time becomes so instinctive in your movement—if you do not maintain this high degree of sportsmanship, this character of the game, it just isn't going to be recognizable.

> *Charles Ufford, champion squash player*

You just shake your head and tip your cap.

> *Ken Griffey, Jr., professional baseball player, remarking on watching opposing player Nomar Garciaparra hit three homers (two of which were grand slams) and chalk up 10 RBIs in one nine-inning game*

Sportswriters

A dark day for sportswriters around the country indeed.

> *Tim Mowry, sled racer and sportswriter, about Brian Patrick O'Donoghue, a political writer, who finished ahead of the former in the Alaska Sled Race*

All newspaper writers have heard that the stuff they compose today has an excellent chance of being used to wrap tomorrow's mackerel.

> *Ira Berkow, sportswriter*

A writer sick—good, I hope they gave the son-of-a-bitch rat poison.

> *Lou Gehrig, Hall of Fame baseball player*

The bias against sportswriting remains large, and any good sportswriter is usually dismissed as the world's tallest midget.

> *Frank Deford, sportswriter*

Considering that most sportswriters I know are drunks, speed freaks, adulterers, hopeless chain smokers, or bad harmonizers (often all five if it's somebody I really want to hang out with), I find it amusing every spring when many of them turn lyrical as they sit down at their typing machines. Baseball does it.

> *Dan Jenkins, writer and best-selling author*

Do you want to know the weirdest thing about being a sportswriter other than, of course, the requirement that you spend much of your time talking to naked men? The other weird thing is that you don't get to be a fan.

Mike Littwin, sportswriter

Give 'em your own story, 'cause if you don't, they're just gonna go ahead and make up their own, and what good'll that do ya?
Casey Stengel, Hall of Fame baseball player and manager, to Whitey Herzog, professional baseball player, executive, and manager

Good to meet you. A writer, huh? What paper you with, Ernie?
Yogi Berra, Hall of Fame baseball player and manager, to Ernest Hemingway, to whom he'd been introduced as an "important writer"

Go up and write a column and a side bar.
Woody Paige, sportswriter, to a woman who said she would do anything for $100

He knew the stars of the baseball team, and he was full of the inside dope, even if he did not always write it. He was also the source of tickets for big games, something of which senior editors were always aware.
David Halberstam, writer, referring to sportswriters in the 1940s

He treats fans with contempt and sportswriters even worse.
Murray Chass, sportswriter, on Graig Nettles, professional baseball player

Hey, you a nice fella. You a sportswriter?
Muhammad Ali, world champion boxer, to Tom Seaver, Hall of Fame baseball player, at dinner one night in New York

I can buy anyone of these sons-of-bitches for a five-dollar steak.

George Weiss, baseball executive

If I ever need a brain transplant, I want one from a sportswriter, because I'll know it's never been used.

Joe Paterno, college football coach

If I had my life to live over again, I'd have ended up a sportswriter.

Richard M. Nixon, president of the United States

If sports writing teaches you anything, and there is much truth to it as well as plenty of lies, it is that for your life to be worth anything you must sooner or later face the possibility of terrible, searing regret. Though you must also manage to avoid it or your life will be ruined.

Richard Ford, writer, from his novel The Sportswriter

If you can't write the truth, you shouldn't write.

Jackie Robinson, Hall of Fame baseball player, to Dick Young, sportswriter

If you want someone to talk, talk, talk, you've come to the right person.

Thomas "Hollywood" Henderson, professional football player, to a sportswriter

I had a migraine the whole year. There weren't a lot of safe harbors. Your fellow staffers resented you, the players thought you were from Mars, and the wives hated you.

Lesley Visser, sportswriter and broadcaster, on being a pioneering female sports reporter

I never had any soaring ambition to be a sportswriter, per se. I wanted to be a newspaperman, and I came to realize I didn't really care which side of the paper I worked on.

Red Smith, sportswriter

I remember that last night in Yankee Stadium when Joe Louis knocked out Billy Conn in the eighth round of a fight that had been tautly dull, the way the slow hours are for reporters sitting on a stoop and waiting for a man to die.

Jimmy Cannon, sportswriter

It's amazing you still got jobs when you can't even write a sentence in English.

Toots Shor, restaurateur, to a group of sportswriters

It is the sportswriters' mission to bring the news from the field; they have more in common with war correspondents than they do with any other kind of writers.

Thomas McGuane, writer

It was like watching a friend of yours being run over by a trolley car, watching it coming and knowing what would happen but looking at it quietly, the curiosity dominating the horror and compelling you to be attentively silent. Maybe it was sudden but it was there all the time, the knockout inevitable and sure. It was there all the time like the rain in the night.

Jimmy Canon, sportswriter

I've just been a reporter.

A. J. McClane, outdoorsman and writer

I was not filled with social purpose. I didn't want to see sports as a "microcosm of real life." I wasn't zeroing in on myths to debunk or muck to rake. I just wanted to get out there and see what was going on and write better stories about it than anyone else.

Robert Lipsyte, writer

Long before I was allowed to eat fish with bones, could go all night without peeing in my bed, or understood *Gilligan's Island* wasn't real, I loved baseball. It's the reason I am a sportswriter.

Jennifer Briggs, sportswriter

Look, Mr. Knight, suppose I wrote three stinkers. I wouldn't have the rest of the week to recover.

Red Smith, sportswriter, to John S. Knight, publisher, refusing the offer to write three columns a week instead of six

Men of letters have always gravitated to sports. Witness yourselves.

A. Bartlet Giamatti, Major League Baseball commissioner, replying to a question as to why a learned man like himself would want to be commissioner of Major League Baseball, to a group of sportswriters

My readers never learned how to write, so I was entirely without contributions, and therefore hard up for material.

Ring Lardner, writer

Never look down at your notepad, or a player might think you're snagging a glimpse of his crotch.

Jennifer Briggs, sportswriter, recounting some of the wisdom passed on to her when she was a rookie sportswriter

Nothing on earth is more depressing than an old baseball writer.

Ring Lardner, writer

Nudity rarely bothered me, but I prefer never to see Nolan Ryan in anything but Ranger white or blue jeans. I have no idea why, except that Nolan Ryan and my daddy are my heroes, and I have no need of seeing either one of their white heinies.

Jennifer Briggs, sportswriter

On days when we're too tired to hunt or fish, play golf or go girl watching, we lie back in an easy chair with a scratch pad on our laps, doze, and stare at the ceiling. Occasionally we scribble down a few words for which our editors pay us incredible sums, and when our wives or children disturb our daydreams we run them the hell out and tell them we are working.

Ted Trueblood, outdoorsman, editor, and writer

The only damn thing you have in your hand is a beer. You haven't written down a word I've said.

Lee Trevino, champion golfer, to a drunken sportswriter who badgered him

Probably a professor of English.
Jimmy Cannon, sportswriter, after being told that fellow sportswriter Gene Ward's house had been burned down, due to arson

Shit-stirrers.

Roger Maris, professional baseball player

Somebody once wrote—another wise guy— that the only dumber thing than a grown-up playing a little kid's game is a grown-up writing about a grown-ups playing a little kid's games. Maybe there's truth in that. All I know is for twenty years I could never imagine doing anything else.

Mike Littwin, sportswriter

The British athletics press has this lazy, imperious attitude towards athletes. We run our guts out on the track, and if we've pleased them enough, we get a demand to attend the press box interview room, like a royal command. But if we don't say what they expect us to say, or we offend their sense of patriotism, then we're branded as arrogant.

Steve Ovett, champion runner

The so-called Golden Age of Sports, the twenties and early thirties, was really the Golden Age of Sportswriting. The Glories of the Babe, the Manassa Mauler, the Four Horsemen, were tunes composed on portable typewriters by gifted, ambitious, often cynical men who set customs and standards of sports journalism that are being dealt with to this day. . . .

Robert Lipsyte, writer

The most difficult aspect of dealing with sportswriters is their assumption of moral superiority. They insist on advising everyone.
Glenn Seaburg, University of Southern California chancellor

The sportswriter whose horizons are no wider than the outfield fences is a bad sportswriter.

Red Smith, sportswriter

Sportswriting is assumed to be second-rate, and, therefore, if any sportswriting is not second-rate, then, ergo, it must not be sportswriting.

Frank DeFord, sportswriter

They'll tell they want a story about one thing and they'll get the quotes they want. But the story comes out a whole different way. They

put your accurate quotes in there, but they change the context.

Maury Wills, professional baseball player, broadcaster, and manager

When they ask you a question, answer it and just keep going. That way they can't ask you another one.

Casey Stengel, Hall of Fame baseball player and manager

Why do I have to talk to these guys who make six thousand dollars a year when I make forty thousand dollars a year?

Yogi Berra, Hall of Fame baseball player, coach, and manager

You guys wouldn't like it if you had a box score on yourselves every day.

Casey Stengel, Hall of Fame baseball player and manager

You guys write this and say this about players, and criticize us, but half the time your information is wrong, and you're hypocrites, too. You guys drive drunk, do drugs, cheat on your wives. But you don't write about that.

Michael Irvin, professional football player

You wouldn't know a three step drop if it grew teeth, jumped up, and bit you in the ass!

Bill Parcells, professional football coach, to a sportswriter

Spouses

Ballplayer's wives live with some uncertainty now. Every time the plane comes back and all the wives go to meet it, some one says, "Oh my God, what if he isn't on the plane."

Margarita Valle, wife of Cuban national baseball player, about husbands defecting to the United States to play baseball

Bill James is a solitary genius in Westchester, Kansas. Well, not entirely solitary. He has, he says, a wife to neglect.

George Will, writer and baseball owner

I'm afraid for them, certainly. It's hard on any woman in a racing family. There's nothing we can do but wait and hope for the best.

Mrs. Elizabeth Petty, wife of Lee Petty and mother of Richard Petty

It's not a game. It's a lifestyle.

Beverlee Schnellenberger, wife of Howard Schnellenberger, college and professional football coach

Look at his eyes real good. There's a lot of sincerity and sweetness in those eyes. I don't know what I would have done without him.

Babe Didrickson Zaharias, professional golfer

That's the trouble. You can't get in the ring with them.

Norma Graziano, wife of Rocky Graziano, world champion boxer

When I played, wives caused as many problems among the players as anything else. They caused more trouble than the media ever could.

Maury Wills, professional baseball player, broadcaster, and manager

Spring Training

Spring training? They don't pay you for spring training!

Rickey Henderson, professional baseball player, when asked about his poor performance in spring training

The way to make coaches think you're in shape in the spring is to get a tan.

Whitey Ford, Hall of Fame baseball player

Squash

Jonathan Power is talented, eccentric, mouthy and wild. He could be the sporting world's next big-time rebel. Too bad he plays squash.

Bruce Grierson, writer

When most people think of squash—if they think of it at all—it's as a pastime enjoyed by toffee-nosed Ivy League seniors, captains of industry, TV psychiatrists. Or just dorks who spend the summers of their youth bouncing balls off the garage and never outgrew the fascination.

Bruce Grierson, writer

I encountered a series of mental hazards: a weakness for exotic, low-percentage shots; a vulnerability to distraction; a lack of patience in developing a point; a fondness for whaling away at ground strokes. I was in sum much more of a hot hitter than I was a cool thinker on the court.

Austin Francis, champion squash player

If you think squash is a competitive activity, try flower arrangement.

Alan Bennett, writer

I love this game. I played when I was a lad and rediscovered it at 41 when there was not enough time for golf and no sensible rationale for returning to rugby.

Sir Michael Edwardes, chairman British Leyland PLC

It's hard to run around your backhand in squash.

Cal MacCracken, champion squash player

Just play one point at a time. Forget everything else; just think about that one point. If you win that point, you move on to the next.

Roland Oddy, champion squash player

Played well, the international game of squash is more physically punishing than tennis and requires far more racquet skill than racquetball. It has all the bending and leaping of top-level badminton, the most aerobically taxing of all racquet sports.

Eliot Barry, sportswriter

Squash is a sport in which one's game constantly grows and evolves while utilizing all of the characteristics and abilities of the individual player. It's a game that can be likened to chess and boxing but has a three-dimensional element to it. It taxes the mind, body and character.

Victor Niederhoffer, champion squash player

Squash is my life.

Jahangir Khan, champion professional squash player

The fitter player usually wins.

Eliot Barry, sportswriter

The game is getting tougher and rougher. With more money coming in, more incentive, more young guys are playing. The concept of the game as a gentleman's game . . . that's changing.

Sharif Khan, champion professional squash player

When I first went on the squash courts, I couldn't believe how dangerous it was. I thought I was going to lose my head. . . .

Goldie Edwards, champion squash
player and badminton player

Winning squash involves good decision making.

John O. Truby and John O. Truby, Jr.,
champion squash players

You can sum up the game of squash in one phrase. Move your legs fast and your racket slow.

George Cummings, legendary squash coach

Stadiums (and Arenas)

Ebbets Field was where one learned to duck a punch and get along with a lot of different people.

Tony LoBianco, actor

If you build it, he will come.

W. P. Kinsella, novelist, from Shoeless Joe

I've built the greatest tribute man ever paid to athlete's foot!

Jack Kent Cooke, owner, referring to the
Los Angeles Forum

Some ballyard!

Babe Ruth, Hall of Fame baseball player,
about Yankee Stadium

The Philadelphia Spectrum . . . has a basic griminess to it that is both inescapable and, in a strange way, charming.

John Feinstein, writer

There is no better place to play basketball than the Boston Garden. When you first walk onto the parquet floor, the moment is frozen in time. You're at the Garden, the place where championships were won.

Bill Walton, college and professional basketball
player and broadcaster

The stadium . . . has only limited parking for those foolhardy motorists who enter the traffic caused by 200,000 spectators.

Janet Lever, sociologist, referring to
Maracana, the world's largest stadium,
in Brazil, which holds 220,000
at capacity

Stanley Cup

Every player who is sitting here who lifted up the Cup the first time will tell you the same thing. There's no feeling like lifting up that Stanley Cup.

Wayne Gretzky, Hall of Fame hockey player

The moment we won it, I felt awesome; it was thrilling, but it didn't give me as much joy as spending time with my daughter. We found the Stanley Cup didn't change our lives.

Steve Yzerman, professional hockey player

Statistics

Baseball fans love numbers. They love to swirl them around their mouths like Bordeaux wine.

Pat Conroy, writer

Do you want the statistics or the facts?

Mark Twain, writer

Every time I hear a ballplayer tell me, "Statistics are for losers," or the other maxim: "The only statistic that matters is win or lose," I wonder why everyone crowds around the bulletin board when the league stats are posted.

John Thorn, writer

The box score, being modestly arcane, is a matter of intense indifference, if not irritation, to the non-fan. To the baseball bitten, it is not only informative, pictorial, and gossipy but lovely in aesthetic structure. It represents happenstance and physical flight exactly translated into figures and history.

Roger Angell, writer

I gotta tell you I lost my scorecard and I'm trying to read McCarver's, but he's got the worst penmanship I've ever seen.

Richie Ashburn, broadcaster, during a baseball broadcast with Tim McCarver

Statistics always remind me of the fellow who drowned in a river whose average depth was only three feet.

Woody Hayes, Hall of Fame college football coach

Up to five goals is journalism. After that, it become statistics.

attributed by Pete Davies to a French journalist, at a match won by Sweden over Cuba, 8-0

What do you want, a higher average for me personally or value to the team? Every day, every at-bat, I do what's good for the team, I move runners around, and I knock runners in. But if you want batting average I'll give it to you next year.

Tommy Heinrich, professional baseball player, negotiating with management

When I was six, my father gave me a bright red scorebook that opened my heart to the game of baseball . . . Night after night he taught me the odd collection of symbols, numbers, and letters that enable a baseball lover to record every action of the game.

Doris Kearns Goodwin, writer and historian

You could look it up.

Casey Stegel, Hall of Fame baseball player and manager

You watch them all year and you say they aren't contributing that much to the team. Then they show you a lot of impressive statistics. They put you to sleep with statistics that don't win games.

Branch Rickey, baseball executive

If you really want to enjoy the game and understand it, you've got to score it.

Warner Fuselle, broadcaster, about scoring a baseball game

No other American sport has anything that genuinely approximates the scorecard—that single piece of paper, simple enough for a child—that preserves the game both chronologically and in toto with almost no significant loss of detail.

Thomas Boswell, sportswriter, on scoring a baseball game

Writing their names in a scorecard made them real to me; recording their exploits made them heroes.

Pat Edelson, sportswriter, on scoring a baseball game

Stealing (bases)

All of you guys, when you get into the locker room I want you to check your lockers. He stole everything out there he wanted today so he might have stole your jockstraps as well.

Casey Stengel, Hall of Fame baseball player and manager, to his team, the New York Yankees, after Jackie Robinson had stolen two bases in an exhibition game

I think that aggressive is an individual thing. You take a lot of pounding, you have to want to be a base stealer, you have to want to be the one to go out there and take that pounding. It's individual, it's not required.

Rickey Henderson, professional baseball player

Steeplechase

The horses treat the timber with the greatest respect and know clearly from experience that one mistake will be too many . . . The fences do not "give" an inch.

Dick Francis, champion jockey and novelist

There is no real equivalent in the United States to our Grand National, but the Maryland Hunt Cup is the most important social event in steeplechasing all year.

Dick Francis, champion jockey and novelist

Steroids

I knew it was all over for me. Every system in my body was shot, my testicles had shrunk to the size of peanuts. It was only a question of which organ was going to explode on me first.

Steve Michalik, world champion bodybuilder

Stickball

Nowadays, the automobiles, parked bumper to bumper, stifle the city boys' development, but in the late 1930s cars were a luxury and parking spaces were plentiful. If a man threatened to park in our stickball field—the distance between three manhole covers—we would say, "Would you mind moving down the street, Mister?" There was a kid named Lefty . . . who could ask that question with exactly the right balance between threat and appeal.

Dick Miles, U.S. tabletop tennis champion

Strikeouts

You mean I traveled 2,500 miles just to do this?

Mickey Mantle, Hall of Fame baseball player, after striking out in his one time at bat in an All-Star Game

Strikes (labor)

I look back on what I did as a contribution. I look back on what I did and realized that I derived a personal gain, too. I receive a pension from Major League Baseball.

Curt Flood, professional baseball player, and first to file for free agency

I love the game, and when it's there, I'm there. If the players and owners want to ruin it for themselves, let them do it.

Fred Klein, New York Knicks fan, referring to the 1998–1999 National Basketball Association strike

Buck Williams does it all: takes the kids to school, washes the dishes.

headline from the New York Times *during the 1998–1999 National Basketball Association strike*

Success

At a certain level, success is determined by mental factors, by dedication and motivation, and these things can't be faked. You either really care, or you don't. You're either happy or your not.

Arnold Schwarzenegger, champion bodybuilder and actor

I envied those who in success clung to a measure of peace and tranquillity—I was always too restless and life was a constant battle against boredom.

Sir Edmund Hillary, mountain climber

Ingenuity, plus courage, plus work, equals miracles.

Bob Richards, pole vaulter

It's harder to stay on top than it is to get there.
Don Shula, Hall of Fame professional football coach

It's important to set goals and work hard—no matter how many people tell you it's useless or that you won't succeed. Without determination, your dreams of a better life won't come true.

Jackie Joyner-Kersee, Olympic gold medalist track and field competitor

I watched the first Ali–Frazier fight in prison. And I promoted the third one.

Don King, boxing promoter

I've had enormous success, but you have to find your own happiness and peace. You can't find it in other things and other people. I'm still searching.

Chris Evert, champion tennis player

Success and failure cannot always be judged . . . All a man can do is walk straight and upright and believe that if behind him things don't look so good, around the corner they must be eye-popping wonderful.

Chuck Knox, professional football coach

Success is like surfing; you're doing what you can to stay on the board, but you really aren't in control of anything.

Kirk Shelmerdine, car racing crew chief

Success is not the result of spontaneous combustion. You must set yourself on fire.

Fred Shero, professional hockey coach

Success is the result of the application of scientific methods of training to the development of natural talents or skill, which we all possess in some degree or another.

Walter Goodall George, champion runner

Sweat plus sacrifice equals success.
Charles O. Finley, Major League Baseball owner

That's really the biggest price you pay. Time and privacy are luxuries that money can't buy me now. In the back of my mind I thought I could handle things becoming this big, but I didn't really envision this whole trip.

Billie Jean King, champion tennis player

The difference between a successful person and others is not a lack of strength, not a lack of knowledge, but rather a lack of will.

Vince Lombardi, professional football player and coach

The pole is slippery from top to bottom. I ought to know. I've been up and down it a few times.

Charlie Whittingham, thoroughbred horse trainer

To succeed in anything at all one should go understandingly about his work and be prepared for every emergency.

Joshua Slocum, sailor, first modern sailor to sail around the world alone

Whatever your goal in life, be proud of every day that you are able to work in that direction.

Chris Evert, champion tennis player

When we look at it, we look at him as still a great player but when he looks at himself, he looks at the time when he was totally dominating the game.

Jaromir Jagr, professional hockey player, about Wayne Gretzky

Willie Mays was my boyhood hero, but not because he was a great baseball player. Because he had a big house.

O.J. Simpson, Hall of Fame football player

You build a successful life a day at a time.
Lou Holtz, professional and college football coach

You can win and still not succeed, still not achieve what you should. And you can lose without really failing at all.

Bobby Knight, basketball coach

Super Bowl

It means $7,500 bucks, which in the whole scheme of life doesn't mean very much. In the final analysis, we're all going to wake up in the morning and be who we are and go where we go.

Alan Page, professional football player and state supreme court justice

Superstars

After scoring touchdowns and dancing in the end zone, after a stadium full of cheering fans had finally gone home, I was still empty inside.

Dion Sanders, professional baseball and football player

Anyone who thinks it's glamorous ought to go out and get the hell beat out of him like I do every Sunday, and then he'll see how glamorous it is.

Alex Karras, Hall of Fame football player

Fans wanted to rip his jersey right off of him. He wasn't a basketball player, he was a rock star.

Orlando Woolridge, professional basketball player, about Michael Jordan

He sits on the bench as if he were a teenager forced to attend an opera.

Bill Libby, sportswriter, referring to Hot Rod Hundley, professional basketball player

Hey, you're somebody too, right?
A fan, while asking Joe DiMaggio for his autograph, to Ernest Hemingway, who was with the sports star. Hemingway replied, "Yeah, I'm his doctor."

I Can't Wait Until Tomorrow 'Cause I Get Better Looking Every Day
> Joe Namath, Hall of Fame football player, the title of his autobiography written with Dick Schaap

If you accept the modern philosophy that there must be a ruthless and selfish motivation to succeed in sport then it could be justly claimed that Tenzing and I were the closest approximations we had on our expedition to the climbing Prima Donnas of today.
> *Sir Edmund Hillary, mountain climber*

In Seattle, they'll tell you Ken Griffey Jr. demands constant attention. He needs to be appreciated, loved, respected, stroked and sweet-talked. If that's the case, he has come to the right place.
> *Bill Koch, sportswriter*

It's incredibly tough on a rookie making $5 million to $7 million. Most of them are coming from families who have never had that type of money, and they can't go ask a successful uncle, "What would you do?"
> *Doc Rivers, National Basketball Association player*

I was never caught up in being a "superstar" because, for me, basketball is all about winning. It has never interested me who got the job done as long as it got done, even if it's not me.
> *Ervin "Magic" Johnson, Hall of Fame basketball player*

It wasn't unusual for me to run by the bench during a game and yell at Coach Wooden as I moved up court, "Get me some rebounders in here." I wanted to win. I was a bit overbearing at times.
> *Bill Walton, college and professional basketball player and broadcaster*

I used to say "I want to be like Mike," but now that I've had a taste of it, I think I'll pass.
> *Cynthia Cooper, Women's National Basketball Association player*

I want you to go out there; I want you to shine up my car. I'm gonna put on a show tonight, and I'm gonna have somebody ridin' home with me.
> *Attributed to Marvin Barnes by Steve Jones, professional basketball players. Barnes was supposed to have said this to the ball boys as he came into the sports complex.*

I wonder how many kids have made it in life—I mean really got to the top—because some son of a bitch made fun of their daddy?
> *A. J. Foyt, champion race car driver*

So famous is the bald pate that it is shaved by contractual agreement with Bic razors. And a particular shiver must have gone through is cranium as he got his customary prematch peck from Laurent Blanc. The defender had said that this would be his international farewell and—whatever the state of play in his on-off romance with Linda Evangelista—Barthez must find it hard to imagine being kissed by another man.
> *Jon Brodkin, sportswriter, about the famous French goalie Fabien Barthez*

The plan for my life had worked, I had it all—fame, money, cars, NFL stardom. The thinking had always been that everything I went through was going to be worth it if I ever made it this far. But when I finally got there, you know what I thought? I thought: "It wasn't worth it."
> *Kerry Collins, professional football player*

The players are richer, the arenas are nicer and the telecasts are better, but the financial and ideological divide has grown.

Harvey Araton, sportswriter

There's not one guy who is bigger than the game.

Wayne Gretzky, Hall of Fame hockey player

This team, it all flows from me. I've got to keep it going. I'm the straw that stirs the drink.

Reggie Jackson, Hall of Fame
baseball player

The Kobe Bryants, the Michael Finleys, the Kevin Garnetts and the Shaquille O'Neals are Internet savvy with many of them owning their own websites. . . . Talk all you want about tattoos and corn rows, the real substance of this new group of players will come with their ability to market themselves digitally.

George Willis, sportswriter

This 30-year-old with the backwards hat, 398 homers, the center-field play of Willie Mays and the pizzazz of Tiger Woods has moved from the back of the stage to the center of the proscenium. And we the audience now get to watch him in the bright lights.

Rick Telander, sportswriter,
referring to Ken Griffey, All-Star professional
baseball player

Throw Me the Damn Ball!
Keyshawn Johnson, professional football player,
the title of the controversial receiver's
autobiography

When Sinatra settled onto a stool and took a mike, all the other singers sat down and shut up. When Mark McGwire takes BP, even the strongest of the bombardiers put down their lumber and watch. And when Tiger Woods plunges a tee into a manicured greensward, coils and cocks—well, this is how you know it is a moment for the ages: Michael Jordan gets goose bumps.

Bill Lyon, sportswriter

Who's Bruce Springsteen?

Larry Bird, Hall of Fame player and coach

You know, they all want me to continue being the great mountain climber, in good condition and pursuing great adventures; yet they also want me to be sitting in their offices, cutting films or writing articles and books.

Reinhold Messner, mountain climber

Superstition

I am not a very superstitious person. I don't go in for rabbit feet or garlic cloves or lucky pennies or any of that. To me, luck is work, preparation, ability, attitude, confidence, skill.

Dennis Conner, businessman and
champion yachtsman

Surfing

All right, so the waves are shitty, so why don't we just settle this thing with an arm wrestling match.

Keith Malloy, surfer, to competitors at the Body
Glove Surfbout XII at Lowers

Alone on a board, speeding over a wave at fifteen or twenty miles an hour, the surfer experiences an ecstatic communication with

natural forces, a delicious isolation, and total freedom from the anxieties and mundane cares of the workaday world.

Peter L. Dixon, surfer and writer

As I paddled I thought, "If I blow this I'll probably drown and no one will know." I only looked over my shoulder once, just to make sure it wasn't going to explode on my head, then it picked me up and sucked me into its vortex, and suddenly I'm flying down the face . . . It sucked me up into it about three times, totally in control of my destiny, then it just blew me apart and spat me out into the channel.

Jeff Hakman, surfer

Backdoor is my dream wave. I mean, I know a lot of magazines have talked about me and my surfer at Backdoor. I truly feel I could close my eyes and surf that place.

Dane Kealoha, surfer

Because of my knee, I had to avoid the lip for almost two years. In retrospect, that was the best thing ever for my surfing, because I learned how to use the entire wave and concentrate on carving.

Garth Dickenson, surfer

Even though it was a strictly female contest, the beach was filled with little boy groupies dying to meet one of the competitors. It was nice to see the roles reversed.

Daize Shane, surfer

Focus on your surfing. Too many kids nowadays are focusing on how many sponsors they have and what they're getting. I think they forgot about the main thing, which is surfing.

Conan Hayes, surfer

For the longboard contingent on the North Shore, winter means many different things. For the younger generation, it's a hurdle representing a time to deal with the fears that keep them up at night, haunt them on the playground, or disrupt their doodling waves on homework assignments. For those who've cleared this barrier, winter offers a chance to prove themselves further, and to demonstrate that they have what it takes to assume a place in the big-league lineup.

Jimmy Barros, writer and surfer

His ability to change his body shape in the deepest of barrels is masterful.

Wayne Lynch, surfer, referring to
Chris Ward, surfer

I did win more money than Kelly Slater last year, so I guess that says something about the state of women's surfing. Even though the sponsorship side of the sport is where the real money is, and the men's side still dominates the competitive arena . . . There are more companies out there today focusing on women's needs, which means there's a lot more opportunities for the girls who are marketable.

Layne Beachley, champion surfer

If I set my goal on being world champion, I'll go all out, but right now I'm going on trips because it's more fun.

Chris Ward, surfer, referring to being a writer in
the meantime

If you asked him when he was twelve what he wanted to be, he would always say world champ. He doesn't say that now because he's getting closer to the real thing.

David Pu'u, surfer, about
Bobby Martinez, surfer

I get to travel so much and surf with all the really good guys—it's humbling.

Saxon Boucher, surfer

I grew up in California during the pre-Curren era. And for that reason all of my early surf heroes were Australian . . . untouchable idols living, or so I thought, in a dreamworld full of clearwater right pointbreaks and topless girls on the beach.

Chris Mauro, writer and surfer

I learned more in a few weeks in Hawaii than all the time I'd been surfing on the East Coast.

Dick Catri, champion surfer

I like single fins because they force you to concentrate on your style. They slow you down a bit, but I like that coming from a longboard.

Joel Tudor, surfer

I love the adrenaline of surfing, enjoy what I do, and have a common bond with other surfers of all ages in that we love to surf.

Herbie Fletcher, surfer

I'm always looking for something new day to day, whether it's surfing or just life in general. Style isn't always something you see on the cover of a magazine; sometimes it's a picture you paint in your head.

Kanoe Uemura, surfer

I take my children surfing every chance I have when I am home, and like all parents, I would like to be reassured that the water they are surfing in, or on any coast, is safe.

Brian Bilbray, U.S. representative, who sponsored HR 999 Beach Bill proposing clean water statutes and penalties

It's ten feet and SMOKING. None of this tiny Backdoor crap; full-on Pipeline, belching rage and fury . . . somehow this has become a huge pivotal moment.

Nick Carroll, writer and surfer

It was sometime in my second summer that one of these Prussian blue dream walls swept in out of Santa Monica Bay and caught everybody off guard except for me, and as the section between First Point and Second pitched over, cutting short some hotdogger's slide, I stroked down the face and felt the inertial transference and hitched onto that sweet gravitational slide.

Drew Kampion, writer and surfer

Kelly Slater, the greatest surfer of all time . . . First, he's in complete domination of the Bonzai Pipeline . . . Next, he has the continual desire to prove he's better than you.

Steve Zeldin, writer and surfer

Like an unwelcome houseguest who won't go away, La Niña's ball-numbing waters are expected to stick around till the end of July, affecting both swells and temperatures this summer.

Blair Mathieson, writer and surfer

Mate, me fire's rekindled, I just spent three months in Hawaii and I've never felt better. Whatever you do, don't ever turn your back on surfing. That was the biggest mistake of my life.

Wayne Lynch, champion surfer, after giving up surfing for many years

More than any other top pro since Mitch Thornson, Pipe master Jake Peterson is the embodiment of all the dust, flies, hazardous

sealife and ass-kicking conditions that make up the rugged West Australian coastline.

Steve Barilotti, writer and surfer

Style is the result of confidence in your ability and your equipment, it shows in the water.

Duane De Soto, surfer

Thirty years ago, the shortboard revolution spread like the Melissa virus through the surf world. Almost overnight, surfers cut a few feet off of their lumbering 10' 0"'s with the hope of surfing like one of those power-turning Aussies.

Chris Mauro, writer and surfer

To me, a bodyboard is something you'd use to slide a dead body into a bag.

Tim Mowery, inventor, created what he insists on calling "Boogie Boards"

Very early in his rise through the amateur ranks, Taj eclipsed most juniors in Australian surfing history as the "chosen one."

Derek Hynd, writer and surfer

Watermen just know the surf and pass it on.

Rabbit Kekai, surfer

We've all had that feeling. We've all paddled out and felt the ocean draw away all our fears and cares, and felt some primitive child spirit rise back to the surface of our beings, some animal beautiful infancy, something most people stop feeling somewhere around the age of twelve and never feel again their whole godforsaken legitimized lives.

Nick Carroll, writer and surfer

When I get depressed I go surf, come in and I'm refreshed.

Rabbit Kekai, surfer

While Cape Canaveral is world famous for its procession of high-flying astronauts, only the surfing population is aware of the astronomical number of champions and incredibly gifted riders launched from this tiny corner of the planet over the last 35 years.

Peter Interland, writer and surfer

While studying Buddhism, I learned to appreciate surfing for what it really is. It's totally humbling. I might get a 10-second tube and do the best cutback in the world, but without the ocean and the earth, I'm just an idiot.

Garth Dickenson, surfer

You need to surf more.

Todd Chesser, surfer, to his mother, Jeanine Chesser, on days when she was uptight

Yup, Briley's back. Put that on the cover with exclamation points.

Shawn Briley, surfer, after taking a year off, to Surfer magazine, which actually followed his suggestion

Sweat

Sweat is the cologne of accomplishment.

Heywood Hale Broun, sportswriter

Swimming

Apart from the Olympics, a swimmer finds it difficult to achieve any fame at all.

Daniel F. Chambliss, swimming coach and writer

A swimmer knows that magical blend of water and being and moment not once but every time he slips through the membrane

from air to liquid—his skin wet and cool, his mind and body suspended, the water pressing against his palms and churning as his feet rise and fall.

Harvey S. Wiener, writer and swimmer

Everyone bad raps the big program, but swimming in the same lane with a world record holder or a world champion made it so much easier for them to accept that they could be like that.

Michael Schubert, U.S. Olympic swimming coach

My training was constant. I would start in the summer, just swimming, maybe going 2,000 yards, then continually building up so that by the end of September I would enter a schedule that was pretty substantial. At that point I was doing 10,000 yards in one workout, which took between two and two-and-a-half hours.

Mark Spitz, Olympic gold medal swimmer

Now I will you to be a bold swimmer. . . .

Walt Whitman, poet

Swimming is essential. It should be as basic to a child's education as learning the ABCs.

Mark Spitz, Olympic gold medal swimmer

There is a complex citizenship to the natural world we are part of when we swim. We have no special human powers, no superior dis-

pensation, then. In its mystery, its profound and changeable reverberations in both the memory and the mind, swimming is a decathlon all by itself.

The New York Times

This is swimming, not turns.

Mark Spitz, Olympic gold medal swimmer, remarking on the difference between indoor- and outdoor-length pools

Which is the ideal sport, the one that's least distressful physically, that uses all the most important muscles vigorously and without strain, and that is just all-around best for you? Swimming is the best exercise.

Harvey S. Weiner, writer

Racing . . . is an exercise in self-discovery. My final time interests me less than the broader revelation of how well my training has prepared me to race on this particular day.

Terry Laughlin, swimmer and swimming coach, editor, and writer

Stroke mechanics play the largest single role in creating a satisfying swimming career.

Mark Schubert, swimming coach and writer

Swimming is the closest thing on this earth to the perfect sport.

Jane Katz, Olympic synchronized swimmer and writer

T

Table Tennis

If you say ping-pong a few times with your eyes closed, you will realize how appropriately, poetically and musically the name describes the game. You can almost hear ping-pong being played.

Ding Shu De, Zhu Qing Zuo,
Chinese national Ping-Pong players

There was a table tennis parlor in the neighborhood, Manhattan's Upper West Side, and I passed it every day when returning from school. One day I courageously entered and saw that my idea of the game—to outlast your opponent in a monotonous duel of close-to-the-table pings and pongs—was completely wrong. Here, grown men and boys my own age played the game with drives and long-range retrieves and made it really look like a sport.

Dick Miles, U.S. table tennis champion

Once giggling young ladies and un-athletic youths tentatively patted a little white ball across the net in a parlor game called Ping-Pong. Today, superfit athletes, coached and trained to a peak, their bodies subjected to special diets and intensive exercises, blast the ball towards opponents at speeds of over 100 m.p.h. and with such violence that the ball has been known to disintegrate.

Chester Barnes, champion table tennis player

Talent

Character will only take you so far. You've got to have talent.

Karl Malone, professional basketball player

Talent is more than hitting the ball and moving well. I'm sick of hearing about guys who had the greatest strokes in the world, could have been champions if they'd felt like it. Feeling like it, even when you don't feel like it—that's talent.

Nikki Pilic, professional tennis player and
German Davis Cup captain

What did it mean for Aaron or Matthews to hit their .350 or their forty homers? Anybody with ability can play in the big leagues.

263

To last as long as I did with the skills I had, with the numbers I produced, was a triumph of the human spirit.

Bob Uecker, professional baseball player and broadcaster

You wonder why teams lose? That's a perfect example, if they can't recognize talent like that.

Fran Tarkington, professional football player, about Amad Rashad, who had been passed up in the draft by three losing franchises

Talk Radio

Talk radio, Philly style. Flak jacket required.

Mike Freeman, New York Times writer, on toughness of Philadelphia fans on local professional athletes

Tanking

I've got to get out of here tomorrow. I've got a flight booked, so I'm tanking and getting out of here.

Alex Antonitsch, professional tennis player, to Glenn Laydendecker, professional tennis player

Tanking—giving up, quitting, just going through the motions—when playing a tournament is a rotten thing to do.

John Feinstein, writer

Team

Ask not what your teammates can do for you.
Ask what you can do for your teammates.

Ervin "Magic" Johnson, Hall of Fame basketball player

A team is as skittish as a herd of animals—like gazelles—and a wrong word or decision can rile them up so they never can really be set straight again.

George Plimpton, writer

I don't like it when everyone wants to interview me and no one pays attention to my teammates. Without them, I'd be nothing. This is a team game, and I'm just one of the guys on the team.

Bill Walton, Hall of Fame basketball player

I don't plan on having any of these guys as friends when I'm finished here.

Bill Laimbeer, professional basketball player, about his teammates as well as his opponents

If I had my druthers, I'd rather have five guys in double figures than two guys averaging 20.

Jim O'Brien, college basketball coach

Individual commitment to a group effort, gentlemen, that's what makes a team work, a company work, a society work, a civilization work.

Vince Lombardi, Hall of Fame football coach

I wanted to lead this crew gently, by example, until this group of twelve women . . . could come together and become a team. After the meeting, I realized we don't have the luxury of waiting for this to happen.

Dawn Riley, yachtswoman

Once a player becomes bigger than the team, you no longer have a team.

Red Auerbach, Hall of Fame basketball coach and executive

Playing time is a problem now. Guys are bitching about their minutes, and if we don't

get it straightened out, we can forget about winning anything.

Larry Bird, Hall of Fame basketball player and coach

Teamwork is the essence of life.

Pat Riley, professional basketball player and coach

The more we play unselfishly, the more everybody gets involved, the better the flow of the game.

Allan Houston, professional basketball player

The only guys I care about are the other 24 guys on my team.

Ken Griffey, Jr., professional baseball player

The secret of winning football games is working more as a team, less as individuals. I play not my eleven best, but my best eleven.

Knute Rockne, college football coach

There's the business side and there's the team. Once the season starts, I just want to win. And I don't care about hurting people's feelings if that's what it takes.

Michael Strahan, National Football League player

There's nothing worse than a sorry, pitiful, whining teammate. . . .

Charles Barkley, professional basketball player

The way a team plays determines its success. You may have the greatest bunch of stars in the world, but if they don't play together, the club won't be worth a dime.

Babe Ruth, Hall of Fame baseball player

They're dedicated, talented, and easy to get along with. This team had no problems, and that had a lot to do with our success.

Andy Petree, crew chief

To make any basket happen, somebody played good defense, somebody boxed out, somebody got the rebound, somebody hustled down the floor, somebody set the pick, somebody got open, somebody passed the ball, and somebody hit the shot. That's a lot of somebodies, but a lot of somebodies equals a team.

Ervin "Magic" Johnson, Hall of Fame professional basketball player

We're a good team, but maybe there are different kinds of good teams. Like good teams, okay teams and teams that screw up. We were okay there for a while. And then we seemed screwed up.

Fred Dryer, professional football player and actor

We were like the strings of a guitar. Each one was different, but we sounded pretty good together.

Willie Worsley, college basketball player

We were too young as a team to understand the tensions of a pennant race. Each days was an adventure. We weren't expected to win.

Ed Kranepool, professional baseball player, referring to the 1969 Miracle Mets

When I can't win and my teammate does, that's good for my team. That's good for me. I truly believe that.

Jimmy Vasser, automobile racer

Working hard individually is what builds a team collectively.

Karch Kiraly, professional volleyball player

Technique

All rods can catch fish; their success depends on that hand that uses them.

Charles Ritz, A Fly Fisher's Life

I don't know, I never think about it. Instinct, I guess.

Evonne Goolagong, champion tennis player, when asked about her technique

I never had technique.

Al Oerter, gold medal–winning track and field star

They have a pretty basic offense. No fancy blocking. Technique at its best.

Erik Howard, professional football player

Tee Time

English clubs are very exclusive . . . You can't get a starting time on Sunday unless you've been knighted.

Bob Hope, comedian

Television

His philosophy is that the networks are just renters. At the end of four years of a contract it's his product again, whereas they can walk away.

Gregg Winnick, television executive, talking about National Basketball Association commissioner David Stern

In baseball, the production toys are many: Bat Track, which measures bat speed; super-slo-mo cameras; CatcherCam and MaskCam; triple-split screens; instant replays; pitch-by-pitch sequences; Hit Zones; radar guns, plus managers, outfield walls, bullpens and bases are all wired for sound.

Richard Sandomir, writer

One team scores, ten guys party for the camera. Big 300-pounders shaking their ass. What the hell does that have to do with football?

Jim Brown, Hall of Fame football player

Roone Arledge, as anyone at ABC will tell you, was born in a manger.

attributed by Sports Illustrated *to an unidentified executive at ABC*

Sometimes, whether you're in the sixth grade or the eighth grade, you're going to make some shots to win the ball game and miss some shots to lose the ball game. Mine just happen to be on national TV.

Kobe Bryant, professional basketball player

Television's overpowering financial leverage must not obscure what I believe to be its greatest importance: its capacity to accelerate change.

James Michener, writer

We think TV exposure is so important to our program and so important to this university that we will schedule ourselves to fit the medium. I'll play at midnight if that's what TV wants.

Paul "Bear" Bryant, Hall of Fame college football coach

Tennis

A perfect combination of violent action taking place in an atmosphere of total tranquillity.

Billie Jean King, professional tennis player

Because she was so unlike any other tennis player in the world, no one ever said that this goddess "played tennis."

Larry Engleman, writer, about Suzanne Lenglen, champion tennis player

I am the best tennis player who cannot play tennis.

Ian Tiriac, professional tennis coach

I guess I was the first Englishman to bring the American attitude to the game of lawn tennis.

Fred Perry, professional tennis champion

In a racquets game, you are like a boxer. You attack and exploit another man's weakness. And a five-set singles match would be like going fifteen rounds.

Stan Hart, writer

It's one-on-one out there, man. There ain't no hiding. I can't pass the ball.

Pete Sampras, professional tennis champion

It seems to me that a primary attraction of the sport is the opportunity it gives to release aggression physically without being arrested for felonious assault.

Nat Hentoff, writer

On clay, you can't just kill the ball, because it's going to come back over and over.

Martina Hingis, professional tennis player

Physically, mentally and tennistically it's coming together.

Martina Hingis, professional tennis player

Tennis is structured, with lots of rules and regulations, but within those confines you can be very artistic, creative and aggressive.

With a racket in your hand, you can be whoever you really are.

Jason Cox, professional tennis player

The game of tennis and the atmosphere around it seem to narrow the intellect of the average good player and reduce his horizon. He tends to become petty and cantankerous.

Bob Considine, sportswriter

For a tennis player the only thing worse than playing in the U.S. Open, is not playing in the U.S. Open.

John Feinstein, writer

Tennis, anyone?

Anonymous

Tennis is my art.

Billie Jean King, champion tennis player

Tennis players start out so bloody young. Twenty-four is approximately the age that most football and baseball players *reach* the pros.

Frank Deford, sportswriter

The dictatorship of the players is deadly dangerous to the sport. The players get tremendous money without 100 percent effort.

Peter Kovarchik, tennis promoter

The list of girls who traded their adolescence for trophies haunts women's tennis.

Linda Robertson, writer

The primary object in match tennis is to break up the other man's game.

Bill Tilden, champion professional tennis player

That's when you know they're in trouble, when they start steering the ball.

Dennis Van Der Meer, professional tennis coach

The life we lead in tennis is most unlike that in any other sport. Tennis knows no season now, and is spectacularly international. I don't really live anywhere.

Arthur Ashe, Hall of Fame tennis champion and writer

There is no doubt in my mind that tennis is *The Ring* [the opera]. As soon as they discover the gold the end was inevitable. Great and godlike as all these players are, the sport will have to be destroyed—before it will ever become sane. Ever since the game's been professional, there's been nothing but chaos.

Ted Tinling, tennis player and umpire

We are merely the stars' tennis balls, struck and bandied which way please them.

John Webster, English playwright

When you can hit a serve 120 mph on the line, there's not much you can do. This was just an old-fashioned street mugging.

Andre Agassi, professional tennis champion, after losing in the finals at the U.S. Open to Pete Sampras

With some noble exceptions among the three genders attracted to top flight tennis—male, female, and neuter—the game seems to draw the oddest characters in sports.

Bob Considine, sportswriter

World-class tennis players are tribal creatures, who regardless of national origin, share the same mores, totems and taboos.

Michael Mewshaw, writer

You're going to win the majority of points on your first serve, but you're only as good as your second serve.

Pete Sampras, champion professional tennis player

Thorpe, Jim

(b. May 28, 1888; d. May 28, 1953)
Olympic pentathlon and decathlon gold medalist (1912); professional baseball player; professional football player; All-American college football player; considered by many as the world's greatest athlete

Jim Thorpe defeated Brown thirty-two to nothing—all by himself. Runs of fifty and sixty yards were nothing . . . the Indian was a tornado.

Michael Thompson, college football referee

Sir, you are the greatest athlete in the world.

King Gustav of Sweden, at the 1912 Olympic Games, during the medal ceremony

We could have won if it hadn't have been for Thorpe. He's the best I've ever seen.

Dwight D. Eisenhower, U.S. president, commander of Allied Forces in Europe during World War II, and college football player, when undefeated Army played the Canton Bulldogs and lost 27–6

Ticket Prices

The cheapest way to see the playoffs is to drive to Indianapolis.

John Tierney, writer, advice to fans in the New York Times, referring to the disparity between playoff ticket prices between the New York Knicks and the Indiana Pacers

The only crimes being committed out here are the ticket prices.

Bronx borough president Fernando Ferrer in response to George Steinbrenner's charges that the neighborhood surrounding the stadium was crime-ridden

Tie(s)

A tie is like kissing your sister.

Paul "Bear" Bryant, Alabama
University football coach

Tilden, Bill

(b. Feb. 10, 1893; d. May 28, 1953) *Hall of Fame tennis champion; won U.S. Open seven times; won Wimbledon three times*

Bill Tilden was a stickler for the rules. He knew them inside out, sideways, what could be done, what could not be done. If you tried to bend the rules a little bit, he jumped you quick.

Fred Perry, professional tennis champion

Bill was stand-offish and show-offish. Proud, sensitive, he craved affection and respect from mature people—just as any man, but received it from few.

Grantland Rice, sportswriter

He's quite something. He's not afraid of work.

Ty Cobb, Hall of Fame baseball player

When he came out and started trotting down the stairs, it was the laird taking possession of his empire. Even if you were going to beat him, you knew you were only a subject.

Jean Borotra, champion tennis player

Who *is* this fruit?

Ty Cobb, Hall of Fame baseball player, upon
meeting Tilden for the first time

Toughness

If me and King Kong went into an alley, only one of us would come out, and it wouldn't be the monkey.

Lyle Alzado, National Football League player

I saw him get hit with a beer bottle right across the forehead, and he just wiped it off. That's all I'm going to say. He just kind of blinked and said, "You shouldn't have done that."

Jack Patera, professional football player, speaking
about Buzz Guy, professional football player

I'm not mean, just aggressive.

Harvey Martin, professional football player

To me being tough includes going into the corners without phoning ahead to see who's there.

Ted Lindsay, professional hockey player

They're so tough that when they finish sacking the quarterback they go after his family in the stands.

Tim Wrightman, on Chicago Bears'
defensive unit

We're not tough enough.

Pete Babcock, National Basketball Association
team executive, on his team's reputation
for being soft

When the going gets tough, the tough get going.

Theodore Roosevelt, president of the United
States, conservationist, and sportsman

Yes, I had a reputation for being tough. You had to be when you were Italian.

Gene Sarazen, champion professional golfer

Track and Field

Almost anyone can run or jump, but few can make a sport of it.

Kathleen McElroy, sportswriter and editor

As long as I'm here, I might as well throw.
Al Oerter, Olympic champion discus thrower, at the 1956 Melbourne Olympics

By breaking the world record every few days, those two Limeys are making a mockery of the mile race, which has traditionally been the core and kernel of any track meet.
Red Smith, sportswriter, referring to Sebastian Coe and Steve Ovett, world record–setting milers

In the next 50 years to 100 years, you'll see tremendous things in the 100 meters, tremendous times. The era started is going to continue and it's going to be great.
Gail Devers, Olympic track and field competitor

Leading is the best way to stay out of trouble.
Mary Decker Slaney, world champion runner

The decathlon is the most social of track events and promotes a strong sense of camaraderie among contestants. There is a lot of time to visit during and between events, much of which is used in helping other participants. Athletes will give and take advice, analyze each other's technique, assist each other in locating and checking take-off points, and even use each other's equipment.
Frank Zarnowski, writer

The strength events—such as the discus throw, hammer throw and shot put—are by and large won on the practice fields.
Al Oerter, Olympic champion discus thrower

The time you won your town the race
We chaired you through the market-place;
Man and boy stood cheering by,
And home we brought you shoulder-high.
A. E. Housman, poet

They weren't going to have a party without me.
Maurice Greene, track and field competitor, after setting a new world record in the 200-meter

Track and field has little in common with major American sports like football and basketball. But on the high school level, there is at least one similarity. If you are very good, you'll get recruited.
Carl Lewis, Olympic gold medalist track and field competitor

Track and field is not ice-skating. It is not necessary to smile and make a wonderful impression on the judges.
Emil Zatopek, Olympic gold medalist runner

We're the only professional sport that is not officially recognized as a professional sport. Track and field are where tennis was 20 years ago. It's time for the rules of the sport to catch up with reality.
David Greifinger, lawyer for Carl Lewis, gold medalist track and field competitor

Trades

I knew ballplayers got traded like horses, but I can't tell you how it felt when they traded me. I was only nineteen, but I made up my mind then it wouldn't ever happen again.
Curt Flood, professional baseball player and the first to file a lawsuit against Major League Baseball that eventually won players free agent rights

In the most lopsided transaction since the island of Manhattan was purchased for $24 worth of beads, Junior jilted Seattle and forced the Mariners to hand him over to the

Cincinnati Reds . . . It was more an extortion than it was a transaction, and if ever a deal screamed that it is not in the best interests of baseball, this one does.

> *Bill Lyon, sportswriter*

I've still got stuff in storage in Philly that I was going to move to Cleveland. I have stuff in storage in Cleveland that I was ready to put in the new place. Now I have no house, and my things—who knows where they are?

> *Jerry Spradlin, professional baseball player, who was traded twice in six months*

I didn't want you. I wouldn't trade 100 Bob Ueckers for one Gary Kolb.

> *Branch Rickey, baseball executive, to Bob Uecker, baseball player and announcer, after Uecker introduced himself to Rickey upon arriving at St. Louis against Rickey's wishes*

The Cowboys got nothing more than a handful of Minnesota smoke.

> *Randy Galloway, sportswriter, commenting on the trade of Herschel Walker to the Minnesota Vikings for eight players, many of whom went on to help Dallas win three more Super Bowls*

There were a great many people who thought the cards had made a great mistake, trading two ballplayers for one Uecker. As the season wore on Uecker proved that they were indeed correct.

> *Mark Stillwell, president of the Bob Uecker Fanclub, from the club newsletter*

Me for Tittle? You mean, just me?

> *Lou Cordileone, offensive lineman, asking about being traded for Hall of Fame quarterback Y. A. Tittle*

Smart managing is dumb. The three-run homer you trade for in the winter will always beat brains.

> *Earl Weaver, professional baseball manager*

The Spurs traded me to the Chicago Bulls for center Will Perdue, a guy with no game. Straight up for Will Perdue, bro. That's how much San Antonio wanted to get rid of me.

> *Dennis Rodman, professional basketball player*

You play bad and you hear you might get traded; you play good and you hear you might get traded.

> *Jack Youngblood, professional football player*

Trainers

Celebrity trainers who look as if they've walked out of the opera more than a smelly barn have become the marketing rage.

> *Harvey Araton, sportswriter, about horse trainers*

He couldn't train a vulture to eat.

> *Kelso Sturgeon,* Guide to Sports Betting, *in response when asked about a professional sports trainer.*

I was taught when I was a little boy that if you never lie, cheat or steal you'll be all right. But it's tough when you're a horse trainer not to steal a little here or there.

> *Charlie Whittingham, thoroughbred horse trainer*

The gift that God gave me is racehorses.

> *Diane Crump, trainer*

They all get beat if you run them often enough.

> *Oft-repeated saying in horse racing, attributed by William Murray, writer*

Trainers are the college basketball and football coaches of thoroughbred racing. They represent The Program. The Program, the continuum, as the horses pass in and out of prominence every few years.

Harvey Araton, sportswriter, about thoroughbred horse trainers

Trainers spend all their time looking for one thing . . . They're looking for *the* horse.

Brendan Boyd, sportswriter

We were compulsive buyers. I still am. You walk a good looking saddle pony by me and I'll want to buy it.

D. Wayne Lukas, thoroughbred horse trainer

When we saw that, everybody patted the trainer on the back.

Chuck Finley, professional baseball player, about seeing Mo Vaughn back in the lineup, coming back from a sprained ankle

You always have to have that big horse, that superstar to get noticed. To remind people we're still out here. And winning.

D. Wayne Lukas, thoroughbred horse trainer

Training

If I had practiced more, trained harder, taken the game more seriously, maybe even put on a big act, like it was a religion to me, I might have done better. But maybe not. You know, sometimes it's a matter of the club you land with.

Hot Rod Hundley, professional basketball player

If you train hard, you'll not only be hard, you'll be hard to beat.

Herschel Walker, professional football player

I never let my social life interfere with my athletic training. I set my standards early so that I would never get wrapped up in that manner.

Mark Spitz, Olympic gold medal swimmer

It is not a matter of how much you train, but how you train.

Rick Niles, triathlon coach

I took for granted that I had to be in good physical shape to win. I ran, cycled, lifted weights, practiced yoga, did everything the . . . trainers said was necessary.

Jean-Claude Killy, Olympic gold medalist skier

Never ask your body to do something it hasn't already done in training—and you'll have confidence that you can actually do it.

Alberto Salazar, champion marathoner

Nothing like the feel of the trail in your hair to make you want to train harder.

John Bass, mountain climber, about falling and getting banged up

The day I don't want to train in the off season, the day I don't want to work as hard as I possibly can, that's the day I'll quit.

Karl Malone, professional basketball player

The five S's of sports training are: stamina, speed, strength, skill, and spirit; but the greatest of these is spirit.

Ken Doherty, track coach

You've got to train.

Cyrille Guimard, cycling coach

Training Camp

The first thing you learn is never to learn their names until the last cut is made. 'Cause you feel bad when they get cut.

Eddie LeBaron, professional football player

Trash Talking

An old-fashioned ass-kicking.

Ervin "Magic" Johnson, Hall of Fame basketball player, about losing in the finals to the Chicago Bulls

Block that, Bitch!

Michael Jordan, professional basketball player, to John Salley, professional basketball player, who was defending against Jordan

Get up and fight, sucker! Get up and fight!

Muhammad Ali, world champion boxer, to Sonny Liston, world champion boxer, after knocking Liston out for the heavyweight crown

He did something stupid, and that's what he does best.

George Foreman, champion boxer, broadcaster, and pitchman, talking about Prince Nassem Hemed's victory over Paul Ingle

He'll have to grow a hell of a lot to get as big as his mouth.

John Nerud, thoroughbred horse trainer and owner, about a competitor

He missed me all night, at the plate and on the mound. That tells you how stupid he is. He's obviously frustrated—that's his problem.

Todd Stottlemeyre, professional baseball player, about Charlie Hayes, with whom he started a fight in the middle of a Giants/Dimondback games

I don't like him. Nobody likes him because he's a————. I'm sick of people like that. Who is he, Sandy Koufax? He's a .500 pitcher, that's all. If he has a problem with me, we can get it settled. I told him I'd knock him out.

Charlie Hayes, professional baseball player, about Todd Stottlemeyre

I don't need to be practicing, I'm leading this tournament. You guys go on and practice, because you're behind.

Lee Trevino, champion golfer, to fellow competitors after a good first round

If you can't hit, you can't run, and can't throw, then you've got to holler at them.

Solly Hemus, professional baseball player and manager

I just gave him a look, and Steve Javie, the ref, told me to stop looking.

Marcus Camby, professional basketball player, about eyeballing Alonzo Mourning during a hotly contested New York Knicks–Miami Heat playoff game

I've been called a racist, a drunk and a quitter. Other than that, I'm fine.

Kerry Collins, professional football player

I will crush you like a grape.

Mark Tuinei, professional football player, the phrase he most liked to tell opposing linemen

Jesse, thanks for the directions.

Mark Tuinei, professional football player, who retorted to friend Jesse Sapulo that the road to the Super Bowl went through Candlestick, after the Cowboys beat the 49ers in the playoffs

273

One's a liar and the other's convicted.
Billy Martin, professional baseball player and manager, about Reggie Jackson and George Steinbrenner, respectively

The Knicks are going to win the East, more than likely, unless they get upset, 'cause they're playing against the Little Sisters of the Poor.
Charles Barkley, professional basketball player

Who's guarding me? Nobody's guarding me. You're supposed to be guarding me?
Larry Bird, to Dennis Rodman, both professional basketball player

This is what you're lookin' for.
Johnny Sample, National Football League player, to an opposing receiver after intercepting the ball and tapping him on the head with it.

You're next, big mouth.
Sonny Liston, world champion, to Muhammad Ali from inside the ring after beating Floyd Patterson a second time

Triple Crown

It's one of those things that is not on my resume. I'd love to have it. The chance comes along so seldom.
D. Wayne Lukas, thoroughbred horse trainer

Now I won't have to worry about a Triple Crown.
Bob Baffert, trainer, after not winning the Kentucky Derby for the first time in three years

We're at a cross roads in racing. Tracks are changing ownership and the business is searching for answers. A Triple Crown winner would be an enormous thing for racing.
D. Wayne Lukas, thoroughbred horse trainer

Trust

The foundation of getting people to do what you want them to do is built on a relationship based on trust. That is the critical element, the glue that holds everything together.
Marty Shottenhimer, professional football coach

Ultra-Marathon

Every year, two or three dozen elite ultra-marathoners come to Badwater, and every year Badwater beats them down.

David Ferrell, sportswriter

For a thin slice of society—zealots who live to train, who measure themselves by their mental toughness—the ultra-marathon is the constant test of human character. No other event in sport, except possibly a prize fight, is as punishing, as demanding of the mind and body.

David Ferrell, sportswriter

Umpires

As an umpire, when you make a call, you're alone.

Bernice Gera, umpire, first female umpire

F——— the safety of the umpires. I've got fifty thousand people out there who want to see baseball!

Bill Veeck, baseball owner and racetrack operator, to the umpires in their locker room, when thousands of rowdy fans had taken the field during a promotional day, and refused to yield for the second game. The game was eventually canceled.

I cursed him out in Spanish, and he threw me out in English.

Lou Pinella, professional baseball player and manager, referring to Armando Rodriquez, umpire, after being thrown out of a game

I don't recall.

Bobby Thompson, professional baseball player, when asked if he remembered who the umpire was when he hit the famous Home Run Heard Round the World

I normally shudder when I think I've really kicked one. I can't sleep that night and I don't feel good until I get back on the field the next day. My early years in umpiring, I might go back to the umpires' room and cry a little after missing a crucial call.

Durwood Merrill, umpire

It's wonderful to be here, to be able to hear the baseball against the bat, ball against the glove, and to be able to boo the umpire.

Douglas MacArthur, U.S. general, commander of Pacific theater in World War II, at a baseball game

I umpired more than two thousand games during my career. I was called every name in the book and then some. I was sworn at in two languages, blackballed by my own peers, ridiculed by fans, and abused by ball players and managers in five different countries.

Pam Postema, female umpire

Lately . . . we've been hearing that the umpires are trying to take over the game and that they're too arrogant and that some of them think they are bigger than baseball. It seems some umpires don't want to argue anymore. They just want to toss you out of the game.

Ken Griffey, Jr., baseball player

Players being more concerned about the next day's umpire than the next day's starting pitcher; there's something wrong there.

Sandy Alderson, league official

That guy has definitely done some wrestling. Only wrestlers know how to do that particular series of actions. It was basically a double leg takedown . . . it was a good three-point move.

Dan Gable, Olympic champion wrestler, on Cuban umpire Cesar Valdez's takedown of an anti-Castro protester during a game between the Baltimore Orioles and the Cuban national team

Today, conscious of the great unseen audience, they play every decision out like the balcony scene from *Romeo and Juliet*. On a strike they gesticulate, they brandish a fist aloft, they spin almost as if shot through the heart, they bellow all four parts of the quartet from *Rigoletto*. On a pitch that misses the plate, they stiffen with loathing, ostentatiously avert the gaze, and render a boot from *Gotterdammerung*.

Red Smith, sportswriter

When you think about it, you've probably spent more time with umpires than you spent with your wife.

Richie Ashburn, broadcaster to Tim McCarver, broadcaster and former baseball catcher

You argue with an umpire because there's nothing else you can do about it.

Leo Durocher, professional baseball player and manager

You're not even supposed to be watching!

Lou Pinella, professional baseball player and manager, to Durwood Merrill, umpire, after Merrill overruled a home run call because he cited fan interference. Merrill was correct, replays showed later

You're out, and you're ugly, too.

Durwood Merrill, umpire

Uniforms

Baseball outfits went through their gaudy period during the disco '70's, when the White Sox looked like softball players and the Athletics looked like "Saturday Night Fever" personified.

George Vecsey, sportswriter

I don't know. I'm not in shape yet.
Yogi Berra, Hall of Fame baseball player and coach, when asked during spring training what his cap size was

Instead of looking like an American flag, I look like a taco.
Steve Garvey, professional baseball player, referring to his new Padres uniform versus his previous Dodgers uniform

I wear a sombrero, silk neckerchief, fringed buckskin shirt, sealskin chaparajos or riding-trousers, and alligator-hide boots, and with my pearl-hilted revolver and beautifully finished Winchester rifle, I feel I can face anything.
Theodore Roosevelt, president of the United States, conservationist, and outdoorsman

Unions
They have no sense of history whatsoever.
Curt Flood, professional baseball player, first to file for free agency

Unknowns
At least I didn't swing and miss.
Mike Stone, rookie golfer, at the 1999 U.S. Open, referring to his first tee shot

You don't know me, I was just a ham-and-egger.

Lew Perez, club fighter

Veterans

Walt, you don't have to run the forties . . . If those rookies ever find out how slow you are and you've been playing six years, they'll think it's a snap to make this team.

Tom Landry, professional football head coach and player, to Walt Garrison, professional football player

Victory

I tried to get away from things tonight by going over to gamble at the Playboy Club, and who should I meet at the blackjack table but Joe Frazier. Frazier had no idea who I was. Other black athletes don't even know me, although the tennis boom has made me much more visible outside the tennis world.

Arthur Ashe, Hall of Fame tennis champion and writer

Everyone has the will to win, but few have the will to prepare to win.

Bobby Knight, basketball coach

Forget about style; worry about results.

Bobby Orr, Hall of Fame hockey player

How vainly men themselves amaze
To win the palm, the oak, or bays.

Andrew Marvell, poet

I am a winner each and everytime I go into the ring.

George Foreman, champion boxer

I don't think we can win every game—just the next one.

Lou Holtz, college and professional football coach

If you believe in yourself and have dedication and pride—and never quit, you'll be a winner. The price of victory is high—but so are the rewards.

Paul "Bear" Bryant, Hall of Fame college football coach

That's the big difference between victory and defeat for us. After a victory we want to be

together . . . When we lose, everyone goes off in his own direction.

Rick Casares, professional football player

The more difficult a victory, the greater the happiness is in winning.

Pelé, soccer player

The price for victory is hard work.

Knute Rockne, college football coach

There is a pleasant taste to victory, and soon I was thinking, why not try for a bigger cup, a longer trip, a more important victory?

Jean-Claude Killy, Olympic gold medalist skier

Victory is not necessarily a gold medal.

Gale Tanger, Olympic figure skating judge, referring to Nancy Kerrigan's winning the silver medal after being attacked by friends of rival skater Tonya Harding

Violence

Despite all the moaning and gnashing of teeth over violence in the NFL over the past few years, I can safely say that anyone who didn't watch us play hasn't seen true violence in sports. In a way, I kind of miss it.

Art "Fatso" Donovan, Hall of Fame football player

I ain't ever liked violence.

Sugar Ray Robinson, champion boxer

I kept thinking about all the guys kneeled down before the game to say the Lord's Prayer. When they were done everyone leaped up, put on their helmets and charged out of the locker room screaming, "Let's kill the bastards."

Rick Sortun, professional football player

Knocking down an offensive lineman and breaking his head open is something that I enjoy.

Alex Karras, Hall of Fame football player

The only time I am really violent is on the football field. I'm going to catch him and knock his block off. It's as simple as that.

Alex Karras, Hall of Fame football player

Volleyball

Beach volleyball is a little like marriage—a doomed one. I don't think there's ever been a team that didn't break up at one point or another. It's inevitable.

Karch Kiraly, professional volleyball player

Between the pass and the attack, the setter is in control.

Doug Beal, volleyball coach and writer

In an ace-to-error ratio, how many mistakes are you willing to give up to score points by the ace? The ace is the easiest way to score. One contact of the ball and you have a point.

Mike Herbert, volleyball coach

The rule is a simple one: If you want to win the Association of Volleyball Professionals' Miller Lite U.S. Championships, you have to go through Karch Kiraly and Adam Johnson. That rule was enforced on Sunday.

Los Angeles Times

The setter has to be the most consistent player on the court, day in and day out.

Lorne Sawula, volleyball coach

Volleyball is among the purest of team sports. It is virtually impossible for one player to

dominate the game as a great running back in football or a tremendous shooter in basketball.

Doug Beal, volleyball coach and writer

When a ball was dug up and put up for one of them, a point was almost automatic.

Karch Kiraly, professional volleyball player,
about Steve Timmons and Pat Powers

Walton, Izaak

(b. Aug. 9, 1593; d. Dec. 15, 1683) *Biographer; fisherman; author of* The Compleat Angler *(1653) which is one of the most frequently reprinted books in the English language according to the* Encyclopaedia Britannica

It is said that many an unlucky urchin is induced to run away from his family and betake himself to a seafaring life, from reading the history of Robinson Crusoe; and I suspect that, in like manner, many of those worthy gentlemen who are given to haunt the sides of pastoral streams with angle rods in hand, may trace the origin of their passion to the seductive pages of honest Izaak Walton.

Washington Irving, writer

Water

Above all to be taken into account were some years of schooling, where I studied with diligence Neputune's laws, and these laws I tried to obey when I sailed over seas; it was worth the while.

Joshua Slocum, first modern sailor to sail around the world alone

A healthy respect of the sea is a must for all sailors, regardless of experience.

Bob Bond, sailor, instructor, and writer

A man who is not afraid of the sea, will soon be drowned, he said, for he will be going out on a day he shouldn't. But we do be afraid of the sea, and we do only be drowned now and again.

John Millington Synge, writer and playwright, from The Aran Islands

A river is like a piece of music. The score is basically the same every time, but everyone who plays it will play it a little differently, and no matter how many times you play it yourself, you'll play it a little differently each time.

Robert Kimber, outdoorsman and writer

But what is the test of a river? Who shall say? "The power to drown a man," replies the river darkly.

R. D. Blackmore, outdoorsman and writer

Each sea is different and because the North Sea is prone to bad weather, it is one of the biggest graveyards in the world.

John Beattie, sailor

I am haunted by waters.

Norman Maclean, writer

If there is magic on this planet, it lies in water.

Loren Eiseley, scientist, naturalist, and writer

If the Southern Ocean represents the consummate challenge for any long-distance sailor, then the Vendee Globe is the pinnacle—one man, one boat against the elements.

Pete Goss, champion solo sailor and writer, commenting on the Vendee Globe race, an around-the-world solo boat race

I had to keep guessing at the channel. I had to discern, mostly by inspiration, the signs of hidden banks; I watched for sunken stones . . . When you have to attend to things of that sort, to the mere incidents of the surface, the reality—the reality, I tell you—fades. The inner truth is hidden—luckily, luckily.

Joseph Conrad, writer, in his novella Heart of Darkness

It has something to do with the infiniteness of water, its vastness; it doesn't inhibit vision.

Stuart Williamson, yachtsman

It was a storm precisely like this one that saved England from the Spanish Armada. Whenever you sail in the English Channel, you've got to be prepared for the return of that storm.

Ted Turner, yachtsman and baseball owner, referring to the storm that struck the 1979 Fastnet Race

It's no worse than the Indianapolis 500 race. The danger is part of it. We were racing all the time.

Dennis Conner, yachtsman

Man marks the earth with ruin; his control stops at the shore.

Lord Byron, poet

Mid-September is not the ideal time to make a passage west through the Straits of Dover and down the English Channel. It's a boisterous stretch of water at the best of times, but during the equinoctial gales it is a 22-carat sod.

Tristan Jones, sailor and writer

Rivers are a constant lure to the adventurous instinct in mankind.

Henry David Thoreau, writer and philosopher

The fact that a man can drown while fishing is obvious . . . the very first lesson every young angler must learn are the techniques of water safety.

A. J. McClane, outdoorsman and writer

The people I respect are the ones who quit the race. The competitive urge can be a very unbalancing thing, and we are all guilty in a way of not respecting the sea enough.

Tom McLoughlin, sailor, participant in the 1979 Fastnet Race

The sea drives truth into a man like salt.

Hilaire Belloc, writer

The sea is a great leveler, and quickly humbles the big-headed sailor.

Alex Rose, yachtsman

The Southern Ocean is teaching us its lessons; respect the sea because I can snap you up like a twig if I want to; never think you are special or too important, because I can be arbitrary and unfair and I don't care who gets in my path of destruction.

Dawn Riley, yachtswoman

There is enough water in the world for all of us.

Annette Kellerman, swimmer and women's rights activist

To face the elements, is to be sure, no light matter when the sea is in its grandest mood. You must know the seas, and know that you know it, and not forget that it was made to be sailed over.

Joshua Slocum, first modern sailor to sail around the world alone

Very few people will actually travel an entire water trail, but the very fact of a water trail's existence is a siren for at least a few days' travel.

Tamsin Venn, kayaker and publisher of Atlantic Coastal Kayaker

Water is the blood of the Earth, and flows through its muscles and veins.

Kuan Tzu, philosopher

Water on the move is nimble as well as subtle. It is apparently made of an infinite series of layers that seem to slip over each other with very little friction. Running water is a truly dynamic medium.

Jay Evans, Olympic kayaker and outdoorsman

Water Polo

If we wanted to win, we had to be in that pool.

John Vargas, coach, U.S. national water polo team

They're different from swimmers. They don't see the world as a concrete prison, a place to swim lap after lap in pain. They like having their heads out of the water, having a good time.

Ted Newland, college water polo coach

Weakness

He doesn't cook very well.

Michael Chang, professional tennis champion, when asked to describe Pete Sampras's weakness

If there's a weakness, you want to exploit that weakness.

Michael Peca, professional hockey player

Weather

A storm never blows in when the action is slow.

Randy Voorhees, fisherman and writer

Depressions are born, reach maturity, and then decline and die. They travel in their youth and stagnate in their retirement; some are feeble from birth and never make a mark on the world, while others attain a vigor which makes them remembered with as much awe as a hurricane.

Ingrid Holford, weather specialist

Did you see it snow again in Scottsdale? That's God's way of telling the Diamondbacks it will snow in hell before they win.

Charlie Hayes, professional baseball player

Don't worry, it's not really raining. This is just Houston humidity.

Walter Bloxsom, chairman of the Pin Oak equestrian event

I couldn't care less about Greenland. I'm here for the golf.

William Starrett II, lawyer and avid golfer, who went to Greenland to golf at the World Ice Golf Championship

I have friends who claim the month of February offers us New Englanders, especially those of us who like to fish and hunt, nothing but memories and hopes. Savor the past, they recommend, or dream of the future. Try to ignore the miserable present.

William G. Tapply, outdoorsman and writer

I know I got loaded last night, but how did I wind up at Squaw Valley?

Jimmy Demaret, champion golfer, on waking up in Pebble Beach to find snow on the ground

Someone call the big man. Tell him to turn the heat on!

Percy Ellsworth, professional football player, referring to cold weather before a game in December

We joked that God's an Irishman because he brought us the weather we left at home.

John Morrin, runner, joking about bad weather at the Penn Relays

We're sorry. Too much snow. Too much indecision.

Bill Veeck, baseball owner and racetrack operator, a sign he had posted outside a racetrack in Massachusetts, because the city wouldn't help him open in a snowstorm.

Whether we could stick it out was not so much a question as whether the storm would allow us to stick it out.

Frank Smythe, mountain climber

Weightlifting

For years, coaches would not allow athletes to lift weights because it made them look muscle-bound. Now weight training is a main part of almost any team's training program.

Lou Ferrigno, champion bodybuilder, professional football player, and actor

Lifting a barbell ain't like eating no watermelon.

Toad, U.S. Olympic weightlifter

Since the earliest days of the human race, physical strength above the ordinary has been admired, envied, and striven for by the majority of men.

D. P. Willoughby, writer

Yuri Vlasov was enormously hardworking, but he underestimated the value of technique and failed to make the most of his potential. Leonid Zhabotinskii was exactly the opposite . . . My advantage over both of them is that I know exactly where I am going, I have a will to win, and I have the ability to keep up an incomparably more intensive training program.

Vasilii Alekseev, Olympic gold medalist weightlifter

Williams, Ted

(b. Aug. 30, 1918) *Hall of Fame baseball player; called the "Splendid Splinter"; won the batting Triple Crown twice (1942 and 1947); last player to bat .400 for a whole season; missed five years of his career as pilot in the air force in World War II and the Korean War; considered one of the great pure hitters in baseball history; also a world-class fisherman*

He's the best fisherman there is—the best. No doubt about it. How many people have ever been the absolute best there is at *two* things?

> *Bobby Knight, champion college basketball coach*

He was sometimes unbearable, but he was never dull.

> *Ed Linn, sportswriter*

Like a feather caught in a vortex, Williams ran around the square of bases at the center of our beseeching screaming. He ran as he always ran out home runs—hurriedly, unsmiling, head down, as if our praise were a storm of rain to get out of.

> *George Plimpton, editor and best-selling author*

Winning

A dream I had worked for so hard had come true, and everything has turned red. Everything around me is going in slow motion. I have proved my point, and my blood is literally exploding in my head.

> *Jean-Claude Killy, Olympic gold medalist skier*

A winner never quits and a quitter never wins.

> *Knute Rockne, college football coach*

Because I wanted to win the game!

> *Roger Maris, professional baseball player, responding to a question about why he bunted in a run instead of swinging for a homer*

He can't hit, he can't run, he can't field, he can't throw, but if there's a way to beat the other team, he'll find it.

> *Branch Rickey, baseball executive, speaking about Ed Stanky, professional baseball player*

How much do you really want to win when you have as much money, attention, and fame as Shaquille O'Neal does?

> *Dennis Rodman, professional basketball player*

I believe there is winning and misery and even when we win I'm miserable.

> *Pat Riley, champion professional basketball coach*

I don't feel like dancing.

> *Tom Warner, triathlete, after winning the 1979 Ironman*

I don't see any point in playing the game if you don't win.

> *Babe Didrikson Zaharias, champion golfer and Olympic track and field competitor*

I don't think it's possible to be too intent on winning.

> *Woody Hayes, college football coach*

In playing or managing, the game of ball is only fun for me when I'm out in front and winning. I don't give a hill of beans for the rest of the game.

> *John J. McGraw, Hall of Fame baseball player and manager*

It's nice to be favored, but it doesn't put you in the winner's circle.

> *Nick Zito, thoroughbred horse trainer*

I've won at every level, except college and pro.

> *Shaquille O'Neal, professional basketball player*

I want to win now. Who cares about 2001? The world could blow up in two years. We could all be dead by then.

> *Jason Kendall, professional baseball player*

That's why I took the extra lap. I wanted to wipe away the tears.

Jeff Gordon, champion race car driver, explaining why he took two victory laps at the 1994 Brickyard 400

The game could have gone either way. It came down to the women on this team having to win.

Tony DiCicco, soccer coach, U.S. women's World Cup team

There's only a little margin between winning and losing. A lot of luck is involved. It's hard to get too excited when you know that you could have lost as easily as you won.

Doug Atkins, professional football player

People always try to jump on you when you're not winning. They try to rattle you . . . but that's part of the game. That's what makes it fun.

Jimmy Vasser, automobile racer

Wanting to win has zero to do with money. You can't buy your way into something that's worthwhile, and the only thing worthwhile out of here is trying to be the best team for one year.

Jeff Van Gundy, professional basketball coach

We can't win at home. We can't win on the road. As general manager, I just can't figure out where else to play.

Pat Williams, Orlando Magic general manager, on his team's 7-27 record

We didn't come up here to ruin their season. We came up here to win. We'll let them ruin their season on their own.

Keyshawn Johnson, professional football player

When you have a particularly good game, the community opens up to you—the key to the city and all that. The downfall is that they close up to you. It's all predicated on what you did on Sunday.

Jerome Bettis, National Football League player

Winning is an attitude.

John Chaney, college basketball coach

Winning is like shaving. You do it every day, or you end up looking like a bum.

Jack Kemp, professional football player and U.S. congressman

Winning isn't everything. It's the only thing.

Vince Lombardi, National Football League Hall of Fame coach

Winning is the only thing there is. Anything below first is losing.

A. J. Kitt, world champion skier

Winning tends to heal uneasiness and promote job security.

Selena Roberts, sportswriter

Winners are different. They're a different breed of cat.

Byron Nelson, champion golfer

You know, the house, the car, the money, the fame . . . I'd give it all away in a second to be cancer free.

Lance Armstrong, champion cyclist, winner of the Tour de France, cancer survivor

You win on Sunday, but you can't expect them to roll over for you next week. You've got to go out there next week and prove you're a winner again.

Sam Huff, Hall of Fame football player

Women

Every city in the league has a group of women who hang around the arenas and know where the players go after the games. They're pros, and a lot of them are sexy as hell.

Dennis Rodman, professional basketball player

I got all that out of my system before I got married. Now, every town I go to, women come chasing after me, calling my room, sending me notes, but I don't pay them any attention. I wouldn't want any woman who chases after me, and I stopped chasing after them once I taught my wife how to fire my pistol.

Bo Jackson, professional baseball and football player

I frequently make my own clothes. And if it interests you, I'm a pretty good cook.

Babe Didrikson Zaharias, Olympian and champion golfer, responding to a jest by Grantland Rice, "How is your sewing?"

Everything a woman does has an emotional level. Paying attention to my emotional side without surrendering to it is one of the toughest parts of playing professional sports.

Gabrielle Reece, professional volleyball player

From the bedroom my wife calls. I grumble intelligibly and she calls again, winsomely. I grumble again and continue my work: I steel-wool the male ferrule of my Thomas and whistle into its mate.

Nick Lyons, outdoorsman, writer, and publisher

Let's face it, women are more interesting than football.

Roy Blount, Jr., wruter and humorist

Men are in danger of thinking everything is winning while women think winning is nothing.

Mariah Burton Nelson, professional basketball player

Mother, when I get a telephone call from a beautiful girl like Miss Margaret Foot, I must leave at once—remember, Mother, never let a pitch hang.

Tiny Tim, musician, sports fan

Real groupies present all kinds of dangers. First, a real groupie will travel around between guys and even different sports teams, bringing with her various sorts of abominable "luggage," or diseases, which she is more than happy to share. Second, for the married scoundrels, a groupie is like a live hand grenade without the pin.

Tim Gree, professional football player, broadcaster, and writer

The only way of preventing civilized men from kicking and beating their wives is to organize games in which they can kick and beat balls.

George Bernard Shaw, writer

We play big matches on tour these days. When more of the public realizes we're no carnival act, they'll be bigger.

Babe Didrikson Zaharias, Olympian and champion golfer

When I hear those foxes squealing, I get all jiggly inside. It makes me feel like I can do anything I want to on the court.

Walt "Clyde" Frazier, Hall of Fame basketball player and broadcaster

When we won the league championship, all the married guys on the club had to thank their wives for putting up with all the stress and strain all season. I had to thank all the single broads in New York.

Joe Namath, Hall of Fame football player

Women are more capable of pushing through the pain.

Robyn Benincasa, extreme athlete,
adventure racer

You will come home with me tonight.

Alberto Tomba, Olympic gold medalist skier,
to many local women in Calgary

Women Athletes

Any trainer will tell you that if a girl has good hands she can handle a fractious horse far better than any man. Especially in those early morning hours. There is a relationship between a female and a horse that transcends anything that can possibly exist between a male and a horse.

Bill Veeck, baseball owner, racetrack operator

As an athlete, I believe I was popular as long as I was demure, appreciative, decorative, obedient, and winning.

Shirley Strickland De La Hunty, Olympic track
gold medalist

As a jockey she went where no female—and a hell of a lot of males before her—had ever gone. She is the only woman to ride a winner in a Triple Crown race. She fought for her mounts in a time when most trainers couldn't deal with the idea of turning over a thoroughbred meal ticket to a lady jockey.

Jerry Izenberg, sportswriter, about
Julie Krone, jockey

Few athletes in any Olympic sport—and certainly none so young—face the unique pressure young female gymnasts and figure skaters do. They must instill an entire childhood of training into one perfect performance, and they must do it on the largest stage in the world.

Joan Ryan, journalist and writer

Fishing gear for woman isn't what it used to be. It used to be there wasn't any.

Laurie Morrow, sportswoman and writer

Girls of all colors, sizes, shapes, gritty kids bonding through hard, clean competition.

John Edgar Wideman, writer

I have never felt—I have a hard time even saying the word—*unfeminine* while playing sports.

Jackie Joyner-Kersey, Olympic gold
medalist track and field competitor

I'm not so sure we have changed the perspective of men, but I do think that women are saying to themselves, "If they can do it, why can't I?"

Dawn Riley, champion yachtswoman

I'm not sure that women know what they want to do with tennis. A lot of the girls, when they quit, they go back to school or try something else. The men don't.

Joan Pennello, Women's Tennis
Association executive

I see elegance and beauty in every female athlete. I don't think being an athlete is unfeminine. I think of it as a kind of grace.

Jackie Joyner-Kersey, Olympic gold medalist
track and field competitor

I wanted to be a major league umpire . . . Turns out I took more than anybody—just because I was a woman, a she instead of a he. In professional baseball, there is no worse crime.

Pam Postema, female umpire

I well remember wearing exotic hairstyles and Chanel No. 5 during my competitive days to reassure myself, as well as everyone else, that I was female.

Shirley Strickland De La Hunty,
Olympic track gold medalist

Men who find women athletes sexy are more apt to accept women in all of their dimensions. Athletic women sweat, blow snot from their noses, grunt and lose their tempers. That is sport.

Steve Marantz, sportswriter

My boyfriend's going to take your husband's job.

Attributed to a girlfriend of Stacey King,
professional basketball player, to Donna Grant,
wife of Horace Grant, professional
basketball player

People say PGA first, then LPGA, like a little behind. I don't like that. We're all professionals. Nothing different, many great players.

Se Ri Pak, professional golfer

She was the sort of woman who took off tight shoes which hurt and wiggled her toes, no matter where she was . . . the first athlete to make people confront the issues of femininity: how much muscle is too much? how much is unfeminine?

Adrianne Blue, writer, about
Babe Didrikson Zaharias

The most rewarding moments have been when little girls, 10 and 11 years old, would run up to me and say things like, "I played soccer with boys and I was the best goalkeeper out there." This has happened hundreds of times.

Julie Krone, jockey

The sooner little boys begin to realize that little girls are equal and that there will be many opportunities for a boy to be tested by a girl, the closer they will be to better mental health.

Sylvia Pressley, hearing officer, in her 1973
decision to integrate Little League

The story of women in sports is a personal story, because nothing is more personal than a woman's bone, sinew, sweat, and desire, and a political story, because nothing is more powerful than a woman's struggle to run free.

Mariah Burton Nelson, writer

There's still more pressure on men. If a girl doesn't make it on the tour, she can always get married and have her husband support her.

Marty Mulligan, sponsor representative

The women walk through the gates and see the men and say, "Why should he get more than me?" It's like a heavyweight and a middleweight in boxing. They might be on the same bill, but no matter how good the middleweight is, the heavyweight gets paid more.

John Curry, tennis grand slam executive

We run with women in road races all the time. It would have seemed strange to run without them.

John Benkert, runner, about competitive
running events

291

With the single exception of the improvement of legal status of women, their entrance into the realm of sports is the most cheering thing that has happened to them in this century just past.

Anne O'Hagen, writer, in 1901

Women athletes are no longer curiosities . . . no longer revolutionaries, pioneers or tokens . . . just another bunch of jocks.

Grace Lichtenstein, writer

Women in sports now receive equal recognition. But they still have to work twice as hard as men to be recognized.

Jackie Joyner-Kersey, Olympic gold medalist track and field

Women tennis players call themselves girls . . . If we go to a party or a function where we have to get all dressed up, we're women, but if we're at the tennis club wearing track suits, we're girls—except when we're bitches, of course.

Pam Shriver, champion professional tennis player

World's Fastest Woman is an Expert Cook

headline from the Daily Telegraph (London) about Francina Blankers-Koen, Olympic track gold medalist

Woods, Tiger

(b. Dec. 30, 1975) *Professional golfer; first African American and youngest golfer to win the U.S. Amateur in 1994 (also won 1995 and 1996); won Masters by record 18 under par (with a 13-stroke lead); won 1999 PGA; won nearly $10,000,000 in prize money on the PGA tour in 2000; possibly the most recognized active athlete in the world today*

Bottom line is that I am an American and proud of it.

Tiger Woods, professional golfer, youngest winner of the U.S. Open

He's got the heart of a lion. He may be the type of player that comes around once in a thousand years.

Tom Watson, champion professional golfer

World Cup

I never thought that the World Cup would be such a test of nerves.

Gustave Sebes, deputy of sports, Hungary, after the Hungarians won a wild final, complete with fights and injuries, beating Brazil 3-2

It was terrible. Everybody was sick about this . . . I had a feeling in my skin the robber was not Brazilian. He has no feeling for patriotism.

Pedro T. Natal, chairman of Kodak Brazil, after the country's retired World Cup Jules Rimet Trophy soccer statue was stolen. The robber was found dead, but the statue was not recovered. A replacement—a duplicate—now stands in its place.

It wasn't a very good final.

Franz Beckenbauer, professional soccer player and manager, after West Germany won the World Cup in a lackluster game against Argentina

The lines go from a base rising in a sphere and covering the world. From the body of the sculpture, two figures stand out—two athletes in a moving celebration of victory.

Silvio Gazzaniga, sculptor, who sculpted the new World Cup trophy

The World Cup is the world's grandest sporting event. Every four years, the best 24 teams in the world come together to celebrate this beautiful game with a spectacular tournament and cultural celebration that cannot be duplicated anywhere.

Pelé, professional soccer player

The World Cup was going on and people who maybe make $1 a day were using all their money to go into town to watch it. They'd been saving up for three years to go there.

Leslie Downer, journalist

You cannot run a bid on the cheap and people are naive if they think otherwise. We were the only campaign which had been open about what it has spent and there is no doubt that some people will say it is money down the drain. But if you look at it properly, £10 million is an amazingly modest investment compared to the rewards.

Alec McGivan, leader of England's 2006 World Cup campaign

World Series

I don't think you play this game for any other reason than to get to the World Series. I've thought about it since Little League, when you dream of hitting that home run in the ninth inning.

Ken Griffey, Jr., professional baseball player

Worry

Earl Monroe was the only man I would dream about. He gave me nightmares.

Walt "Clyde" Frazier, champion professional basketball player

Wrestling

As a kid, I remember Archie the Stomper mauling my dad in the ring. Then later, I'd see Archie the Stomper come to get his check, and hug my mom. I couldn't figure it out.

Brett Hart, second-generation professional wrestler

Give a good wrestler a microphone, push him out the door, ask him for ten minutes and you'll get ten great minutes. Who else can do that?

Michael Braverman, agent

I don't want to say that wrestling has taken over this country, but pretty soon I expect my accountant to be wearing a diaper and boots.

Mitch Albom, sportswriter and best-selling writer

I have very hard feelings towards the W.W.F. because they continued the show after Owen's death. It was very cold-blooded.

Brett Hart, second generation professional wrestler, whose brother Owen (also a professional wrestler) fell to his death during a bout

In wrestling you never see anybody get seriously hurt. When was the last time you heard of a wrestler who was out for the season with a knee injury?

Darryl Dawkins, professional basketball player

I saw *Shakespeare in Love,* how the Elizabethan actors and stagehands set up the stage and set. It sounds bizarre, but wrestling's much like that.

Bret Hart, second generation professional wrestler

The professional wrestling addiction that has afflicted segments of my family began in the early 1950s. First to drink at the early fountain of television fraud was a widow in her 60s, whose only flirtation with danger until then had been puffing a single Viceroy filter tip after each meal. She bristled at suggestions she was committing her emotions and several hours a week to a game phony as a three-dollar bill even in the days when TV reception was so poor it was difficult to tell.

Bill Conlin, sportswriter

This business is a lot like Hollywood in the 30s and 40s, when the studios had all the power.

Al Snow, professional wrestler

People told me I could get into wrestling and make millions. I did it for about 12, 13, 14 years. It was tough work, and I didn't make millions.

Brocko Nagurski, Hall of Fame football player and professional wrestler

Pro wrestlers are wondrous athletes, traditionally in better shape than baseball players and even most football players, and they work harder at entertaining us.

Robert Lipsyte, writer

When a guy comes into the ring, he's fair game. You've got to take him out.

Goldberg, champion professional wrestler

Yachting

Certainly America's Cup is the pinnacle of yachting and the Holy Grail of our sport.

Dennis Conner, businessman and champion yachtsman

I can't tell you why, but I wanted very much to do the race. I don't know whether it was vanity, escapism, the zest for competition, a hoped-for sense of independence, or what. Something deep within me said that I should throw all caution and common sense aside and try it.

Hal Roth, yachtsman, about the solo sailing race BOC Challenge

If young Joe and Jack ever lost a sailboat race, his rage was a caution; the only way to avoid it was to win.

William Manchester, writer, referring to Joseph Kennedy, Sr.'s, passion for victory and his attitude toward his sons Joseph Kennedy, Jr., and John Fitzgerald Kennedy, president of the United States

If we still value the qualities of daring, comradeship, and endurance in our national life we should cherish the sports which foster them with the risks they carry . . . they can never expel the danger from yachting and the conviction that it will be a sad and bad day when this seafaring people declines the challenge of the ocean.

The Daily Telegraph *(London)*

If you want to win in heavy weather, you've got to keep thinking. No matter if you're tired, wet, or even seasick, if you want to keep going, you've got to pull yourself together and use all your resources.

Theodore A. Jones, yachtsman

I hereby publicly retract anything and everything I have ever said about inland sailing.

Ted Turner, champion yachtsman, after hitting a storm during the 1970 Chicago–Mackinac race, after having made several derogatory comments about "lake sailing"

In a survival gale of Force 10 or over, perhaps gusting at hurricane strength, wind and sea become the masters. For skipper and crew it is then a battle to keep the yacht afloat.

K. Adlard Coles, yachtsman

I remember very clearly how astonished we all were during that first encounter with *Australia III* . . . We all looked at each other with insolent amazement, but no one dared utter a word even though we were all thinking the same thing . . . She turned faster than any boat I had ever seen.

Dennis Conner, businessman
and champion yachtsman

It only blew there for five hours. During Sydney-to-Hobart, it blew for two straight days.

Andrew Buckland, champion sailor, comparing the tragic 1979 Fastnet race to the tragic 1998 Sydney-to-Hobart race, as he had sailed competitively in both storm-racked races

Everyone gets to Hobart and comments on how they beat the Bass Strait. But deep inside they know the Strait allowed them to win.

Adrian von Friedberg, champion sailor, about the Sydney-to-Hobart race

Fifteen men died, not in wartime, or on a hunt for whales, or in a typhoon on the South China Sea, but during a yacht race only seventy miles off the coast of England.

John Rousmaniere, yachtsman and writer, about the 1979 Fastnet Race

Frankly, I knew *Freedom* was a better boat than *Courageous,* and I knew we were far more prepared than Ted and his crew. There was little doubt we'd kill them, but I certainly wasn't going to say that.

Dennis Conner, businessman
and champion yachtsman

Like Jupiter among the gods, *America* is first and there is no second.

Daniel Webster, author, about the ship for which the America's Cup is named, after having beaten all comers in races off Newport

Most expert seamen I know sail fast. They don't know any other way. To sail slowly or inefficiently is to be unseamanlike.

Theodore A. Jones, yachtsman

Newspapers crowing over the victory of the Stevens yacht, which has beaten everything in the British seas. Quite creditable to Yankee shipbuilding, certainly, but not worth the intolerable, vainglorious vaporings that make every newspaper I take up now so ridiculous. One would think yachtbuilding were the end of man's existence on earth.

George Templeton Strong, lawyer
and diarist, 1851

No matter how good the helmsman the most brilliant tactics will look ridiculous if your boat is not moving fast enough through the water.

John Oakley, yachtsmen

People who say that ocean racing is boring have never worked hard at it.

John Rousmaniere, yachtsman and writer

Perhaps as never before in 100 years of challenges had a series been fought so directly on the water, rather than having already been settled on the designer's board, towing tank or sail loft.

Bill Robinson, sportswriter, referring to Intrepid's victory over Gretel II in the America's Cup

Racing is meant to be difficult, yes. Dangerous, no. Life threatening, definitely not. I wouldn't go out there again if I lived to be a thousand years.

Larry Ellison, American industrialist and champion sailor, after surviving the tragic 1998 Sydney-to-Hobart race

Stop surviving and race.
Bruce Kirby, yachtsman

The captain was the cook, the navigator, the dishwasher, the sail changer, the radio operator, the plumber, and the bed-maker.
Hal Roth, yachtsman, referring to his solo trip around the world in the BOC Challenge

There may have been some moaning at the bars by those who mourn the passing of the gentler age of big boat racing, but the cries of despair were unheard in the excitement along the Fremantle waterfront. Here was a real international competition, a really world-class event. Whatever exclusivity had still surrounded 12-meter racing at Newport had disappeared at Fremantle.
Walter Cronkite, journalist and sailor

The tops of the waves were breaking and toppling over in the wind. We could imagine what they could do to a small boat. We continued racing, but it was survival conditions, really.
Gerry McGarry, yachtsman, referring to the 1979 Fastnet Race

Those that built a single boat and sent a single crew to Australia never were seriously in the running, although they gave the big boys a scare now and again. Their expenditure of only seven, eight, or nine million dollars wasn't nearly enough. The "serious" syndicates with multiboat programs spent fifteen or twenty million, maybe even more, to make their bid.
Walter Cronkite, journalist and sailor

When the mast was jammed into the trough we stopped like we hit a brick wall. Food exploded out of the refrigerator and flew into the navigation station. Cottage cheese became a lethal weapon.
John Tuttle, yachtsman

Yachtsmen generally tend to over-complicate and surround their tuning problems with highly technical and confusing discussion that has no bearing on the immediate issue.
Mike Fletcher, sailor and journalist

Yankees, New York
The residents of other cities who hate the Yankees really only hate New York.
Leonard Koppett, writer

It is impossible for anyone who does not live in New York to know what it truly is to hate the Yankees.
Murray Kempton, Back at the Polo Grounds

The Yankees are only interested in one thing, and I don't know what it is.
Luis Polonia, professional baseball player

Youth
The key to success for any pro team is young players, unformed, eager, ready to learn, playing on legs not yet pounded and broken.
Peter Golenboch, sportswriter

Zone (the)

He's playing real, real, real good.

Ed Gray, professional basketball player, about
Latrell Sprewell

I can tell you right now, I'm soooo on a different wavelength.

Tara Lipinski, after winning the
U.S. Skating Championships

It is not merely mechanical, it is not only spiritual; it is something of both, on a different plane and a more remote one.

Arnold Palmer, champion professional golfer

I was rising above myself, doing things I had no right to be doing.

Bruce Jenner, Olympic gold medalist
decathlon competitor

There comes that moment when I have lost myself and only the play finds me.

Brett Hull, professional hockey player

————. *Days of Grace.* New York: Knopf, 1993.

Asinov, Eliot. *Eight Men Out.* New York: Holt, Rhinehart & Winston, 1963.

Axthelm, Pete. *The City Game.* New York: Harper & Row, 1970.

Auerbach, Red (with Joe Fitzgerald). *On and Off the Court.* New York: Macmillan, 1988.

Babcock, Havilah. *The Best of Babcock.* New York: Holt, Rinehart and Winston, 1974.

Baily, Anthony. *The Coast of Summer.* New York: HarperCollins, 1994.

Barber, Red. *1947 When All Hell Broke Loose in Baseball.* Garden City: Doubleday, 1982.

Barnes, Chester. *Advanced Table Tennis Techniques.* New York: Arco, 1977.

Barzini, Luigi. *Peking to Paris.* Chicago: The Library Press, 1973.

Bergman, Ray. *Fishing with Ray Bergman.* New York: Knopf, 1970.

Berkow, Ira. *Pitchers Do Get Lonely.* New York: Atheneum, 1988.

Berra, Yogi (with Tom Horton). *Yogi: It Ain't Over . . .* New York: McGraw-Hill, 1989.

Bird, Larry. *Bird Watching.* New York: Warner Books, 2000.

————. *Drive.* New York: Doubleday, 1990.

Bissinger, H. G. *Friday Night Lights.* Boston: Addison-Wesley, 1990.

Boliteri, Nick and Schaap, Dick. *My Aces, My Faults.* New York: Avon Books, 1996.

Bradley, Bill. *Values of the Game.* New York: Artisan, 1999.

Brander, Michael. *The Roughshooter's Dog.* London: The Sportsman's Press, 1989.

Brennan, Christine. *Inside Edge.* New York: Scribner, 1996.

————. *The Edge of Glory.* New York: Scribner, 1998.

Brokhin, Yuri. *The Big Red Machine.* New York: Random House, 1978.

Brown, Jim (with Steve Delsohn). *Out of Bounds.* New York: Zebra Books, 1989.

Brown, Nigel. *Ice-Skating: A History.* New York: A.S. Barnes, 1959.

Boukareeve, Anatoli. *The Climb.* New York: St. Martin's Press, 1997.

Bouton, Jim. *Ball Four.* 20th Anniversary Edition. New York: Macmillan, 1990.

Burfoot, Amby. *The Complete Book of Running.* Emmaus, Penn.: Rodale, 1997.

Bursey, Kevin. *Icestars.* Chicago: Triumph, 1999.

Cannon, Jimmy (edited by Jack and Tom Cannon). *Nobody Asked Me, But . . .* New York: Holt, Rinehart & Winston, 1978.

Cantor, Andres. *Goooal!* New York: Fireside, 1996.

Capstick, Peter Hathaway. *Death in the Tall Grass.* New York: St. Martin's Press, 1977.

————. *Death in the Silent Places.* New York: St. Martin's Press, 1981.

Caras, Roger. *Death as a Way of Life.* Boston: Little Brown, 1970.

Casio, Chuck. *Soccer U.S.A.* Washington: Robert L. Bruce, 1975.

Casper, Billy. *My Million Dollar Shots.* New York: Grossett and Dunlap, 1971.

Charlton, James and Thompson, William. *Croquet.* New York: Scribner, 1977.

Coe, Sebastian. *Running Free.* New York: St. Martin's Press, 1981.

Connor, Dennis. *Comeback.* New York: St. Martin's Press, 1987.

Cooke, Alistair. *Fun and Games with Alistair Cooke.* New York: Arcade, 1994.

Cosell, Howard (with Mickey Herskowitz). *Cosell.* New York: Playboy Press, 1973.

Crist, Steven. *The Horse Traders.* New York: W. W. Norton, 1986.

Crowe, Phillip A. *Sporting Journals.* Barre, Mass.: Barre Publishers, 1966.

Dawidoff, Nicholas. *The Catcher Was a Spy.* New York: Pantheon, 1994.

Dawkins, Darryl (with George Wirt). *Chocolate Thunder.* Chicago: Contemporary Books, 1986.

De, Ding Shu, et al. *The Chinese Book of Table Tennis.* New York: Atheneum, 1981.

De Ford, Frank. *Big Bill Tilden.* New York: Simon & Schuster, 1976.

————. *The World's Tallest Midget.* Boston: Little Brown, 1987.

Dent, Jim. *The Junction Boys.* New York: St. Martin's Press, 2000.

Dickson, Paul. *The Joy of Keeping Score.* New York: Walker, 2000.

Didinger, Ray. *Game Plans for Success.* New York: Little Brown, 1995.

Dodson, James. *Final Rounds.* New York: Bantam, 1996.

Dugard, Martin. *Knockdown.* New York: Pocket Books, 1999.

Durocher, Leo (with Ed Lynn). *Nice Guys Finish Last.* New York: Simon & Schuster, 1975.

Elliott, James Francis. *Jumbo Elliott.* New York: St. Martin's Press, 1982.

Elman, Robert and Seybold, David. *Seasons of the Hunter.* New York: Knopf, 1985.

Englade, Ken. *Hot Blood.* New York: St. Martin's Press, 1996.

Eskenazi, Gerald. *Gang Green.* New York: Simon & Schuster, 1999.

Evans, George Bird. *The Upland Shooting Life.* New York: Knopf, 1971.

Fassi, Carlo. *Figure Skating with Carlo Fassi.* New York: Scribner, 1980.

Feinstein, John. *A Good Walk Spoiled.* New York: Little Brown, 1995.

————. *A March to Madness.* New York: Little Brown, 1998.

————. *A Season Inside.* New York: Villard Books, 1988.

————. *Forever's Team.* New York: Villard Books, 1989.

————. *Hard Courts.* New York: Villard Books, 1991.

————. *The Majors.* New York: Little Brown, 1999.

Fergus, Jim. *The Sporting Road*. New York: St. Martin's Press, 1999.

Fischler, Stan. *Cracked Ice*. Chicago: Masters Press, 1999.

Firestone, Roy (with Scott Ostler). *Up Close*. New York: Hyperion, 1993.

Fitzpatrick, Frank. *And the Walls Came Tumbling Down*. New York: Simon & Schuster, 1999.

Fleming, Peggy. *The Long Program*. New York: Pocket Books, 1999.

Foreman, George and Engle, Joel. *By George*. New York: Villard Books, 1995.

Foyt, A. J. (with William Neely). *A. J.* New York: Times Books, 1983.

Francis, Austin. *Smart Squash*. Philadelphia: J.B. Lippincott, 1977.

Francis, Dick. *The Sport of Queens*. New York: Harper & Row, 1969.

Freidman, Arthur. *The World of Sports Statistics*. New York: Atheneum, 1978.

Frey, Darcy. *The Last Shot*. New York: Houghton Mifflin, 1994.

Gallwey, W. Timothy. *Inner Skiing*. New York: Random House, 1977.

———. *Inner Tennis*. New York: Random House, 1976.

———. *The Inner Game of Golf*. New York: Random House, 1981.

Garagiola, Joe and Quigley, Martin. *Baseball Is a Funny Game*. Philadelphia: J.B. Lippincott, 1960.

Garvey, Cynthia. *The Secret Life of Cyndy Garvey*. New York: Doubleday, 1989.

George, Nelson. *Elevating the Game*. New York: HarperCollins, 1992.

Giamatti, A. Bartlett. *A Great and Glorious Game*. N.C.: Algonquin Books of Chapel Hill, 1998.

Gibson, Bob and Wheeler, Lonnie. *Stranger to the Game*. New York: Viking, 1994.

Glanville, Jerry. *Elvis Don't Like Football*. New York: Macmillan, 1991.

Golenbock, Peter. *American Zoom*. New York: Macmillan, 1993.

———. *Personal Fouls*. New York: Carroll & Graff, 1989.

Goodwin, Doris Kearns. *Wait Till Next Year*. New York: Simon & Schuster, 1997.

Goolagong, Evonne (with Bud Collins). *Evonne!* New York: E.P. Dutton, 1975.

Gordeeva, Ekaterina. *My Sergei*. New York: Warner Books, 1997.

Gordon, Herb. *Essential Skiing*. New York: Lyons & Burford, 1996.

Greene, Bob and Jordan, Michael. *Hang Time*. New York: Doubleday, 1992.

Green, Tim. *The Dark Side of the Game*. New York: Warner Books, 1996.

Greenlaw, Linda. *The Hungry Ocean*. New York: Hyperion, 1999.

Halberstam, David. *The Amateurs*. New York: William Morrow, 1985.

———. *The Breaks of the Game*. New York: Knopf, 1981.

———. *October '64*. New York: Villard Books, 1994.

————. *Summer of '49.* New York: Villard Books, 1990.

————. *For Keeps.* New York: Random House, 1999.

Hamilton, Scott. *Landing It.* New York: Kensington, 1999.

Hanks, Stephen. *The Game That Changed the World.* New York: Carol Publishing, 1989.

Harding, Anthony, ed. *The Race and Driver's Reader.* New York: Arco Publishing, 1972.

Hart, Stan. *Once a Champion.* New York: Dodd, Mead & Co., 1985.

Heisler, Mark. *The Lives of Riley.* New York: Macmillan, 1994.

Hemingway, Ernest. *The Dangerous Summer.* New York: Scribner, 1985.

————. *Death in the Afternoon.* New York: Scribner, 1936.

————. *Green Hills of Africa.* New York: Scribner, 1930.

Herne, Brian. *White Hunters.* New York: Henry Holt, 1999.

Hill, Graham (with Neil Ewart). *Graham.* New York: St. Martin's Press, 1977.

Hogaan, Marty and Turner, Ed. *Skills and Strategies for Winning Racquetball.* Chicago: Leisure Press, 1988.

Hollis, David W. *National to National.* New York: Howell Book House, 1992.

Hope, Bob. *Confessions of a Hooker.* New York: Doubleday, 1985.

Hornung, Paul. *Woody Hayes.* Champaign, Ill.: Sagamore Publishing, 1991.

Hovdey, Jay. *Whittingham.* Lexington, Ky.: The Blood-Horse Inc., 1993.

Hurt, Harry. *Chasing the Dream.* New York: Avon, 1997.

Izenberg, Jerry. *No Medals for Trying.* New York: Macmillan, 1988.

————. *The Jerry Izenberg Collection.* Dallas: Taylor Publishing, 1989.

Jackson, Phil and Delehanty, Hugh. *Sacred Hoops.* New York: Hyperion, 1995.

Jacobs, Barry. *Three Paths to Glory.* New York: Macmillan, 1993.

James, Bill. *The Politics of Glory.* New York: Macmillan, 1994.

Javorsky, Ben. *Hoop Dreams.* Atlanta: Turner Publishing, 1995.

Jenkins, Dan. *Fairways and Greens.* New York: Doubleday, 1994.

————. *Saturday's America.* New York: Little Brown, 1970.

————. *You Call It Sports, But I Say It's a Jungle Out There.* New York: Simon & Schuster, 1989.

Jenner, Bruce (and Phillip Fitch). *Decathlon Challenge.* New York: Prentice-Hall, 1977.

Jones, Tristan. *One Hand for Yourself, One Hand for the Ship.* New York: Macmillan, 1982.

————. *Yarns.* Boston: Sail Books, 1983.

Kahn, Roger. *The Games We Used to Play.* New York: Ticknor & Fields, 1992.

————. *The Boys of Summer.* New York: Harper & Row, 1972.

————. *A Flame of Pure Fire.* New York: Harcourt Brace, 1999.

Kardong, Don. *30 Phone Booths to Boston.* New York: Macmillan, 1985.

Karras, Alex (with Herb Gluck). *Even Big Guys Cry.* New York: Holt, Rinehart and Winston, 1977.

Katz, Jane. *Swimming for Total Fitness.* New York: Doubleday, 1992.

Kerasote, Ted. *Bloodties.* New York: Random House, 1993.

Killy, Jean-Claude. *Skiing . . . The Killy Way.* New York: Simon & Schuster, 1971.

———— (with Al Greenberg). *Comeback.* New York: Macmillan, 1974.

Kimble, Martha Lowder. *Robin Cousins.* Baltimore: Gateway Books, 1998.

King, Billie Jean (with Frank Deford). *Billie Jean.* New York: Viking Press, 1982.

King, Peter. *The Season After.* New York: Warner Books, 1989.

————. *Inside the Helmet.* New York: Warner Books, 1993.

Kislevitz, Gail Waesche. *First Marathons.* New York: Breakaway Books, 1998.

Klapisch, Bob and Harper, John. *The Worst Team That Money Could Buy.* New York: Random House, 1993.

Kleinbaum, Nancy H. *The Magnificent Seven.* New York: Bantam Books, 1996.

Kowalchik, Dagny. *The Complete Book of Running for Women.* New York: Pocket Books, 1999.

Krakauer, John. *Into Thin Air.* New York: Villard Books, 1997.

Krich, John. *El Beisbol.* New York: Atlantic Monthly Press, 1989.

Krone, Julie (with Nancy Ann Richardson). *Riding for My Life.* New York: Little, Brown, 1995.

Ladew, Harvey S. *Random Collections on Fox-hunting.* Monkton, Md.: Ladew Topiary Gardens Foundation.

Lane, Mills. *Let's Get It On.* New York: Crown, 1998.

Lardner, Ring. *You Know Me, Al.* New York: Collier, reprint 1991.

Laughlin, Terry and Delves, John. *Total Immerson.* New York: Fireside, 1996.

Lee, Spike. *Best Seat in the House.* New York: Crown, 1997.

Lever, Janet. *Soccer Madness.* Chicago: Univ. of Chicago Press, 1983.

Levine, David. *Life Above the Rim.* New York: Macmillan, 1989.

Lewis, Carl (with Jeffrey Marx). *Inside Track.* New York: Simon & Schuster, 1990.

Lewis, Fredrick (edited by Dick Johnson). *Young At Heart.* Waco, Tex.: WRS Publishing, 1992.

Lewis, Michael. *World Cup Soccer.* London: Moyer, Bell, 1994.

Libby, Bill. *Great American Race Drivers.* New York: Cowles Books, 1970.

———— (with Richard Petty). *King Richard.* New York: Doubleday & Co., 1977.

Lipsyte, Robert and Levine, Peter. *Idols of the Game.* Atlanta: Turner Publishing, 1995.

————. *Sports World.* New York: Quadrangle Books, 1975.

Louganis, Greg. *Breaking the Surface.* New York: Random House, 1995.

Luchiano, Ron and Fisher, David. *The Umpire Strikes Back.* New York: Bantam Books, 1982.

Lyons, Nick. *Fisherman's Bounty.* New York: Crown, 1970.

MacCambridge, Michael, et al. *Eson Sports Century.* New York: Hyperion, 2000.

Madden, John (with Dave Anderson). *Hey, Wait a Minute (I Wrote a Book).* New York: Villard Books, 1985.

———— (with Dave Anderson). *One Knee Equals Two Feet.* New York: Villard Books, 1986.

Mahony, Devin. *The Challenge.* Chicago: Contemporary Books, 1989.

Manley, Dexter. *Educating Dexter.* Nashville, Tenn.: Rutledge Hill Press, 1992.

Mantle, Mickey and Pepe, Phil. *My Favorite Summer 1956.* New York: Doubleday, 1991.

Maraniss, David. *When Pride Still Mattered.* New York: Simon & Schuster, 1999.

Mathias, Bob and Tassin, Myron. *Bob Mathias.* New York: St. Martin's Press, 1983.

McCullagh, James C. *Cycling.* New York: Dell, 1995.

McGuane, Thomas. *An Outside Chance.* New York: Farrar, Straus and Giroux, 1980.

McLaggan, Doug and Torbet, Laura. *Squash.* Garden City, N.Y.: Doubleday, 1978.

McManus, Patrick F. *They Shoot Canoes, Don't They?.* New York: Holt, Rhinehart and Winston, 1981.

McIntyre, Thomas. *Days Afield.* New York: E. P. Dutton, 1994.

McPhee, John. *A Sense of Where You Are.* New York: Farrar, Straus and Giroux, 1965.

Merrill, Durwood. *You're Out, And You're Ugly Too!* New York: St. Martin's Press, 1998.

Mewshaw, Michael. *Ladies of the Court.* New York: Crown, 1993.

Michener, James A. *Sports in America.* New York: Random House, 1976.

Millburn, Frank. *Polo.* New York: Knopf, 1994.

Miller, Peter. *The 30,000 Mile Ski-race.* New York: Dial Press, 1972.

Merrill, Christopher. *The Grass of Another Country.* New York: Henry Holt, 1993.

Miles, Dick. *The Game of Table Tennis.* Philadelphia: J. B. Lippincott, 1968.

Mitchell, John G. *The Hunt.* New York: Knopf, 1980.

Morris, Willie. *The Courting of Marcus Dupree.* New York: Doubleday, 1983.

Mosconi, Willie and Cohen, Steve. *Willie's Game.* New York: Macmillan, 1993.

Multi-Media Partners. *Grace & Glory.* Chicago: Triumph Books, 1996.

Murphy, Michael and White, Rhea A. *In the Zone.* New York: Penguin Books, 1995.

Murray, Jim. *Jim Murray.* New York: Macmillan, 1993.

Murray, William. *The Wrong Horse.* New York: Simon & Schuster, 1992.

Nicholson, T. R. *The Wild Roads.* New York: W. W. Norton, 1969.

Oates, Joyce Carol. *On Boxing.* New York: Viking Press, 1985.

Oates, Joyce Carol and Halpern, Daniel. *Reading the Fights.* New York: Henry Holt, 1988.

O'Connor, Jack. *The Big Game Rifle.* Long Beach, Calif.: Safari Press, 1952.

Olajuwon, Hakeem. *Living the Dream.* New York: Little Brown, 1996.

Oriard, Michael. *Reading Football.* Chapel Hill, N.C.: University of North Carolina Press, 1993.

Ortega y Gasset, José. *Meditations on Hunting.* New York: Charles Scribners, 1972.

Osius, Alison. *Second Ascent.* Chicago: Stackpole Books, 1991.

Pennick, Harvey (with Bud Shrake). *For All Those Who Love the Game.* New York: Simon & Schuster, 1995.

———. *Harvey Pennick's Little Red Book.* New York: Simon & Schuster, 1992.

Petty, Richard. *King Richard I.* New York: Macmillan, 1986.

Pitino, Rick (with Dick Weiss). *Full Court Pressure.* New York: Hyperion, 1992.

——— (with Bill Reynolds). *Born to Coach.* New York: NAL Books, 1988.

Plimpton, George. *Paper Lion.* New York: Harper & Row, 1966.

Reaske, Christopher R. *Crouquet.* New York: E. P. Dutton, 1988.

Reese, Paul and Henderson, Joe. *Ten Million Steps.* Waco, Tex.: WRS Publishing, 1993.

Reeves, Dan (with Dick Connor). *Dan Reeves.* Chicago: Bonus Books, 1988.

Rice, Grantland. *The Tumult and the Shouting.* New York: A. S. Barnes & Co., 1954.

Richardson, Donald Charles. *Crouquet*. New York: Harmony Books, 1988.

Riley, Pat. *The Winner Within*. New York: Putnam, 1993.

Ritter, Lawrence S. *The Glory of Their Times*. New York: William Morrow, 1984.

Robinson, Ray. *The Home Run Heard 'Round the World*. New York: HarperCollins, 1991.

Robyns, Gwen. *Wimbledon*. New York: Drake Publishers, Inc., 1974.

Rodman, Dennis (with Tim McKeown). *Bad As I Wanna Be*. New York: Delacourt Press, 1991.

Rogers, Bill (with Joe Concannon). *Marathoning*. New York: Simon & Schuster, 1980.

Roosevelt, Theodore. *Hunting Trips of a Ranchman & the Wilderness Hunter*. New York: Modern Library, 1996.

Roth, Hal. *Chasing the Rainbow*. New York: W. W. Norton, 1990.

Rousmaniere, John. *Fastnet, Force 10*. New York: W. W. Norton, 1980.

Rust, Art. *Art Rust's History of the Black Athlete*. Garden City, N.Y.: Doubleday, 1985.

———. *Get That Nigger Off the Field*. New York: Delacourt Press, 1976.

Ryan, Bob and Pluto, Terry. *Forty-eight Minutes*. New York: Macmillan, 1987.

Sampson, Curt. *The Masters*. New York: Villard Books, 1998.

Schulberg, Budd. *Sparring with Hemingway*. Chicago: Ivan R. Dee, 1995.

Schubert, Mark. *Competitive Swimming*. Lanham, Md.: Sports Illustrated Books, 1996.

Schwarzenegger, Arnold. *The New Encyclopedia of Modern Bodybuilding*. New York: Fireside, 1999.

Seidel, Michael. *Ted Williams*. Chicago: Contemporary Books, 1991.

Sheed, Wilfred. *Baseball and Lesser Sports*. New York: HarperCollins, 1991.

Sheehan, George. *Running and Being*. New York: Simon & Schuster, 1978.

———. *The Running Life*. New York: Simon & Schuster, 1980.

Silverman, Al. *The Best of Sport 1946–1971*. New York: Viking Press, 1971.

Simpson, Joe. *Touching the Void*. New York: Harper & Row, 1988.

Sisco, Peter, et al. *Ironman's Ultimate Bodybuilding Encyclopedia*. Chicago: Contemporary Books, 1999.

Siner, Harold. *Sports Classics*. New York: Coward-McCann, 1983.

Smith, Lissa. *Nike Is a Goddess*. New York: Atlantic Monthly Press, 1998.

Smith, Red. *The Red Smith Reader*. New York: Random House, 1982.

———. *To Absent Friends*. New York: Atheneum, 1982.

Smith, Robert. *A Social History of the Bicycle*. New York: American Heritage Press, 1972.

Smith, Sam. *The Jordan Rules.* New York: Pocket Books, 1994.

Spitz, Mark and LeMond, Alan. *The Mark Spitz Complete Book of Swimming.* New York: Thomas Y. Crowell, 1976.

Sports Illustrated. *Sports Illustrated Book of Badminton.* Philadelphia: J.B. Lippincott, 1967.

Stump, Al. *Cobb.* Chapel Hill, N.C.: Algonquin Books, 1994.

Sturgeon, Kelso. *Guide to Sports Betting.* New York: Harper and Row, 1974.

Sugar, Bert. *Hit the Sign and Win a Free Suit of Clothes from Harry Finklestein.* Chicago: Contemporary Books, 1978.

Suster, Gerald. *Champions of the Ring.* London: Robson Books, 1992.

Swan, James A. *In Defense of Hunting.* San Francisco: HarperSanFrancisco, 1995.

Tapply, William G. *Those Hours Spent Outdoors.* New York: Scribner's, 1988.

Tatum, Jack (with Bill Kushner). *They Call Me Assassin.* New York: Everest House, 1979.

Thorn, John. *The Armchair Quarterback.* New York: Scribner's, 1982.

Thorne, Gerard and Embleton, Phil. Ontario, Canada: MuscleMag International, 1997.

Torrez, Danielle Gagon (and Ken Lizotte). *High Inside.* New York: G.P. Putnam, 1983.

Trueblood, Ted. *The Ted Trueblood Hunting Treasury.* New York: David McKay Company, 1978.

Unsworth, Walt, ed. *Peaks, Passes and Glaciers.* Seattle: The Mountaineers, 1981.

Valerio, Anthony. *Bart.* San Diego: Harcourt, Brace, Jovanovich, 1991.

Walton, Izaak. *The Compleat Angler.* New York: Modern Library, 1996.

Wartman, William. *Playing Through.* New York: William Morrow, 1990.

Waterman, Jonathan. *In the Shadow of Denali.* New York: Delta Books, 1994.

Watson, J. N. P. *The Book of Foxhunting.* New York: Arco Publishing, 1976.

Weaver, Earl (with Berry Stainback). *It's What You Learn After You Know It All That Counts.* Garden City, N.Y.: Doubleday and Co., 1982.

Weider, Joe (with Joe Reynolds). *Joe Weider's Ultimate Bodybuilding.* Chicago: Contemporary Books, 1988.

Weld, Philip S. *Moxie.* New York: Little Brown, 1981.

Williams, Doug (with Bruce Hunter). *Quarterblack.* Chicago: Bonus Books, 1990.

Wills, Maury and Celizic, Mike. *On the Run.* New York: Carroll & Graf, 1991.

Whiting, Robert. *You Gotta Have Wa.* New York: Macmillan, 1989.

Whittingham, Richard. *The Meat Market*. New York: Macmillan, 1992.

Wideman, John Edgar. *Brothers and Keepers*. New York: Holt, Rinehart and Winston, 1984.

———. *Philadelphia Fire*. New York: Henry Holt, 1990.

Wiener, Harvey S. *Total Swimming*. New York: Simon & Schuster, 1980.

Willoughby, David P. *The Super Athletes*. New York: A.S. Barnes, 1970.

Wilson, Mike. *Right on the Edge of Crazy*. New York: Times Books, 1993.

Wiltse, David. *It Only Hurts When I Serve*. Norwalk, Conn.: A Tennis Magazine Book, 1980.

Wind, Herbert Warren. *The Realm of Sport*. New York: Simon & Schuster, 1966.

Wolf, Warner. *Let's Go to the Videotape*. New York: Warner Books, 2000.

Wulff, Joan. *Joan Wulff's Fly Fishing*. Harrisburg, Pa.: Stackpole Books, 1991.

Woog, Dan. *Jocks*. Los Angeles: Alyson Books, 1998.

Zafferano, George J. *Handball Basics*. New York: Sterling Publishing, 1977.

Index

Boldface page numbers denote main topics.

796
ULT

The ultimate
dictionary of sports
quotations.

$45.00

42028

DATE			

ACKNOWLEDGMENTS

FROM TODD:

An immeasurable thanks to my wife, Lara, for your unending well of belief, your constant nurturing, and for shouldering the load while I was sending so much energy elsewhere. I can't thank you enough, but I look forward to trying for the rest of my life. Thanks to my daughter, Elowyn, for bringing me breakfast in the morning when I was too attached to the computer to eat. Thanks to Jessica and Kristin, for keeping me laughing, for "continental" wisdom, and for your dedication to bad puns and the making of tacos. And thanks to Joss Whedon, for creating the most unfairly truncated series, *Firefly*, which I must have watched about eighteen times while seeking inspiration for this book.

FROM GILES:

First and foremost, I need to thank my wife, Tanya, for her unwavering faith in my ability and her gratuitous suffering from my procrastination. Also a big thanks to my semi-neglected children, Liefke and Luna, for brightening my days and sort-of leaving me alone to write. And a special salute to Glenn Mullen for letting me camp at his desk for weeks on end.

FROM BOTH OF US:

Thanks to our advance readers Aaron Brown, Laren Crawford, Megan Foss, Liana Holmberg, Chris Mandeville, Kristin Maresca, Jessica Meltzer, and Morgan Thomas. Without your wit, insight, enthusiasm, encouragement, and occasional outright disgust, this book would have been much less fun to write (and read). Thanks again to Langdon Foss for his wonderful work on the drawings of Ohndarien and The Floating Palace. Thanks to the "Clan," for being the largest group of best friends in the world. A big thanks to our agent, Donald Maass, for his continual support of these books, and for answering all of the little questions. And all hail Marie Lu, our shameless self-promoter and directrix of the über-spiffy flash movie on our website. *No animals were harmed in the writing of this book.*